COLLECTED WORKS OF

BERNARD LONERGAN

VOLUME 9

*THE REDEMPTION*

Part 2: Redemption denotes not only an end but also a mediation. / 35
Part 3: Redemption as mediation is seen in the payment of the price. / 39
Part 4: Redemption as mediation is seen in Christ's vicarious passion and death because of sins and for sinners. / 45
Part 5: Redemption as mediation is seen in the sacrifice offered by our high priest in his own blood. / 53
Part 6: Redemption as mediation is seen in obedience. / 59
Part 7: Redemption as mediation is seen both in the power of the risen Lord and in the intercession of the eternal priest. / 65
*A note on the modes and effects of redemption* / 77

**Thesis 16**: Christ's satisfaction. Christ made not only condign but even superabundant satisfaction for our sins. This satisfaction is understood according to a sacramental analogy, and therefore it adds to Christ's vicarious passion and death an expression of the utmost detestation of all sins and of the greatest sorrow for all offense against God. / 79
*Terminology* / 79
*Church teaching* / 81
*Theological note* / 81
*Meaning of the thesis* / 83
*Opinions* / 87
[*Preliminary notes*] / 107
Preliminary note 1: Anselm's opinion / 107
Preliminary note 2: Either satisfaction or punishment / 111
Preliminary note 3: Either pardon or punishment / 113
Preliminary note 4: Fault, offense, punishment / 117
Preliminary note 5: Satisfaction, pardon, remission of punishment / 123
Preliminary note 6: Vicarious satisfaction / 127
Preliminary note 7: The justice of God / 133
Preliminary note 8: The reintegration or restoration of the order of divine justice / 139
Preliminary note 9: The problem of integration / 143
Preliminary note 10: The problem of coherence / 153
Preliminary note 11: The symbolic mentality / 169
*The argument* / 171
1 Christ materially made satisfaction for our sins. / 171

2 Christ formally made satisfaction for our sins. / 171
3 Christ made condign satisfaction for our sins. / 177
4 Christ made superabundant satisfaction for our sins. / 179
5 God directly willed Christ's satisfaction. / 181
6 It must be acknowledged that there is a certain transformative principle operative throughout the entire work of redemption. / 183
7 Christ's satisfaction is to be understood according to a sacramental analogy. / 185
8 Christ's satisfaction adds to his vicarious passion and death an expression of the utmost detestation for all sins and of extreme sorrow for all offense against God. / 191

**Thesis 17**: [Understanding the Mystery: The Law of the Cross.] This is why the Son of God became man, suffered, died, and was raised again: because divine wisdom has ordained and divine goodness has willed, not to do away with the evils of the human race through power, but to convert those same evils into a supreme good according to the just and mysterious law of the cross. / 197

*Meaning of the thesis, terms* / 197
*Theological note* / 207
*Opinions* / 207
*Preliminary note: The analogy of this question* / 219
*The argument* / 223
1 The law of the cross, first element: sin and death / 223
2 The law of the cross: the transformation of death / 225
3 The transformation of death has a twofold significance. / 225
4 This same transformation of death, understood in several ways, is required of us. / 227
5 The law of the cross is the law of the redemption. / 233
6 It was fitting for the Son of God to make the law of the cross his own. / 241
*Scholion 1: The purpose of the incarnation* / 251
*Scholion 2: The cause of sin* / 257

**Part Two: The Redemption: A Supplement** / 265

**1 Good and Evil** / 267
**Article 1**: On the good in general / 269
**Article 2**: The human good of order / 275

1 The good of order in human affairs / 275
2 How the human good of order progresses / 277
3 What is meant by 'higher culture'? / 281
**Article 3**: Signs / 289
**Article 4**: The comparison of goods / 295
**Article 5**: Evil / 301
**Article 6**: From evil, good / 317
**Article 7**: Human impotence / 327
**Article 8**: Original sin / 343

**2 The Justice of God** / 347
**Article 9**: The notion of divine justice / 349
**Article 10**: The just order of reality / 353
**Article 11**: The historical order of justice / 365
**Article 12**: The personal order of justice / 369
**Article 13**: The just will of God / 379
**Article 14**: Voluntarism and related errors / 393
**Article 15**: Recapitulation of the foregoing / 403

**3 The Death and Resurrection of Christ** / 411
**Article 16**: The death of Christ / 411
**Article 17**: The payment of the price / 419
**Article 18**: The sacrifice of the new covenant / 425
**Article 19**: Meritorious obedience / 431
**Article 20**: Vicarious suffering / 437
**Article 21**: The power of the resurrection / 441

**4 The Cross of Christ** / 449
**Article 22**: The meaning of the cross / 449
**Article 23**: The law of the cross / 455
**Article 24**: The mystery of the cross / 465
**Article 25**: The justice of the cross / 479

**5 The Satisfaction Made by Christ** / 495
**Article 26**: Division of the question / 495
**Article 27**: The notion of necessity / 501
**Article 28**: The notion of punishment / 503
**Article 29**: The punishment of Christ / 515
**Article 30**: Transference of punishment to Christ / 527
**Article 31**: The sacramental analogy / 537

**Article 32**: The sorrow of Christ / 543
**Article 33**: The satisfaction made by Christ / 547
**Article 34**: Superabundant satisfaction / 555

**6 [The Effects of the Redemption]** / 563
**Article 35**: The work of Christ / 563
**Article 36**: Agents acting through intellect / 571
**Article 37**: Social agents / 577
**Article 38**: Historical agents / 581
**Article 39**: Christ as agent / 587
**Article 40**: Christ the exemplar / 593
**Article 41**: Christ the head / 599
**Article 42**: Christ the historical agent / 609
**Article 43**: The mediator in heaven / 621
**Article 44**: The purpose of the incarnation / 625
**Article 45**: Why did God become man? / 631

**Appendix** / 645
**Article 44**: The purpose of the incarnation / 645

Abbreviations / 661

Bibliography of Modern Authors / 663

Scriptural Passages / 669

Index / 681

LATIN TEXT

**Pars V: De Redemptione** / 2
**[Introductio]** / 2
*Nota bibliographica* / 2

**Thesis 15**: Redemptio non solum finem dicit sed etiam mediationem, solutum nempe pretium, vicariam Christi mediatoris passionem et mortem propter peccata et pro peccatoribus, sacrificium a pontifice nostro in suo sanguine oblatum, meritoriam obedientiam, resuscitati Domini virtutem, et aeterni sacerdotis intercessionem. / 4

*Notiones* / 4
*Sensus theseos* / 4
*Termini* / 8
*Nota* / 8
*Adversarii* / 8
[*Praenotamina*] / 16
Praenotamen I: De morte Christi / 16
Praenotamen II: De voce 'redemptionis' / 24
Praenotamen III: De sensu vocis 'redemptionis' in NT / 26
[*Argumentum*] / 30
Pars prima: Redemptio dicit finem. / 30
Pars secunda: Redemptio non solum finem dicit sed etiam mediationem. / 34
Pars tertia: Redemptio-mediatio perspicitur in soluto pretio. / 38
Pars quarta: Redemptio-mediatio perspicitur in vicaria Christi passione et morte propter peccata et pro peccatoribus. / 44
Pars quinta: Redemptio-mediatio perspicitur in sacrificio a pontifice nostro in suo sanguine oblato. / 52
Pars sexta: Redemptio-mediatio perspicitur in obedientia. / 58
Pars septima: Redemptio-mediatio perspicitur tum in virtute Domini resuscitati tum in intercessione aeterni sacerdotis. / 64
*Scholion: De modis et effectibus redemptionis* / 76

**Thesis 16**: De Satisfactione Christi. Christus pro peccatis nostris non solum condigne sed etiam superabundanter satisfecit; quae quidem satisfactio secundum analogiam sacramentalem intelligitur; et ideo vicariae passioni et morti addit expressionem summae detestationis omnium peccatorum et summi doloris de omni offensa Dei. / 78
*Termini* / 78
*Magisterium* / 80
*Nota* / 80
*Sensus theseos* / 82
*Sententiae* / 86
[*Praenotamina*] / 106
Praenotamen I: Sententia Anselmiana / 106
Praenotamen II: Aut satisfactio aut poena / 110
Praenotamen III: Aut venia aut poena / 112
Praenotamen IV: Culpa, offensa, poena / 116
Praenotamen V: Satisfactio, venia, remissio poenae / 122

Praenotamen VI: Satisfactio vicaria / 126
Praenotamen VII: De Dei iustitia / 132
Praenotamen VIII: De ordine divinae iustitiae redintegrando seu reparando / 138
Praenotamen IX: Problema integrationis / 142
Praenotamen X: Problema cohaerentiae / 152
Praenotamen XI: De mentalitate symbolica / 168
*Argumentum* / 172
1 Christus materialiter satisfecit pro peccatis nostris. / 172
2 Christus formaliter pro peccatis nostris satisfecit. / 172
3 Christus pro nostris peccatis condigne satisfecit. / 176
4 Christus pro nostris peccatis superabundanter satisfecit. / 178
5 Deus directe voluit satisfactionem Christi. / 180
6 In toto redemptionis opere agnoscendum est quoddam quasi principium transformationis. / 182
7 Satisfactio Christi intelligitur secundum analogiam sacramentalem. / 184
8 Satisfactio Christi vicariae passioni et morti addit expressionem summae detestationis omnium peccatorum et summi doloris de omni offensa Dei. / 190

**Thesis 17**: Dei Filius ideo homo factus, passus, mortuus, et resuscitatus est, quia divina sapientia ordinavit et divina bonitas voluit, non per potentiam mala generis humani auferre, sed secundum iustam atque mysteriosam crucis legem eadem mala in summum quoddam bonum convertere. / 196

*Sensus theseos, termini* / 196
*Nota* / 206
*Sententiae* / 206
*Praenotamen: De analogia huius quaestionis* / 218
*Argumentum* / 222
1 Lex crucis, primum elementum: de peccato et morte / 222
2 Lex crucis: mortis transformatio / 224
3 Mortis transformatio duo importat / 224
4 Eadem mortis transformatio multipliciter intellecta nobis praecipitur. / 226
5 Lex crucis est lex redemptionis. / 232
6 Quod convenienter Dei Filius legem crucis suam fecit. / 240

*Scholion I: De fine incarnationis* / 250
*Scholion II: De causa peccati* / 256

**[Part Two: The Redemption]** / 265

1 **Caput Primum: De Bono et Malo** / 266
**Articulus I**: De bono in genere / 268
**Articulus II**: De bono ordinis humano / 274
*1 Quale sit bonum ordinis in rebus humanis* / 274
*2 Quemadmodum humanum ordinis bonum proficiat* / 276
*3 Quaenam sit quae dicitur cultura superior* / 280
**Articulus III**: De signis / 288
**Articulus IV**: De comparatione bonorum / 294
**Articulus V**: De malo / 300
**Articulus VI**: E malis bonum / 316
**Articulus VII**: De impotentia humana / 326
**Articulus VIII**: De peccato originali / 342

2 **Caput Alterum: De Iustitia Dei** / 346
**Articulus IX**: De notione divinae iustitiae / 348
**Articulus X**: De iusto rerum ordine / 352
**Articulus XI**: De ordine iustitiae historico / 364
**Articulus XII**: De ordine iustitiae personali / 368
**Articulus XIII**: De iusta Dei voluntate / 378
**Articulus XIV**: De voluntarismo affinibusque erroribus / 392
**Articulus XV**: Praecedentium recapitulatio / 402

**Caput Tertium: De Christo Mortuo et Resurrecto** / 410
**Articulus XVI**: De morte Christi / 410
**Articulus XVII**: De pretii solutione / 418
**Articulus XVIII**: De sacrificio Novi Testamenti / 424
**Articulus XIX**: De obedientia meritoria / 430
**Articulus XX**: De vicaria passione / 436
**Articulus XXI**: De virtute resurrectionis / 440

**Caput Quartum: De Cruce Christi** / 448
**Articulus XXII**: De ratione crucis / 448
**Articulus XXIII**: De lege crucis / 454
**Articulus XXIV**: De mysterio crucis / 464
**Articulus XXV**: De iustitia crucis / 478

**Caput Quintum: De Satisfactione Christi** / 494
**Articulus xxvi**: Dividitur quaestio / 494
**Articulus xxvii**: De ratione necessitatis / 500
**Articulus xxviii**: De ratione poenae / 502
**Articulus xxix**: De poena Christi / 514
**Articulus xxx**: De poenis in Christum translatis / 526
**Articulus xxxi**: De analogia sacramentali / 536
**Articulus xxxii**: De dolore Christi / 542
**Articulus xxxiii**: De satisfactione Christi / 546
**Articulus xxxiv**: De satisfactione superabundante / 554

**Caput Sextum** / 562
**Articulus xxxv**: De opere Christi / 562
**Articulus xxxvi**: De agente per intellectum / 570
**Articulus xxxvii**: De agente sociali / 576
**Articulus xxxviii**: De agente historico / 580
**Articulus xxxix**: De Christo agente / 586
**Articulus xl**: De Christo exemplari / 592
**Articulus xli**: De Christo capite / 598
**Articulus xlii**: De Christo agente historico / 608
**Articulus xliii**: De mediatore caelesti / 620
**Articulus xliv**: De fine incarnationis / 624
**Articulus xlv**: Cur Deus homo / 630

**Appendix** / 644
**Articulus xliv**: De fine incarnationis / 644

# General Editors' Preface

Volume 9 in Collected Works of Bernard Lonergan combines two distinct texts.

Part 1 presents theses 15 to 17 from Lonergan's 1964 text *De Verbo incarnato.* The first fourteen theses of *De Verbo incarnato* constitute volume 8 in the Collected Works, *The Incarnate Word.* Those theses make up parts 1 to 4 of the original Latin text: The Teaching of the New Testament on the Hypostatic Union (thesis 1), The Teaching of the Ecumenical Councils on the Hypostatic Union (theses 2 to 5), Theological Conclusions regarding the Hypostatic Union (theses 6 to 10), and What Belongs Properly to Christ (theses 11 to 14). Part 5, The Redemption, comprises the three theses included here.

Part 2 of this volume presents a distinct manuscript on the redemption that Lonergan wrote in the late 1950s, completing it probably in 1958. Frederick E. Crowe has made my work in composing this Preface easy. In fact, a much more complete 'General Editors' Preface' to part 2 can be found on pages 99–125 in Frederick E. Crowe's *Christ and History,*[1] and especially on pages 99–102, where Crowe presents all but definitive evidence on the date of this manuscript and background information regarding its title. I cannot improve on Crowe's comments regarding the date of the manuscript, and so I leave it to readers to consult them. Lonergan left the title somewhat ambiguous, and the editors have adapted Michael Shields's

1 Frederick E. Crowe, *Christ and History: The Christology of Bernard Lonergan from 1935 to 1982* (Toronto: University of Toronto Press, 2015).

suggestion of 'De redemptione supplementum quoddam' and have simply called it 'De redemptione' and, in English, 'The Redemption.'

In addition to Crowe's treatment of the 1958 manuscript in *Christ and History*, attention must be called to a dissertation written at Marquette University by John Volk and defended there in 2011, 'Lonergan on the Historical Causality of Christ: An Interpretation of *The Redemption*: A Supplement to *De Verbo Incarnato*.' Between Crowe's treatment and Volk's much longer interpretation, readers will find quite sufficient commentary on the manuscript that forms part 2 of the present volume. Volk's dissertation can be found on the website www.lonerganresource.com, under 'Scholarly Works/Dissertations.'

Why are the two texts combined here into one volume? The answer is quite simple. At some point in the development of the prospectus for the Collected Works, Frederick Crowe and I realized that the full text of *De Verbo incarnato*, with Latin and English facing pages, would be an enormously large publication, most likely over a thousand pages, and at that point we decided to place theses 15 to 17, which treat the topic of redemption, together with Lonergan's distinct text on the same topic.

Several hands and heads have gone into the production of this volume. Michael Shields went over the work of translating part 2 several times, and H. Daniel Monsour worked with him on the text of part 2, editing the translation, tracking down references, and providing most of the editorial comments found in footnotes. Michael Shields also worked on a translation of part 1. Even though Charles Hefling had already provided a quite adequate translation of part 1 that has been circulating privately in Lonergan circles for some time, Shields thought that consistency with his translation of part 2 called for his own work on part 1. I have been over the entire manuscript many times, and each time have made some changes in the translation and added further editorial comments. Jeremy Wilkins provided the final editorial work, once again, as he did with volume 8, making the volume a far better production than it would have been without his contribution. As I wrote in the General Editors' Preface to volume 8, 'The final product is the work of many hands, but as General Editor I take responsibility, for better or for worse, for adjudicating the various contributions.'

Lonergan did not put any footnotes in his text of the theses from *De Verbo incarnato*, and so all footnotes in part 1 of the present volume are editorial. The autograph of part 2 contains references in the margins, and footnotes for some of the chapters are also provided in separate items

found in the Archives. Editorial additions to the footnotes in part 2 are placed in brackets.

We have used the New Revised Standard Version as the default translation of the Bible unless reason was found to supply an alternate translation. In general the *Oxford American Dictionary* and the *Chicago Manual of Style* were relied on throughout, though not rigidly.

Once again I thank Marquette University for allowing me to remain for so many years in the Emmett Doerr Chair in Systematic Theology, where I have had the time needed to do the work of bringing these volumes to completion.

ROBERT M. DORAN
Marquette University

PART ONE

# Theses 15–17 of *De Verbo Incarnato* (Part 5: The Redemption)

PARS V

# De Redemptione

## [Introductio]

Tria praecipue considerantur themata. Primo, ipsa NT doctrina exponitur (thesi 15a). Deinde, ad dogma[1] de satisfactione Christi proceditur (thesi 16a). Tertio, quaestiones moventur theologicae quae ad imperfectam quandam mysterii intelligentiam acquirendam proponi solent (thesi 17a).

### *Nota bibliographica*

Bibliographia fundamentalis: J. Rivière, *Le dogme de la Rédemption dans la théologie contemporaine* (Albi, 1948) v–xix. Eadem bibl. sed minus recens apud DTC XIII (26) 1992–2004.

Bibliographia acatholica anglice: T.H. Hughes, *The Atonement*, London, 1949, 325–26.

B. Xiberta, *De Verbo Incarnato*, Madrid, 1954, II, 719–31.

# PART 5

# [of *De Verbo Incarnato*]: The Redemption

**[Introduction]**

Three main themes will be considered here. In the first thesis (15), we present the teaching of the New Testament on the redemption; in the second (16), we proceed to the dogma[1] concerning the satisfaction made by Christ; in the third (17), we take up theological questions that are customarily raised in order to acquire some understanding, however imperfect, of this mystery.

***Bibliographical note***

Basic bibliography: Jean Rivière, *Le dogme de la Rédemption dans la théologie contemporaine* (Albi: Chanoine Lombard, 1948) v–xix. The same bibliography, though less recent, can be found in Jean Rivière, 'Rédemption,' DTC XIII (26) 1992–2004 [henceforth Rédemption'].

For English bibliography of non-Catholic authors, see: Thomas Hywel Hughes, *The Atonement: Modern Theories of the Doctrine* (London: George Allen & Unwin, 1949) 325–26.

Bartholomeus M. Xiberta, *Tractatus de Verbo Incarnato*, vol. 2: *Soteriologia* (Madrid: Consejo Superior de Investigaciones Científicas, Instituto 'Franciscus Suárez,' 1954) 719–31.

1 Although Lonergan uses the word 'dogma' here, this should be qualified by what he says in the theological note for the next thesis. See below, p. 81.

G. Oggioni, *Problemi e orientamenti di teologia dommatica,* Milano, 1957, II, 329–43.

D. Bertetto, *Gesù redentore,* Firenze, 1958, 552–53, 634–36, 714, 778.

L. Richard, *Le mystère de la Rédemption,* Desclée, 1959, v–vii.

## THESIS 15

**Redemptio non solum finem dicit sed etiam mediationem, solutum nempe pretium, vicariam Christi mediatoris passionem et mortem propter peccata et pro peccatoribus, sacrificium a pontifice nostro in suo sanguine oblatum, meritoriam obedientiam, resuscitati Domini virtutem, et aeterni sacerdotis intercessionem.**

### *Notiones*

*Redemptio ut finis:* est status redemptorum; redempti autem sunt qui, a praeteritis malis liberati, collatis bonis fruuntur.

*Redemptio ut mediatio:* respicit processum ad finem (medium = id quod est ad finem); dicit interventum personae ut finis attingatur.

*Vicarius:* (1) communiter, is qui agit vice alterius, pro alio, loco alterius; (2) specialiter, is qui patitur vice alterius, pro alio, quodammodo loco alterius.

### *Sensus theseos*

1 Thesis affirmat redemptionem ut finem: exsistit nempe status redemptorum, qui a potestate tenebrarum, a timore mortis, a peccatis, a poenis liberati, repromissionem Abrahae factam accipiunt, Deo reconciliantur, iustificantur, inhabitantem Spiritum sanctum et filiorum adoptionem habent, cum fiducia ad Deum accedunt, spe sunt salvati, resurrectionem carnis, gloriae coronam, aeternam cum Christo vitam exspectant.

Giulio Oggioni, 'Il mistero della redenzione,' in *Problemi e orientamenti di teologia dommatica*, vol. 2 (Milan: Marzorati, 1957) 237–343 [at 329–43].

Domenico Bertetto, *Gesù redentore: cristologia* (Florence: Libreria Editrice Fiorentina, 1958) 552–53, 634–36, 714, 778.

Louis Richard, *Le mystère de la Rédemption* (Tournai: Desclée, 1959) v–vii. [English translation: *The Mystery of the Redemption*, trans. Joseph Horn, with a foreword by Frank B. Norris (Baltimore and Dublin: Helicon Press, 1966) 353–56; suggested additional readings 357–58.]

## THESIS 15

**'Redemption' denotes not only an end but also a mediation, namely, the payment of the price, Christ the mediator's vicarious passion and death on account of sins and for sinners, our high priest's sacrifice offered in his blood, his meritorious obedience, the power of the risen Lord, and the intercession of the eternal priest.**

### *Notions*

*Redemption considered as an end* is the state of the redeemed; the redeemed are those who, having been delivered from past evils, are enjoying the good things given to them.

*Redemption as a mediation* regards the process towards the end (a 'means' is that which is to or for an end) and refers to the intervention of a person in order to attain the end.

*Vicarious*: (1) in a general sense, one who acts in the stead of another, for another, in place of another; (2) in a special sense, one who suffers in the stead of another, for another, in some way in place of another.

### *Meaning of the thesis*

1 This thesis affirms redemption as an end; namely, there exists the state of the redeemed, those who, having been delivered from the power of darkness, from the fear of death, from sins, from punishments, receive the promise made to Abraham, are reconciled to God, are justified, enjoy the indwelling Holy Spirit and adoptive filiation, approach God with confidence, are saved in hope, and await the resurrection of the body, the crown of glory, and everlasting life with Christ.

2 Thesis affirmat redemptionem non solum ut finem sed etiam ut mediationem. Passio ergo et mors, resurrectio et Domini resuscitati potentia atque intercessio sunt in ordine ad finem. Neque sunt in ordine ad finem tantummodo per modum cuiusdam medii sed etiam per modum interventus personalis. Quo in interventu elucent habitudines interpersonales inter Christum et Deum Patrem, inter Christum et peccatores, inter Christum et iustificatos.

3 Thesis affirmat mediationem vicarii non solum agentis sed etiam patientis. Agit quidem vicarius qui ipse pretium solvit; sed idem patitur quia pretium solvendum est 'dare animam suam.' Agit ut peccata tollantur, auferantur, deleantur; sed patitur quia peccatum est, peccatur, peccabitur. Agit pro peccatoribus, h.e., in beneficium peccatoribus collatum quorum peccata remittuntur; sed etiam patitur pro peccatoribus secundum mysterium crucis. Agit ut sacerdos qui sacrificium offert; sed patitur ut victima quae offertur. Agit per meritum suae obedientiae ut iusti constituantur multi; sed etiam patitur quia passio obedienti praecepta est. Agit ut Dominus sedens ad dexteram Patris; sed intercessio aeterni sacerdotis victimam semel oblatam recolit.

4 Tria quae in thesi asseruntur non pari attentione considerantur.

Redemptio ut finis in aliis tractatibus theologicis secundum varios eius aspectus plenius consideratur, ubi de ecclesia, de peccato originali, de impotentia morali peccatoris, de gratia et virtutibus, de novissimis, de sacramentis. Quae sane omnia non hic sunt iteranda sed potius praesupponenda.

Factum mediationis prout in scripturis clare et explicite proponitur est principale nostrum obiectum, et cum aspectus vicarii agentis facilius intelligatur, ad vicarium qua patientem magis quodammodo est attendendum.

Neque tamen nunc agitur de vicaria passione intelligenda, sed de certitudine ipsius facti ex textibus scripturisticis attingenda. Quam ob causam, non solum speculationes theologorum ab hac thesi excluduntur, sed etiam ipsum dogma Catholicum de satisfactione Christi nisi implicite hic non proponitur.

Denique tandem contra tendentiam rationalisticam non sane patentem sed facile latentem lectores monemus. Non eatenus in scripturis vel ab ecclesia docetur vicaria Christi passio, quatenus haec doctrina clare, distincte,

2 The thesis affirms redemption not only as an end but also as a mediation. Thus, the passion and death of Christ, his resurrection, and the power and intercession of the risen Lord are ordered to the end. They are ordered to the end not only as means but also by way of a personal intervention. In this intervention are clearly revealed the interpersonal relations between Christ and God the Father, between Christ and sinners, and between Christ and the justified.

3 The thesis affirms the mediation on the part of one who not only acts vicariously but also suffers vicariously. He acts vicariously in paying a price himself, but he also suffers because the price to be paid is 'to give his own life.' He acts in order to cancel, take away, wipe out sins; but he suffers because sins have been committed, are being committed, are going to be committed. He acts for sinners, that is, in order to confer a benefit upon sinners whose sins are forgiven; but he also suffers for sinners in accord with the mystery of the cross. He acts as the priest who offers a sacrifice; but he suffers as the victim who is offered. He acts by virtue of the merit of his obedience in order that many may be made just; but he also suffers because suffering was commanded for the obedient one. He acts as the Lord sitting at the right hand of the Father; but the intercession of the eternal Priest recalls the victim offered once.

4 The three assertions made in this thesis are not given equal attention.

Various aspects of redemption as an end are considered more fully in other theological treatises, those dealing with the church, original sin, the moral impotence of the sinner, grace and the virtues, the last things, and the sacraments. Here, all these will be presupposed rather than repeated.

Our main concern is with the fact of mediation as it is clearly and explicitly presented in scripture, and since the aspect of a vicarious agent is more easily understood than that of the vicarious sufferer, we need to pay somewhat more attention to the latter.

Neither are we concerned, at this point, with understanding vicarious suffering, but rather with reaching certitude about the simple fact of it from the biblical texts. For this reason, not only are the speculations of theologians excluded from this thesis, but also the Catholic dogma itself concerning Christ's satisfaction is presented here only implicitly.

Finally, we would warn our readers against what may easily be a covert if not an overt tendency towards rationalism. The vicarious suffering of Christ is not taught in scripture or by the church in such a manner that this

exacte, cohaerenter intelligitur atque explicatur. Mysteriorum plena intelligentia est non fidelium sed Dei; neque eatenus sunt credenda mysteria quatenus intelliguntur; sed simpliciter sunt credenda sive aliquatenus sive nullatenus intelliguntur.

Neve quis tale monitum iudicet superfluum. Qui enim arbitrantur vicariam Christi passionem subsumi sub principio quodam per se noto quoad nos, ii negant hanc vicariam passionem esse mysterium. Qui facilius rem explicant atque in explicando deficiunt, occasionem haereticis praebent ut vera revelata facilius impugnent. Quod quidem iam esse factum, non sine probabilitate diceretur, si quidem doctrinae Lutheranae ex scholasticismo decadente originem quoddammodo ducunt, et a doctrinis Lutheranis reactio socinianorum, rationalistarum, liberalium, modernistarum aliquatenus intelligitur.

### *Termini*

In genere termini sunt scripturistici atque in illo sensu concreto intelligendi qui e scripturis clare habetur et in probatione exponetur.

*finis, mediatio, vicarius*: iam supra sunt explicata.

*peccatum*: actus humanus malus; ubi malitia praecipue attendenda est theologica, et in offensa Dei consistit.

*peccator*: qui peccavit.

*meritum*: opus praemio dignum.

*virtus*: potentia, potestas, quae a Domino sedente ad dexteram Patris exercetur.

### *Nota*

De fide divina et catholica. I.e., clare in scripturis continetur et in universali praedicatione ecclesiae auditur.

### *Adversarii*

1 Plura e bibliographiis facile colliguntur. Prima pars operis L. Richard historica est, ad quam remittimus. Opus acatholicum utile invenimus: R.S. Franks, *A History of the Doctrine of the Work of Christ*, 2 vol., London, New York, Toronto, 1918.

doctrine is clearly, distinctly, exactly, coherently understood and explained. Full understanding of mysteries belongs not to believers but to God. Nor are the mysteries to be believed only to the extent that they are understood; they are simply to be believed whether they are understood to some degree or not understood at all.

This is no idle warning. Those who think that the vicarious suffering of Christ falls under a principle that is self-evident to us deny that this vicarious suffering is a mystery. Those who explain matters in too facile a manner and fail in so explaining provide heretics with an occasion for more easily attacking revealed truths. It may indeed be said with considerable probability that this has happened already, if indeed the doctrines of the Lutherans in some way owe their origin to a decadent Scholasticism, and the doctrines of the Socinians, rationalists, liberals, and modernists can to some extent be understood as a reaction against Lutheranism.

### *Terms*

In general, the terms are scriptural and are to be understood in that concrete sense that they clearly have in scripture and that will be set out in the proof.

*end, mediation, vicarious*: as explained above.

*sin*: a morally evil human act; the evil considered here is chiefly theological and consists in an offense against God.

*sinner*: one who has committed sin.

*merit*: a deed deserving of reward.

*power*: might, strength, exercised by the Lord sitting at the right hand of the Father.

### *Theological note*

The thesis is of divine and Catholic faith; that is, it is clearly contained in scripture and preached throughout the church.

### *Opponents of the thesis*

1 One may easily gather a lot from the works cited in the bibliography. The first part of Richard's book is historical, and we refer the reader to it. *A History of the Doctrine of the Work of Christ in Its Ecclesiastical Development*, 2 vols. (London, New York, Toronto: Hodder & Stoughton, 1918), by Robert S. Franks, a non-Catholic, is a work we have found useful.

2 Sententiarum radices in Nestorianismo et Pelagianismo iam habebantur.

Qui enim Christi divinitatem negant, Christi opus intelligere recteque aestimare nequeunt. Vide damnationem Theodori Mopsuesteni (DB 225, DS 435), ubi Christiani ad Christum comparantur, sicut Platonici ad Platonem, Manichaei ad Manichaeum, Epicurei ad Epicurum, Marcionistae ad Marcionem.

Qui autem necessitatem gratiae qua sanantis et qua elevantis negant etiam necessitatem redemptionis haud explicare possunt. Unde si nihilominus redemptionem quandam agnoscunt, eam tum ut finem tum ut mediationem tum maxime ut mediationem vicarii patientis secundum haereticam quandam simplificationem exponere solent.

Ne tamen concludas, Nestorianos et Pelagianos de facto perspexisse nexum inter suas sententias et falsam de redemptione doctrinam et ideo explicite ipsam redemptionem impugnasse. Cf. J. Rivière, RHE 41 (1946) 5–43.

3 *Abaelardus*, ob. 1142; Richard, 137–39; Franks, I, 185–92.

Damnatus a c. Senonensi et ab Innocente II (DB 387, DS 721) quia negavit Christum carnem assumpsisse ut nos a iugo diaboli liberaret (DB 371, DS 723), nos non solum poenam sed etiam culpam ex Adamo contraxisse (DB 376, DS 728).

Postea a liberalibus praesertim celebratus est tamquam praecursor *theoriae moralis influentiae* seu *theoriae subiectivae* de redemptione.

Docuit quidem Christum nos redimere inquantum divinum amorem nobis manifestavit, unde nos ad amorem excitati remissionem peccatorum attingimus. Expositio in Epist. ad Romanos, lib. II, ML 178, 833–36, praesertim 836 B: 'Redemptio itaque nostra est illa summa in nobis per passionem Christi dilectio, quae non solum a servitute peccati liberat sed veram nobis filiorum Dei libertatem acquirit, ut amore eius potius quam timore cuncta impleamus.'[2]

2 The roots of the opposed opinions were already present in Nestorianism and Pelagianism.

Those who deny the divinity of Christ cannot understand and correctly judge Christ's work. See the condemnation of Theodore of Mopsuestia (DB 225, DS 435, [ND 621]), who taught that Christians are to Christ as Platonists to Plato, Manicheans to Manes, Epicureans to Epicurus, and Marcionists to Marcion.

On the other hand, those who deny the necessity of grace as healing and as elevating are quite incapable of explaining the need for redemption. Hence, if nonetheless they do acknowledge some sort of redemption, they usually explain it – as an end and as a mediation, and especially as the mediation of a vicarious sufferer – in reliance on some heretical simplification.

Nevertheless, one must not conclude that Nestorians and Pelagians in fact saw the connection between their opinions and a false doctrine on the redemption and therefore explicitly rejected the redemption itself. See J. Rivière, 'Hétérodoxie des Pélagiens en fait de rédemption?' *Revue d'Histoire Ecclésiastique* 41 (1946) 5–43.

3 *Peter Abelard* (1079–1142). See Richard, *Le mystère de la Rédemption* 137–39 [*The Mystery of the Redemption* 183–85]; Franks, *A History of the Doctrine of the Work of Christ*, vol. 1, 185–92.

Abelard was condemned at the Council of Sens and by Innocent II (DB 387, DS 721) for having denied that Christ assumed flesh in order to free us from the yoke of the devil (DB 371, DS 723), and that we have contracted from Adam not only punishment but also fault (DB 376, DS 728).

Subsequently he was hailed especially by liberals as a precursor of *the theory of moral influence*, or *the subjective theory* of redemption.

He taught that Christ redeems us in that he has manifested to us God's love, so that we, having been aroused to love, attain forgiveness for our sins. See his commentary on Romans, book 2 (ML 178, 833–36), especially the following (836 B): 'Our redemption is that deeper affection in us through Christ's suffering which not only frees us from slavery to sin but also wins for us the true liberty of sons of God, so that we do all things out of love of him rather than fear.'[2]

2 *Library of Christian Classics*, vol. 10, *A Scholastic Miscellany: Anselm to Ockham*, ed. and trans. Eugene R. Fairweather (Philadelphia: Westminster, 1956) 284, slightly modified.

Quae gravior simplificatio aliquatenus intelligitur ubi recolitur eo tempore (1) nondum inter gratiam habitualem et actualem communiter distingui, (2) nondum esse excogitatum theorema de duobus ordinibus, naturali et supernaturali, et (3) nondum esse evolutam consequentem distinctionem inter methodum philosophicam et theologicam.

4 *Unitarii*, seu *Sociniani*. Richard 161–63; Franks, II, 13–33.

Damnati implicite a Paulo IV, anno 1555 (DB 993, DS 1880); haec damnatio renovata est a Clemente VIII, anno 1603 (vide n. 2 ad DB 993, DS 1880); etiam damnati sunt a Calvino.

Nominantur a Lelio Sozzini, ob. 1562, et a Fausto Sozzini, prioris nepote, ob. 1604.

SS. Trinitatem, DNIC divinitatem, BVM perpetuam virginitatem negaverunt; insuper docuerunt 'eundem Dominum et Deum nostrum non subiisse acerbissimam crucis mortem ut nos a peccatis et ab aeterna morte liberaret et Patri ad vitam aeternam reconciliaret.'

5 *Rationalistae* christianam de redemptione doctrinam secundum principia generalia et anthropologica et omnibus religionibus communia intelligunt atque explicant. Ita communiter hodie inter infideles psychologos, anthropologicos, historicos, religionis philosophos.

6 *Liberales* a rationalistis differunt quatenus traditione christiana imbuti valorem quendam specialem, immo supremum, in christianismo reponunt. Qui tamen valor qualis sit, alii aliter explicant ut tamen Christus sit homo quidam eximius et vita christiana sit excellentia quaedam humana.

*Schleiermacher*, 1768–1834; Richard 165–66; Franks, II, 225–59. Religionem ad conscientiam religiosam reduxit; Christo plenitudinem conscientiae religiosae attribuit; redemptionem posuit in communicatione conscientiae religiosae a Christo in fideles.

This very serious simplification is somewhat understandable when we recall that at that time (1) habitual and actual grace had not yet been generally distinguished, (2) the theorem concerning two orders, the natural and the supernatural, had not yet been thought through, and (3) the consequent distinction between philosophical and theological method had not yet been developed.

4 *Unitarians,* or *Socinians.* See Richard, *Le mystère de la Rédemption* 161–63 [*The Mystery of the Redemption* 215–17]; Franks, *A History of the Doctrine of the Work of Christ,* vol. 2, 13–33.

They were implicitly condemned by Paul IV in 1555 (DB 993, DS 1880, [ND 648]); this condemnation was repeated by Clement VIII in 1603 (DB 993, note 2, DS 1880). They were also condemned by Calvin.

They are named after Lelio Sozzini (1525–1562) and his nephew Fausto Sozzini (1539–1604).

They denied the Trinity, the divinity of Christ, and the perpetual virginity of Mary. Moreover, they taught that 'the same Lord our God did not undergo a most bitter death on the cross in order to free us from sins and from eternal death and to reconcile us to the Father for life everlasting.'

5 *Rationalists* understand and explain the Christian doctrine of redemption by way of general anthropological principles that are common to all religions. Today this is the usual approach among unbelieving psychologists, anthropologists, historians, and philosophers of religion.

6 *Liberals* differ from rationalists in that, being steeped in Christian tradition, they attach a special, indeed the highest, value to Christianity. What this value may be is explained in various ways, yet so that Christ is an outstanding human being and the Christian life a human excellence.

Friedrich Schleiermacher (1768–1834). See Richard, *Le mystère de la Rédemption* 165–66 [*The Mystery of the Redemption* 219–20]; Franks, *A History of the Doctrine of the Work of Christ,* vol. 2, 225–59. He reduced religion to religious consciousness, attributed to Christ the fullness of religious consciousness, and located redemption in a communication of religious consciousness from Christ to believers.

A. Ritschl, 1822–1889, *Unterricht in der christlichen Religion*;[3] *Die christliche Lehre von der Rechtfertigung und Versöhnung*, 3 vols., edit. 1, 1870 et 1874.[4] Richard 166, n. 1; Franks, II, 329–51.

Doctrinam Schleiermacher perfecit quatenus ad dimensionem socialem conscientiae religiosae attendit; communitatem in conscientia religiosa fundatam cum regno Dei biblico identificavit; Christus mediator remissionem peccatorum efficit quatenus ipse quam arctissime cum Deo coniungitur et ex suo munere habet alios ita in similem habitudinem ad Deum recipiendos, ut recepti non iam a fiducia in Deum et a communione cum Deo per propria peccata impediantur.

A. Réville, *De la rédemption. Études historiques et dogmatiques*, Paris, 1859. A. Sabatier, *La doctrine de l'expiation et son évolution historique*, Paris, 1903, anglice, 1904. Vide Richard 166–67.

Distinguunt tria stadia: stadium mythicum (iura diaboli); stadium iuridicum (satisfactio Anselmiana); et stadium morale (opinio liberalium). Non datur essentialis differentia inter mortem Christi et mortem Socratis. Ex solidaritate humana peccaminosa mortuus est Christus ut nos de nostris peccatis poeniteat et a Deo Patre per fidem peccatorum remissionem habeamus.

H. Rashdall, *The Idea of the Atonement in Christian Theology*, 1915 (Bampton Lectures). R. S. Franks, *A History of the Doctrine of the Work of Christ*, 1918; *The Atonement*, 1934. D.M. Edwards, *Bannau'r Ffydd*. Vix breviter exponuntur;

Albrecht Ritschl (1822–1829), author of *Unterricht in der christlichen Religion*[3] and *Die christliche Lehre von der Rechtfertigung und Versöhnung* (3 volumes, 1870–74).[4] See Richard, *Le mystère de la Rédemption* 166, n. 1 [*The Mystery of the Redemption* 221, n. 27]; Franks, *A History of the Doctrine of the Work of Christ*, vol. 2, 329–51.

Ritschl improved upon Schleiermacher's doctrine in directing attention to the social dimension of religious consciousness. He identified a community founded upon religious consciousness with the biblical reign of God; Christ the mediator brings about the remission of sins inasmuch as he is joined most intimately to God and from his service is able to receive others into a similar relationship with God, so that those received are no longer prevented by their sins from trusting in God and from communion with God.

Albert Réville [1826–1906], author of *De la rédemption: Études historiques et dogmatiques* (Paris: Joel Cherbuliez, 1859) and *Auguste Sabatier* [1839–1901], author of *Le doctrine de l'expiation et son évolution historique* (Paris: Librairie Fischbacher, 1903) [in English, *The Doctrine of the Atonement and Its Historical Evolution* (New York: Putnam, 1904)]. See Richard, *Le mystère de la Rédemption* 166–67 [*The Mystery of the Redemption* 221–23].

They distinguish three stages: the mythic stage (the devil's rights), the juridical stage (Anselmian satisfaction), and the moral stage (the opinion of the liberals). There is no essential difference between the death of Christ and the death of Socrates. Out of solidarity with sinful humanity Christ died so that we might repent of our sins and through faith receive forgiveness from God the Father.

No brief exposition can be given of the works of H. Rashdall, *The Idea of Atonement in Christian Theology* (Bampton Lectures, 1915; London: Macmillan, 1925), R.S. Franks, *A History of the Doctrine of the Work of Christ* (1918 [see above,

3 Albrecht Ritschl, *Unterricht in der christlichen Religion* (Bonn: A. Marcus, 1875). Lonergan's text referred to a third edition published in 1886 (Bonn: A. Marcus). There is an English translation by Alice Mead Swing of a fourth, 1895 edition in Albert Temple Swing, *The Theology of Albrecht Ritschl, Together with Instruction in the Christian Religion* (London and New York: Longmans, Green, 1901). There is a more recent German version edited from the first, 1875 edition by Gerhard Ruhbach (Gütersloh: Gütersloher Verlagshaus Gerd Mohn, 1966).

4 Albrecht Ritschl, *Die christliche Lehre von der Rechtfertigung und Versöhnung*, 3 vols. (Bonn: A. Marcus, 1870–74). In English, Albrecht Ritschl, *The Christian Doctrine of Justification and Reconciliation: The Positive Development of the Doctrine*, trans. and ed. H.R. Mackintosh and A.B. Macaulay (Edinburgh: T.&T. Clark, 1900).

sunt tendentiae liberalis secundum T.H. Hughes, 200–29; de Rashdall tamen dicit Rivière, bibliographie, vii, 'd'inspiration plutôt ecclésiastique et traditionnelle.'

6 *Modernistae* (DB 2038, DS 3438) negaverunt piacularem Domini nostri mortem esse doctrinam evangelicam; eam a S. Paulo inventam habuerunt.

***[Praenotamina]***

PRAENOTAMEN I: DE MORTE CHRISTI

1 Cum mors Christi multipliciter consideretur, operae pretium esse videtur quam brevissime ea praemittere quae sunt et clara et certa et communiter agnita.

2 Mortem Christi effecerunt causae secundae: proditor Iudas (Mc 14.21, 14.43), summi sacerdotes (Mc 14.55–64), turba Hierosolymitana a pontificibus concitata (Mc 15.11–14), Pilatus volens populo satisfacere (Mc 15.15), milites (Mc 15.16, 15.21–24), et si consentientes secundum Paulum (Rom 1.32) addis, praetereuntes et blasphemantes (Mc 15.29–31).

3 Eiusdem mortis causalitatem historicam exhibet S. Ioannes, qui non solum continuam Iudaeorum oppositionem narrat (Io 5.16–18, 6.52–53, 6.60, 6.66, 6.70, 7.12–13, 7.20, 7.31–32, 7.45–49, 7.51–52, 8.48–59, 9.16, 9.22, 9.30–34, 10.19–21, 10.31, 10.39, 11.46–53, 11.56, 12.19, 12.42–43), sed etiam ea altiora principia proponit quae hanc oppositionem communi rerum humanarum cursu fere necessariam fuisse suadent.

Christus enim Dei Verbum erat lux vera quae illuminat omnem hominem (1.9), lux mundi (8.12), in hoc natus est et ad hoc venit in mundum ut testimonium perhiberet veritati (18.37), et testimonium quidem perhibuit, Ioanne Baptista maius, testimonium nempe Dei Patris, scripturarum, Moysis (5.36–46).

At homines magis tenebras quam lucem diligunt; mala enim sunt opera eorum (3.19–21, 7.7); ideo dixit Dominus, 'Sermo meus non capit in vobis'

p. xxx]) and *The Atonement* (Oxford: Oxford University Press, 1934), and D.M. Edwards, *Bannau'r Ffydd* (Wrexham: Hughes & Son, 1929). According to T.H. Hughes (*The Atonement: Modern Theories of the Doctrine* 200–29) they have liberal tendencies, but Rivière (p. vii of his bibliography) says of Rashdall's book that 'its inspiration is thoroughly ecclesiastical and traditional.'

7 The *Modernists* (DB 2038, DS 3438, [ND 650/38]) denied that our Lord's atoning death is a gospel teaching; they held it was invented by Paul.

**[*Preliminary notes*]**

PRELIMINARY NOTE 1: THE DEATH OF CHRIST

1 Since there are many different ways to consider the death of Christ, it seems desirable to indicate here as briefly as possible those aspects that are clear and certain and commonly acknowledged.

2 Christ's death was brought about by secondary causes: Judas his betrayer (Mark 14.21, 14.43), the chief priests (Mark 14.55–64), the Jerusalem mob stirred up by the priests (Mark 15.11–14), Pilate, wishing to satisfy the people (Mark 15.15), the soldiers (Mark 15.16, 15.21–24), and, if you add those who, according to Paul (Romans 1.32), showed their approval, then also the passersby who jeered at him (Mark 15.29–31).

3 The Gospel of John lays out the historical causality that led to Christ's death. Not only does it show the Jewish leaders' constant opposition (John 5.16–18, 6.52–53, 6.60, 6.66, 6.70, 7.12–13, 7.20, 7.31–32, 7.45–49, 7.51–52, 8.48–59, 9.16, 9.22, 9.30–34, 10.19–21, 10.31, 10.39, 11.46–53, 11.56, 12.19, 12.42–43); it also presents the higher principles that lead one to think this opposition was all but inevitable in the ordinary course of human affairs.

For Christ, the Word of God, was the true light who enlightens everyone (1.9), the light of the world (8.12), was born for this and for this he came into the world, to give testimony to the truth (18.37), and he did give this testimony, a testimony greater than that of John the Baptist, that is, the testimony of God the Father, of the scriptures, and of Moses (5.36–46).

But people love darkness more than light, for their deeds are evil (3.19–21, 7.7). Hence the Lord said, 'There is no place in you for my word' (8.37),

(8.37); ideo oppositionem delineavit inter Deum et diabolum, veritatem et mendacium, fidem et homicidium (8.37–47).

Neque necessitas gratiae (6.44–45, 6.65) neque Iudaeorum caecitas eos excusat; qui culpabiliter (9.41), maiori peccato (19.11), gravissimo odio (15.24–25) erant excaecati (12.39–41).

4 At agnitis causis secundis, agnita causalitate historica, nihilominus Deus omnipotens per causas secundas et secundum leges historicas omnia regit atque gubernat.

Unde ulterius docet NT Christum 'definito consilio et praescientia Dei traditum' (Act 2.23) nec quidquam fecisse Herodem et Pontium Pilatum cum gentibus et populis Israel quam quod 'manus tua et consilium tuum decreverunt fieri' (Act 4.28); immo, oportuisse Christum pati (Lc 24.26, 24.46) secundum scripturas (Mt 26.54, 1 Cor 15.3, Act 3.18). Quibus accedunt quae de mandato Patris narrantur (Io 10.18), praedictiones ipsius Christi de sua passione et morte (Mc 9.12, 9.31 10.33–34), voluntaria eiusdem passionis et mortis acceptatio (Mc 14.36), et laudata Christi obedientia (Rom 5.19, Phil 2.8, Heb 5.8, 10.5–7).

5 Ipsa passio et mors Christi est illa eventuum series in quattuor evangeliis narrata.

Qui quidem eventus considerari possunt tum aliter tum praecipue (1) ut eventus physici, et (2) ut voluntarii.

Physice, idem eventus est et actio et passio: actio quidem ut procedens ab agente; passio autem ut receptus in patiente. Cf. *In III Phys.*, lect. 5, § 308; *Sum. theol.*, I, q. 28, a. 3, ad 1m.

Haec tamen identitas physica minime excludit diversitatem voluntariam: alia enim est voluntas agentis; alia autem est voluntas patientis. Unde in eodem eventu habentur et gravissimum scelus et opus excellentissimum: pessima enim erat actio Iudaeorum qui Christum affligebant; optima autem erat passio Christi qui iniustam inflictionem ex caritate et obedientia patienter acceptabat et sustinebat: Petrus Lombardus, 3, d. 20; *Sum. theol.* I-II, q. 20, a. 6, ad 2m; III, q. 47, aa. 1, 2, 4, 6.

and described the opposition between God and the devil, between truth and lies, between faith and murder (8.37–47).

Neither the necessity of grace (6.44–45, 6.65) nor the blindness of the Jewish leaders excuses them; it was by their own fault (9.41), by their greater sin (19.11), by their extreme hatred (15.24–25) that they were blinded (12.39–41).

4 But while we acknowledge secondary causes and historical causality, it is still almighty God who directs and governs all things through the secondary causes and according to the historical laws.

Thus the New Testament also teaches that Christ was handed over 'according to the definite plan and foreknowledge of God' (Acts 2.23), and that Herod and Pontius Pilate along with the Gentiles and the people of Israel did nothing other than what 'your hand and your plan had predestined to take place' (Acts 4.28), and in fact that Christ had to suffer (Luke 24.26, 24.46) in accordance with the scriptures (Matthew 26.54, 1 Corinthians 15.3, Acts 3.18). To this there is added mention of the command of the Father (John 10.18), the predictions by Christ himself concerning his passion and death (Mark 9.12, 9.31, 10.33–34), his willing acceptance of his passion and death (Mark 14.36), and his praiseworthy obedience (Romans 5.19, Philippians 2.8, Hebrews 5.8, 10.5–7).

5 The passion and death of Christ is a series of events related in the four gospels.

These events can be considered in different ways and especially (1) as physical events and (2) as voluntary.

Physically, the same event is both action and passion: action as proceeding from the agent, passion as received in the thing or person affected. See Thomas Aquinas, *In III Phys.*, lect. 5, § 308; *Summa theologiae,* 1, q. 28, a. 3, ad 1m.

This physical identity, however, does not at all exclude a diversity of wills: the will of the agent and the will of the one acted upon are not the same. Hence in the same event there is a most serious crime and a work most excellent. The action of the Jewish leaders in afflicting Christ was the worst of actions, but the passion of Christ in patiently accepting and bearing this unjust treatment out of love and obedience was most noble. See Peter Lombard, *Libri III Sententiarum,* d. 20; Thomas Aquinas, *Summa theologiae,* 1-2, q. 20, a. 6, ad 2m; 3, q. 47, aa. 1, 2, 4, 6.

6 Proinde tum Iudaei peccantes tum Christus homo suberant divinae providentiae et divinae gubernationi. Et quamvis unus actus purus est et divina sapientia ordinans et divina bonitas volens, non tamen eodem modo se habet Deus ad bona, ad alia mala, et ad malum culpae.[5]

Bona enim directe vult Deus.

Malum naturalis defectus et malum poenae nisi indirecte non vult Deus; scilicet, quia Deus vult ordinem universi (quod est magnum quoddam bonum et rebus ordinatis quodammodo excellentius: *Sum. theol.*, 1, q. 103, a. 2, ad 3m; q. 47, a 1 c. ad fin.; q. 93, a. 2, ad 3m), per consequens Deus ea vult quae ex ordine consequuntur, nempe, naturales defectus et poenas.

Malum culpae Deus nullo modo vult neque directe neque indirecte: *Sum. theol.*, 1, q. 19, a. 9 c.

6 Thus both the Jews who sinned and the human Christ were subject to divine providence and divine governance. And although the divine wisdom that ordains and the divine goodness that wills is one pure act, nevertheless God is not related in the same way to what is good, to other evils, and to culpable evil.[5]

God directly wills the good.

God only indirectly wills the evil of natural defect and the evil of punishment; that is to say, because God wills the order of the universe (which is a great good and, in a way, more excellent than the things that are ordered [*Summa theologiae,* 1, q. 103, a. 2, ad 3m; q. 47, a. 1 c.; q. 93, a. 2, ad 3m]), it follows that God wills those things that are a consequence of that order, namely, natural defects and punishments.

God in no way wills culpable evil, either directly or indirectly (*Summa theologiae,* 1, q. 19, a. 9 c.).

5 'Culpable evil' translates *malum culpae,* literally, the 'evil of fault,' the voluntary defect that is the formal element of sin. The terminology is from Thomas Aquinas, who divides evil, in voluntary matters, into fault (*malum culpae*) and punishment (*malum poenae*): fault is the absence of due order in voluntary action; punishment is the consequent corruption of one's moral being (see *De malo,* q. 1, aa. 4–5; *Summa theologiae,* 1, q. 48, aa. 5–6); for Lonergan's exposition of Aquinas on this matter, see Bernard Lonergan, *Grace and Freedom: Operative Grace in the Thought of St Thomas Aquinas,* vol. 1 in Collected Works of Bernard Lonergan, ed. Frederick E. Crowe and Robert M. Doran (Toronto: University of Toronto Press, 2000) 111–16. In *Insight,* Lonergan transposed these distinctions to 'basic sin' and 'moral evil.' Basic sin is a 'contraction of consciousness,' 'the failure of free will to choose a morally obligatory course of action or its failure to reject a morally reprehensible course of action,' while the consequent moral evil includes both the moral corruption of oneself and others (*malum poenae* in Aquinas's sense), and, as well, the morally corrupt acts of omission and commission. Bernard Lonergan, *Insight: A Study of Human Understanding,* vol. 3 in Collected Works of Bernard Lonergan, ed. Frederick E. Crowe and Robert M. Doran (Toronto: University of Toronto Press, 1992) 689; see 689–91; compare *Summa theologiae,* 1-2, q. 79, a. 2. In his Latin here, Lonergan retained the Thomist vocabulary but evidently intended his own meanings: *malum culpae,* culpable evil, is basic sin, while *malum poenae,* the evil of punishment, is moral evil. 'From the basic sin of not willing what one ought to will, there follow moral evils of omission and a heightening of the temptation in oneself or others to further basic sins. From the basic sin of not setting aside illicit proposals, there follows their execution and a more positive heightening of tension and temptation in oneself or in one's social milieu.' Lonergan, *Insight* 689. See below, thesis 17, pp. 198–99; and chapter 4 in the supplement, pp. 450–53.

Unde, ibid. ad 3m: Deus igitur neque vult mala fieri neque vult mala non fieri sed vult permittere mala fieri. Et hoc est bonum. Cf. q. 23, a. 3, ob. 2 et ad 2m: 'perditio tua ex te Israel.'[6]

7 Quae quidem tria in passione Christi coniunguntur.

Primo, enim, Deus nullo modo vult malum culpae, seu peccatum interius, in Iuda, sacerdotibus, turba, Pilato, militibus, consentientibus. Quod tamen nullo modo vult sive fieri sive non fieri, idem permittere vult. Quae quidem permissio est bona.

Deinde, Deus indirecte vult quod ex ordine universi et ex interiori peccato consequitur, nempe, actio Iudaeorum quae erat afflictio Christi.

Tertio, Deus directe vult bonum, nempe obedientiam et caritatem Christi.

8 Quod Deus nullo modo voluit malum culpae manifestatur ubi dicitur: haec est hora vestra, et potestas tenebrarum (Lc 22.53; cf. Col 1.13).

Quod Deus indirecte voluit afflictionem Christi manifestatur ubi dicitur: 'qui etiam proprio Filio non pepercit' (Rom 8.32).

Quod Deus directe voluit obedientiam et caritatem Christi constat tum ex speciali doctrina de mandato Patris, tum etiam ex generali doctrina NT quae legem talionis reprobat et dilectionem inimicorum praecipit (Mt 5.38–48), quae malorum perpessionem propter iustitiam summopere laudat (Mt 5.10–12), quae passionem Domini, qua iniuste inflictam et patienter toleratam, exemplum a nobis sequendum proponit (1 Pet 2.19–24).

9 At haec tria unitatem quandam faciunt: sicut enim unum faciunt et peccatum Iudaeorum et consequens afflictio Christi et consequens Christi patientia, ita etiam unum faciunt et bona Dei permissio et bona Dei volitio indirecta et bona Dei volitio directa.

Sapientis autem est ordinare. Unde et Apostolus: 'Nos autem praedicamus Christum crucifixum, Iudaeis quidem scandalum, gentibus autem stultitiam, ipsis autem vocatis Iudaeis atque Graecis Dei virtutem et Dei sapientiam' (1 Cor 1.23–24). Et paulo post: 'in Christo Iesu, qui factus est

Hence (ibid. ad 3m) God neither wills that evils occur nor wills that evils not occur, but he wills to permit evils to occur. And this is good. See *Summa theologiae,* 1, q. 23, a. 3, ob. 2 and ad 2m: 'Your downfall is you own doing, Israel.'[6]

7 These three positions come together in the passion of Christ.

First, then, God in no way wills culpable evil, that is, the interior sin in Judas, in the priests, in the crowd, in Pilate, in the soldiers, in those who expressed their approval. Still, what God in no way wills, either to occur or not to occur, he does will to permit. And this permission is good.

Second, God indirectly wills what results from the order of the universe and from the interior sin, namely, the action of the Jewish leaders, which was Christ's affliction.

Third, God directly wills what is good, namely, Christ's obedience and love.

8 That God in no way willed culpable evil is clear from the words, 'This is your hour, and the power of darkness' (Luke 22.53; see Colossians 1.13).

That God indirectly willed Christ's affliction is clear from the words, 'He ... did not withhold his own son' (Romans 8.32).

That God directly willed Christ's obedience and love is clear both from the particular teaching about the command of the Father and also from the general teaching of the New Testament which condemns the *lex talionis,* the law of retaliation, and commands love of one's enemies (Matthew 5.38–48), highly praises suffering evils for justice's sake (Matthew 5.10–12), and proposes the Lord's sufferings, unjustly inflicted and patiently borne, as an example for us to follow (1 Peter 2.19–24).

9 Yet these three form a certain unity; for as the sin of the Jewish authorities and the consequent affliction of Christ and the consequent endurance of Christ form a unity, so also do the good that is God's permission, the good that is God's indirect volition, and the good that is God's direct volition form a unity.

To order is the work of the wise. Hence the words of St Paul, 'We proclaim Christ crucified, a stumbling block to Jews and foolishness to Gentiles, but to those who are the called, both Jews and Greeks, Christ the power of God and the wisdom of God' (1 Corinthians 1.23–24). And a little further

6 This is the reading of Hosea 13.9 cited in 'q. 23, a. 3, ... ad 2m.'

nobis sapientia a Deo' (1 Cor 1.30). Et iterum: 'sed loquimur Dei sapientiam in mysterio' (1 Cor 2.7).

PRAENOTAMEN II: DE VOCE 'REDEMPTIONIS'

1 Ubi in Vulgata leguntur 'redimere,' 'redemptio,' 'redemptor,' in originali leguntur:

λύτρον: Mc 10.45, Mt 20.28.[7]
ἀντίλυτρον: 1 Tim 2.6.
λύτρωσις: Lc 1.68, 2.38, Heb 9.12.

ἀπολύτρωσις: Lc 21.28, Rom 3.24, 8.23, 1 Cor 1.30, Eph 1.7, 1.14, 4.30, Heb 9.15, (Heb 11.35).

λυτροῦσθαι: Lc 24.21, Tit 2.14.
λυτρωτής: Act 7.35.

2 Mediante versione LXX ad usum hebraicum ascenditur, ubi inveniuntur verba et nomina correspondentia: *Pâdâh, pidyôn*; *Gâ'al, ge'ûllah*; *Kipper, kôfer*.

*Pâdâh,* redimere, occurrit in contextu liberationis populi electi ex Aegypto. Deut 7.8, 9.26, 13.5, 15.15, 21.8, 24.18; cf. Act 7.35.

*Gâ'al,* liberare, occurrit in contextu liberationis ex captivitate Babylonica (Ier 31.7–11, Is 43.1, 43.14) sed etiam applicatur liberationi ex Aegypto (Ps 73.2, 76.16, 77.35).[8]

*Kipper,* extinguere (forte tegere), occurrit in contextu liberationis a morbo vel a peccato. Unde fit vehiculum profundioris sensus in liberationibus politicis figurati.

on, 'in Christ Jesus, who became for us wisdom from God' (1 Corinthians 1.30); and again, 'But we speak God's wisdom, secret and hidden' (1 Corinthians 2.7).

PRELIMINARY NOTE 2: THE WORD 'REDEMPTION'

1 In the Vulgate, the words *redimere, redemptio, redemptor* translate the following words of the original Greek:

λύτρον: Mark 10.45, Matthew 20.28 [Latin, *redemptio*; English, 'ransom'].[7]

ἀντίλυτρον: 1 Timothy 2.6 [*redemptio*; 'ransom'].

λύτρωσις: Luke 1.68 [*redemptio*; 'redeemed' ('wrought redemption')], Luke 2.38, Hebrews 9.12 ['redemption'].

ἀπολύτρωσις: Luke 21.28, Romans 3.24, 8.23, 1 Corinthians 1.30, Ephesians 1.7, 1.14, 4.30, Hebrews 9.15 [*redemptio*; 'redemption'], (Hebrews 11.35) [*redemptio*; 'release'].

λυτροῦσθαι: Luke 24.21, Titus 2.14 [*redimere*; 'redeem'].

λυτρωτής: Acts 7.35 [*redemptor*; 'liberator'].

2 Going back to the Hebrew terms by way of the Septuagint, we find the corresponding verbs and nouns: *Pâdâh, pidyôn*; *Gâ'al, ge'ûllah*; *Kipper, kôfer.*

*Pâdâh,* 'redeem,' occurs in the context of the liberation of the chosen people from Egypt (Deuteronomy 7.8, 9.26, 13.5, 15.15, 21.8, 24.18; see Acts 7.35).

*Gâ'al,* 'liberate,' occurs in the context of the liberation from the Babylonian captivity (Jeremiah 31.7–11, Isaiah 43.1, 43.14) but is also used with reference to the liberation from Egypt (Psalms 73.2 [EVV 74.2], 76.16 [EVV 77.16], 77.35 [EVV 78.35]).[8]

*Kipper,* 'extinguish' (or perhaps 'cover'), occurs in the context of liberation from sickness or from sin. Hence it came to bear the deeper meaning prefigured in political liberations.

7 The word 'redeem' means 'to buy back,' Latin, *redimere* (*re-emere*). Where persons are concerned, the usual English word for the transaction and the price to be paid is 'ransom.' The English equivalents offered here are those found in the New Revised Standard Version.

8 Lonergan follows the Vulgate's numbering of the Psalms. The numbering used in English bibles is often different and has been added in square brackets, preceded by EVV.

Nomina significant medium redemptionis seu liberationis: *pidyôn* bis occurrit; *ge'ûllah,* 14ies; *kôfer,* 13ies. Ubi medium est argentum, LXX vertunt per λύτρον; ita *kôfer* 6ies.

3 Thema liberationis a peccato profundius exploratur.
Brevissime: extollitur Dei sanctitas (Is 6.1–5); doletur de offensa Dei (Ps 50.6); celebratur redemptio a Deo peracta (Is 40.1–5, 43.1, 43.3–4, 44.22, 45.1, 45.4–5, 50.1, 52.3, 54.5–8); promittitur novum foedus (Is 55.3–8, Ier 31.31–34; cf. Heb 8.8–12); annuntiatur servus Iahwe patiens (Is 42.1–7, 49.1–6, 50.4–9, 52.13 – 53.12, Ps 21).

4 Plura vide apud: S. Lyonnet, *De peccato et redemptione*: I. *De notione peccati,* Romae 1957; II. *De vocabulario redemptionis,* Romae 1960; idem opus per partes apud *Verbum Domini* et etiam MS, Romae 1956.

L. Richard 13–37. C. Novel, *Essai sur le développement de l'idée biblique de rédemption.*, diss. fac. theol., Lyon, 1954 (mimeogr.). Acath. J. Stamm., *Erlösen und Vergeben im Alten Testament,* Bern, 1940. DBS. TWNT.

PRAENOTAMEN III: DE SENSU VOCIS 'REDEMPTIONIS' IN NT

1 Omissis Act 7.35 et Heb 11.35, sensus vocis in NT semper connectitur cum Domino nostro.

2 Ubi 'redemptio' vertit λύτρον, ἀντίλυτρον, sensus est quod Christus dat animam suam, dat semetipsum, pro multis, pro omnibus. Ita Mc 10.45, Mt

The nouns signifying the means of redemption or liberation: *pidyôn* occurs twice, *ge'ûllah* 14 times, *kôfer* 13 times. In cases where the means is the payment of money, the Septuagint translates it as λύτρον; in this sense *kôfer* occurs six times.

3 The theme of liberation from sin is explored more deeply.

Very briefly: the holiness of God is extolled (Isaiah 6.1–5); sorrow for offending God is expressed (Psalm 50.6 [EVV 51.4]); redemption wrought by God is celebrated (Isaiah 40.1–5, 43.1, 43.3–4, 44.22, 45.1, 45.4–5, 50.1, 52.3, 54.5–8); a new covenant is promised (Isaiah 55.3–8, Jeremiah 31.31–34; see Hebrews 8.8–12); the suffering servant of Yahweh is announced (Isaiah 42.1–7, 49.1–6, 50.4–9, 52.13–53.12, Psalm 21 [EVV 22]).

4 For more on this matter see Stanislas Lyonnet, *De peccato et redemptione*: vol. 1, *De notione peccati* (Rome: Pontifical Biblical Institute, 1957); vol. 2, *De vocabulario redemptionis* (Rome: Pontifical Biblical Institute, 1960). [An English translation of both volumes is contained in Stanislas Lyonnet and Léopold Sabourin, *Sin, Redemption, and Sacrifice: A Biblical and Patristic Study* (Rome: Pontifical Biblical Institute, 1970).] This work was published serially in *Verbum Domini*, and also in manuscript, Rome, 1956 [*Theologia biblica Novi Testamenti: De peccato et redemptione* (Rome: Pontifical Biblical Institute, 1956)].

Richard, *Le mystère de la Rédemption* 13–37 [*The Mystery of the Redemption* 35–64]. Charles Novel, *Essai sur le développement de l'idée biblique de rédemption* (doctoral thesis, Faculté de Théologie de Lyon, 1954, mimeographed). By a non-Catholic author, Johann Jakob Stamm, *Erlösen und Vergeben im Alten Testament: Eine begriffsgeschichtliche Untersuchung* (Bern: A. Francke, 1940). See also *Dictionnaire de la Bible, Supplément* (DBS) and *Theologisches Wörterbuch zum Neuen Testament* (TWNT) [*Theological Dictionary of the New Testament* (TDNT).]

### PRELIMINARY NOTE 3: THE MEANING OF THE WORD 'REDEMPTION' IN THE NEW TESTAMENT

1 Apart from Acts 7.35 and Hebrews 11.35, the meaning of the word 'redemption' in the New Testament is always connected with our Lord.

2 When the Greek words λύτρον and ἀντίλυτρον are translated in Latin as *redemptio* [and in English as 'ransom'], the meaning is that Christ gives his

20.28, 1 Tim 2.6. Qui sensus exploratur in parte tertia de pretio soluto, parte quarta de morte vicaria, parte quinta de sacrificio, et parte sexta de obedientia meritoria.

3 Ter refertur ad statum a piis Iudaeis exspectatum: ita λύτρωσις, Lc 1.68, 2.38; λυτροῦσθαι, Lc 24.21.

4 Quater vel quinquies refertur ad redemptionem eschatologicam: ita λύτρωσις, Heb 9.12; ἀπολύτρωσις, Lc 21.28, Rom 8.23, Eph 4.30, Eph 1.14.

5 Ter significat effectum sanguinis Christi vel mortis Christi, nempe, peccatorum remissionem; ita ἀπολύτρωσις, Eph 1.7, Col 1.14, Heb 9.15.

6 Semel significat productionem huius effectus a Christo qui dedit semet ipsum; ita λυτροῦσθαι, Tit 2.14.

7 Semel significat causam omnis redemptionis; ita uti videtur ἀπολύτρωσις, 1 Cor 1.30.

8 Semel ita dicitur ἀπολύτρωσις ut trahi possit sive ad sensum sub 2, sive ad sensum sub 5–7. Ita Rom 3.24.

9 Cum tamen eadem realitas sub diversis aspectibus per unum redemptionis nomen designari soleat, distinguimus: finem ultimum (supra, 4), finem proximum (supra, 5), ipsam finis productionem (supra, 6, 7), et fundamentum huius productionis (supra, 2). Quia vero omnes sensus ad Christum referuntur distinguimus redemptionem ut finem (pars prima) et redemptionem ut mediationem (pars secunda) quae in morte est magis passiva (partes tertia ad sextam) et in Christo caelesti est magis activa (pars septima).

life, gives himself, for many, for all. Thus Mark 10.45, Matthew 20.28, and 1 Timothy 2.6. This meaning is explored in part 3 concerning the price paid, in part 4 concerning vicarious death, in part 5 concerning sacrifice, and in part 6 concerning meritorious obedience.

3 Three times 'redemption' refers to the state awaited by devout Jews: λύτρωσις in Luke 1.68, 2.38, and λυτροῦσθαι in Luke 24.21.

4 Four or five times it refers to the eschatological redemption: λύτρωσις in Hebrews 9.12 and ἀπολύτρωσις in Luke 21.28, Romans 8.23, Ephesians 4.30, and Ephesians 1.14.

5 Three times 'redemption' signifies the effect of the blood of Christ or the death of Christ, that is, the forgiveness of sins: so ἀπολύτρωσις in Ephesians 1.7, Colossians 1.14, Hebrews 9.15.

6 In one occurrence it signifies the production of this effect by Christ, who gave himself for us [in order to redeem us]: λυτροῦσθαι [λυτρώσηται] in Titus 2.14.

7 In one occurrence it seems to signify the cause of all redemption: ἀπολύτρωσις, 1 Corinthians 1.30.

8 In one occurrence (Romans 3.24), ἀπολύτρωσις is used in such a way that it could refer either to the meaning given in (2) above or in a sense that would fall under (5) through (7).

9 Since, however, the same reality is designated under different aspects by the one word 'redemption,' we distinguish an ultimate end (4, above), a proximate end (5), the production of the end (6 and 7), and the foundation of this production (2). But because all these meanings refer to Christ, we distinguish redemption as end (part 1) and redemption as mediation (part 2), which is more passive in the death of Christ (parts 3 to 6) and more active in Christ in glory (part 7).

[*Argumentum*]

PARS PRIMA: REDEMPTIO DICIT FINEM.

1 Ipse finis communi nomine dicitur 'salus'; de ea agitur de qua in NT; cf. S. Lyonnet, *Verbum Domini* 36 (1958) 3–15 (= *De vocabulario redemptionis* 7–23), ubi loca de salute collecta invenies.

2 Rom 8.24: spe enim salvi facti sumus. Quare ipse finis in duo stadia dividitur, terrestre et caeleste. Stadium caeleste quod speratur est salus definitiva, ubi iam non cum metu et tremore nostram salutem operabimur (Phil 2.12). Stadium terrestre quo iam salvi facti sumus vera bona confert: remissio peccatorum, iustificatio, Spiritus sanctus effusus in corda, caritas, pax ad Deum, vita vestra abscondita cum Christo in Deo, etc.

3 Vox 'redemptio' in NT dicit finem, nempe, illud divinae liberationis beneficium, in VT praefiguratum et tempore Christi a piis Iudaeis exspectatum. Loca VT collecta apud S. Lyonnet, *Verbum Domini* 36 (1958) 136–40; *De vocabulario redemptionis* 35–40. NT: Lc 1.68 (λύτρωσις); 2.38 (λύτρωσις); 24.21 (λυτροῦσθαι). Cf. Act 7.35 ubi Moyses est λυτρωτής. Sensus huius redemptionis maxime ex canticu *Benedictus* colligitur, Lc 1.68–79.

4 Vox 'redemptio' in NT dicit finem, nempe, salutem NT secundum stadium definitivum.

*Lc 21.28*: His autem fieri incipientibus ... appropinquat redemptio vestra. *Rom 8.23*: exspectantes redemptionem corporis nostri. *Eph 4.30*: in quo signati estis in diem redemptionis. *Heb 9.12*: aeterna redemptione inventa. *Eph 1.14*: in redemptionem adquisitionis (περιποιήσεως). His locis, semper adhibetur ἀπολύτρωσις, excepto Heb., ubi λύτρωσις.

**[*The argument*]**

PART 1: REDEMPTION DENOTES AN END.

1 This end is expressed by the common word 'salvation.' We are concerned here with its usage in the New Testament. For a collection of the various texts concerned with salvation see Stanislas Lyonnet, 'De notione salutis in Novo Testamento,' *Verbum Domini* 36 (1958) 3–15 ([roughly equivalent to] *De peccato et redemptione*, vol. 2, *De vocabulario redemptionis* 7–23 [*Sin, Redemption, and Sacrifice* 63–78]).

2 'For in hope we were saved' (Romans 8.24). Hence the end is divided into two stages, earthly and heavenly. The heavenly stage that is hoped for is definitive salvation, where we shall no longer work out our salvation with fear and trembling (Philippians 2.12). The earthly stage in which we are already saved brings us true goods: the forgiveness of sins, justification, the outpouring of the Holy Spirit into our hearts, charity, peace with God, your life hidden with Christ in God, and so on.

3 In the New Testament the word 'redemption' denotes an end in the sense of the benefit of the divine liberation prefigured in the Old Testament and awaited by devout Jews at the time of Christ. For the Old Testament texts on redemption see Stanislas Lyonnet, 'De notione redemptionis,' *Verbum Domini* 36 (1958) 129–46, at 136–40; *De peccato et redemptione*, vol. 2, *De vocabulario redemptionis* 35–40 [*Sin, Redemption, and Sacrifice* 90–95]. In the New Testament, Luke 1.68 (λύτρωσις), 2.38 (λύτρωσις), and 24.21 (λυτροῦσθαι). See Acts 7.35, where Moses is called a liberator (λυτρωτής). The meaning of this redemption can best be gathered from the Canticle of Zechariah, the 'Benedictus,' Luke 1.68–79.

4 In the New Testament the word 'redemption' denotes an end which is the definitive stage of salvation in its New Testament sense.

*Luke 21.28*: 'Now when these things begin to take place ... your redemption is drawing near.' *Romans 8.23*: 'waiting for ... the redemption of our bodies.' *Ephesians 4.30*: 'marked with a seal for the day of redemption.' *Hebrews 9.12*: 'obtaining eternal redemption.' *Ephesians 1.14*: 'toward redemption as God's own people' (περιποιήσεως, literally, 'of acquisition'). In these texts the word ἀπολύτρωσις is always used, except in Hebrews, where the word is λύτρωσις.

Alia manifeste de stadio finali agunt, sed Eph 1.14 difficultatem quandam facere potest. Quo sensu dicitur 'adquisitio': cf. 1 Pet 2.9: λαὸς εἰς περιποίησιν; Tit 2.14: λαὸν περιούσιον; et praeter contextum horum locorum, multa e VT collecta apud S. Lyonnet, *Verbum Domini* 36 (1958) 261–62; *De vocabulario redemptionis* 56–57. Historia exegeseos: Daniel a Conchas, *Verbum Domini* 30 (1952) 14–29, 81–91, 154–69. Unde colligi videtur: adquisitio est illa qua Deo adquiritur populus electus proprius, Dei peculium.

Utrum agatur de stadio finali? E contextu, Eph 1.14: 'signati estis Spiritu promissionis sancto, qui est pignus haereditatis nostrae, in redemptionem adquisitionis, in laudem gloriae ipsius,' ubi redemptio concipitur ut finis vel terminus doni Spiritus, pignoris iam habiti; unde Eph 4.30: 'in diem redemptionis' et loca parallela.

5 Redemptio in NT dicit finem (vel ipsam finis productionem) secundum stadium terrestre.

*Eph 1.7* et *Col 1.14*: in quo habemus redemptionem (ἀπολύτρωσις) per sanguinem eius, remissionem peccatorum. Ubi redemptio non est pretium, nempe, sanguis, sed est per sanguinem; et dicitur quaenam sit haec redemptio, nempe, remissio peccatorum, quae ad stadium finis terrestre pertinet.

*Tit 2.14*: qui dedit semetipsum pro nobis, ut nos redimeret (λυτροῦσθαι) ab omni iniquitate et mundaret sibi populum acceptabilem. Ubi 'dedit semetipsum' est solutio pretii, cuius finis est liberatio, redemptio, ab omni iniquitate, mundatio populi acceptabilis.

*Heb 9.15*: morte intercedente in redemptionem (ἀπολύτρωσις) earum praevaricationum quae erant sub priori testamento. Ubi redemptio ut pretii solutio est mors quae intercedit; cuius finis est liberatio, redemptio, a prioribus praevaricationibus.

6 Redemptio in NT dicit finem seu effectum secundum quod in causa sua continetur.

The other texts clearly refer to a final stage, but Ephesians 1.14 can present a difficulty. What is the meaning of 'acquisition'? Compare 1 Peter 2.9 (λαὸς εἰς περιποίησιν, 'God's own people' or more literally 'a people for possession') and Titus 2.14 (λαὸν περιούσιον, 'a people of his own' or 'a people [his] own possession'). In addition to the context of these passages, many Old Testament texts have been collected by Stanislas Lyonnet, 'De notione emptionis seu acquisitionis,' *Verbum Domini* 36 (1958) 257–69, at 261–62, and *De peccato et redemptione*, vol. 2, *De vocabulario redemptionis* 56–57 [*Sin, Redemption, and Sacrifice* 110–12]. For a history of the exegesis, see Daniel a Conchas, '"Redemptio acquisitionis" ad Historiam Exegeseos Eph 1:14b et Loc. Par.,' *Verbum Domini* 30 (1952) 14–29, 81–91, 154–69. From all this it seems that 'acquisition' is that means by which a chosen people is acquired for God to be his own, his personal possession.

Does this refer to the final stage? It seems so, from the context of Ephesians 1.13–14: 'You ... were marked with the seal of the promised Holy Spirit; this is the pledge of our inheritance toward redemption as God's own people, to the praise of his glory.' In this passage redemption is conceived as the end or goal of the gift of the Spirit, the pledge we already possess; hence Ephesians 4.30, 'for the day of redemption,' and parallel texts.

5 'Redemption' in the New Testament denotes an end, or the production of the end, with respect to the earthly stage.

*Ephesians 1.7* and *Colossians 1.14*: In him we have redemption (ἀπολύτρωσις) through his blood, the forgiveness of our sins. Here 'redemption' is not the price paid, that is, blood, but what is had through the blood; and it states in what this redemption consists, namely, the forgiveness of sins, which belongs to the earthly stage of the end.

*Titus 2.14*: 'He it is who gave himself for us that he might redeem (λυτροῦσθαι [λυτρώσηται]) us from all iniquity and purify for himself a people of his own ...' Here 'he gave himself' is the payment of the price, the end of which is liberation, redemption, from all iniquity, the purification of a people acceptable to him.

*Hebrews 9.15*: through the intervention of a death for their redemption (ἀπολύτρωσις) from the transgressions under the first covenant. Here redemption as the payment of the price is the death that intervenes; its end is liberation, redemption, from previous transgressions.

6 Redemption in the New Testament denotes an end in the sense of the effect considered as contained in its cause.

*1 Cor 1.30*: qui factus est nobis sapientia a Deo et iustitia et sanctificatio et redemptio. Sicut Christus nobis exprimit divinam sapientiam et communicat iustitiam et sanctificationem, ita etiam communicat redemptionem, i.e., liberationem, salutem. Cf. Heb 5.9.

7 Remanet locus forte ambiguus.

*Rom 3.24*: iustificati gratis per gratiam ipsius, per redemptionem (ἀπολύτρωσις) quae est in Christo Iesu. Ubi 'per redemptionem' idem dicere videtur ac 'per sanguinem,' per solutum pretium, per vitam pro nobis datam. Attamen non dicitur λύτρον vel ἀντίλυτρον sed ἀπολύτρωσις; et sensus esse potest idem ac supra nn. 5 et 6.

8 Unde concludes: redemptio significat (1) finem secundum stadium definitivum, (2) finem secundum stadium terrestre, (3) productio effectus qui est finis et, uti mox videbimus, (4) medium adhibitum in ordine ad finem.

### PARS SECUNDA: REDEMPTIO NON SOLUM FINEM DICIT SED ETIAM MEDIATIONEM.

1 Haec pars plenius declaratur et probatur in sequentibus, ubi de soluto pretio, de vicaria passione, de sacrificio, etc.

2 Christus est unus mediator inter Deum et homines, et quidem ut homo (1 Tim 2.5): Unus enim Deus, unus et mediator Dei et hominum, homo Christus Iesus. Cf. *Sum. theol.*, III, q. 26, aa.1 et 2; C. Spicq, art. 'Médiation,' DBS, fasc. 28, 1955. Gal 3.20 ponit Moysen mediatorem legis.

3 Christus est mediator relate ad redemptionem ut finem, nam est mediator novi testamenti (Heb 9.15, 12.24), melioris testamenti (Heb 8.6) ubi impletur prophetia Ieremiae (Heb 8.8–12).

4 Christus est mediator per redemptionem ut medium, solutum pretium (1 Tim 2.5–6): unus et mediator Dei et hominum, homo Christus Iesus, qui

*1 Corinthians 1.30*: '... who became for us wisdom from God, and righteousness and sanctification and redemption.' Just as Christ is an expression for us of God's wisdom and communicates to us righteousness and sanctification, so also he communicates redemption, that is, liberation, salvation. See also Hebrews 5.9.

7 There remains a text that is perhaps ambiguous.

*Romans 3.24*: 'they are now justified by his grace as a gift, through the redemption (ἀπολύτρωσις) that is in Christ Jesus.' 'Through the redemption' seems here to mean the same as 'through his blood,' that is, by means of the price paid, through the life that has been given for us. Still, the Greek word is not λύτρον or ἀντίλυτρον but ἀπολύτρωσις, and the meaning could be the same as in §§ 5 and 6 above.

8 Hence we conclude: 'redemption' signifies (1) an end with respect to the definitive stage, (2) an end with respect to the earthly stage, (3) the production of the effect that is the end, and, as we shall now see, (4) the means employed to attain the end.

PART 2: REDEMPTION DENOTES NOT ONLY AN END BUT ALSO A MEDIATION.

1 This part is explained more fully and is proven in what follows, concerning the price paid, vicarious suffering, sacrifice, and so on.

2 Christ is the one mediator between God and the human race, and indeed is so as human: 'there is one God; there is also one mediator between God and humankind, Christ Jesus, himself human' (1 Timothy 2.5). See Thomas Aquinas, *Summa theologiae*, 3, q. 26, aa. 1 and 2. Ceslaus Spicq, 'Médiation – IV: Dans le Nouveau Testament,' DBS V, 1020–83. Galatians 3.20 makes Moses the mediator of the law.

3 Christ is mediator with respect to redemption as end, for he is the mediator of the new covenant (Hebrews 9.15, 12.24), of a better covenant (Hebrews 8.6), where the prophecy of Jeremiah is fulfilled (Hebrews 8.8–12).

4 Christ is mediator through redemption as the means, the price paid: 'there is ... one mediator between God and humankind, Christ Jesus,

dedit semet ipsum redemptionem (ἀντίλυτρον) pro omnibus. Circa ἀντίλυτρον, cf. Mc 10.45;[9] plura in parte tertia.

5 Christus, non ut Deus, sed ut homo mediator, uti constat ex 1 Tim 2.5, ex S. Augustino apud S. Thomam, ex ipso S. Thoma, loc. cit, super no. 2.

6 Christus ut homo est persona divina in humana natura subsistens, et quidem in humana natura quae passionem mortemque subiit.

Christus homo mediator relate ad redemptionem ut finem inquantum est fundamentum proportionatum ut ille finis habeatur. Qui quidem finis considerari potest dupliciter: primo modo, *essentialiter*, et sic est regnum Dei et civitas caelestis ubi creaturae rationales donis gratiae et gloriae fruuntur; alia modo, *concrete*, et sic est idem regnum eademque civitas prout in genere humano lapso atque peccaminoso per Christum est productum.

Inquantum finis consideratur essentialiter, mediatio Christi in ipsa Incarnatione perspici potest, secundum ea quae supra[10] diximus de Christo tamquam fundamento omnis gratiae. Unde solemne est apud Patres tum Graecos tum Latinos, Deum esse factum hominem ut homines faceret deos. Vide L. Richard 106–12, ubi citantur S. Athanasius, SS. Gregorius Nazianzenus et Gregorius Nyssenus, Ioannes Chrysostomus, Cyrillus Alexandrinus, S. Hilarius, S. Ambrosius, S. Augustinus, S. Leo Magnus. Plura de singulis his Patribus apud E. Mersch, *Le corps mystique du Christ*, 2 vol., 1936.[11]

Inquantum autem finis consideratur concrete, non gratis sed sub onerosa conditione passionis et mortis Christus nos in finem-redemptionem

himself human, who gave himself a ransom (ἀντίλυτρον; Vulgate, *redemptio*) for all' (1 Timothy 2.5–6). On the meaning of ἀντίλυτρον, see Mark 10.45;[9] more in part 3.

5 Christ is mediator not as God but as human, as is clear from 1 Timothy 2.5, from St Augustine as quoted by St Thomas, and from St Thomas himself (*Summa theologiae*, 3, q. 26, aa. 1 and 2).

6 Christ as human is a divine person subsisting in a human nature, indeed in a human nature that underwent suffering and death.

The human Christ is mediator with respect to redemption as end in that he is the proportionate foundation of having that end. There are two ways of considering this end: first, *essentially*, and as such it is the reign of God and the heavenly city where rational creatures enjoy the gifts of grace and glory; second, *concretely*, and as such it is the same reign and the same city as produced by Christ in a fallen and sinful human race.

Inasmuch as the end is considered essentially, Christ's mediation can be seen in the incarnation itself, according to what we said above[10] about Christ as the foundation of all grace. Hence the saying common to both the Greek and Latin Fathers, 'God became man so that men might become gods.' See Richard, *Le mystère de la Rédemption* 106–12 [*The Mystery of the Redemption* 141–49] for quotations from Athanasius, Gregory of Nazianzus, Gregory of Nyssa, John Chrysostom, Cyril of Alexandria, Hilary, Ambrose, Augustine, and Leo the Great. For more on each of these Fathers, see Emile Mersch, *Le corps mystique du Christ.*[11]

Insofar as the end is considered concretely, however, Christ brings us to the end that is our redemption not without cost but under the crushing

9 Lonergan's meaning seems to be that ἀντίλυτρον in 1 Timothy 2.6 means what λύτρον means in Mark 10.45.

10 Lonergan is referring to thesis 11 in Bernard Lonergan, *The Incarnate Word*, vol. 8 in Collected Works of Bernard Lonergan, trans. Charles Hefling, ed. Robert M. Doran and Jeremy D. Wilkins (Toronto: University of Toronto Press, 2016). The original is *De Verbo incarnato* (Rome: Gregorian University Press, 1964; earlier editions 1960, 1961).

11 Emile Mersch, *Le corps mystique du Christ: Études de théologie historique*, 2 vols., 2nd ed., rev., corr. and considerably augm. (Paris: Desclée de Brouwer, 1936 [3rd ed., rev. and augm., 1951]). [English translation of the 2nd French edition, *The Whole Christ: The Historical Development of the Doctrine of the Mystical Body in Scripture and Tradition*, trans. John R. Kelly (London: Dennis Dobson, and Milwaukee: Bruce Publishing Co., 1938; reprint Dennis Dobson, 1962). A line of print containing the first four Fathers' names was omitted in the 1964 text.]

producit. Quamvis enim (καίπερ) Filius Dei esset, didicit ex iis quae passus est obedientiam, et consummatus factus est omnibus obtemperantibus sibi causa salutis aeternae (Heb 5.8–9).

PARS TERTIA: REDEMPTIO-MEDIATIO PERSPICITUR IN SOLUTO PRETIO.

1 Mc 10.45, Mt 20.28: Nam et Filius hominis non venit ut ministraretur ei sed ut ministraret et daret animam suam redemptionem pro multis (δοῦναι τὴν ψυχὴν αὐτοῦ λύτρον ἀντὶ πολλῶν).

(a) Idem est contextus apud Mt et Mc: petitio pro filiis Zebedaei; indignatio duodecim; praeceptum Domini ut inter discipulos suos primi sint servi et maiores sint ministri; quod exemplo ipsius Filii confirmatur; unde 1 Pet 5.3: non ut dominantes in cleris.

(b) 'Dare animam suam': semitismus qui mortem significat; cf. Io 10.11, 10.15, 10.17: ponere animam meam.

(c) 'Redemptio' (λύτρον) clare significat medium redemptionis; nam dare animam suam non est ille redemptorum status ubi a praeteritis malis habetur liberatio bonorumque collatorum fruitio; praeterea, Filium hominis animam suam dare dicitur, non 'pro multis' tantum, sed 'redemptionem pro multis.'

(d) 'Pro' (ἀντὶ)[12] multi sensus possibiles ex usu NT elucent:

(a´) loco alterius: regnare pro patre suo (Mt 2.22);

(b´) substitutio: pro pisce dare serpentem (Lc 11.11);

(c´) retributio: oculum pro oculo, malum pro malo (Mt 5.38, Rom 12.17, 1 Thess 5.15, 1 Pet 3.9); quod in NT non laudatur;

(d´) electio: proposito sibi gaudio, sustinuit crucem (Heb 12.2);

(e´) in utilitatem: dare staterem de ore piscis sumptum pro me et te (Mt 17.27).

(e) 'Pro multis': pro populo, pro multitudine, pro 'massa.' Cf. Is 53.11: iustificabit ipse iustus servus meus *multos* et inquitates eorum ipse portabit.

condition of suffering and death. For 'although (καίπερ) he was Son [of God], he learned obedience through what he suffered; and having been made perfect, he became the source of eternal salvation for all who obey him' (Hebrews 5.8–9).

PART 3: REDEMPTION AS MEDIATION IS SEEN IN THE PAYMENT OF THE PRICE.

1 Mark 10.45, Matthew 20.28: 'For the Son of man came not to be served but to serve, and to give his life as a ransom for many' (δοῦναι τὴν ψυχὴν αὐτοῦ λύτρον ἀντὶ πολλῶν).

(a) The context in Mark and Matthew is the same: the request on behalf of the sons of Zebedee, the indignation of the Twelve, the Lord's precept that among his disciples those who are first should be slaves and the greater among them should be servants. The Son himself confirmed this precept by his example; hence 1 Peter 5.3, 'Do not lord it over those in your charge.'

(b) 'To give his life' is a Semitic expression signifying death; see John 10.11, 10.15, 10.17, 'lay down my life.'

(c) 'Ransom' (λύτρον) clearly signifies the means of redemption, for 'to give his life' is not that state of the redeemed in which they are delivered from past evils and enjoy the good things given them. Besides, the Son of man is said to give his life not only 'for many' but 'as a ransom for many.'

(d) Greek ἀντὶ, Latin *pro*,[12] can have many meanings in the New Testament:

(a′) in place of another: Archelaus reigned '*in place of* his father' (Matthew 2.22);

(b′) substitution: 'will give a snake *instead of* a fish' (Luke 11.11);

(c′) retribution: 'an eye *for* an eye,' 'evil *for* evil' (Matthew 5.38, Romans 12.17, 1 Thessalonians 5.15, 1 Peter 3.9), which the New Testament does not praise;

(d′) choice: '*for the sake of* the joy that was set before him endured the cross' (Hebrews 12.2);

(e′) for a purpose: give the coin from the mouth of the fish '*for* you and me' (Matthew 17.27).

(e) 'For many': for the people, for the multitude, for the 'masses.' See Isaiah 53.11: my just servant will make *many* righteous and will bear their iniquities.

12 In the following passages the italicized word or words correspond to ἀντὶ in the Greek and *pro* in the Vulgate. English has no similarly versatile preposition.

2 1 Tim 2.5–6: unus mediator ... qui dedit redemptionem (ἀντίλυτρον) semet ipsum pro (ὑπέρ) omnibus.

Quod adeo premit Mc 10.45, Mt 20.28, ut fere commentarium diceres. Cf. 'dare animam suam' et 'dedit semet ipsum'; λύτρον ἀντὶ πολλῶν et ἀντίλυτρον ὑπέρ παντῶν.

Conferri potest cum λύτρον ἀντὶ et ἀντίλυτρον, quod alibi ponitur ἀντάλλαγμα: Quid enim prodest homini si mundum universum lucretur, animae vero suae detrimentum patiatur? Aut quam dabit homo commutationem (ἀντάλλαγμα) pro anima sua? Mt 16.26, Mc 8.37. Unde concludendum esse videtur Christum dedisse semet ipsum, animam suam, commutationem pro multis, pro omnibus.[13]

3 1 Pet 1.18: non corruptibilibus auro vel argento redempti estis (ἐλυτρώθητε) ... sed pretioso sanguine quasi agni immaculati Christi et incontaminati.

4 Accedunt varia loca ubi adhibentur, non λύτρον, ἀντίλυτρον, λυτροῦσθαι, sed τίμη, ἀγοράζειν, ἐξαγοράζειν.

Corinthii pretio empti esse dicuntur, ut corpora sua non sua sed Christi sint, ut ipsi non sui sed Spiritus sancti sint (1 Cor 6.15–20), ut qui liberi vocati sint, servi hominum fieri nolint, cum servi sint Christi (1 Cor 7.22–23).

Christus dicitur nos coemisse de maledicto legis (Gal 3.13), eosque qui sub lege erant coemisse (Gal 4.5).

Reprobat S. Petrus eos qui 'eum qui emit eos Dominum negant' (2 Pet 2.1).

In Apocalypsi emptio fit Deo in sanguine Christi ex omni tribu, populo, natione (Apoc 5.9); 144, 000 de terra (Apoc 14.3); virginum (Apoc 14.4).

5 Plenior horum locorum discussio: S. Lyonnet, *Verbum Domini* 36 (1958) 129–46; 257–69; *De vocabulario redemptionis* 24–66. Circa manumissionem sacram inter paganos, ibid. 258–61; *De vocabulario redemptionis* 50–56.

2 1 Timothy 2.5–6: 'one mediator ... who gave himself as a ransom (ἀντίλυτρον) for (ὑπέρ) all.'

This text is so close to Mark 10.45 and Matthew 20.28 that it might almost be said to be a commentary on them. Compare 'to give his life' with 'he gave himself,' and 'λύτρον ἀντὶ πολλῶν,' 'a ransom for many,' and 'ἀντίλυτρον ὑπέρ παντῶν,' 'a ransom for all.'

The word ἀντάλλαγμα (Matthew 16.26, Mark 8.37) can be compared with λύτρον ἀντὶ and ἀντίλυτρον: 'What will it profit them if they gain the whole world but forfeit their life? Or what will they give *in return for* their life?' From this the evident conclusion is that Christ gave himself, his life, in exchange for many, for all.[13]

3 1 Peter 1.18–19: 'you were ransomed (ἐλυτρώθητε) ... not with perishable things like silver and gold, but with the precious blood of Christ, like that of a lamb without defect or blemish.'

4 There are various other texts where τίμη [price], ἀγοράζειν [to buy], ἐξαγοράζειν [to buy up, buy from] are used instead of λύτρον, ἀντίλυτρον, λυτροῦσθαι.

The Corinthians are said to have been bought at a price (τίμη), so that their bodies belong not to themselves but to Christ, and they are not their own but belong to the Holy Spirit (1 Corinthians 6.15–20); and those who were free when called must not become slaves of human masters, since they are slaves of Christ (1 Corinthians 7.22–23).

Christ is said to have bought (ἐξαγοράζειν) us from the curse of the law (Galatians 3.13), and to have bought (ἐξαγοράζειν) those who were under the law (Galatians 4.5).

Peter rebukes those who 'deny the Master who has bought (ἀγοράζειν) them' (2 Peter 2.1).

In Revelation the purchase (ἀγοράζειν) is made to God in the blood of Christ from every tribe, people, nation (Revelation 5.9); 144,000 from the earth (14.3), virgins (14.4).

5 For a fuller discussion of these texts, see Lyonnet, 'De notione redemptionis,' *Verbum Domini* 36 (1958) 129–46 [*De peccato et redemptione*, vol. 2, *De*

13 The Latin of 1960 and 1961 has been restored. The 1964 edition reads '... Christum dedisse semet ipsum, animam suam commutatione pro multis, pro omnibus.'

6 Quid pro certo ex his locis retinendum sit?

Inquantum negotiatio quaedam commercialis significatur per τίμη, ἀγοράζειν, ἐξαγοράζειν, inquantum negotiatio significari potest per λύτρον, ἀντίλυτρον, sensus non litteralis sed metaphoricus esse videtur; uti enim dixit S. Petrus, non auro vel argento (1 Pet 1.18).

At sensus ille metaphoricus quid significet? Significat nexum, connexionem. Omnes enim homines intelligunt nexum, non forte in sensu metaphysico vel scientifico, sed certe in negotiis: si vis mercem, solve pretium. Sicut ergo habetur nexus inter mercem et pretium, ita simili quodam modo habetur nexus inter 'dare animam suam,' 'dare semet ipsum,' 'pretiosum sanguinem,' et, alia ex parte, redemptionem-finem seu salutem.

Quod aliter declarari potest. Redemptio-finis non habetur *gratis*, habetur sub conditione (ergo cum alio connectitur); quae quidem conditio est 'dare animam suam.'

7 Hic sensus minimus est, et dupliciter augeri potest. *Uno modo*, ut 'ἀντὶ' significet quandam quasi substitutionem, ut loco peccatorum Christus subire debeat mortem, peccati poenam, ut peccatores liberet. *Alio modo*, ut quaeratur cuinam pretium sit solutum.

Circa primum, dicendum est hunc sensum quodammodo esse verum, ut postea ex aliis locis stabilietur et clarius explicabitur. Utrum vero ex solis verbis λύτρον ἀντὶ, ἀντίλυτρον, habeatur, disputatur. Longe enim facilius ex usu pagano quam ex usu scripturistico concluditur; vide Lyonnet, loc. cit. supra, § 5. Neque convenit NT imponere sensum magis paganum quam qui ex VT et LXX habetur.

Circa alterum, si ita premitur aspectus commercialis, dupliciter respondetur. Uno modo, cum Patribus, et sic pretium solvitur diabolo. Alio modo, cum theologis, et sic pretium solvitur Deo.

*vocabulario redemptionis* 24–48; *Sin, Redemption, and Sacrifice* 79–103]; 'De notione emptionis seu acquisitionis,' *Verbum Domini* 257–69 [*De vocabulario redemptionis* 49–66; *Sin, Redemption, and Sacrifice* 104–19]; concerning sacred manumission among pagans, see 'De notione emptionis seu acquisitionis,' *Verbum Domini* 258–61; *De vocabulario redemptionis* 50–56 [*Sin, Redemption, and Sacrifice* 105–10].

6 What must we hold for certain from these texts?

Inasmuch as a business transaction is signified by the words τίμη, ἀγοράζειν, and ἐξαγοράζειν, and inasmuch as the transaction can be signified by λύτρον and ἀντίλυτρον, the meaning is evidently not literal but metaphorical. For, as Peter said, redemption was not by silver or gold (1 Peter 1.18).

But what does this metaphorical meaning signify? It signifies a nexus, a connection. Everyone understands what a connection means – not, perhaps, in a metaphysical or scientific sense, but certainly in business: if you want the goods, pay the price. Just as there is a connection between the goods and the price, then, so there is, in like manner, a connection between 'to give his life,' 'to give himself,' the 'precious blood,' and, on the other side, redemption as end, that is, salvation.

To put this in another way, redemption as end is *not had for nothing*; it is had on a condition (and is connected, therefore, with something else); and this condition is 'to give his life.'

7 The meaning here is minimal, and it can be expanded in two ways: *first,* by taking ἀντὶ to signify a kind of substitution, so that Christ was to suffer death, the penalty for sin, in place of sinners in order to ransom them; *second,* by asking to whom the ransom was paid.

With regard to substitution, it must be said that it is true in a way, as will be established later and explained more clearly from other texts. But whether this meaning can be had from the words λύτρον ἀντὶ and ἀντίλυτρον alone is disputed. For it is much easier to derive it from pagan than from scriptural usage; see Lyonnet as cited under § 5 above. Nor is it right to impose upon the New Testament a meaning that is more pagan than that which is found in the Old Testament and the Septuagint.

As for the question to whom the ransom was paid, if its commercial reference is pressed, two answers are given: the first, with the Fathers, that the ransom is paid to the devil; the second, with the [Scholastic] theologians, that the ransom is paid to God.

De mente Patrum hac in re non dubitandum est, quamvis alii aliter loquantur. Cf. Richard 112–17; Rivière, DTC XIII (26) 1939–41; Xiberta, Index, 796; exquisitiora quaedam apud Daniel a Conchas, *Verbum Domini* 30 (1952) 14–29, 81–91.

Non tamen dicendum est et Patres et theologos de eadem re sub eodem respectu esse locutos. Quod solvitur Deo est sacrificium quod Deo offertur, scilicet passio et mors Christi qua voluntate Christi voluntariae; quod autem diabolo solvitur, est quod tenebris conceditur (cf. Lc 22.53, Heb 2.14–15), scilicet malum culpae quod Deus nullo modo vult, et malum poenae seu Christi afflictionem quam Deus indirecte tantum vult. Cf. supra, praenotamen 1, §§ 7–9.

PARS QUARTA: REDEMPTIO-MEDIATIO PERSPICITUR IN VICARIA CHRISTI PASSIONE ET MORTE PROPTER PECCATA ET PRO PECCATORIBUS.

1 Christus mortuus est, dedit animam suam, se dedit, se tradidit, traditus est pro peccatoribus, pro peccatis.

Mortuus est pro omnibus (2 Cor 5.15, Heb 2.9), pro singulis (Rom 14.15, 1 Cor 8.11), pro impiis (Rom 5.6), pro nobis (Rom 5.8, 1 Thess 5.10), et pro nostris peccatis (1 Cor 15.3, 1 Pet 3.18).

Dedit animam suam redemptionem pro multis (Mc 10.45, Mt 20.28) et pro omnibus (1 Tim 2.6).

Se dedit pro nobis (Tit 2.14) et pro nostris peccatis (Gal 1.4).

Se tradidit pro nobis (Eph 5.2), pro ecclesia (Eph 5.25), et pro me (Gal 2.20).

Traditus est pro nobis omnibus (Rom 8.32) et propter nostra delicta (Rom 4.25).

2 Christus est vicarius agens ad peccata tollenda et in beneficium seu utilitatem peccatorum quorum peccata auferuntur.

There is no doubt about the thought of the Fathers on this matter, although various Fathers express it in different ways. See Richard, *Le mystère de la Rédemption* 112–17 [*The Mystery of the Redemption* 149–56]; J. Rivière, 'Rédemption' 1939–41; Bartholomé María Xiberta, *Enchiridion de Verbo Incarnato, fontes quos ad studia theologica collegit* (Madrid: Consejo Superior de Investigaciones Cientificas, Patronato 'Raimundo Lulio' – Instituto 'Francisco Suárez,' 1957), Index doctrinarum 796 [XXVIII – 'Redemptionis excellentia']; for some of the finer points on this, see Daniel a Conchas, '"Redemptio acquisitionis" ...' *Verbum Domini* 30 (1952) 14–29, 81–91.

However, it must not be said that the Fathers and the theologians spoke about the same thing under the same aspect. What is paid to God is the sacrifice that is offered to God, that is, Christ's passion and death as voluntarily accepted by the will of Christ. What is paid to the devil is what is conceded to darkness (Luke 22.53, Hebrews 2.14–15), namely culpable evil, which God in no way wills, and the evil of punishment, Christ's sufferings, which God wills only indirectly. See above, preliminary note 1, pp. 22–25, §§ 7–9.

### PART 4: REDEMPTION AS MEDIATION IS SEEN IN CHRIST'S VICARIOUS PASSION AND DEATH BECAUSE OF SINS AND FOR SINNERS.

1 Christ died, gave his life, gave himself, handed himself over, was handed over for sinners and for sins.

Christ died for all (2 Corinthians 5.15, Hebrews 2.9), for each (Romans 14.15, 1 Corinthians 8.11), for the ungodly (Romans 5.6), for us (Romans 5.8, 1 Thessalonians 5.10), and for our sins (1 Corinthians 15.3, 1 Peter 3.18).

He gave his life as a ransom for many (Mark 10.45, Matthew 20.28) and for all (1 Timothy 2.6).

He gave himself for us (Titus 2.14) and for our sins (Galatians 1.4).

He handed himself over for us (Ephesians 5.2), for the church (Ephesians 5.25), and for me (Galatians 2.20).

He was handed over for us all (Romans 8.32) and because of our sins (Romans 4.25).

2 Christ acts vicariously to take away sins and for the benefit or utility of sinners whose sins are taken away.

Vide supra 'Sensus theseos' 3, ubi distinguuntur vicarius agens et vicarius patiens.

Nam redemptio-finis includit remissionem peccatorum: Eph 1.7, Col 1.14; cf. Mt 26.28, Heb 9.22, 10.18, 1 Cor 6.11, Act 2.38, Io 20.23; plura in tractatu de baptismo et de poenitentia.

*Io 1.29*: Ecce agnus Dei, ecce qui tollit peccatum mundi. *Heb 2.17*: ut repropitiaret delicta populi (ἱλάσκεσθαι). *1 Io 2.2*: ipse est propitiatio (ἱλασμός) pro peccatis nostris, non pro nostris autem tantum, sed etiam pro totius mundi. *1 Io 4.10*: ipse prior dilexit nos et misit Filium suum propitiationem (ἱλασμὸν) pro peccatis nostris. *Rom 3.25*: in Christo Iesu, quem proposuit Deus propitiationem (ἱλαστήριον) per fidem in sanguine ipsius, ad ostensionem iustitiae suae propter remissionem praecedentium delictorum.

N.B. Circa voces proptiare, propitiatio, (ἱλάσκεσθαι, ἱλασμός, ἱλαστήριον) omnino distinguendum esse videtur inter sensum paganum et sensum in usu LXX. Inter paganos homo deos propitiat, propitios reddit, placat, ex iratis vel infensis in pacatos et benevolos mutat. In usu LXX sacerdos vel sacrificium propitiat peccata, scilicet, ea delet, aufert, tollit, tegit, ut actio sit non in Deum sed in peccata; uti clarum est in Heb 2.17; similiter actio in Deum excluditur apud 1 Io 4.10, ubi dicitur 'ipse prior dilexit nos'; neque alia est mens S. Pauli: 2 Cor 5.19, Rom 5.6–8, 8.32.

Quaestionem exegeticam abunde tractavit S. Lyonnet, *De vocabulario redemptionis* 67–117. Cf. L. Moraldi, *Verbum Domini* 26 (1948) 257–76; *Espiazione: sacrificale e riti espiatori nell'ambiente biblico e nell'Antico Testamento* (Roma, 1956) 182–221.

3 Christus non solum agit in utilitatem peccatoris ut peccata deleantur sed etiam patitur propter peccata commissa et pro peccatoribus.

(a) In primis habetur factum manifestum: Christus passus et mortuus est. Non solum pretium solvit, sed dare animam suam est ipsum pretium solvendum. Non solum dicit 'remittuntur tibi peccata tua' per modum agentis peccata auferentis, sed pro omnibus et singulis peccatoribus et pro peccatis

For the distinction between acting vicariously and suffering vicariously, see *Meaning of the thesis* § 3 above, p. 7.

For redemption as end includes the forgiveness of sins: Ephesians 1.7, Colossians 1.14; see Matthew 26.28, Hebrews 9.22, 10.18, 1 Corinthians 6.11, Acts 2.38, John 20.23; more in the treatises on baptism and on penance.

*John 1.29*: Behold the Lamb of God, behold him who takes away the sin of the world. *Hebrews 2.17*: to make a sacrifice of atonement (ἱλάσκεσθαι) for the sins of the people. *1 John 2.2*: He himself is the atoning sacrifice (ἱλασμός) for our sins, and not for ours only, but also for the sins of the whole world. *1 John 4.10*: God loved us first and sent his Son as the atoning sacrifice (ἱλασμός) for our sins. *Romans 3.25*: in Christ Jesus, whom God put forward as a sacrifice of atonement (ἱλαστήριον) by faith in his blood. He did this to show his righteousness by remission of the sins previously committed.

Note: Regarding the words 'propitiate,' 'propitiation' (ἱλάσκεσθαι, ἱλασμός, ἱλαστήριον [in Latin, *propitiare, propitiatio*]), one must distinguish altogether between the pagan meaning of these words and their meaning in the Septuagint. Among pagans, humans propitiate the gods, render them propitious, placate them, change them from being angry and hostile to being peaceable and benevolent. According to Septuagint usage, the priest or the sacrifice propitiates (atones for) sins, that is, wipes out sins, cancels them, takes them away, covers them, so that the object of the action is not God but sins, as is clear in Hebrews 2.17. Similarly, action directed to God is excluded in 1 John 4.10, where it is stated that 'He first loved us.' St Paul is of the same mind: 2 Corinthians 5.19, Romans 5.6–8, 8.32.

Lyonnet has abundantly treated the exegetical question in *De peccato et redemptione*, vol. 2, *De vocabulario redemptionis* 67–117 [*Sin, Redemption, and Sacrifice* 120–66]. See also Luigi Moraldi, 'Sensus vocis ἱλαστήριον in Rom. 3, 25,' *Verbum Domini* 26 (1948) 257–76; *Espiazione sacrificale e riti espiatori: nell'ambiente biblico e nell'Antico Testamento* (Rome: Pontifical Biblical Institute, 1956) 182–221.

3 Christ not only acts for the benefit of sinners so that their sins be wiped away but also suffers because of the sins committed, and on behalf of sinners.

(a) First of all, there is the obvious fact: Christ suffered and died. Not only did he pay the price, but the very price to be paid was to give his life. Not only does he say, 'Your sins are forgiven,' as one who acts to take away sins, but he died, he gave himself, he handed himself over, he was handed

mortuus est, se dedit, se tradidit, traditus est (cf. supra § 1). Et uti mox dicetur, Christus non solum fuit sacerdos hostiam offerens, sed etiam ipse erat hostia oblata.

(b) Neque eo tantum sensu ex peccatis passus est Christus quia individui quidam peccaverunt, uti Iudas, sacerdotes, turba, Pilatus, milites, vel quia secundum quandam quasi legem tenebrae lucem tolerare non possunt (cf. praenotamen I, §§ 2, 3).

Nam definito Dei consilio (ibid. § 4) mortuus est Christus. Immo, ipse Pater omnipotens 'proprio Filio suo non pepercit, sed pro nobis omnibus tradidit illum' (Rom 8.32). Inquantum Pater peccata sacerdotum et Pilati permisit, proprio Filio non pepercit. Inquantum indirecte voluit consequentem Christi afflictionem usque ad mortem, pro nobis omnibus tradidit illum. Sed quaeri potest cur permiserit et cur indirecte voluerit. Quaeri potest cur non oportuerit Salvatorem mundi cum gloria et virtute venire, cur oportuerit eum in carne passibili venire, in carne patiente opus consummare, et sic intrare in regnum suum (Lc 24.26, 24.46). Sane res non ita fuisset, si nemo umquam peccavisset. Egit ergo vicarius pro nobis ad peccata tollenda; sed passus est vicarius pro nobis propter peccata commissa.

(c) Quod obscure annuntiatum est apud Isaiam 53.4–12.

Ubi narratur de quodam iusto (9cd, 11c) atque tacente (7d), qui propter iniquitates alienas (5abc, 7a, 8d, 11d, 12e) divina voluntate (6c, 10a) vulneratur, atteritur, conteritur, laborat, ponit animam suam, tradit in mortem animam suam (5ab, 10ab, 12c), unde fructum duraturum meret et multorum iustificationem (10cd, 11bc, 12ab).

Locus habetur ut messianicus inde ab ipso NT. Non applicatur passioni (Mt 8.17, 10.6); obvia allusio ad passionem (Act 8.32–36, Mc 15.28, Lc 22.37, 23.34, Rom 4.25); longior applicatio indubitata, 1 Pet 2.22–25.

Exegetae abundantissime (bibliographia apud C. North, *The Suffering Servant in Deutero-Isaiah: An Historical and Critical Study* [Oxford: Oxford University Press, 1950]).[14] Recenter: H. Cazelles, *RechScRel* 43 (1955) 5–55; D. Stanley, *CathBibQuar* 16 (1954) 385–425; proxime ad rem nostram, S.

over for each and every sinner, and for sins (see above, § 1). And, as we will shortly indicate, Christ was not only the priest offering the victim, but he himself was also the victim offered.

(b) Nor did Christ suffer because of sins only in the sense that he suffered from the sinful acts of certain individuals, such as Judas, the chief priests, the crowd, Pilate, and the soldiers, or because, in accordance with some sort of law, darkness cannot tolerate the light. See above, preliminary note 1, §§ 2 and 3.

For it was by the definite plan of God that Christ died. See above, preliminary note 1, § 4. Indeed, the almighty Father 'did not withhold his own Son, but gave him up for all of us' (Romans 8.32). In permitting the sins of the chief priests and of Pilate, the Father did not spare his own Son. In indirectly willing the consequent affliction of Christ to the point of death, he handed him over for all of us. But it may be asked why God permitted and indirectly willed these events to occur. It may be asked why the Savior of the world should not have come with glory and power, why he had to come in flesh that could suffer, in the suffering of his flesh to complete his work and so enter into his kingdom (Luke 24.26, 24.46). This would certainly not have happened had no one ever sinned. Therefore, he acted vicariously for us to take away our sins; but he suffered vicariously for us on account of the sins committed.

(c) This was dimly announced in Isaiah 53.4–12.

This passage tells of a just (9cd, 11c) and silent (7d) one, who, on account of the iniquity of others (5abc, 7a, 8d, 11d, 12e) and by the divine will (6c, 10a), is wounded, bruised, crushed, burdened, lays down his life, and surrenders himself to death (5ab, 10ab, 12c), whereby he merits lasting fruit and the justification of many (10cd, 11bc, 12ab).

This passage has been accepted as messianic from the time of the New Testament itself. In Matthew 8.17 and 10.6 there is no reference to the passion; but there is an obvious allusion to the passion in Acts 8.32–36, Mark 15.28, Luke 22.37, 23.34, and Romans 4.25, and a longer and unmistakable allusion in 1 Peter 2.22–25.

There is abundant exegesis on this passage. See the bibliography in Christopher R. North, *The Suffering Servant in Deutero-Isaiah: An Historical and Critical Study* (Oxford: Oxford University Press, 1950) 223–35.[14] Later,

14 Lonergan's text had 'C. North, *The Servant Songs in Deutero-Isaiah*, Lund, Gleerup, 1951.' He seems to have conflated information from two different books: the North book that is here substituted in the text for Lonergan's

Lyonnet, *De peccato et redemptione,* 1956, 264: 'Certo ex his assertis concludere licet nostra propria peccata causam fuisse passionis et mortis Christi; immo Christum aliquid passum esse, quod erat partialis poena nobis (non vero sibi) propter peccata nostra debita.'

Immo, vix dubitatur Iesum hunc locum de se ipso intellexisse (1) cum propriam passionem praedixerit (Mc 9.12, 9.31, 10.33–34, 10.45), (2) cum mortem declinare potuerit et propter scripturas noluerit (Mt 26.53–54), et (3) cum se mori oportuisse explicaverit (Lc 24.26, 24.46).

(d) Explicatur passio morsque Christi per peccata:

1 Pet 2.24: peccata nostra ipse pertulit in corpore suo super lignum.

2 Cor 5.21: eum qui non noverat peccatum pro nobis peccatum fecit, ut nos efficeremur iustitia Dei in ipso. Uti Lyonnet, *In II Cor,* 1956, 256–66, sicut non ipsa divina iustitia efficimur sed effectum eius recipimus, ita Christus non ipsum peccatum efficitur sed effectum peccati recepit.[15]

Rom 8.3: Deus Filium suum mittens in similitudine carnis peccati et de peccato damnavit peccatum in carne. Ubi videtur haberi iudicium divinum adversus peccatum in carne Christi quae propter peccata passa est.

Gal 3.13 (cf. Deut 21.23) argumentum sat subtile ex lege ducit. Vide Lyonnet, *De peccato et redemptione* 260. Agnus, sane symbolum passivitatis, est Christus: Is 53.7, 1 Pet 1.19, Io 1.29, Apoc 7.14, 12.11.

Henri Cazelles, 'Les poèmes du seriteur: leur place, leur structure, leur théologie,' *Recherches de science religieuse* 43 (1955) 5–55; David M. Stanley, 'The Theme of the Servant of Yahweh in Primitive Christian Soteriology and Its Transposition by St. Paul,' *Catholic Biblical Quarterly* 16 (1954) 385–425. More to our point is Lyonnet, *Theologia biblica Novi Testamenti: De peccato et redemptione* 264: 'From these statements one may conclude with certainty that our own sins were the cause of the passion and death of Christ; indeed, what Christ suffered was part of the punishment due to us, not to him, on account of our sins.'

In fact, there is no doubt that Jesus understood this passage as referring to himself since (1) he predicted his own passion (Mark 9.12, 9.31, 10.33–34, 10.45), (2) he could have avoided death but refused to do so because of the scriptures (Matthew 26.53–54), and (3) he explained that it was necessary for him to die (Luke 24.26, 24.46).

(d) The passion and death of Christ is explained by sin.

1 Peter 2.24: 'He himself bore our sins in his body on the cross.'

2 Corinthians 5.21: 'For our sake [God] made him to be sin who knew no sin, so that in him we might become the righteousness of God.' As Lyonnet suggests, just as we do not become divine righteousness itself but receive its effect, so Christ does not become sin itself but receives the effect of sin.[15]

Romans 8.3: 'by sending his own Son in the likeness of sinful flesh, and to deal with sin, [God] condemned sin in the flesh.' Here, it seems, we have the judgment of God upon sin in the flesh of Christ that suffered on account of sins.

Galatians 3.13 (compare Deuteronomy 21.23) takes a rather subtle argument from the Law. See Lyonnet, *Theologia biblica Novi Testamenti: De peccato et redemptione* 260–61 [see *Sin, Redemption, and Sacrifice* 250]. The lamb, surely a symbol of passivity, is Christ: Isaiah 53.7, 1 Peter 1.19, John 1.29, Revelation 7.14, 12.11.

---

reference, and Johannes Lindblom, *The Servant Songs in Deutero-Isaiah: A New Attempt to Solve an Old Problem* (Lund: C.W.K. Gleerup, 1951). Lindblom begins by saying that his study would not have been written if North's book 'had not appeared.' There is also a bibliography in Lindblom's book on pp. 105–109.

15 'Inde sicuti homo dicitur fieri "iustitia Dei" quatenus beneficos effectus istius activitatis Dei in seipsum recipit; ita Christus dicitur factus esse "peccatum," quatenus maleficos effectus istius potentiae ... ipse subiit.' Stanislas Lyonnet, *Exegesis epistulae secundae ad Corinthios* (Romae: Pontificium Institutum Biblicum, 1955–56) 256–66 [at 263].

De omnibus his locis, vide L. Sabourin, *Rédemption sacrificielle. Une enquête exégetique*, Desclée de Brouwer, 1961.

(e) Notate, sicut vicaria passio et mors illuminant atque complent quae iam de soluto pretio sunt dicta, ita etiam ipsam vicariam passionem et mortem illuminant atque complent quae mox de sacerdote agente et victima patiente dicenda sunt.

PARS QUINTA: REDEMPTIO-MEDIATIO PERSPICITUR IN SACRIFICIO A PONTIFICE NOSTRO IN SUO SANGUINE OBLATO.

1 In sacrificiis distinguuntur (1) *effectus*: peccatorum remissio, sanctificatio, accessus ad Deum cum fiducia; (2) effectum *recipiens*: populus pro quo fit sacrificium; (3) *agens*: sacerdos, pontifex; (4) *patiens*: hostia, victima, oblatum; (5) *actio*: oblatio victimae a sacerdote; (6) *fundamentum*: foedus, testamentum, quo constituitur sancta illa societas in qua assumuntur sacerdotes de populo ut pro populo sacrificia Deo offerant (Heb 5.1–2).

2 Caeteris fundamentis praestat foedus divinitus institutum.

Praeterea, ipsum foedus sacrificio iniri potest. Ita vetus testamentum in sanguine initum est (Exod 24.8, Heb 9.19–21).

Quod tamen veterandum novumque ineundum annuntiavit Ieremias, quo (l) omnes intime Deum Deique legem scirent, quo (2) 'ero eis in Deum, et ipsi erunt mihi in populum,' quo (3) 'propitius ero iniquitatibus eorum et peccatorum eorum iam non recordabor' (Heb 8.8–12, Ier 31.31–34).

Quod promissum atque novum testamentum initum est et sancitum in sanguine Christi. Mc 14.24: Hic est sanguis meus novi testamenti, qui pro multis effundetur (cf. Mt 26.28, Lc 22.20, 1 Cor 11.25).

Unde Dominus dicitur melioris et novi testamenti sponsor atque mediator (Heb 7.22, 8.6, 9.15, 12.24; cf. C. Spicq, DBS, art. 'Médiation,' v, 1020–83).

3 Quantum veteri novum praestet testamentum, fere tota ad Hebraeos epistola exponit, comparatis (l) *mediatoribus* Moyse (Gal 3.20) et Filio, (2) *sacerdotiis* Levi et Melchisedech, (3) *sacrificiis* ad emundationem carnis et ad emundationem conscientiae.

On all these passages, see Léopold Sabourin, *Rédemption sacrificielle: Une enquête exégétique* (Bruges and Paris: Desclée de Brouwer, 1961) [especially 328–40].

(e) Note that just as the vicarious passion and death illumine and complement what has been said about the price paid, so also what is shortly to be said about the priest as acting and the victim as suffering illumines and complements this same vicarious passion and death.

## PART 5: REDEMPTION AS MEDIATION IS SEEN IN THE SACRIFICE OFFERED BY OUR HIGH PRIEST IN HIS OWN BLOOD.

1 In sacrifices the following elements may be distinguished: (1) the *effect*: the forgiveness of sins, sanctification, access to God with confidence; (2) the *recipient* of the effect: the people for whom the sacrifice is offered; (3) the *agent*: the priest, high priest; (4) the *sufferer*, the *patient*: the victim, the one offered; (5) the *action*: offering of the victim by the priest; (6) the *foundation*: the compact, covenant, by which is constituted that holy society in which priests are taken from among the people to offer sacrifices to God for the people (Hebrews 5.1–2).

2 A divinely instituted covenant is superior to all other foundations.

Besides, the covenant itself can be established by a sacrifice. Thus the old covenant was established in blood (Exodus 24.8, Hebrews 9.19–21).

Yet Jeremiah proclaimed that this covenant was to become old and a new covenant entered into, in which (1) all would know God and God's law inwardly, in which (2) 'I will be their God and they shall be my people,' and in which (3) 'I will be merciful towards their iniquities and I will remember their sins no more' (Hebrews 8.8–12, Jeremiah 31.31–34).

This promised new covenant was established and ratified in the blood of Christ: 'This is my blood of the new covenant, which is poured out for many' (Mark 14.24; see also Matthew 26.28, Luke 22.20, 1 Corinthians 11.25).

Hence the Lord is said to be the guarantor and mediator of a new and better covenant (Hebrews 7.22, 8.6, 9.15, 12.24). See Spicq, 'Médiation – IV: Dans Le Nouveau Testament,' DBS V, 1020–83.

3 Almost the whole Letter to the Hebrews expounds the superiority of this new covenant over the old, comparing (1) the *mediators*, Moses (Galatians 3.20) and the Son, (2) the *priesthoods*, of Levi and Melchizedek, (3) the *sacrifices*, for the purification of the flesh and for the purification of conscience.

(a) Comparantur mediatores.

Fidelis quidem erat Moyses, sed sicut famulus in domo Dei.

Fidelis autem est Christus sicut Filius in domo sua quae sumus nos (3.2–6). Ipse enim Filius, splendor gloriae et figura divinae substantiae, heres constitutus universorum, per quem Deus fecit et saecula (1.2–3), participavit carni et sanguini (2.14) per omnia nobis assimilatus absque peccato (2.17, 4.15). Nam ut misericors fieret et fidelis pontifex ad Deum (2.17, 4.15, 5.2), passionibus eum perfici decuit (2.10), et passus est et tentatus per omnia pro similitudine (2.18, 4.15), unde et ex iis quae passus est didicit obedientiam, et perfectus factus est omnibus obtemperantibus sibi causa salutis aeternae (5.8–9).

(b) Comparantur sacerdotia.

Postquam sacerdotium secundum Melchisedech sacerdotio Levitico demonstratum est superius, introducitur individualis quidem sacerdos secundum similitudinem Melchisedech, 'qui non secundum legem mandati carnalis factus est, sed secundum virtutem vitae insolubilis' (7.16). Qui quidem divino iuramento constituitur sacerdos (5.4–6, 7.17, 7.21), dum Levitici sine iuramento erant (7.20). Qui sempiternum habet sacerdotium et in aeternum manet (7.24, 7.3), sed Levitici, quia moriebantur, erant multi (7.23). Qui innocens, sanctus, impollutus, segregatus a peccatoribus et excelsior caelis factus est (7.26), dum Levitici pro propriis delictis offerre debebant (5.3, 7.27). Qui semel in ipsum caelum per suam hostiam apparuit (9.24–26), sed Levitici saepe in tabernaculum manufactum introierunt (9.6–7, 9.25). Qui Filius est in aeternum perfectus (7.28), dum lex nihil ad perfectum adduxit (7.11, 7.18–19).

(c) Comparantur sacrificia.

Sacrificia legis nisi umbram non habebant futurorum bonorum (10.1), nisi emundationem carnis non efficiebant (9.10, 9.13), non poterant iuxta conscientiam perfectum facere servientem (9.9, 10.1–2) neque peccata auferre (10.4, 10.11).

Quibus reprobatis, ipse Filius corpore sibi aptato venit ad faciendam voluntatem Dei (10.5–7), in qua voluntate sanctificati sumus per oblationem corporis Iesu Christi semel (10.10, 7.27). Cuius sanguis emundat conscientiam nostram ab operibus mortuis ad serviendum Deo viventi (9.14), tollit praevaricationes quae erant sub priori testamento (9.15).

Christus enim semel in consummatione saeculorum ad destitutionem peccati per hostiam suam apparuit (9.26); semel oblatus est ad exhaurienda

(a) The mediators are compared.

Moses was indeed faithful, but as a servant in the household of God.

But Christ was faithful as a Son in his own house, which house we are (Hebrews 3.2–6). For the Son himself, the radiance of God's glory and the imprint of God's very being, the appointed heir of all things, through whom God made the ages (1.2–3), shared in our flesh and blood (2.14), is like us in all things but sin (2.17, 4.15). That he might become a merciful and faithful high priest before God (2.17, 4.15, 5.2) it was fitting that he be made perfect through suffering (2.10), and so he suffered and was tested in every way that we are (2.18, 4.15), whereby through what he suffered he learned obedience, and having thus been made perfect, he became for all who obey him the source of eternal salvation (5.8–9).

(b) The priesthoods are compared.

After the priesthood according to Melchizedek was shown to be superior to the Levitical, an individual priest in the likeness of Melchizedek is introduced, 'one who has become a priest, not through a legal requirement concerning physical descent, but through the power of an indestructible life' (7.16). He was constituted priest by a divine oath (5.4–6, 7.17, 7.21), while the Levites were priests without an oath (7.20). He has an everlasting priesthood and abides forever (7.24, 7.3), but the Levitical priests, because they died, were many in number (7.23). He was innocent, holy, undefiled, separated from sinners, and raised above the heavens (7.26), while the Levitical priests had to offer sacrifices for their own sins (5.3, 7.27). He appeared once for all in heaven itself through his sacrifice (9.24–26), but the Levitical priests enter many times into a tabernacle made by human hands (9.6–7, 9.25). He is the Son made perfect for ever (7.28), while the law brought nothing to perfection (7.11, 7.18–19).

(c) The sacrifices are compared.

The sacrifices of the law were merely a shadow of the good things to come (10.1), effected only a purification of the flesh (9.10, 9.13), and could neither perfect the conscience of the worshiper (9.9, 10.1–2) nor take away sin (10.4, 10.11).

Rejecting these, the Son himself came with the body fitted to him to do God's will (10.5–7); by this will 'we have been sanctified through the offering of the body of Jesus Christ once for all' (10.10, 7.27). His blood purifies 'our conscience from dead works to serve the living God' (9.14) and takes away the transgressions under the former covenant (9.15).

For Christ 'has appeared once for all at the end of the age to remove sin by the sacrifice of himself' (9.26); he has been 'offered once to bear the

multorum peccata (9.28); unam pro peccatis offerens hostiam in sempiternum sedet in dextera Dei (10.12), nam una oblatione consummavit in aeternum sanctificatos (10.14). Impletum ergo est verbum propheticum: 'et peccatorum et iniquitatum eorum non iam recordabor amplius. Ubi autem horum remissio, iam non est oblatio pro peccato' (10.17–18).[16]

(d) Christus ergo novi testamenti non solum sponsor et mediator (7.22, 8.6, 9.15, 12.24) sed etiam sacerdos est atque hostia; purgationem peccatorum effecit (1.3), et per suum sanguinem populum sanctificavit (13.12).

4 Quod brevius inculcat reliquum NT.

Institutio Eucharistiae: Mt 26.28, Mc 14.24, Lc 22.20, 1 Cor 11.25, ubi omnes memorant sanguinem novi testamenti effusum; Mt addit in remissionem peccatorum; Lc dicit corpus quod pro vobis datur; Paulus dicit corpus quod pro vobis tradetur.[17]

Accedit quod pascha nostrum immolatus est Christus (1 Cor 5.7; cf. Io 1.29, Act 8.32, Is 53.7, 1 Pet 1.19, 1 Io 3.5).

Christus factus est sanctificatio nostra (1 Cor 1.30; cf. Heb 2.3, 13.12, Io 17.19).

Christus dilexit nos, et tradidit semet ipsum pro nobis oblationem et hostiam Dei in odorem suavitatis (Eph 5.2, Ps 39.7, Exod 29.18, Ezech 20.41). Unde et dicitur missus propitiatio pro peccatis nostris (1 Io 4.10) et pro peccatis totius mundi (1 Io 2.2) et propositus a Deo propitiatorium (Rom 3.25).

5 Propter sacrificium singularis efficacia ascribitur sanguini Christi, in quo iustificamur (Rom 5.9), per quem habemus redemptionem, remissionem peccatorum (Col 1.14,[18] Eph 1.7), pacificationem (Col 1.20), in quo Christus nos redemit Deo (Apoc 5.9) et lavit a peccatis nostris (Apoc 1.5,

sins of many' (9.28); having offered 'for all time a single sacrifice for sins, "he sat down at the right hand of God"' (10.12), 'for by a single offering he has perfected for all time those who are sanctified' (10.14). Thus was fulfilled the word of the prophet: '"I will remember their sins and their lawless deeds no more." Where there is forgiveness of these, there is no longer any offering for sin' (10.17–18).[16]

(d) Christ, therefore, was not only the guarantor and mediator of the new covenant (7.22, 8.6, 9.15, 12.24) but also its priest and victim; he effected the purification of sins (1.3), and sanctified the people through his own blood (13.12).

4 There are briefer expositions of this doctrine elsewhere in the New Testament.

The institution of the Eucharist: Matthew 26.28, Mark 14.24, Luke 22.20, 1 Corinthians 11.25. All these passages mention the outpouring of the blood of the new covenant; Matthew adds 'for the forgiveness of sins,' Luke has 'my body which is given for you,' and Paul 'my body that is for you.'[17]

'Our paschal lamb, Christ, has been sacrificed': 1 Corinthians 5.7; see John 1.29, Acts 8.32, Isaiah 53.7, 1 Peter 1.19, 1 John 3.5.

Christ 'became ... for us ... sanctification': 1 Corinthians 1.30; see Hebrews 2.3, 13.12, John 17.19.

'Christ loved us and gave himself up for us, a fragrant offering and sacrifice to God': Ephesians 5.2, Psalm 39.7 [EVV 40.6], Exodus 29.18, Ezekiel 20.41. Hence he is also said to be sent as 'the atoning sacrifice for our sins' (1 John 4.10) and 'for the sins of the whole world' (1 John 2.2), and 'whom God put forward as a sacrifice of atonement' (Romans 3.25).

5 Because of his sacrifice, a singular efficacy is attributed to the blood of Christ, in which we are justified (Romans 5.9), through which we have redemption, the forgiveness of sins (Colossians 1.14,[18] Ephesians 1.7), and peace (Colossians 1.20), in which Christ redeemed us for God (Revelation 5.9) and washed away our sins (Revelation 1.5, 7.14), in which 'you who once were far off have been brought near' (Ephesians 2.13), which 'cleanses us from all sin' (1 John 1.7), the sprinkling of which 'speaks a better

16 See Jeremiah 31.34.

17 This last is the literal reading of the current Greek critical editions; see NRSV. Lonergan's text follows the Vulgate, which itself, following an older received Greek text, inserts the verb *tradetur*, 'will be handed over.'

18 Vulgate: *redemptionem per sanguinem eius*, 'redemption through his blood.'

7.14), in quo qui erant longe facti sunt prope (Eph 2.13), qui emundat nos ab omni peccato (1 Io 1.7), cuius aspersio melius loquitur quam sanguis Abel (Heb 12.24; cf. 1 Pet 1.2), quo adquiritur ecclesia (Act 20.28), propter quem habetur victoria (Apoc 12.11).

### PARS SEXTA: REDEMPTIO-MEDIATIO PERSPICITUR IN OBEDIENTIA.

1 Missio Filii a Deo Patre in opus nostrae salutis (Gal 4.4–5, Rom 8.3–4) tum ipsam Filii personam respicit tum actus eius humanos.

Quatenus missio ipsam personam respicit, dicit aeternam Filii processionem a Patre, addito ad extra termino conveniente (cf. *Divinarum personarum* 206–12, *De Deo trino II* 226–32).[19]

Quatenus missio actus humanos a Filio perficiendos respicit, illam dependentiam dicit quam obedientiam nominamus. Sicut enim praecipere est alium per rationem et voluntatem movere (*Sum. theol.*, II-II, q. 104, a. 1), ita etiam obedire est ab alia moveri per rationem et voluntatem (ibid. III, q. 47, a. 2, ad 1m; a. 3 c.).

2 Testatus est Christus se habere mandata a Patre tum alia (Io 15.10), tum mandatum quid dicat et quid loquatur (Io 12.49), tum denique mandatum ponendi animam suam et iterum sumendi eam (Io 10.17–18).

Quibus mandatis correspondet impletio. Docuit enim Christus non suam doctrinam sed eius qui misit eum (Io 7.16–18, 8.28, 14.24). Descendit de caelo ut faceret voluntatem non suam sed eius qui misit eum (Io 6.38). Quaesivit voluntatem non suam sed eius qui eum misit (Io 5.30). Cibus suus erat facere voluntatem eius qui misit eum opusque eius implere (Io 4.34). Semper fecit quae placita erant Patri (Io 8.29). Mandata Patris servabat et

word than the blood of Abel' (Hebrews 12.24; see 1 Peter 1.2), by which he acquired the church (Acts 20.28), and through which victory has been won (Revelation 12.11).

PART 6: REDEMPTION AS MEDIATION IS SEEN IN OBEDIENCE.

1 The mission, the sending of the Son by God the Father for the work of our salvation (Galatians 4.4–5, Romans 8.3–4), regards both the person of the Son and his human acts.

As far as the mission of the Son regards his person, it refers to his eternal procession from the Father, with the added appropriate external term. See *Divinarum personarum conceptionem analogicam evolvit Bernardus Lonergan, S.I.* (Rome: Gregorian University Press, 1959) 206–12. Later included in Bernard Lonergan, *De Deo trino II: Pars systematica* (Rome: Gregorian University Press, 1964) 226–32.[19]

As far as his mission regards the human acts to be performed by the Son, it refers to that dependence we call 'obedience.' For just as 'to command' means to move another through reason and will (*Summa theologiae*, 2-2, q. 104, a. 1), so 'to obey' means to be moved by another person through reason and will (ibid. 3, q. 47, a. 2, ad 1m; a. 3 c.).

2 Christ testified that he has other commands from the Father (John 15.10), the command about what he should say and speak (John 12.49), and finally the command to lay down his life and take it up again (John 10.17–18).

To these commands there corresponds fulfilment. For Christ taught not his own doctrine but that of the one who sent him (John 7.16–18, 8.28, 14.24). He came down from heaven not to do his own will but the will of the one who sent him (John 6.38). He did not seek his own will but the will of the one who sent him (John 5.30). His food was to do the will of the one who sent him and to complete his work (John 4.34). He always did what was pleasing to the Father (John 8.29). He kept the Father's commands,

19 See Bernard Lonergan, *The Triune God: Systematics*, vol. 12 in Collected Works of Bernard Lonergan, trans. Michael G. Shields, ed. Robert M. Doran and H. Daniel Monsour (Toronto: University of Toronto Press, 2007) 454–67.

in dilectione Patris manebat (Io 15.10). Unde in articulo mortis dicere potuit: Consummatum est (Io 19.30).

3 Obedientiam Christi in acceptanda passione et morte memorant tum evangelia (Mc 14.36 et loca parallela) tum S. Paulus (Phil 2.8; cf. Rom 5.19).

4 Epistola ad Hebraeos obedientiam Christi ab ingressu in mundum docet (Heb 10.5–7; cf. Ps 39.7).

Sed addit quod mirum videri potest decuisse Patrem Filium passionibus perficere (Heb 2.10) ipsumque Filium ex iis quae passus est obedientiam didicisse et perfectionem attigisse (Heb 5.8).

In cuius intelligentiam notari possunt:

(a) Sicut homo non solum anima sed etiam corpore constituitur, ita etiam actus humanus plenus et perfectus non solum interiori voluntatis actu sed etiam actu exteriori et corporali componitur.

(b) Obedientia dicit non solum interiorem rationis et voluntatis motum secundum placita praecipientis sed etiam corporalem exsecutionem.

(c) In natura lapsa ubi spiritus promptus esse potest etsi caro infirma, manifestum est quantum intercedat inter velle et perficere, quantoque perfectior sit ipse interior voluntatis actus cum non solum velimus bonum facere sed etiam ita velimus ut faciamus.

(d) Quod autem in natura lapsa augetur fundari tamen videri in ipsa diversa proportione naturae intellectivae et naturae sensitivae: quatenus enim natura intellectualis est, in totum ens totumque bonum naturaliter tendit; quatenus autem natura est sensitiva in ea obiecta tendit naturaliter quae sensibus et appetitibus sensitivis proportionantur.

(e) Unde, etiam praecisione facta a lapsa natura et ab indigentia gratiae sanantis, ex ipsa natura rei in homine augetur perfectio interioris actus ex eo quod non solum bonum facere volumus sed etiam in difficilibus ita volumus ut faciamus.

(f) Iam vero Dei Verbum caro factum (Io 1.14) ita corpus sibi aptatum habuit (Heb 10.5), ita carni et sanguini communicavit et participavit (Heb 2.14), ut fratribus per omnia similaretur (Heb 2.17) tentatus per omnia pro similitudine absque peccato (Heb 4.15). Cumque opus supremum caritatis

abiding in the Father's love (John 15.10). Hence at the moment of his death he could say, 'It is finished' (John 19.30).

3 Both the gospels (Mark 14.36 and par.) and Paul (Philippians 2.8; see Romans 5.19) note the obedience of Christ in accepting his passion and death.

4 The Letter to the Hebrews (10.5–7; see Psalm 39.7 [EVV 40.6]) affirms the obedience of Christ from the time of his coming into the world.

But it adds what may seem strange, namely, that it was fitting for the Father to perfect the Son through suffering (2.10), and for the Son himself to have learned obedience and reached perfection through what he suffered (5.8).

To understand this, the following points may be noted:

(a) Just as a human being is made up not only of a soul but of a body as well, so also a full and complete human act comprises not only the interior act of the will but also the exterior bodily action.

(b) Obedience means not only the interior movement of the reason and will in accordance with the orders of the one who commands but also the bodily execution of the command.

(c) In the state of fallen nature, where the spirit can be willing while the flesh is weak, it is obvious how great a distance there is between willing and performing, and how much more perfect is that interior act of the will when we are not only willing to do a good deed but also will in such a way that we do it.

(d) This distance is increased in our fallen nature, yet its basis can be seen in the different proportions (respectively) of our intellectual nature and our sensitive nature. For insofar as our nature is intellectual, it tends to all being and all good; but insofar as our nature is sensitive, it naturally tends towards those objects that are proportioned to the senses and the sense appetites.

(e) Hence, even prescinding from our fallen nature and the need of healing grace, from the very nature of the case in a human being the perfection of an interior act is enhanced when we not only will to do the good but also so will to do it in difficult circumstances that we actually do it.

(f) Now, the Word of God made flesh (John 1.14) had a body fitted to him (Hebrews 10.5) and took part in flesh and blood (Hebrews 2.14), so that he was like his brethren in every way (Hebrews 2.17) and was tested like us in every respect, yet without sin (Hebrews 4.15). And since his

(Io 15.13) non sola mente sed etiam corpore perfecturus fuerit, mirari non possumus quam narrant evangelia coartationem (Lc 12.50) quam animae conturbationem (Io 12.27), quod desiderium (Lc 22.15), quem pavorem, quod taedium, quam tristitiam usque ad mortem (Mc 14.34).

(g) Quibus perspectis, dici posse videtur ideo Christum passionibus esse consummatum seu perfectum (Heb 2.10), ideo ex iis quae passus est obedientiam didicisse (Heb 5.8), non quasi virtutes ei infusae ulterius perficerentur, sed quia ex iisdem virtutibus eliciebantur operationes quae ipsam earundem summam perfectionem summo gradu exercebant.

Sicut enim omnis operatio seu actus secundus perfectior est habitu seu actu primo, ita etiam tota quaedam operationum complexio, earumque maxime difficilium, perfectione excedit totam virtutum complexionem e quibus procedunt.

(h) Dixerit tamen quispiam Christum obedisse quidem inquantum praeceptum opus perfecit et inquantum tota voluntate illud opus perficere interius voluit; at necessario defuisse Christo, summa scientia ornato, tertium et supremum obedientiae gradum qui in subordinatione proprii intellectus ad iudicium superioris consistit.

Quod quidem verum est inquantum Christus Deum per essentiam cognovit et ideo certissime concludere potuit actualem rerum ordinem, in quo ipse tot tantaque pati debuit, ex infinita sapientia ordinante et infinita bonitate decernente procedere.

Attamen, cum Christus homo non cognoverit omnia quae sunt in potentia creatoris (*Sum. theol.*, III, q. 10, a. 2), comparare non potuit actualem rerum ordinem cum omnibus aliis ordinibus possibilibus; qua comparatione deficiente, iudicare non potuit ex propria scientia meliorem esse hunc rerum ordinem in quo ipse 'vir dolorum' fore destinabatur.

Iam vero obedientia intellectus (vide plura in cursu theologiae asceticae) in eo consistit quod subditus ex propria scientia ignorat totam excellentiam eorum quae superiores, quatenus divinae providentiae instrumenta, praecipiunt. Et ideo non simpliciter verum est Christum non intellectu sed sola voluntate et exsecutione obedisse.

5 Hanc Christi obedientiam fuisse liberam probant tum explicita Christi affirmatio (Io 10.17), tum repetita oratio atque submissio (Mt 26.39–44), tum declinandi passionem possibilitas (Mt 26.53–54).

supreme act of love (John 15.13) was to be performed not in his mind alone but also in his body, it is no wonder the gospels relate his anguish (Luke 12.50), his troubled soul (John 12.27), his longing (Luke 22.15), his fear, his weariness, his sorrow even unto death (Mark 14.34).

(g) From these considerations it seems possible to say that Christ was made perfect through suffering (Hebrews 2.10) and to have learned obedience by what he suffered (Hebrews 5.8), not as if his infused virtues were further perfected, but because by them he elicited operations that exercised the greatest perfection of these virtues to the very highest degree.

For just as every operation or second act is more perfect than its habit or first act, so also a whole complex of operations, and of them the most difficult, is of greater perfection than the whole complex of virtues from which they proceed.

(h) Still, one could say that Christ did indeed obey insofar as he carried out the command given him and insofar as he willed interiorly with his entire will to perform that work fully, but that in possessing all knowledge he necessarily lacked the third and highest degree of obedience, which consists in subordinating one's own understanding to the judgment of the superior.

This indeed is true inasmuch as Christ knew God through his essence and therefore most certainly could have concluded that the actual order of events, in which he had to suffer so greatly and so much, proceeded from the ordering of infinite wisdom and the decree of infinite goodness.

However, since the human Christ did not know everything that is in the power of the creator (*Summa theologiae,* 3, q. 10, a. 2), he could not have compared the actual order of events with all other possible orders; and without this comparison he could not have judged from his own knowledge that the order of events in which he was destined to be the 'Man of Sorrows' was the better order.

Obedience of the understanding (which is treated fully in ascetical theology) consists in the fact that a subordinate does not know from his own knowledge the full excellence of what his superiors, as instruments of divine providence, command. Hence it is not true without qualification that Christ obeyed only in will and execution and not with his understanding.

5 That this obedience of Christ was free is proven from his explicit statement (John 10.17), from his repeated prayer and his submission (Matthew 26.39–44), and from the possibility of avoiding his passion (Matthew 26.53–54).

Eam fuisse meritoriam est de fide definita (DB 790, 799, 820, 842, 843; DS 1513, 1529, 1560, 1582, 1583).

Meritum enim est opus praemio dignum. Sed S. Paulus obedientiam Christi usque ad mortem crucis proponit tamquam fundamentum exaltationis subsequentis (Phil 2.9). Epistola ad Hebraeos affirmat eum 'propter passionem mortis gloria et honore coronatum' (Heb 2.9). Epistola ad Romanos docet quod 'per unius obeditionem iusti constituentur multi' (Rom 5.19). Unde S. Thomas (*Sum. theol.*, III, q. 48, a. 1) et omnes theologi docent Christum per modum meriti nostram salutem causavisse.

6 Dixerit tamen quispiam non solum opera obedientiae sed etiam omnia opera Christi sub omni aspectu fuisse meritoria.

Quod tamen praesupponit Christum alia ex propria voluntate et alia ex voluntate Patris facere; quod reconciliari non posse videtur cum iis quae ipse Christus de se testatus est (cf. supra § 2). Unde optime S. Thomas ita caritatem et obedientiam Christi comparavit ut in unum quodammodo reducerentur: 'praecepta caritatis nonnisi ex obedientia implevit; et obediens fuit ex dilectione ad Patrem praecipientem' (*Sum. theol.*, III, q. 47, a. 2, ad 3m).

Specialis autem videtur convenientia in eo quod meritum ad obedientem refertur, tum quia scriptura talem connexionem innuit (Rom 5.19, Phil 2.8), tum quia operatio, praecepto alterius facta, speciali quodam modo a praecipiente praemiari convenit. Attamen de conditionibus meriti necessariis, vide DB 809, DS 1545–46, et tractatum de gratia. Neve opinaris non operationem interiorem sed solam exteriorem esse meritoriam, neve rationem obedientiae a Heb 10.5–10 excludas.

## PARS SEPTIMA: REDEMPTIO-MEDIATIO PERSPICITUR TUM IN VIRTUTE DOMINI RESUSCITATI TUM IN INTERCESSIONE AETERNI SACERDOTIS.

1 Quanta sit potestas atque virtus eius qui sedet ad dexteram Patris, iam in thesi 1a recitavimus.[20]

That this obedience was meritorious is defined as a matter of faith (DB 790, 799, 820, 842, 843; DS 1513, 1528–29, 1560, 1582, 1583; [ND 510, 647, 1960, 1982, 1983]).

Merit is a deed that is worthy of reward. But Paul puts forth Christ's obedience unto death as the foundation for his subsequent exaltation (Philippians 2.9). The Letter to the Hebrews states that he 'was crowned with glory and honor because of the suffering of death' (Hebrews 2.9). The Letter to the Romans teaches that 'by the one man's obedience the many will be made righteous' (Romans 5.19). Hence Thomas Aquinas (*Summa theologiae,* 3, q. 48, a. 1) and all theologians teach that Christ has caused our salvation by way of merit.

6 But one could object that not only Christ's works of obedience were meritorious but also all his works in every respect.

This objection, however, presupposes that Christ did some things by his own will and others by the Father's will. But this, it seems, cannot be reconciled with what Christ said about himself (see § 2, above). Hence, Thomas Aquinas best compared Christ's love and obedience by reducing them to a kind of unity: 'He did not fulfill the commands of love except out of obedience; and he was obedient out of love for the Father who commanded' (ibid. q. 47, a. 2, ad 3m).

A special fittingness is evident in the fact that merit is connected with obedience, both because scripture indicates such a connection (Romans 5.19, Philippians 2.8), and because an operation carried out upon the command of another is in a special way fittingly rewarded by the one who commanded it. However, concerning the conditions necessary for merit, see DB 809, DS 1545–46, [ND 1946–47], and the treatise on grace. Do not suppose that no interior operation but only an exterior one is meritorious, and do not exclude the note of obedience from Hebrews 10.5–10.

### PART 7: REDEMPTION AS MEDIATION IS SEEN BOTH IN THE POWER OF THE RISEN LORD AND IN THE INTERCESSION OF THE ETERNAL PRIEST.

1 In the first thesis [of *De Verbo incarnato, The Incarnate Word*] we described the greatness of the power and might of the one who sits at the right hand of the Father.[20]

20 See Lonergan, *The Incarnate Word* 72–75.

Quod autem aeternus sacerdos pro nobis interpellat, explicite habetur apud Heb 7.25, Rom 8.34, 1 Io 2.1.

Quam mediationem memorat omnis oratio liturgica quae a Deo Patre non petit nisi per Dominum nostrum Iesum Christum.[21]

2 Dubitari tamen potest utrum ipsa resurrectio ad redemptionem pertineat.

Sed hoc dubium non fundatur nisi in erronea abstractione: aliud enim ab alio non abstrahitur ubi intelligentia alterius ab alio dependet; ita si 'pes' ab 'animali' abstrahitur, a 'pede' tolluntur omnes functiones organicae quae ipsam 'pedis' naturam faciunt et non relinquitur nisi nomen intelligentia vacuum. Cf. S. Thomam, *In Boet. de Trin.*, q. 5, a. 3. Iam vero patet resurrectionem a morte abstrahi non posse: nemo enim resurgere potest nisi qui mortuus est; neque mors Domini ab eius resurrectione abstrahi

That the eternal Priest intercedes on our behalf is stated explicitly in Hebrews 7.25, Romans 8.34, and 1 John 2.1.

This mediation is observed in the liturgy, where prayers are addressed to the Father only 'through Jesus Christ our Lord.'[21]

2 Still, there can be some doubt whether the resurrection itself pertains to redemption.

Such a doubt, however, is based solely on an erroneous abstraction: *B* is not abstracted from *A* when understanding *B* depends upon *A*. For example, if 'foot' is abstracted from 'animal,' then all the organic functions that are part of the nature of a foot are removed from it and nothing is left but a word empty of meaning. See Thomas Aquinas, *In Boethium de Trinitate*, q. 5, a. 3. Now it is clear that resurrection cannot be abstracted from death: no one can rise again except one who has died, and neither can the death of

21 The 1960 and 1961 texts have 'quae semper a Patre petit ...,' 'where prayers are always addressed to the Father ...' And the Durrwell references that appear in 1964 in point 2 are found at this point in those texts.

The next point and the beginning of point 3 were revised by Lonergan between 1961 and 1964. The earlier text (1960 and 1961) reads as follows, in Latin, followed by a translation.

'2 Quamvis clare perspiciatur mediatio tum in intercessione Sacerdotis tum in actione Domini (e.g. effundendi Spiritum sanctum, Act 2.23), dubitari potest utrum iam agatur de redemptione.

'Iam vero in Christo caelesti non perspicitur "redemptio" eo sensu quo vertit λύτρον (Mt 20.28; Mc 10.45) vel ἀντίλυτρον (1 Tim 2.6). Nam "Christus resurgens ex mortuis iam non moritur, mors illi ultra non dominabitur," Rom 6.9.

'At optime perspicitur "redemptio" in sensu activo quo Christus dicitur nos redimere ab omni iniquitate et mundare sibi populum acceptabilem (Tit 2.14; cf. partem 1m, nn. 5, 6).

'3 Convenienter autem in consideratione redemptionis ad Dominum sedentem ad dexteram Patris et ad Sacerdotem intercedentem attenditur.'

'2 Although mediation is clearly evident both in the intercession of the Priest and in the action of the Lord (e.g., the outpouring of the Spirit, Acts 2.23), there can be doubt as to whether this still concerns redemption.

'Now what is evident in Christ in glory is not "redemption" in the sense that translates λύτρον (Matthew 20.28, Mark 10.45) or ἀντίλυτρον (1 Timothy 2.5). For "Christ, being raised from the dead, will never die again; death no longer has dominion over him" (Romans 6.9).

'Yet what is evident above all is "redemption" in the active sense in which Christ is said to "redeem us from all iniquity and purify for himself a people of his own" (Titus 2.14; see part 1, points 5 and 6).

'3 It is appropriate, however, in a consideration of redemption to attend to the Lord seated at the Father's right hand and to the Priest who intercedes.'

potest; non enim mortuus est Dominus ut videret corruptionem (Act 2.31), sed ideo posuit animam suam *ut* iterum sumat eam (Io 10.17) qui tam sumendi quam ponendi potestatem habuit (Io 10.18). Cf. F.X. Durrwell, *La résurrection de Jésus,* Le Puy – Paris, 1950, 1954;[22] 'Christus victor mortis,' *Gregorianum* 39 (1958).

Quapropter, sicut mors Christi ad redemptionem pertinet, ita etiam ipsa resurrectio Christi ad redemptionem pertinet. Qui enim mortem Christi dicit neque mortem in corruptionem dicit neque mortem quandam abstractam dicit, sed concretam eam mortem quam intendebat et elegit et passus est Dominus: quae mors in resurrectionem fuit ut mors per mortem vinceretur et destrueretur.

3 Attamen, exclusa erronea abstractione, convenienter alibi ad alia attenditur. Ubi superius cum ecclesia diximus solutum esse pretium per mortem, cum ecclesia pariter intelleximus non abstractam mortem neque mortem in corruptionem sed mortem resurrecturi. Et idem cogita de morte propter delicta ubi intendebantur tum Christi resurrectio tum nostra iustificatio (Rom 4.25); de sacrificio quod obtulit Sacerdos in aeternum (Heb 6.20, 7.24–28, 9.24); de meritoria obedientia propter quam exaltatus est Dominus (Phil 2.8–11). Et vicissim, ubi infra de spiritu vivificante et de sacerdote intercedente agetur, non cogitandus est resuscitatus quasi numquam mortuus esset; neque tamen ideo omittenda sunt quae facilius in resuscitato perspiciantur.

Primo, enim, quamvis in passione et morte Domini adsit actio nostri vicarii qui obedire elegit, sacrificium obtulit, pretium solvit, facilius tamen ad aspectum passivum, in moriente multo magis clarum, attenditur; et ideo convenienter ad Dominum sedentem ad dexteram Patris mens nostra dirigitur, ut aspectus pure activus consideretur.

the Lord be abstracted from his resurrection, for the Lord did not die in such a way as to experience corruption (Acts 2.31), but he who had the power to lay down his life and take it up again (John 10.18) laid down his life precisely *in order to* take it up again (John 10.17). See François-Xavier Durrwell, *La résurrection de Jésus, mystére de salut; étude biblique* (Le Puy and Paris: Xavier Mappus, 1950; 2nd ed., rev. and augm., 1954–55).[22] See also the series of articles on the resurrection by various authors from a conference held at the Gregorian University, Rome, from 23rd to 27th September, 1957, under the general heading 'Christus Victor Mortis,' published in *Gregorianum* 39 (1958) 201–524.

Therefore, just as Christ's death pertains to redemption, so also does his resurrection. To speak of Christ's death is to speak not of a death that leads to corruption, nor of some abstract death, but of that concrete death which the Lord intended, chose, and suffered. This death was a dying into resurrection, so that death might be conquered and destroyed by death.

3 Nevertheless, having ruled out this erroneous abstraction, it will be appropriate to consider other points in order. When with the church we said above that the price was paid by death, we likewise with the church understood not an abstract death nor death into corruption but the death of one who was to rise again. And the same is to be thought of the death on account of sin, in which both Christ's resurrection and our justification were intended (Romans 4.25), of the sacrifice offered by the eternal Priest (Hebrews 6.20, 7.24–28, 9.24), and of the meritorious obedience on account of which the Lord was exalted (Philippians 2.8–11). Conversely, when we deal later with the life-giving spirit and with priestly intercession, one must not think that Jesus was raised up as if he had never died; nor yet should we omit those realities that are more easily grasped in the risen one.

First, then, although vicarious action is present in the passion and death of the Lord who chose to obey, offered the sacrifice, and paid the price, it is easier to attend to the passive aspect, which is much more obvious in his dying; and therefore our minds appropriately turn to the Lord sitting at the right hand of the Father in order to consider the purely active aspect.

22 English translation, *The Resurrection: A Biblical Study*, trans. Rosemary Sheed (New York: Sheed and Ward, 1960; 10th ed. of French, 'entièrement refondue,' Paris: Éditions du Cerf, 1976).

Deinde, quamvis in passione et morte adfuerit aspectus personalis mediationis, si quidem persona divina propter mandatum Patris pro nobis passa et mortua est, tamen hic aspectus mediationis personalis clarius perspicitur in Sacerdote caelesti interpellante.

Tertio, ipsa redemptio ut finis duplici stadio peragitur, si quidem nunc cum metu et tremore nostram salutem operamur (Phil 2.12); et cum Dominus Christus non solum opus nostrae salutis inceperit sed etiam nunc in ultimam perfectionem producat, minime praetereundum[23] est hoc redemptoris munus quo 'tamquam caput in membra et tamquam vitis in palmites in ipsos iustificatos iugiter virtutem influat' (DB 809, DS 1546).

Quarto, redemptio peccato opponitur. Sed peccatum non est tantummodo actus humanus malus in tali genere et specie collocatus; nam et est offensa Dei et tamquam inimicitia cum Deo perdurat. Similiter, redemptio non est tantummodo transactio quaedam olim peracta, sed est mediatio Filii qui carnem assumpsit ut nostram carnem mundaret et resuscitatam secum in caelos elevaret, ubi primogenitus ex multis fratribus cum Deo Patre in Spiritu sancto in aeternum regnabit.

4 *Sanctificatio.* Christus ergo, mortificatus quidem carne, vivificatus autem spiritu (1 Pet 3.18), non iam cognoscitur secundum carnem (2 Cor 5.16), cum factus sit spiritus vivificans (1 Cor 15.45; cf. Io 6.62–64) et Filius Dei in virtute secundum spiritum sanctificationis ex resurrectione mortuorum (Rom 1.4; cf. Act 13.33).

Secundum hanc virtutem sanctificatricem 'traditus est propter delicta nostra et resurrexit propter iustificationem nostram' (Rom 4.25); secundum hanc iustificationem 'vita vestra est abscondita cum Christo in Deo' (Col 3.3); et sine hac resurrectione et iustificatione iam in peccatis nostris essemus, nam 'si Christus non resurrexit, vana est fides vestra; adhuc enim estis in peccatis vestris' (1 Cor 15.17).

Quorum locorum sensus videtur obvius, quamvis sint qui in 1 Cor vanam ideo futuram fuisse fidem censeant, non quia non haberetur iustificatio sed quia non haberetur argumentum apologeticum ex resurrectione. Vide S. Lyonnet, *Gregorianum* 39 (1958) 297–318; *Exegesis epist. ad Rom.*, MS, 1960, 294–96; D. Stanley, *Verbum Domini* 29 (1951) 257–74; J.M. Gonzalez Ruiz, *Biblica* (1959) 837–58; B. Vawter, *CathBibQuar* 15 (1953) 17–23.

Second, although the aspect of personal mediation was present in his passion and death, since it was a divine person who by the Father's command suffered and died for us, nevertheless this aspect of personal mediation is more clearly seen in the Priest in glory interceding on our behalf.

Third, the redemption as end is accomplished in two stages, since in this life we work out our salvation with fear and trembling (Philippians 2.12); and since Christ our Lord not only began the work of our salvation but also now is bringing it to final perfection, we must by no means omit[23] this work of the redeemer by which he 'continually infuses strength into the justified, as the head into the members and the vine into the branches' (DB 809, DS 1546, [ND 1947]).

Fourth, redemption and sin are opposites. But sin is not only an evil human act, classified in such and such a genus and species; it is an offense against God and continues as an ongoing enmity with God. Similarly, redemption is not just a transaction performed long ago, but is the mediation of the Son who assumed flesh in order to purify our flesh and raise it up to heaven with him, where, as 'the firstborn of many children' [Romans 8.29], he will reign for ever with God the Father in the Holy Spirit.

4 *Sanctification.* Thus, Christ, 'put to death in the flesh, but made alive in the Spirit' (1 Peter 3.18), is no longer known 'according to the flesh' (2 Corinthians 5.16), since he has become 'a life-giving spirit' (1 Corinthians 15.45; see John 6.62–64) and 'Son of God with power according to the spirit of holiness by resurrection from the dead' (Romans 1.4; see Acts 13.33).

In accordance with this sanctifying power he 'was handed over to death for our trespasses and was raised for our justification' (Romans 4.25), and through this justification 'your life is hidden with Christ in God' (Colossians 3.3). Without this resurrection and justification, we should still be in our sins, for 'if Christ has not been raised, your faith is futile and you are still in your sins' (1 Corinthians 15.17).

The meaning of these texts seems quite clear, although there are those who think that in 1 Corinthians 15.17 faith would have been futile, not because there would be no justification, but because there would be no apologetic argument for faith based upon the resurrection. See Stanislas Lyonnet, 'La valeur sotériologique de la résurrection du Christ selon saint Paul,' *Gregorianum* 39 (1958) 295–318, at 297–318; *Exegesis Epistulae ad*

23 Reading 'praetereundum' for Lonergan's 'praeterendum.'

5 *Sacerdos.* Idem Filius in virtute secundum spiritum sanctificationis sanctificat, quia factus est pontifex in aeternum (Heb 6.20, 7.28), melius sortitus ministerium (Heb 8.6), consedens in dextera sedis magnitudinis in caelis, sanctorum minister et tabernaculi veri, quod fixit Deus et non homo (Heb 8.1–2), ubi apparet nunc vultui Dei pro nobis (Heb 9.24), unde et facit sanguinis aspersionem melius loquentem quam Abel (Heb 12.24).[24]

Nam qui per aeternum spiritum semet ipsum obtulit immaculatum Deo, et aeternam redemptionem invenit, eius sanguis emundabit conscientiam nostram ab operibus mortuis ad serviendum Deo viventi (Heb 9.14, 9.12); vivit enim (Heb 7.8) et sacerdos est, non secundum legem mandati carnalis, sed secundum virtutem vitae insolubilis (Heb 7.16), et eo quod manet in aeternum, sempiternum habet sacerdotium (Heb 7.24) quo proximamus ad Deum (Heb 7.19).

Obiecerit tamen quispiam superfluere hanc multiplicem activitatem aeterni Sacerdotis. Nam mors Christi est principium omnino sufficiens nostrae salutis; et applicatio mortis Christi per ecclesiam, sacrificium Missae, et sacramenta sufficienter obtinetur.

R. Obiciens tripliciter errare videtur. Primo enim ea seiungit quae nisi simul non intelligantur.[25] Deinde, quamvis instrumentalia in suo ordine omnino sufficiant, immo superabundent, non ideo tollitur operatio causae principalis. Tertio, quamvis gratia sit quoddam accidens, vel permanens vel etiam transiens, in anima et in potentiis receptum, tamen hoc non est

*Romanos, cap. I ad IV*, 3rd ed. rev. and augm. (Rome: Pontifical Biblical Institute, 1963) 294–96; David M. Stanley, 'Ad historiam exegeseos Rom 4, 25,' *Verbum Domini* 29 (1951) 257–74; José María González Ruiz, '"Muerto por nuestros pecados y resucitado por nuestra justificación,"' *Biblica* 40 (1959) 837–58; Bruce Vawter, 'Resurrection and Redemption,' *Catholic Biblical Quarterly* 15 (1953) 12–23 at 17–23.

5 *Priest.* This same 'Son of God with power according to the spirit of holiness' [Romans 1.4] sanctifies because he has been made High Priest forever (Hebrews 6.20, 7.28), has been allotted a far higher ministry (Hebrews 8.6), sits at the right hand of the throne of majesty in the heavens, the minister in the sanctuary and the true tent that the Lord, and not any mortal, has set up (Hebrews 8.1–2), where he appears now in the presence of God on our behalf (Hebrews 9.24), with a sprinkling of blood that speaks more effectively than the blood of Abel (Hebrews 12.24).[24]

For the one who through the eternal spirit offered himself immaculate to God and won eternal redemption cleansed by his blood our conscience from dead works to serve the living God (Hebrews 9.14, 9.12); for he lives (Hebrews 7.8) and is a priest, not on the basis of a regulation as to his ancestry but on the basis of the power of an indestructible life (Hebrews 7.16), and because he lives forever, he has an eternal priesthood (Hebrews 7.24) by which we draw near to God (Hebrews 7.19).

Still, one might object that all this activity of the eternal Priest is superfluous. For the death of Christ is the principle that is entirely sufficient for our salvation; and the application of Christ's death is sufficiently obtained through the church, the sacrifice of the Mass, and the sacraments.

In reply we would say that the objector seems to err in three ways. First, he separates what can only be understood when taken together.[25] Second, although instrumental causes be wholly sufficient, even superabundant, in their own order, the operation of the principal cause does not thereby disappear. Third, although grace is an accident, either permanent or transient, received in the soul and in its powers, nonetheless this is not to be understood to the exclusion of the interpersonal relationship by which we

24 The 1960 and 1961 editions add 'Gen 4.10' and '1 Pet 1.2' to 'Heb 12.24.' The 1964 version omits the following paragraph, which has here been restored.

25 This sentence does not appear in the earlier versions, where the objector 'seems to err in two ways,' not three. Thus what here is second there is first, and what here is third there is second.

intelligendum ad exclusionem habitudinis interpersonalis secundum quam in amicitiam cum Deo Patre per Filium suum carnem factum in Spiritu sancto reducimur. Cf. *Divinarum personarum* 229–39, *De Deo trino II* 249–59.

6 *Intercessio.* Qualis autem sit interpellatio aeterni Sacerdotis et advocati (Heb 7.25, Rom 8.34, 1 Io 2.1) narravisse videtur S. Ioannes ubi Iesum exhibet dicentem: 'et iam non sum in mundo,' et 'cum essem cum illis, ego servabam eos' (Io 17.11–12).

Quo in loco, postquam pro se (Io 17.1–5) et pro apostolis (vv. 6, 19) oravit, etiam eos memorat 'qui credituri sunt per verbum eorum in me' (v. 20). Pro quibus orat 'ut unum sint, sicut tu Pater in me et ego in te, ut ipsi in nobis unum sint' (vv. 21–22). Affirmat se iis illam dedisse claritatem quam Pater ipsi Christo dedit (v. 22); Patrem eos diligere sicut et Christum diligit (vv. 23, 26). Orat 'ut ubi sum ego et illi sint mecum, ut videant claritatem meam quam dedisti mihi, quia dilexisti me ante constitutionem mundi' (v. 24; cf. v. 5, 1 Io 3.2, Col 3.4).

Neque dubitare potest Christum, sicut se ipsum sanctum seu sacrum fecit pro apostolis, ita etiam se sacrum fecit pro credituris (v. 19) quos etiam Deo offert (1 Pet 3.18; cf. 2.5).

7 *Missio S. Spiritus.* Ante glorificationem Iesu non est datus Spiritus (Io 7.39); 'si enim non abiero, Paraclitus non veniet ad vos; si autem abiero, mittam eum ad vos' (Io 16.7).

Dominus autem resuscitatus in apostolos insufflavit ut Spiritum sanctum acciperent et potestatem remittendi peccata haberent (Io 20.22–23). Die autem Pentecostes, apertum et manifestum Spiritus sancti donum a S. Petro attribuitur Iesu (Act 2.33).

Tam in nomine Domini Iesu quam in Spiritu Dei sumus abluti, sanctificati, iustificati (1 Cor 6.11). Et quia filii adoptionis facti sumus, misit Deus Spiritum Filii sui in corda nostra clamantem, Abba, Pater (Gal 4.6, Rom 8.15). Unde apud Paulum ad idem redit sive dicimur in Christo sive dicimur in Spiritu. Cf. Prat, *La théologie de S. Paul,* II, note M, p. 479, edit. 9, 1925.[26]

are brought into friendship with God the Father through his incarnate Son in the Holy Spirit. See *Divinarum personarum* 229–39; *De Deo trino II: Pars systematica* 249–59 [*The Triune God: Systematics* 500–21].

6 *Intercession.* The nature of the intercession of the eternal Priest and advocate (Hebrews 7.25, Romans 8.34, 1 John 2.1) seems to have been described by St John where he depicts Jesus saying, 'And now I am no longer in the world,' and 'while I was with them, I protected them' (John 17.11–12).

In this passage, after he prayed for himself (John 17.1–5) and for the apostles (vv. 6, 19), he also mentions 'those who will believe in me through their word' (v. 20). For these he prays 'that they may all be one. As you, Father, are in me and I am in you, may they also be one in us' (vv. 21–22). He declares that he has given them the glory that the Father has given to him (v. 22), and that the Father loves them just as he loves Christ (vv. 23, 26). He prays 'that those also, whom you have given me, may be with me where I am, to see my glory, which you have given me because you loved me before the foundation of the world' (v. 24; see v. 5, 1 John 3.2, Colossians 3.4).

It cannot be doubted that Christ, just as he sanctified or consecrated himself for the apostles, so also he consecrated himself for those who were to believe in him (John 17.19) and whom he also offers to God (1 Peter 3.18; see 2.5).

7 *The mission of the Holy Spirit.* Prior to the glorification of Jesus, the Spirit was not given (John 7.39); 'for if I do not go away, the Advocate will not come to you; but if I go, I will send him to you' (John 16.7).

The risen Lord breathed upon the apostles that they might receive the Holy Spirit and have the power to forgive sins (John 20.22–23). On the day of Pentecost, St Peter attributed to Jesus the public and manifest gift of the Holy Spirit (Acts 2.33).

We are washed, sanctified, justified (1 Corinthians 6.11) as much in the name of the Lord Jesus as in the Spirit of God. And because we have become the adopted children of God, he has sent the Spirit of his Son into our hearts crying out, 'Abba, Father!' (Galatians 4.6, Romans 8.15). Hence, in Paul it comes to the same thing whether we are said to be in Christ or in the Spirit. See Ferdinand Prat, *La théologie de S. Paul*, vol. 2 (Paris: Gabriel Beauchesne, Éditeur, 1925) 479–80, note m.[26]

26 English translation: *The Theology of Saint Paul*, vol. 2, trans. John L. Stoddard from the 10th French edition (Westminster, MD: Newman Bookshop 1952) 394–95, note m.

***Scholion: De modis et effectibus redemptionis***

Cum S. Thomas de convenientia Incarnationis tractaverit (*Sum. theol.*, III, q. 1, a. 2), enumeratis quinque rationibus quantum ad promotionem hominis in bono et aliis quinque additis quantum ad remotionem mali, conclusit denique: 'Sunt autem et aliae plurimae utilitates quae consecutae sunt supra comprehensionem sensus humani.'

Similiter, cum de redemptione disputaverit non unam quandam rationem quasi totius mysterii essentiam exposuit, sed et multos modos et multos effectus enumeravit. Quorum caetera ita alte in mente Catholica fixa sunt ut ad paginam S. Doctoris aliud addere haud necessarium est; cum tamen de satisfactione qualis sit, non una sit omnium sententia, thesin ponemus distinctam et proximam.

Q. 48,[27] a. 1: de merito. Cf. supra de obedientia meritoria.

Q. 48, a. 3: de sacrificio. Cf. supra de sacrificio et etiam tractatum de Eucharistia ubi plenius ratio sacrificii explorari solet.

Q. 48, a. 4: de redemptione. Cf. supra de soluto pretio.

Q. 48, a. 6: de efficientia. Cf. supra de mediatione Christi caelesti, et etiam tractatum de sacramentis in genere, ubi de causalitate sacramentorum quae sunt instrumenta humanitatis Christi.

Q. 49,[28] aa. 1 et 3: de liberatione a peccato et a poena. De qua modo generali tota thesis 15a; magis particularia in tractatu de baptismo qui ab omni reatu culpae et poenae liberat.

Q. 49, a. 2: de liberatione a potestate diaboli, Heb 2.14–15, Col 1.13; cf. damnationem Abaelardi, DB 371, DS 723. Patres, qui hoc thema elaborare solebant: J. Rivière, DTC XIII (26) 1939–41; L. Richard 104, 112–17. Vide tractatum de gratia: de necessitate gratiae et de morali impotentia peccatoris, *Sum. Theol.*, I-II, q. 109, tractatum de peccato originali, DB 2318, DS 3891.

Q. 49, a. 4: de reconciliatione. Rom 5.10–11, 11.15, 2 Cor 5.18–19, 1 Cor 7.11. Thema reconciliationis totum aspectum personalem tum peccati ut offensae Dei tum redemptionis ut mediationis complectitur. Vide tractatum de paenitentia.

### *A note on the modes and effects of redemption*

When St Thomas was treating the fittingness of the incarnation (*Summa theologiae*, 3, q. 1, a. 2), after listing five ways in which it was conducive to human progress in moral good and then five ways in which it was helpful in removing moral evil, he concluded, 'It has many other advantageous consequences, which are beyond human comprehension.'

In a similar way, when discussing the redemption, he did not put forth some single concept as the essence of the entire mystery, but enumerated both many modes and many effects. All but one of these are so deeply fixed in the Catholic mind that it is quite unnecessary to add anything to what the Angelic Doctor has written; but concerning the nature of satisfaction there is a variety of opinions, and therefore we will add a separate treatment of it in the next thesis.

*Summa theologiae*, 3, q. 48,[27] Article 1: on merit. See above, on meritorious obedience [pp. 64–65].

Article 3: on sacrifice. See above, on sacrifice [pp. 52–59], and see also the treatise on the Eucharist, where the notion of sacrifice is more fully explored.

Article 4: on redemption. See above, on price paid [pp. 40–45].

Article 6: on efficient causality. See above, on the mediation of Christ in glory [p. 71], and also the treatise on the sacraments in general concerning the causality of the sacraments as instruments of the humanity of Christ.

Question 49,[28] articles 1 and 3: on deliverance from sin and from punishment. The whole of this present thesis has dealt with this in a general way. There is more in particular in the treatise on baptism, which releases one from every liability for fault and punishment.

Article 2: on deliverance from the power of the devil, Hebrews 2.14–15, Colossians 1.13; see the condemnation of Abelard, DB 371, DS 723. Concerning the Fathers of the church, who wrote extensively on this theme, see Rivière, 'Rédemption' 1939–41, and Richard, *Le mystère de la Rédemption* 104, 112–17 [*The Mystery of the Redemption* 138–39, 149–56]. See the treatise on grace; on the necessity of grace and the moral impotence of the sinner, *Summa theologiae* 1-2, q. 109; on original sin, DB 2318, DS 3891.

Article 4: on reconciliation. Romans 5.10–11, 11.15, 2 Corinthians 5.18–19, 1 Corinthians 7.11. The theme of reconciliation embraces the whole personal aspect both of sin as an offense against God, and of redemption as a mediation. See the treatise on the sacrament of penance.

27 This question treats the efficacy of Christ's passion.
28 Question 49 deals with the effects of the passion of Christ.

**THESIS 16**

**De Satisfactione Christi.[1] Christus pro peccatis nostris non solum condigne sed etiam superabundanter satisfecit; quae quidem satisfactio secundum analogiam sacramentalem intelligitur; et ideo vicariae passioni et morti addit expressionem summae detestationis omnium peccatorum et summi doloris de omni offensa Dei.**

***Termini***

*Christus*: scil., homo; persona divina in natura humana subsistens.

*peccatum*: actus humanus malus; malitia attenditur praecipue theologica, quae in offensa Dei consistit.

*nostra*: loquentes sunt omnes homines; agitur de omni peccato, originali et actuali, omnium hominum.

*satisfacere*: 'Ille proprie satisfacit pro offensa qui exhibet offenso id quod aeque vel magis diligit quam oderit offensam' (*Sum. theol.*, III, q. 48, a. 2).

*condigne*: qui exhibet quod aeque placet.

*superabundanter*: qui exhibet quod offensus magis diligit.

*sacramentum*: scil., paenitentiae. DB 893a–906, 911–25; DS 1667–93, 1701–15.

*analogia sacramentalis*: scil., analogia est petenda non ex iure Romano vel Germanico[2] sed ex complexione notionum quae in sacramento paenitentiae et usu ecclesiae inveniuntur.

*expressio*: manifestatio sensibilis.

*vicaria passio et mors*: vide thesin 15m.

*detestatio*: respicit peccatum ut malum; supponit iudicium valoris: dicit odium voluntatis.

*dolor*: dolor se habet ad malum praesens sicut delectatio ad bonum praesens. Notio doloris plene evolvitur, *Sum. theol.*, I-II, qq. 35–39.

## THESIS 16

**Christ's satisfaction.[1] Christ made not only condign but even superabundant satisfaction for our sins. This satisfaction is understood according to a sacramental analogy, and therefore it adds to Christ's vicarious passion and death an expression of the utmost detestation of all sins and of the greatest sorrow for all offense against God.**

### *Terminology*

*Christ*: that is, the human Christ, a divine person subsisting in a human nature.

*sin*: a morally evil human act; the evil considered here is chiefly theological, which consists in an offense against God.

*our*: all human beings are speaking here; every sin, original and actual, of all human beings, is taken into account.

*satisfaction*: 'one properly gives satisfaction for an offense who presents something the offended one loves equally, or even more than he detested the offense' (*Summa theologiae*, 3, q. 48, a. 2).

*condign*: equally pleasing to the person offended.

*superabundant*: more pleasing to the person offended.

*sacrament*: the sacrament of penance. DB 893a–906, 911–25; DS 1667–93, 1701–15; [ND 1615–34, 1641–55].

*sacramental analogy*: the analogy is to be taken not from Roman or Germanic law[2] but from the complex of notions found in the sacrament of penance and in the practice of the church.

*expression*: a sensible manifestation.

*vicarious passion and death*: see thesis 15.

*detestation*: regards sin as evil; it presupposes a judgment of value: it denotes a willful hatred.

*sorrow*: sorrow stands to a present evil as delight to a present good. The notion of sorrow is fully developed in *Summa theologiae*, 1-2, qq. 35–39.

1 In the 1960 edition, the thesis is preceded by a full page headed 'De Satisfactione Christi,' and containing an outline of the major divisions: Termini, Magisterium, Nota, Sensus theseos, Sententiae, all eleven Praenotamina, and the seven assertions that make up the argument of the thesis.

2 On Roman law, see Richard, *Le mystère de la Rédemption* 134 [*The Mystery of the Redemption* 179–80]. On Germanic law, see below, p. 185, note 40.

*dolor de offensa Dei*: supponit caritatem erga Deum, detestationem peccati, et factum peccati contra Deum; unde caritas facit ut quis doleat de offensa Dei sicut de malo sibi praesente, seu sicut de malo suo.

### *Magisterium*

*Tridentinum*: 'sua sanctissima passione in ligno crucis nobis iustificationem meruit et pro nobis Deo Patri satisfecit' (DB 799, DS 1529).

Ibid.: '... dum satisfaciendo patimur pro peccatis, Christo Iesu, qui pro peccatis nostris satisfecit ... conformes ... efficimur' (DB 904, DS 1690).

*Leo XIII*: '... violato Patris numini cumulatissime pro hominibus uberrimeque satisfecit de sanguine suo ...' ASS 33 (1900–1901) 275.

Secundum schema c. Vaticani I, in capite positum esset quod Christus divinae iustitiae pro nobis satisfecit, in canonibus quod satisfacere potuit et quod vere et proprie satisfecit. Col. Lac., VII, 561a, 566c.[3] Plenior citatio apud L. Richard, 187, 189.[4] Mens theologorum: Col. Lac., VII, 543bc.

*Pius XII* repraehendit perversionem notionis satisfactionis pro nobis a Christo exhibitae (DB 2318, DS 3891).

### *Nota*

Ipsum factum quod Christus homo pro nobis et propter nostra peccata Deo satisfecit (1) supponitur a Tridentino sed non proprie definitur, (2) est implicite in scripturis et explicite in magisterio ordinario, (3) dicitur a Galtier proximum fidei, 372, § 469.[5]

*sorrow for offense against God*: presupposes charity for God, detestation for sin, and the fact of sin against God; hence charity makes one sorrow for an offense against God as one would sorrow over an evil present to oneself, or over one's own evil.

### *Church teaching*

*Council of Trent*: '... by his most holy passion on the wood of the cross he merited justification and made satisfaction for us to God the Father' (DB 799, DS 1529, [ND 647]).

And: '... when we suffer in satisfaction for our sins, we become conformed to Christ Jesus, who made satisfaction for our sins' (DB 904, DS 1690, [ND 1631]).

*Leo XIII*: '... by his blood he has satisfied for men the Father's violated majesty most abundantly and most richly' (ASS 33 [1900–1901] 275).

According to a schema of the First Vatican Council, it would have been stated in a chapter [of a Constitution] that Christ satisfied divine justice for us, and in the canons, that he was able to make satisfaction and that he truly and properly did so. (See *Collectio Lacensis Conciliorum Recentiorum*, VII, 561a, 566c;[3] for further citations, Richard, *Le mystère de la Rédemption* 187, 189;[4] for the mind of the theologians, *Collectio Lacensis*, VII, 543bc.

*Pius XII* censured a distortion of the notion of the satisfaction made for us by Christ (DB 2318, DS 3891).

### *Theological note*

The fact that the human Christ made satisfaction to God for us and because of our sins (1) is presupposed by Trent but not strictly defined, (2) is implicit in scripture and explicit in the ordinary magisterium, and (3) is said by Galtier to be proximate to faith.[5]

3 *Acta et decreta sacrosancti oecumenici Concilii Vaticani: cum permultis aliis documentis ad concilium eiusque historiam spectantibus* (Freiburg im Breisgau: Herder, 1892).

4 These citations are not included in the English translation of Richard's book.

5 Paul Galtier, *De incarnatione ac redemptione*, new ed. (Paris: Beauchesne, 1947) 372, § 469. *Sententia fidei proxima* refers to teachings generally accepted as divine revelation but not defined as such by the church.

***Sensus theseos***

1 Satisfactio materialiter est illa vicaria passio et mors Christi propter peccata et pro peccatoribus, de qua egimus thesi 15a, parte 4a; ubi 'propter peccata' consideratur non secundum finem peccata delendi sed secundum motivum cur Christum pati et mori oportuerit; ubi 'pro peccatoribus' consideratur non secundum finem, qui utilitatem peccatorum includit, sed secundum motivum, quia peccatores poenas meruerunt.

Materialiter ergo satisfactio est quaedam expiatio propter peccata commissa secundum aliquem sensum expiationis; et est expiatio vicaria quia est pro aliis secundum aliquem sensum istius 'pro.'

2 Satisfactio formaliter est nudum factum supra expositum secundum aliquam interpretationem, secundum aliquem contextum intelligibilem. Pro variis enim interpretationibus seu contextibus intelligibilibus, alii aliter intelligunt illum sensum, quem superius reliquimus indeterminatum, secundum quem in Christo patiente et moriente verificatur expiatio quaedam pro peccatis alienis.

3 Iam vero eiusmodi interpretatio seu contextus intelligibilis nihil est aliud quam theologia quaedam systematica; neque fit theologia systematica per frusta. Involvitur theologia de peccatis et poenis; involvitur theologia de iustitia Dei; et denique tandem non est praetermittenda theologia de redemptione.

4 Sicut in aliis quaestionibus etiam in hac numquam desunt qui dicant omittenda esse disputata et clare esse dicenda quae omnes boni Catholici profiteantur.

Sed quaero utrum haec omissio atque selectio sint faciendae ab aliquo intelligente vel ab aliquo non intelligente, ab aliquo sapiente vel ab aliquo insipiente. Sane nemo vult insipientem et non intelligentem audire. Volunt ergo intelligentem et sapientem, neque intelligentem et sapientem de aliis quibuscumque rebus, sed intelligentem et sapientem de theologia peccati et poenae, de theologia iustitiae, de theologia redemptionis.

***Meaning of the thesis***

1 Considered materially, satisfaction is that vicarious passion and death of Christ because of sins and for sinners which we dealt with in part 4 of thesis 15. Here, 'because of sins' is understood, not from the standpoint of the end, the wiping away of sins, but from the standpoint of motive, that is, why Christ had to suffer and die; and also 'for sinners' is understood, not from the standpoint of the end, which includes the benefit of sinners, but from the standpoint of motive, because sinners deserved punishment.

Materially, therefore, satisfaction is expiation for sins committed, in some sense of the word 'expiation'; and it is a vicarious expiation because it is for others, in some sense of the word 'for.'

2 Considered formally, satisfaction is the simple fact just referred to as understood according to some interpretation, some intelligible context. Depending upon the various interpretations or intelligible contexts, various theologians understand differently that meaning which we have left indeterminate, according to which there is verified in Christ's suffering and death an expiation for the sins of others.

3 Now, such an interpretation or intelligible context is nothing other than an instance of systematic theology, and systematic theology is not put together piecemeal. The theology of sin and punishment is involved, as well as the theology of the justice of God; and lastly, the theology of redemption must not be omitted.

4 In this question as in others, there are never lacking those who say that disputed points should be ignored and that what all good Catholics profess should be stated clearly.

But, I ask, is this omission and this selection to be made by someone who understands or by someone who does not understand, by someone who is wise or by someone who is not? Surely no one wants to listen to one who is unwise or does not understand. Hence they want someone understanding and wise, and not understanding and wise in any other matters whatever, but understanding and wise concerning the theology of sin and punishment, the theology of justice, and the theology of redemption.

Quid autem est illud intelligere? Est quaedam nexuum perspicientia secundum quam habitui intellectus attribuitur quod, positis terminis, perspiciuntur principia.[6]

Quid autem est illud sapere? Est illa omnium ordinatio secundum quam quis bene seligit et definit ipsos terminos fundamentales e quibus conflantur principia. Vide *Sum. theol.*, I-II, q. 66, a. 5, ad 4m.

Quid denique est intelligere vel sapere theologicum? Est quod describitur in Vaticano, DB 1796, 1800, DS 3016, 3020. Est quod veris revelatis, magisterio ecclesiae, Patribus, theologis inhaeret. Neque, uti patet, ita ad inhaesionem attendit ut intelligentiam et sapientiam parvi faciat, contra c. Vaticanum (DB 1800, DS 3020).

5 Quae cum ita sint, post indicatas sententias non pauca addemus praenotamina quibus, uti speramus, ad aliquam huius quaestionis intelligentiam et ad quoddam iudicium sapiens perveniri potest.

6 At quamvis praenotamina longiora sint, sensus eorum brevis et simplex est.

'Poenas pro peccatis dare' in duplici contextu poni potest. Poni potest in contextu in quo nulla est quaestio de venia petenda vel concedenda, in quo unice agitur de illa iustitia quae retributiva vel vindicativa dicitur. Sed etiam poni potest in contextu in quo principaliter agitur de venia petenda et concedenda, de detestatione et dolore circa offensam, de remissione tum culpae tum poenae. Vide praenotamina IV et V.

Iam vero 'poenas dare' in primo contextu non est satisfactio; et 'poenas dare' in altero contextu est satisfactio.

Proinde sive in primo contextu sive in altero poenae dantur, hoc secundum divinam iustitiam est et ad reparandum seu redintegrandum ordinem divinae iustitiae fit. Quia autem non unus sed duo sunt contextus in quibus

What, then, is this understanding? It is a grasping of connections; hence, it is attributed to the habit of understanding that, when terms are posited, the principles are grasped.[6]

What is wisdom? It is that ordering of all things by which one rightly selects and defines the fundamental terms themselves from which principles [for understanding] are gathered. See Thomas Aquinas, *Summa theologiae*, 1-2, q. 66, a. 5, ad 4m.

What, finally, is theological understanding or wisdom? It is what is described by Vatican I, DB 1796, 1800, DS 3016, 3020; [ND 132, 136]. It holds fast to revealed truths, the teaching of the church, the Fathers and theologians, but obviously not in such a way as to belittle – against the teaching of the council – understanding and wisdom (DB 1800, DS 3020, [ND 136]).

5 Accordingly, we will indicate the various opinions on this matter, and then add a number of preliminary notes whereby, we hope, one who is wise can arrive at some understanding of this question and at a judgment.

6 But although these preliminary notes are rather lengthy, their meaning is short and simple.

'Paying the penalty for sin' can take place in two contexts. It can take place in a context in which there is no question of asking or granting pardon, in which what is at stake is that justice that is called retributive or vindictive. But it can also take place in a context in which the main concern is asking and granting pardon, detestation and sorrow for offense, the remission of fault and punishment. See preliminary notes 4 and 5 [below, pp. 116–27].

Now, 'to pay the penalties' in the former context is not satisfaction; in the latter context, it is.

So then, whether penalties are paid in the former context or in the latter, it is in accord with divine justice and takes place to repair or reintegrate the order of divine justice. But because there are not one but two contexts in

6 Aquinas followed Aristotle in distinguishing intellectual from moral virtues, and identified three virtues of speculative intellect, that is, habits for contemplating truth: wisdom, science, and understanding (see *Summa theologiae*, 1-2, q. 57, a. 2). Understanding grasps principles, science is of conclusions, and wisdom orders and judges both. See Lonergan's discussion of understanding (*nous*) in *Verbum: Word and Idea in Aquinas*, vol. 2 in Collected Works of Bernard Lonergan, ed. Frederick E. Crowe and Robert M. Doran (Toronto: University of Toronto Press, 1997) 193–94; also, see the parallel discussion at Lonergan, *The Triune God: Systematics* (CWL 12) 20–31.

poenae dantur, etiam duo sunt modi quibus reparatur seu redintegratur ordo divinae iustitiae. Quia denique duo sunt contextus et duo sunt reparationis modi, tripliciter dicitur ipsa divina iustitia, nempe (1) secundum quod poenae dantur in contextu iustitiae vindicativae, (2) secundum quod poenae dantur in contextu satisfactionis, reconciliationis, remissionis, et (3) secundum quod de facto hoc in rerum ordine sunt hi duo contextus, sunt hi duo modi, et tertius non datur. Vide praenotamina II, III, VII, et VIII.

7 Quae tam brevia et clara sunt ut, quis quaerere possit cur tam longa sint praenotamina. Et ultro fatemur praenotamina futura fuisse superflua si de thesi philosophica ageretur. At theologiam tractamus, et ideo sententiarum ortum et evolutionem et conflictus pensare debemus antequam iudicare possimus utrum haec brevis et simplex notionum declaratio traditioni Catholicae sit conformis.

***Sententiae***

1 Satisfactionis notio non est nisi conceptio quaedam exprimens intelligentiam fidei circa passionem et mortem Christi.

2 Habetur materialiter haec notio inquantum creditur Christum hominem divino iudicio propter peccata et pro peccatoribus esse passum et mortuum, se Deo sacrificium obtulisse, in ordine ad remissionem totius peccati et ad reconciliationem omnium peccatorum cum Deo, huncque finem suo sanguine esse adeptum.

3 Habetur formaliter satisfactionis notio inquantum ad gravitatem peccati ut offensam Dei ('Nondum considerasti quanti ponderis sit peccatum,' S. Anselmus., *Cur Deus homo,* I, 21; edit. Schmitt II, 88)[7] attenditur et sub hoc aspectu passio et mors Christi intelliguntur. Quod quid significet sic forte declaratur.

which penalties are paid, there are also two ways in which the order of divine justice is repaired or reintegrated. Since, then, there are two contexts and two ways of reparation, we speak of divine justice in three ways, namely, (1) when penalties are paid in the context of retributive justice, (2) when penalties are paid in the context of satisfaction, reconciliation, and forgiveness, and (3) as it is in the actual order of this world in which there are these two contexts and two ways of reparation, and there is no third. See preliminary notes 2, 3, 7, 8 [below, pp. 110–17, 132–43].

7 These points are so brief and so clear that one may wonder why the preliminary notes that follow are so long. We readily admit that they would be superfluous if this were a philosophical thesis. But we are engaged in theology, and so we must carefully consider the origin and the development of various opinions and the conflicts between them before we can judge whether this short and simple statement of notions is in keeping with Catholic tradition.

### *Opinions*

1 The notion of satisfaction is simply a conception expressing an understanding of faith concerning the passion and death of Christ.

2 This notion is expressed materially in the belief that the human Christ, by divine decree, suffered and died because of sins and for sinners, offered himself as a sacrifice to God for the forgiveness of all sin and the reconciliation of all sinners to God, and that he achieved this end by his blood.

3 This notion of satisfaction is expressed formally in attending to the gravity of sin as an offense against God, – 'You have not as yet estimated the great burden of sin' (Anselm, *Cur Deus homo*, book 1, c. 21; Schmitt, vol. 2, 88)[7] – and the passion and death of Christ is understood in the light of this. What this means might be clarified as follows.

7 The Schmitt reference is to Anselm, *Opera omnia ad fidem codicum recensuit Franciscus Salesius Schmitt*, vol. 2 (Edinburgh: Nelson, 1946–61). An electronic version of this edition is available: http://archive.org/details/sanselmicantuario2anse. The English translation here is from *St. Anselm: Basic Writings*, 2nd ed., trans. S.N. Deane, with an introduction by Charles Hartshorne (La Salle, IL: Open Court Publishing Company, 1962) 242.

Heb 10.17: et peccatorum et iniquitatum eorum iam non recordabor amplius.

Quod si passus non esset Christus pro peccatis, dicere forte quis posset: Deum facere quod nobis faciendum esse praecipit; Mt 6.12: dimitte nobis debita nostra, sicut et nos dimittimus debitoribus nostris.

Cui interpretationi obstant passio et mors Domini. Non enim venisset Dominus in carne passibili, non tot et tanta passus esset, nisi 'Deus Filium suum mittens in similitudinem carnis peccati et de peccato damnavit peccatum in carne' (Rom 8.3).

Unde Christiano passionem Domini meditanti elucent duo: primo, gravitas peccati, gravitas offensae Dei, si quidem Dominus divino iudicio tot tantaque passus est et pati oportebat, neque alia huius passionis ratio assignari potest nisi peccatum; deinde, perspecta gravitate peccati, novo quodam lumine circumfunditur ipsa Domini passio, nam si tanta est passus Dominus propter gravitatem peccati, ideo est passus Dominus ut pro peccato satisfaceret.

Quid ergo est haec satisfactio? Est quod offensae Dei opponitur quantum concipi potest. Est quasi compensatio pro offensa, ubi compensatio cogitatur non ad modum negotii commercialis sed ad modum habitudinum interpersonalium. E.g., si quis offenditur, alius dicere potest, 'Bene, accepit quod meruit'; et sic non tollitur sed augetur offensa. Sed alius indignari potest de offensa, eius iniustitiam reprehendere, omnibus modis monstrare se stare non a parte offendentis sed a parte offensi; et sic quodammodo minuitur offensa, pro offensa compensatur, fit satis.

4 Sed praeter formalem satisfactionem (compensationem pro offensa) alia est consideratio passionis et mortis Domini sub ratione poenae.

Propter peccata mortalia debentur poenae aeternae; propter venialia debentur poenae temporales; quae tamen poenae eatenus auferuntur quatenus peccatori applicantur merita Christi, prout in tractatu de baptismo et de paenitentia docetur.

Quamvis tamen peccatori remittantur poenae, quas non remissas ipse iuste ex iustitia Dei vindicativa solveret, tamen Christo Domino et inculpabili non sunt remissae poenae; ipse passus est et ita passus ut inde moreretur; eius livore sanati sumus (1 Pet 2.24).

Hebrews 10.17: 'I will remember their sins and their lawless deeds no more.'

Now if Christ had not suffered for sins, one could perhaps say that God is doing what he commanded us to do: 'forgive us our debts, as we also have forgiven our debtors' (Matthew 6.12).

The Lord's passion and death contradict this interpretation. For the Lord would not have come in flesh capable of suffering, would not have suffered so many and such grievous afflictions, unless 'God ... by sending his own Son in the likeness of sinful flesh, and to deal with sin, ... condemned sin in the flesh' (Romans 8.3).

For the Christian, then, meditating on the passion of the Lord, two things are clear: first, the seriousness of sin, the seriousness of offending God, if indeed by divine decree the Lord suffered and had to suffer so much, and no other reason for this suffering can be given except sin; second, when the gravity of sin is grasped, the Lord's passion itself is bathed in a new light, for if he suffered so much on account of the gravity of sin, it follows that he suffered in order to make satisfaction for sin.

What, then, is this satisfaction? It is what is as opposed to an offense against God as can be conceived. It is, so to speak, compensation for an offense, where compensation is thought of, not in the manner of a commercial transaction, but rather in the manner of interpersonal relationships. For example, if someone is offended, someone else could say, 'Good, he got what he deserved.' That would actually add to the offense, not remove it. But another person could be indignant at the offense, denounce the injustice of it, and in every way show that he is on the side of the offended party, not that of the offender. And in this way the offense is somewhat lessened, some compensation is made for the offense, some satisfaction.

4 But besides formal satisfaction (compensation for an offense), the passion and death of the Lord can be considered under the formality of punishment.

Mortal sins are deserving of eternal punishment; venial sins are deserving of temporal punishment. But these punishments are remitted to the extent that the merits of Christ are applied to the sinner; this is taught in the treatises on baptism and penance.

But although the punishments are remitted for the sinner, which otherwise the sinner would justly undergo in accordance with divine retributive justice, nevertheless these punishments were not remitted for Christ the Lord, who was without fault. He suffered, and suffered unto death; by his wounds we have been healed (see 1 Peter 2.24).

5 Quibus perspectis, elucet satisfactionem Christi fuisse quidem compensationem pro offensa, sed non fuisse tantummodo compensationem formalem supra descriptam (§ 3). Ita satisfecit Christus ut etiam pateretur. Ita principaliter ad offensam Dei attenditur, ut tamen non praetermittatur factum poenae.

Quae quidem duo ita a S. Thoma componuntur ut poenae a Domino nostro toleratae concipiantur ut materia satisfactionis, cuius tamen principium fuit caritas Christi. Vide *Sum. theol.*, III, q. 14, a. 1 c., ad 1m et 3m; a. 3 c., ad 1m, 2m, et 3m; a. 4 c., ad 2m; quae ideo non exscripsi, non quasi non essent necessaria ad rei intelligentiam, sed quia sunt longiora.

6 Omnium tamen non est sapientia Aquinatis, et ideo ut multiplex sententiarum diversitas intelligatur, breviter considerari oportet quotupliciter ab hac supra exposita conceptione recedi possit.

7 Primo modo sed improprie dicto receditur, quatenus notio satisfactionis nondum plene erat evoluta.

Qua in evolutione duplex distinguitur stadium: (1) ante opus Anselmi (cf. praenotamen I), et (2) post Anselmum sed ante *Summam* S. Thomae (cf. praenotamen IX). Brevissime: S. Anselmus maxime ad compensationem pro offensa Dei attendit; S. Thomas hanc mysterii intelligentiam cum doctrina traditionali de poenis Christi integravit.

8 Altero modo receditur quatenus doctrina Anselmiana cum contextu theologico minus laudabili integratur.

Quae quidem recessio maioris momenti esse non videtur. Illustratur a Scoto, qui sicut de caeteris ita etiam de satisfactione Christi, de absoluta possibilitate huius vel illius rei, de valore huius vel illius demonstrationis, diligenter inquisivit, ut praetermissa rerum intelligibilitate quae de facto haberi potest, ad voluntarismum denique tandem recurreret. Iterum illustratur solutionibus quae in contractibus iuridicis hypotheticis fundantur: e. g., Christus libere mortem acceptavit et tamen Christus mori debuit; quae duo reconciliantur ex eo quod Christus libere inivit contractum quendam ut postea obligaretur ad id quod antea libere acceptavit. Cf. Suárez, *In IIIm*, 1, 2; disp. 4, sect. 3, § 7; Paris, 1866; XVII, 54.

5 From this it is clear that Christ's satisfaction was indeed compensation for the offense, but that it was not only the formal compensation described above in § 3. Christ made satisfaction in such a way that he also suffered. Hence, the focus of attention is offense against God, yet one must not overlook the fact of punishment.

These two aspects are brought together by St Thomas in conceiving the punishment borne by our Lord as the material element of satisfaction, the principle of which was Christ's love. See *Summa theologiae*, 3, q. 14, a. 1 c., ad 1m, ad 3m; a. 3 c., ad 1m, ad 2m, ad 3m; a. 4 c., ad 2m. I have not transcribed these texts here, not because they are not necessary for an understanding of the matter, but because they are too long.

6 However, not everyone possesses the wisdom of Aquinas, and therefore in order to understand the many diverse opinions it is necessary to consider briefly how many ways there are in which it is possible to fall short of the conception presented above.

7 A first way of falling short is when the notion of satisfaction was not yet fully developed. Only in an improper sense can this be called 'falling short.'

Distinguish two stages in its development: (1) before the work of Anselm (see preliminary note 1); and (2) after Anselm but before Thomas's *Summa* (see preliminary note 9). To put it briefly: Anselm directed his attention most of all to compensation for the offense against God; Thomas integrated this understanding of the mystery with the traditional teaching on Christ's punishments.

8 A second way of falling short was the integration of Anselm's doctrine into a less praiseworthy theological context.

This shortcoming does not seem to be very important. It is illustrated by Scotus, who, as in other matters, so also in regard to Christ's satisfaction persistently asked about the absolute possibility of this or that, about the value of this or that demonstration, so that in ignoring the intelligibility that in fact could be found he eventually had recourse to voluntarism. This shortcoming is illustrated also in solutions that are based upon hypothetical legal contracts: for example, that Christ freely accepted death and yet that Christ had to die; these two statements are reconciled by saying that Christ freely entered into a contract that subsequently obliged him to do what he had previously freely accepted to do. See Suárez, *In IIIm*, 1, 2; disp. 4, sect. 3, § 7 (in the Paris edition of 1866, XVII: 54).

9 Tertio modo receditur quatenus ipsa satisfactionis notio pervertitur.

Supra vidimus satisfactionem Christi principaliter fuisse compensationem pro peccatis; cui compensationi morali accedit modo subordinato passionem pro poenis a nobis debitis. At ipsa haec conceptio ita inverti potest ut principale elementum habeatur compensatio pro poenis; eatenus pro offensa satisfecit Christus quatenus pro poenis satis est passus.

Cui satispassionis notioni necessario fere annectitur notio cuiusdam substitutionis. Christus locum tenet omnium peccatorum; satis pro omnibus omnium peccatis patitur vel punitur, ut Deus iustus caeteris hominibus et peccata et poenas iuste dimittere possit.

Quae substitutionis et satispassionis theoria tripliciter proponi potest: uno modo, ab haereticis et sic apud veteres Protestantes; alio modo, ab oratoribus Catholicis qui hanc conceptionem suis artibus magis adaptatam invenerunt; tertio modo, a theologicis Catholicis qui hanc notionem censuisse videntur nihil aliud esse quam veram et genuinam doctrinam Catholicam.

10 Quarto modo et improprie dicto receditur quatenus theologia Catholica a notione satispassionis et substitutionis purificatur, ita tamen ut per excessum vel defectum non omnis error excludi videatur. Vide infra, § 19.

11 Quibus praemissis ut sententiarum diversitas intelligi possit, iam de ipsis sententiis aliquid est dicendum.

12 Circa auctores priores remittimus ad praenotamina: *S. Anselmus,* I; IX, 7; *Hugo Victorinus,* IX, 2; *Petrus Lombardus,* II, 3; IX, 2, 5; X, 2; *Gulielmus Alvernus,* IX, 2; *Ioannes de Rupella,* II, 3; IX, 2, 6; *S. Thomas,* II, 3; IV, 4–7, 10; V, 3; VI, 3, 4, 6, 8;[8] VII, 1–6, VIII, 1, 3, 4; IX, 7; X, 2, 4, 9, 10.

9 A third way of falling short distorts the very notion of satisfaction.

We saw above that Christ's satisfaction was mainly compensation for sins. To this moral compensation is added, in a subordinate role, Christ's suffering in place of the punishment that we have deserved. But this conception can be inverted so that the principal element is held to be compensation in place of our punishment: Christ made satisfaction for the offense to the extent that he suffered sufficiently in place of this punishment.

To this notion of satispassion, there is connected, almost by necessity, the notion of a kind of substitution. Christ takes the place of all sinners; he suffers enough, or is punished enough, for all the sins of all people, so that a just God might justly forgive others their sins and their punishments.

This theory of substitution and satispassion finds expression in three ways: first, by heretics, and this is the case among the early Protestants; secondly, by Catholic preachers who have found this conception better adapted to their rhetoric; thirdly, by those Catholic theologians who seem to have held this notion to be nothing other than the true and genuine Catholic doctrine.

10 There is a fourth way of falling short – again, not properly so called – insofar as Catholic theology is purged of the notion of satispassion and substitution, but in such a way that either by excess or by defect not all error seems to be excluded. See below, § 19.

11 Having prefaced these observations in order to be able to understand the diversity of opinions, we must now say something about these opinions themselves.

12 We will deal with the opinions of the earlier theologians in the preliminary notes, as follows: *Anselm,* preliminary notes 1 and 9, § 7; *Hugh of St Victor,* 9, § 2; *Peter Lombard,* 2, § 3; 9, §§ 2 and 5; 10, § 2; *William of Auvergne,* 9, § 2; *John of Rupella,* 2, § 3; 9, §§ 2 and 6; *Thomas,* 2, § 3; 4, §§ 4–7 and 10; 5, § 3; 6, §§ 3, 4, 6, and 8;[8] 7, §§ 1–6; 8, §§ 1, 3, and 4; 9, § 7; 10, §§ 2, 4, 9, and 10.

8 The 1960 edition mentioned '6' here, but not the 1961 and 1964 editions. It has been restored.

13 Circa scholasticos posteriores saec. XVI ad XIX, lamentamus eruditorum silentium. Breviter notavit J. Rivière: 'De ces longues controverses ... l'importance n'égale pas l'ampleur,' DTC XIII (26) 1951. At lacuna in historia doctrinae de redemptione agnoscenda esse videtur; quam viginti post annos nondum adimpletam demonstrare videtur recens atque diligens bibliographia a G. Oggioni confecta, *Problemi e Orientamenti,* II, 337–38.

14 Veteres Protestantes

(a) In intelligentiam eorum doctrinae, vide supra § 9; sed adde sequentia.

Negata satisfactione sacramentali, sublata est analogia fundamentalis ad satisfactionem Christi intelligendam (cf. DB 922–25; DS 1712–15).

Negata vera et reali peccatorum remissione et introducta opinione de meritis Christi nobis quodammodo imputatis, aperta est via ut demerita nostra Christo imputarentur.

Quod si per imputationem omnium peccatorum Christus quasi maximus quidam peccator erat habendus, poenas peccati ut peccator dare debuit.

(b) Apud Lutherum adsunt notiones substitutionis et satispassionis. Christus pati et mori debuit quia omnia peccata quodammodo portavit. Richard 156–61. Franks, I, 353–88.

(c) Melanchthon. Christus fuit victima ad iram divinam placandam; debuit tantam iram tantis in doloribus ita sustinere ut iustitiam divinam simul laudaret. Quibus laudibus omissis, punitio Christi non fuisset Dei placatio. Neque merus homo potuit tantos ita perferre dolores ut simul tamen Deum laudaret. Franks, I, 412.

(d) Calvinus. Caro humana pretium fuit quod divinae iustitiae satisfaceret; caro Christi debitum a nobis contractum solvit; in ordine actuali iustus Deus gratiam non confert nisi expiatio iram divinam placat; neque suffecit ipsa Christi mors, sed et anima eius ad inferos descendit ut divinae vindictae sentiret severitatem et damnatorum subiret tormenta. Attamen contra Christum Deus non est iratus. Richard 160–61. Franks, I, 427–28, 431, 434.

13 As for the later Scholastics from the sixteenth to the nineteenth centuries, regrettably very little scholarly work has been done. As Jean Rivière has noted, 'The importance of these long drawn out controversies is not commensurate with their length' (Rivière, 'Rédemption' 1951). It seems we must acknowledge this gap in the history of the doctrine on the redemption, a gap that even after twenty years has not yet been filled, as the recent bibliography diligently compiled by G. Oggioni, 'Il mistero della redenzione,' in *Problemi e orientamenti*, vol. 2, 337–38, seems to demonstrate.

14 The early Protestants

(a) For an understanding of their teaching, see above, § 9, with the following additional observations.

Once sacramental satisfaction was denied, the fundamental analogy for understanding Christ's satisfaction was destroyed. See DB 922–25, DS 1712–15, [ND 1652–55].

Once the true and real remission of sin was denied, and the opinion that the merits of Christ are somehow imputed to us introduced, the way was opened for our demerits to be imputed to Christ.

But if by the imputation of all sins Christ had to be considered the greatest sinner, then as a sinner he had to be punished for sin.

(b) The notions of substitution and satispassion are present in Luther's thought. Christ had to suffer and die because in some way he bore all sins. Richard, *Le mystère de la Rédemption* 156–61 [*The Mystery of the Redemption* 208–15]. Franks, *A History of the Doctrine of the Work of Christ*, vol. 1, 353–88.

(c) According to Melanchthon, Christ was a victim for placating the wrath of God. He had to bear this great wrath in such great suffering while simultaneously praising the justice of God. Without this praise, Christ's punishment would not have placated God. Nor was it possible for a mere human being to undergo such great suffering and be praising God at the same time. Franks, *A History of the Doctrine of the Work of Christ*, vol. 1, 412.

(d) For Calvin, human flesh was the price that would satisfy divine justice. The flesh of Christ paid the debt contracted by us; in the present order, a just God does not confer grace unless expiation has placated the divine wrath. Nor was Christ's death itself sufficient, but his soul also descended into hell in order to experience the severity of divine retribution and undergo the torments of the damned. Nevertheless, God is not angry with Christ. Richard, *Le mystère de la Rédemption* 160–61 [*The Mystery of the Redemption* 214–15]. Franks, *A History of the Doctrine of the Work of Christ*, vol. 1, 427–28, 431, 434.

(e) Quenstedt, 1617–1688, cuius expositio haberi videtur ut 'classica' inter Lutheranos.

Deus per ipsam divinam iustitiam tenetur ut solutionem totius debiti ex peccatis contracti exigat. Quo pretio non soluto, Deus peccata remittere absolute non potest.

Christus tam pro omnibus peccatis quam pro omnibus poenis satisfecit, qui voluntarie totum nostrum debitum suscepit sibique habuit imputatum, et secundum rigorem iustitiae exsolvit, cum ipsa inferni tormentata (non tamen in inferno nec aeternaliter) subierit. Franks, II, 81–84.

15 Fausto Sozzini, una cum SS. Trinitate, DNIC incarnatione, BB Mariae virginitate, etiam Christi satisfactionem negavit. Cf. DB 993, DS 1880.

Contextum historicum huius negationis in Calvino habes. Ex scripturis, ex nominalium theologia, ex iuris prudentia, quot et quanta potuit Sozzini coacervavit argumenta ad hanc duplicem probandam thesin: (1) Christus pro nobis nostrisque peccatis non satisfecit; (2) Deus Pater a Christo Domino nullam requisivit satisfactionem. Richard 161–63. Franks, II, 13–33.

16 H. Grotius, 1583–1645, Iacobi Arminii sequax, iuris peritus, sententiam Protestanticam quodammodo mitigavit ut eam cum iuris principiis reconciliaret.

Redemptio erat amnestia quaedam generalis, hac tamen concessa conditione, ut Christus pro nostris peccatis puniretur.

Ne homines enim, propter gratuitam prorsus peccatorum remissionem, et levius peccarent et parvi peccatum facerent, necessarium erat insigne quoddam exemplum atque divinae iustitiae manifesta quaedam demonstratio. Quod exemplum, quae demonstratio, non tantum afflictio Christi erat sed vera eiusdem punitio.

Huius punitionis iustitiam tam ex scripturis quam ex principiis iuris defendit. Admisit punitionem iustam esse non posse nisi propter delictum. Negavit autem, saltem in casu Christi, iniustitiam Dei qui innocentem pro nocentibus puniret. Franks, II, 57.

(e) The exposition of Johann Andreas Quenstedt (1617–1688) seems to be regarded as the 'classic' among Lutherans.

God, by reason of divine justice itself, is bound to demand payment of the entire debt contracted because of sin. If the price is not paid, God absolutely cannot forgive sins.

Christ made satisfaction for all sins as well as for all punishments, by voluntarily assuming our entire debt and having it imputed to himself, and discharged it in accord with strict justice, since he suffered the torments of hell – not in hell itself, however, nor eternally. Franks, *A History of the Doctrine of the Work of Christ*, vol. 2, 81–84.

15 Fausto Sozzini, in addition to denying the Trinity, the incarnation of our Lord, and the virginity of Mary, denied the satisfaction made by Christ. See DB 993, DS 1880, [ND 648].

The historical context of this denial you will find in Calvin. From scripture, from nominalist theology, and from jurisprudence Sozzini amassed as many arguments as he could in order to prove this twofold thesis: (1) Christ did not make satisfaction for us and for our sins, and (2) God the Father did not seek satisfaction from Christ the Lord. Richard, *Le mystère de la Rédemption* 161–63 [*The Mystery of the Redemption* 215–17]. Franks, *A History of the Doctrine of the Work of Christ*, vol. 2, 13–33.

16 Hugo Grotius (1583–1645), a follower of Jacob Arminius and a jurist, softened to some extent the Protestant position in order to reconcile it with the principles of law.

Redemption was a general amnesty, granted on condition that Christ be punished for our sins.

For in order that people, noting the completely gratuitous forgiveness of sins, might not too easily commit sins and take sin too lightly, there was needed a conspicuous example and an open demonstration of divine justice. This example, this demonstration, was not only Christ's affliction but his true punishment as well.

Grotius defended the justice of this punishment, arguing from scripture and from principles of law. He admitted that punishment where there is no offense cannot be just. Yet he denied, at least in the case of Christ, that God was unjust in punishing an innocent person in place of the guilty. Franks, *A History of the Doctrine of the Work of Christ*, vol. 2, 57. [Franks's discussion of Grotius's position extends from p. 48 to p. 73.]

Notate differentiam huius theoriae a praecedentibus. Qui dicit Christum eas ipsas poenas peccatis debitas ex iustitia Dei vindicativa solvisse, concludere debet cum Calvino Christum poenas infernales dedisse; hae enim sunt quae peccatis debentur. Praeterea, cum idem poenae debitum ex iustitia vindicativa non bis solvatur, ubi remittitur culpa per Christum ibi etiam remittitur poena, contra Tridentinum (DB 922, DS 1712), et praeterea ubi non remittitur poena, ibi Christus non satisfecit, contra Innocentium X (DB 1096, DS 2005). Quas consequentias evitat theoria Grotii quatenus Christus punitur per modum exempli insignis, seu uti hodie diceretur per modum terrorismi.

17 Theologi Catholici

(a) Deesse videtur studium historicum circa motum idearum inter Catholicos huius temporis. Vide supra § 13.

(b) J. Rivière, DTC XIII (26) 1973, citat consultores synodi Tridentinae, Maldonatum, Suárezium, S. Franciscum Salesium, S. Bellarmino contra extremam consequentiam theoriae Protestanticae, nempe, Christum dedisse poenas infernales.

(c) Etiam (ibid.) citat cum S. Bonaventura Suárezium et S. Bellarmino tamquam contrarios opinioni quae faceret perpessionem mali obiectum directum divinae voluntatis.

(d) Nota est quaestio disputata utrum Christus ex rigore iustitiae Deo satisfecisset. Billot, thesis 52, ed. 7, 1927, 501;[9] Parente, 211–12;[10] Galtier, 407, § 513.[11]

Quae quidem quaestio respicere videtur non causam seu motivum satisfactionis Christi sed potius effectum. Scilicet non subsunt supposita Lutherana ut quaeratur utrum ex rigore iustitiae vindicativae punitus sit Christus; sed subest doctrina Catholica de satisfactione Christi; accedit conclusio hanc satisfactionem fuisse condignam; et ulterius quaeritur quo usque haec condigna pretii solutio dicenda sit ad aequalitatem iustitiae pervenire.

Notice the difference between this theory and the preceding ones. One who holds that Christ suffered the punishment due to sin by reason of God's retributive justice must conclude, with Calvin, that Christ suffered the punishments of hell, for these are what sins deserve. Besides, since in retributive justice the same debt of punishment is not paid twice, then, where fault is remitted through Christ, punishment also is remitted, contrary to the Council of Trent (DB 922, DS 1712, [ND 1652]); and furthermore, where there is no remission of punishment, Christ has not made satisfaction, contrary to Pope Innocent X (DB 1096, DS 2005, [ND 1989/5]). Grotius's theory avoids these consequences in holding that Christ was punished as a conspicuous example, or, as we might say today, by way of terrorism.

17 Catholic theologians

(a) There seems to be no historical study of the movement of ideas among Catholic theologians during this period; see above, § 13.

(b) Rivière ('Rédemption' 1973) quotes advisers to the Council of Trent, Maldonado, Suárez, St Francis de Sales, and St Robert Bellarmine, as rejecting the extreme consequence of the Protestant theory, namely, that Christ suffered the torments of hell.

(c) He also (ibid.) quotes Suárez and Bellarmine as agreeing with St Bonaventure in rejecting the opinion that would make the suffering of evil a direct object of the divine will.

(d) There is also the well-known disputed question whether Christ made satisfaction to God out of strict justice. Billot, thesis 52 (in the 7th edition [1927] 501);[9] Parente 211–12;[10] Galtier 407, § 513.[11]

This question seems to regard not the cause or motive of Christ's satisfaction but rather its effect. That is to say, the basis for the question whether Christ was punished out of strict retributive justice is not the suppositions of the Lutherans but the Catholic teaching of Christ's satisfaction, with the added conclusion that this satisfaction was condign; and the further question arises as to what extent this condign payment of the price can be said to measure up fully to the demands of justice.

9 The reference is to L. Billot, *De Verbo incarnato: Commentarius in tertiam partem S. Thomae*, 7th ed. (Rome: Gregorian University Press, 1927).

10 The reference is to P. Parente, *L'Io di Cristo* (Brescia: Morcelliana, 1951, 1955).

11 See above, note 5.

(e) At perdifficillima redditur inquisitio historica de hac re ubi auctores (e.g., Suárez) quaestionem de redemptione non seorsum tractant sed eam expediunt in disputationibus subtilioribus de fine incarnationis.

18 Oratores Catholici

Theoriam fere Protestanticam substitutionis et satispassionis praesupposuisse videntur: Bossuet, Bourdaloue, Monsabré, Gay, d'Hulst, Grimal, Fouard.

Cf. G. Oggioni, *Problema e Orientamenti,* II, 311–12. L. Richard 179–81. J. Rivière, *Le dogme de la Rédemption. Etude théologique* (Paris, 1914) 230–49.

19 Quaestiones recentiores

(a) Permulta studia a J. Rivière peracta statum quaestionis inter Catholicos renovasse videntur.

Classicum fere factum esse videtur quod in DTC XIII (26) 1969–75 composuit de elementis castigationis, expiationis, reparationis, quae diversimode a diversis auctoribus et scholis coniunguntur.

(b) Ipse Rivière impugnatus est: a C. Pesch, *Das Sühneleiden unseres göttlichen Erlösers* (Freiburg i. B., 1916); ab A. d'Alès, *Rev. du clergé fran.*, 15 nov., 1919; t. 100, pp. 294–99.[12]

Quibus respondit R., *Le dogme de la Rédemption dans la théologie contemporaine* 147–60.[13]

(e) But the historical investigation of this matter is rendered extremely difficult by the fact that the authors (Suárez, for example) did not treat redemption as a separate question but dealt with it in overly subtle disputations on the purpose of the incarnation.

18 Catholic preachers

Jacques-Bénigne Bossuet [1627–1704], Louis Bourdaloue [1632–1704], Jacques-Marie Louis Monsabré [1827–1907], Charles Louis Gay [1815–1892], Maurice Le Sage d'Hautroche d'Hulst [1841–1896], Julius Leo Grimal [1867–1953], and Constant Henri Fouard [1837–1904] seem to have taken for granted a virtually Protestant theory of substitution and satispassion.

See Oggioni, *Problema e orientamenti*, vol. 2, 311–12; L. Richard, *Le mystère de la Rédemption* 179–81 (*The Mystery of the Redemption* 237–40); Rivière, *Le dogme de la Rédemption: Etude théologique* (Paris: J. Gabalda, 1914) 230–49.

19 More recent questions

(a) The numerous studies by Rivière seem to have revived the question among Catholics.

In his article in the *Dictionnaire de théologie catholique* XIII (26) 1969–75, which seems to have become an almost classic treatment of the question, he has brought together the elements of chastisement, expiation, and reparation that are connected to one another in various ways by different authors and schools of thought.

(b) Rivière himself was attacked by C. Pesch in *Das Sühneleiden unseres göttlichen Erlösers* (Freiburg im Breisgau: Herder, 1916), and by A. d'Alès, *Revue du clergé français* 100 (15 November 1919) 294–99.[12]

To these criticisms Rivière replied in *Le dogme de la Rédemption dans la théologie contemporaine* 147–60.[13]

12 The reference to *Revue du clergé français* 100 (15 Nov. 1919) 294–99 has to do with a review article by Rivière, under the heading, 'Chronique d'Apologétique et de Théologie,' which begins on p. 277 and ends on p. 300. At the beginning of the article, on pp. 277–78, a series of works are listed, and among these d'Alès is mentioned in connection with the *Dictionnaire apologétique de la Foi catholique.* Pesch is expressly mentioned within the pages Lonergan cites in his reference, but there is no express mention of d'Alès within these pages. A further piece of information is that on p. 402 of the first of the Solano articles mentioned two paragraphs later, we read: 'Las ideas de Rivière suscitaron una enérgica crítica por parte del P. Adh. D'Alès,' giving as a reference d'Alès's article, 'Le dogme catholique de la Rédemption,' *Etudes* 1935 (1913) 170–97. Could Lonergan have this article in mind?

13 See above, p. 3.

Recentius impugnatus est vel ipse Rivière vel tendentia ab eo incepta: J. Solano, *Est. ecl.* 20 (1946) 399–414; 24 (1950) 43–69; Basilio de San Pablo, XI Semana esp. teol. (Madrid, 1952) 455–503.

De quibus vide G. Oggioni, *Problemi e orientamenti*, II, 312–14, 318. Circa exegesin Rom 3.21–26, vide S. Lyonnet, *Verbum Domini* 25 (1947) 23, 118, 129, 193, 257.[14] Etiam infra, praenotamen X.

(c) Quae nobis videntur quam maxime clarificatione indigere sunt haec:

Primo, cum Deus directe malum poenae non velit (*Sum. theol.*, I, q. 19, a. 9; Rivière, DTC XIII [26] 1973), quemadmodum fiat ut directe satisfactionem Christi velit.

Deinde, utrum Christus homo non solum poenam nostram susceperit sed etiam quodammodo culpam, ut vere et realiter dici possit eum esse passum ex iustitia Dei vindicativa.

Circa priorem quaestionem vide probationem, § 5: Deus directe voluit satisfactionem Christi.

(d) Circa alteram quaestionem notate sententias sequentes:

Theologi annotationes in schema c. Vaticani I: 'Christus Agnus immaculatus utique non in se suscepit nec potuit suscipere ipsa formaliter peccata nostra, ut sua essent; nec ergo homo Christus punitus est eo sensu quo poena proprie significat malum inflictum reo in vindictam culpae ab ipso contractae.' Col. Lac., VII, 543 b. Circa sensum verborum 'suscipere,' 'contrahere,' vide *Sum. theol.*, III, q. 14, a. 3, unde sensum technicum in Christologia habent.

J. Rivière circa systema castigationis quod prorsus reiciendum iudicat, haec habet: 'D'ordinaire, c'est la justice vindicative qui est mise au premier plan. Parce qu'il est un désordre, le péché appelle une sanction. Exigence tellement sacrée que, même en pardonnant, Dieu n'a pas renoncé – et l'on ajoute souvent qu'il ne le pouvait – à rétablir l'ordre par ce moyen.' DTC XIII (26) 1970.

Either Rivière himself or the tendency he initiated has been attacked by Jesús Solano, 'El sentido de la muerte redentora de Nuestro Señor Jesucristo y algunas corrientes modernas,' *Estudios eclesiásticos* 20 (1946) 399–414; 'Actualidades cristológico-soteriológicas,' *Estudios eclesiásticos* 24 (1950) 43–69; by Basilio de San Pablo, 'Irenismo en soteriología. Un caso típico de relativismo dogmático,' in *Semana Española de Teología, XI, 17–22 Sept., 1951: La encíclica "Humani generis"* (Madrid: Consejo Superior de Investigaciones Científicas, Instituto 'Francisco Suárez,' 1952) 455–503.

On this topic, see Oggioni, *Problemi e orientamenti,* vol. 2, 312–14, 318. On the exegesis of Romans 3.21–26, see S. Lyonnet, *Verbum Domini* 25 (1947) 23, 118, 129, 193, 257;[14] also preliminary note 10 below.

(c) It seems to us that the following points are most in need of clarification:

First, since God does not directly will the evil of punishment (*Summa theologiae,* 1, q. 19, a. 9; Rivière, 'Rédemption' 1973), how is it that he directly wills Christ's satisfaction?

Second, did the human Christ take upon himself not only our punishment but also in some way our fault, so that it can really and truly be said that he suffered in accordance with God's retributive justice?

As to the first question, see the proof, § 5, below: God directly willed Christ's satisfaction.

(d) As to the second question, note the following opinions:

The first is an annotation of a theologian [Franzelin] on a schema of Vatican I: 'Christ, the spotless Lamb, did not and indeed could not formally take upon himself our sins, so as to make them his; therefore the human Christ was not punished in the sense in which punishment properly means an evil inflicted upon a guilty person in retribution for a fault personally incurred' (*Collectio Lacensis,* VII, 543b). For the meaning of the words 'take upon oneself' (*suscipere*) and 'incur' (*contrahere*), see *Summa theologiae,* 3, q. 14, a. 3, from which they acquire a technical meaning in Christology.

Regarding the system of chastisement, which he utterly rejects, Rivière states as follows: 'As a rule, it is retributive justice that is foremost. Because sin is a disorder, it calls for a sanction. Such a sacred demand God, even in pardoning, has not waived – and it is often said that he could not do so – in restoring order by this means.' Rivière, 'Rédemption' 1970.

14 For further information on these articles, see below, p. 137.

P. Galtier, 391, § 492 (vide nota 1 ibid.) simpliciter reicit tamquam perversionem Protestanticam opinionem secundum quam Christus 'umquam a Deo habitus est ut iniquitatum nostrarum reus propertereaque expertus sit vindictam divinae iustitiae in se saevientis ...' Circa saevitiam, vide *Sum. theol.*, II-II, q. 159, a. 2.[15]

Philippe de la Trinité, 'La Rédemption par le Sang,' *Encycl. XXième Siècle* (Paris, 1959) 55–58, vehementer eos impugnat qui dictitant Christum ex iustitia Dei vindicativa poenas dedisse.[16]

J. Solano, BAC III, ita negat Christum a Deo esse punitum ut tamen dicat dolores Christi Deo esse gratos (282) et 'elementum iustitiae Dei vindicativae omnino esse retinendum' (283).[17]

Ipsi censemus: (1) minoris momenti esse mera nomina uti punitionis vel castigationis; (2) seriam quaestionem esse utrum ex iustitia Dei vindicativa Christus pro nobis poenas pro peccatis dederit; (3) Christum poenas pro peccatis debitas suscepisse sed non contraxisse; (4) ideo poenas, quas suscepit, Christum non contraxisse quia culpam propriam vel originalem vel actualem non habuit et culpam alienam nullatenus suscepit sed 'omnino peccatum nescivit' (DB 122, DS 261); (5) quia Christus poenas non contraxit, ideo ex iustitia Dei vindicativa eum poenas dedisse dici non posse; nam (6) delicti exsistentiam ad iustitiam vindicativam non sufficere ubi, in eo qui poenas dat, nulla est culpa propria sive originalis sive actualis et nulla est culpa aliena quomodocumque suscepta; et (7) dicere solam delicti exsistentiam sufficere ad rationem iustitiae vindicativae nihil aliud esse quam iustitiam vindicativam concipere vel immoraliter vel amoraliter. Vide praenotamina VII ad XI, praesertim X.

Galtier simply rejects as a Protestant distortion the opinion according to which Christ 'was at any time held by God to be guilty of our sins and for that reason experienced the retribution of a divine justice brutal in itself ...' *De incarnatione ac redemptione*, 391, § 492, and note 1. On brutality (*saevitia*) [as opposed to cruelty], see *Summa theologiae*, 2-2, q. 159, a. 2.[15]

Philippe de la Trinité severely criticizes those who maintain that Christ was punished in accordance with the retributive justice of God. *La Rédemption par le Sang* (Paris: Libraire Arthème Fayard, 1959) 55–58.[16]

J. Solano denies that Christ was punished by God, yet says Christ's sufferings were pleasing to God and that 'an element of *God's retributive justice* must by all means be retained.'[17]

Our position is as follows: (1) mere words such as 'punishment' or 'chastisement' are less important; (2) the serious question is whether it was out of God's retributive justice that Christ was punished for us and for our sins; (3) Christ took on but did not incur the punishment due to sins; (4) therefore the punishments that he took on Christ did not incur, because he had no fault of his own, either original or actual, and in no way took on the fault of others, but 'he knew no sin' whatever (DB 122, DS 261, [ND 606/10]); (5) since Christ did not incur punishments, it cannot therefore be said that he was punished out of God's retributive justice; for (6) the existence of a crime calling for retributive justice does not suffice when the one who is punished has incurred no fault of his own, either original or actual, and has taken no one else's fault upon himself in any way whatsoever; and (7) to say that the mere existence of a crime is sufficient for retributive justice in the true and proper sense is nothing else than an immoral or amoral conception of retributive justice. See preliminary notes 7–11, especially note 10.

15 'Both cruelty (*crudelitas*) and brutality (*saevitia*) are excessive, but brutality disregards guilt or innocence out of sheer delight in inflicting pain.'

16 English translation, *What Is the Redemption?* trans. Anthony Armstrong (New York: Hawthorn Books and London: Burns & Oates, 1961) 70–74.

17 See Jesús Solano, *De Verbo incarnato*, in vol. 3 of *Sacrae Theologiae Summa*, 3rd ed. (Matriti: Biblioteca de Autores Cristianos, 1956) 282, § 671 and 283, § 673. Italics appear in the Latin text that Lonergan quotes.

## [*Praenotamina*]

### PRAENOTAMEN I: SENTENTIA ANSELMIANA

1 *Cur Deus homo*, ed. F.S. Schmitt, *Opera Omnia*, II, 37–133. Cuius articulum de S. Anselmo, vide LTK I, 592–94

2 Quamvis eruditi hic illic indicia sese invenisse doceant alios ante S. Anselmum de satisfactione Christi cogitasse, nullum videtur dubium ipsum Anselmum primum hanc sententiam elaborasse.

3 Ipsius tamen Anselmi intentio fuit non dogmatica sed speculativa, neque tam de redemptione quam de fine incarnationis erat eius inquisitio. Quod ex ipso titulo, *Cur Deus homo*, satis elucet. Accedunt obiectiones quae in ore interlocutoris Bosonis ponuntur neque plene solvuntur, contra (1) theoriam *recapitulationis* ex S. Irenaeo haustam et per S. Augustinum medio aevo traditam, quippe quae potius picturam quam rationem praestaret, (2) theoriam demonstrati *amoris* divini, cum multis et aliis modis potuisset Deus suum amorem nobis demonstrare, (3) theoriam *redemptionis* ex potestate diaboli, cum Deus, etiam diaboli omnipotens Dominus, diabolo nihil prorsus debuerit (I, 3–10).

4 His ergo theoriis praetermissis, invenienda erat ratio, quam Anselmus necessariam nominavit, cur Deus homo.

Porro, quamvis interdum argumentis convenientiae usus sit (I, 12; II, 11), quamvis inter necessitatem cogentem et non cogentem distinxerit (II, 17), simpliciter tamen urget hoc argumentum: 'Necesse est ergo ut aut ablatus honor solvatur aut poena sequatur. Alioquin aut sibi Deus iustus non erit aut ad utrumque impotens erit: quod nefas est vel cogitare' (I, 13; Schmitt 71, lin. 24).

Hac in disiunctione 'necessaria,' nempe, *aut satisfactio aut poena*, fundatur tota theoria, quae sequentibus breviter exponi potest.

(a) Merus homo omnia prorsus Deo debet, et ideo satisfactionem simpliciter supererogatoriam peragere non potest (I, 19–24).

## [*Preliminary notes*]

### PRELIMINARY NOTE 1: ANSELM'S OPINION

1 *Cur Deus homo,* Schmitt 37–133. See also Schmitt's article on St Anselm in *Lexikon für Theologie und Kirche* I, 592–94 [see below, Bibliography, at 'Schmitt'].

2 Although scholars say that here and there they have found indications that others before Anselm had thought of Christ's satisfaction, there seems to be no doubt that Anselm himself was the first to have elaborated this position.

3 Anselm's intention, however, was not dogmatic but speculative, and his inquiry was not so much about the redemption as about the purpose of the incarnation, as the title of his book, *Cur Deus homo,* clearly indicates. As well, there are objections that are put in the mouth of Boso, his interlocutor, and not fully solved. These reject (1) the theory of *recapitulation,* taken from Irenaeus and transmitted by Augustine to the Middle Ages, on the grounds that it presents a picture rather than a rational argument, (2) the theory of the demonstration of divine *love,* since God could have demonstrated his love for us in many other ways, and (3) the theory of *ransom* from the power of the devil, since God, who is the omnipotent Lord even of the devil, owes the devil absolutely nothing (book 1, cc. 3–10).

4 Having discarded these theories, Anselm had to find a reason, which he called a necessary reason, why God became man.

So, although sometimes he used arguments of fittingness (book 1, c. 12; book 2, c. 11), and although he distinguished between compelling and non-compelling necessity (book 2, c. 17), he simply advanced this argument: 'It is therefore necessary either for the honor that has been removed to be repaid or else for punishment to result. Otherwise, either God would not be just towards himself, or else he would be powerless to do the one or the other: heinous things, these, even to think about' (book 1, c. 13; Schmitt 71, lines 24–26).

His whole theory is based on this 'necessary' disjunction, namely, *either satisfaction or punishment,* which we shall now briefly explain.

(a) A mere human being owes absolutely everything to God, and therefore cannot make satisfaction that is simply supererogatory (book 1, cc. 19–24).

(b) Deus-homo mori non debet, et ideo moriendo eiusmodi satisfactionem praestare potest (II, 11).

(c) Haec Dei-hominis satisfactio omnibus prorsus peccatis maior exsistit (II, 14, 15).

(d) Haec Dei-hominis satisfactio omnium peccatorum remissionem meret (II, 19).

5 Circa methodum Anselmianam notandum est eo tempore nondum fuisse excogitatum theorema systematicum quod duos ordines entitativos, naturalem et supernaturalem, distinguit; et ideo nondum deduci potuisse corollarium quod theologiam et philosophiam distinguit earumque methodos proprias elaborat.

Quam ob causam, quamvis in opere Anselmiano inveniantur quae, si alio et posteriori tempore scripta fuissent, crimen semi-rationalismi fundare viderentur, non ideo tamen est ipse Anselmus ob errorem arguendus sed potius suum tempus ob defectum nondum superatum.

6 Deinde, circa notionem quae satisfactionem et meritum in operibus simpliciter supererogatoriis fundat notandum est eiusmodi opinionem inde a Tertulliano exstitisse sed inde a saec. XIII, ratione supernaturalitatis perspecta, superatam esse.

7 Uti iam diximus, Anselmus simul duas quaestiones consideravit: (1) quaestionem de fine incarnationis, et (2) quaestionem quae mortem Domini tamquam satisfactionem respicit.

Iam vero haec duo iam pridem inter theologos prorsus distinguuntur, et, hac in thesi, de satisfactione Christi vicaria agitur, in subsequenti vero de fine incarnationis quaedam proponentur.

8 Quemadmodum denique sententia Catholica de satisfactione Christi sit intelligenda, maxime per duas quaestiones, uti nobis videtur, elucebit.

Doctrina enim Anselmiana hoc fere disiunctione continetur, Aut satisfactio aut poena. Cf. *Cur Deus homo,* I, 15 (Schmitt, 74). Quaeritur ergo primo utrum haec disiunctio secundum doctrinam Catholicam ita sit intelligenda *ut tertium quid negetur.* Quaeritur deinde utrum verus disiunctionis sensus sit, *aut poena aut poena,* ut scilicet satisfactio et poena ad idem redeant, neque membra disiunctionis opposita aliud significent quam hoc, aut poena a Christo his in terris est danda, aut poena a nobis in infernis est danda.

(b) A God-man is not obliged to die, and therefore in dying renders satisfaction that is supererogatory (book 2, c. 11).

(c) This satisfaction made by a God-man is greater than all sins whatsoever (book 2, cc. 14–15).

(d) This satisfaction made by a God-man merits the forgiveness of all sins (book 2, c. 19).

5 It should be noted in connection with Anselm's method that in his time the systematic theorem distinguishing two entitative orders, the natural and the supernatural, had not yet been worked out. Hence it was not yet possible to deduce a corollary that would distinguish between theology and philosophy and between the methods proper to each.

Thus, although there are found in Anselm's work certain expressions that, had they been written at a later time, would seem to be grounds for the charge of semi-rationalism, rather than charge Anselm with error we should charge his age with a deficiency not yet overcome.

6 Further, with respect to the notion that bases satisfaction and merit on works that are simply supererogatory, it should be noted that that sort of opinion had existed since Tertullian. But since the thirteenth century, with the grasp of the idea of the supernatural, it has been superseded.

7 As we have said, Anselm considered two questions together: (1) the question of the purpose of the incarnation, and (2) the question that regards the death of the Lord as satisfaction.

Now, these two questions have long been distinguished by theologians. In the present thesis we will treat Christ's vicarious satisfaction, and in the next thesis make some observations concerning the purpose of the incarnation.

8 Finally, in our opinion the Catholic position on Christ's satisfaction will become clear mainly through a consideration of two questions.

For the Anselmian doctrine is pretty well summed up in the disjunction 'either satisfaction or punishment' (*Cur Deus homo,* book 1, c. 15, at Schmitt 74). Hence the first question is whether according to Catholic teaching this disjunction is to be understood *as excluding a third alternative.* The next question is whether the true meaning of the disjunction is *either punishment or punishment,* so that satisfaction and punishment come to the same thing, and the opposed members of the disjunction mean simply this: either Christ is to be punished in this life or we are to be punished in hell.

## PRAENOTAMEN II: AUT SATISFACTIO AUT POENA

1 Quaeritur utrum ita completa sit disiunctio ut tertium excludatur.

Respondetur per distinctionem inter ordinem rerum actualem et ordines alios possibiles. Supposito enim actuali rerum ordine, affirmative est respondendum; supposita autem quolibet possibili, negative.

2 Nam in actuali rerum ordine de facto Christus pro nostris peccatis satisfecit (DB 799, 904, DS 1529, 1690). Neque in alio aliquo datur salus hominibus (Act 4, 12). Unde docuit c. Tridentinum non per aliud remedium tolli peccatum originale quam per meritum unius mediatoris Domini nostri Iesu Christi (DB 790, DS 1513).

3 Si autem quaeritur utrum Deus omnipotens aliter potuisset nos salvos facere quam per mortem Christi, sententia affirmativa est communis et certa (cf. d'Alès 342).[18] Allegari autem solent:

S. Augustinus, *De Trin.*, XIII, X, 13; ML 42, 1024; *De Agone Christiano,* XI, 12; ML 40, 297.

Petrus Lombardus, 3, d. 20, c. 1, qui S. Augustinum sequens sententiam Anselmianam alto silentio praetermittit.

Ioannes de Rupella (*Summa fratris Alexandri* [Halensis], Ad claras aquas, IV/1, 16), Lib. 3, tr. 1, q. 1, c. 4.

S. Thomas, *Sum. theol.*, III, q. 46, aa. 1 et 2.

Scotus, *In III Sent.*, d. 20.

Suárez, *In Sum. theol.*, III, q. 1, a. 2; disp. 4, sect. 2, § 2; ed. Breton, XVII, 51.

4 Immo, non solum potuisset Deus gratis omnia peccata condonare sed etiam, si satisfactionem voluisset, suffecisset una minima Christi passio.

## PRELIMINARY NOTE 2: EITHER SATISFACTION OR PUNISHMENT

1 Is this disjunction complete so that a third alternative is excluded?

In reply, we distinguish between the actual order of reality and all other possible orders. Granted the order that actually exists, the answer is yes; on some other supposition, no.

2 For in the actual order of things Christ has in fact made satisfaction for our sins (DB 799, 904; DS 1529, 1690; [ND 647, 1631]), and in no one else is salvation given to us (Acts 4.12). Hence the Council of Trent taught that original sin is taken away through no other remedy than the merit of the one mediator, our Lord Jesus Christ (DB 790, DS 1513, [ND 510]).

3 If, however, one asks whether God in his omnipotence could have saved us in some other way than through the death of Christ, an affirmative answer is common and certain (see d'Alès 342).[18] The authorities usually referred to are the following:

Augustine, *De Trinitate*, XIII, X, 13; ML 42, 1024; *De agone Christiano*, XI, 12; ML 40, 297.

Peter Lombard, *Sententiae*, 3, d. 20, c. 1, who follows Augustine, passing over Anselm's opinion in deep silence.

John of Rupella [de la Rochelle], *Summa fratris Alexandri* [*Halensis*], edd. PP. Collegii S. Bonaventurae, 4 vols. (Quaracchi: Collegium S. Bonaventurae, 1924–48), book 3, tract. 1, q. 1, c. 4, in vol. IV/1, 14–17, at 16.

Thomas Aquinas, *Summa theologiae*, 3, q. 46, aa. 1 and 2.

Scotus, *In 3 Sententiarum*, d. 20, the only question.

Suárez, *Commentaria ac disputationes in tertiam partem D. Thomae*, in *Opera omnia*, vol. XVII, q. 1, a. 2; disp. 4, sect 2, no. 2, 51–52, at 51.

4 In fact, not only could God have by his grace pardoned all sins, but even if he had wanted satisfaction, a minimal suffering on the part of Christ would have sufficed.

18 The reference is to Adhémar d'Alès, *De Verbo incarnato*, 2nd ed. (Paris: Gabriel Beauchesne, 1930) 342. The discussion of the thesis, '*Redemptio generis humani nulla absoluta necessitate requirebatur, sed fuit purum divinae gratiae beneficium,*' extends from p. 341 to p. 346.

Quod contineri videtur in doctrina S. Thomae: 'secundum sufficientiam una minima passio Christi suffecisset ad redimendum genus humanum ab omnibus peccatis' (*Sum. theol.*, III, q. 46, a. 5, ad 3m).

Et idem videtur concludendum ex simili doctrina Clementis VI (DB 550, DS 1025), et ex communi theologorum doctrina de satisfactione Christi superabundante. Si enim actualis satisfactio superabundat, minor suffecisset.

5 Utrum haec agnitio tertiae possibilitatis sit sententia ipsius S. Anselmi.

In talem sensum Suárez censuit Anselmum benigne esse interpretandum (loc. cit., p. 52).

Contradixit Rivière, DTC XIII (26) 1943, ubi remittit ad suum opus, *Le dogme de la Rédemption: Études critiques et documents* 313–47.

Caeterum satis constare videtur hanc tertiam possibilitatem dupliciter afficere sententiam Anselmianam. Nam ex alia parte nullatenus nocet doctrinae Anselmianae circa factum satisfactionis Christi; et ex alia parte vulnus quoddam inferri videtur systemati Anselmiano speculativo.

Cuius vulneris exsistentia in eo perspicitur quod, ubi dixerat Anselmus *necessariam*, communiter docent theologi *convenientissimam* fuisse satisfactionem Christi ad salutem generis humani.

### PRAENOTAMEN III: AUT VENIA AUT POENA

1 Quaeritur deinde utrum idem dicat satisfactio quod poena, utrum sensus disiunctionis, aut satisfactio aut poena, nihil aliud sit quam sensus huius disiunctionis, aut poena a Christo danda aut poena a nobis omnibus in infernis danda.

2 In sensum affirmativum manifeste tendebant veteres Protestantes, a quibus dissentiunt communiter Catholici auctores. Catholicorum tamen non una est omnium sententia, cum alii propius ad opinionem Protestanticam accedant et alii magis ab ea recedant, neque ab his neque ab illis, quantum perspicere potui, plena claritate exponitur vel quid sit satisfactio vel quid sit poena vel quemadmodum haec ab illa distinguatur. Eminet Galtier 384–98, §§ 485–500.

This seems part of St Thomas's teaching: 'so far as sufficiency is concerned, the slightest suffering of Christ would have sufficed to redeem the human race from all its sins' (*Summa theologiae,* 3, q. 46, a. 5, ad 3m).

And the same conclusion seems to follow from a similar teaching of Clement VI (DB 550, DS 1025, [ND 643]), and from the common doctrine of theologians concerning the superabundant satisfaction made by Christ. For if the actual satisfaction is superabundant, less would have been sufficient.

5 Did Anselm's position acknowledge a third possibility?

Suárez felt that Anselm should be benignly interpreted in this sense (*Commentaria ac disputationes in tertiam partem D. Thomae,* in *Opera omnia,* vol. 17, q. 1, a. 2; disp. 4, sect 2, §2, 51–52, at 52).

Rivière disagrees, 'Rédemption' 1943–44, where he refers to his book, *Le dogme de la Rédemption. Études critiques et documents* (Louvain: Bureaux de la Revue, 1931) 313–47.

However, it seems clear enough that this third possibility affects the Anselmian doctrine in two ways. On the one hand, it does no harm to Anselm's doctrine about the fact of Christ's satisfaction, but on the other hand it does seems to wound his speculative system.

The existence of this wound is seen in the fact that where Anselm had said that Christ's satisfaction was *necessary* for the salvation of the human race, [later] theologians commonly teach that is was *most fitting.*

PRELIMINARY NOTE 3: EITHER PARDON OR PUNISHMENT

1 The second question [posed at the end of preliminary note 1] is whether satisfaction means the same as punishment, whether the meaning of the disjunction 'either satisfaction or punishment' is the same as the meaning of this disjunction, 'either punishment borne by Christ or punishment borne by us all in hell.'

2 The early Protestants clearly tended to give an affirmative answer to this question, and Catholic authors generally disagreed with them. Still, Catholics were not all of the same mind, since some inclined towards the Protestant opinion while others moved farther away from it; and as far as I have been able to determine, none of them has a completely clear explanation of what satisfaction is or what punishment is or how these two are to be differentiated. Galtier, *De incarnatione ac redemptione,* stands out; see §§ 485–500, pp. 384–98.

3 Circa vocabulum 'satisfactio,' vide A. Deneffe, *Zeitschrift für katholische Theologie* 43 (1919) 158–75.

Circa historiam doctrinae, principalia sunt permulta opera J. Rivière; brevior elenchus apud L. Richard, plenior in bibliographia ipsius Rivière.[19]

Circa notiones nunc communes, vide distinctionem inter castigationem, expiationem, et reparationem (DTC XIII [26] 1969–70) a J. Rivière expositam sed ex L. Heinrichs mutuatam.[20] Notate huic triplici distinctioni addidisse J. Solano (BAC, III, 245) quartam quandam 'reparationis expiativae' categoriam.[21]

4 De praesenti nihil aliud intendimus nisi ipsius notionis intelligentiam quandam attingere. Probatio, quatenus in re disputata haberi possit, in ipsa thesi exponetur.

5 Dicemus (1) duas esse notionum complexiones, (2) quarum prima culpam, offensam, et poenae reatum, inflictionem, atque solutionem complectitur, (3) altera autem satisfactionem, veniae et petitionem et concessionem, poenae denique remissionem, (4) has duas notionum complexiones esse formaliter seu conceptione distinctas, sed (5) in concreta rerum humanarum complexitate eas saepe commisceri et raro simpliciter separari, unde (6) nisi quis sobrie, pie, sedulo rei intelligentiam quaerit (DB 1796, DS 3016), facillime in profunda quadam quasi palude notionum indistinctarum et casuum semper magis complexorum submergitur.

6 Duas notionum complexiones (2 et 3) brevissime apud Tertullianum indicatas invenies, *De pudicitia*, 2: 'Omne delictum aut venia expungit aut poena: venia, ex castigatione; poena, ex damnatione' (ML 2, 985).[22]

3 On the word 'satisfaction,' see August Deneffe, 'Das Wort *satisfactio*,' *Zeitschrift für katholische Theologie* 43 (1919) 158–75.

On the history of the doctrine, the chief works are the many writings of Jean Rivière. There is a short list of writings in L. Richard, and a longer one in Rivière's own bibliography.[19]

On the notions that are now common, see the distinction between chastisement, expiation, and reparation given by Rivière ('Rédemption' 1969–70) but borrowed from Ludwig Heinrichs.[20] Note that J. Solano has added to these a fourth category, 'expiative reparation.'[21]

4 At this point we are intent only upon acquiring some understanding of the notion itself. A proof, insofar as one is possible in a disputed question, will be set forth in the thesis proper.

5 Our position will be as follows: that (1) there are two sets of notions, (2) the first comprises fault, offense, and liability to punishment, its imposition and payment, (3) while the second comprises satisfaction, pardon sought and granted, and the remission, finally, of punishment, that (4) these two sets of notions are distinct, formally, in their conception, (5) but in the concrete complexity of human affairs are often confused and seldom completely separated, (6) as a result of which, unless you soberly, devoutly, and earnestly seek to understand the matter (DB 1796, DS 3016, [ND 132]), you will very easily sink into a deep swamp of murky notions and ever more complicated cases.

6 The two sets of notions stated in (2) and (3) above were briefly touched upon in Tertullian: 'Every sin is expunged either by pardon or punishment: by pardon, as a result of chastisement; by punishment, as a result of condemnation' (*De pudicitia*, 2 [ML 2, 985]).[22]

19 On the bibliographies of Rivière and Richard, see above, p. 3.
20 See Ludwig Heinrichs, *Die Genugtuungstheorie des hl. Anselmus von Canterbury* (Paderborn: Schöningh, 1909).
21 Solano, *De Verbo incarnato*, in vol. 3 of *Sacrae Theologiae Summa*, 3rd ed., § 584, p. 245; more fully in his thesis 27, §§ 666–93, pp. 279–92.
22 'Venia, ex castigatione; poena, ex damnatione': see W.P. Le Saint's discussion of this typically pithy passage in *Tertullian: Treatises on Penance*, Ancient Christian Writers, vol. 28 (Westminster, MD: Newman, 1959) 201–202, notes 76 and 77.

7 Quantum ad exempla concreta attinet, si tribunalia humana (omissis exceptionibus) vel ultimum omnium iudicium divinum consideras, clarum est, ubi de delicto non dubitatur, nullatenus de venia deliberari sed, lata damnationis sententia, ad exsecutionem poenae procedi.

Si autem Christum Dominum nostrum consideras, in quo nullum fuit peccatum sive originale sive actuale, certum est ipsum a Deo propter propriam culpam ad poenas non damnari; si autem NT vel breviter cognoscis, non minus est certum passionem et mortem Domini immediate atque expresse in veniam, in remissionem peccatorum, fuisse.

Si denique ordinariam hominum vitam respicis, ubi neque simpliciter inculpabiles inveniuntur, neque cum frigida tribunalium iustitiae proceditur, facillime commisceri et rarius simpliciter separari illa duo a Tertulliano posita, nempe, veniam ex castigatione et poenam ex damnatione.

8 Quibus perspectis, elucet quid intenderit disiunctio in hoc tertio praenotamine exposita, aut venia aut poena, nempe aliam esse intelligentiam et aliam conceptuum complexionem ubi de damnatione et poena agitur, et aliam ubi de castigatione et venia.

Quod tamen nisi initium solutionis non facit, et ideo paulo accuratius declarandum est quemadmodum duae notionum complexiones quoad intelligentiam et conceptionem inter se differant. Neque satis est has complexiones distingui nisi ulterius comparantur ad divinam iustitiam, quae vindicativa est in poenis a damnatis exigendis, redemptiva in venia post satisfactionem concedenda, severa denique (*Sum. theol.*, III, q. 47, a. 3, ad 1m) propter ipsam hanc disiunctionem, aut satisfactio aut poena.

## PRAENOTAMEN IV: CULPA, OFFENSA, POENA

1 Quaeritur de prima notionum complexione qualis sit. Et de ipsa notionum intelligentia, non de earum applicatione concreta agitur, nisi quis casus rariores attendit vel mundum quendam abstractum ubi nulla umquam fuisset quaestio de venia petenda vel concedenda, sed unice regnasset lex talionis secundum Mt 5.38: 'Audistis quia dictum est: Oculum pro oculo, et dentem pro dente.'

7 As for concrete examples, if you consider human tribunals (with some exceptions) or the Last Judgment, it is clear that when there is no doubt about the offense there is no discussion about pardon, but once sentence is pronounced, the punishment is carried out.

But if you consider the case of Christ our Lord, in whom there was no sin, either original or actual, it is certain that he was not condemned to punishment by God for any fault of his own. However, if you have even a slight knowledge of the New Testament, it is no less certain that the Lord's passion and death was directly and expressly for obtaining pardon, the forgiveness of sins.

Finally, if you look at ordinary human life, where no one totally blameless is to be found and trials are not conducted in cold justice, the two notions mentioned by Tertullian are very easily confused and almost never simply separated, namely, pardon after chastisement and punishment after condemnation.

8 In light of all this, the intent of the disjunction stated in this third preliminary note, either pardon or punishment, is clear, namely that there is one understanding and one set of concepts when condemnation and punishment are concerned and another set when chastisement and pardon are concerned.

Still, this is only the beginning of a solution, and therefore we must express more accurately how these two sets of notions differ from each other as to understanding and conception. Nor is it enough to distinguish them without further relating them to divine justice, which is retributive in requiring punishment of the condemned, redemptive in granting pardon after satisfaction, and severe, finally, by reason of this very disjunction, either satisfaction or punishment. (On the severity of divine justice, see *Summa theologiae*, 3, q. 47, a. 3, ad 1m).

## PRELIMINARY NOTE 4: FAULT, OFFENSE, PUNISHMENT

1 Here we are inquiring about the nature of the first set of notions. And it is the understanding of these notions, not their concrete application, that is our concern, unless one is considering very rare cases or some abstract world where there had never been a question of asking or granting pardon, but where the only law was the *lex talionis*, as in Matthew 5.38: 'You have heard that it was said, "An eye for an eye and a tooth for a tooth."'

2 *Malum* est privatio boni.

*Culpa* est malum in ipsa voluntate; dividitur culpa in actualem et originalem; culpa actualis est privatio boni in ipsa voluntatis operatione; culpa originalis est privatio boni ex mala operatione voluntatis Adae (DB 376, DS 728).

3 Ad culpam sequitur *offensa*.

Nam voluntas ad omnia bona proportionatur quae ab intellectu apprehenduntur; et obiectum intellectus adaequatum est totum ens.

At concrete dantur tantummodo determinata quaedam bona actualia et possibilia, quae omnia possunt esse obiecta multarum et diversarum voluntatum.

Unde, ubi circa eadem bona aliae voluntates alia volunt oritur conflictus; et ubi haec vel illa voluntas culpabiliter vult atque agit, sequitur aliarum iusta offensa.

Quod quidem in rebus humanis facile perspicitur; nam quo magis circa eadem bona aliae voluntates alia volunt, eo frequentiores et graviores oriuntur conflictus; et ubi voluntates quaedam culpabiliter procedunt, caeterae iuste offenduntur, iniustitiam denuntiant atque reprehendunt, litigationes et bella parant.

Sed ulterius Deus est omnium rerum creator atque gubernator; de omnibus et singulis secundum infinitam suam sapientiam ordinavit, et secundum iustissimam suam voluntatem elegit. Et ideo ubi quilibet culpabiliter vult, contra voluntatem Dei vult, et offensae contra Deum esse reus analogice sed vere dicitur.

4 *Poena* (latius) est privatio boni in rebus exterioribus, in bonis corporis, vel in bonis animae. Quibus in privationibus attenditur gradatio cum, caeteris paribus, gravior est privatio in bonis corporis quam in rebus exterioribus, et gravior est in bonis animae quam in bonis corporis.

5 *Poena* (strictius) est privatio boni inflicta: 'de ratione enim poenae est quod sit contraria voluntati' (*Sum. theol.*, I, q. 48, a. 5).

6 Ulterius dividitur poena in poenam simpliciter et poenam secundum quid.

2 *Evil* is the privation of good.

*Fault* is evil in the will. It is divided into personal fault and original fault. Personal fault is the privation of good in an act of one's own will; original fault is the privation of good resulting from the evil act of Adam's will (DB 376, DS 728).

3 *Offense* follows upon fault.

For the will is proportionate to all the goods that are apprehended by the intellect; and the adequate object of the intellect is the totality of being.

Concretely, however, there exist only certain determinate actual and possible goods, all of which can be objects of many and diverse wills.

Hence, when different wills will different things concerning the same good, a conflict arises; and when one of them wills and acts culpably, the others rightly take offense.

This can be easily seen in human affairs. The more times different wills will different things concerning the same goods, the more frequent and more serious are the conflicts that arise; and when some wills proceed culpably, the others are rightly offended, they denounce and condemn the injustice, and resort to litigation and war.

But further, God is the creator and ruler of all things: in his infinite wisdom he has put each and all in order, and has chosen them by his most just will. Whoever, therefore, wills something culpably wills what is contrary to the will of God, and is analogously but truly said to be guilty of an offense against God.

4 *Punishment,* in a broader sense, is the privation of a good in external things, of a good of the body, or of a good of the soul. There is a gradation among these privations, since, all other things being equal, a privation in the goods of the body is more serious than a privation of external goods, and a privation of the goods of the soul is more serious than of the goods of the body.

5 *Punishment,* in a stricter sense, is an inflicted privation of good: 'It is of the essence of punishment that it be contrary to one's will' (*Summa theologiae,* 1, q. 48, a. 5).

6 Punishment is further divided into punishment simply so called, and punishment in a qualified sense.

*Poena simpliciter* privat etiam de bonis animae. Et ideo ubi voluntas est bona et recta, haec poena est simpliciter contra voluntatem.

*Poena secundum quid* (medicinalis) privat a bono minori ut augeatur bonum maius. Quae quidem poena, ubi voluntas est bona et recta, simpliciter est secundum voluntatem quae bonum maius vult, sed secundum quid est contra voluntatem quae minus malum non vult. Quatenus autem voluntas a bonitate deficit, eatenus poena secundum quid est contra voluntatem simpliciter; sed cum ipsa poenae inflictio dispositionem patientis mutare soleat, etiam eiusdem voluntatem per accidens mutare potest (cf. *De Malo,* q. 16, a. 5), et secundum hoc (suppositis bonis quibusdam dispositionibus initialibus) poena medicinalis in conversionem voluntatis quodammodo tendit.

7 *Reatus* seu debitum poenae ex culpa oritur.

Quare, poena simpliciter non iuste infligitur nisi propter propriam culpam vel originalem vel actualem.

Poena autem medicinalis iuste infligi potest praeter culpam propriam actualem; sed ipsa haec possibilitas in culpam originalem reducitur.

*Sum. theol.*, I-II, q. 87, aa. 7 et 8; II-II, q. 108, a. 4.

8 Solutio et inflictio poenae differunt sicut passio et actio: una eademque est mutatio quae in patiente est solutio et ab agente est inflictio.

Solutio poenae ad reatum seu debitum poenae sequitur et quidem secundum iustitiam commutativam in civilibus et secundum iustitiam vindicativam in criminalibus.

Ad solutionem poenae reducitur quae in iure Romano nominabatur satisfactio et a solutione iuridica distinguebatur. Satisfacit enim qui debitum solvit non secundum contractum sed alio modo qui placet creditori. Quae sane satisfactio, quae nihil est aliud quam species quaedam solutionis, non minus ad iustitiam commutativam reducitur quam solutio contractu determinata.

Unde concludes: ubi satisfactio intelligitur, uti in iure Romano, tamquam poenae quaedam solutio, non est dubitandum disiunctionem S. Anselmi nihil aliud significare quam hoc, aut poenae solutio aut poenae solutio.

*Punishment simply so called* deprives one even of the goods of the soul. Thus in the case when the will is good and upright, this punishment is simply contrary to the will.

*Punishment in a qualified sense*, 'medicinal' punishment, deprives one of a lesser good in order to increase a greater good. Such punishment, when the will is good and upright, is absolutely speaking in accord with a will that wills the greater good, but in a qualified sense is contrary to a will that does not will the lesser evil. However, insofar as a will is lacking in goodness, this medicinal punishment is simply contrary to that will; but since the inflicting of punishment often changes the disposition of the one being punished, it can *per accidens* change even that person's will (see Thomas Aquinas, *De malo*, q. 16, a. 5), and in this way, presupposing some good dispositions to begin with, medicinal punishment in a way tends to a conversion of the will.

7 *Guilt*, the liability to punishment, the debt of punishment, results from fault.

Hence punishment simply so called is justly inflicted solely on account of one's fault, either personal or original.

Medicinal punishment, on the other hand, can be justly inflicted apart from one's personal fault; but this possibility itself is reducible to original fault.

*Summa theologiae*, 1-2, q. 87, aa. 7 and 8; 2–2, q. 108, a. 4.

8 Paying a penalty and imposing it differ from each other as passion and action: one and the same change is payment in the one punished and imposition from the one punishing.

Paying the penalty is consequent upon one's debt of punishment; in civil matters it takes place according to commutative justice, and in criminal matters according to retributive justice.

What in Roman law used to be termed 'satisfaction' was ultimately a matter of paying the penalty and was distinguished from a juridical payment. For one who pays a debt not strictly in accordance with the contract but in some other way that is acceptable to his creditor gives satisfaction. This satisfaction, which is nothing other than a kind of payment, is reducible to commutative justice no less than a payment stipulated in a contract.

From this one may conclude that when satisfaction is understood, as in Roman law, to be a certain payment of a penalty, there is no doubt that St Anselm's disjunction means simply this: 'either payment of the penalty or payment of the penalty.'

9 Sicut reatum seu debitum poenae consequitur poenae solutio, ita etiam offensam sequitur poenae inflictio.

Quod non est intelligendum quasi ipse offensus poenam infligeret: ad tale opus deputantur ministri legitimi secundum ordinatissimam eorum hierarchiam, e. g., custodes platearum, iudices et iuris periti, carnifices.

10 Circa poenarum inflictionem distinguuntur:

Saevitia: infligere poenam praeter culpam. Crudelitas: infligere poenam ultra culpam. Vindicatio illicita: infligere poenam secundum culpam sed modo indebito, e.g., delectando in malo alterius. Vindicatio licita: infligere poenam secundum culpam, debito fine, debitis adiunctis. Vide *Sum. theol.*, II-II, q. 108, a. 1; q. 159, a. 2.

## PRAENOTAMEN V: SATISFACTIO, VENIA, REMISSIO POENAE

1 Quaeritur deinde de altera notionum complexione; et iterum de notionibus intelligendis agitur, non de earum concreta applicatione.

2 *Venia* est offensae remissio.

Mt 5.23–26: Si ergo offers munus tuum ad altare et ibi recordatus fueris quia frater tuus habet aliquid adversum te, relinque ibi munus tuum ante altare, et vade prius reconciliari fratri tuo, et tunc veniens offeres munus tuum. Esto consentiens adversario tuo cito, dum es in via cum eo; ne forte tradat te adversarius iudici, et iudex tradat te ministro, et in carcerem mittaris. Amen dico tibi, non exies inde, donec reddas novissimum quadrantem.

Ubi agitur de veniae petitione et concessione (aliquid adversum te, reconciliari, esto consentiens), quae distinguitur a poenae inflictione (iudex, minister, carcer, novissimus quadrans).

Cf. Mt 6.12, 6.14–15, 18.21–35, Mc 11.25–26, Lc 7.47, 17.3–4, ubi fortissime inculcatur doctrina Christiana omnibus nota.

9 Just as paying the penalty is consequent upon liability to punishment, so also inflicting punishment is consequent upon an offense.

This is not to be understood as if the person offended is to inflict the punishment himself; legitimate officials are appointed for this task according to an appropriate hierarchical order, such as the police, judges and lawyers, and executioners.

10 Note the following distinctions regarding the infliction of punishment.

Brutality or savagery is inflicting punishment where no fault warrants it. Cruelty is inflicting punishment beyond what is warranted by the fault. Illicit retribution is inflicting punishment warranted by the fault, but in an inappropriate manner, such as taking pleasure in the other's suffering. Licit retribution means inflicting punishment proportionate to the fault, for the right purpose, and in proper circumstances (*Summa theologiae,* 2-2, q. 108, a. 1; q. 159, a. 2).

PRELIMINARY NOTE 5: SATISFACTION, PARDON, REMISSION OF PUNISHMENT

1 We go on now to inquire about the second set of notions; and again, we are concerned with understanding these notions, not with their concrete application.

2 *Pardon* is the forgiveness of an offense.

Matthew 5.23–26: 'So when you are offering your gift at the altar, if you remember that your brother or sister has something against you, leave your gift there before the altar and go; first be reconciled to your brother or sister, and then come and offer your gift. Come to terms quickly with your accuser while you are on your way to court with him, or your accuser may hand you over to the judge, and the judge to the guard, and you will be thrown into prison. Truly I tell you, you will never get out until you have paid the last penny.'

Here it is a matter of asking and granting pardon ('something against you,' 'be reconciled,' 'come to terms'), which is different from inflicting punishment ('judge,' 'guard,' 'prison,' 'the last penny').

See Matthew 6.12, 6.14–15, 18.21–35, Mark 11.25–26, Luke 7.47, 17.3–4, passages where the well-known Christian teaching is forcefully set forth.

3 *Satisfactio* est poenae susceptio voluntaria ut convenienter petatur et concedatur venia. Ad terminos:

*Poena*: boni privatio, et quidem boni minoris privatio, nempe, in bonis exterioribus vel in bonis corporis non autem in bonis animae. Intelligitur ergo poena latius dicta et ad modum poenae secundum quid (praenotamen IV, §§ 4 et 6).

*Susceptio voluntaria*: scilicet, satisfaciens vult simpliciter manifestationem voluntatis concordis, quamvis a malo minori secundum quid refugiat. Uti patet, toto caelo quoad conceptum differunt (1) poenae susceptio voluntaria ubi perfecta voluntate suscipitur et (2) poenae inflictio quae nullo modo sustineretur nisi vi infligeretur. In concreto, tamen, ubi imperfectae sunt hominum voluntates, et alia alterius imperfectio, inter susceptionem pure voluntariam et inflictionem simpliciter contrariam voluntati, commixtiones intermediae sine fine distingui possunt. Sed de praesenti de conceptibus agitur, et ideo agnoscendum est poenam satisfactoriam, quia voluntarie et libere suscipitur, omnino distingui a poena strictius dicta de cuius ratione est quod sit voluntati contraria.

Vide *Sum. theol.*, I-II, q. 87, a. 7 c. et ad 3m; a. 8; III, q. 47, a. 3, ad 1m; q. 48, a. 5.

*In ordine ad veniam*: scilicet, in ordine ad remissionem offensae (quod minime est confundendum cum remissione poenae); agitur enim de offensa amovenda, de concordia renovanda, de reconciliatione. Iterum, uti patet, quoad conceptum omnino differunt poenae susceptio voluntaria in ordine ad veniam et poenae inflictio invito imposita propter offensam quam septagesies septies repetere vult. In concreto, tamen, non minus patet inter haec extrema dari casus intermedios et permultos.

*Convenienter*: voluntarie suscipitur poena ut conveniens sit veniae tam petitio quam concessio. Quid sit convenientia? Neque necessitas est, neque mera contradictionis absentia, sed positiva quaedam intelligibilitas secundum sapientem et prudentem rerum ordinationem, e.g., in scientiis empiricis perspicitur intelligibilitas quae absolute posset esse alia sed de facto est haec. Qualis sit haec convenientia, hac in thesi non dicitur sed ad sequentem remittitur; notate tamen statim quod agitur de imperfecta mysteriorum intelligentia (DB 1796, DS 3016).

3 *Satisfaction* is the voluntary acceptance of punishment in order that pardon may fittingly be asked and granted. These terms are explained as follows:

*Punishment*: a privation of a good, and indeed of a lesser good, that is, an external good or a good of the body, not a good of the soul. Hence punishment here is understood broadly and in the manner of a qualified punishment: see preliminary note 4, §§ 4 and 6.

*Voluntary acceptance*: in other words, the one making satisfaction wants simply to manifest a harmonious will, although in a sense he shrinks from the lesser evil. As is quite obvious, there is a world of difference conceptually between (1) the voluntary acceptance of punishment when it is accepted with complete willingness, and (2) the infliction of punishment that would in no way be submitted to if it were not imposed by force. Concretely, however, where human wills are imperfect and different persons have different imperfections, there is a whole range of intermediate combinations between the purely voluntary acceptance of suffering and the infliction of suffering that is simply against one's will. But at this point we are concerned with concepts, and so it must be recognized that satisfactory punishment, willingly and freely accepted, is altogether different from punishment strictly so called, which by its very essence is contrary to the will.

See *Summa theologiae*, 1-2, q. 87, a. 7 c. and ad 3m; a. 8; 3, q. 47, a. 3, ad 1m; q. 48, a. 5.

*In order that pardon may be asked and granted*: that is to say, with a view to forgiveness, the remission of the offense (which is not at all to be confused with the remission of punishment). It is a question of canceling the offense, re-establishing harmony, reconciliation. Again, conceptually, as is clear, the voluntary acceptance of punishment with a view to pardon is altogether different from punishment forcibly inflicted upon an unwilling person for an offense which that person is ready and willing to repeat seventy times seven. Concretely, however, it is no less clear that between these extremes there are a great many intermediate cases.

*Fittingly*: punishment is accepted voluntarily in order that both the asking and the granting of pardon may be fitting. What is fittingness? It is not necessity, nor the mere absence of contradiction, but a positive intelligibility in accordance with a wise and prudent order of things. In the empirical sciences, for example, an intelligibility is grasped that absolutely speaking might be otherwise than in fact it is. We will postpone to the following thesis a discussion of the nature of this fittingness. But for now, however, note that we are dealing with an imperfect understanding of the mysteries (DB 1796, DS 3016, [ND 132]).

4 Veniae concessio convenienter sequitur veniae petitionem eoque magis quo manifestior est dolor de offensa culpaeque detestatio.

Quod tamen ita in se est conveniens ut tamen praecepto novae legis imponitur. Mt 5.38–48, 18.21–35, 1 Pet 2.18–25. Ubi sensus intentus omne excludit dubium, neque ulla est difficultas nisi in exsecutione.

5 Poenae remissio convenienter sequitur veniam seu offensae remissionem. Si enim quis re vera de corde suo (Mt 18.35) fratri remittit offensam et cum eo reconciliatur, non amplius de poena exigenda cogitat.

Attamen non idem eodem modo fit indifferenter in omnibus casibus: in baptismo enim ita remittuntur omnia peccata ut simul omnis poena remittatur, sed in sacramento paenitentiae ita peccata remittuntur ut tamen non totalis poena remittatur (DB 922, DS 1712).

## PRAENOTAMEN VI: SATISFACTIO VICARIA

1 Expressio 'satisfactio vicaria' ad saeculum XIX pertinet (Deneffe, *ZeitKathTheol* 43 [1919] 174). Uti vidimus tamen thesi 15a ipso NT contineri doctrinam de passione et morte Christi vicaria; et praesenti thesi probatur hanc passionem et mortem rationem satisfactionis habuisse; quibus coniunctis habetur vicaria satisfactio.

2 Satisfactio vicaria est poenae susceptio voluntaria ut convenienter et petatur et concedatur venia offensae non propriae sed alienae.

3 Fundamentum satisfactionis vicariae est voluntatum unio secundum amorem.

De hac unione: *Sum. theol.*, I-II, q. 28, aa.1 et 2.

Quod est fundamentum: 'Et quia contingit eos qui differunt in reatu poenae, esse unum secundum voluntatem unione amoris, inde est quod interdum aliquis qui non peccavit, poenam voluntarius pro alio portat: sicut etiam in rebus humanis videmus quod aliquis in se transfert alterius debitum' (*Sum. theol.*, I-II, q. 87, a. 7 c.).

4 Granting pardon fittingly follows upon the request for pardon, and is all the more fitting the more manifest is one's sorrow for the offense and detestation for the sin.

Still, fitting as this is in itself, it is nevertheless enjoined by a precept of the new law: see Matthew 5.38–48, 18.21–35, 1 Peter 2.18–25. The meaning intended is beyond all doubt. It is difficult only in practice.

5 It is fitting that the remission of punishment be consequent upon pardon, the forgiveness of the offense. For if one truly in one's heart (Matthew 18.35) forgives the offense and is reconciled with the offender, there is no further thought of exacting punishment.

Nevertheless, this same process is not carried out in the same way in every case. In baptism all sins and all punishment are remitted at the same time, whereas in the sacrament of penance sins are remitted but not all punishment (DB 922, DS 1712, [ND 1652]).

PRELIMINARY NOTE 6: VICARIOUS SATISFACTION

1 The expression 'vicarious satisfaction' was introduced in the nineteenth century (Deneffe, 'Das Wort *satisfactio*' 174). But as we saw in the previous thesis, the New Testament itself contains the doctrine of the vicarious passion and death of Christ, and in the present thesis this passion and death is shown to fit the definition of satisfaction. Combining these, we have vicarious satisfaction.

2 Vicarious satisfaction is the voluntary acceptance of punishment in order that it may be fitting to ask and be granted pardon for an offense that is not one's own but that of another.

3 The basis of vicarious satisfaction is the union of wills through love.

On this union, see Thomas Aquinas, *Summa theologiae,* 1-2, q. 28, aa. 1 and 2.

This is the basis: 'And since it can happen that those who have unequal liability to punishment are of one will through their union in love, occasionally someone who has not committed an offense bears voluntarily the punishment for it in place of the one who has, just as also in human affairs we see a person taking on someone else's debt' (*Summa theologiae,* 1-2, q. 87, a. 7 c.).

4 Obiecerit tamen quispiam: satisfactio vicaria probat bonam voluntatem amici qui non offendit; sed nihil facit ut manifestetur bona voluntas eius qui offendit; et ideo non videtur conveniens ut propter satisfactionem vicariam remittatur offensa eius qui et offendit et, quantum scitur, iterum offendet.

R. Obiciens praetermittere videtur fundamentum satisfactionis vicariae quod, uti diximus, est unio voluntatum secundum amorem. Audi S. Thomam:

> Quae autem per amicos facimus, per nos ipsos facere videmur (Arist., *Eth.*, III, iii, 13, 1112b): quia amicitia ex duobus facit unum per affectum, et praecipue dilectio caritatis. Et ideo, sicut per se ipsum, ita et per alium potest aliquis satisfacere Deo: praecipue cum necessitas fuerit. Nam et poenam quam amicus propter ipsum patitur, reputat aliquis ac si ipse pateretur: et sic poena ei non deest, dum patienti amico compatitur; et tanto amplius, quanto ipse est ei causa patiendi. Et iterum affectio caritatis in eo qui pro amico patitur facit magis satisfactionem Deo acceptam quam si pro se pateretur: hoc enim est promptae caritatis ... Ex quo accipitur quod unus pro alio satisfacere potest, dum uterque in caritate fuerit. Hinc est quod Apostolus dicit, Gal 6.2: 'Alter alterius onera portate.' *C. Gent.*, III, 158, ¶7.[23]

5 Quae quidem ita generaliter de satisfactione vicaria dicta sunt ut applicari possunt tum satisfactioni vicariae ipsius Christi tum illi satisfactioni quae communiter 'reparatio' nominatur, e.g., in cultu SS. Cordis Iesu. Vide praesertim Pium XI, 'Miserentissimus Redemptor,' AAS 20 (1928) 165–78. A. Bea, alii, redact., *Cor Jesu*, 2 vol., Romae, 1959.[24]

4 One may object here that vicarious satisfaction is a proof of the good will of the friend who has not offended, but does nothing to manifest good will on the part of the one who has committed the offense, and therefore it does not seem fitting because of vicarious satisfaction to forgive the offense of the one who has offended and, as far as anyone knows, may well re-offend.

In answer to this we point out that the objector seems to overlook the basis of vicarious satisfaction, which is, as we have said, the union of wills through love. Listen to St Thomas:

> What we do through our friends we are considered to do ourselves (Aristotle, *Nicomachean Ethics,* III, iii, 13, 1112b 22–23), since friendship makes two persons one through their affection, and especially through the love that is charity. Hence, just as one can make satisfaction to God by himself, one can also do this through another, especially where there is some urgent need. For anyone counts the punishment suffered by a friend on one's own account as though he were suffering it himself, and therefore he is not without some punishment in suffering along with his friend – all the more so insofar as he is the cause of his friend's suffering. Again, the affection in charity in the one who suffers in place of a friend makes satisfaction more acceptable to God than if he were suffering on account of himself, for it is an outstanding display of charity … From this, it is accepted that one person can make satisfaction on behalf of another, so long as both abide in charity. Hence the Apostle says, Galatians 6.2: 'Bear one another's burdens' (*Summa contra Gentiles,* 3, c. 158, ¶7, § 3311).[23]

5 What is said here in general terms concerning vicarious satisfaction can be applied both to Christ's vicarious satisfaction and to the kind of satisfaction that is commonly called 'reparation' – in the devotion to the Sacred Heart, for example. See especially Pius XI, 'Miserentissimus Redemptor,' *Acta Apostolicae Sedis* 20 (1928) 165–78; also *Cor Jesu,* ed. A. Bea and others (Rome, 1959).[24]

23 Lonergan tended to count paragraphs in the Leonine manual edition of the *Summa contra Gentiles.* Hence, ¶7.

24 Augustin Bea, Hugo Rahner, Henri Rondet, and Friedrich Schwendimann, eds., *Cor Iesu: Commentationes in Litteras Encyclicas PII PP. XII 'Haurietis Aquas':* vol. 1: *Pars Theologica;* vol. 2: *Pars Historica et Pastoralis* (Rome: Herder, 1959).

6 Sed in utroque casu omnino cavendum est ne mente Pelagiana legantur. Non enim de qualibet amicitia agitur sed de illa quae in communicatione divinae beatitudinis consistit (*Sum. theol.*, II-II, q. 23, a. 1), et ideo absolute supernaturalis est.

Quam ob causam, ita in unione amoris fundatur satisfactio vicaria Christiana ut ille ipse amor in Christo habeatur propter plenitudinem gratiae ei propriam, neque ab ullo alio habeatur nisi per ipsam satisfactionem atque meritum Christi.

7 Unde concludes analogice inter se comparari satisfactionem vicariam quae ex amicitia naturali procedit, satisfactionem vicariam quae ab ipso Christo est facta, et satisfactionem vicariam quae a fidelibus virtute Christi fit.

In ordine enim naturali amicitia offendentis et satisfacientis non solum fundat sed etiam praecedit satisfactionem.

In ordine autem supernaturali dilectio caritatis in satisfaciente conducit in similem dilectionem in offendente. Quod tamen aliter fit in Christo satisfaciente et in fideli satisfaciente: Christus enim habet dilectionem caritatis quia est persona divina in humana natura subsistens; et per suam satisfactionem et meritum pro aliis impetrat similem dilectionem. Fidelis autem sicut ipse per Christum habet dilectionem caritatis, ita etiam per Christum satisfaciendo petit similem dilectionem in offendente.

8 Quibus differentiis accedunt aliae non paucae quae ex iam dictis magis sunt concludendae quam hic explicite ponendae. Breviter haec notamus. (Quae de Christo dicemus etiam de Beata Virgine propter immaculatam conceptionem quodammodo sunt intelligenda).

In Christo, satisfactio est simpliciter vicaria: ita pro aliis satisfecit ut pro se nihil satisfaciendum habuerit (Io 14.30, Heb 7.27). In peccatoribus autem satisfactio non est simpliciter vicaria; ita enim pro aliis satisfaciunt ut tamen pro se etiam satisfaciant; et quamvis haec duo, nempe, pro aliis et pro se, conceptu distingui possint, non tam facile re separantur.

In Christo satisfactio non solum simpliciter vicaria sed etiam simpliciter satisfactio est. Etsi enim in peccatoribus satisfactio ita sit conveniens veniae

6 Yet neither of these should be taken in a Pelagian sense. For it is not any sort of friendship that is involved here but that which consists in the communication of divine beatitude (*Summa theologiae,* 2-2, q. 23, a. 1) and is therefore absolutely supernatural.

For this reason, Christian vicarious satisfaction is based upon union in love in such a way that the very same love that Christ has on account of the plenitude of grace proper to him alone is had by no one else except through Christ's satisfaction and merit.

7 From this you will infer that the vicarious satisfaction that proceeds from natural friendship, the vicarious satisfaction made by Christ, and the vicarious satisfaction made by Christians in virtue of Christ are related analogically.

In the natural order the friendship between the offender and the one who makes satisfaction for the offense is not only the basis of satisfaction but precedes it.

In the supernatural order, however, the love that is charity in the one who makes satisfaction induces a similar love in the offender. Still, this occurs differently in Christ making satisfaction and in the faithful making satisfaction; for Christ has the love of charity because he is a divine person subsisting in a human nature, and it is through his satisfaction and merit that he wins for others a similar love. But just as the faithful have the love of charity through Christ, so also it is through Christ that by making satisfaction they pray for a similar love in the offender.

8 Besides these differences there are several others, which are to be inferred from what we have said rather than explicitly stated here. We shall briefly mention the following. (What we say here concerning Christ is also to be understood, in a way, of the Blessed Virgin on account of her immaculate conception.)

Christ's satisfaction is purely and simply vicarious. He made satisfaction for others while having no need to make satisfaction for himself (John 14.30, Hebrews 7.27). In the case of sinners, however, satisfaction is not purely vicarious, for the satisfaction they makc for others also entails satisfaction for themselves. And although these two, 'for others' and 'for themselves,' can be distinguished conceptually, they are not so easily separated in reality.

Christ's satisfaction is not only simply vicarious but is also simply satisfaction. In sinners satisfaction is a fitting petition for pardon, in such a way that

petitio ut etiam sit poena propter culpam praeteritam et medicina contra futuram (DB 905, DS 1692; *Sum. theol.*, I-II, q. 87, a. 6; II-II, q. 108, a. 4), in Christo impeccabili sicut defuit culpa praeterita etiam defuit possibilitas culpae futurae. Quam ob causam in Christo ita adfuit satisfactio ut simpliciter excludatur illa poena quae est vel propter praeteritam vel contra futuram culpam propriam.

PRAENOTAMEN VII: DE DEI IUSTITIA

1 Deus potest facere quodcumque rationem entis habet, i.e., quodcumque internam contradictionem non continet. *Sum. theol.*, I, q. 25, a. 3.

2 Quaecumque Deus potest facere absolute (cf. § 1 supra), eadem potest facere secundum infinitam suam sapientiam; non enim aliud est divina potentia et aliud divina sapientia, sed idem realiter sunt; unde 'divina sapientia totum posse potentiae comprehendit' (ibid. a. 5 c.).

Praeterea, Deus nihil facit nisi secundum infinitam suam sapientiam; et eadem est ratio, nempe, idem realiter esse et sapientiam et potentiam. Ibid. a. 5, ad 1m.

3 Ideo voluntas est bona quia intellectum sequitur; sed voluntas Dei necessario est bona; et ideo fieri non potest ut divina voluntas agat praeter ordinem divinae sapientiae. Ibid. q. 21, a. 1, ad 2m. Cf. *De veritate*, q. 23, a. 6, ubi addiscis sententiam contrariam esse blasphemiam.

Quod minime opponitur libertati divinae voluntatis. Ita enim omnia possibilia ordinat infinita sapientia ut in sua essentia Deus cognoscat omnes omnium mundorum ordines possibiles, usquequaque determinatos, quorum nullum vel quemlibet eligere potest divina bonitas quin praeter ordinem divinae sapientiae agat.

4 Iustitia Dei in eo consistit quod divina voluntas secundum ordinem divinae sapientiae eligit. *Sum. theol.*, I, q. 21, a.1, ad 2m.

5 Aristoteles triplicem distinxit iustitiam: commutativam, quae regulat operationes inter subditos seu concives; legalis, quae regulat operationes subditorum vel civium erga gubernatorem seu civitatem; distributiva, quae regulat operationes gubernantis erga cives vel subditos.

it is also punishment for previous fault and a preventive medicine against future fault (DB 905, DS 1692, [ND 1633]; *Summa theologiae*, 1-2, q. 87, a. 6; 2–2, q. 108, a. 4). In Christ, however, who was incapable of sinning, just as there was no previous fault, so there was also no possibility of a future fault. Hence Christ's satisfaction was such that it simply excludes the punishment that one receives on account of one's own fault, whether past or future.

### PRELIMINARY NOTE 7: THE JUSTICE OF GOD

1 God can do whatever has the formality of being, that is, whatever does not contain an internal contradiction (*Summa theologiae*, 1, q. 25, a. 3).

2 Whatever God can do absolutely (see § 1, above) he can do in accordance with his infinite wisdom. For God's power and wisdom are not two different things, but are the same in reality; hence 'divine wisdom comprehends all that is within the divine power' (ibid. a. 5 c.).

Besides, God does nothing except in accordance with his infinite wisdom; and the reason is the same, namely, that in God wisdom and power are really identical (ibid. a. 5, ad 1m).

3 A will is good when it follows the intellect; but the will of God is necessarily good, and therefore it cannot be that the divine will should act apart from the order of divine wisdom (ibid. q. 21, a. 1, ad 2m; see also Thomas Aquinas, *De veritate*, q. 23, a. 6, where you will find that the opposite opinion is blasphemous).

This is in no way opposed to the freedom of the divine will. For infinite wisdom orders all possible beings in such a way that God knows in his essence every possible order of every possible world, down to the least detail, and divine goodness can choose none of these orders or any of them without acting outside the order of divine wisdom.

4 The justice of God consists in this, that the divine will chooses in accordance with the order of divine wisdom (*Summa theologiae*, 1, q. 21, a. 1, ad 2m).

5 Aristotle distinguished three kinds of justice: commutative, which regulates actions among subjects or citizens; legal, which regulates the actions of subjects or citizens towards the governor or city; and distributive, which regulates the actions of the governing authority towards the citizens or subjects.

Quod si Deo analogice applicatur, dicendum est iustitiam Dei non esse commutativam, quia non est alius ei aequalis, neque esse legalem, quia ipse non est subditus, sed esse distributivam, quia ipse est fons omnis boni et omnis legis et omnis iudicii. *Sum. theol.*, I, q. 21, a. 1. Notate iustitiam qua iustificamur esse secundum Aristotelem metaphorice dictam. I-II, q. 113, a. 1.[25]

6 Ordo divinae sapientiae seu divinae iustitiae omnem alium ordinem actualem in se includit, aliter tamen et aliter, secundum quod Deus bona directe vult, mala naturalis defectus et mala poenae indirecte vult, malum autem culpae nullo modo vult sed tantummodo permittit. Ibid. q. 19, a. 9 c. et ad 3m.

7 Ordinationes autem quae intra unam Dei iustitiam inveniuntur quadrupliciter dividi possunt, secundum quod (1) e bonis fit bonum, (2) e malis fit malum, (3) e bonis fit malum, et (4) e malis fit bonum.

Et prima et secunda ordinatio, quamvis in multis aliis inveniantur, maxima claritate in iudicio finali perspiciuntur ubi iudex venturus Dominus noster et bonos gloria praemiabit et malos ad poenas aeternas condemnabit.

Tertia ordinatio est ubicumque Deus malum culpae in iustis permittit.

Quarta autem ordinatio est tum nostra redemptio tum iustificatio impii tum omnis profectus spiritualis in quo mala deponuntur et bona augentur.

Praeterea, prima et secunda ordinatio sunt secundum iustitiam retributivam prout ordinarie concipitur.

Tertia autem et quarta ordinatio, quamvis omnino inter se oppositae videantur, nihilominus ab Augustino tamquam connexae perspiciebantur: 'Melius enim iudicavit (Deus) de malis bene facere, quam mala nulla esse permittere.' *Enchiridion*, c. XXVII; ML 40, 245. Neque aliud significari videtur,

If this is applied to God analogously, divine justice cannot be said to be commutative, since there is no one else equal to him, nor legal, since God is not a subject; but it can be said to be distributive, since God is the source of all good and all law and all judgment (*Summa theologiae,* 1, q. 21, a. 1). Note that the justice by which we are justified is for Aristotle justice only in a metaphorical sense (ibid. 1-2, q. 113, a. 1).[25]

6 The order of divine wisdom or divine justice includes within itself all the other actual orders, though in different ways, so that God directly wills what is good, indirectly wills the evil of natural defect and the evil of punishment, and absolutely does not will culpable evil but merely permits it (ibid. 1, q. 19, a. 9 c. and ad 3m).

7 The orderings that are found within the one justice of God can be divided into four: (1) good from good, (2) evil from evil, (3) evil from good, and (4) good from evil.

The first and the second of these orderings, although they are found in many other instances, are most apparent in the last judgment when the future Judge, our Lord, will reward the good with glory and condemn the wicked to eternal punishment.

The third ordering obtains whenever God permits culpable evil in the just.

The fourth ordering is our redemption and the justification of the unjust and all spiritual progress in which evil is forsaken and goodness increased.

Furthermore, the first and second orderings are in accordance with retributive justice, as ordinarily conceived.

The third and the fourth orderings, however, although they seem to be totally opposite to each other, were nevertheless perceived by Augustine to be connected: '(God) judged it better to draw good out of evil than to permit no evil to exist' (*Enchiridion,* c. XXVII; ML 40, 245). This also seems to be

25 On Aquinas's account, justice concerns the relations among persons and is governed by the virtue of justice, which is an attitude of willingness. Metaphorically, it concerns the relations among the internal principles of action within a person (rational, irascible, and concupiscible). That is, these principles are taken metaphorically, as if they were agents related to one another. The grace of justification establishes rectitude among these principles within the soul, and so is called justice according to this metaphor. This reordering involves the infusion of virtues that reorient us to other agents. See, in addition to the passage Lonergan notes, *Summa theologiae,* 2-2, q. 58, a. 2.

ubi in vigilia paschali canitur: 'O certe necessarium Adae peccatum, quod Christi morte deletum est. O felix culpa, quae talem ac tantum meruit habere Redemptorem.'

8 Ulterius, quam distinctionem posuit Tertullianus inter veniam ex castigatione et poenam ex damnatione, quam distinctionem voluit Anselmus inter satisfactionem et poenam, nihil aliud est quam distinctio inter ordinationem secundam superius positam atque ordinationem quartam cum tertia connexam. Ubi enim habetur poena ex damnatione seu a non satisfaciente poenae exactio (*Cur Deus homo,* I, 15), ibi habetur secunda ordinatio secundum quam e malis fit malum, et quidem e malo culpae malum poenae. Ubi autem habetur venia ex castigatione seu perversitatis spontanea satisfactio (ibid.), ibi supponitur tertia ordinatio quae est peccati permissio et habetur quarta ordinatio quae est e malis in bonum.

9 Neque in ipsis scripturis deesse videtur similis distinctio. Quam enim iram Dei exposuit S. Paulus ad Rom 1.18 usque ad 3.20 ad secundam ordinationem pertinet. Quam autem Dei iustitiam ibidem, 3.21 et deinceps laudat, ad quartam pertinet ordinationem. Haec enim Dei iustitia secundum eruditos est illa divina sanctitas atque fidelitas Hebraeis notissima (testificata a lege et prophetis), nunc autem manifestata quatenus, omnibus tam Iudaeis quam gentibus in peccato exsistentibus, gratis (ne quis glorietur) per sanguinem Iesu et per fidem Iesu Christi datur propitiatio, redemptio, iustificatio, ut Deus sit iustus et iustificans. Vide S. Lyonnet, *Verbum Domini* 25 (1947) 23–34, 118–21, 129–44, 193–203, 257–63.

10 Intra unum ordinem divinae sapientiae et iustitiae diversas distinximus ordinationes. Quibus tamen distinctis, ad earum coniunctionem nunc attendendum est.

Quae sane coniunctio nihil est aliud quam illa disiunctio iam pridem considerata, nempe, inter veniam ex castigatione et poenam ex damnatione, inter satisfactionem et poenam, inter divinam iustitiam quae e malis facit bonum absolute supernaturale et divinam iram quae impaenitentes reprobat.

the meaning in the canticle that is sung in the Easter Vigil: 'O truly necessary sin of Adam, destroyed completely by the death of Christ! O happy fault, that earned so great, so glorious a Redeemer!'

8 Moreover, Tertullian's distinction between pardon after chastisement and punishment after condemnation, and the distinction that Anselm intended between satisfaction and punishment, is simply the distinction between the second ordering above and the fourth ordering taken in conjunction with the third. For where there is punishment after condemnation, or punishment exacted from one who has not made satisfaction (*Cur Deus homo*, book 1, c. 15), the second ordering obtains, according to which evil comes out of evil, the evil of punishment resulting from culpable evil. But where there is pardon after chastisement, or spontaneous satisfaction for one's perversity (ibid.), the third ordering, which is the permission of sin, is supposed, and the fourth ordering, good from evil, obtains.

9 A similar distinction seems to be present in the scriptures themselves. The wrath of God that St Paul expounds in Romans 1.18–3.20 pertains to the second ordering. The justice of God, praised from 3.21 onward, pertains to the fourth ordering. According to the scholars, this justice of God is that divine holiness and fidelity, esteemed by the Hebrews (as attested in the law and the prophets), and now made manifest, inasmuch as to all who are in sin, Jews and Gentiles alike, expiation, redemption, and justification are given gratis (lest anyone boast) through the blood of Jesus and through faith in Jesus Christ, so that God may be just and justifying. See Lyonnet, 'De "Iustitia Dei" in Epistola ad Romanos 1, 17 et 3, 21–22,' *Verbum Domini* 25 (1947) 23–34; 'De "Iustitia Dei" in Epistola ad Romanos 10, 3 et 3, 5,' ibid. 118–21; 'De "Iustitia Dei" in Epistola ad Romanos 3, 25–26,' ibid. 129–44, 193–203, 257–63.

10 We have distinguished various orderings within the one order of divine wisdom and divine justice. Having distinguished them, however, we must now consider the connection among them.

This connection is nothing other than the disjunction we have been considering, namely, between pardon after chastisement and punishment after condemnation, between satisfaction and punishment, between divine justice that draws absolutely supernatural good from evil and the divine wrath that condemns the unrepentant.

Sed ipsa haec coniunctio, uti vidimus, ita in actuali rerum ordine verificatur ut tamen absolute non necessaria sed conveniens est dicenda. Quod enim in epistola ad Hebraeos de VT docetur, 'Et omnia paene in sanguine secundum legem mundantur, et sine sanguinis effusione non fit remissio' (Heb 9.22), non legem facit cui Deus obtemperare tenetur, sed legem dicit secundum quam hoc in rerum ordine populum suum salvum fieri Deo placuit.

## PRAENOTAMEN VIII: DE ORDINE DIVINAE IUSTITIAE REDINTEGRANDO SEU REPARANDO

1 Ordo divinae iustitiae est ille ordo divinae sapientiae de facto a divina voluntate infinite iusta electus. Qui quidem ordo etiam est ordo divinae providentiae, ordo secundum quem Deus totum universum secundum omnem suam determinationem gubernat, ordo qui in ipso universo infallibiliter, efficaciter, irresistibiliter efficitur, et denique tandem ita productus est finis ipsi universo intrinsecus seu gloria Dei externa obiectiva.

*Sum. theol.*, I, q. 15, a. 2; q. 19, a. 4; q. 21, a. 1, ad 2m; q. 22, a. 1; q. 103, a.1; a. 2, ad 3m; q. 47, a. 1. Plura apud J. Wright, *The Order of the Universe* (Romae, PUG, 1957).

2 Qui sane ordo non eo sensu redintegrari vel reparari potest quod aliquis Deo sapientior, melior, potentior opus divinum corrigit; et ideo necesse est dicere quamcumque redintegrationem vel reparationem fieri inquantum ab aeterno intra ordinem divinae sapientiae continetur et a Deo volente atque primo agente efficitur.

3 Nihilominus verissimo quodam sensu dicitur quod ordo divinae iustitiae reparatur vel redintegratur.

Quem enim diximus ordinem non solum ea continet quae Deus directe vult sed ea etiam quae Deus nullo modo vult, ut malum culpae, et ea quae Deus indirecte tantum vult, ut malum naturalis defectus et malum poenae. Et secundum hoc praedestinatio et reprobatio dicuntur partes divinae providentiae. *Sum. theol.*, I, q. 23, aa. 1 et 3.

At idem ordo, in mente divina exsistens, est lex aeterna (*Sum. theol.*, I-II, q. 91, a. 1) et a creaturis rationalibus participata est lex naturalis (ibid. a. 2);

But as we have seen, in the present order of things this conjunction is verified in such a way that it must be said to be not absolutely necessary but rather fitting. For what the Letter to the Hebrews (9.22) teaches concerning the old covenant, 'Indeed, under the law almost everything is purified with blood, and without the shedding of blood there is no forgiveness of sins,' does not constitute a law that God is bound to obey, but states a law according to which in this present order of things God has seen fit to save his people.

### PRELIMINARY NOTE 8: THE REINTEGRATION OR RESTORATION OF THE ORDER OF DIVINE JUSTICE

1 The order of divine justice is that order of divine wisdom that has in fact been chosen by the infinitely just divine will. This order is also the order of divine providence, the order according to which God governs the entire universe in all its particular details, an order that is implemented in this universe infallibly, efficaciously, and irresistibly, and finally, as thus carried out, is the intrinsic end of the universe, or the external objective glory of God.

*Summa theologiae,* 1, q. 15, a. 2; q. 19, a. 4; q. 21, a. 1, ad 2m; q. 22, a. 1; q. 103, a. 1 and a. 2, ad 3m; q. 47, a. 1. For more on this, see John H. Wright, *The Order of the Universe in the Theology of St. Thomas Aquinas* (Rome: Gregorian University Press, 1957).

2 This order certainly cannot be reintegrated or restored in the sense that someone wiser, better, and more powerful than God corrects God's work. Hence it is necessary to say that any reintegration or reparation whatsoever takes place inasmuch as it is from all eternity contained within the order of divine wisdom and implemented by God, who wills it and is its first agent.

3 Nevertheless, it is very true to say that there is a restoration or reintegration of the order of divine justice.

For the order we have been speaking of contains not only those things that God directly wills, but also those that God in no way wills, that is, culpable evil, and those that God wills only indirectly, the evil of natural defect and the evil of punishment. And it is according to this that predestination and reprobation are said to be parts of divine providence (*Summa theologiae,* 1, q. 23, aa. 1 and 3).

This same order as existing in the divine mind is the eternal law (ibid. 1-2, q. 91, a. 1), and as participated in by rational creatures is the natural law

neque ex alio fonte processerunt vel praecepta VT vel mandata Domino Christo a Patre data vel mandata nobis a Christo per apostolos et ecclesiam data.

Quam ob causam, etsi nihil praeter ordinem divinae gubernationis contingere possit (*Sum. theol.*, I, q. 103, a. 7), fieri tamen potest ut aliquid contra eundem ordinem reniti possit (ibid. a. 8). Nam ordo divinae providentiae dupliciter consideratur: uno modo, secundum quod a divina sapientia et electione procedit; alio modo, secundum quod a causa proxima finem quendam proximum intendente procedit. Et primo quidem modo nihil contra divinum ordinem reniti potest; sed alio modo iniqui, particulare quoddam bonum intendentes, peccant (ibid. c. et ad 1m).

Iam vero, inquantum iniqui peccant, habentur violationes ordinis divinae iustitiae; sed inquantum omnia divinae providentiae atque gubernationi subduntur (ibid. q. 22, a. 2; q. 103, a. 5), etiam fit ut ordo violatus reparetur seu redintegretur.

4 Quemadmodum vero ordo divinae iustitiae reparetur, tripliciter consideratur: primo modo, in individuis; altero modo, in Christo capite corporis sui et in diabolo qui est caput omnium iniquorum; tertio modo, in Deo qui est omnis reparationis et redintegrationis auctor et agens primum.

Quantum ad singulos peccatores pertinet, aliud est omnibus commune et aliud in aliis diversum. Et commune omnibus est debitum poenae, quae est quaedam recompensatio ad aequalitatem iustitiae 'ut scilicet qui plus suae voluntati indulsit quam debuit, contra mandatum Dei agens, secundum ordinem divinae iustitiae aliquid contra illud quod vellet spontaneus vel invitus patiatur.' *Sum. theol.*, I-II, q. 87, a. 6.

Quod autem ad debitum poenae sequitur, aliud est in aliis. Quorum enim caput est diabolus (*Sum. theol.*, III, q. 8, a. 7) poenas non subeunt nisi inflictas, easque propter mortalia peccata aeternas, propter autem venialia quodammodo temporales. Unde in iis reparatur seu redintegratur ordo divinae iustitiae inquantum secundum iustam Dei vindictam poenas peccatis debitas luunt.

Quorum autem caput est Christus, non eodem sed alio modo debitum poenae solvunt. In cuius intelligentiam recolendum est quod delictum expungit non solum poena ex damnatione sed etiam venia ex castigatione. Nam 'dilectio ad Deum sufficit mentem hominis firmare in bono, praecipue si vehemens fuerit: displicentia autem culpae praeteritae, cum fuerit

(ibid. a. 2). Nor is there any other source from which have issued either the precepts of the Old Testament or the commands given to Christ by the Father or the commands given to us by Christ through the apostles and the church.

Hence, although nothing can happen outside the order of divine governance (ibid. 1, q. 103, a. 7), it is possible that something could go against this order (ibid. a. 8). For the order of divine providence can be considered in two ways: first, as proceeding from divine wisdom and choice, and second, as proceeding from a proximate cause that intends some proximate end. Considered in the first way, there is nothing that can go against the divine order; but in the second way the wicked, intent upon some particular good, commit sin (ibid. c. and ad 1m).

Now, insofar as the wicked sin, there are violations of the order of divine justice; but inasmuch as all things are subject to divine providence and governance (ibid. q. 22, a. 2; q. 103, a. 5), it also happens that the order that has been violated is repaired or reintegrated.

4 The manner in which the order of divine justice is repaired can be considered in three ways: first, in individuals; second, in Christ the head of his body, and in the devil the head of all the wicked; and third, in God the author and first agent of all reparation and reintegration.

As regards individual sinners, there is something common to all and something that is different in each one. What is common to all is the debt of punishment, which is a compensation to be made towards restoring the balance of justice, 'so that one who, going against the commandment of God, has indulged his will more than is right, in accordance with the order of divine justice suffers, willingly or unwillingly, something opposite to what he wants' (ibid. 1-2, q. 87, a. 6).

The consequences of the debt of punishment are different in different cases. Those whose head is the devil (ibid. 3, q. 8, a. 7) suffer only the punishments that are inflicted upon them, whether eternal punishment because of mortal sins or in some way temporal in the case of venial sins. In them, therefore, the order of divine justice is repaired or reintegrated insofar as the punishments due to sin are suffered in accordance with God's retributive justice.

But those whose head is Christ do not pay the debt of punishment in the same way but in another way. To understand this, recall that what cancels sin is not only punishment after condemnation but also pardon after chastisement. For, 'love for God suffices to strengthen the mind of a person in goodness, especially if it is very fervent; while displeasure over one's past

intensa, magnum affert dolorem. Unde per vehementiam dilectionis Dei, et odii peccati praeteriti, excluditur necessitas satisfactoriae vel purgatoriae poenae: et si non sit tanta vehementia quod totaliter poenam excludat, tamen, quanto vehementius fuerit, tanto minus de poena sufficiet' (*C. Gent.*, III, 158, § 66). Quod sane mente pelagiana non est intelligendum, cum de dilectione supernaturali agatur, quae a peccatore nisi per Christum et in Christo non habetur. Ipse enim est caput corporis sui quod est ecclesia 'et se ipsum tradidit pro ea, ut illam sanctificaret' (Eph 5.25–26); quam sanctificationem tum aliis modis effecit tum etiam satisfaciendo pro membris suis quibus unitur secundum unionem amoris (*Sum. theol.*, III, q. 48, a 2, ad 1m); et ideo in baptizatis omnis poena remittitur, in paenitentia autem poena minuitur (DB 905, DS 1692). Unde in Christo per eius satisfactionem atque meritum ita redintegratur ordo divinae iustitiae ut e malis gravissimis educat Deus maximum illud bonum quod est corpus Christi et ecclesia militans, patiens, triumphans.

Remanet ut prima causa omnis reparationis atque redintegrationis memoretur. Qui secundum altissimum mysterium suae voluntatis et mundum creare potuit in quo nulla fuissent mala, et tamen mundum creare voluit in quo ita mala fieri permisit, ut et electi e peccatis reversi, Christo compatientes cum Christo conglorificentur (DB 904, DS 1690), et reprobi in peccatis indurati (*De malo*, q. 16, a. 5) pro peccatis suis poenas dent aeternas. Neque vel in electis vel in reprobis ita redintegratur ordo divinae iustitiae ut dici possit in alteris eum non vere redintegrari; hic enim ordo multiformem Dei sapientiam exhibet.

5 Unde concludes quam gravis esset error si quis censeret ordinem divinae iustitiae redintegrari, non per satisfactionem in ordine ad veniam, sed solummodo per ipsum poenarum debitum secundum vindicativam Dei iustitiam solutum.

### PRAENOTAMEN IX: PROBLEMA INTEGRATIONIS

1 Quae de redemptione revelata sunt, eorum intelligentiam ita auxit Anselmus ut tamen theologis determinandum manserit quemadmodum haec nova intelligentia cum traditionali doctrina integrari posset.

sin, when it is intense, evokes great sorrow. Hence on account of the fervor of one's love for God and of hatred of past sin, the necessity of satisfactory or purgative punishment is excluded; and even if one's fervor is not so great as to exclude punishment totally, still, the greater the fervor, the less is the punishment that will suffice' (*Summa contra Gentiles*, 3, c. 158, ¶6, § 3310). This is certainly not to be understood in a Pelagian sense, since it is a question here of supernatural love, which a sinner does not have except through Christ and in Christ. For Christ is the head of his body that is the church, 'and gave himself up for her, in order to make her holy' (Ephesians 5.25–26). He produces this sanctification, among other ways, by making satisfaction for the members of his body with whom he is united in a union of love (*Summa theologiae*, 3, q. 48, a. 2, ad 1m), and in this way all punishment is forgiven in baptism, while in the sacrament of penance it is reduced (DB 905, DS 1692, [ND 1633]). Hence in Christ, through his satisfaction and merit, the order of divine justice is so well reintegrated that from the very gravest evils God draws that greatest good of all, which is the body of Christ and the church militant, suffering, and triumphant.

It remains now to mention the first cause of all reparation and reintegration. God, in accordance with the most profound mystery of his will, could have created a world in which there would have been no evil, but willed instead to create a world in which evils are allowed to occur, yet in which the elect, after turning away from sin, by suffering with Christ might be glorified with Christ (DB 904, DS 1690, [ND 1631]), and the reprobate, hardened in sin (*De malo*, q. 16, a. 5), suffer eternal punishment for their sins. And neither in the elect nor in the reprobate is the order of divine justice restored in a way that would make it possible to say that only in the one but not in the other is that order truly restored, for it is an order that displays God's multiform wisdom.

5 From this one may conclude how serious an error it would be if one were to think that the order of divine justice is reintegrated, not through satisfaction ordered to pardon, but solely through payment of the debt of punishment in accordance with the retributive justice of God.

### PRELIMINARY NOTE 9: THE PROBLEM OF INTEGRATION

1 The understanding of what has been revealed about redemption was advanced by Anselm, but in such a way as to leave theologians with the task of determining how this new understanding could be integrated with traditional doctrine.

2 Ipsum integrationis processum illustrant:

Hugo Victorinus (ob. 1141; DTC VII, 279; Franks, I, 203–14) qui sententiam Anselmianam cum traditione circa partes diaboli ita coniunxit ut Christum exhibuerit intervenientem, non inter Deum et hominem, sed inter Deum, hominem, et diabolum.

Petrus Lombardus (c. 1150) totam Anselmianam sententiam de satisfactione Christi alto silentio praetermisit.

Gulielmus Alvernus (ob. 1249; ep. Parisiensis) cum multas et diversas in redemptione rationes perspexit opus composuit *De causis cur Deus homo* (E. Weis, diss. dact. 2720, PUG).[26] Cf. modum procedendi S. Thomae, *Sum. theol.*, III, q. 1, a. 2; qq. 48, 49.

Ioannes de Rupella, seu auctor *Summae fratris Alexandri* (Halensis), ita diligens fuit Anselmi sequax, ut tamen minus de morte Christi, dono supererogatorio, quam de passione et poenis Domini tractavit. Cf. S. Thomam, III, qq. 48 et 49 de passione, q. 50 de morte. Edita est *Summa fratris Alexandri,* Ad claras aquas, 1948;[27] identificatio auctoris tertiae partis, IV/1, Prolegomena, p. ccclxv; text., IV/2, Lib. III, tr. 1, et 3–6; Franks, I, 227–57.[28]

3 Generale integrationis problema ad thesin sequentem remittimus. Particulare iam consideravimus, utrum tertium quid detur vel dari possit praeter satisfactionem et poenam. Aliud autem particulare nunc exponi debet.

2 The following illustrate this process of integration:

Hugh of St Victor (d. 1141; see F. Vernet, 'Hughes de Saint-Victor,' DTC VII (13) 240–308, at 279; Franks, *A History of the Doctrine of the Work of Christ,* vol. 1, 203–14), in linking Anselm's opinion with the tradition about the role of the devil, presented Christ as intervening, not between God and human beings, but between God, human beings, and the devil.

Peter Lombard (c. 1150) passed over in deep silence the whole of the Anselmian opinion on Christ's satisfaction.

William of Auvergne (bishop of Paris; d. 1249) grasped many different aspects in the redemption and composed his work, *De causis cur Deus homo* (E. Weis, doctoral dissertation 2720, Gregorian University Press).[26] Compare St Thomas's way of proceeding, *Summa theologiae,* 3, q. 1, a. 2, and qq. 48 and 49.

John of Rupella, or the author of the *Summa fratris Alexandri* (*Halensis*), was a close follower of Anselm, who nevertheless wrote much less on the death of Christ as a supererogatory gift than on the Lord's passion and punishments. Compare St Thomas, *Summa theologiae,* 3, qq. 48 and 49 on the passion, and q. 50 on Christ's death. An edition of the *Summa fratris Alexandri* has been published (Quarrachi, 1948);[27] for the identity of the author of its third part, see IV/1, p. ccclxv; in the text, IV/2, Book III, tr. 1 and 3–6; Franks, *A History of the Doctrine of the Work of Christ,* vol. 1, 227–57.[28]

3 We leave the general problem of integration to the following thesis. We have already considered a particular problem, that is, whether there is or can be a third alternative besides satisfaction and punishment. Now we must examine another particular problem.

26 Earl Augusto Weis, *The Anselmian Tradition in William of Auvergne's De Causis Cur Deus Homo* (Rome: Gregorian University Press, 1958). This is an extract from the dissertation.

27 Alexander of Hales (?), *Summa theologica: seu Sic ab Origine dicta 'Summa Fratris Alexandri',* edd. PP. Collegii S. Bonaventurae, 4 vols. (Quaracchi: Collegium S. Bonaventurae, 1924–48).

28 One view of the authorship is presented by H. Daniel Monsour: '*Summa Fratris Alexandri,* in its present form, is a compilation, the product of a collaborative effort of theologians who garnered and adapted material from a variety of sources. The project commenced under Alexander's direction probably sometime after 1240; it remained unfinished at the time of his death in 1245; and was completed by his collaborators and disciples, at the express behest of Pope Alexander IV, during the following fifteen to twenty years.' H. Daniel Monsour, 'The Halesian *Summa*'s Specification of the Relation between Uncreated and Created Grace within the Speculative Development of Medieval Theology,' unpublished essay (Toronto, 1999) 2.

4 Distinxit enim Anselmus inter satisfactionem et poenam, et Christum docuit non poenam dedisse sed satisfactionem obtulisse. At proh dolor, tota traditio docuerat Christum poenas subiisse, neque tanta umquam fuit Anselmi auctoritas ut hic traditionalis loquendi modus deponeretur.

5 Nam secundum scripturas (Gen 2.17, 3.19, Sap 2.24, Rom 5.12, 6.23; cf. 1 Cor 15.21–22, 15.26, Heb 2.14–15) mors est poena peccati. Sed Christus mortuus est. Ergo Christus poenam peccati dedit.

Pro traditione loquantur Augustinus et Petrus Lombardus. Augustinus: 'Suscipiendo poenam et non suscipiendo culpam, et culpam delevit et poenam' (*Sermo* 171, 3; ML 38, 934).

Lombardus fuse exposuit Christum suscepisse, non nostram culpam, sed nostras infirmitates, peccati poenas (3, d. 15); ulterius, eo sensu intellexit 1 Pet 2.24 ut concluderet Christum portasse poenas nostrorum peccatorum super lignum, et propter has poenas a Christo toleratas tum omnem poenam in baptismo tolli tum partem in paenitentia (3, d. 19, c. 7).

N.B. Cum Lombardus sententiam Anselmi silentio praeterierit, concludi posse videtur tum Lombardum ex traditione prae-Anselmiana esse locutum tum theologos posteriores, qui cum Anselmo expresse consentiebant et tamen Christi poenas dictitabant, non solum ex ipso Anselmo sed etiam ex littera magistri sententiarum suam doctrinam hausisse.[29]

6 Ex duplici hoc fonte, prae-Anselmiano et Anselmiano, ortum est problema distinguendi inter varios poenae sensus.

*Summa fratris Alexandri* (supra, § 2) distinxit duplicem poenam, aliam reatum separationis a Deo, aliam exercitium virtutis ad meritum et praemium (IV/1, p. 67); passionem Christi maxime poenalem habuit quia maxime erat contraria tum naturae tum voluntati sensualitatis (ibid. 193).

Hanc Christi passionem duxit de convenientia divinae iustitiae 'ut numquam peccatum dimittatur sine poena,' et ideo 'aut ergo peccatum

4 Anselm made a distinction between satisfaction and punishment and taught that Christ was not punished but offered satisfaction. But alas, the entire tradition had taught that Christ underwent punishment, and the authority of Anselm has never been so great that this traditional way of speaking has been abandoned.

5 For according to scripture (Genesis 2.17, 3.19, Wisdom 2.24, Romans 5.12, 6.23; see also 1 Corinthians 15.21–22, 15.26, Hebrews 2.14–15), death is the punishment for sin. But Christ died. Therefore Christ received the punishment for sin.

Let Augustine and Peter Lombard speak for the tradition. Augustine: 'By accepting our punishment and not our fault, he wiped away both fault and punishment' (*Sermo* 171, 3; ML 38, 934).

Peter Lombard explained at considerable length that Christ took on, not our fault, but our weaknesses, as the punishments for sin (*Sententiae*, 3, d. 15); further, from his understanding of 1 Peter 2.24 he concluded that Christ on the cross had borne the punishments for our sins, and that by these punishments suffered by Christ our punishment is canceled both totally in baptism and partially in the sacrament of penance (3, d. 19, c. 7).

Note that since Peter Lombard passed over Anselm's opinion in silence, it seems that one could conclude both that Lombard was speaking out of the pre-Anselmian tradition, and that later theologians who expressly agreed with Anselm and still emphasized Christ's punishments derived their doctrine not only from Anselm himself but also from the writings of the Master of the Sentences.[29]

6 It was from these two sources, pre-Anselmian and Anselmian, that the problem of distinguishing between the various meanings of punishment arose.

The author of the *Summa fratris Alexandri* (§ 2, above) distinguished two kinds of punishment, the debt of separation from God and the exercise of virtue to obtain merit and reward (IV/1, p. 67); he held Christ's suffering to be the most punitive because it was most contrary to nature as well as to sensual desire (ibid. 193).

He deemed this suffering of Christ to be appropriate to divine justice 'that no sin might be forgiven without punishment,' and therefore that 'sin

29 Franks discusses Peter Lombard in *A History of the Doctrine of the Work of Christ*, vol. 1, 214–26.

ordinatur de destricta iustitia, ut puniatur aeternaliter, aut de iustitia cum misericordia, ut puniatur temporaliter. Et sic passio est de iustitia, quia non poterat reatus solvi per purum hominem, secundum quod probat Anselmus' (ibid. 212).

Ubi habetur poena quae est (1) exercitium virtutis ad meritum et praemium, (2) contraria naturae et voluntati sensualitatis, (3) de convenientia divinae iustitiae, (4) punitio temporalis ex misericordia, (5) distincta a poena separationis, (6) propugnata ex auctoritate S. Anselmi.

Contra talem poenam obicitur: innocentem condemnare non est iustum. Respondit auctor: primo, Christus voluntarie mortem subiit, et volenti nulla fit iniuria; deinde, secundum Rom 9.21, absolute posse Deum punire innocentem; tertio, Deum iuste punire posse innocentem ut bonum inde eliciat, et sic punitum esse Iob pro bono proprio, et Christum pro bono alieno (ibid. 212).

Alibi fortius docuit: Pater Filium et Filius se ipsum tradidit ad hoc ut poenam sustineret pro liberatione humani generis; quod tradere erat malum ex genere et malum absolute, sed bonum erat ex fine (ibid. 225).

E quibus elucet non sine difficultate fieri integrationem tum intelligentiae Anselmianae tum traditionalis doctrinae; quam difficultatem non credimus plus quam terminologicam, sed quam facile theologus incautus inconvenientia proferre potuerit in auctore huius *Summae* perspicitur.

7 *S. Thomas* post Lombardum (3, d. 19, c. 7) connectit satisfactionem Christi cum nostra liberatione a reatu poenae (*Sum. theol.*, III, q. 48, a. 6, ad 3m); docet nos liberari a reatu poenae dupliciter: directe, ex satisfactione Christi, indirecte, ex eo quod passio Christi est causa remissionis peccati (ibid. q. 49, a. 3, ad 3m).

Praeterea, cum Lombardo (3, d. 15, c. 1) docet Christum suscepisse defectus humanae naturae qui sunt peccati poenae, nempe, mors, fames, sitis, et huiusmodi; ubi Lombardus docuit Christum haec suscepisse non conditionis necessitate sed miserationis voluntate (3, d. 15, c. 5), ipse modo technico distinguit inter defectus ex peccato contractos et defectus (eosdem materialiter) voluntate susceptos; sed ultra Lombardum procedens Aquinas integrationem cum sententia Anselmiana perfecit; unde addidit Christum hos defectus, peccati poenas, non contraxisse sed ea voluntate suscepisse ut

either falls under strict justice and so is punished eternally, or falls under justice tempered with mercy, and so is punished temporally. Thus the passion is a matter of justice, since the debt could not be paid by a mere mortal, as Anselm proves' (ibid. 212).

In this case the punishment is (1) an exercise of virtue to obtain merit and reward, (2) contrary to nature and to sensual desire, (3) appropriate to divine justice, (4) temporal punishment because of mercy, (5) different from the pain of separation, and (6) defended by the authority of St Anselm.

Against such punishment it is objected that it is unjust to condemn an innocent person. The author's answer is, first, that Christ went willingly to his death, and no injustice is done to one who is willing; second, that according to Romans 9.21 absolutely speaking God could punish an innocent person; and third, that God can justly punish an innocent person in order to bring about some good, as Job was punished for his own good and Christ was punished for the good of others (ibid. 212).

He stated the case more forcefully elsewhere: the Father handed over the Son and the Son handed himself over in order to suffer punishment for the liberation of the human race; this handing over was evil from its genus and evil absolutely, but was good on account of its end (ibid. 225).

From this it is clear that integration of Anselm's understanding with that of the traditional doctrine is not without difficulty. We believe this difficulty to be no more than a matter of terminology, but the author of this *Summa* is an example of how easily an unwary theologian can make inappropriate statements.

7 St Thomas, following Lombard (*Sententiae*, 3, d. 15, c. 1), connects Christ's satisfaction with our liberation from liability to punishment (*Summa theologiae*, 3, q. 48, a. 6, ad 3m). He teaches that we are freed from this liability in two ways: directly, as a result of Christ's satisfaction, and indirectly, from the fact that the passion of Christ is the cause of the forgiveness of sin (ibid. q. 49, a. 3, ad 3m).

Furthermore, with Lombard (*Sententiae*, 3, d. 19, c. 7) he teaches that Christ took on the defects of human nature that are the penalties for sin, namely, death, hunger, thirst, and the like. While Lombard taught that Christ took on these things not by the necessity of his human condition but out of voluntary compassion (*Sententiae*, 3, d. 15, c. 5), Thomas made a technical distinction between defects contracted from sin and defects (materially the same defects) voluntarily assumed. But Aquinas went beyond Lombard in perfecting integration with the Anselmian opinion, adding

materiam satisfactionis pro peccato humani generis haberet. *Sum. theol.*, III, q. 14, a. 1 c., ad 1m, ad 3m; a. 3 c., ad 1m, ad 2m, ad 3m; a. 4 c., ad 2m.

Ubi notas distinctionem explicitam inter *materiam* satisfactionis et *principium* quo quis inclinatur ad satisfaciendum et ex quo ipsa satisfactio efficaciam habet; materia est poena et quidem in Christo non ex peccato contracta sed libere suscepta; principium autem est caritas (ibid. a. 1, ad 1m).

Ubi ulterius notas commentum implicitum in illud Augustini: 'suscipiendo poenam et non suscipiendo culpam'; nam affirmavit Aquinas Christum sicut naturam humanam absque culpa ita etiam absque poena suscipere potuisse; eumque de facto poenam suscepisse propter opus nostrae redemptionis implendum (ibid. a. 3, ad 1m).

Plura de poenis in genere apud Aquinatem: *Sum. theol.*, I, q. 48, a. 5, ubi habetur mala in rebus voluntariis dividi sufficienter in culpam et poenam; I-II, q. 87, a. 6, ubi de debito poenae et poena satisfactoria; ibid. aa. 7 et 8, de poena simpliciter et secundum quid, et de habitudine inter culpam et poenam; II-II, q. 108, a. 4, de vindicatione; ibid. q. 159, aa. 1 et 2, de crudelitate et saevitia. Quae superius exposuimus, praenotamen IV.

Ulterius, satisfactio ad mentem Anselmi concipitur.

Quamvis enim satisfactio ab Anselmo distinguatur a poena et rationem doni (*dare* animam suam) habuerit, dum Aquinas communiter nomen poenae passioni et morti Christi applicet, tamen in ipsa notionis structura invenitur mira conformitas.

Anselmus: '... nulla ratione se ipsum morti *ex debito* ... dedit ad honorem Dei, et tamen facere debuit quod fecit' (*Cur Deus homo*, II, 18; Schmitt, II, p. 129, lin. 14[–16]).[30] Quibus correspondent quae supra vidimus de poena contracta et suscepta; et ulterius ea quae docentur de libertate, caritate, et obedientia Christi, de necessitate et convenientia redemptionis (*Sum. theol.*, III, q. 1, a. 2; q. 46, aa. 1–3; q. 18, a. 4; q. 47, aa. 2 et 3; q. 48, a. 2).

that Christ did not contract these defects, the penalties for sin, but assumed them with the intention that he might have the material element of satisfaction for the sin of humanity (*Summa theologiae,* 3, q. 14, a. 1 c., ad 1m, ad 3m; a. 3 c., ad 1m, ad 2m, ad 3m; a. 4 c., ad 2m).

Note here the explicit distinction between the *matter* of satisfaction and the *principle* that inclines one to make satisfaction and by reason of which satisfaction itself has its efficacy. The matter is the punishment, and in Christ, of course, it was not contracted from sin but freely assumed; but its principle is charity (ibid. a. 1, ad 1m).

Note also the implication in Augustine's remark, 'by accepting our punishment but not our fault,' quoted above; for Aquinas affirmed that just as Christ could take on a human nature without taking on fault, he could also have done so without taking on punishment; but in fact he did take on punishment in order to carry out the work of our redemption (ibid. a. 3, ad 1m).

For more on punishment in Aquinas, see *Summa theologiae,* 1, q. 48, a. 5, where evil in volitional matters is divided into fault and punishment; 1-2, q. 87, a. 6, on the debt of punishment and satisfactory punishment; ibid. aa. 7 and 8, on punishment simply so called and punishment in a qualified sense, and on the relationship between fault and punishment; 2-2, q. 108, a. 4, on retribution; ibid. q. 159, aa. 1 and 2, on cruelty and brutality. We have treated these points above, in preliminary note 4.

Further, satisfaction is conceived according to the mind of Anselm.

Although satisfaction is distinguished from punishment by Anselm and has the note of gift (to *give* one's life) while Aquinas usually applies the word 'punishment' to the passion and death of Christ, nevertheless there is a remarkable conformity in the very structure of the notion.

Anselm: '... in no way did he give himself up for the honor of God *out of debt,* and yet he ought to have done what he did' (*Cur Deus homo,* book 2, c. 18; Schmitt, vol. 2, p. 129, lines 14–16).[30] To this there correspond what we have seen above concerning punishment contracted and punishment taken on, as well as the doctrine about the freedom, love, and obedience of Christ and the necessity and fittingness of the redemption in the *Summa theologiae,* 3, q. 1, a. 2; q. 46, aa. 1–3; q. 18, a. 4; q. 47, aa. 2 and 3; q. 48, a. 2.

30 In the dialogue, these words are spoken by Boso, not Anselm. It is not easy to retain in translation the etymological connection between the Latin 'debitum' (debt) and 'debuit' (what he ought to do).

Anselmus: '... vita haec plus est amabilis, quam sint peccata odibilia ...' (II, 14); et consequens impetratio Filii a Patre pro hominibus 'ut eis dimittatur quod pro peccatis debent, et detur quo propter peccata carent ...' (II, 19; p. 131, lin. 2). Unde Aquinas: 'ille proprie satisfacit pro offensa qui exhibet offenso id quod aeque vel magis diligit quam oderit offensam. Christus autem, ex caritate et obedientia patiendo, maius aliquid Deo exhibuit quam exigeret recompensatio totius offensae humani generis' (III, q. 48, a. 2).

At longe ultra Anselmum progressus est Aquinas inquantum explicavit satisfactionem vicariam secundum illam unionem amoris quae est inter Christum caput eiusque membra. Cf. praenotamen VI.

### PRAENOTAMEN X: PROBLEMA COHAERENTIAE

1 Iam vidimus (praenotamen IX) problema quoddam exsistere integrationis, quemadmodum videlicet aucta per Anselmum veri revelati intelligentia cum traditionali in ecclesia modo loquendi sit componenda. Cui problemati non fit satis si tantummodo nomen 'poenae' consideratur et inter poenam contractam et poenam susceptam distinguatur. Nam tota quaedam exsistit nominum verborumque series quae similem vel connexam ambiguitatem habere possunt.

Problema ergo cohaerentiae est ut omnes eiusmodi ambiguitates secundum principia clara, bene definita, et quantum quis bene iudicare possit etiam certa, resolvantur.

2 Christus non suscepit culpam.

Sensus est (1) Christum nullam habuisse culpam actualem vel originalem et (2) Christum nullo modo in se culpam alienam suscepisse, sive per imputationem Lutheranam, sive per contractum quendam iuridicum, sive per dictam solidaritatem.

Augustinus: 'suscipiendo poenam et non suscipiendo culpam' (*Sermo* 171, 3; ML 38, 934; cf. Lombardus, 3, d. 15, c. 1 et 5); unde Aquinas, *Sum. theol.*, III, q. 14, ubi systematica distinctio inter defectus seu poenas susceptas et contractas in eo erat quod defectus vel poenae in Christo non erant ex debito peccati; vide praesertim a. 3.

Anselm: '… this life is more lovable than the sins are detestable …' (*Cur Deus homo,* book 2, c. 14, Schmitt, vol. 2, p. 114, line 27); and the consequent prayer of the Son to the Father on behalf of humans 'to forgive them what is owing for their sins, and give them what they lack on account of their sins' (*Cur Deus homo,* book 2, c. 19; Schmitt, vol. 2, p. 131, lines 1–2). Hence Aquinas: 'One properly gives satisfaction for an offense who presents something the offended one loves equally, or even more than he detested the offense. Now Christ, by suffering out of love and obedience, offered to God a greater recompense than was required for all the offense of the human race' (*Summa theologiae,* 3, q. 48, a. 2).

But Aquinas went far beyond Anselm in explaining vicarious satisfaction by the union of love between Christ the head and his members. See preliminary note 6.

### PRELIMINARY NOTE 10: THE PROBLEM OF COHERENCE

1 In the previous preliminary note we have seen that there exists a problem of integration, that is, how Anselm's contribution to the understanding of revealed truth is to be combined with the church's traditional way of speaking. In dealing with this problem it is not enough to consider only the term 'punishment' and distinguish between punishment contracted and punishment assumed, for there is a series of nouns and verbs that can have a similar or related ambiguity.

The problem of coherence, therefore, is to resolve all such ambiguities according to principles that are clear and well defined and, as far as one can reasonably judge, certain.

2 Christ did not assume fault.

This means that (1) Christ had neither personal nor original fault, and (2) in no way took upon himself the fault of others, whether by Lutheran imputation or through some legal contract or through what is termed 'solidarity.'

Augustine: '… by accepting our punishment but not our fault' (*Sermo* 171, 3; ML 38, 934; compare Lombard, *Sententiae,* 3, d. 15, cc. 1 and 5); hence Aquinas, *Summa theologiae,* 3, q. 14, where the systematic distinction between defects or punishments that are assumed and those that are contracted consisted in the fact that in the case of Christ defects or punishments were not due to sin; see especially q. 14, a. 3.

Cf. Annotationes in primum schema c. Vaticani: 'Christus Agnus immaculatus utique non in se suscepit nec suscipere potuit ipsa formaliter peccata nostra ut sua essent' (Col. Lac., VII, 543b).

Quaeritur tamen quemadmodum Christus pro nobis satisfecerit si culpam nostram nullatenus suscepit. Christus enim pro nobis fecit quod ipsi pro nobis facere non potuimus (*Sum. theol.*, III, q. 1, a. 2, ad 2m; q. 46, a. 1, ad 3m; a. 5, ad 3m; a. 6, ad 6m; q. 47, a. 3, ad 1m; q. 48, a. 2; q. 49, a. 3).

Respondetur personam divinam sufficienter cum nobis connecti ut pro nobis satisfacere possit ex eo quod humanam naturam ex stirpe Adae assumpsit, inter nos vixit, et pro nobis egit ut novissimus Adam (1 Cor 15.45), ut sponsor melioris testamenti (Heb 7.22), ut caput corporis sui (Eph 5.25; *Sum. theol.*, III, q. 48, a. 2, ad 1m; q. 49, a. 3, ad 3m). Unde et theologus in annotationibus ad schema c. Vaticani, quamvis de substitutione, vade, vadimonio loquatur, denique tandem cum S. Thoma dixit: 'Christus novissimus Adam (1 Cor 15.45) constitutus caput humani generis reparandi satisfecerit pro suis membris, et suis membris meruerit restitutionem gratiae quam in primo Adam perdiderant' (Col. Lac., VII, 543c).

Quam explicationem et solidam censemus et bene fundatam. Si quis eam perficiendam ducit per hypotheticum quendam contractum iuridicum, pro suo lubitu faciat; sed nobis videntur vanae esse hypotheses quarum nulla est possibilis verificatio. Caeterum, de hac quaestione nunc non agitur. Dicimus Christum satisfecisse pro omnibus, non quia culpam omnium suscepit, sed quia est novissimus Adam et sponsor novi testamenti et caput ecclesiae, ad quam omnes vocantur.

Dices: si Christus satisfecit ut caput ecclesiae, pro solis fidelibus satisfecit.

Respondetur: Christus caput ecclesiae ita satisfecit ut omnes ad ecclesiam accedere possint et debeant; sicut et pro omnibus mortuus est (DB 1096, DS 2005) et tamen extra ecclesiam nulla salus (DB 1000, DS 1870).[31]

3 Dupliciter dicitur quod (1) divino iudicio oportet aliquem pati, (2) redintegratur ordo divinae iustitiae, (3) reparatur divinae iustitiae ordo violatus, (4) divinae iustitiae satisfit, (5) expiantur peccata, (6) fit compensatio

See the annotations on the first schema of Vatican I: 'Christ the spotless lamb indeed did not take upon himself and could not have taken upon himself our formal sins to be his own' (*Collectio Lacensis*, VII, 543b).

Nevertheless, we may ask how Christ made satisfaction for us if he did not in any way take on our fault. For Christ did for us what we could not have done for ourselves (*Summa theologiae*, 3, q. 1, a. 2, ad 2m; q. 46, a. 1, ad 3m; a. 5, ad 3m; a. 6, ad 6m; q. 47, a. 3, ad 1m; q. 48, a. 2; q. 49, a. 3).

The answer is that a divine person is sufficiently connected with us as to be able to make satisfaction for us by the fact that he assumed human nature from Adam's stock, lived among us and acted for us as the last Adam (1 Corinthians 15.45), as the guarantor of a better covenant (Hebrews 7.22), and as head of his body, the church (Ephesians 5.25; *Summa theologiae*, 3, q. 48, a. 2, ad 1m; q. 49, a. 3, ad 3m). Hence the theologian annotating the schema of the Vatican Council, although he mentions substitution, surety, and bail, finally, with St Thomas, said that 'Christ the last Adam (1 Corinthians 15.45), constituted head of the human race to be repaired, made satisfaction for his members and merited for his members the restoration of the grace that was lost in the first Adam' (*Collectio Lacensis*, VII, 543c–544a).

We consider this explanation to be solid and well founded. Anyone who thinks it should be improved upon by the addition of some hypothetical legal contract is perfectly free to do so; but it seems to us that unverifiable hypotheses are worthless. At any rate, that is not at issue here. We say that Christ has made satisfaction for all, not because he assumed the fault of all but because he is the last Adam and the guarantor of the new covenant and the head of the church, to which all are called.

But, you may say, if Christ made satisfaction as the head of the church, then he did so only for believers.

In reply we say that Christ as head of the church made satisfaction so that all could and should enter the church, just as he died for all (DB 1096, DS 2005, [ND 1989/5]) and nevertheless 'outside the church there is no salvation' (DB 1000, DS 1870, [ND 38]).[31]

3 The following statements can be taken in two ways: (1) by the judgment of God it is necessary for someone to suffer, (2) the order of divine justice is reintegrated, (3) the violated order of divine justice is restored, (4)

31 The understanding of 'extra eccclesiam nulla salus' developed considerably after the Second Vatican Council. Lonergan's expression followed suit.

pro peccatis debita, (7) debitum pro peccatis solvitur, (8) solvuntur poenae, (9) dantur poenae, (10) debitae poenae exsolvuntur, (11) et si quid aliud huiusmodi.

Nam alia est venia ex castigatione, et alia est poena ex damnatione; alia est perversitatis spontanea satisfactio, et alia est a non satisfaciente poenae exactio; alia est poena sine paenitentia uti in daemonibus perspicitur, et alia est poenae satisfactoria quae in Christo Domino et in sanctis invenitur; alius est diabolus caput malorum, et alius est Christus caput corporis sui, qui a iugo diaboli nos liberavit.

Iam vero omnia sunt secundum illam divinam iustitiam, quae est ordo divinae sapientiae a divina bonitate electus, a divina providentia intentus, a divina gubernatione productus, et in ipsis rebus ut ordo universi inventus.

Sed non omnium est una ratio, si quidem aliud dicit divina praedestinatio, et aliud divina reprobatio, et aliud lex aeterna, quae tamen omnia ad Deum sapientem et iuste eligentem reducuntur, secundum quod bona quidem directe vult Deus, et mala naturalis defectus malaque poenae indirecte vult Deus, et mala culpae nullo modo vult Deus sed permittit tantum. Cf. praenotamina VII et VIII; *Theol. Stud.* 3 (1942) 547–52.[32]

4 Ubi dicitur poena satisfactoria, vel satisfactio, Deum placare, divinam iram avertere, Deum benevolum reddere, facere ut quiescant irae caelestes, duplex esse potest dicti intelligentia.

Primo modo, quasi assignaretur causa divinae voluntatis, ut Deus propter hoc vellet illud; alia modo, ut dicatur ordo eorum quae Deus unico voluntatis actu et vult et inter se ordinata vult. Et primus quidem modus a S.

divine justice is satisfied, (5) sins are expiated, (6) due compensation is made for sins, (7) the debt of sin is paid, (8) penalties are paid, (9) punishments are meted out, (10) the debt of punishment is discharged, and (11) any other statements of the sort.

For pardon following chastisement and punishment following condemnation are quite different. Ready satisfaction for wrongdoing is one thing, punishment imposed on one who does not amend is something else. Punishment without repentance, as seen in demons, is quite different from satisfactory punishment as found in Christ the Lord and in the saints. On the one hand there is the devil, the head of all evildoers, and on the other is Christ, the head of his body, who has freed us from the devil's yoke.

Now, all this is in accordance with that divine justice which is the order of divine wisdom as chosen by divine goodness, intended by divine providence, implemented by divine governance, and present in things themselves as the order of the universe.

But there is not the one same intelligibility in all of these, since divine predestination is not the same as divine reprobation, and the eternal law is something else again; yet all these are traced back to God, who is wise and just in his choice, according to which God directly wills all that is good, indirectly wills the evils of natural defect and the evil of punishment, and in no way whatsoever wills culpable evils but merely permits them to occur. See preliminary notes 7 and 8; see also Bernard Lonergan, 'St. Thomas' Thought on *Gratia Operans*,' *Theological Studies* 3 (1942) 547–52.[32]

4 Satisfactory punishment, or satisfaction, placating God, turning aside divine wrath, rendering God benevolent, appeasing the wrath of heaven – such expressions can be understood in two ways.

In one way they are understood as if they were being assigned as the cause of God's will, so that God would will *B* because of *A*; in another way, it can be understood as referring to the order of things that God, in a single act of will, both wills and wills to be ordered among themselves. The first way St Thomas rejects, and explains the second way thus: 'Therefore [God]

32 Available now in Lonergan, *Grace and Freedom* 111–16. A thorough treatment of these issues may be found in Bernard Lonergan, 'God's Knowledge and Will,' in *Early Latin Theology*, vol. 19 in Collected Works of Bernard Lonergan, trans. Michael G. Shields, ed. Robert M. Doran and H. Daniel Monsour (Toronto: University of Toronto Press, 2011) 256–411.

Thoma reprobatur, alter autem explicatur, *Sum. theol.*, I, q. 19, a. 5: 'Vult ergo hoc esse propter hoc: sed non propter hoc vult hoc.'[33]

Quod non aestimari debet mera subtilitas theologica, si quidem et verum est et, ubi praetermittitur, etiam praetermitti solet quod in scripturis clare docetur.

Ita enim Deus placatur et benevolus redditur et divina ira avertitur et quiescit, ut tamen verum est quod 'ipse prior dilexit nos et misit Filium suum propitiationem pro peccatis nostris' (1 Io 4.10, 4.19), et 'Deus erat in Christo mundum reconcilians sibi, non reputans illis delicta ipsorum' (2 Cor 5.19), et 'Deus autem qui dives est in misericordia, propter nimiam caritatem suam qua dilexit nos, et cum essemus mortui peccatis, convivificavit nos in Christo' (Eph 2.4–5), et 'Commendat autem caritatem suam Deus in nobis, quoniam cum adhuc peccatores essemus, secundum tempus Christus pro nobis mortuus est' (Rom 5.8).

Plura in Litt. Encycl., *Haurietis aquas*, DS 3922–25, AAS 48 (1956) 309–53; ubi finis esse videtur 'ut Divinum Amorem amore nostro redamemus' (p. 311).[34] Vide S. Augustinum de pari amore et Patris et Filii erga nos peccatores (*De Trin.*, XIII, xi, 15; ML 42, 1025).

5 Divina iustitia comparatur tripliciter ad poenam et dupliciter ad satisfactionem.

Nam fit poena sine paenitentia, e.g., in daemonibus; et fit poena satisfactoria in paenitentia, e.g., tamquam pars sacramenti paenitentiae (DB 905, DS 1692); et fit poena satisfactoria a non paenitente, uti in Christo Domino qui culpam non habuit.

Quod autem fit poena sine paenitentia, hoc est ex divina iustitia vindicativa. Et quamvis etiam ibi appareat divina misericordia quatenus Deus puniat citra condignum (*Sum. theol.*, I, q. 21, a. 4, ad 1m), tamen dici potest

wills that *B* should exist because of *A*, but it is not because he wills *A* that he wills *B*' (*Summa theologiae*, 1, q. 19, a. 5 c.).[33]

This must not be considered a mere theological subtlety, since not only is it true, but when it is overlooked, the clear teaching of scripture is usually overlooked as well.

For while God is placated and rendered benevolent and the divine anger appeased, it is still also true that he loved us first and sent his Son to be the propitiation for our sins (1 John 4.10, 4.19), and 'in Christ God was reconciling the world to himself, not counting their trespasses against them' (2 Corinthians 5.19), and 'God, who is rich in mercy, out of the great love with which he loved us, even when we were dead through our trespasses, made us alive together with Christ' (Ephesians 2.4–5), and 'God proves his love for us in that while we still were sinners Christ died for us' (Romans 5.8).

For more on this, see the encyclical 'Haurietis aquas,' DS 3922–25, [ND 664–67]; *Acta Apostolicae Sedis* 48 (1956) 309–53, where the point seems to be 'that we may love in return for God's love' (p. 311).[34] See St Augustine on the equal love on the part of both Father and Son towards us sinners (*De Trinitate*, XIII, xi, 15; ML 42, 1025).

5 Divine justice is related in three ways to punishment and in two ways to satisfaction.

There is punishment without repentance, as in the case of the demons, for example, and there is satisfactory punishment with repentance, as in part of the sacrament of penance (DB 905, DS 1692, [ND 1633]); and there is the satisfactory punishment of one who is not a penitent, as in the case of Christ our Lord in whom there is no fault.

Punishment without repentance is a matter of divine retributive justice. And although even there God's mercy is present insofar as God punishes less than is condign (*Summa theologiae*, 1, q. 21, a. 4, ad 1m), still it can be said that this is a case of retributive justice pure and simple, and also that it

33 See ibid. 309, and in the same volume, 'The Notion of Fittingness' 495: 'God does not will *B* to exist because he wills *A*; rather, he wills that *B* exist because of *A*. That is to say, it is the order of things that God wills, and consequently he wills both that which is ordered and that to which it is ordered.' See also below, p. 381.

34 The encyclical by Pope Pius XII is published in English translation in *Heart of the Saviour: A Symposium on Devotion to the Sacred Heart*, ed. Josef Stierli (New York: Herder and Herder, 1957) 212–59. See 214: 'that we should ourselves make a return of love to the Divine Love.'

hic agi de iustitia vindicativa simpliciter; et iterum quod agitur de illa Dei ira, de qua Rom 1.18–3.20 (cf. praenotamen VII, § 9).

Ubi autem fit poena satisfactoria in paenitentia, quia ipse satisfaciens etiam culpam habuit et ideo poena non est tantum suscepta sed etiam contracta, ibi invenitur ratio quaedam iustitiae Dei vindicativae. Vide DB 905, DS 1692: satisfactio paenitenti imponitur in vindictam et castigationem praeteritorum peccatorum. Etiam *Miserentissimus Redemptor*: 'Deo iusto vindici satisfaciamus oportet "pro innumerabilibus peccatis et offensionibus et negligentiis" nostris' (AAS 20 [1928]) 169.

At haec iustitia vindicativa ita cum misericordia coniungitur ut etiam adsit illa iustitia Dei qua Deus est iustus et iustificans (Rom 3.26); quae quidem iustitia omnino distinguitur contra iram Dei de qua in capitibus ad Rom. praecedentibus (praenotamen VII, § 9).

Ubi denique fit satisfactio a non paenitente, uti in Christo Domino qui culpam habuit neque actualem neque originalem neque quomodocumque susceptam (cf. supra § 2), ibi habetur poena nullatenus contracta sed tantummodo suscepta; et ideo de ira vel de vindicta vel de iustitia Dei Patris vindicativa contra Filium suum dilectissimum vel intenta vel exercita nullatenus est loquendum. Cf. Sententias, § 19.

6 Totum cohaerentiae problema resolvi videtur ubi expresse agnoscitur Christum ex iustitia quidem Dei sed non ex iustitia Dei vindicativa poenas dedisse.

Nam ubi fit haec agnitio, necessario fit distinctio inter poenam ex damnatione et veniam ex castigatione.

Pariter, necessario agnoscitur Deum placari non per meram malorum perpessionem, quae etiam in damnatis invenitur, sed per malorum perpessionem in finem redemptionis, nempe, peccatorum remissionem et cum Deo reconciliationem.

Pariter, necessario agnoscitur dupliciter reparari seu redintegrari ordinem divinae iustitiae, alio modo sicut in damnatis et alio modo in Christo capite et in suis membris.

Pariter, necessario agnoscitur iustitiam vindicativam non esse unicam iustitiam proprie dictam quae Deo attribui potest.

Pariter, necessario agnoscitur divinae iustitiae satisfieri non solum inquantum divinae iustitiae vindicativae satisfit sed etiam inquantum satisfit illi divinae iustitiae quae redemptionem in remissionem peccatorum et in reconciliationem cum filiis Adae decrevit.

is an instance of the wrath of God described in Romans 1.18–3.20 (see preliminary note 7, § 9).

However, there is also an element of God's retributive justice in the case of punishment with repentance, because the one making satisfaction was also guilty and therefore the punishment is not only assumed but also contracted. See DB 905, DS 1692, [ND 1633]: satisfaction is imposed on the penitent in retribution and chastisement for sins of the past. See also 'Miserentissimus Redemptor': 'we are obliged to make satisfaction to God, the just avenger, "for our innumerable sins, offenses, and negligences"' (*Acta Apostolicae Sedis* 20 [1928] 169).

But this retributive justice is so conjoined with mercy that here also there is that justice of God whereby God is just and justifying (Romans 3.26), and this justice is altogether different from the wrath of God mentioned in the previous chapters of Romans (see preliminary note 7, § 9).

Lastly, when satisfaction is made by one who is not a penitent, as in the case of Christ our Lord who had neither personal nor original sin and did not assume them in any way whatsoever (see § 2, above), the punishment is not at all contracted but only assumed; and therefore one must by no means speak of the wrath or vengeance or the retributive justice of God the Father either intended or carried out against his beloved Son. See *Opinions*, § 19, above.

6 The whole problem of coherence appears to be solved when it is expressly acknowledged that Christ was punished according to God's justice but not according to God's retributive justice.

For when this is acknowledged, the distinction is necessarily made between punishment following condemnation and pardon following chastisement.

It is likewise necessarily acknowledged that God is placated not through the mere endurance of evils, which is found even among the damned, but through the endurance of evils with a view to redemption, namely, the forgiveness of sins and reconciliation with God.

It is likewise necessarily acknowledged that the order of divine justice is restored or reintegrated in two different ways, in the damned and in Christ the head and his members.

It is likewise necessarily acknowledged that retributive justice is not the only justice in the proper sense of the word that can be attributed to God.

It is likewise necessarily acknowledged that divine justice is satisfied not only inasmuch as divine retributive justice is satisfied but also inasmuch as satisfaction is made to that divine justice which decreed redemption, the forgiveness of sins, and reconciliation with the children of Adam.

7 E contra, ubi urgetur Deum Patrem de Filio suo ex iustitia vindicativa poenas peccatis debitas voluisse et Filium ex iustitia vindicativa eas dedisse, statim emergit tota illa errorum et confusionum complexio quae inde a saec. XVI hanc quaestionem obscuravit.

(a) Nam poenae quae ex iustitia vindicativa peccatis debentur sunt poenae infernales. Unde Calvinus et alii e veteribus Protestantibus concluserunt Christum poenas infernales dedisse.

(b) Praeterea, poenae ex iustitia vindicativa debitae non bis sed semel tantum solvuntur. Unde concludendum esset numquam per merita Christi remitti culpam quin tota poena remittatur, contra Tridentinum (DB 922, DS 1712); et ulterius Christum pro solis electis esse mortuum (cf. DB 1096, DS 2005–2006), secus reproborum poenae non essent in infernis luendae si quidem iam a Christo solutae sunt.

(c) Praeterea, quamvis per defectum logicae evitari possint conclusiones aperte Protestanticae, eiusmodi defectus non est laudandus simpliciter. Bonum sane est ab haereticis dissentire. Sed cohaerentiae defectus ipsam Catholicam doctrinam obscurat, neque leviter verendum est ne hanc ob causam 'nomen Dei per vos blasphematur inter gentes' (Rom 2.24).

8 Non est doctrina Anselmiana quod Christus poenas ex iustitia Dei vindicativa dedit.

Nam de essentia satisfactionis Anselmianae est ut sit donum adeo supererogatorium ut solus Deus-homo illud offerre possit. Cf. praenotamen 1, 4.

Eiusmodi de facto fuisse mortem Christi tandem confessus est ipse Boso: 'Aperte nunc video quia nulla ratione se ipsum morti ex debito, sicut ratio mea videbatur monstrare, dedit ad honorem Dei, et tamen fecit quod debuit' (*Cur Deus homo,* II, 18; Schmitt, p. 129, lin. 14–16).[35]

7 On the contrary, when it is insisted that God the Father willed that his Son should suffer the punishment due to sins out of retributive justice and that the Son was punished out of retributive justice, there immediately emerge that whole host of errors and welter of opinions that have clouded this issue since the sixteenth century.

(a) For the punishment due to sin out of retributive justice is the punishment of the damned. Hence Calvin and others among the early Protestants concluded that Christ suffered the pains of hell.

(b) Besides, punishment due out of retributive justice is not suffered twice but only once. From this one would have to conclude that sin is never remitted through the merits of Christ without its entire punishment being remitted, which is contrary to Trent (DB 922, DS 1712, [ND 1652]); further, one would have to conclude that Christ died only for the elect (DB 1096, DS 2005–2006, [ND 1989/5]), otherwise the damned would not have to pay their penalty in hell since Christ had already paid it.

(c) Again, although overtly Protestant conclusions could be avoided through defective logic, this sort of defect is not praiseworthy in itself. Certainly, it is good to disagree with heretics; but a defect of coherence obscures Catholic doctrine itself, and we should greatly fear lest for this reason 'the name of God is blasphemed among the Gentiles because of you' (Romans 2.24).

8 It is not Anselm's doctrine that Christ was punished out of God's retributive justice.

For it is of the essence of the Anselmian idea of satisfaction that it be a gift so supererogatory that only a God-man could offer it. See preliminary note 1, § 4.

Even Boso himself finally admitted that this is the way it was with Christ's death: 'Now I see clearly that in no way did he give himself up to death for God's honor out of a debt, as my reasoning seemed to show, and yet he did what he ought to do' (*Cur Deus homo,* book 2, c. 18; Schmitt, vol. 2, p. 129, lines 14–16).[35]

35 Anselm writes: '... et tamen facere debuit quod fecit,' 'he ought to have done what he did.' This is how it is transcribed and translated at p. 88 above. But here, we have what seems to be a transcription error: '... et tamen fecit quod debuit,' 'he did what he ought [to do].' Our translation follows Lonergan's Latin even where that departs from the text he is quoting.

Quod si *nulla ratione ex debito* mortuus est Christus, sane non est mortuus ex iustitia Dei vindicativa.

*Dices*: si non ex debito, cur debuerit?

*Respondeat Aquinas*: Christus ex caritate et obedientia satisfecit (*Sum. theol.*, III, q. 48, a. 2).

9 Non est doctrina S. Thomae quod Christus ex iustitia Dei vindicativa poenas dedit.

Nam hoc fecit ex caritate et obedientia (ibid.); obedivit autem Patris severitati qui noluit sine poena peccatum dimittere (ibid. q. 47, a. 3, ad 1m); quod autem Pater sic voluit, fuit 'abundantioris misericordiae quam si peccata absque satisfactione dimisisset' (ibid. q. 46, a. 1, ad 3m).

E contra qui poenas dat ex iustitia vindicativa, ille poenas non suscipit sed contrahit; neque Christus poenas contrahere potuit, quin culpam quodammodo suscepisset; manifeste autem apud Aquinatem susceptio culpae excluditur (vide ibid. q. 14, aa. 1 et 3).

Qui sentiunt Christum ex iustitia vindicativa poenas dedisse, vehementissime impugnantur apud Philippe de la Trinité, 'La Rédemption par le Sang,' *Encycl. XXième Siècle*, 25 (Paris, 1959) 55–58. Ubi plurima loca e S. Thoma collecta invenies.

10 Principia S. Thomae non adiuvant eos qui volunt iustam vindictam Dei Patris contra Filium.

Docet quidem S. Thomas poenas medicinales iuste et ex vindicta infligi posse praeter culpam actualem propriam (*Sum. theol.*, I-II, q. 87, aa. 7 et 8; II-II, q. 108, a. 4).

At haec doctrina Christo applicari non potest.

Primo, quia Christus peccatum originale non habuit; et ad peccatum originale hae poenae reducuntur: 'hoc ipsum quod est poenale in talibus reducitur ad originalem culpam sicut ad causam' (I-II, q. 87, a. 7 c.).

Deinde, quia Christus erat impeccabilis, et in impeccabili haberi non potest poena quae est vel sanativa peccati praeteriti vel praeservativa a peccato futuro; sed eiusmodi est poena medicinalis de qua agitur (II-II, q. 108, a. 4 c.); et ideo in Christo esse non potest.

But if *in no way out of debt* Christ died, surely he did not die out of God's retributive justice.

*You may object*: if it was not out of debt, why ought he?

*Let Aquinas reply*: Christ satisfied out of charity and obedience (*Summa theologiae*, 3, q. 48, a. 2).

9 It is not the teaching of St Thomas that Christ was punished out of God's retributive justice.

For he accepted punishment out of charity and obedience (ibid.); he submitted to the severity of the Father, who refused to remit sin without punishment (ibid. q. 47, a. 3, ad 1m); but what the Father thus willed was 'of a more abounding mercy than if he had dismissed sins without satisfaction' (ibid. q. 46, a. 1, ad 3m).

On the contrary, one who is punished out of retributive justice does not accept but rather incurs punishment. And Christ could not have incurred punishment without having accepted fault in some way; but it is clear that in Aquinas accepting fault is clearly ruled out (see ibid., q. 14, aa. 1and 3).

Those who hold that Christ was punished out of retributive justice were vigorously attacked by Philippe de la Trinité, *La Rédemption par le Sang* 55–58 [*What Is the Redemption?* 70–74], where many texts from St Thomas are collected.

10 The principles of St Thomas's doctrine are of no help to those who hold that God the Father punished his Son according to retributive justice.

St Thomas does indeed teach that medicinal punishments can be inflicted for an offense that is not one's own personal fault (*Summa theologiae*, 1-2, q. 87, aa. 7 and 8; 2-2, q. 108, a. 4).

But this teaching cannot be applied to Christ.

First, it cannot be applied to Christ because Christ did not have original sin, and these punishments are reducible to original sin: 'the element of punishment in such cases goes back to the original fault as its cause' (ibid. 1-2, q. 87, a. 7 c.).

Second, it cannot be applied to Christ because Christ was incapable of sin. For one incapable of sin, there can be no punishment that is either a remedy for past sin or a safeguard against future sin; but this is the sort of medicinal punishment in question (ibid. 2-2, q. 108, a. 4 c.), and therefore it cannot apply in the case of Christ.

11 C. Tridentinum non adiuvat eos qui volunt vindictam iustam Patris contra Filium.

DB 904, DS 1690; docetur assimilatio paenitentis per satisfactionem ad Christum satisfacientem; et ulterius (DB 905, DS 1692) docetur paenitenti satisfactio imponi in vindictam peccatorum.

At manifeste Christus non habuit peccata propria remittenda et remissa quidem quoad culpam sed non quoad poenam totam; et ideo nisi quis credit Christum suscepisse aliorum culpam ut aliorum poenam non solum susciperet sed etiam contraheret, concludi non potest ad iustam vindictam contra Filium.

12 Litt. Encycl. *Miserentissimus Redemptor* non adiuvant eos qui volunt iustam vindictam Dei Patris contra Filium dilectionis suae.

Deo iusto vindici nos sane pro peccatis nostris satisfacimus (AAS 20 [1928] 169); sed Christus satisfecit non pro suis peccatis sed pro alienis; neque aliorum culpam suscepit ut aliorum poenas contraheret; sed poenam suscepit et culpam non suscepit.

13 Dices: iuste poenas dat innocens ex iustitia vindicativa si ipse consentit; nam volenti non fit iniuria; atque manifestum est Christum consensisse.

R. Si adest iustitia vindicativa, iuste poenas dat sive consentit sive dissentit. Obiciens arguit non ex principio 'volenti non fit iniuria' sed ex errore 'stat pro ratione voluntas.' Quam suam voluntatem sine probatione Christo attribuit.

14 Unde brevissime: Qui dicit Deum Filium ex iustitia Dei vindicativa esse flagellatum, crucifixum, mortuum, *aut* supponit Filium culpam vel habuisse vel suscepisse, *aut* supponit iustitiam Dei vindicativam secundum solam delicti exsistentiam procedere et omnem excludere culpae considerationem vel originalis vel actualis vel susceptae in eo qui poenas dat. Primum suppositum non est Catholicum. Alterum suppositum aut immorale aut amorale est. Unde ipsa conclusio a blasphemia non facile discernitur.

11 The Council of Trent is of no help to those who hold that God the Father punished his Son according to retributive justice.

The Council teaches that in the sacrament of penance the penitent, in performing the imposed satisfactory penance, is conformed to Christ making satisfaction for sin (DB 904, DS 1690, [ND 1631]). And the Council further teaches that the satisfactory penance is imposed upon the penitent as retributive punishment for past sins (DB 905, DS 1692, [ND 1633]).

But obviously Christ had no sins of his own to be forgiven, and forgiven indeed with respect to fault but not with respect to their entire punishment. Hence unless one believes that Christ accepted the fault of others in such a way that he not only accepted but also incurred their punishment, one cannot conclude that just retribution was imposed upon the Son.

12 The encyclical 'Miserentissimus Redemptor' is of no help to those who hold that God the Father punished his beloved Son according to retributive justice.

Certainly it is true that we make satisfaction for our sins to God, who retributes justly (*Acta Apostolicae Sedis* 20 [1928] 169). But Christ made satisfaction not for any sins of his own but for the sins of others. He did not take on the fault of those others and so incur their punishment; rather, he took on their punishment and did not take on fault.

13 One may object that an innocent person is justly punished out of retributive justice if that person consents; for *volenti non fit iniuria*: where the sufferer is willing, no injury is done; and clearly Christ did consent.

In reply we would say that if the justice is retributive, one is justly punished whether one consents or not. The objector is arguing not from the principle, *volenti non fit iniuria*, but from the erroneous dictum, *stat pro ratione voluntas*: the will stands in place of a reason; and without proof he attributes this will of his to Christ.

14 Very briefly, then: one who says that it is out of retributive justice that God the Son was scourged, crucified, and died *either* supposes that the Son incurred or accepted fault *or* supposes that the retributive justice of God proceeds solely according to the existence of an offense to the exclusion of any consideration of the fault, original or personal or assumed, in the one being punished. The first supposition is not Catholic. The second supposition is either immoral or amoral. Hence this conclusion is hard to distinguish from blasphemy.

## PRAENOTAMEN XI: DE MENTALITATE SYMBOLICA

1 Perpauca de mentalitate symbolica dicenda esse videntur, ne quis credat nos contra adversarios vel non exsistentes vel amentes arguere.

2 Mentalitatem symbolicam intelligimus eum intelligendi, iudicandi, loquendi modum in quo magis secundum leges imaginationis et affectus proceditur quam secundum illam logicam a Graecis evolutam et hellenistica cultura diffusam.

In mentalitate symbolica evanescunt (vel nondum sunt evolutae) distinctiones. Loco generum et specierum inveniuntur figurae repraesentativae; loco univocitatis uni nomini multi sunt sensus; loco exclusi medii (aut *A* aut non-*A*) simul intenduntur multa; loco probationis habentur repetitiones, enumerationes, contrastus, variationes; loco simplicis negationis contrariis quasi obruitur quod negatur; loco unici thematis simul multa condensantur.

Quae tamen dicta sunt de mentalitate symbolica secundum oppositionem suam ad modum procedendi logicum. At mentalitas symbolica ipsam suam quasi logicam habet, suam propriam causalitatis notionem, suam propriam explicandi methodum, quae quidem omnia quasi connaturalia sunt ordini humano sensitivo seu psychico quatenus hic ordo minus quam in cultura graeca a parte hominis intellectuali et rationali gubernatur atque quasi informatur.

3 De se, mentalitas symbolica est quid indifferens. In homine etiam cultissimo minime deest. Magis tamen perspicitur in somniantibus quam in vigilantibus, in multitudine excitata quam in individuis, in artibus quam in scientiis, in vita affectiva quam in vita practica, etc. Denique tandem gravissimus erat rationalistarum error quod mentalitatem symbolicam iam esse superatam crediderunt. Semper viget mentalitas symbolica, semper praepotens est, sive ad verum et bonum, sive ad falsum et malum.

4 Conceptio passionis et mortis Domini per modum substitutionis et satispassionis de se nihil est aliud quam apprehensio symbolica. Quatenus enim dominantur imagines et affectus aliter vix apprehenditur passio Christi atque mors nisi tamquam Domini substitutio pro peccatoribus et Domini satispassio pro peccatis. Sed statim est illud addendum, nempe, quamdiu

## PRELIMINARY NOTE 11: THE SYMBOLIC MENTALITY

1 It seems advisable to make a few remarks about the symbolic mentality, lest anyone think that we are arguing against opponents who are either nonexistent or out of their mind.

2 By the symbolic mentality we understand that way of understanding, judging, and speaking which proceeds more according to the laws of the imagination and affectivity than according to that logic developed by the Greeks and disseminated through Hellenistic culture.

In the symbolic mentality distinctions vanish, or else are not yet developed. Instead of genera and species, there are representative figures; instead of univocal meanings, one word has many meanings; instead of the excluded middle ('either *A* or not-*A*'), many things are intended at the same time; instead of proof, there are repetitions, enumerations, contrasts, variations; instead of a simple denial, what is denied is almost overwhelmed by contrary notions; and instead of a single theme, many themes are compressed.

What we have said, however, applies to the symbolic mentality in contradistinction to the logical way of proceeding. But the symbolic mentality has, as it were, a logic of its own; it has its own notion of causality and its own method of explication, which indeed are all in a way connatural to the order of human sensibility, or psyche, where this order is less controlled and, as it were, less informed by the intellectual and rational part than it is in Greek culture.

3 In itself, the symbolic mentality is a matter of indifference. It is by no means absent even in a highly educated person. It is observed in dreamers more than in those who are awake, in an excited crowd more than in individuals, in the arts more than in the sciences, in the affective more than in the practical life, and so forth. The most serious error of the rationalists, finally, was that they believed the symbolic mentality to be a thing of the past. The symbolic mentality is ever vigorous, ever powerful, whether for the true and good or for the false and evil.

4 The conception of the passion and death of the Lord as substitution and satispassion is in itself only a symbolic apprehension. For to the extent that images and affects are predominant, the passion and death of Christ can hardly be apprehended except as the Lord's substitution for sinners and his satispassion for sins. But this point must immediately be added, namely,

dominantur imagines et affectus, etiam deest systema quoddam logicum conceptionum et theorematum; et quamdiu deest tale systema, etiam deest omnis conclusio falsa. Quam ob causam, apprehensionem symbolicam passionis et mortis Domini per modum substitutionis et satispassionis non semper et in omnibus esse impugnandam censemus cum pericula aberrationis per alia elementa doctrinae, devotionis, vitae practicae excludi possint.

5 Omnino tamen distinguendum esse nobis videtur inter ipsam apprehensionem symbolicam et eiusdem transpositionem in categorias apprehensionis logicae. Ubi enim fit illa transpositio, ibi incipit aberratio. Nam eiusmodi transpositio sibi pro criterio atque norma assumit, non doctrinam scripturae, non doctrinam patrum, non doctrinam theologorum, non doctrinam magisterii, sed fidelitatem erga propriam experientiam psychicam atque efficaciam in tali experientia aliis communicanda.

Sic intelliguntur aberrationes haereticorum de satisfactione Christi. Sic intelligi possunt aberrationes, multo minus graves, in oratoribus Catholicis qui ipsa sua fide ab excessibus haereticorum retinebantur. Sic intelligi possunt sentimenta theologorum qui sensisse[36] videntur non genuinam doctrinam Catholicam de satisfactione Christi proponi, ubi a notionibus substitutionis et satispassionis earumque implicationibus receditur.

6 Quibus perspectis, commentum quoddam addere velim censurae a G. Oggioni propositae circa theoriam expiationis poenalis (substitutionis et satispassionis), nempe, 'teoria che, se non è eterodossa, è però oramai superata' (*Problemi e orientamenti*, II, 311, Milano, 1957).

Forte enim exactius dici potest: (1) aliam esse theoriam et aliam esse apprehensionem symbolicam; (2) theoriam esse aberrationem impugnandam; (3) apprehensionem symbolicam de se esse indifferentem et in concreto contextu doctrinae et vitae Catholicae vel esse vel esse posse laudabilem.

that as long as images and affects are in charge, there is no logical system of concepts and theorems; and as long as there is no such system, so also are there no false conclusions. For this reason we judge that a symbolic apprehension of the passion and death of the Lord as substitution and satispassion is not always and in all aspects to be rejected, since the danger of aberration can be precluded through other elements of doctrine, of devotion, and of practical living.

5 However, we consider it to be of the utmost importance to distinguish between a symbolic apprehension itself and the transposition of such apprehension to the categories of logical apprehension. Aberration begins when this transposition occurs. For this sort of transposition assumes as its criterion and norm, not the teachings of scripture, not the teachings of the Fathers, not the teachings of the theologians, not the teachings of the magisterium, but fidelity to its own psychic experience and its effectiveness in communicating this experience to others.

This is how the aberrations of heretics concerning Christ's satisfaction are to be understood. This is how we can understand the much less serious aberrations among Catholic preachers, whose faith kept them from the more blatant errors of the heretics. This is how we can understand the sentiments of theologians who seemingly have felt[36] that authentic Catholic teaching on Christ's satisfaction is not communicated when we draw back from the notions of substitution and satispassion and all that they imply.

6 In view of this, I should like to add a comment to the censure proposed by G. Oggioni concerning the theory of penal expiation (substitution and satispassion), 'a theory that, if not unorthodox, is, however, now obsolete' (Oggioni, 'Il mistero della redenzione,' in *Problemi e orientamenti,* vol. 2, 311).

This point can perhaps be stated more accurately as follows: (1) theory and symbolic apprehension are two different things; (2) the theory in question is an aberration to be refuted; (3) a symbolic apprehension in itself is indifferent, and in the concrete context of Catholic teaching and life it is or can be praiseworthy.

36 In 1960 the word is 'censisse' (who seemingly have *thought*); Lonergan changed this to 'sensisse,' which appears in 1961 and 1964.

***Argumentum***

1 CHRISTUS MATERIALITER SATISFECIT PRO PECCATIS NOSTRIS.

(a) Hoc iam est probatum in thesi 15a, parte quarta, ubi de vicaria passione et morte Christi propter peccata et pro peccatoribus, ubi 'propter peccata' consideratur non secundum finem peccata auferendi sed secundum motivum cur divino iudicio oportuerit Christum pro peccatis pati et mori, et ubi similiter 'pro peccatoribus' consideratur non secundum finem utilitatis peccatoribus obventurum sed secundum motivum cur divino iudicio oportuerit Christum pati et mori.

(b) Haec pars est de fide ex scripturis, uti ex probatione alibi iam facta constat. Etiam manifeste continetur in magisterio ordinario.

(c) Doctrina patrum hunc aspectum mortis Christi minime praetermittit. Vide L. Richard 117–20; J. Rivière, DTC XIII (26) 1941; *Le Dogme de la Rédemption. Étude historique* 111, 115, 132–33, 135–38, 168, 173, 175–76, 183–84, 216–17, 219, 230, 235–36, 243, 255–57.

(d) Doctrina theologorum manifesta est ex praenotamine IX, cum theologi poenas Christi omittere noluerint.

(e) Haec materialis satisfactio convenienter 'expiatio' nominari potest secundum sensum huius nominis hodie, uti videtur, communem. De sensu tamen scripturistico vide quae in thesi 15a diximus de propitiatione (ἱλάσκεσθαι), p. 46.

2 CHRISTUS FORMALITER PRO PECCATIS NOSTRIS SATISFECIT.

(a) Primo, argui potest sumendo satisfactionem formaliter secundum definitionem S. Thomae.

Ille proprie satisfacit pro offensa qui exhibet offenso id quod aeque vel magis diligit quam oderit offensam. *Sum. theol.*, III, q. 48, a. 2 c. Cf. *Cur Deus homo*, II, 14: haec vita plus est amabilis quam sunt peccata odibilia.

### *The argument*

1 CHRIST MATERIALLY MADE SATISFACTION FOR OUR SINS.

(a) This was proved in the previous thesis, part 4, in dealing with the vicarious passion and death of Christ on account of sin and for sinners, where 'on account of sin' was considered, not in terms of the aim, the canceling of sins, but as the motive from which by divine judgment Christ had to suffer and die for sins, and where similarly 'for sinners' was considered not in terms of the aim, the benefit sinners would receive, but as the motive from which by divine judgment Christ had to suffer and die.

(b) This part is a matter of faith from the scriptures, as is clear from the proof given previously. It is also clearly contained in the ordinary magisterium.

(c) The teaching of the Fathers by no means ignores this aspect of Christ's death. See Richard, *Le mystère de la Rédemption* 117–20 [*The Mystery of the Redemption* 156–60]; Rivière, 'Rédemption' 1941; *Le dogme de la Rédemption: Essai d'étude historique* (Paris: Victor Lecoffre, 1905) 111, 115, 132–33, 135–38, 168, 173, 175–76, 183–84, 216–17, 219, 230, 235–36, 243, 255–57 [English translation: *The Doctrine of the Atonement: A Historical Essay*, vol. 1, trans. Luigi Cappadelta (London: Kegan Paul, Trench, Trübner & Co., and St Louis, MO: B. Herder, 1909) 131–32, 136–37, 154–57, 159–63, 198–99, 204–205, 206–209, 216–18, 252–55, 256–57, 268–69, 274–76, 283–84, 296–99.]

(d) The teaching of theologians is manifest from preliminary note 9, since theologians have refused to omit the punishments Christ suffered.

(e) This material satisfaction can fittingly be called 'expiation' according to what seems to be the common meaning given to this word today. As for its meaning in scripture, see what appears in the previous thesis on 'propitiation,' ἱλάσκεσθαι, p. 47.

2 CHRIST FORMALLY MADE SATISFACTION FOR OUR SINS.

(a) First, it can be argued by taking 'satisfaction' formally according to St Thomas's definition.

One properly gives satisfaction for an offense who presents something to the offended one that he equally, or even more than he detested the offense (*Summa theologiae*, 3, q. 48, a. 2 c.; see Anselm, *Cur Deus homo,* book 2, c. 14: This life is more lovable than sins are detestable).

Atqui Christus ex caritate et obedientia patiendo maius aliquid Deo exhibuit quam exigeret recompensatio totius offensae humanae generis. *Sum. theol.*, III, q. 48, a. 2 c. *Cur Deus homo*, II, 19.

Ergo Christus proprie satisfecit pro offensa tota humani generis.

Maior: probatur ex auctoritatibus S. Anselmi et S. Thomae quos citamus et quibuscum theologi consentiunt.

Minor: probatur ex iisdem; ex documentis magisterii, DB 799, 2318; DS 1529, 1690, 3891; ex magisterio ordinario. Ex scripturis autem argui potest ex effectu secuto: nisi enim aeque Deo placeret quod Christus obtulit, non iugiter diceretur nos habere remissionem peccatorum et reconciliationem cum Deo per Christum, per sanguinem Christi, per mortem Christi. E.g., Rom 5.10, Eph 1.7.

(b) Deinde, argui potest sumendo satisfactionem formaliter tamquam opus in honorem Dei factum, tamquam compensationem pro peccatis.

Nam Christus obtulit sacrificium, hostiam, et oblationem Deo in odorem suavitatis (Eph 5.2), et ideo opus in honorem Dei fecit. Vide thesin 15m, partem 5m.

Praeterea, pretium solvit nostrae redemptionis, nempe, dare animam suam, et ideo ratio compensationis non defuit. Vide thesin 15m, partem 3m.

(c) Tertio, argui potest sumendo satisfactionem formaliter sicut in praenotaminibus determinatum est.

Ibi habetur satisfactio formaliter ubi dantur poenae, non in contextu pure iuridico (culpae, offensae, reatus poenae, poenae inflictionis et solutionis; praenotamen IV) sed in contextu ubi inveniuntur compensatio pro offensa, culpae remissio, et consequens poenae vera remissio (praenotamen V).

Atqui ita iniquitates nostras nostrasque poenas Christus portavit ut Deo offeratur sacrificium et a Deo habeatur remissio peccatorum, reconciliatio Dei cum peccatoribus, et vera ipsarum poenarum remissio.

Quoad remissionem peccatorum, Eph 1.7, Col 1.14, etc. Quoad reconciliationem, Rom 5.10, 2 Cor 5.19. Quoad remissionem poenarum notate in contextu pure iuridico (praenotamen IV) fieri non posse ut reus ad decem annos damnatus et per decem annos incarceratus denique post decem annos remissionem earundem poenarum accipiat; peracta enim poenae solutione, nulla est quaestio de remissione. Sed in contextu evangelico ita

But Christ, by suffering out of love and obedience, offered to God something greater than the compensation demanded for all the offense of the human race (*Summa theologiae*, 3, q. 48, a. 2 c.; *Cur Deus homo*, book 2, c. 19).

Therefore, Christ made proper satisfaction for all the offense of the human race.

The major premise is proven on the authority of St Anselm and St Thomas, whom we cite and with whom the theologians are in agreement.

The minor premise is proven from the same authorities, from the documents of the magisterium, DB 799, 2318; DS 1529, 1690, 3891; [ND 647, 1631], and from the ordinary magisterium. From scripture one can argue from the effect that followed: if what Christ offered were not equally pleasing to God, it would not constantly be said that we have forgiveness of our sins and reconciliation with God through Christ, through the blood of Christ, through the death of Christ; for example, Romans 5.10, Ephesians 1.7.

(b) Second, one can argue by understanding satisfaction in the formal sense as a work done for the honor of God in compensation for sins.

For Christ presented a fragrant sacrifice, victim, and offering to God (Ephesians 5.2), and therefore performed a work in honor of God. See the previous thesis, part 5.

Also, he paid the price for our redemption, namely, giving his life; therefore, the idea of compensation was not lacking. See the previous thesis, part 3.

(c) Third, one can argue by taking satisfaction in the formal sense as determined in the preliminary notes.

Satisfaction in the formal sense is made when punishment is suffered, not in a purely juridical context (fault, offense, liability to punishment, penalty imposed and paid – see preliminary note 4), but in the context in which there are found compensation for an offense, the remission of fault, and the consequent true remission of punishment (preliminary note 5).

But Christ bore our iniquities and our punishment so that a sacrifice might be offered to God and that there might be received from God forgiveness of sins, reconciliation of God with sinners, and true remission of the punishment itself.

Regarding the forgiveness of sins, see Ephesians 1.7, Colossians 1.14, among other texts. Regarding reconciliation, see Romans 5.10 and 2 Corinthians 5.19. As to the remission of punishment, note that in a purely juridical context (preliminary note 4) an offender sentenced to ten years and imprisoned for ten years cannot receive after those ten years are up the remission of that same punishment; for once the penalty has been paid, there

poenas nostras portavit Christus ut tamen vere dicatur Deus et baptizatis totam poenam et paenitentibus poenam aeternam remittere. Cf. Mt 6.12.

### 3 CHRISTUS PRO NOSTRIS PECCATIS CONDIGNE SATISFECIT.

(a) Condigna est satisfactio ad aequalitatem secundum proportionem quandam.

(b) Condignam fuisse satisfactionem Christi concluditur ex pretio soluto (thesi 15a, parte 3a) et ex valore sacrificii Christi prout in epistola ad Hebraeos exponitur, 9.9–14, 10.1–4, 10.10–14. Ibi enim docetur insufficientia sacrificii VT et inculcatur sufficientia sacrificii Christi qui 'una enim oblatione consummavit in sempiternum sanctificatos' (Heb 10.14).

(c) Quod condignitas fuit non ex sola acceptatione Dei sed etiam ex ipsa satisfactione a Christo facta (1) negatur a Durando, Scotistis, nominalibus, (2) a caeteris affirmatur theologis Catholicis. Vide *Sum. theol.*, III, q. 46, a. 6, ad 6m.

(d) Ut haec condignitas ab intrinseco aliquatenus intelligatur, notantur sequentia:

Non eadem est ratio in poenis simpliciter et in poenis satisfactoriis, et ideo non est mensurandus valor satisfactionis Christi per comparationem dolorum Christi ad dolores infernales peccatis debitos. Sed ad intrinsecam rationem poenae satisfactoriae attendendum est, quae quidem ratio est talis ut, quo magis augetur caritas, eo minus requiratur poena satisfactoria seu purgatoria. Cf. *C. Gent.*, III, 158, § 6, quod supra citavimus, praenotamen VIII, 4.

Iam vero in Christo habebantur dolores maximi (*Sum. theol.*, III, q. 46, aa. 5–7), habebantur virtutes et dona secundum plenitudinem gratiae, habebatur operatio interior quae totam perfectionem habitualem exercebat (cf. thesin 15m, partem 6m, ubi quaeritur intelligentia circa Heb 2.10, 5.8). E quibus concludendum est satisfactionem Christi tantam ab intrinseco fuisse quantam concipi potest.

Sed et ulterius ex excellentia effectus iure concluditur ad excellentiam causae sine qua non haberetur effectus. Iam vero satisfactio Christi est principium omnis alterius satisfactionis (DB 904, DS 1690), et quidem modo quodam valde intrinseco (cf. loca S. Thomae, praenotamen VI), unde et passiones sanctorum quodammodo adimplent quae desunt passionum

is no question of remission. But in the context of the gospel Christ so bore our punishment that it is truly said God remits all punishment to the baptized and eternal punishment to the repentant. See Matthew 6.12.

### 3 CHRIST MADE CONDIGN SATISFACTION FOR OUR SINS.

(a) That satisfaction is condign in which there is equivalence according to some due measure.

(b) We conclude that Christ's satisfaction was condign from the price paid (see previous thesis, part 3) and from the value of Christ's sacrifice as expounded in Hebrews 9.9–14, 10.1–4, 10.10–14. In this passage the sacrifices of the Old Testament are declared to be insufficient and the sacrifice of Christ is affirmed to be sufficient, for he 'by a single offering has perfected for all time those who are sanctified' (Hebrews 10.14).

(c) That this satisfaction was condign not only by reason of God's acceptance but also by virtue of Christ's satisfaction itself is denied by Durandus, the Scotists, and the nominalists, but affirmed by the rest of Catholic theologians. See *Summa theologiae*, 3, q. 46, a. 6, ad 6m.

(d) For some understanding of this satisfaction as intrinsically condign, note the following points.

Punishment simply so called and satisfactory punishment are different in nature, and so the value of Christ's satisfaction is not to be measured by comparing Christ's sufferings to the pains of hell which sins deserve. Rather, one must attend to the intrinsic nature of satisfactory punishment, in which the greater the increase in love, the less the need for satisfactory or purgatorial punishment. See *Summa contra Gentiles*, 3, c. 158, ¶6, § 3310, quoted above in preliminary note 8, § 4.

Now, Christ's sufferings were extreme (*Summa theologiae*, 3, q. 46, aa. 5–7). He possessed the virtues and gifts of grace to the fullest, and he possessed an interior life in which he exercised the fullness of habitual perfection (see the previous thesis, part 6, where we are seeking understanding concerning Hebrews 2.10 and 5.8). From this we must conclude that Christ's satisfaction was as great interiorly as can possibly be conceived.

But further, from the excellence of an effect we rightly conclude to the excellence of the cause without which the effect would not exist. Now Christ's satisfaction is the source of all other satisfaction (DB 904, DS 1690, [ND 1631]), and is so indeed in a very intrinsic manner (see the passages from St Thomas quoted in preliminary note 6); hence the sufferings of the saints complete in some way what is lacking in the sufferings of Christ

Christi (Col 1.24). Et ideo tota quaedam excellentia redemptionis in satisfactione Christi praecontinetur tamquam in causa. Cf. Heb 5.9.

Quibus perspectis, ad condignitatem satisfactionis Christi concluditur secundum dicta S. Thomae (*Sum. theol.*, III, q. 48, a. 2).

Quod enim exigit recompensatio totius offensae generis humani est totalitas quaedam poenarum (ibid. I-II, q. 87, a. 6).

Quae totalitas, si secundum iustitiam vindicativam solveretur, non esset nisi totalitas poenarum simpliciter quam Deus nisi indirecte non vult (ibid. I, q. 19, a. 9).

Sed Deus non vult mortem peccatoris sed magis ut convertatur et vivat. Et totalis cuiusdam conversionis principium in perfectissima Christi satisfactione Deo exhibitum est. Unde iure cum S. Thoma concluditur quod 'Christus ex caritate et obedientia patiendo maius aliquid Deo exhibuit quam exigeret recompensatio totius offensae humani generis' (ibid. III, q. 48, a. 2).

(e) Quibus accedit quod, quamvis peccatum sit malum infinitum ratione Dei offensi, eadem infiniti ratio in satisfactione Christi invenitur cum Christus sit divina persona. Sicut enim peccatum mensuratur pro dignitate personae offensae, ita et satisfactio mensuratur pro dignitate personae pro offensa satisfacientis.

Vide DB 550, 552, DS 1025, 1027, ubi clare docentur infinita Christi merita et infinitus thesaurus ecclesiae adquisitus; at ibidem tot dicuntur de passione Christi ut ad infinitam satisfactionem concludi posse videatur.

### 4 CHRISTUS PRO NOSTRIS PECCATIS SUPERABUNDANTER SATISFECIT.

(a) Rom 5.15, 5.20: multo magis gratia abundavit; gratia superabundavit. Quae superabundantia attribuitur uni homini Christo, sicut et delictum est per unum hominem Adam. Alibi autem gratia, iustificatio, remissio peccatorum attribuuntur morti vel sanguini Christi. Unde ad satisfactionem superabundantem concludendum est.

(b) Clemens VI: propter unionem ad Verbum modica gutta sanguinis suffecisset ad redemptionem totius generis humani (DB 550, DS 1025).

(Colossians 1.24). And therefore the entire excellence of the redemption is precontained in Christ's satisfaction as in its cause. See Hebrews 5.9.

Understanding all this, we conclude that the satisfaction made by Christ was condign, in accordance with the teaching of St Thomas (*Summa theologiae*, 3, q. 48, a. 2).

Recompense for the whole offense of the human race requires a certain totality of punishment (ibid. 1-2, q. 87, a. 6).

This totality, if it were paid according to retributive justice, would come simply to a totality of punishments that God, except indirectly, does not will (ibid. 1, q. 19, a. 9).

Yet God does not will the death of the sinner, but rather that the sinner be converted and live. And the principle of this total conversion is displayed in the perfect satisfaction Christ made to God. Accordingly, in the words of St Thomas we rightly conclude that 'by suffering out of love and obedience, Christ offered God something greater than what was demanded in recompense for all the offense of the human race' (ibid. 3, q. 48, a. 2).

(e) In addition to this there is the fact that although sin is an infinite evil by reason of its being an offense against God, the same note of infinity is present in Christ's satisfaction, since Christ is a divine person. For just as sin is measured according to the dignity of the person offended, so also is satisfaction measured according to the dignity of the person making satisfaction for the offense.

See DB 550, 552; DS 1025, 1027; [ND 1681, 1683], which clearly speak of the infinite merits of Christ and the infinite treasure given to the church. So many points are made in these statements concerning the passion of Christ that it seems possible to conclude that his satisfaction is infinite.

### 4 CHRIST MADE SUPERABUNDANT SATISFACTION FOR OUR SINS.

(a) Romans 5.15, 5.20: grace was more abundant; grace was superabundant. This superabundance is attributed to one human being, Christ, just as sin has come through one human being, Adam. And in other texts, grace, justification, and the forgiveness of sins are attributed to the death or the blood of Christ. Hence we must conclude that his satisfaction was superabundant.

(b) Pope Clement VI: because of Christ's union with the Word, a tiny drop of his blood would have sufficed for the redemption of the whole human race (DB 550, DS 1025, [ND 643]).

(c) S. Thomas: 'una minima passio Christi suffecit ad redimendum genus humanum ab omnibus peccatis' (*Sum. theol.*, III, q. 46, a 5, ad 3m. Cf. q. 48, a. 2, ubi superabundantia concluditur.)

5 DEUS DIRECTE VOLUIT SATISFACTIONEM CHRISTI.

(a) Quaestio oritur ex argumento a J. Rivière proposito contra systema (non factum) expiationis, q.v., DTC XIII (26) 1973.

(b) Clara est doctrina S. Thomae. In rebus voluntariis mala dividuntur in culpam et poenam (*Sum. theol.*, I, q. 48, a. 5); Deus nisi indirecte non vult malum naturalis defectus et malum poenae (ibid. q. 19, a. 9). Similis doctrina invenitur apud S. Bonaventuram, Suárez, S. Bellarmino (Rivière, loc. cit.).

(c) Notate secundum Aristotelem actionem esse in passo, et ideo eundem physice actum fuisse et actionem Iudaeorum et passionem Christi; quod etiam ad dolores sensibiles in Christo ab affligentibus productos extenditur (*In III de Anima*, lect. 2, § 592).[37] At haec identitas non se extendit ad ordinem moralem, et ideo simpliciter differunt actio voluntaria Iudaeorum et passio voluntaria Christi (*Sum. theol.*, I-II, q. 20, a. 6, ad 2m).

(d) Recole quae dicta sunt de divina intentione circa seriem actuum seu effectuum (thesi 15a, praenotamen I, de morte Christi; hac thesi, praenotamina VII, VIII). Unde dicendum est:

(a′) Quia Deus nullo modo vult malum culpae, nullo modo voluit vel peccatum Pilati vel maius peccatum Iudaeorum (Io 19.11).

(b′) Permisso peccato, nisi indirecte non vult Deus actiones consequentes eorum qui Christum affligebant; nisi forte dicendum est Deum etiam has actiones non tam indirecte voluisse quam permisisse (*Sum. theol.*, I, q. 19, a. 9, ad 3m).

(c′) Similiter iudicandum est de eo quod realiter est idem cum actione affligentis, nempe, de physica et sensibili passione Christi, praecisione facta ab aspectu voluntarietatis.

St Thomas: 'The slightest suffering of Christ would have sufficed to redeem the human race from all its sins' (*Summa theologiae*, 3, q. 46, a. 5, ad 3m. See q. 48, a. 2, where Aquinas concludes to the superabundance of Christ's satisfaction.)

5 GOD DIRECTLY WILLED CHRIST'S SATISFACTION.

(a) This question arises from the argument made by Rivière in *Rédemption* 1973, against the system (not the fact) of expiation.

(b) St Thomas's teaching is clear. In volitional matters, evil is divided into fault and punishment (*Summa theologiae*, 1, q. 48, a. 5); God wills the evil of natural defect and the evil of punishment only indirectly (ibid. q. 19, a. 9). In his article Rivière notes that a similar teaching is found in St Bonaventure, St Robert Bellarmine, and Suárez.

(c) Note that according to Aristotle, action is in that which is acted upon, and therefore the same physical act was both the action of the Jewish leaders and the passion of Christ; and this extends also to the sensible sorrows produced in Christ by his afflictions (*In 3 De Anima*, lect. 2, § 592).[37] But this identity does not extend to the moral order, and therefore the voluntary action of the Jewish leaders and the voluntary passion of Christ are absolutely different (*Summa theologiae*, 1-2, q. 20, a. 6, ad 2m).

(d) Recall what was said on the death of Christ, about God's intention concerning a series of acts or effects (in the preceding thesis, preliminary note 1 and in this thesis, preliminary notes 7 and 8). The following points, therefore, are to be noted:

(a′) Because God in no way wills culpable evil (the evil of fault), he in no way willed either the sin of Pilate or the greater sin of the Jewish authorities (John 19.11).

(b′) Having permitted the sin, only indirectly did God will the consequent actions of those who afflicted Christ – unless, perhaps, one is to say that these actions, too, God did not so much indirectly will as simply permit that they be done (*Summa theologiae*, 1, q. 19, a. 9, ad 3m).

(c′) A similar judgment must be made concerning that which is really identical with the action of those who afflicted Christ, that is, his painful physical suffering, prescinding from its voluntary aspect.

37 See also Lonergan's extended discussion of action and passion in *Grace and Freedom* 253–67.

(d′) At hae passiones, quatenus Christus eas acceptabat et patienter sustinebat ex obedientia et caritate, etiam sunt pars materialis in actibus Christi voluntariis; et sic sunt simpliciter bonae. Et similiter eaedem passiones erant quasi materia (*Sum. theol.*, III, q. 14, a. 1, ad 1m) in satisfactione Christi cuius principium erat caritas (ibid.); et ideo etiam satisfactio erat simpliciter bona et directe Deus eam voluit. Quod confirmatur ex praecepto sequendi exemplum Christi patientis (1 Pet 2.18–24).

6 IN TOTO REDEMPTIONIS OPERE AGNOSCENDUM EST QUODDAM QUASI PRINCIPIUM TRANSFORMATIONIS.

(a) Nuperrime vidimus quemadmodum nequissima Iudaeorum actio transmutata est in satisfactionem Christi Deo acceptissimam. Sed idem in aliis multis observatur.

(b) Mors enim est poena peccati: Gen 2.17, 3.19, Sap 2.24, Rom 5.12, 6.23. Sed in Christo mors facta est principium salutis: quod manifestum est tum ex multis locis explicitis, tum etiam Heb 2.14: 'carni et sanguini ... participavit ut per mortem destrueret eum qui habebat mortis imperium'; similiter Praefatio paschalis: 'qui mortem nostram moriendo destruxit et vitam nostram resurgendo reparavit'; cf. Rom 4.25. Vide articulos in thema, 'Christus Victor Mortis,' *Gregorianum* 1958.[38]

(c) Unde intelligi potest mira illa differentia inter Patres et theologos. Ubi enim theologi laudant satisfactionem a Christo peractam, Patres de partibus diaboli loqui solebant (Richard 112–17). Sed in eodem eventu coniungebantur tum 'haec est hora vestra et potestas tenebrarum' (Lc 22.53), tum 'oblatio et hostia Deo in odorem sauvitatis' (Eph 5.2), tum illud in hoc transformatum, nam 'absorpta est mors in victoria' (1 Cor 15.54) 'ut per mortem destrueret eum qui habebat mortis imperium, id est diabolum' (Heb 2.14).

(d) Secundum idem transformationis principium intelligenda esse videntur Gal 3.13–14 et 2 Cor 5.21. In Gal 3 agitur de transformatione ex maledicto legis in benedictionem Abrahae; in 2 Cor agitur de transformatione ex effectibus peccati in effectus iustitiae Dei. Exegetarum sententiae

(d′) But insofar as Christ accepted these sufferings and bore them patiently out of obedience and love, they are also the material element in Christ's voluntary acts and thus are good without qualification. Likewise these same sufferings were like the matter (*Summa theologiae*, 3, q. 14, a. 1, ad 1m) in Christ's satisfaction, the principle of which was love (ibid.); and therefore his satisfaction also was good without qualification and directly willed by God. This is confirmed by the precept to follow the example of Christ in his suffering (1 Peter 2.18–24).

6 IT MUST BE ACKNOWLEDGED THAT THERE IS A CERTAIN TRANSFORMATIVE PRINCIPLE OPERATIVE THROUGHOUT THE ENTIRE WORK OF REDEMPTION.

(a) We have just seen how the most vile action of the Jewish authorities was transformed into Christ's most pleasing satisfaction to God. But the same can be observed in many other instances.

(b) Death is the penalty for sin: Genesis 2.17, 3.19, Wisdom 2.24, Romans 5.12, 6.23. But in Christ, death became the source of salvation, as is explicitly stated in many places in scripture, such as Hebrews 2.14: He himself shared flesh and blood so that through death he might destroy the one who has the power of death. Similarly, the Easter preface: 'Dying, he destroyed our death, rising he restored our life'; also Romans 4.25. See the articles on the theme 'Christus Victor Mortis,' in *Gregorianum*, 1958.[38]

(c) From this we can understand the strange difference between the Fathers and theologians. Where theologians praise the satisfaction made by Christ, the Fathers generally mention the role of the devil (Richard, *Le mystère de la Rédemption* 112–17 [*The Mystery of the Redemption* 149–56]). But together in the same event we read both 'This is your hour, and the power of darkness' (Luke 22.53) and 'a fragrant offering and sacrifice to God' (Ephesians 5.2), and the transformation of the former into the latter, for 'death has been swallowed up in victory' (1 Corinthians 15.54), 'so that through death he might destroy the one who has the power of death, that is, the devil' (Hebrews 2.14).

(d) It seems that Galatians 3.13–14 and 2 Corinthians 5.21 are to be understood according to this same principle of transformation. Galatians 3 speaks of the transformation from the curse of the law into Abraham's blessing, and 2 Corinthians speaks of the transformation of the effects of sin into the effects of the justice of God. For the opinion of exegetes, see

38 See p. 69 above for an earlier reference to these articles.

apud S. Lyonnet, *De peccato et redemptione,* MS 1956, 259–64, ubi etiam de Col 2.14. L. Sabourin, *Rédemption sacrificielle.*[39]

(e) Idem transformationis principium videtur esse de essentia redemptionis quae nihil est aliud quam hoc quod Deus de malis permissis facit bonum excellentius. Vide praenotamen VII.

(f) Quo principio agnito, necesse est distinguere duplicem poenam et duplicem iustitiam divinam: debentur enim peccatorum poenae ex iustitia Dei vindicativa; sed solvuntur a Christo ex obedientia et caritate ut Deus sit iustus et iustificans (Rom 3.26). Cf. praenotamen VIII.

### 7 SATISFACTIO CHRISTI INTELLIGITUR SECUNDUM ANALOGIAM SACRAMENTALEM.

(a) Etiam a liberalibus (Harnack, Loofs) iam pridem agnitum est (contra H. Cremer) satisfactionem a S. Anselmo esse conceptam secundum notiones et usum ecclesiae. J. Rivière, DTC XIII (26) 1943. Franks, I, 175–78.[40]

Quod tamen nisi remote ad hoc nostrum assertum pertinet, nam quaerimus non de conceptione Anselmiana sed de doctrina Catholica.

(b) Disputari solent theologi de effectu satisfactionis Christi, scilicet, posita hac satisfactione, quo usque teneatur Deus ad remissionem peccatorum concedendam. Vide sententias, § 17.

Hic non quaeritur de effectu sed de ipsa satisfactione a Christo peracta quemadmodum intelligenda sit.

(c) Duo asseruntur. Primo, quod satisfactio Christi est secundum analogiam satisfactionis sacramentalis. Deinde, quod agitur de analogia et non de perfecta similitudine.

Lyonnet, *Theologia biblica Novi Testamenti: De peccato et redemptione* (MS 1956) 259–64, where Colossians 2.14 is also discussed. See also Sabourin, *Rédemption sacrificielle*.[39]

(e) This transformative principle appears to be of the essence of the redemption. It is simply the fact that God brings a more excellent good out of the evils that are permitted to occur. See preliminary note 7.

(f) Once this principle is acknowledged, it is necessary to distinguish two kinds of punishment and two kinds of divine justice: the punishment for sin is owed according to God's retributive justice, but it is paid by Christ out of obedience and love, that God might be both just and justifying (Romans 3.26). See preliminary note 8.

### 7 CHRIST'S SATISFACTION IS TO BE UNDERSTOOD ACCORDING TO A SACRAMENTAL ANALOGY.

(a) Even liberal theologians (Harnack, Loofs) recognized long ago (contrary to Hermann Cremer [1834–1903]) that St Anselm conceived satisfaction in terms of the ideas and practices current in the church. Rivière, 'Rédemption' 1943; Franks, *A History of the Doctrine of the Work of Christ*, vol. 1, 175–85.[40]

This, however, is only remotely relevant to our position, for we are inquiring not about Anselm's conception but about Catholic doctrine.

(b) There is a dispute among theologians concerning the effect of Christ's satisfaction, namely, to what extent God, given this satisfaction, is bound to grant forgiveness of sins. See *Opinions*, no. 17, above [p. 99].

Here, we are not asking about the effect of Christ's satisfaction but about how this satisfaction itself is to be understood.

(c) We make two assertions: first, that the satisfaction of Christ is understood by analogy with sacramental satisfaction; second, that it is a question of analogy, not a perfect likeness.

39 The discussion of Colossians 2.14 begins on p. 261 in Lyonnet's manuscript. Lonergan does not here cite particular pages from Sabourin's work. For bibliographical details on the work of Lyonnet cited here, see below, p. 421, note 9.

40 On p. 178, Franks refers to two essays by Cremer, 'Die Wurzeln des Anselmischen Satisfaktionsbegriffs,' *Studien und Kritiken* (1880) 7–21, and 'Der germanische Satisfaktionsbegriff in der Versöhnungslehre,' *Studien und Kritiken* (1893) 316–45. According to Franks (p. 178), Cremer claimed that Anselm was influenced by 'the ideas of German law.' See above, p. 79, at n. 2.

(d) Sensus prioris asserti colligitur ex praenotaminibus III, IV, V; quibus, si de iustitia Dei quaeritur, accedunt praenotamina VII et VIII.

Concrete ponatur quaestio quo sensu valeat disiunctio, aut satisfactio aut poena. Certo valet tum ratione subiecti et libertatis tum ratione poenarum materialiter sumptarum. Si enim est satisfactio, Christus libere est subiectum quod poenas dat; si autem est non satisfactio sed poena, peccatores inviti sunt subiecta quae poenas dant. Iterum, si est satisfactio, poenae sunt flagellatio, crucifixio, mors; si autem non satisfactio sed poena est, tunc poenae sunt ignis aeternus et poena damni. Sed ulterius quaeritur utrum ulla alia differentia discerni possit inter satisfactionem et poenam, utrum forte formalis ratio satisfactionis et formalis ratio poenae inter se differant. Cui quaestioni respondemus affirmative.

(e) Adversarii huius prioris asserti sunt qui satisfactionem Christi concipiunt quasi esset substitutio Christi pro peccatoribus et satispassio Christi donec debitum poenae per passionem solvatur satis. Vide sententias 14, 16, 18. J. Rivière, DTC XIII (26) 1970–71, 1973–74, de notione et systemate expiationis.

(f) Quatenus contra veteres Protestantes, doctrina est certa et communis; quatenus contra auctores Catholicos, eorum sententia est dicenda 'teoria che, se non è eterodossa, è però oramai superata' (G. Oggioni, *Problemi e orientamenti*, II, 311).

(g) Primum assertum sic probatur.

Ibi invenitur formalis differentia ubi alia et alia est notionum complexio.

Atqui alia et alia est notionum complexio si comparantur poenae in infernis datae et poenae a Christo datae.

Ergo intercedit formalis differentia inter poenas in infernis datas et poenas a Christo datas.

Maior: videtur evidens; est fere definitio differentiae formalis.

Minor: circa poenas in infernis datas invenitur illa notionum complexio praenotamine IV exposita de culpa, offensa, reatu poenae, inflictione poenae, solutione poenae; sed circa poenas a Christo datas invenitur illa notionum complexio praenotamine V exposita de satisfactione, venia, et poenae remissione.

(d) The meaning of the first assertion can be gathered from preliminary notes 3, 4, and 5, to which, if God's justice is in question, are added preliminary notes 7 and 8.

In concrete terms, we are asking in what sense the disjunction 'either satisfaction or punishment' is valid. There is no doubt that it is valid both by reason of the subject and his freedom and by reason of punishment taken materially. For if there is satisfaction, Christ is freely the subject who is punished; but if there is not satisfaction but punishment, then unwilling sinners are the subjects who are punished. Again, if there is satisfaction, the punishments are flagellation, crucifixion, death; but if there is not satisfaction but punishment, then the punishments are eternal fire and the pain of loss. But a further question is whether any other difference can be discerned between satisfaction and punishment, whether perhaps the formal meaning of satisfaction is different from the formal meaning of punishment. This question we answer in the affirmative.

(e) The adversaries of this first assertion are those who conceive Christ's satisfaction as if it were the substitution of Christ for sinners and satispassion on his part until the punishment due to sin should be paid in full through his suffering. See opinions 14, 16, and 18 above. See Rivière, 'Rédemption' 1970–71, 1973–74, on the notion and system of expiation.

(f) As against the early Protestants, this doctrine is certain and common; as against Catholic authors, their opinion must be said to be 'a theory that, if not unorthodox, is, however, now obsolete' (Oggioni, 'Il mistero della redenzione,' in *Problemi e orientamenti*, vol. 2, 311).

(g) The first assertion is proved as follows.

A difference is formal when there are two different sets of notions.

But there are two different sets of notions when one compares the pains of hell with the punishment Christ suffered.

Therefore there is a formal difference between the pains of hell and the punishment Christ suffered.

The major premise is evident, as almost a definition of 'formal difference.'

As to the minor premise: regarding the pains of hell, there is the set of notions laid out in preliminary note 4 concerning fault, offense, liability to punishment, the imposition of punishment, and payment of the punishment; but regarding Christ's punishment, there is the set of notions laid out in preliminary note 5 concerning satisfaction, pardon, and the remission of punishment.

Quae sane differentia est manifesta in magisterio ordinario ecclesiae, quod negat de infernis esse redemptionem, et praedicat (1) Christum passum in remissionem peccatorum et in reconciliationem peccatorum cum Deo et (2) per baptismum remissionem omnis poenae et per paenitentiam remissionem poenae aeternae.

(h) Unde concludes contra adversarios: quamvis et Christus satis sit passus, quamvis et damnati satis sint passuri, alia tamen et alia est ratio istius 'satis.' In damnatis non dicit nisi pati secundum sententiam iudicis condemnantis. Sed in Christo 'satis' pati dicit pati secundum satisfactionem pro offensa in ordine ad remissionem peccati, reconciliationem, et remissionem poenae.

(i) Unde ulterius concludes ad similitudinem quandam inter satisfactionem Christi et satisfactionem sacramentalem.

Nam satisfactio sacramentalis etiam est in contextu satisfactionis pro offensa Dei, remissionis offensae, et remissionis poenae aeternae. Et praeterea accedit auctoritas c. Tridentini: '... dum satisfaciendo patimur pro peccatis, Christo Iesu, qui pro peccatis nostris satisfecit ... conformes efficimur, certissimam quoque inde arrham habentes, quod, si compatimur, et conflorificabimur' (DB 904, DS 1690).

(j) At analogice inter se comparantur satisfactio Christi et satisfactio sacramentalis.

Nam analogica sunt quae partim similia et partim dissimilia sunt. Differt autem satisfactio Christi a satisfactione paenitentis, tum quia satisfactio Christi est causa omnis alterius satisfactionis (DB 904, DS 1690), tum quia Christus nullam propriam culpam vel originalem vel actualem vel etiam susceptam habuit et ideo nullatenus pro se satisfecit 'qui peccatum omnino nescivit' (DB 122, DS 261), sed paenitens propriam culpam etiam actualem habuit unde et poenam non tantum suscepit sed et contraxit et, etiam remissa culpa, totius contractae poenae remissionem non sine satisfactione accipit (DB 922, DS 1712).

(k) Qua perspecta analogia, concludi non potest ex c. Tridentino Christum ex iustitia Dei vindicativa poenas dedisse. Verum est concilium docuisse (DB 905, DS 1692) paenitentem satisfacere debere 'ad praeteritorum peccatorum vindictam et castigationem.' Sed Christus praeteritam culpam propriam vel originalem vel actualem vel susceptam non habuit, et ideo non est simile.

This difference is certainly very clear in the ordinary magisterium of the Church, which denies any redemption from hell and proclaims (1) that Christ suffered for the forgiveness of sins and to reconcile sinners with God, and (2) that through baptism all punishment is remitted, and through the sacrament of penance eternal punishment is remitted.

(h) Hence we may conclude against our opponents that although Christ suffered enough, and although the damned will suffer enough, the word 'enough' here has different meanings. In the case of the damned it simply means suffering according to the sentence passed by the condemning judge; but in the case of Christ, suffering 'enough' means suffering in satisfaction for the offense with a view to the forgiveness of sin, reconciliation, and the remission of punishment.

(i) From this we may further conclude to a similarity between Christ's satisfaction and sacramental satisfaction.

For sacramental satisfaction also is in the context of satisfaction for an offense against God, of forgiveness of the offense, and of the remission of eternal punishment. Then, too, there is the authority of the Council of Trent: '... when we suffer in satisfaction for our sins, we conform ourselves to Christ Jesus, who made satisfaction for our sins, giving us the surest pledge that, if we suffer with him, we shall also be glorified with him' (DB 904, DS 1690, [ND 1631]).

(j) The comparison between Christ's satisfaction and sacramental satisfaction is analogical.

Things that are partly the same and partly different are analogous. Now Christ's satisfaction is different from the satisfaction of a penitent both in that Christ's satisfaction is the cause of all other satisfaction (DB 904, DS 1690, [ND 1631]) and in that Christ had no fault of his own, either original or actual or even assumed, and therefore in no way did he make satisfaction for himself 'who knew no sin' (DB 122, DS 261, [ND 606/10]); but a penitent is one who has accrued actual fault and so has not only taken on but also incurred punishment, and even with the remission of fault does not receive the remission of all the punishment incurred without making some satisfaction (DB 922, DS 1712, [ND 1652]).

(k) In the light of this analogy one cannot conclude from the Council of Trent that Christ suffered punishment out of the retributive justice of God. It is true that the Council taught that a penitent ought to make satisfaction 'in retribution and castigation for past sins'(DB 905, DS 1692, [ND 1633]). But Christ had no past sin of his own, either original or actual or assumed, and therefore the cases are not alike.

## 8 SATISFACTIO CHRISTI VICARIAE PASSIONI ET MORTI ADDIT EXPRESSIONEM SUMMAE DETESTATIONIS OMNIUM PECCATORUM ET SUMMI DOLORIS DE OMNI OFFENSA DEI.

(a) Thesi 15a, parte 4a, probatum est Christum vicarie esse passum et mortuum propter peccata et pro peccatoribus, non eo solo sensu ut in utilitatem peccatorum peccata deleantur, sed etiam quia peccatum est, peccatur, peccabitur, et quia peccatores poenas meruerunt.

Quod verum hac in thesi probanda (supra § 1) assumptum est et nominatum satisfactio materialis seu expiatio.

Quod autem formaliter aderat satisfactio et quid satisfactio formaliter sit variis modis (§§ 2–7) statutum est. Quae omnia nunc colligentes dicimus satisfactionem materialem fieri formalem ex eo quod exprimuntur detestatio peccati et de peccato dolor.

(b) Quod Christus homo omnia peccata detestatus est, sequitur (1) ex visione beata qua Deum per essentiam cognovit et etiam, per modum obiecti secundarii, omnia peccata et (2) ex perfectissima caritate qua Deum dilexit.

Quod Christus de omnibus peccatis summopere doluit, ex iisdem sequitur praemissis. Vide terminos iam pridem definitos initio huius theseos. Notate nullum viatorem vel visione beata gavisum esse vel caritate Christi Deum dilexisse, et ideo nullum alium viatorem potuisse sicut potuit et fecit Christus peccata omnia detestari et de iis dolere.

(c) Quod Christus homo 'propter peccata' passus et mortuus est, hoc veritatem habet non solum secundum voluntatem divinam sed etiam secundum voluntatem Christi humanam.

Quod hoc veritatem habet secundum voluntatem divinam, vide thesin 15m, partem 4m: propter peccata commissa oportebat Christum pati et mori, divina ordinatione atque iudicio.

Quod hoc veritatem habet secundum voluntatem Christi humanam constat ex scientia Christi et perfectissima eius obedientia qui non solum fecit quod praeceptum est sed etiam ob eam rationem fecit propter quam praeceptum est.

(d) Eatenus Christus homo secundum voluntatem suam humanam propter peccata passus et mortuus est, quatenus peccata detestatus est et de peccatis dolet.

Nam 'propter peccata' dicit motivum; et eatenus hoc motivum movet, quatenus quis peccata detestatur et de iis dolet.

8 CHRIST'S SATISFACTION ADDS TO HIS VICARIOUS PASSION AND DEATH AN EXPRESSION OF THE UTMOST DETESTATION FOR ALL SINS AND OF EXTREME SORROW FOR ALL OFFENSE AGAINST GOD.

(a) In part 4 of the previous thesis it was proved that Christ vicariously suffered and died because of sins and for sinners, not only in the sense that sins might be wiped away for the benefit of sinners, but also because sins have been committed, are being committed, and are going to be committed, and because sinners have deserved punishment.

This truth was assumed in proving the present thesis (see above, *The argument,* § 1) and was termed material satisfaction, or expiation.

The presence also of formal satisfaction and the meaning of formal satisfaction have been stated in various ways (§§ 2–7). Taking all of these statements together, we say that material satisfaction becomes formal satisfaction from the fact that it expresses detestation for sin and sorrow for sin.

(b) The fact that the human Christ detested all sins follows (1) from his beatific vision in which he knew God through God's essence and also, as secondary objects, all sins, and (2) from the most perfect love that he had for God.

The fact that Christ had extreme sorrow for all sins follows from the same premises. See the terms defined at the beginning of this thesis. Note that no one in this life has either enjoyed the beatific vision or has loved God with Christ's love, and therefore no other human being could have detested all sins and felt sorrow for them as Christ was able to do and did.

(c) That the human Christ suffered and died 'because of sins' has its truth not only from the divine will but also from Christ's human will.

That it has its truth from the divine will, see the previous thesis, part 4: because of sins that have been committed it was incumbent upon Christ to suffer and die, by divine ordination and judgment.

That it has its truth from Christ's human will is evident from Christ's knowledge and the most perfect obedience of one who not only did what was commanded but also did it for the very reason for which it was commanded.

(d) The human Christ according to his human will suffered and died because of sins to the extent that he detested and grieved for sins.

For 'because of sins' expresses the motive; and this motive moves one to the extent that one has detested sins and grieved for them.

(e) Ad idem ergo redit, sive dicis Christum propter peccata esse passum et mortuum, sive dicis Christum esse passum et mortuum quia peccata detestatus est et de peccatis doluit.

Ubi enim primum dicis, ad motivum attendis; ubi autem alterum dicis, ad voluntatem motivo motam attendis.

(f) Quaecumque de satisfactione Christi dicuntur, nisi magis explicite non declarant quod iam ex scripturis cognoscitur, nempe, propter peccata Christum esse passum et mortuum.

Nam evolutio dogmatis et evolutio theologica eiusmodi sunt ut nisi transitum de implicito in explicitum non faciunt. Et quod in scripturis de satisfactione Christi habetur, brevi compendio est Christum propter peccata esse passum et mortuum.

(g) Et idem a posteriori colligitur.

Nam concipi solet satisfactio vel cum S. Thoma tamquam id quod Deus magis diligit quam odit peccata, vel cum S. Anselmo tamquam opus in honorem Dei, vel cum aliis theologis tamquam compensatio quaedam propter offensam Dei, vel secundum praenotamina nostra tamquam susceptio poenae in contextu veniae petendae et concedendae. Quae quidem omnia implicite continentur in hoc quod Christus propter peccata passus et mortuus est.

(h) Quare, quaecumque de satisfactione Christi dicuntur, etiam in hoc implicite continentur, quod Christus ideo est passus et mortuus quia peccata detestatus est et de peccatis doluit.

Nam ex (e) habetur aequivalentia, inter 'propter peccata' et 'quia peccata detestatus est et de iis doluit.'

(i) Passio et mors Christi est expressio interioris Christi detestationis et doloris de peccatis.

Quod dupliciter manifestatur. Primo modo, quia Christi hominis detestatio et dolor de peccatis dicunt voluntatem Christi qua motam per motivum acceptandae passionis et mortis. Altero modo, quia omnes Christiani, Christum patientem et morientem contemplantes, intelligunt motivum istius passionis et mortis tum secundum quod motivum est tum secundum quod movet Christi voluntatem.

(j) Satisfactio Christi formaliter est actus exterior.

Nam hanc ob causam satisfactio vicaria esse potest (*Sum. theol.*, III, q. 48, a. 2, ad 1m; cf. q. 48, a. 6, ad 3m).

Praeterea, actus Christi interiores, uti caritas Christi, nominantur a S. Thoma 'principium' satisfactionis (ibid. q. 14, a. 1, ad 1m).

(e) It comes to the same thing, therefore, whether one says that Christ suffered and died because of sins or that Christ suffered and died because he detested sins and was grieved by them.

In making the first statement one is attending to the motive; in the second statement one is attending to his will as moved by the motive.

(f) Whatever is said about Christ's satisfaction simply expresses more explicitly what is already known from scripture, namely, that Christ suffered and died because of sins.

For development in dogma and development in theology are simply transitions from the implicit to the explicit. And so what scripture says concerning the satisfaction made by Christ is, briefly put, that Christ suffered and died because of sins.

(g) The same point may be gathered from what comes later.

For satisfaction is conceived either following St Thomas as that which God loves more than God hates sin, or following St Anselm as a work to give honor to God, or along with other theologians as a kind of compensation for offense against God, or according to our preliminary notes as the acceptance of punishment in the context of pardon to be asked for and granted. All of these are contained implicitly in the statement that Christ suffered and died because of sins.

(h) Whatever, therefore, is said about Christ's satisfaction is also implicitly contained in this statement, that Christ suffered and died because he detested sins and was grieved by them.

For from (e), above, 'because of sins' is seen to be equivalent to 'because he detested sins and was grieved by them.'

(i) The passion and death of Christ is an expression of his interior detestation of and sorrow for sins.

This is evident in two ways: first, because the detestation of and sorrow for sins on the part of the human Christ express the will of Christ as moved by the motive for accepting his passion and death; second, because all Christians, in contemplating Christ in his suffering and dying, understand the motive for this passion and death both as a motive and as moving the will of Christ.

(j) Christ's satisfaction in the formal sense is an exterior act.

This is the reason why satisfaction can be vicarious (*Summa theologiae*, 3, q. 48, a. 2, ad 1m; see a. 6, ad 3m).

Besides, Christ's interior acts, such as his love, are called a 'principle' of satisfaction by St Thomas (ibid. q. 14, a. 1, ad 1m).

Notate actum exteriorem non ita dividi contra interiorem ut exterior non sit voluntarius (*Sum. theol.*, I-II, q. 20, a. 2, ad 3m).

(k) Non ergo ipsa Christi detestatio peccatorum eiusque de peccatis dolor, sed huius detestationis atque doloris expressio facit satisfactionem Christi formalem.

Nam ipsa detestatio ipseque dolor sunt actus interiores; eorum autem expressio est actus exterior; et ex dictis (j), satisfactio formaliter est actus exterior.

(l) Quibus collectis, habetur intentum: satisfactionem Christi vicariae passioni et morti addere expressionem summae detestationis omnium peccatorum et summi doloris de omni offensa Dei.

(m) Quam autem peccati detestationem Christus per acceptam passionem et mortem expressit, eandem etiam Deus expressit.

Nam in Christo homine quasi 'visibiliter Deum cognoscimus' (Praefatio nativitatis Domini).

Rom 8.3–4: '... Deus Filium suum mittens in similitudinem carnis peccati et de peccato damnavit peccatum in carne, ut iustificatio legis impleretur in nobis, qui non secundum carnem ambulamus sed secundum spiritum.' Nam quod Deus suum iudicium de peccato in passione et morte Christi expressit, intelligi posse videtur in illis verbis, 'damnavit peccatum in carne.'

Et idem concluditur ex eo quod iam est probatum: divina praeordinatione Christum, esse morti traditum, eum pati oportuisse, etc., cuius praeordinationis ratio est peccatum, nam Deus misit Filium suum de peccato.

(n) Unde concludi possunt omnia quae de satisfactione dicuntur.

Si enim satisfactio est passio et mors Christi qua expressio detestationis peccati et doloris de peccato, sequitur (1) Christum esse vicarie passum et mortuum ex motivo quod in peccatis et peccatoribus invenitur, quod in NT docetur, (2) Christi dolorem de offensa Dei fuisse opus in honorem Dei, quod a S. Anselmo propositum est, (3) hoc Christi opus magis Deo placere quam displicent peccata, quod a S. Thoma conceptum est, (4) satisfactionem ita ad genus meriti reduci ut pro demeritis compenset, uti ab aliis concipitur, (5) satisfactionem esse poenae susceptionem ut venia convenienter petatur et concedatur, uti in praenotaminibus diximus.

Note that distinguishing exterior act from interior act does not imply that an exterior act is not voluntary (ibid. 1-2, q. 20, a. 2, ad 3m).

(k) Hence it is not Christ's detestation of sins and his sorrow for them but the expression of this detestation and sorrow that render his satisfaction formal.

For this detestation and this sorrow are interior acts; their expression is an exterior act; and from what we have said in (j) above, satisfaction taken formally is an exterior act.

(l) With all of this taken together, we have reached our objective: the satisfaction made by Christ adds to his vicarious suffering and death an expression of the utmost detestation for all sins and of extreme sorrow for all offense against God.

(m) The very same detestation for sin Christ expressed in accepting his passion and death was also expressed by God.

For, in the words of the Preface of the Nativity of the Lord, in the human Christ 'we know God visibly.'

Romans 8.3–4: God, 'by sending his own Son in the likeness of sinful flesh, and to deal with sin, ... condemned sin in the flesh, so that the just requirement of the law might be fulfilled in us, who walk not according to the flesh but according to the Spirit.' For the fact that God delivered his judgment upon sin in the passion and death of Christ can, it seems, be understood in the words, 'God ... condemned sin in the flesh.'

And we reach the same conclusion from what has already been proved: that God foreordained that Christ be handed over to death, that he had to suffer, and so on; and the reason for this foreordination is sin, for God sent his Son to deal with sin.

(n) From all this we can conclude to all that is said about satisfaction.

For if satisfaction is the passion and death of Christ as an expression of detestation and sorrow for sin, it follows (1) that Christ vicariously suffered and died out of the motive that is found in sins and in sinners, as the New Testament teaches, (2) that Christ's sorrow for offense against God was a work in honor of God, as St Anselm proposed, (3) that this work of Christ is more pleasing to God than sins are displeasing, as St Thomas conceived it, (4) that satisfaction is reduced to the genus of merit to compensate for demerits, as some others conceive it, and (5) that satisfaction is the acceptance of punishment so that pardon may be fittingly asked and granted, as we have stated in the preliminary notes.

## THESIS 17[1]

**Dei Filius ideo homo factus, passus, mortuus, et resuscitatus est, quia divina sapientia ordinavit et divina bonitas voluit, non per potentiam mala generis humani auferre, sed secundum iustam atque mysteriosam crucis legem eadem mala in summum quoddam bonum convertere.**

### *Sensus theseos, termini*

1 Thesis supponit facta: Dei Filium esse hominem factum, passum, mortuum, resuscitatum (DB 2, 6, 54, 86; DS 11, 30, 125, 150). Quorum tamen quaerit intelligentiam: DB 1796, 1800; DS 3016, 3020.

2 *Ideo … quia …*: intelligentia quae quaeritur non est vel mera nonrepugnantia vel necessitas absoluta vel necessitas conditionata, sed positiva illa convenientia quae de facto in revelatis et traditis invenitur. Cf. *Sum. theol.*, III, q. 1, aa. 1–3; q. 46, aa. 1 et 2. Vide Sententias.

3 *Divina sapientia ordinavit et divina bonitas voluit*: nam omnia, etiam minima, secundum omnes eorum determinationes reducuntur in divinam sapientiam et in divinam voluntatem; in divinam sapientiam quatenus convenienter inter se et ad finem ordinantur; in divinam voluntatem quae hunc ordinem prae omnibus aliis possibilibus de facto elegit. Cf. *C. Gent.*, II, 23, 24; III, 97; *Sum. theol.*, I, q. 25, aa. 3 et 5.

4 *Bonum* et ens convertuntur. Quare sicut sunt entia realia et entia rationis, ita sunt bona realia et bona rationis (e.g., cognoscere bonum et non facere; praecipere bonum sine effectu).

## THESIS 17

**[Understanding the Mystery: The Law of the Cross.][1] This is why the Son of God became man, suffered, died, and was raised again: because divine wisdom has ordained and divine goodness has willed, not to do away with the evils of the human race through power, but to convert those same evils into a supreme good according to the just and mysterious law of the cross.**

### *Meaning of the thesis, terms*

1 The thesis supposes the following facts: that the Son of God was made man, suffered, died, and was raised from the dead (DB 2, 6, 54, 86; DS 11, 30, 125, 150; [ND 5, 7, 12]). It seeks an understanding of those facts (DB 1796, 1800; DS 3016, 3020 [ND 132–136]).

2 *This is why … because*: the understanding sought is neither a mere absence of internal incoherence nor an absolute necessity nor a conditioned necessity, but rather that positive fittingness which, de facto, is found in revelation and tradition. See *Summa theologiae*, 3, q. 1, aa. 1–3; q. 46, aa. 1–2. See *Opinions* below.

3 *Divine wisdom has ordained and divine goodness has willed*: all things, even the very least, are reducible in all their details to the wisdom of God and the will of God: to God's wisdom, in their being fittingly ordered among themselves and to their end, and to God's will, which, de facto, has chosen this order in preference to all other possible orders. See *Summa contra Gentiles*, 2, cc. 23–24; 3, c. 97; *Summa theologiae*, 1, q. 25, aa. 3 and 5.

4 *Good* and being are interchangeable. Therefore, just as there are real beings and conceptual beings, so also are there real goods and conceptual goods (for example, to know the good and not do it; to command the good without effect).

1 Lonergan gave the title 'Understanding the Mystery' to this thesis in the index at the end of part 5 in *De Verbo incarnato*; the subtitle, 'The Law of the Cross,' has been added because he often referred to the thesis in that way, for example in 'The Transition from a Classicist World-View to Historical-Mindedness,' written in 1966 (in Bernard Lonergan, *A Second Collection*, vol. 13 in Collected Works of Bernard Lonergan, ed. Robert M. Doran and John D. Dadosky [Toronto: University of Toronto Press, 2016] 8).

Sicut ens est vel per essentiam vel per participationem, ita bonum est vel per essentiam (Deus) vel per participationem (ens finitum). Quibus accedunt bona per communicationem in quibus ipse Deus enti finito communicatur, uti in incarnatione, in dono increato Spiritus sancti, in ipsa divina essentia intellectui beato coniuncta (*Sum. theol.*, 1, q. 12, aa. 4 et 5).

Bona per participationem dividuntur in bona particularia (hoc est huic bonum) et bonum ordinis (ipsam complexionem potentiarum, habituum, relationum interpersonalium, ordinationum, cooperationum, quibus fiunt bona particularia). Cf. *Divinarum personarum* 189–90, 224–28; *De Deo trino* II 209–10, 244–49.

*Summum quoddam bonum* in quod convertuntur mala humana est Christus totus, caput et membra, tum hac in vita tum in vita futura, secundum omnes eorum determinationes et relationes concretas. Quod summum quoddam bonum includit (1) bona per communicationem, (2) bonum ordinis in illa unitate quasi organica quae est Christus et ecclesia, (3) bona particularia tum Christi capitis tum membrorum.

5 *Malum* est boni privatio. In rebus voluntariis dividitur in malum culpae et malum poenae (*Sum. theol.*, 1, q. 48, a. 5), ut malum poenae sit ex malo culpae et etiam in malum culpae inclinet. Quae quidem inclinatio invenitur tum in individuo, inquantum peccata generant vitia et vitia inclinant ad peccata ulteriora, tum in societate humana, inquantum peccata situationes humanas corrumpunt et situationes corruptae vehementissime in peccata inclinant. Vide *Insight*, cc. 7, 18, 20.[2]

Quae mala generis humani secundum doctrinam Catholicam reducuntur in peccatum originale. Vide tractatum de Deo creante et elevante.[3]

Just as being is either being by essence or being by participation, so good is either good by essence (God) or good by participation (finite being). To these are added goods by communication, in which God *in se* is communicated to a finite being, as in the Incarnation, in the uncreated gift of the Holy Spirit, and in the divine essence itself united to the intellect of the blessed (*Summa theologiae,* 1, q. 12, aa. 4–5).

Goods by participation are divided into particular goods (this is good for that) and the good of order – the complex of potencies, habits, interpersonal relationships, arrangements, cooperative efforts, by which particular goods are produced. See *Divinarum personarum* 189–90 and 224–28 or *De Deo trino: Pars systematica* 209–10 and 244–49 [*The Triune God: Systematics* 422–25 and 490–99].

*The supreme good* into which human evils are converted is the whole Christ, head and members, in this life as well as in the life to come, in all their details and concrete relations. This supreme good includes (1) goods by communication, (2) the good of order in that quasi-organic unity that is Christ and the church, and (3) the particular goods of both Christ the head and his members.

5 *Evil* is the privation of good. In voluntary matters, evil is divided into culpable evil and the evil of punishment (*Summa theologiae,* 1, q. 48, a. 5), which arises from culpable evil and also inclines towards culpable evil. This inclination is found both in individuals, inasmuch as sins generate vices and vices incline towards further sins, and in human societies, in which sins corrupt human situations and these corrupt situations are in turn a most powerful inducement to further sins. See *Insight,* chapters 7, 18, and 20.[2]

According to Catholic teaching, these evils of the human race are traceable to original sin. See the treatise on God the creator and restorer.[3]

2 On *malum culpae, malum poenae,* and the corresponding terms used in the book *Insight,* see above, thesis 15, p. 21, note 5, and below, p. 451.

3 One instance of such a treatise is a translation of Joseph Pohle's *De Deo creante et elevante* entitled *God: The Author of Nature and the Supernatural,* ed. and trans. Arthur Preuss (St Louis: Herder, 1916).

6 *Per potentiam auferre*: quod intelligi potest vel generaliter vel particulariter.

(a) Intelligitur generaliter speculando de potentia Dei, qui potest facere quodcumque internam contradictionem non dicit (*Sum. theol.*, I, q. 25, a. 3) et ideo multis aliis modis potuit genus humanum reparari (ibid. III, q. 1, a. 2; q. 46, aa. 1 et 2).

Ita alium modum redemptionis exspectavit messianismus iudaicus (Act 1.6, Lc 24.21, etc.); neque postea defuerunt qui quaerebant num potuisset Deus aliter facere; quibus et brevissime et iustissime respondit Augustinus: 'Poterat omnino; sed si aliter faceret, similiter vestrae stultitiae displiceret' (*De agone Christiano*, XI, 12; ML 40, 297).

Cuius responsi acumen minime est praetermittendum. Nam Deus infinite sapiens omnes ordines omnium mundorum possibilium secundum omnem et minimam eorum determinationem cognoscit; unde infinita sua sapientia circa hos ordines optime iudicare potest. Sed de iisdem ordinibus creatus intellectus nihil fere cognoscit vel sapit nisi hoc quod sunt possibiles, quod infinita sapientia sunt ordinati, quod infinita bonitate eligi possunt, quod omnes simul sumpti continent quaecumque internam contradictionem non dicant. Unde, ubi creatura de his ordinibus iudicare praesumit, non sapientia sed stultitia iudicat; quare si actualis ordo huic stultitiae non placet, ita alius et possibilis similiter displiceret.

(b) Sicut generaliter contra totam oeconomiam salutis ita particulariter contra hunc vel illum eiusdem aspectum intelligitur illud 'per potentiam auferre.'

Ita Patres laudant modum nostrae redemptionis quae facta est per Iesum, mitem et humilem corde (Mt 11.29), qui venit non ut ministraretur ei sed ut ministraret et daret animam suam (Mc 10.45). Cui contraponunt modum diaboli et humanae superbiae secundum quem bonum est faciendum per acquisitionem atque exercitium potestatis. Vide Augustinum, *De Trin.*, XIII, xiii, 17; ML 42, 1026–27; J. Rivière, DTC XIII (26) 1939–40, ubi alia plura invenies.

Similiter contra actualem salutis oeconomiam esset si quis praetermittere vellet quod salus singulis venit per praedicationem evangelii, per fidem et paenitentiam; qui quidem modus supponit et antiquam confusionem religionis et status esse sublatam et individualismum libertatemque iam aliquatenus esse evolutos; unde et ulterius quodammodo intelligitur illa temporis plenitudo de qua Gal 4.4, Eph 1.10, Mc 1.15. Quare non inconvenienter

6 *To do away with through power*: this can be understood in general and in particular.

(a) It is understood in a general way by speculating about the power of God, who can do whatever does not involve an internal contradiction (*Summa theologiae*, 1, q. 25, a. 3) and therefore could have restored the human race by many other means (ibid. 3, q. 1, a. 2; q. 46, aa. 1 and 2).

Thus, Jewish messianism expected redemption by a different means (Acts 1.6, Luke 24.21, etc.). And later, there were those who were asking whether God could not have done it differently. To them Augustine curtly and to the point replied, 'Of course he could have; but if he had, your foolishness would be just as unhappy' (*De agone Christiano*, XI, 12; ML 40, 297).

The acuteness of this retort should by no means go unnoticed. For God in his infinite wisdom knows every order of every possible world in its every detail down to the very least; hence in his infinite wisdom he can best judge concerning these orders. But about these same orders, a created intellect has practically no knowledge or wisdom except that they are possible, that they are ordered by infinite wisdom, that they can be chosen by infinite goodness, and that all of them together contain no internal contradiction. Hence, when a creature presumes to make a judgment about these orders, it is not wisdom but folly judging; and if this folly is not pleased with the actual order of reality, any other possible order would be just as displeasing.

(b) Just as 'doing away with by power' is understood in a general way as being contrary to the economy of salvation as a whole, so also it is understood to be contrary to this or that particular aspect of it.

Thus the Fathers praise the manner in which our redemption was accomplished by Jesus, gentle and humble of heart (Matthew 11.29), who came not to be served but to serve and give his life (Mark 10.45). With this they contrast the ways of the devil and of human pride, according to which the good is to be done by getting and exercising power. See Augustine, *De Trinitate*, XIII, xiii, 17; ML 42, 1026–27. See also Rivière, 'Rédemption' 1939–40, for further on this point.

Similarly, it would be contrary to the actual economy of salvation if anyone wished to ignore the fact that the salvation comes to each by the preaching of the gospel, by faith and repentance. This way supposes that the ancient confusion between religion and the state has been dissolved, and that individualism and freedom are already fairly well advanced; hence we further understand, in a way, that 'fullness of time' alluded to in Galatians 4.4, Ephesians 1.10, and Mark 1.15. It was quite fitting, then, for Irenaeus to state

Irenaeus nos redemptos docuit non per violentiam sed per persuasionem. Vide Richard 103–104.

7 *Mala in bonum convertere.* Scilicet, redemptio fit, non auferendo mala per potentiam, sed ipsa mala subeundo atque per Dei gratiam et bonam voluntatem in bona transformando. Vide thesin 16m, conclusionem 6m, de principio transformationis. Exemplum clarissimum est in ipsa Christi morte: de se enim mors est poena peccati; sed in Christo mors est facta medium salutis.

8 *Lex crucis.* Tres quasi gressus complectitur quorum primus est ex malo culpae in malum poenae, alter est voluntaria transformatio poenae in bonum, et tertius est transformationis benedictio a Deo Patre.

Dicitur lex tum ex convenientia quae in singulis gressibus perspicitur tum ex generalitate quam in hac oeconomia salutis habet.

Nam invenitur in Domino nostro tamquam in homine individuo, qui ex peccato Iudaeorum passus et mortuus est, qui malum passionis et mortis per caritatem et obedientiam acceptum in bonum morale transformavit, unde et Deus Pater eum a mortuis resuscitavit.

Sed etiam invenitur in Domino nostro tamquam in novissimo Adam, capite corporis sui quod est ecclesia. Nam ideo Deus permisit peccatum Iudaeorum et afflictionem Christi quia homines peccant et poenas merent; et ideo Christus homo passionem et mortem acceptavit ut pro omnibus peccatis satisfaceret et sacrificium Deo Patri offerret; et ita Deus Filium suum a mortuis resuscitavit ut inde etiam nos a peccatis revivificaret et mortalia nostra corpora in vitam aeternam resuscitaret.

Quod autem in Christo factum est, legem facit generalem pro membris suis: quos praescivit et praedestinavit conformes fieri imaginis Filii sui (Rom 8.29); et si tamen compatimur ut et conglorificemur (Rom 8.17). Unde lex crucis nobis inculcatur tum praeceptis tum exemplis secundum totam suam generalitatem, ut omne malum in rebus humanis et voluntariis tamquam peccati poena habeatur (*Sum. theol.*, 1, q. 48, a. 5), ut cotidie unusquisque tollat crucem suam (Mt 16.24) et ea adimplet quae desunt passionum Christi (Col 1.24) unde 'diligentibus Deum omnia cooperantur in bonum' (Rom 8.28).

that we have been redeemed not by force but by persuasion. See Richard, *Le mystère de la Rédemption* 103–104 [*The Mystery of the Redemption* 137–39].

7 *To convert evils into good*: that is to say, redemption is accomplished, not by doing away with evils through power but by submitting to those very evils and, by the grace of God and by good will, transforming them into good. See § 6 of the concluding argument of the previous thesis, on the principle of transformation. The outstanding example of this is the death of Christ: death as such is the punishment for sin, but in Christ death has been made the means of salvation.

8 *The law of the cross* comprises three steps, so to speak, the first of which is the progression from culpable evil to the evil of punishment, the second is the voluntary transformation of punishment into good, and the third is the blessing of this transformation by God the Father.

It is called a law both because of the fittingness grasped in each step and because of the generality it has in this present economy of salvation.

For it is found in our Lord as an individual human being who suffered and died through the sin of the Jewish authorities, who transformed the evil of his passion and death, accepted in love and obedience, into a moral good, whereupon God the Father raised him from the dead.

But also it is found in our Lord as the last Adam, the Head of his body the church. For it was because human beings sin and deserve punishment that God permitted the sin of the Jewish leaders and the sufferings of Christ; and therefore the human Christ accepted his passion and death in order to make satisfaction for all sins and to offer a sacrifice to God the Father; and God raised his Son from the dead so that thenceforth he might bring us, too, back to life from our sins and raise up our mortal bodies unto eternal life.

What took place in Christ becomes a general law for his members: whom God foreknew and predestined to be conformed to the image of his Son (Romans 8.29) – if, that is, we suffer with him, so that we may also be glorified with him (Romans 8.17). Hence, the law of the cross is instilled into us by both precept and example in its full generality, so that every evil in matters human and voluntary is held to be punishment for sin (*Summa theologiae,* 1, q. 48, a. 5), and so that all should take up their cross daily (Matthew 16.24) and 'complete what is lacking in Christ's afflictions' (Colossians 1.24), whence 'all things work together for good for those who love God' (Romans 8.28).

At eadem crucis lex aliter in Christo et aliter in membris observatur: in illo enim invenitur tamquam in principio redimente, qui 'factus est omnibus obtemperantibus sibi causa salutis aeternae' (Heb 5.9); in membris autem invenitur tamquam in materia redimenda, non sane tamquam in materia inerti vel mere biologica vel tantummodo sensitiva, sed tamquam in materia rationali quae addiscere et credere debet, quae ex caritate libenter Christo consentit, in Christo vivit, per Christum operatur, cum Christo consociatur, ut Christo morienti et resurgenti assimiletur atque conformetur.

9 *Iusta* et *mysteriosa* dicitur lex crucis secundum quod ex divina sapientia et bonitate procedit, et ipsam infinitam sapientiam et infinitam bonitatem nobis in Christo et quodammodo etiam in ipsis nobis revelat.

Iusta autem est quia divina iustitia in eo consistit quod divina voluntas ordinem divinae sapientiae sequitur (*Sum. theol.*, 1, q. 21, a. 1, ad 2m).

Mysteriosa autem dicitur tripliciter: *primo modo*, inquantum a sapientia infinita procedit et ideo intellectum creatum simpliciter excedit (cf. DB 1795–96, DS 3015–16); *altero modo*, inquantum praeter divinum mysterium etiam oppositum humanae iniquitatis mysterium respicit; et *tertio modo*, inquantum, secundum alium vocis 'mysterii' sensum, in mysteriis vitae Domini nostri etiam per sensibilitatem atque affectum humanum contemplamur quemadmodum divina sapientia et bonitas ad mysterium humanae iniquitatis se habeat.

10 Quibus dictis, haud obscurum est vel qualis sit sensus theseos vel qualis significatio terminorum.

Supponimus enim facta, Dominum nostrum incarnatum, passum, mortuum, et resuscitatum.

Quorum intelligentiam quaerimus, non speculando de possibilibus, non deducendo necessaria, sed illam stabiliendo positivam intelligibilitatem quae convenientia nominari solet, quae in ipsis factis perspicitur prout in NT et in magisterio ordinario intelliguntur.

Quam convenientiam in lege crucis invenimus, quae de se est sequentia quaedam vel consecutio tribus constans gressibus, quae in Domino nostro reperitur tum inquantum est homo quidam individualis tum inquantum est caput corporis sui quod est ecclesia; quae conveniens lex etiam in membris Christi secundum voluntatem Dei Patris et secundum praeceptum et exemplum Christi adesse debet et per gratiam et operationem Christi de facto adest.

But the same law of the cross is observed in one way in Christ and in another way in his members. For it is present in Christ as in the redeeming principle, 'who became the source of eternal life for all who obey him' (Hebrews 5.9); but it is found in his members as the matter to be redeemed – not, of course, as matter that is inert or merely biological or only sensitive, but as rational material that has to learn and believe, that out of charity gladly feels together with Christ, lives in Christ, works through Christ, is one with Christ, so as to be assimilated and conformed to Christ in his dying and rising.

9 The law of the cross is said to be *just* and *mysterious* in that it proceeds from divine wisdom and goodness, and reveals to us that infinite wisdom and infinite goodness present in Christ and in some way also in ourselves.

It is just, because divine justice consists in the fact that the divine will follows the order of divine wisdom (*Summa theologiae,* 1, q. 21, a. 1, ad 2m).

It is said to be mysterious in three ways: *first,* in that it proceeds from infinite wisdom and therefore absolutely surpasses the created intellect (DB 1795–96, DS 3015–16; [ND 131–32]); *second,* in that besides the mystery of God, it is concerned with the opposite mystery of human iniquity; and *third,* in that, according to another meaning of the word 'mystery,' through our sensibility and affectivity we contemplate in the mysteries of the life of our Lord how the divine wisdom and goodness stand in relation to the mystery of human iniquity.

10 From the foregoing remarks, the meaning of the thesis and of its terms is quite clear.

For we take for granted these facts, namely, that our Lord was incarnate, suffered, died, and was raised up again.

What we are seeking is an understanding of these facts, not by speculating about possibilities, not by deducing necessary conclusions, but by establishing that positive intelligibility, generally termed 'fittingness,' which is grasped in the facts themselves as understood in the New Testament and in the ordinary magisterium of the church.

We find this fittingness in the law of the cross, which in itself is a sequence or succession consisting of three steps that are found in our Lord both as an individual human being and as head of his body, the church. This fitting law also ought to be present in the members of Christ in accordance with the will of God the Father and through the precept and example of Christ, and is actually present in them through grace and the work of Christ.

***Nota***

Quatenus thesis simpliciter colligit ea quae in NT et in magisterio manifeste docentur, dicenda est de fide divina et Catholica. Quatenus autem ipsa collectio non sine aliqua intelligentia perficitur, videtur sententia solide probabilis.

***Sententiae***

1 Qui intelligentiam incarnationis atque redemptionis quaesierunt, sex maxime modis procesisse videntur. Quorum primus est qui apud Patres reperitur. Alter autem in deductione 'necessaria' S. Anselmi illustratur. Tertius in deductionibus hypothetico-necessariis qui deductioni Anselmianae successerunt. Quartus autem incepit ex quaestione Ruperti abbatis Tuitiensis, utrum Filius Dei incarnatus esset si Adam non peccasset. Quintus ex modificata Ruperti quaestione habebatur utrum incarnationis primarius finis fuerit peccatorum redemptio an Filii exaltatio. Sextus denique in enumeratis convenientiis consistit, uti apud S. Thomam, *Sum. theol.*, III, q. 1, a. 2, ubi quinque narrantur convenientiae secundum promotionem hominis in bono, aliae quinque secundum remotionem a malo, ut denique addatur plurimas et alias esse utilitates quae comprehensionem sensus humani superant.

Qui sane sex modi non omnes sunt mutuo exclusivi, sed alius aliam theologiae methodum supponit et alius est alterius fructus.

2 In primis, quod a Patribus enuntiatum est et in symbolis depositum (DB 2, 6, 54, 86; DS 11, 30, 125, 150) est de fide definita et ab omnibus Catholicis agnitum, Filium esse hominem factum 'propter nos homines et propter nostram salutem' (DB 54, 86; DS 125, 150). Unde certo concluditur finem incarnationis fuisse redemptionem generis humani.

3 Quod thema fundamentale maxime quadrupliciter Patres illustraverunt. *Primo modo*, docuerunt Filium Dei nostra assumpsisse ut sua nobis daret; quod thema divinizationis etiam a S. Thoma memoratur (*Sum. theol.*, III, q. 1, a. 2 c., versus medium), et hodie retinetur inquantum Christus habetur tamquam causa omnis gratiae tum huius vitae tum futurae. *Altero modo*, docuerunt Christum nos redimisse a iugo diaboli non per potentiam sed secundum iustitiam; quod invenies etiam tum in damnatione Abaelardi (DB

### *Theological note*

Insofar as this thesis simply gathers together what is clearly taught in the New Testament and in the magisterium, it is a matter of divine and Catholic faith; but insofar as this gathering together is not made without some understanding, the thesis appears to be a solidly probable opinion.

### *Opinions*

1 It seems that those who have sought to understand the incarnation and the redemption have proceeded mainly in six different ways. The first of these ways is found among the Fathers. The second is exemplified in St Anselm's 'necessary' deduction. The third is in the hypothetically necessary deductions which succeeded Anselm's. The fourth begins with the question raised by Rupert, Abbot of Deutz, whether the Son of God would have been incarnate had Adam not sinned. The fifth, from a modification of Rupert's question, asks whether the primary purpose of the incarnation was redemption from sin or the exaltation of the Son. The sixth, finally, consists in enumerating appropriate or fitting reasons, as when St Thomas gives five reasons with respect to our advancement in the good and another five with respect to our drawing away from evil, adding that there are many other benefits which exceed human comprehension (*Summa theologiae*, 3, q. 1, a. 2).

These six ways are not all mutually exclusive, but they suppose different theological methods and bear different fruit.

2 To begin with, what is stated by the Fathers and set down in the creeds (DB 2, 6, 54, 86; DS 11, 30, 125, 150; [ND 5, 7, 12]) is defined as a matter of faith acknowledged by all Catholics, namely, that the Son became man 'for us and for our salvation' (DB 54, DS 125, [ND 7]). From this we conclude with certainty that the purpose of the incarnation was the redemption of the human race.

3 The Fathers illustrated this basic theme in four main ways. *First,* they taught that the Son of God assumed what is ours in order to give us what is his. This theme of divinization is also recalled by St Thomas (*Summa theologiae,* 3, q. 1, a. 2 c, towards the middle) and is maintained today inasmuch as Christ is held to be the cause of all grace in both the present and the future life. *Second,* they taught that Christ redeemed us from the yoke of the devil not by power but in accordance with justice; this point you will also

371, DS 723), tum apud S. Thomam (*Sum. theol.*, III, q. 46, a. 3, ad 3m; a. 6, ad 6m; q. 48, a. 4, ad 2m et ad 3m; q. 49, a. 2 c. et ad 1m). *Tertio modo,* docuerunt expiationem pro peccatis a Christo factam, quae in subsequenti doctrina de satisfactione Christi continetur tamquam pars materialis. *Quarto modo,* docuerunt sacrificium Christi, quod manifeste in NT et tota traditione continetur. Plura apud J. Rivière, DTC XIII (26) 1938–42; L. Richard 106–30, ubi alia afferuntur.

4 S. Anselmus incarnationem deducere voluit. Probavit ergo Deum et hominem redimere velle, et sine satisfactione hoc non facere, et sufficientem non esse aliam satisfactionem praeter eius qui et Deus et homo esset. Cf. thesin 16m, praenotamen I.

5 Cum tamen S. Anselmi argumentum non ex necessitate sed ex convenientia processisse omnes sint confessi (thesin 16m, praenotamen II), transmutata est deductio Anselmiana ex necessaria in hypothetico-necessariam. Unde communius docetur in hypothesi condignae satisfactionis necessariam fuisse incarnationem. Quod a S. Thoma approbatur (*Sum.theol.*, III, q. 1, a. 2, ad 2m), sed a Scotistis distingui solet ut habeatur hypothetica illa necessitas non de potentia Dei absoluta sed solummodo de potentia Dei ordinaria.[4] Praeter Scotistas etiam dubitare videntur Caietanus et Vásquez, sed communior doctrina (1) praesupponitur a Catechismo Romano, (2) exponitur explicite a c. Coloniensi (AD 1860), et (3) dicitur certa a Galtier, q.v., p. 409, § 514.

6 In intelligentiam huius quaestionis, recolenda sunt principia S. Thomae: '... absolute loquendo, possibile fuit Deo alio modo hominem liberare quam per passionem Christi ... Sed ex aliqua suppositione facta, fuit impossibile. Quia ... supposita praescientia et praeordinatione Dei de passione

find both in the condemnation of Abelard (DB 371, DS 723) and in St Thomas (*Summa theologiae*, 3, q. 46, a. 3, ad 3m; a. 6, ad 6m; q. 48, a. 4, ad 2m, ad 3m; q. 49, a. 2 c., ad 1m). *Third*, they taught that Christ made expiation for sin, which is contained, as its material element, in the later teaching on Christ's satisfaction. *Fourth*, they taught the sacrifice of Christ, which is manifestly contained in the New Testament and in the whole of tradition. More on this in Rivière, 'Rédemption' 1938–42; see Richard, *Le mystère de la Rédemption*, 106–30 [*The Mystery of the Redemption* 141–74] for further references.

4 St Anselm wanted to deduce the incarnation. Therefore, he proved that God wanted to redeem the human race, that he did not want to do this without satisfaction, and that no other satisfaction was sufficient than that made by one who was both God and man. See the previous thesis, preliminary note 1.

5 But since, as all admit, St Anselm's argument proceeded not from necessity but from fittingness (previous thesis, preliminary note 2), the Anselmian deduction is transformed from a necessary into a hypothetically necessary deduction. Hence, it is more commonly taught that the incarnation was necessary, on the hypothesis of condign satisfaction. This is approved by St Thomas (*Summa theologiae*, 3, q. 1, a. 2, ad 2m), but the Scotists generally make the distinction that this hypothetical necessity is not based upon God's absolute power but only upon God's ordained power.[4] In addition to the Scotists, Cajetan and Vásquez also apparently had their doubts, but the more common teaching (1) is presupposed by the Roman Catechism, (2) is explicitly set forth by the Council of Cologne (1860), and (3) is affirmed as certain by Galtier, *De incarnatione ac redemptione*, p. 409, § 514.

6 To understand this question, recall the principles of St Thomas: '... absolutely speaking, it was possible for God to liberate mankind in some other way than through the passion of Christ ... But once a certain supposition is made, this was not possible. Because ... supposing God's foreknowledge

4 Much more common than *potentia ordinaria* is *potentia ordinata*, but *potentia ordinaria* does occur in later Latin discussions of this topic, as a synonym for *potentia ordinata*. See Francis Oakley, 'The Absolute and Ordained Power of God and the King in the Sixteenth and Seventeenth Centuries: Philosophy, Science, Politics, and Law,' *Journal of the History of Ideas* 59 (1998) 669–90.

Christi, non erat simul possibile Christum non pati, et hominem alio modo quam per eius passionem liberari. Et est eadem ratio de omnibus his quae sunt praescita et praeordinata a Deo: ut in Parte Prima habitum est' (*Sum. theol.*, III, q. 46, a. 2). Cf. quae thesi 14a de libertate Christi disputavimus.[5]

Iam vero ubicumque ponitur quodlibet quod incarnationem praesupponit, ad necessitatem incarnationis concluditur. Semper enim de principio non-contradictionis agitur sive dicitur (1) incarnationem non posse et esse et non esse, sive (2) si est incarnatio, fieri non posse ut incarnatio non sit, sive (3) si est quod incarnationem praesupponit, fieri non potest ut non sit incarnatio. Ita in hypothesi personae divinae ridentis, necessaria est incarnatio; et similiter in hypothesi cuiuslibet alterius quod personam divinam cum proprietate humana coniungit, necessaria est incarnatio.

Ulterius, in hypothesi omnium quae tum divinam personam tum etiam naturam assumptam simul praesupponunt, necessaria est incarnatio. Eiusmodi autem sunt omnia quae gratiam Christi dicunt; nam gratia Christi ex una parte proportionem naturae assumptae excedit et ex alia parte speciali quodam modo divinae personae et convenit et competit; et ideo hypothesis gratiae eiusmodi praesupponit tum naturam assumptam, ut gratia sit gratuita, tum divinam personam, ut gratia ei competat. Quare dicendum est quod in hypothesi talis gratiae necessaria est incarnatio.

Praeterea, meritum gratiam sequitur et, sicut gratia Christi est singularis, ita etiam meritum Christi est singulare; et ideo in hypothesi meriti Christi necessaria est incarnatio.

Praeterea, mediatio Christi est singularis; et ideo in hypothesi quod Deus voluit per talem mediationem filios sibi adoptare, necessaria est incarnatio.

Praeterea, ex singularitate gratiae et meriti et mediationis Christi sequitur singularitas eius sacerdotii et sacrificii; et ideo in hypothesi talis sacerdotii, vel in hypothesi talis sacrificii, necessaria est incarnatio.

Praeterea, ex his omnibus sequitur singularitas intercessionis Christi; et ideo in hypothesi quod Deus talem intercessionem voluit, necessaria est incarnatio.

and foreordination concerning the passion of Christ, it was not simultaneously possible that Christ not suffer and that humankind be liberated otherwise than through his suffering. And this same reason holds for all other things that are foreknown and foreordained by God, as was said in the first part' (*Summa theologiae*, 3, q. 46, a. 2 c.). See also our position on the freedom of Christ in *The Incarnate Word*, thesis 14.[5]

Now, whenever anything that presupposes the incarnation is posited, the conclusion follows that the incarnation is necessary. For the principle of non-contradiction is always involved whether it is asserted (1) that the incarnation cannot both be and not be, or (2) if there is the incarnation, the incarnation cannot not be, or (3) if there exists something that presupposes the incarnation, the incarnation cannot not be. Thus on the hypothesis of a divine person laughing, the incarnation is necessary; and similarly on the hypothesis of anything else that connects a divine person with a properly human attribute, the incarnation is necessary.

Furthermore, on the hypothesis of everything that presupposes both a divine person and also an assumed nature together with it, the incarnation is necessary. Everything that refers to the grace of Christ is of this sort, for on the one hand the grace of Christ exceeds the proportion of the assumed nature, and on the other hand is, in a sense, especially fitting and due to a divine person. Thus the hypothesis of such a grace presupposes both the assumed nature, so that the grace is gratuitous, and a divine person, to whom the grace is due. It must be said, therefore, that on the hypothesis of such a grace the incarnation is necessary.

Furthermore, merit follows from grace and, just as the grace of Christ is unique, so also is his merit; hence on the hypothesis of Christ's merit, the incarnation is necessary.

Again, Christ's mediation is unique, and therefore on the hypothesis that God willed the adoption of children by such a mediation, the incarnation is necessary.

Further, from the uniqueness of Christ's grace, merit, and mediation follow the uniqueness of his priestood and sacrifice; and therefore on the hypothesis of such a priesthood, or on the hypothesis of such a sacrifice, the incarnation is necessary.

Moreover, the uniqueness of Christ's intercession follows from all these, and therefore on the hypothesis that God willed such intercession, the incarnation is necessary.

5 Lonergan, *The Incarnate Word* 726–65.

Quibus perspectis, omnino vana videntur dubia eorum qui non affirmant in hypothesi condignae satisfactionis necessariam esse incarnationem. Condigna enim fuit satisfactio Christi, uti supra probavimus (thesi 16a, conc. 3a); neque eodem sensu condigna esse potest satisfactio purae creaturae. Et ideo hac in disputatione non immorandum esse censemus: aut enim ita concipitur condigna satisfactio ut incarnationem necessario praesupponat, aut ita concipitur ut non necessario incarnationem praesupponat; si primo modo concipitur, tunc in hypothesi talis satisfactionis manifeste necessaria est incarnatio; si altero modo concipitur, tunc in hac altera hypothesi non necessaria est incarnatio.

7 Quae cum ita sint, ulterius concludi potest disputationes de hypothetice necessariis nisi remote non conferre ad intelligentiam fidei. Hanc sane utilitatem habent quod conceptus claros, definitiones exactas, deductiones rigorosas exigunt. Quae tamen omnia nisi instrumenta logica non constituunt. Nam primo ad intelligentiam fidei acceditur quando quaeritur, non quid sequeretur ex tali et tali hypothesi, sed utrum conveniat Deum hanc hypothesim et non aliam eligere. Aliis verbis, eatenus actu augetur fidei intelligentia, quatenus perspicitur cur de facto Deus voluerit nos salvos fieri per Christum, per gratiam Christi, per meritum Christi, per mediationem Christi, per sacerdotium et sacrificium Christi, per intercessionem et satisfactionem et efficientiam Christi. Qua convenientia perspecta, utiles sunt hypotheticae necessitates ad reliquam materiam ordinandam, quae tamen per se solae vim principii non-contradictionis non excedunt.

8 Quibus adiungi placet conclusionem circa methodum theologiae. In litt. encycl. *Humani generis*, docemur quod 'sacrorum fontium studio sacrae disciplinae semper iuvenescunt; dum contra speculatio, quae ulteriorem sacri depositi inquisitionem neglegit, ut experiundo novimus, sterilis evadit' (DB 2314, DS 3886).

Iam vero ubi convenientia facti quaeritur, necessario ad fontes revelationis reditur tum ut ipsa facta cognoscantur tum ut in ipsis factis eorum intelligibilitas perspiciatur.

In the light of all of this, the doubts of those who do not affirm the necessity of the incarnation on the hypothesis of condign satisfaction seem to be altogether groundless. For Christ's satisfaction was condign, as we have demonstrated in the previous thesis, conclusion § 3, and the satisfaction of a mere creature cannot be condign in the same sense. And therefore we feel there is no point in prolonging this discussion. For condign satisfaction is conceived either as necessarily presupposing the incarnation or as not necessarily presupposing it; if it is conceived in the first way, then on the hypothesis of such satisfaction, the incarnation is obviously necessary; if it is conceived in the second way, then on this second hypothesis the incarnation is not necessary.

7 This being the case, we may further conclude that disputes about hypothetical necessities only remotely contribute to an understanding of the faith. True, they are useful in that they demand clear concepts, exact definitions, and rigorous deductions; but all these are only logical tools. For the first approach to understanding the faith occurs when one asks, not what would follow from such or such a hypothesis, but whether it was fitting for God to choose this hypothesis and not some other. In other words, the understanding of the faith actually increases to the extent that one grasps why in fact God willed to save us through Christ, through the grace of Christ, through the merit of Christ, through the mediation of Christ, through the priesthood and sacrifice of Christ, and through the intercession, satisfaction, and efficient causality of Christ. Once this fittingness is grasped, hypothetical necessities are helpful in ordering the remaining material, yet by themselves alone they do not exceed the force of the principle of non-contradiction.

8 It would be good here to add a conclusion regarding the method of theology. In the encyclical *Humani generis,* we read that 'through the study of the sacred sources, the sacred sciences are kept ever fresh and vigorous; while speculation, on the other hand, that neglects the further investigation of the deposit of faith becomes sterile, as we know by experience' (DB 2314, DS 3886, [ND 859]).

When we ask about the fittingness of a fact, we necessarily return to the sources of revelation to learn about those facts and to grasp, in the facts themselves, an understanding of them.

E contra, ubi unice de hypothetice necessariis disputatur, non solum facta negligi possunt (nam de hypothesibus agitur) sed etiam facta praetermittere convenit (nam ipsa sola facta non includunt illas claras conceptiones et exactas definitiones quae solae rigidis demonstrationibus inserviunt). Unde in mundos mere possibiles transitur et, cum intellectus creatus de possibilitate parum cognoscat (vide supra, sensus theseos, § 6), cum ipse Christus homo omnia quae sunt in potentia creatoris etiam per perfectissimam suam visionem beatam non cognoverit (*Sum. theol.*, III, q. 10, a. 2), mirum esse non potest eiusmodi disputationes de possibilibus necessario connexis facile evadere steriles.

9 Praeter deductionem Anselmianam 'necessariam' et aliorum deductiones hypothetice necessarias, etiam memoranda est quaestio a Ruperto abbate Tuitiensi posita (v. Deutz, ob. 1139, ML 167–70; LTK 9 [1937] 15; Franks, I, 200–202) quae postea facta est classica, nempe, utrum Filius incarnatus esset si Adam non peccasset.

Cui quaestioni respondit S. Thomas: (1) de supernaturalibus concludi non potest ubi deest revelatio, (2) secundum scripturas Filius homo est factus propter peccatum primi hominis, et ideo (3) convenientius dicitur, non exsistente peccato, incarnationem futuram non fuisse, quamvis (4) Dei potentia per hoc minime limitetur, cum etiam sine peccato Filius incarnari potuisset (*Sum. theol.*, III, q. 1, a. 3).

10 Alia deinde est quaestio de fine incarnationis primario et secundario quae potest vel seorsum poni vel cum praecedente coniungi.

Si seorsum ponitur, quaeritur utrum incarnationis finis primarius fuerit Christi exaltatio an peccatorum reconciliatio. Et primarium fuisse Christi exaltationem tueri solent Scotistae; unde recenter, J.-F. Bonnefoy, O.F.M., *La primauté du Christ selon l'écriture et la tradition*, Romae, 1959.[6]

On the other hand, when all the discussion is about hypothetical necessities, not only can the facts be overlooked (for what is at stake is hypothetical), but it is even fitting to set aside the facts (for the facts by themselves do not include those clear concepts and exact definitions which alone serve rigorous proofs). From here the discussion shifts to merely possible worlds, and since a created intellect knows little about possibilities, as we said above (see *Meaning of the thesis, terms* § 6), and since the human Christ himself, even through his most perfect beatific vision, did not know all that is within the power of the creator (*Summa theologiae*, 3, q. 10, a. 2), it is not surprising that this sort of discussion about necessarily connected possibilities easily becomes sterile.

9 In addition to Anselm's 'necessary' deduction and the hypothetically necessary deductions of other theologians, we must also keep in mind the question raised by Rupert, Abbot of Deutz (who died in 1139), which later became a classic, namely, whether the Son would have been incarnate had Adam not sinned. See ML 167–70; 'Rupert v. Deutz,' *Lexikon für Theologie und Kirche* 9 (1937) 15; Franks, *A History of the Doctrine of the Work of Christ*, vol. 1, 200–202.

To this question St Thomas replies: (1) no conclusions can be drawn about matters supernatural in the absence of revelation, (2) according to the scriptures the Son became man because of the sin of the first man, and therefore (3) it is more appropriate to say that in the absence of sin the incarnation would not have taken place, even though (4) the power of God is in no way limited by this, since even apart from sin the Son could have been incarnate (*Summa theologiae*, 3, q. 1, a. 3).

10 Next there is the question of the primary and secondary purpose of the incarnation, which can be considered either separately or in conjunction with the preceding question.

As considered separately, the question is whether the primary purpose of the incarnation was the exaltation of Christ or the reconciliation of sinners. The Scotists generally maintain that the primary purpose was the exaltation of Christ. Thus recently, Jean-François Bonnefoy, *La primauté du Christ selon l'écriture et la tradition* (Rome: Herder, 1959).[6]

6 English translation, *Christ and the Cosmos*, ed. and trans. Michael D. Meilach (Paterson, NJ: St Anthony Guild Press, 1965).

Huic quaestioni respondendum videtur et finem fuisse Christi exaltationem (Col. 1.18: 'in omnibus ipse primatum tenens') et finem fuisse peccatorum reconciliationem (Col. 1.20: 'per eum omnia reconciliare in ipsum'). Quemadmodum vero haec duo inter se comparentur, dupliciter responderi potest: uno modo, inveniendo definitiones finis primarii et secundarii et eas ad hunc casum applicando; alio modo, ipsum bonum quod est incarnationis finis considerando. Quod si quis primum modum eligit, sat facile definitiones invenit atque applicat sed difficilius probat suas definitiones ex ea sapientia procedere quae per divinam revelationem nobis innotescit. Si autem altero modo proceditur, et facta considerantur et aliqua eorum intelligentia gignitur. Iam vero per sex saecula secundum primum modum disputatum est, et ideo non sine probabilitate censere quis posset alterum modum forte fructuosiorem fore.

11 At quaestio de fine primario et secundario cum quaestione Ruperti coniungi potest, et tunc quaeritur utrum exaltatio Christi ita sit finis primarius incarnationis ut etiam, Adamo non peccante, Filius incarnatus esset.

Quam quaestionem melius omitti censemus, tum quia multas simul ponat quaestiones, tum quia de possibilibus agitur de quibus iudicandis intellectus creatus non videtur esse principium sufficiens (supra, sensus theseos, § 6), tum quia de possibilibus supernaturalibus agitur de quibus prudens est consilium Aquinatis ut, ubi silet revelatio, convenienter sileat etiam theologus (cf. supra § 9).

12 Remanet denique ut methodum Aquinatis recolamus qui *primo* finem statuit, nempe, reparationem generis humani, *deinde* duplicem distinxit necessitatem alicuius ad finem, nempe, necessitatem eius sine quo finis esse non potest, sicut cibi ad conservationem vitae, et necessitatem eius sine quo minus bene et minus convenienter finis attingitur, sicut equi ad iter, *tertio* affirmavit necessariam esse incarnationem ad reparationem generis humani, non ut sit sed ut melius et convenientius sit, *quarto* hanc convenientiam ex auctoritatibus probavit tum secundum quod finis est promotio in bono tum secundum quod finis est remotio mali (*Sum theol.*, III, q. 1, a. 2).

The answer to this question seems to be both: the purpose was the exaltation of Christ ('so that he might come to have first place in everything,' Colossians 1.18), and the purpose was the reconciliation of sinners ('through him to reconcile all things to himself,' Colossians 1.20). The question of how these two are related to each other can be answered in two ways: first, by finding the definitions of 'primary' and 'secondary' and applying them to this case; second, by considering that good itself that is the purpose of the incarnation. If one chooses the first way, it is quite easy to find definitions and apply them, but more difficult to prove that one's definitions proceed from that wisdom that is made known to us through divine revelation. If, however, one chooses the second way, the facts are considered, and some understanding of them emerges. Now, for six centuries disputes have marked the discussions conducted according to the first way, and therefore one might conclude with some degree of probability that the second way would perhaps be more productive.

11 But the question about the primary and secondary purpose can be linked with Rupert's question, and then one asks whether the exaltation of Christ is the primary purpose of the incarnation such that, even had Adam not sinned, the Son would have become incarnate.

In our opinion, it is better to omit this question, because it raises many questions at the same time, because it deals with possibilities about which a created intellect seems unqualified to judge (see above, *Meaning of the thesis, terms*, § 6), and because in discussing supernatural possibilities, we have the prudent advice of Aquinas, that when revelation is silent it is better for a theologian to be silent too (see above, § 9).

12 Finally, it remains to recall the method of Aquinas. *First,* he established the end, namely, the restoration of the human race; *second,* he distinguished a twofold necessity of something for an end, that is, the necessity for that without which the end is impossible to attain, for example, the necessity of food for the preservation of life, and the necessity of that without which the end is less well or less fittingly attained, for example, the necessity of a horse for a journey; *third,* he affirmed that the incarnation was necessary, not in order to restore the human race but that it be restored in a better and more fitting way; and *fourth,* from authorities he proved this fittingness both with respect to the end that is the advancement of good and with respect to the end that is the elimination of evil (*Summa theologiae,* 3, q. 1, a. 2).

Quam methodum sequendam esse censemus, tum quia a possibilibus parum notis abstrahit ut ad facta attendat, tum quia non sola necessaria considerat sed etiam convenientia, et ideo non meram partem sed totam huius quaestionis intelligibilitatem attingere potest.

At quamvis methodum Aquinatis laudemus, quaestionem paulo diversam movemus ut non solius incarnationis sed etiam Domini nostri passionis et mortis et resurrectionis imperfectam quandam atque analogicam intelligentiam (DB 1796, DS 3016) adipiscamur.

### Praenotamen 1 De analogia huius quaestionis[7]

1 Qui intelligit, multa per unum perspicit. Ad quam perspicientiam in difficilioribus attingendam multum iuvat adhibita simpliciorum analogia. Et ideo a quattuor causis aristotelicis ita incipimus ut, perspecta earum applicatione in domo aedificanda, ad intelligentiam oeconomiae salutis procedamus.

2 Quattuor ergo causae sunt: finis, agens, materia, forma.

Et in domo aedificanda finis quidem est forma in materia producenda; agens autem ad hanc formam producendam proportionatur; materia vero lignis, lapidibus, caemento, et si quid aliud, constat; forma denique est stabilis ille partium ordo atque dispositio quae ex materiis adductis, collocatis, transformatis pedetentim efficitur.

Quae quidem omnia ita in oeconomia salutis observantur ut tamen propter rationalitatem materiae et supernaturalitatem formae et singularitatem agentis multae et magnae sint differentiae.

3 Materia ergo in oeconomia salutis est genus humanum peccato originali infectum, actualibus peccatis oneratum, peccati poenis irretitum, a Deo alienatum, et in se divisum tam individualiter quam socialiter.

We believe that this is the method to be followed, both because it leaves aside possibilities that are scarcely known in order to attend to the facts, and because it takes into consideration not only what is necessary but also what is fitting, and so is able to attain not just a partial but a complete understanding of this question.

But while we praise Aquinas's method, we are asking a slightly different question in order to obtain an imperfect and analogical understanding (DB 1796, DS 3016, [ND 132]), not of the incarnation alone, but also of the passion, death, and resurrection of the Lord.

PRELIMINARY NOTE: THE ANALOGY OF THIS QUESTION[7]

1 One who understands grasps several objects in a single view. In order to attain this grasp when more difficult matters are concerned, it will be very helpful to make use of an analogy from simpler matters. Accordingly, we begin with Aristotle's four causes, in order that having seen how they apply in building a house, we may proceed to an understanding of the economy of salvation.

2 These four causes, then, are: end or purpose, agent, matter, and form.

In building a house, the end is the form that is to be produced in the matter; the agent is one who is proportioned to producing this form; the matter consists of the materials: the wood, the stone, the cement, and anything else of the sort; and the form is that stable order and arrangement of the various parts that is produced step by step through the process of gathering together, allocating, and transforming the materials.

In the economy of salvation, all of these elements are present, yet with many great differences owing to the fact that the matter is rational, the form supernatural, and the agent unique.

3 The matter, then, in the economy of salvation is the human race infected by original sin, burdened by actual sins, enmeshed in the penalties of sin, estranged from God, and divided within itself both individually and socially.

7 Although Lonergan designates this the first preliminary note, there are no others.

4 Finis autem est duplex, extrinsecus et intrinsecus; et finis universo creato extrinsecus est ipsum bonum per essentiam seu bonum universale; finis autem universo creato intrinsecus est ordo ipsius universi (*Sum. theol.*, 1, q. 103, a. 2 c. et ad 3m).

Quae magis particulariter sunt declaranda, cum in actuali rerum ordine genus humanum supernaturaliter in finem producatur, et quidem secundum apprehensionem rationis et bonitatem voluntatis.

Quare, finis extrinsecus non est simpliciter extrinsecus sed ipse se creaturae communicat, tum substantialiter in unione hypostatica, tum accidentaliter in dono increato Spiritus sancti et in dono sui ipsius a beatis videndi.

Praeterea, finis intrinsecus ita est ordo universi, ut ipse ordo sit personarum in communicatione boni divini, ut hic ordo efficiatur per sapientiam apprehensionis (sapientis enim est ordinare) et per caritatem voluntatis, ut denique sapientia huius apprehensionis hac in vita sit per fidem sed in vita futura per visionem Dei.

Unde et duo stadia in adeptione finis distinguuntur: primum enim est stadium viatorum, in quo sapientia per fidem habetur; alterum autem est comprehensorum, in quo sapientia per visionem Dei communicatur.

5 Forma proinde in oeconomia salutis est Christus totus, caput et membra. Nam in Christo toto perspiciuntur tum triplex illa communicatio ipsius boni divini, tum ille ordo qui est personarum in communicatione boni divini et qui efficitur per sapientiam apprehensionis et caritatem voluntatis sive secundum stadium huius vitae sive secundum stadium vitae futurae.

6 Quae quidem forma seu finis adeptio in materia humana et peccaminosa non producitur nisi secundum remotionem mali et promotionem in bono. Et cum homines sint creaturae rationales, in iis haec forma non producitur convenienter nisi secundum legem crucis ut, scilicet, mala ex peccatis orta non miraculose secundum potentiam Dei auferantur sed patienter tolerata in occasionem boni maioris transformentur, unde et bonus Pater secundum suam mensuram 'confertam et coagitatam et supereffluentem' (Lc 6.38) convenienter eos in omnibus adiuvet secundum illud, 'Diligentibus Deum omnia cooperantur in bonum' (Rom 8.28).

4 The end is twofold, extrinsic and intrinsic. The extrinsic end of the created universe is the good by essence, the universal good; the intrinsic end of the created universe is the order of the universe itself (*Summa theologiae,* 1, q. 103, a. 2 c. and ad 3m).

This needs to be explained more particularly, since in the actual order of reality the human race is brought to its end supernaturally, and indeed in a way that accords with the apprehension of reason and the goodness of the will.

Therefore, the extrinsic end is not absolutely extrinsic but communicates himself to creation, both substantially in the hypostatic union and accidentally in the uncreated gift of the Holy Spirit and in the gift of himself that is the beatific vision.

Furthermore, the intrinsic end is the order of the universe in a way such that (1) it is an order of persons in the communication of the divine good, (2) this order is brought about through the wisdom of apprehension (to put things in order is the work of the wise) and through the charity of the will, and, finally, (3) the wisdom of this apprehension is attained in this life through faith, and in the life to come through the vision of God.

Thus there are two stages in the attainment of the end: the first is the stage of the wayfarers, in which wisdom is had through faith; the second is the stage of the blessed, in which wisdom is communicated by the vision of God.

5 The form in the economy of salvation is the whole Christ, head and members. For in the whole Christ we grasp both the threefold communication of the divine good and the order brought about among persons in this communication of the divine good through the wisdom of apprehension and charity of will, whether in the stage of this life or in that of the life to come.

6 This form, this attainment of the end, is produced in sinful human matter solely through the elimination of evil and the advancement of good. And since human beings are rational creatures, this form is not produced in them in an appropriate way except through the law of the cross; that is to say, the evils resulting from sin are not miraculously banished through the power of God, but are patiently tolerated and made into an occasion for greater good. Thus does the good Father, following his own good measure, 'pressed down, shaken together and flowing over' (Luke 6.38), help them in fitting ways in all things, according to the scripture, 'all things work together for good for those who love God' (Romans 8.28).

7 Iam vero quae materiam, finem, formam,[8] et convenientem modum formae in materia efficiendae respiciunt ad alios tractatus theologicos pertinent, uti de peccatis, de novissimis, de gratia, de virtutibus, de ecclesia, de re morali, ascetica, et pastorali. Et ideo in praesenti thesi haec non probanda sunt sed brevissime memoranda et deinceps praesupponenda.

Attamen, praeter finem et materiam et formam, alia etiam est causa quae agens dicitur; et in consideratione huius causae quis sit, et qualiter ad formam inducendam proportionetur, et quemadmodum in hunc finem procedat, tota perspicitur convenientia eius quod Dei Filius homo factus, passus, mortuus, et resuscitatus est.

Quis autem sit hic agens, thesi 1a ad 10m, consideravimus ubi de unione hypostatica; qualiter vero ad formam inducendam proportionetur, thesi 11a ad 14m consideravimus, ubi de gratia, scientia, impeccabilitate, et libertate Christi egimus; quemadmodum denique ad hanc formam inducendam de facto processerit, patiendo, moriendo, resurgendo, nunc secundum summam suam convenientiam, quantum possumus, intelligere volumus.

## *Argumentum*

### 1 LEX CRUCIS, PRIMUM ELEMENTUM: DE PECCATO ET MORTE

(a) Factum peccati universale, tam in Iudaeis quam in gentibus, descripsit S. Paulus, Rom 1.18–3.20.

(b) Hominem carnalem sub peccato venumdatum descripsit idem, Rom 7.14–24; unde 'nos omnes aliquando conversati sumus in desideriis carnis nostrae, facientes voluntatem carnis et cogitationum, et eramus natura filii irae sicut et caeteri' (Eph 2.3).

(c) Mortem esse poenam peccati, diabolum autem et Adam fuisse originem tum peccati tum poenae, docent scripturae: 'in quocumque die comederis ex eo, morte morieris' (Gen 2.15, 3.19); 'invidia autem diaboli mors intravit in orbem terrarum' (Sap 2.24); 'per unum hominem peccatum in hunc mundum intravit, et per peccatum mors' (Rom 5.12); 'finis illorum mors est; stipendia peccati mors' (Rom 6.21–23).

7 However, what pertains to the matter, the end, the form,[8] and the suitable ways of producing the form in the matter, is dealt with in other theological treatises, such as the treatise on sin, on eschatology, on grace, on the virtues, on the church, and on moral, ascetical, and pastoral theology. In this present thesis, therefore, these doctrines need not be proved but briefly noted and henceforth presupposed.

Still, in addition to matter and form there is another cause, which is called the agent. And by considering who this cause is, how he is the one who is qualified to induce the form, and how he proceeds to attain this end, we grasp how entirely fitting it is that the Son of God became man, suffered, died and rose again.

But we have already considered who this agent is, in the first ten theses in *The Incarnate Word*, where we treated the hypostatic union; and we considered how he is proportioned to inducing the form in theses 11 through 14, which dealt with Christ's grace, knowledge, sinlessness, and freedom. How as a matter of fact he did go about inducing this form, by his suffering, dying, and rising, is what we wish to understand now in its supreme appropriateness, so far as we are able to do so.

### *The argument*

#### 1 THE LAW OF THE CROSS, FIRST ELEMENT: SIN AND DEATH

(a) The universal fact of sin, in both Jews and Gentiles, has been described by St Paul, Romans 1.18–3.20.

(b) The same writer described the carnal human being as being in bondage to sin (Romans 7.14–24); hence, 'All of us once lived ... in the passions of our flesh, following the desires of flesh and senses, and we were by nature children of wrath, like everyone else' (Ephesians 2.3).

(c) Scripture teaches that death is the penalty for sin, and that the devil and Adam were the source of both sin and its penalty: 'in the day that you eat of it you shall die' (Genesis 2.17; see 3.19); 'through the devil's envy death entered the world' (Wisdom 2.24); 'just as sin came into the world through one man, and death came through sin' (Romans 5.12); 'the end of those things is death ... the wages of sin is death' (Romans 6.21–23).

8 The 1960 edition has 'formam,' but 1961 and 1964 omit it. It has been restored.

## 2 LEX CRUCIS: MORTIS TRANSFORMATIO

(a) Antithesis primi et novissimi Adam: 1 Cor 15.20–22, Rom 5.12–21. Peccato et morti in Adamo successerunt resurrectio et gratia in Christo.

(b) Quae quidem successio non saltus est in novas res sed ipsius mortis transformatio.

Mors enim Christi erat ut resurgeret: 'pono animam meam ut iterum sumam eam' (Io 10.17). Propter obedientiam usque ad mortem Deus exaltavit eum et dedit ei nomen quod est super omne nomen (Phil 2.9). Propter passionem mortis gloria et honore est coronatus (Heb 2.9).

(c) Quae mortis in vitam transformatio non solum Christi causa fuit sed etiam nostri.

Nam 'traditus est propter delicta nostra et resurrexit propter iustificationem nostram' (Rom 4.25). Carni et sanguini participavit 'ut per mortem destrueret eum qui habebat mortis imperium, id est diabolum, et liberaret eos qui timore mortis per totam vitam obnoxii erant servituti' (Heb 2.14–15). 'Reconciliati sumus Deo per mortem Filii eius' (Rom 5.10); 'in quo habemus redemptionem per sanguinem eius, remissionem peccatorum' (Eph 1.7; cf. Col 1.14); 'qui dedit semet ipsum pro nobis, ut nos redimeret ab omni iniquitate et mundaret sibi populum acceptabilem, sectatorem bonorum operum' (Tit 2.14; cf. Eph 5.25–27).

(d) Neque transformatio mortis per Christum ita propter bona nostra spiritualia fuit ut excluderentur bona corporalia.

Nam 'mori lucrum' (Phil 1.21); et 'cum ... mortale hoc induerit immortalitatem, tunc fiet sermo, qui scriptus est: "Absorpta est mors in victoria"' (1 Cor 15.55). Unde in symbolis fidem profitemur in resurrectionem carnis seu mortuorum (DB 2, 6, 86; DS 11, 30, 150).

## 3 MORTIS TRANSFORMATIO DUO IMPORTAT.

(a) Mortis transformatio in Christo peracta considerari potest vel (1) tamquam in homine singulari vel (2) tamquam in capite corporis sui; et utroque modo inveniuntur duo, nempe (1) voluntaria mali vel poenae susceptio et (2) subsequens benedictio Dei Patris.

## 2 THE LAW OF THE CROSS: THE TRANSFORMATION OF DEATH

(a) The antithesis between the first and the last Adam: 1 Corinthians 15.20–22; Romans 5.12–21. Sin and death in Adam are succeeded by resurrection and grace in Christ.

(b) This succession is not a jump to something new but the transformation of death itself.

For Christ died with a view to rising again: 'I lay down my life in order to take it up again' (John 10.17). Because of his obedience even unto death, 'God highly exalted him and gave him the name that is above every name' (Philippians 2.9). '... crowned with glory and honor because of the suffering of death' (Hebrews 2.9).

(c) This transformation of death into life was not only for Christ's sake but also for ours.

For 'he was handed over to death for our trespasses and was raised for our justification' (Romans 4.25). He shared our flesh and blood 'so that through death he might destroy the one who has the power of death, that is, the devil, and free those who all their lives were held in slavery through the fear of death' (Hebrews 2.14–15). 'We were reconciled to God through the death of his Son' (Romans 5.10); 'in him we have redemption through his blood, the forgiveness of our trespasses' (Ephesians 1.7; see Colossians 1.14). 'He it is who gave himself for us, that he might redeem us from all iniquity and purify for himself a people of his own who are zealous for good deeds' (Titus 2.14; see Ephesians 5.25–27).

(d) The transformation of death through Christ was for the goods of the body as well as for those of the spirit.

For 'to die is gain' (Philippians 1.21); and 'when this mortal body puts on immortality, then the saying that is written will be fulfilled: "Death has been swallowed up in victory"' (1 Corinthians 15.54). Hence in the creeds we profess our faith in the resurrection of the body, that is, of the dead (DB 2, 6, 86; DS 11, 30, 150; [ND 5, 12]).

## 3 THE TRANSFORMATION OF DEATH HAS A TWOFOLD SIGNIFICANCE.

(a) The transformation of death accomplished in Christ can be considered in two ways: (1) in Christ as an individual human being, or (2) in Christ as the head of his body; and in each of these ways there are two aspects, (1) his voluntary acceptance of evil or punishment, and (2) the subsequent blessing of God the Father.

(b) Nam in Christo homine singulari inveniuntur mandatum Patris (Io 10.18), Filii obedientia (Phil 2.8–9, Heb 2.9), calicis acceptatio (Mt 26.38–44), tum aliorum malorum tum mortis perpessio (Mt 26.45–27.50). Quibus successerunt Pater suscitans Iesum a mortuis (Rom 8.11), eumque exaltans (Phil 2.9) et gloria et honore coronans (Heb 2.9) eique dicens, 'Sede a dextris meis donec ponam inimicos tuos scabellum pedum tuorum' (Act 2.34–35). Plura ...

(c) Sed inquantum idem Christus homo est caput corporis sui, impletum est tempus ut Pater mitteret Filium suum (Gal 4.4, Rom 8.3); obedientia Christi est per quam iusti constituentur multi (Rom 5.19); acceptatio Christi est dare animam suam redemptionem pro multis (Mc 10.45, Mt 20.28); mors Christi est oblatio et hostia in odorem suavitatis (Eph 5.2).

Quibus successerunt ex parte Dei Patris per Filium mediatorem effectus universales qui redemptionem ut finem tum hac in vita tum in vita futura constituunt: remissio peccatorum (Act 2.38, Eph 1.7, Col 1.14), reconciliatio (Rom 5.10, 2 Cor 5.19), iustificatio (Rom 3.24, 3.28, 5.1, 8.1, 1 Cor 6.11), et caetera omnia pro quibus gratias agimus Deo Patri 'qui dignos nos fecit in partem sortis sanctorum in lumine, qui eripuit nos de potestate tenebrarum et transtulit in regnum Filii dilectionis suae' (Col 1.12–13).

### 4 EADEM MORTIS TRANSFORMATIO MULTIPLICITER INTELLECTA NOBIS PRAECIPITUR.

(a) Multipliciter intelligitur.

Nam intelligitur secundum sacramentum: 'Consepulti enim sumus cum illo per baptismum in mortem, ut quomodo Christus surrexit a mortuis per gloriam Patris, ita et nos in novitate vitae ambulemus' (Rom 6.4; cf. Col 2.12, 1 Cor 11.26).

Intelligitur moraliter: 'Ita et vos existimate vos mortuos quidem esse peccato, viventes autem Deo in Christo Iesu Domino nostro' (Rom 6.11; cf. Col 3.1–4).

Intelligitur ascetice: 'Si enim secundum carnem vixeritis, moriemini; si autem spiritu facta carnis mortificaveritis, vivetis' (Rom 8.13; cf. 1 Cor 9.27).

(b) In Christ as an individual human being are found the Father's commandment (John 10.18), the obedience of the Son (Philippians 2.8–9; Hebrews 2.9), the acceptance of the chalice (Matthew 26.38–44), and the suffering of many evils, including death (Matthew 26.45–27.50). Following upon all this, we find the Father raising Jesus from the dead (Romans 8.11), exalting him (Philippians 2.9), crowning him with glory and honor (Hebrews 2.9), and saying to him, 'Sit at my right hand until I make your enemies your footstool' (Acts 2.34–35). For a fuller exposition of these points, see *The Incarnate Word* 72–77.

(c) But inasmuch as the same human Christ is the head of his body, the time was fulfilled for the Father to send his Son (Galatians 4.4, Romans 8.3). Through Christ's obedience many would be made just (Romans 5.19). Christ's acceptance is the giving of his life as a ransom for many (Mark 10.45, Matthew 20.28); Christ's death is a fragrant offering and sacrifice (Ephesians 5.2).

Upon all of these there followed the universal effects flowing from God the Father through his Son as mediator, which constitute redemption as end both in this life and in the life to come. These effects are the forgiveness of sins (Acts 2.38, Ephesians 1.7, Colossians 1.14), reconciliation (Romans 5.10, 2 Corinthians 5.19), justification (Romans 3.24, 3.28, 5.1, 8.1, 1 Corinthians 6.11), and all other things for which we give thanks to God the Father, 'who has enabled us to share the inheritance of the saints in the light ... [who] rescued us from the power of darkness and transferred us into the kingdom of his beloved Son' (Colossians 1.12–13).

### 4 THIS SAME TRANSFORMATION OF DEATH, UNDERSTOOD IN SEVERAL WAYS, IS REQUIRED OF US.

(a) It is to be understood in several ways.

It is understood sacramentally: 'Therefore we have been buried with him by baptism into his death, so that just as Christ was raised from the dead by the glory of the Father, so we too might walk in newness of life' (Romans 6.4; see Colossians 2.12, 1 Corinthians 11.26).

It is understood morally: 'So also you must consider yourselves dead to sin and alive to God in Christ Jesus' (Romans 6.11; see Colossians 3.1–4).

It is understood ascetically: 'For if you live according to the flesh, you will die; but if by the Spirit you put to death the deeds of the body, you will live' (Romans 8.13; see 1 Corinthians 9.27).

Intelligitur physice: 'Nostra autem conversatio in caelis est, unde etiam salvatorem exspectamus Dominum nostrum Iesum Christum, qui reformabit corpus humilitatis nostrae configuratum corpori claritatis suae, secundum operationem qua etiam possit subicere sibi omnia' (Phil 3.20–21).

(b) Nobis praecipitur.

Praecipitur ut dilectio inimicorum (Mt 5.28–48), ut cotidiana crucis acceptatio (Mc 8.34, Mt 16.24, Lc 9.23), ut sapientia perdendi animam propter Christum et evangelium ut reapse anima salvetur (Mc 8.35, Mt 16.25, Lc 9.24), secundum exemplum seminis morientis et fructificantis (Io 12.24–25), secundum beatitudinem patientibus promissam (Mt 5.11–12).

(c) Unde ipsa Christi mors nobis est exemplum imitandum.

In primis, ipsa redemptionis revelatio a Domino nostro non est facta nisi ut exemplum differentiae inter mundanos, qui dominari et potestatem exercere volunt, et discipulos suos in quibus maior est minister et primus est omnium servus (Mc 10.42–45, Mt 20.25–28).

S. Petrus eos laudavit, non qui iuste puniuntur, sed qui immerito castigantur, quia sic in vestigiis Domini sequuntur (1 Pet 2.18–25).

S. Paulus, exemplum humilitatis et caritatis quaerens, illud proposuit ex Christo Iesu qui, cum in forma Dei esset, semet ipsum exinanivit formam servi accipiens et obediens factus usque ad mortem crucis (Phil 2.6–8).

Idem nos monet: 'si tamen compatimur ut et conglorificemur' (Rom 8.17). Ipse quaerit iustitiam, non quae ex lege est, sed quae ex fide est Christi Iesu, quae ex Deo est iustitia in fide ad cognoscendum illum et virtutem resurrectionis eius et societatem passionum eius, configuratus morti eius, si quo modo occurrat ad resurrectionem quae est ex mortuis (Phil 3.9–11). Unde et voluit adimplere ea quae desunt passionum Christi (Col 1.24). Nam qui praesciti sunt, ii praedestinantur conformes fieri imaginis Filii sui (Rom 8.29); et ideo communicantes Christi passionibus gaudent, ut et in revelatione gloriae eius exsultent (1 Pet 4.13).

It is understood physically: 'Our citizenship is in heaven, and it is from there that we are expecting a Savior, the Lord Jesus Christ. He will transform the body of our humiliation that it may be conformed to the body of his glory, by the power that also enables him to make all things subject to himself' (Philippians 3.20–21).

(b) This transformation is required of us.

It is required of us as love of one's enemies (Matthew 5.28–48), as the daily acceptance of our cross (Mark 8.34, Matthew 16.24, Luke 9.23), and as the wisdom of losing our life for the sake of Christ and the gospel so as to truly save it (Mark 8.35, Matthew 16.25, Luke 9.24), according to the example of a seed dying and producing fruit (John 12.24–25) and the promise of beatitude to those who have suffered persecution (Matthew 5.11–12).

(c) Hence the death of Christ is an example for us to imitate.

First of all, our Lord himself revealed the very meaning of the redemption on the occasion when he pointed out the difference between the worldly, who want to dominate and wield power, and his disciples, among whom the one who is great is a servant and the one who is first is the slave of all (Mark 10.42–45, Matthew 20.25–28).

St Peter praises, not those who are justly punished, but those who patiently suffer harsh treatment undeservedly, because in that way they are following in the footsteps of the Lord (1 Peter 2.18–25).

Looking for an example of humility and charity, St Paul finds it in Christ Jesus, 'who, though he was in the form of God ... emptied himself, taking the form of a slave ... and became obedient to the point of death – even death on a cross' (Philippians 2.6–8).

Paul also reminds us that if we suffer with Christ we shall be glorified with him (Romans 8.17). He seeks righteousness, not that which comes from the law but through faith in Christ Jesus, the righteousness which is from God based on faith, in order to know Christ and the power of his resurrection and to share in his sufferings by becoming like him in his death, if somehow he may attain resurrection from the dead (Philippians 3.9–11). Thus he also desired to complete what is lacking in Christ's afflictions (Colossians 1.24). For those whom he foreknew he also predestined to be conformed to the image of his Son (Romans 8.29), and therefore they are glad to share in the sufferings of Christ so that they may rejoice exultantly when his glory is revealed (1 Peter 4.13).

(d) Quod exemplum discipuli sequuntur, immo evitare non possunt.

Etsi enim restitutionem Israel exspectabant (Lc 24.21, Act 1.6), tamen virtute supervenientis Spiritus sancti suscepta (Act 1.8, 2.1–4), mox ibant gaudentes a conspectu concilii quia digni habiti sunt pro nomine Iesu contumeliam pati (Act 5.41).

Sed 'omnes qui pie volunt vivere in Christo Iesu persecutionem patientur' (2 Tim 3.12). Nam 'si mundus vos odit, scitote quia me priorem vobis odio habuit. Si de mundo fuissetis, mundus quod suum erat diligeret; quia vero de mundo non estis, sed ego elegi vos de mundo, propterea odit vos mundus' (Io 15.18–19).

Accepto ergo Spiritu sancto, quem mundus non potest accipere (Io 14.17), praedicabant 'Christum crucifixum, Iudaeis quidem scandalum, gentibus autem stultitiam, ipsis autem vocatis, Iudaeis et Graecis, Christum Dei virtutem et Dei sapientiam' (1 Cor 1.23–24). Quae sapientia a Deo (1 Cor 1.30) in mysterio (1 Cor 2. 7) per Spiritum Dei revelatur unde sensum Christi habemus; sed eadem sapientia ab homine animali non percipitur (1 Cor 2.10–16).

In quibus elucet legem crucis duplicem exhibere antithesim, inter carnem nempe humanam atque spiritum et inter sapientiam huius mundi et sapientiam Spiritus Dei (Rom 6.12–23, 8.5–17, 1 Cor 1.18–31).

(e) Sed resurrectionis non minus quam mortis exemplum proponitur.

'Si enim complantati (σύμφυτοι) facti sumus similitudini mortis eius, simul et resurrectionis erimus' (Rom 6.5). Immo, 'Deus omnis gratiae, qui vocavit nos in aeternam suam gloriam in Christo Iesu, modicum passos ipse perficiet, confirmabit, solidabitque' (1 Pet 5.10). Neque sunt condignae passiones huius temporis ad futuram gloriam quae revelabitur in nobis (Rom 8.18). 'Id enim quod in praesenti est momentaneum et leve tribulationis nostrae, supra modum in sublimitate aeternum gloriae pondus operatur in nobis' (2 Cor 4.17). Quamquam enim 'oculus non vidit, nec auris audivit, nec in cor hominis ascendit, quae praeparavit Deus iis qui diligunt illum' (1 Cor 2.9), etiam hac in vita addiscere possumus quo 'diligentibus Deum omnia cooperantur in bonum' (Rom 8.28).

(d) The disciples follow this example; indeed, they cannot avoid it.

Even though they were expecting the restoration of Israel (Luke 24.21, Acts 1.6), nevertheless they received power when the Holy Spirit came upon them (Acts 1.8, 2.1–4), and soon afterwards went out from the Sanhedrin rejoicing that they had been deemed worthy to suffer ignominy for the sake of the name of Jesus (Acts 5.41).

But 'all who want to live a godly life in Christ Jesus will suffer persecution' (2 Timothy 3.12). 'If the world hates you, be aware that it hated me before it hated you. If you belonged to the world, the world would love you as its own. Because you do not belong to the world, but I have chosen you out of the world, therefore the world hates you' (John 15.18–19).

So then, after receiving the Holy Spirit, whom the world cannot receive (John 14.17), they preached Christ crucified, 'a stumbling block to Jews and foolishness to Gentiles, but to those who are called, both Jews and Greeks, Christ the power of God and the wisdom of God' (1 Corinthians 1.23–24). This wisdom sent from God (1 Corinthians 1.30), secret and hidden (1 Corinthians 2.7), is revealed by the Spirit of God, so that we have the mind of Christ; but this wisdom is not grasped by the unspiritual (1 Corinthians 2.10–16).

From this it is clear that the law of the cross presents two antitheses, between the flesh and the spirit, and between the wisdom of this world and the wisdom of the Spirit of God (Romans 6.12–23, 8.5–17, 1 Corinthians 1.18–31).

(e) But the resurrection of Christ no less than his death is proposed to us as an example.

'For if we have been united (σύμφυτοι) with him in a death like his, we will certainly be united with him in a resurrection like his' (Romans 6.5). 'After you have suffered a little while, the God of all grace, who has called you to his eternal glory in Christ, will himself restore, strengthen, and establish you' (1 Peter 5.10). And the sufferings of this present time are not worth comparing with the glory about to be revealed in us (Romans 8.18). For 'this slight momentary affliction is preparing us for an eternal weight of glory beyond all measure' (2 Corinthians 4.17). Although 'no eye has seen, nor ear heard, nor the human heart conceived what God has prepared for those who love him' (1 Corinthians 2.9), still we are able to learn that even in this life, 'all things work together for good for those who love God' (Romans 8.28).

5 LEX CRUCIS EST LEX REDEMPTIONIS.

(a) Lex multipliciter dicitur.

Per legem enim intelligi potest nexus qui aliter esse non potest, uti in logica et in metaphysica. Iterum, per legem intelligi potest nexus, qui quidem aliter esse potest, sed in se est positive intelligibilis seu conveniens, et de facto in omnibus particularibus semper verificatur; et eiusmodi sunt leges naturales quae in scientiis empiricis investigantur. Tertio, lex ad ordinem spiritualem pertinere potest, et ita quidem ut neque sit absolute necessaria neque in omnibus particularibus verificatur; et hoc tripliciter. Nam primo modo lex in ordine spirituali potest esse merum praeceptum, quod scilicet non convenit et magis voluntatem et potestatis exercitium quam sapientiam rectamque rationem exprimit. Altero modo, lex in ordine spirituali potest esse praeceptum omnino bonum et conveniens, quod tamen inefficax manet, cum non observetur. Tertio denique modo, lex in ordine spirituali potest esse praeceptum et bonum et efficax et universale, quamvis possibilitatem peccati non excludat; et eiusmodi est lex crucis.

(b) Lex crucis non est absolute necessaria.

Nam absolute potuit Deus non creare et, etiam supposita creatione, potuit Deus mundum facere in quo nulla essent mala; nam potest Deus omne facere quod contradictionem internam non dicit et, quod creatura non peccat, non dicit internam contradictionem.

(c) Lex crucis non habet universalitatem legis empiricae.

Nam eiusmodi leges observantur vi naturae et ideo, ubi exceptio apparet, aut ipsa lex demonstratur hypothesis erronea, aut exceptio probatur esse tantummodo apparens; nisi forte de miraculo agitur.

Sed lex crucis nisi per Spiritum sanctum non agnoscitur (1 Cor 1.18–31, 2.10–16; cf. supra § 4, d). Unde et multi sunt inimici crucis Christi (Phil 3.18) et ii, nostris temporibus, non solum sunt quorum Deus venter est (Phil 3.19) sed etiam quorum philosophia directe et explicite contra crucem Christi elaboratur. Ita humilitas atque mansuetudo christiana a Nietzsche aestimabantur quasi religio servorum qui, ex inveterata sed tacita invidia contra virtutem dominorum, ipsam servilem ignaviam pro virtute habere voluerunt. Ita longanimitas atque patientia christiana a Marx aestimabantur non ex Dei sapientia derivatae sed ex ideologia a divitibus excogitata, quo facilius et divites bonis huius vitae frui possent et pauperes inani spe vitae futurae deciperentur. Qui sane errores eo magis sparguntur

5 THE LAW OF THE CROSS IS THE LAW OF THE REDEMPTION.

(a) 'Law' has several meanings.

'Law' can be understood as a connection that cannot be otherwise, as in logic and in metaphysics. Next, it can be understood as a connection that could indeed be otherwise, but in itself is positively intelligible or fitting, and, de facto, is actually always verified in all particular instances; such are the laws of nature that are investigated by the empirical sciences. Thirdly, there can be laws belonging to the spiritual order that are neither absolutely necessary nor verified in all instances, and this is so in three ways. First, a law in the spiritual order can be a precept and nothing more, one that is simply inappropriate, an expression of will and an exercise of power rather than of wisdom and right reason. Second, a law in the spiritual order can be an entirely good and appropriate precept but one that remains ineffectual, since it is not observed. Third, a law in the spiritual order can be a precept that is good and effective and universal even though not excluding the possibility of sin, and such is the law of the cross.

(b) The law of the cross is not absolutely necessary.

Absolutely speaking, God could have not created, and even supposing creation, God could have made a world in which there would be nothing bad or evil. For God can do anything that does not involve an internal contradiction, and a creature that is sinless is not self-contradictory.

(c) The law of the cross does not have the universality of an empirical law.

Such laws are observed by force of nature, and therefore, when an exception appears, either the law itself is shown to be an erroneous hypothesis or the exception is proven to be only apparent – unless, perhaps, there is question of a miracle.

But the law of the cross is not acknowledged except through the Holy Spirit (1 Corinthians 1.18–31 and 2.10–16; see above, § 4, d). Hence there are many who are enemies of the cross of Christ (Philippians 3.18), and these, in our day, are not only those whose god is the belly (Philippians 3.19), but also those whose philosophy is directly and explicitly devised to counter the cross of Christ. Thus Nietzsche looked upon Christian humility and gentleness as the religion of slaves who, as a result of their deep-seated but silent envy of the power of their masters, have chosen to consider their servile cowardice as a virtue. Marx held that Christian forbearance and patience were derived not from the wisdom of God but from an ideology concocted by the rich in order that they might more easily enjoy the good things of this life and that the poor might be deluded by the empty hope of

et eo altius radices agunt quo manifestius atque saepius ii ipsi qui nomen Christianum profitentur de lege vitae Christianae parum curant.

(d) Lex crucis est et conveniens et efficax.

*Est conveniens.* 'Venit enim Filius hominis quaerere et salvum facere quod perierat' (Lc 19.10). Sed ad gloriam divinam participandam aliter convenit naturam puram vel integram conducere et aliter naturam lapsam. Fieri sane posset de potentia Dei absoluta ut natura lapsa in momento, in ictu oculi, in novissima quadam tuba, ad statum naturae purae vel integrae transmutaretur. Eiusmodi forte erat exspectatio messianica inter Iudaeos olim sparsa. Sed de facto aliter redemptio nostra facta est; et hic alius atque actualis modus sane peccatoribus convenit ut, scilicet, non solum a Deo convertantur sed etiam laboriose se ad Deum convertant, ut ex uno omnes, ex peccatore peccatores, peccatorum stipendia tam socialia quam individualia sustineant et sustinentes in occasionem maioris virtutis cum Christo transmutent. Hoc enim est quod Apostolus praecepit: 'Noli vinci a malo, sed vince in bono malum' (Rom 12.21).

*Est efficax.* Nam lex crucis non est praeceptum a legislatore quodam determinatum atque promulgatum quod aures quidem afficit sed cor immutatum relinquit. Lex crucis praecipitur a Domino nostro atque ab apostolis suis in scripturis sacris; lex crucis inculcatur non verbis tantum sed maxime exemplis iisque maximis; lex crucis in capite ita observata est ut pro omnibus poenis satisfactum sit, pro omnibus peccatis sacrificium oblatum sit, pro omnibus gratiae donis meritum acquisitum sit infinitum, pro omni alienatione a Deo interveniat mediator, sacerdos aeternus, Dominus noster, Patris Filius ut in filios adoptionis recipiamur. Petite et accipietis.

(e) Lex crucis propriam universalitatem habet.

Habet scilicet illam universalitatem quae competit, non legibus quae vi naturae caecae exseruntur, sed legibus qui liberum spiritum in finem conducunt.

'Sicut in Adam omnes moriuntur, ita et in Christo omnes vivificabuntur' (1 Cor 15.22; cf. Rom 5.12–21). Sicut portavimus imaginem terreni, portemus et imaginem caelestis (1 Cor 15.49; cf. supra de schemate Paulino ... Et ipse Dominus noster, non paucis et selectis discipulis legem crucis praecepit, sed 'convocata *turba* cum discipulis suis, dixit eis: "Si quis vult me

a future life. And no doubt these errors become more widespread and deep-rooted the more openly and frequently those who call themselves Christians disregard the law of the Christian life.

(d) The law of the cross is fitting and efficacious.

*It is fitting.* For 'the Son of man came to seek out and to save the lost' (Luke 19.10). But a way fitted to bring fallen nature to share in divine glory differs from a way fitted to pure or integral nature. It is, of course, quite within God's absolute power, 'in a moment, in the twinkling of an eye, at the last trumpet' [1 Corinthians 15.52], to transform fallen nature into the state of pure or integral nature. Such was perhaps the messianic expectation once widely held among the Jews. But in fact our redemption has been accomplished in a different way. And this other way, the actual way, is surely fitting for sinners, because in it they are not only converted by God but also painstakingly convert themselves to God; so that, as all have the same origin and are sinners through the sin of one, all might endure the wages of sin, social as well as individual, and by their endurance change them into occasions of greater virtue in union with Christ. This is what the apostle Paul prescribed: 'Do not be overcome by evil, but overcome evil with good' (Romans 12.21).

*It is efficacious.* For the law of the cross is not a precept drawn up and promulgated by a lawgiver that strikes the ears but leaves the heart unmoved. The law of the cross is enjoined by our Lord and his apostles in sacred scripture. The law of the cross is inculcated not by words alone but especially by example, indeed the most compelling of examples. The law of the cross has been so fully observed on the part of the head that satisfaction has been made for all punishment, sacrifice offered for all sins, infinite merit acquired for all the gifts of grace, and a mediator, the eternal priest, our Lord, the Son of the Father, intercedes on behalf of all who are alienated from God, so that we might be received as children by adoption. Ask and you shall receive.

(e) The law of the cross has its proper universality.

That is to say, it has the sort of universality that is proper not to laws that are enforced by blind nature, but to laws that lead free spirits to their end.

'As all die in Adam, so all will be made alive in Christ' (1 Corinthians 15.22; see Romans 5.12–21). 'Just as we have borne the image of the man of dust, we will also bear the image of the man of heaven' (1 Corinthians 15.49; see 'Paul's Synthetic Pattern,' *The Incarnate Word* 52–65). And our Lord himself taught the law of the cross, not to a few select disciples, but

sequi, deneget semet ipsum et tollat crucem suam et sequatur me'" (Mc 8.34).[9]

(f) Lex crucis est intrinseca redemptionis intelligibilitas.

Intelligibilitas aut extrinseca est aut intrinseca. Et extrinseca intelligibilitas. rei ex fine, ex exemplari, ex agente, et universim ex alio petitur. Sed intrinseca intelligibilitas in ipsa re per se sola perspicitur, sicut et definitio in definito, vel constans rerum nexus in ipsis rebus constanter et convenienter connexis.

Iam vero legem crucis invenimus intrinsece intelligibilem, ut ex peccato sequatur poena, ut poena voluntarie suscepta in medium salutis convertatur, ut ex medio salutis in salutem perveniatur.

Quam intrinsecam intelligibilitatem invenimus non nudam possibilitatem neque vacuam speculationem sed factum, et quidem tum in Christo capite tum in omnibus ei obtemperantibus quibus factus est causa salutis aeternae (Heb 5.9) secundum sacramentalem participationem mortis eius, et moralem, et aesceticam, et physicam (supra, § 4 a), cum ea universalitate quae legi non naturali sed spirituali atque efficaci convenit (supra, § 5 d, e).

(g) Lex crucis est essentia redemptionis.

Essentia enim alicuis est intrinseca eius intelligibilitas. Sed redemptionis intelligibilitas intrinseca est lex crucis, sive Christum caput respicis qui est redemptionis mediator atque causa proportionata, sive membra Christi respicis quae erant redimenda et sunt redempta quoad causam in omnibus, quoad effectum plenum in beatis, et quoad effectum huius vitae in iis qui adhuc peregrinantur a Domino.

(h) Lex crucis aliter in capite et aliter in membris verificatur.

Nam inquantum lex crucis dicit mali seu poenae perpessionem, ex peccato derivatur; sed Christus omnino peccatum nescivit (DB 122, DS 261) et ideo culpam habuit neque originalem neque actualem neque ullo modo

rather, 'He called the *crowd* with his disciples, and said to them, "If any want to become my followers, let them deny themselves and take up their cross and follow me"' (Mark 8.34).[9]

(f) The law of the cross is the intrinsic intelligibility of the redemption.

Intelligibility is extrinsic or intrinsic. The extrinsic intelligibility of a thing is sought from its end, from its exemplary cause, from its agent, and universally from something else. But intrinsic intelligibility is grasped solely in the thing itself per se, as the definition is grasped in the defined, or the regular relation among things is grasped in the things themselves as regularly and fittingly connected.

Now, we find the law of the cross to be intrinsically intelligible in this, that punishment is consequent upon sin, that punishment willingly accepted is converted into the means of salvation, and that through those means salvation is attained.

We find this intrinsic intelligibility to be not a mere possibility nor idle speculation, but a fact: a fact that is verified both in Christ the head and in all those who obey him for whom he has been made the cause of eternal salvation (Hebrews 5.9), through sacramental participation in his death, and through moral, ascetical, and physical participation (§ 4, a, above), having the universality belonging to a law that is not natural but spiritual and efficacious (§ 5, d, e, above).

(g) The law of the cross is the essence of the redemption.

The essence of anything is its intrinsic intelligibility. But the intrinsic intelligibility of the redemption is the law of the cross, whether you are considering Christ the head, the mediator and proportionate cause of the redemption, or the members of Christ who were to be redeemed and have been redeemed – to all of the members, with respect to the cause of the redemption, to the blessed with respect to its full effect, and to those who are pilgrims, away from the Lord [2 Corinthians 5.6], with respect to its effect in this life.

(h) The law of the cross is verified differently in the head and in the members.

For inasmuch as the law of the cross speaks of the endurance of evil or of punishment, it is derived from sin; but Christ knew no sin (DB 122, DS 261, [ND 606/10]) and therefore had no fault, either original or actual, nor did

9 In the 1961 edition, 'turba' ('crowd') was italicized, but not in 1960 or 1964. That emphasis has been restored here: ... not to a few select [but] ... the *crowd*.

susceptam (thesis 16a, praenotamen x); et ideo in Christo mors, peccati poena, non dicitur contracta sed ex propria voluntate suscepta (*Sum. theol.*, III, q. 14, a. 3); et sicut de morte poenarum maxima, ita et de aliis Christi poenis ratiocinandum est.

Inquantum autem lex crucis dicit voluntariam et liberam mali perpessionem, unde malum quodammodo in bono vincitur (Rom 12.21), iam de virtute atque perfectione Christo propria agitur. Quae Christi perfectio per aliam viam quam per malorum perpessionem esse potuit, si quidem ipse culpam habuit nullam. Attamen ita nobis assimilari in omnibus voluit ut sibi eam perfectionis speciem eligeret quam nobis necessariam novit. Et ita intelligi posse videtur quod dicitur decuisse eum passionibus perfici (Heb 2.10) et ex iis quae passus est obedientiam didicisse (Heb 5.8).

Inquantum denique lex crucis dicit bona vincentibus divinitus data, uti sunt omnia dona gratiae et gloriae, haec ita naturam humanam a Filio assumptam excedunt, ut tamen Unigenito Patris ratione personae conveniunt atque competunt. Vide theses 11m et 12m.

Et ideo in Christo homine particulari lex crucis non ex necessitate vel ex debito fuit, si quidem (1) poenam non contraxit sed libere suscepit, et (2) aliam habere potuit perfectionem praeter eam quae in passionibus gignitur atque consummatur, et (3) titulo personae divinae omnia dona gratiae et gloriae ei conveniebant atque competebant.

In nobis autem peccatoribus res omnino aliter se habet.

Non enim malum poenae libere suscipimus sed ex peccato originali et actuali contrahimus.

Neque alia est perfectio nobis propria quam ea quae laboriose attingitur per amotionem mali et ad bonum conversionem.

Neque dona gratiae et gloriae ullo titulo nostra sunt, cum absolute supernaturalia inveniantur et proportionem cuiuslibet purae creaturae simpliciter excedant.

Quibus perspectis, diceres forte legem crucis esse non Christi sed nostram.

Quod aliquatenus veritatem habet inquantum non Christus sed nos poenae debitum contraximus. Sed lex crucis alios melioresque habet aspectus, unde de cruce Domini nostri loqui solemus. Crux enim proprie Christi est, primo, quia ipse fortiter atque perfecte crucem suscepit, deinde, quia per eum et per eius meritum et satisfactionem et sacrificium et mediationem et

he accept fault in any way. See the previous thesis, preliminary note 10. Christ, therefore, did not incur death as punishment for sin, but took it upon himself willingly (*Summa theologiae,* 3, q. 14, a. 3). And the same reasoning holds for his other punishments as for death, the greatest of them all.

However, inasmuch as the law of the cross speaks of the voluntary and freely chosen endurance of evil whereby evil is in some way overcome by good (Romans 12.21), the question now is about the virtue and perfection proper to Christ alone. His perfection could have followed a different path from the endurance of evil, since he was without sin. Yet he willed to be like us in all things, and so he chose for himself the kind of perfection that he knew to be necessary for us. And in this way it seems possible to understand the words of scripture that he was made perfect through his sufferings (Hebrews 2.10) and that he learned obedience through what he suffered (Hebrews 5.8).

Finally, inasmuch as the law of the cross speaks of good things bestowed by God upon the victorious, such as all the gifts of grace and glory, these far surpass the human nature assumed by the Son, and yet they are fitting and suitable to the Father's only Son by reason of his person. See *The Incarnate Word,* theses 11 and 12.

Therefore, in Christ as a particular human being the law of the cross was not a matter of necessity or obligation, since (1) he did not incur punishment but freely took it on, (2) he could have had a perfection other than that born and perfected in suffering, and (3) as a divine person all the gifts of grace and glory were fittingly and rightly his.

In us sinners, however, the matter is altogether different.

We do not freely take the evil of punishment upon ourselves but incur it through original and actual sin.

Nor is any other perfection proper to us than that which is painstakingly achieved by forsaking evil and turning to what is good.

Nor are the gifts of grace and glory ours on any grounds, since they are absolutely supernatural and simply exceed the proportion of any mere creature.

This being so, you may say, perhaps, that the law of the cross is not Christ's but ours.

There is some truth to this, inasmuch as it is not Christ but we who have incurred the debt of punishment. But there are other and nobler aspects to the law of the cross; hence we are accustomed to speak of our Lord's cross. For the cross is properly Christ's, first, because he bravely and perfectly embraced the cross, and secondly, because through him and through his

efficientiam cruci annectuntur tum gratia Dei in cruce perferenda tum gloria cuius spe crux perfertur.

## 6 QUOD CONVENIENTER DEI FILIUS LEGEM CRUCIS SUAM FECIT.

(a) Quod Dei Filius est homo factus, est passus, est mortuus, est resuscitatus, ex symbolis fidei novimus.

Intelligibilitatem intrinsecam huius facti iam addiscimus: haec enim successio incarnationis, mortis, et resurrectionis, nihil est aliud quam lex crucis secundum casum principalem.

At eadem successio ita summa iustitia et summa misericordia peccatoribus convenit ut sine maxima admiratione eam in Domino nostro non deprehendimus. Et ideo de convenientia crucis in Christo quaerimus, ne videamur non sapere ea quae Dei sunt sed ea quae hominum (Mt 16.23).

(b) Iam vero, sicut omnia in sapientiam divini intellectus et in bonitatem divinae voluntatis reducuntur, ita qui convenientiam intelligere quaerit maxime ad sapientiam et ad caritatem attendere debet.

Quae quidem duo ita sunt distinguenda ut tamen neque separentur neque opponantur. Sapientis enim est ordinare, et divinae sapientiae est ordinare omnia. Quae autem ordinantur entia sunt et, cum ens et bonum convertantur, etiam bona sunt; et quidem singularia sunt bona particularia, sed ordinata et simul sumpta ordinem universi eiusque finem intrinsecum faciunt; neque ita a divina sapientia inter se ordinantur ut finem universo extrinsecum praetermittant, si quidem omnia Deum in primis appetunt. Proinde, amare seu diligere est velle bonum alicui; et qui iuste diligit, omnibus et singulis illud bonum vult quod divina sapientia ordinavit et secundum modum atque mensuram a divina sapientia determinatam. Quam ob causam, ita coniunguntur sapientia et caritas ut sine caritate sapientia effectu careat et sine sapientia caritas a recto iustitiae ordine deficit.

(c) Iam vero in lege crucis a Christo suscepta maxime perspicitur convenientia caritatis.

Amicus enim ab amico apprehenditur tamquam 'aliter ipse,' ut scilicet amico bona velit sicut et ipse sibi (Arist. *Eth.*, IX, 1166a 31, 1169b 6). Similiter, S. Augustinus: 'Bene quidam dixit de amico suo, dimidium animae meae' (*Conf.*, IV, 6; ML 32, 698).[10] Et eadem est doctrina S. Thomae qui

merit and satisfaction and sacrifice and mediation and power there are attached to the cross both the grace of God in carrying the cross and the glory in the hope of which the cross is carried.

## 6 IT WAS FITTING FOR THE SON OF GOD TO MAKE THE LAW OF THE CROSS HIS OWN.

(a) The fact that the Son of God was made man, suffered, died, and was raised we know from the creeds.

We have now come to learn the intrinsic intelligibility of this fact: this sequence of events, the incarnation, death, and resurrection, is nothing else than the law of the cross as verified in its principal instance.

But this very sequence so befits sinners in supreme justice and supreme mercy that we marvel to discern it in our Lord. And therefore we ask about the fittingness of the cross in Christ's case, lest we should seem to be wise in human things but not in the things of God (Matthew 16.23).

(b) Now, just as all things are reducible to the wisdom of the divine mind and the goodness of the divine will, so those who seek to understand fittingness must pay attention above all to wisdom and to charity.

These two are to be distinguished without being separated or opposed to each other. For it is the work of the wise to order, and the work of divine wisdom to order all things. But the things that are ordered are beings, and since being and good are convertible, they are also good. And individual beings are particular goods, but when ordered and taken together they constitute the order of the universe and its intrinsic end; nor are they ordered among themselves by divine wisdom to the neglect of the extrinsic end of the universe, since all things seek God above all else. Now, to love is to will good to another; and one who loves justly wills to each and every one that good which divine wisdom has ordained, and does so according to the manner and measure determined by divine wisdom. Wisdom and charity, therefore, are so conjoined that wisdom without charity is ineffective, and charity without wisdom falls short of the right order of justice.

(c) Now in the law of the cross taken up by Christ, the fittingness of charity is seen most clearly.

Friends look upon each other as 'another self,' and so wish good things for their friends just as they do for themselves (Aristotle, *Nicomachean Ethics*, IX, 1166a 31, 1169b 6). So also St Augustine says, 'Someone has rightly described his friend as *dimidium animae meae*, "half of my soul"' (*Confessions*,

effectum amoris docuit esse unionem atque mutuam inhaesionem (*Sum. theol.*, I-II, q. 28, aa. 1 et 2).

Quanta ergo et qualis fuerit dilectio Filii erga nos perspicitur (1) ex eius assimilatione ad nos et ad nostrum statum, (2) ex amore quo pro nobis operatus sit, et (3) ex eo quod nostra crux ita sua facta est ut in nostris perferendis malis cum eo consociari et conformari et coniungi reputemur.

(d) Primo, ergo, Filius nobis assimilari voluit.

Cum enim in forma Dei esset (Phil 2.6), Verbum caro factum est (Io 1.14). Neque caelestem nescio quam carnem assumpsit (Aug., *De Trin.*, XIII, xviii, 23), sed ex muliere (Gal 4.4), ex semine David secundum carnem (Rom 1.3), ex Israelitis, Pauli cognatis, secundum carnem (Rom 9.4–5).

Formam ergo servi accepit (Phil 2.7) et similitudinem carnis peccati (Rom 8.3). Quodammodo corpus peccati habuit, nam in eo corpus peccati destructum est (Rom 6.6), in sua carne damnatum est peccatum (Rom 8.3), et pro nobis peccatum factus est (2 Cor 5.21).

Sub dominio mortis quodammdo erat, nam semel peccato mortuus non iam sub dominio mortis est (Rom 6.9–11). Sub lege factus est (Gal 4.4) ut maledictionem legis subire et benedictio Abrahae fieri posset (Gal 3.13–14). Carnis infirmitatem habuit ut ex ea crucifigeretur (2 Cor 13.4); unde et dictus est carne mortificatus sed spiritu vivificatus (1 Pet 3.18).

Quia pueri communicaverunt carni et sanguini, et ipse similiter participavit eisdem (Heb 2.14), per omnia fratribus assimilatus (Heb 2.17), per omnia pro similitudine tentatus absque peccato (Heb 4.15); quem passionibus perfici decuit (Heb 2.10), ex passionibus obedientiam didicit (Heb 5.8), clamore valido salutem impetravit (Heb 5.7), et redemptionem invenit aeternam (Heb 9.12). Qui enim sanctificat et qui sanctificantur, ex uno omnes (Heb 2.11).

IV, 6; ML 32, 698).[10] And St Thomas's teaching is the same, namely, that the effect of love is union and abiding in one another (*Summa theologiae,* 1-2, q. 28, aa. 1 and 2).

How great and how excellent the Son's love is for us is clearly seen (1) from his becoming like us in our human nature and our human condition, (2) from the love with which he labored on our behalf, and (3) from the fact that our cross has so become his that in bearing the evils afflicting us we are reckoned to be joined with Christ, conformed to him, and united with him.

(d) First, then, the Son willed to become like us.

For though he was in the form of God (Philippians 2.6), the Word was made flesh (John 1.14). And it was not some sort of celestial flesh that he assumed (Augustine, *De Trinitate,* XIII, xviii, 23 [ML 42, 1032–33]), but flesh from a woman (Galatians 4.4), from the seed of David according to the flesh (Romans 1.3), from Paul's people, the Israelites, according to the flesh (Romans 9.4–5).

He took the form of a slave (Philippians 2.7) and the likeness of sinful flesh (Romans 8.3). He had, in some sense, a sinful body, for the sinful body was destroyed in him (Romans 6.6), in his flesh sin was condemned (Romans 8.3), and he was made sin for our sake (2 Corinthians 5.21).

He was also in some way under the dominion of death, for since he died to sin once for all, death no longer has dominion over him (Romans 6.9–11). He was born under the law (Galatians 4.4) so that he might undergo the curse of the law and be able to become the blessing of Abraham (Galatians 3.13–14). He had the weakness of the flesh so that by means of it he might be crucified (2 Corinthians 13.4); hence it was said that he was put to death in the flesh but made alive in the spirit (1 Peter 3.18).

Since, therefore, the children share flesh and blood, he himself likewise shared the same things (Hebrews 2.14), became like his brothers in every respect (Hebrews 2.17), tested as we are in every way, yet without sin (Hebrews 4.15). It was fitting for him to be perfected through his sufferings (Hebrews 2.10); he learned obedience through what he suffered (Hebrews 5.8), he won salvation with a loud cry (Hebrews 5.7), and obtained eternal redemption (Hebrews 9.12). For the one who sanctifies and the ones who are sanctified all have the same Father (Hebrews 2.11).

10 The 'someone' is the poet Horace, speaking of Virgil, *Odes* I, 3, 8.

(e) Nobis assimilatus pro nobis ex dilectione sese obtulit.

Quod et ipse testatus est: 'Maiorem hac dilectionem nemo habet, ut animam suam ponat quis pro amicis suis' (Io 15.13). Quam autem intima, quam tenera fuerit fortissima illa dilectio, explicavit Apostolus comparans dilectionem Christi erga ecclesiam cum dilectione viri erga uxorem et hominis erga carnem propriam (Eph 5.25–30).

Quam dilectionem sicut intus sensit ita foris monstravit. Nos enim novit stultos et tardos corde ad credendum (Lc 24.25). Sed etiam novit quod 'ego si a terra exaltatus fuero, omnia traham ad me ipsum' (Io 12.32).

(f) Ex qua assimilatione atque dilectione factum est ut nos nostram crucem feramus, non soli, non ipsi nobis relicti, sed Christo consociati, Christo conformati, Christo coniuncti.

Praedestinati enim fieri conformes imaginis Filii sui (Rom 8.29), non patimur ut glorificemur, sed compatimur ut conglorificemur (Rom 8.17). Unde illud paradoxon christianis proprium: in passionibus gaudere. Gaudebant discipuli quia digni habiti sunt pro nomine Iesu contumeliam pati (Act 5.41). Gaudebat Paulus in passionibus pro Colossensibus et adimplebat quae deerant passionum Christi in carne sua pro corpore eius quod est ecclesia (Col 1.24). Omnes christiani communicantes Christi passionibus nunc quidem gaudent ut in revelatione gloriae eius exsultent (1 Pet 4.13); socii passionum eius, configurantur morti eius, si quomodo occurrant ad resurrectionem quae est ex mortuis (Phil 3.10–11); 'semper mortificationem Iesu in corpore nostro circumferentes, ut et vita Iesu manifestetur in corporibus nostris' (2 Cor 4.10; cf. vv 7–14, 5.14–15, 6.3–10, Rom 8.35–39, Gal 2.19–20, 3.26–28, 4.19); 'exspoliantes veterum hominem cum actibus suis et induentes novum, eum qui renovatur in agnitionem secundum imaginem eius qui creavit illum; ubi non est gentilis et Iudaeus, circumcisio et praeputium, barbarus et Scytha, servus et liber, sed omnia in omnibus Christus' (Col 3.9–11; cf. Eph 4.22–24).

(g) Quae Filii caritas caritatem Dei revelat atque commendat.

Neque ita Filius nos dilexit ut Pater nos odio habuerit, sed ambo uno Spiritu pariter nos dilexerunt (Aug., *De Trin.*, XIII, xi, 15; ML 42, 1025). Nam ipse Pater prior dilexit nos (1 Io 4.10); cum essemus mortui peccatis, propter nimiam caritatem qua dilexit nos, dives in misericordia (Eph 2.4–5) in Christo erat mundum reconcilians sibi (2 Cor 5.19); et Christum

(e) Having become like us, he offered himself for us out of love.

He himself testifies to this: 'No one has greater love than this, to lay down one's life for one's friends' (John 15.13). The intimacy and tenderness of that most powerful love was explained by Paul by comparing Christ's love for the church to the love of a husband for his wife and of everyone for his or her own body (Ephesians 5.25–30).

As he felt this love within himself, so he manifested it outwardly. For he knew that we were foolish and slow of heart to believe (Luke 24.25). But he also knew that 'I, when I am lifted up from the earth, will draw all things to myself' (John 12.32).

(f) It is by reason of this likeness and this love that we carry our cross, not alone, not left to ourselves, but joined with Christ, conformed to Christ, united with Christ.

For we are predestined to be conformed to the image of his Son (Romans 8.29); we do not suffer that we may be glorified, but we suffer with him that we may be glorified with him (Romans 8.17). Hence the paradox proper to Christians: rejoicing in one's sufferings. The disciples rejoiced that they were deemed worthy to suffer ignominy for the sake of the name of Jesus (Acts 5.41). Paul rejoiced in his sufferings for the sake of the Colossians and in his flesh completed what was lacking in Christ's afflictions for the sake of his body, that is, the church (Colossians 1.24). All Christians sharing the sufferings of Christ rejoice now, that they may rejoice exultantly when his glory is revealed (1 Peter 4.13). They are companions in his sufferings, becoming configured to his death, if somehow they may obtain resurrection from the dead (Philippians 3.10–11); 'always carrying in the body the death of Jesus, so that the life of Jesus may also be made visible in our bodies' (2 Corinthians 4.10; see vv. 7–14, 5.14–15, 6.3–10, Romans 8.35–39, Galatians 2.19–20, 3.26–28, 4.19); stripping off the old self with its practices and clothing themselves with the new self that is being renewed in knowledge according to the image of him who created it; where there is no longer Gentile and Jew, circumcised and uncircumcised, barbarian and Scythian, slave and free, but Christ is all and in all (see Colossians 3.9–11; see also Ephesians 4.22–24).

(g) This love of the Son reveals and demonstrates the love of God.

It is not as if the Son loved us and the Father hated us, but both have loved us equally in the one Spirit (Augustine, *De Trinitate*, XIII, xi, 15; ML 42, 1025). For the Father loved us first (1 John 4.10); even when we were dead through our sins, out of the great love with which he has loved us, being rich in mercy (Ephesians 2.4–5), he was in Christ reconciling the world to

proposuit propitiationem ad ostensionem iustitiae suae ut sit ipse iustus et iustificans (Rom 3.25–26); unde 'commendat caritatem suam Deus in nobis, quoniam cum adhuc peccatores essemus, secundum tempus Christus pro nobis mortuus est' (Rom 5.8).

(h) Quae caritatis convenientia ipsam sapientiae convenientiam demonstrat.

Eatenus enim voluntas est bona, recta, iusta, quatenus ordinem sapientiae ab intellectu determinatum sequitur (*Sum. theol.*, 1, q. 21, a 1, ad 2m). Sed caritas pertinet ad voluntatem. Et ideo excellentia et convenientia caritatis ex excellentia et convenientia sapientiae derivatur.

(i) Sed divina sapientia etiam suam quasi propriam convenientiam habet, quam tamen sacra scriptura magis demonstrat atque laudat quam explicita analysi exponit.

Thema principale videtur esse mysterium divinae voluntatis; cf. D. Deden, *EphTheolLov* 13 (1936) 414; E. Vogt, *Biblica* 37 (1956) 247–57; K. Prümm, *Biblica* 37 (1956) 135–61; art. 'Mystère,' DBS VI, 151–225; ubi alia allegantur. Conclusio generalis: in NT mysterium (sensu principali) dicit secretum Dei consilium.

Quod secretum consilium, aeternis temporibus tacitum, nunc secundum praeceptum aeterni Dei ad obeditionem fidei patefactum et in cunctis gentibus cognitum est (Rom 16.25–26). Quod pietatis mysterium 'manifestum est in carne, iustificatum est in spiritu, apparuit angelis, praedicatum est in gentibus, creditum est in mundo, assumptum est in gloria' (1 Tim 3.16). Quod est 'Christus in vobis, spes gloriae, quem nos annuntiamus' (Col 1.27–28); quod est Dei Patris et Christi Iesu, in quo sunt omnes thesauri sapientiae et scientiae absconditi (Col 2.2–3). Quod est omnia instaurare in Christo (Eph 1.9–10), et temporalem esse caecitatem in Israel (Rom 11.25–32), et gentes esse coheredes et concorporales et comparticipes promissionis eius (Eph 3.3–4, 3.6). Quod regni mysterium ab excaecatis non agnoscitur (Mc 4.11–12, Is 6.9–10, Io 12.40, Act 26.28), sicut crucis mysterium mundanae sapientiae opponitur (1 Cor 1.23–25) et per Spiritum sanctum revelatur (1 Cor 2.10–16).

Unde et S. Paulus: 'O altitudo divitiarum sapientiae et scientiae Dei, quam incomprehensibilia sunt iudicia eius et investigabiles viae eius. Quis enim

himself (2 Corinthians 5.19); and he put forward Christ as a sacrifice of atonement to show his justice, that he might be both just and justifying (Romans 3.25–26). Thus, 'God proves his love for us in that while we were still sinners Christ died for us' (Romans 5.8).

(h) The fittingness of charity shows the fittingness of wisdom.

For the will is good, upright, and just insofar as it follows the order of wisdom determined by the intellect (*Summa theologiae,* 1, q. 21, a. 1, ad 2m). But charity pertains to the will, and therefore the excellence and fittingness of charity flows from the excellence and fittingness of wisdom.

(i) But divine wisdom also has in a way its own proper fittingness, which, however, sacred scripture demonstrates and praises rather than expounds in an explicit analysis.

Its principal theme seems to be the mystery of the divine will. See D. Deden, 'Le "mystère" paulinien,' *Ephemerides theologicae Lovanienses* 13 (1936) 405–42, at 414; E. Vogt, '"Mysteria" in textibus Qumrān,' *Biblica* 37 (1956) 247–57; K. Prümm, 'Zur Phänomenologie des paulinischen Mysterion und dessen seelischer Aufnahme. Eine Übersicht,' *Biblica* 37 (1956) 135–61; K. Prümm, 'Mystères,' DBS VI, 151–225, where further references are given. The general conclusion is that in the New Testament *mysterium* in its primary meaning refers to the hidden plan of God.

This hidden plan 'was kept secret for long ages but is now disclosed … made known to all the Gentiles, according to the command of the eternal God, to bring about the obedience of faith' (Romans 16.25–26). This 'mystery of our religion … was revealed in flesh, justified in spirit, seen by angels, proclaimed among Gentiles, believed in throughout the world, taken up in glory' (1 Timothy 3.16). This mystery 'is Christ in you, the hope of glory, … whom we proclaim' (Colossians 1.27–28). It is the mystery of God the Father and Christ Jesus, in whom are hidden all the treasures of wisdom and knowledge (Colossians 2.2–3). It is the plan for the restoration of all things in Christ (Ephesians 1.9–10) and for the temporary blindness of Israel (Romans 11.25–32), and for the Gentiles to be coheirs, members of the same body, and sharers in the same promise with Christ (Ephesians 3.3–4, 3.6). This mystery of the kingdom is not acknowledged by those who have been blinded (Mark 4.11–12, Isaiah 6.9–10, John 12.40, Acts 26.28), just as the mystery of the cross is opposed to worldly wisdom (1 Corinthians 1.23–25) and is revealed through the Holy Spirit (1 Corinthians 2.10–16).

As St Paul exclaims, 'O the depth of the riches and the wisdom and knowledge of God! How unsearchable are his judgments and how

cognovit sensum (νοῦν) Domini? Aut quis consiliarius eius fuit? Aut quis prior dedit illi, et retribuetur ei? Quoniam ex ipso et per ipsum et in ipso (εἰς αὐτὸν) sunt omnia; ipsi gloria in saecula. Amen' (Rom 11.33–36).

Et tamen idem Paulus: 'Quis cognovit sensum (νοῦν) Domini, qui instruat eum? Nos autem sensum (νοῦν) Christi habemus' (1 Cor 2.16). Unde et Ephesios adhortatus est 'virtute corroborari in interiorem hominem, Christum habitare per fidem in cordibus vestris; in caritate radicati et fundati, ut possitis comprehendere cum omnibus sanctis ... scire etiam supereminentem scientiae caritatem Christi, ut impleamini in omnem plenitudinem Dei' (Eph 3.16–19).

(j) Quam Dei sapientiam sic exposuit S. Augustinus:

'Neque enim omnipotens Deus ... rerum cui summa potestas, cum summe bonus sit, ullo modo sineret mali aliquid esse in operibus suis, nisi usque adeo esset omnipotens et bonus, ut bene faceret et de malo.' *Enchiridion*, c. XI, ML 40, 236.

Et iterum idem: 'Melius enim iudicavit de malis bene facere quam mala nulla esse permittere.' *Enchiridion*, c. XXVII, ML 40, 245.

Quo quid profundius ab homine dici posset? Potuit Deus mundum creare in quo nulla essent mala, sed melius iudicavit de malis bene facere quam mala nulla esse permittere. Et quid aliud est 'de malis bene facere' praeter legem crucis? Maluit ergo Deus legem crucis quam mala nulla esse permittere. Et ita maluit ut tamen proprio Filio suo non pepercisset sed pro nobis omnibus tradidisset illum (Rom 8.32). Eo pervenimus ut quodammodo videamus unum esse mysterium et divinae sapientiae et divinae caritatis. Eo pervenimus ut quodammodo videamus unam esse et divinam severitatem quae disiunctionem, aut satisfactio aut poena, decrevit (*Sum. theol.*, III, q. 47, a. 3, ad 1m) et abundantiorum illam misericordiam (ibid., q. 46, a. 1, ad 3m) quae proprium Filium nobis dedit (et cum eo omnia, Rom 8.32) ut pro nobis et per nos et nobiscum satisfaceret.

(k) Sed ad alium aspectum divinae sapientiae transeundum est. Nam ipsa lex crucis impossibilitatem quandam dicere videtur: non potest arbor bona malos fructus facere, neque arbor mala bonos fructus facere (Mt 7.18); vel, uti dicunt philosophi, nihil in potentia se reducit in actum, et multo minus de potentia obedientiali in actum supernaturalem; quemadmodum ergo

inscrutable his ways! "For who has known the mind (νοῦν) of the Lord? Or who has been his counselor?" "Or who has given a gift to him, to receive a gift in return?" For from him and through him and to him (εἰς αὐτὸν) are all things. To him be the glory forever. Amen' (Romans 11.33–36).

And yet Paul also says, 'Who has known the mind (νοῦν) of the Lord so as to instruct him? But we have the mind of Christ' (1 Corinthians 2.16). Thus he also exhorted the Ephesians 'that you may be strengthened in your inner being with power ... and that Christ may dwell in your hearts through faith, as you are being rooted and grounded in love. I pray that you may have the power to comprehend with all the saints ... and to know the love of Christ that surpasses knowledge, so that you may be filled with all the fullness of God' (Ephesians 3.16–19).

(j) St Augustine explains this wisdom of God as follows:

'The all-powerful God ... who has supreme power over all things, since he is supremely good, would by no means allow anything evil in his works, unless he were so all-powerful and so good as to produce good even out of evil' (*Enchiridion*, c. XI, ML 40, 236).

And again: '[God] judged that it was better to produce good out of evils than to let no evils occur' (ibid. c. XXVII, ML 40, 245).

What could anyone say that is more profound? God could have created a world in which there would be no evils, but he thought it better to draw good things out of evil than to allow no evils to be. And what is it 'to draw good out of evil' if not the law of the cross? God, therefore, preferred the law of the cross to prohibiting all evils. And yet in so preferring he did not spare his own Son but handed him over for the sake of us all (Romans 8.32). We have reached the point now where we see in some way that the mystery of divine wisdom and that of divine love are one and the same. We have reached the point, too, where we see, in some way, that one and the same are both the divine severity which decreed the disjunction 'either satisfaction or punishment' (*Summa theologiae*, 3, q. 47, a. 3, ad 1m) and that more abundant divine mercy (ibid. q. 46, a. 1, ad 3m) which has given us his own Son (and with him all things, Romans 8.32) in order to make satisfaction for us and through us and with us.

(k) But we must go on to consider another aspect of divine wisdom. The law of the cross itself seems to express an impossibility: a good tree cannot produce bad fruit, nor a bad tree good fruit (Matthew 7.18); or, in philosophical parlance, nothing that is in potency reduces itself to act, much less obediential potency to supernatural act. How, then, would it be possible for

fieri possit ut natura lapsa et peccatrix per voluntatem bonam mala vincat et ad gloriam Dei participandam perveniat.

Sane sine Deo, primo agente, reparatio generis humani fieri non potuit: non enim de spinis colliguntur uvae aut de tribulis ficus (Mt 7.16). Sed apud Deum possibile est omne verbum (*Sum. theol.*, I, q. 25, a. 3). Non autem placuit Deo ut ipse immediate secundum suam omnipotentiam de malis arboribus bonos fructus colligeret; sed olivam voluit in qua insereretur oleaster (Rom 11.17), et vitem voluit in qua manerent palmites (Io 15.1–6), et Christum caput voluit in quo viverent membra et implerentur in omnem plenitudinem Dei. Iam supra diximus (§ 5, h) aliter in Christo esse legem crucis et aliter in nobis; quibus differentiis nunc et alia est addenda, nempe eam in Christo fuisse uti in causa redemptionis sed in nobis uti in effectu.

Voluit enim divinam sapientiam non solum salutem nobis dare sed etiam causam salutis (Heb 5.9). Filios adoptare voluit mediante Filio dilecto (Io 16.27, 17.23, 17.26); Spiritum veritatis (Io 14.17, 16.13) et caritatis (Rom 5.5) effundere voluit mediante Filio (Act 2.33) qui Spiritum mittere potuit (Io 15.26); gratiam et gloriam dare voluit mediante persona divina in assumpta natura, cui gratia et gloria proprie convenirent et competerent (thesibus 11a et 12a); indignis et peccatoribus dare voluit, sed non qua indignis neque qua peccatoribus, et ideo per proprium Filium iis procuravit et obedientiae meritum et redemptionem a servitute culpae et satisfactionem pro reatu poenae et sacrificium reconciliationis (*Sum. theol.*, III, q. 48, a. 6, ad 3m).

### *Scholion 1: De fine incarnationis*

1 De fide est Filium esse incarnatum propter nos homines et propter nostram salutem (DB 86, DS 150). Et ideo docent omnes Catholici finem incarnationis fuisse redemptionem.

Disputatur autem de fine primario et secundario utrum sit exaltatio Christi an peccatorum reconciliatio. Vide Sententias, 9–11.

fallen and sinful nature to overcome evils through a good will and come to share in the glory of God?

Certainly without God, the first agent, there could be no restoration of the human race: grapes are not gathered from thorns or figs from thistles (Matthew 7.16). But with God all things are possible (*Summa theologiae,* 1, q. 25, a. 3). But God did not wish to collect good fruit directly from bad trees through his omnipotence; rather, he willed that there should be an olive tree in which the wild olive would be inserted (Romans 11.17) and a vine in which branches would abide (John 15.1–6), and willed that Christ be the head in which the members would live and would be filled with all the fullness of God. We said above (§ 5, h) that the law of the cross is in Christ and in us in different ways; and to these we must add a further difference, namely, that it was in Christ as in the cause of the redemption and is in us as in the effect.

God willed that divine wisdom give us not only salvation but also the cause of salvation (Hebrews 5.9). He willed to adopt children through the mediation of his beloved Son (John 16.27, 17.23, 17.26); he willed to pour out the Spirit of truth (John 14.17, 16.13) and of charity (Romans 5.5) through the mediation of the Son (Acts 2.33), who was able to send the Spirit (John 15.26). He willed to give grace and glory through the mediation of a divine person in an assumed nature, to whom grace and glory are properly fitting and due (*The Incarnate Word,* theses 11 and 12). He willed to give them to unworthy sinners, but not as unworthy nor as sinners, and therefore through his own Son he procured for them the merit of obedience, redemption from slavery to sin, satisfaction for the guilt of punishment, and the sacrifice of reconciliation (*Summa theologiae,* 3, q. 48, a. 6, ad 3m).

### *Scholion 1: The purpose of the incarnation*

1 It is an article of faith that the Son became man for us and for our salvation (DB 86, DS 150, [ND 12)]. Hence all Catholics teach that the end or purpose of the incarnation was the redemption.

There is a dispute, however, as to which end is primary and which secondary, the exaltation of Christ or the reconciliation of sinners. See *Opinions,* above, §§ 9–11.

2 Ad solutionem huius quaestionis praemittendum esse videtur quod (1) bonum ordinis est bonum quoddam atque finis, et (2) institui haud potest comparatio inter bonum ordinis est bona ordinata.

3 Primo, ergo, bonum ordinis est bonum quoddam atque finis.

Exemplo sit res oeconomica in qua facile distinguuntur bona particularia et bonum ordinis. Bona enim particularia sunt vel res vel rerum usus vel ministeria quae pretio venumdantur. Bonum autem ordinis est tota illa complexio omnium operationum oeconomicarum quae ita inter se ordinantur et ita mutuo se complent ut totus processus feliciter devolvatur.

Ubi notas: bonum ordinis non consistit in materiis, in lapidibus, lignis, ferro, etc.; non consistit in instrumentis, in viis ferreis, officinis, machinis, etc.; non consistit in vigore vel bona voluntate opificum, in sollertia artificum, in astutia vendentium et ementium, in proprietate disponibili capitalistarum, etc.; non consistit in bonis rationis, in libris de re oeconomica, in legibus, praeceptis, exhortationibus, in habitu scientiae apud professores; sed in eo consistit quod haec omnia sunt actualiter talia ut de facto habeatur non depressio sed felix processus.

4 Quod particulariter in re oeconomica illustravimus, omnino generaliter dici potest.

Bonum inde ab Aristotele dicitur id quod omnia appetunt.

Quod tamen dupliciter considerari potest: uno modo, inquantum singula appetibilia ad singulos appetitus referuntur, et sic concipiuntur bona particularia; alio modo, inquantum ex ordine particulari practico appetendi et attingendi transitur in ordinem universalem ubi intellectu apprehenduntur ut bona non solum ipsa appetibilia sed etiam appetitus et appetens et appetitiones et recta in his omnibus subordinatio et coordinatio, et sic concipitur bonum a bonis particularibus non sane separatum sed tamen distinctum, quod bonum ordinis nominatur.

Unde S. Thomas ordinem universi reputavit bonum et finem intrinsecum ipsius universi (*Sum. theol.*, 1, q. 103, a. 2, ad 3m) et optimum in rebus exsistens (ibid. q. 15, a. 2); immo, iudicavit quod perfectius participat divinam bonitatem et repraesentat eam totum universum quam alia quaecumque creatura (ibid. q. 47, a. 1 c.; cf. tamen q. 93, a. 2, ad 3m).

2 It seems that the solution to this question should be prefaced by the following points: (1) the good of order is a good and an end, and (2) no comparison can be made between the good of order and the goods that are ordered.

3 First, then, the good of order is a good and an end.

Take economics as an example, in which it is easy to distinguish between particular goods and the good of order. Particular goods are either things or the use of things or services for which payment is made. But the good of order is that entire complex of all economic operations that are so ordered among themselves and so mutually complementary that the whole process prospers.

Note that the good of order does not consist in materials such as stone, wood, iron, and such, nor in tools, railways, factories, machinery, and so forth, nor in an energetic and willing work-force, the skill of craftsmen, the shrewdness of buyers and sellers, or the disposable assets of capitalists; nor does it consist in intellectual property, in books on economics, in legislation, regulations, or exhortations, or in the store of knowledge had by professors. Rather, it consists in this: that all these things are actually such that there is in fact prosperity instead of a depression.

4 What we have illustrated in particular from economics can be applied quite generally.

Ever since Aristotle, 'good' has been said to be that which all things desire.

This can be considered in two ways: (1) inasmuch as particular desirable goods are related to particular desires, whence we have the concept of particular goods; (2) inasmuch as there is a transition from the particular practical order of desiring and obtaining to a universal order where the intellect apprehends as goods not only the desirable things themselves but also the desires, the desirers, and their desiring, and the correct subordination and coordination of all of these. Thus we conceive a good that is distinct, but not separate, from particular goods, which is called the good of order.

Hence St Thomas considered the order of the universe to be a good and the intrinsic end of the universe itself (*Summa theologiae,* 1, q. 103, a. 2, ad 3), indeed to be the highest good existing among all created things (ibid. q. 15, a. 2). He judged that the universe as a whole more perfectly shares in divine goodness and more perfectly represents it than does any individual creature whatsoever (ibid. q. 47, a. 1 c.; but see q. 93, a. 2, ad 3m).

5 Proinde, agnito bono ordinis, statim constat inter se non comparari bonum ordinis et bona particularia. Aliud bonum particulare alio particulari melius esse potest, et ita iure praeponuntur bona animae bonis corporis, et bona corporis bonis exterioribus. Similiter, aliud ordinis bonum alio melius esse potest, et sic inter se comparari possunt capitalismus et socialismus, systema docendi in hac universitate et in illa, etc. Sed nisi ineptorum non est quaerere utrum melior sit via ferrea quam capitalismus, vel hic professor quam illud docendi systema.

6 Iam vero redemptio est restitutio ordinis lapsi.

Qua in restitutione primatum omnem tenet Christus. Ipse enim est caeteris causa salutis. Ipse in salute adepta et primum locum et omnem praeeminentiam iure habet. Omnibus ergo modis bona particularia Christi sunt excellentiora quam bona particularia aliis quibuslibet creaturis concessa.

Quod tamen Christus primum locum habet tum in causando tum in fruendo, hoc ex ordine est. Sine ordine non datur primus sicut non datur ultimus vel medius. Sine ordine non datur causa sicut non datur effectus vel medium. Caput sane membris praecellit, sed sine ordine neque caput neque membra distinguuntur vel ordinantur.

7 Quaerenti ergo de fine incarnationis respondendum est Deum intendisse bonum ordinis universi restitutum, et secundum hoc vere dicitur redemptio fuisse finis primarius incarnationis; praeterea, eo ipso quod Deus hoc ordinis bonum intendit, etiam bona particularia et ordinata intendit; et si haec bona particularia inter se comparantur, sicut excellentius est bonum Christo intentum quam bona caeteris creaturis intenta, ita dicendum esse finem particularem primarium fuisse bonum Christi et fines particulares secundario fuisse bona aliorum.

8 Denique, cum voluntaristae de sapientia et ordine parum intelligant, mirum non est hanc quaestionem e Scotistis provenisse.

5 So then, once the good of order is recognized, it is immediately clear that the good of order and particular goods are incommensurable. One particular good can be better than another particular good, and so the goods of the soul are rightly preferred to the goods of the body, and the goods of the body to external goods. Similarly, one good of order can be better than another good of order, and so one can compare capitalism and socialism, or the curriculum of this university and that of another, and so on. But it is silly to ask whether a railway is better than capitalism, or this professor better than that curriculum.

6 Now, redemption is the restoration of a fallen order.

In this restoration Christ has the whole primacy, for he is the cause of the salvation of all the rest. He rightly holds the first place and every preeminence in the salvation accomplished. In every way, therefore, the particular goods belonging to Christ are more excellent than the particular goods granted to any other creature whatsoever.

But the fact that Christ has first place both in causing and in enjoying is because of order. For without order there is no first, just as there is no last or middle. Without order there is no cause, just as there is no effect or means. The head, no doubt, is more excellent than the members, but without order head and members can neither be distinguished nor ordered.

7 To one, therefore, who asks about the end of the incarnation, the answer must be that God intended the restoration of the good of order of the universe, and accordingly it is truly said that redemption was the primary end of the incarnation; furthermore, by the very fact that God intended this good of order, he also intended the ordered and particular goods [that belong to it]; and if these particular goods are compared with one another, then just as the good intended for Christ is more excellent than the goods intended for other creatures, so it must be said that the primary particular end was Christ's good and the secondary particular ends were the goods of the others.

8 Finally, since voluntarists have little understanding of wisdom and order, it is not surprising that this question came from the Scotists.

### *Scholion II: De causa peccati*

1 Saepius diximus omnia ex infallibili Dei scientia, ex efficaci eius voluntate, et irresistibili eius actione necessitate conditionata provenire. Unde concludendum esse videtur Deum esse causam infallibilem, efficacem, irresistibilem omnis peccati. Quod non solum in se inconveniens est sed etiam non parum obscurat illam divinam sapientiam atque caritatem quam in redemptione et in lege crucis laudavimus.

2 Cuius difficultatis solutio in eo esse videtur quod exacte perspicitur quo sensu peccatum habeat causam. Quatenus enim peccatum causam habet, eatenus in Deum omnium causatorum causam reducitur. Quatenus autem ab intelligibilitate causae et causati deficit peccatum, eatenus in Deum reduci non potest. Quatenus denique peccatum in Deum reduci non potest, eatenus intelligitur quod S. Thomas docet Deum neque directe neque indirecte malum culpae velle sed id tantummodo permittere (*Sum. theol.*, I, q. 19, a. 9 c. et ad 3m).

3 Causa ergo aut intrinseca aut extrinseca est.

Iam vero peccatum (intellige formale formalis peccati seu malum culpae) non est ens et bonum sed entis et boni privatio.

Neque est rationalis quaedam et intelligibilis boni privatio. Haec enim privatio in voluntate est: neque in voluntate invenitur quatenus appetitus rationalis est et intellectum sequitur, sed solummodo quatenus voluntas a rationalitate sua deficit et dictamen rectae rationis non sequitur. Similiter, quod in voluntate est etiam in ipso volente est; sed peccatum in volente est, non quatenus est creatura rationalis, sed quatenus a rationalitate creaturae rationalis deficit.

Quam ob causam, quaerenti cur peccatores peccent, cur Adam peccaverit, cur angeli peccaverint, breviter respondendum est quod, quamvis pro peccatoribus excusationes forte inveniri possint, tamen vera ratio dici non potest. Si enim vera ratio adfuisset, non contra rationem egissent; et si contra rationem non egissent, actum voluntarium non malum sed bonum perfecissent.

Unde et S. Thomas, quando quaesiverit utrum falsitas esse posset non tantum in mente sed etiam in rebus, admisit ipsas res deficere posse ab intentione humana sed non ab intentione divina, et ideo res falsas esse posse per comparationem ad mentem humanam sed non per comparationem ad mentem divinam; et tamen relate ad ipsam mentem divinam exceptionem

### *Scholion 2: The cause of sin*

1 We have often stated that all things proceed by conditioned necessity from God's infallible knowledge, his efficacious will, and his irresistible action. Hence it seems we must conclude that God is the infallible, efficacious, and irresistible cause of all sin. This is not only unfitting in itself, but also greatly obscures the divine wisdom and charity that we extolled in the redemption and the law of the cross.

2 The solution to this difficulty seems to lie in grasping precisely in what sense sin has a cause. For inasmuch as sin has a cause, it is reducible to God as the cause of all that is caused. However, inasmuch as sin lacks the intelligibility of cause and of the caused, it cannot be reduced to God. Finally, insofar as sin cannot be reduced to God, St Thomas's teaching is intelligible, namely, that God neither directly nor indirectly wills culpable evil but merely permits it (*Summa theologiae,* 1, q. 19, a. 9 c. and ad 3m).

3 Causes are either intrinsic or extrinsic.

Sin, understood as the formal element of formal sin, that is, as culpable evil, is not a being and a good but the privation of being and of good.

Nor is it a rational and intelligible privation of good. For this privation is in the will; and it is in the will, not insofar as the will is a rational appetite and follows the intellect, but solely insofar as the will defects from its rationality and does not follow the dictate of right reason. Likewise, what is in the will is also in the one who wills; but sin is in the one who wills, not insofar as that person is a rational creature, but insofar as he or she defects from the rationality of a rational creature.

That is why when someone asks why people sin, why Adam sinned, why the angels sinned, the short answer has to be that, although excuses may possibly be found for sinners, no true reason can be given. Had there been a true reason, they would not have been acting contrary to reason; and if they had not been acting contrary to reason, they would have performed a voluntary act that was not evil but good.

Hence also, St Thomas, when he asked whether falsity can be not only in the mind but also in things, admitted that things themselves can fall short of human intention but not of divine intention, and therefore things can be false in relation to a human mind but not in relation to the divine mind. And yet even with regard to the divine mind he admitted an exception 'in

admisit 'in voluntariis agentibus tantum, in quorum potestate est subducere se ab ordinatione divini intellectus, in quo malum culpae consistit, secundum quod ipsa peccata falsitates et mendacia dicuntur in scripturis' (*Sum. theol.*, I, q. 17, a. 1).

Peccatum ergo secundum constitutionem suam intrinsecam non solum est privatio boni sed etiam est irrationalis quaedam privatio boni. Caeterae quidem privationes ita ab ente et bono deficiunt ut tamen negativam quandam veritatem ontologicam habeant. Sed peccata ita ab ente et bono deficiunt ut etiam a vero ontologico et ab intrinseca intelligibilitate deficiant. Cur sint? Si vere esset 'cur,' rationem peccati non haberent.

4 Hactenus de causa peccati intrinseca, sed iam de causa eiusdem extrinseca quaerendum est.

Omne enim ens finitum, quatenus intelligibile est, in causas extrinsecas reducitur: in finem, qui est causa causarum; in exemplar, secundum quod agens agit; in agentem, a quo fit.

Pariter omne non-ens seu entis privatio, quatenus intelligibile est, in causas extrinsecas modo quodam negativo reducitur: in finem, quatenus non intenditur; in exemplar, quatenus non repraesentatur; in agentem, a quo non est factum.

At quo iure, quo titulo, qua ratione entis et boni privationes non intelligibiles et irrationales in finem, in exemplar, in agentem reducere velis? Nullam aliam non dico rationem sed causam huius viae invenio praeter caecam quandam consuetudinem. Solemus sane intelligibilia in causas reducere; ergo etiam quae in se non sunt intelligibilia in causas pariter reducimus!

Quam reductionem simpliciter erroneam duco. Ens reducitur in causam agentem; non-ens reducitur in causam non agentem; sed non-intelligibile non reducitur sive in agentem sive in non agentem.

Pariter, sicut ens reducitur in divinam sapientiam ordinantem, ita non-ens reducitur in divinam sapientiam non ordinantem; sed non-intelligibile non reducitur in divinam sapientiam sive ordinantem sive non ordinantem sed quodammodo in prohibentem et re-ordinantem.

Similiter, sicut ens reducitur in bonitatem divinam volentem, ita non-ens reducitur in divinam bonitatem non volentem, sed non-intelligibile non reducitur sive in volentem sive in non volentem sed in permittentem.

the case of voluntary agents only, who have it in their power to withdraw themselves from what has been ordained by the divine intellect. It is in this that culpable evil consists, and accordingly scripture calls sins falsehoods and lies' (*Summa theologiae,* 1, q. 17, a. 1).

In its intrinsic constitution, then, sin is not only a privation of good but also an irrational privation of good. Other privations indeed are deficient in being and goodness yet have a certain negative ontological truth. But sins are deficient in being and goodness in such a way that they are also deficient in ontological truth and intrinsic intelligibility. Why do they occur? If there truly were a 'why,' a reason, they would not fulfil the definition of 'sin.'

4 So far we have been dealing with the intrinsic cause of sin, but now we must ask about its extrinsic cause.

Every finite being, insofar as it is intelligible, is reducible to its extrinsic causes: to its end, which is the cause of causes; to its exemplar, in accordance with which the agent acts; and to its agent, by which it is made or done.

In similar fashion every non-being or privation of being, insofar as it is intelligible, is reducible to extrinsic causes in a negative way: to its end, insofar as it is not intended, to its exemplar, insofar as it is not represented, and to its agent, by which it is not made or done.

But, by what right, what entitlement, what reason would you reduce non-intelligible and irrational privations of being and good to an end, an exemplar, or an agent? I find no other cause – I do not say reason – than blind habit. We are, of course, accustomed to reducing intelligible beings to their causes; therefore, we likewise reduce to their causes even what in themselves are not intelligible!

Such reduction I hold to be simply mistaken. Being is reducible to a cause that acts; non-being is reducible to a cause that is not acting; but what is nonintelligible is reducible neither to an agent nor to a non-agent.

Similarly, just as being is reducible to divine wisdom as ordering, so non-being is reducible to divine wisdom as not ordering; but the nonintelligible is not reducible to divine wisdom either as ordering or as not ordering but, in a way, as prohibiting and re-ordering.

Again, just as being is reducible to divine goodness willing, so non-being is reducible to divine goodness not willing; but the nonintelligible is reducible neither to its willing nor non-willing but to its permitting.

Quam ob causam vere dicitur 'Perditio tua ex te, Israel.' Vide *Sum. theol.*, 1, q. 23, a. 3, ob. 2a et ad 2m; *Theol. Stud.* 3 (1942) 547–52.

5 Quae sane non ideo sunt dicta ut 'problema mali' solvatur. Aliud enim non intenditur nisi ut mens fiat et reflexa et critica unde se a fallaciis purgare possit. Sicut enim supra diximus, ubi de libertate Christi ..., nihil probatur nisi hoc quod obiectio non probat.

Obicientis autem fallacia in eo est quod credit disiunctionem completam se habere quia contradictorie opposita in obliquo ponit. Sed, uti notavit S. Thomas, contradictorie opponuntur et 'mala fieri' et 'mala non fieri'; sed non contradictorie opponuntur 'vult mala fieri' et 'vult mala non fieri' (*Sum. theol.*, 1, q. 19, a. 9, ad 3m). Similiter, contradictorie opponuntur (1) ordinantem et non ordinantem, (2) volentem et non volentem, (3) agentem et non agentem, sed non ideo contradictorie opponuntur (1) reducitur in ordinantem et reducitur in non ordinantem, (2) reducitur in volentem et reducitur in non volentem, (3) reducitur in agentem et reducitur in non agentem. Quod enim contradictorie opponitur reductioni est non-reductio; et ubi deest intelligibilitas, pariter desit reductio necesse est.

6 Sicut autem supra ex impossibilitate validi argumenti contra contingentiam vel libertatem ad proprietatem exclusive divinam transcendentiae conclusimus ..., ita nunc ex impossibilitate reducendi peccata in Deum ad profundiorem quandam, non dico intelligentiam, sed admirationem divinae sanctitatis pervenire possumus. Non enim sine causa clamant Seraphim: 'Sanctus, Sanctus, Sanctus' (Is 6.2–3), cum Deus ab omni peccato alienissimus ita tamen peccata permittat ut peccati nullatenus sit auctor, et ita de malis bene faciat ut proprium Filium miserit ad nostra mala nobiscum perferenda, et ad nos per mortem in resurrectionem vitae conducendos.

7 Video tamen mihi audire quempiam dicentem haec nimis esse abstrusa. Qui autem argumenta non capiunt, narrationibus erudiri possunt. Audiant ergo scripturas docentes e serpente ortum esse peccatum et peccati poenas (Gen. 3.1–15): invidia diaboli mortem in hunc mundum intrasse (Sap 2.24); Christi adversarios ex patre diabolo esse et desideria huius patris facere velle (Io 8.44); eorum horam fuisse potestatem tenebrarum (Lc 22.53); Christum, per mortem destruxisse eam qui tenebat mortis imperium, id est diabolum (Heb. 2.14); Deum Patrem nos eripuisse de potestate

Hence it is truly said, 'Your downfall is your own doing, O Israel' [Hosea 13.9 Vulgate]. See *Summa theologiae,* 1, q. 23, a. 3, obj. 2 and ad 2m; *Theological Studies* 3 (1942) 547–52 [*Grace and Freedom* 111–16].

5 All this, of course, is not meant to solve the 'problem of evil.' Our sole aim is that the mind become reflective and critical so it can purge itself of fallacies. As we said in discussing Christ's freedom (*The Incarnate Word* 742–45), nothing is proved except that the objection proves nothing.

The fallacy of the objector lies in believing that there is a complete disjunction when statements are made that posit indirect contradictories. But as St Thomas noted, 'evils exist' and 'evils do not exist' are contradictories, but 'wills evils to exist' and 'wills evils not to exist' are not contradictories (*Summa theologiae,* 1, q. 19, a. 9, ad 3m). Likewise, the following are contradictories: (1) ordering and not ordering, (2) willing and not willing, and (3) acting and not acting; but that does not mean therefore that the following are contradictories: (1) reducible to the one ordering and reducible to the one not ordering, (2) reducible to the one willing and reducible to the one not willing, and (3) reducible to the one acting and reducible to the one not acting. For contradictory to reduction is non-reduction, and where there is no intelligibility, there is likewise no need for a reduction.

6 Just as from the impossibility of a valid argument against contingency or freedom we concluded to the exclusively divine property of transcendence (*The Incarnate Word* 744–47), so now from the impossibility of reducing sins to God we are able to arrive at a more profound, not understanding, but admiration of the holiness of God. The Seraphim have every reason to cry out, 'Holy, holy, holy' (Isaiah 6.2–3), since God, though utterly foreign to all sin, nonetheless permits sin without in the least being its author, and draws good out of evil by sending his own Son to bear our evils with us and to lead us through death to the risen life.

7 Still, it seems to me I hear someone saying that this is all too abstruse. Well, those who cannot grasp arguments can learn from stories. Let them therefore go to the scriptures, which teach that sin and the punishments for sin came from the serpent (Genesis 3.1–15); that sin entered into this world through the envy of the devil (Wisdom 2.24); that Christ's adversaries were those whose father was the devil, and their desire was to do the will of this father of theirs (John 8.44); that their hour was the power of darkness (Luke 22.53); that Christ through his death destroyed the one who has the

tenebrarum et transtulisse in regnum Filii dilectionis suae (Col 1.13); nostram colluctationem esse non adversus carnem et sanguinem sed adversus principes et potestates, adversus mundi rectores tenebrarum harum (Eph 6.12), de quibus tamen Christus triumphum reportavit (Col 2.14). His ergo omnibus manifestum est non Deum sed diabolum esse auctorem peccati, unde et Patres convenientissime de partibus diaboli in passione et morte Christi non silebant.

Sane qui peccatum et peccati poenam in serpentem reducit, ad ultimum 'cur' non pervenit. Ulterius enim quaeri potest cur bonus Deus serpentem creaverit. Attamen non pauci esse videntur qui iam ante mentem defatigentur quam ad ultimum 'cur' perveniatur. Quorum causa salutare est et altiora omittere et clariora narrare. Secus verendum est ne in passione et morte Christi non satis distinguant inter partes Dei Patris et partes Iudae cui diabolus misit in cor ut traderet Christum (Io 13. 2, 13.27, Lc 22.3). Secus etiam verendum est ne, cum excellentiam crucis didicerint, non solum Christum in cruce perferenda imitentur sed etiam Pharisaeos et Pilatum sequantur in cruce aliis imponenda.

power of death, that is, the devil (Hebrews 2.14); that God the Father has rescued us from the power of darkness and transferred us into the kingdom of his beloved Son (Colossians 1.13); that our struggle is not against enemies of flesh and blood but against the rulers, against the authorities, against the cosmic powers of this present darkness (Ephesians 6.12), over whom Christ has nevertheless triumphed (Colossians 2.14–15). In all these it is clear that it is not God but the devil who is the author of sin, and so it was quite right and fitting that the Fathers were not silent about the part the devil played in the passion and death of Christ.

Certainly, one who reduces sin and the punishment for sin to the serpent has not arrived at the ultimate 'why.' For one can further ask why a good God created the serpent. Still, there seem to be not a few who are already mentally fatigued before arriving at the ultimate 'why.' For their sake it is best to leave aside loftier matters and talk about those that are clearer. Otherwise it is to be feared that when speaking of the passion and death of Christ they fail to distinguish clearly enough between the role of God the Father and that of Judas, into whose heart the devil put the intention to betray Christ (John 13.2, 13.27; Luke 22.3). Otherwise, too, it is to be feared that, after learning about the excellence of the cross, they might imitate not only Christ in bearing the cross but also the Pharisees and Pilate in imposing the cross on others.

# PART TWO

## *The Redemption*

# Caput Primum: De Bono et Malo[1]

Notum nobis factum est divinae voluntatis sacramentum 'omnia in Christo instaurare sive quae in caelis sive quae in terris sunt in ipso' (Eph 1.9–10). Quod si his in terris parum perspicimus quemadmodum caelestia in Christo instaurentur, haud forte mirandum est. Sed gravius esse videtur si pariter praetermittamus quemadmodum instaurentur ipsa terrestria, cum nostri sit collaborare ut omnis aedificatio constructa crescat in templum sanctum in Domino (Eph 2.21).

Quam ob causam, diligenter imprimis considerandum esse duximus quale sit bonum, quemadmodum humanum bonum praecipue in ordine ponatur, qua lege humanum ordinis bonum peccato corrumpatur, quaenam denique sit humana potentia ad humanum ordinis bonum restaurandum. Haec enim si perspecta habuerimus, et plenius et fructuosius intelligemus quanti momenti sit in omnibus et singulis hodiernae vitae problematibus magnum illud Dei Patris beneficium quod per Dominum nostrum crucifixum et resurrectum in sancto Spiritu accepimus.

# 1 Good and Evil[1]

To us has been revealed the mystery of God's will, 'to gather up all things in Christ, things in heaven and on earth' (Ephesians 1.9–10). While it is hardly surprising that we here below have little inkling about how heavenly things might be gathered in Christ, it would seem to be a rather more serious matter if we were to neglect the question of how earthly realities are to be brought together, especially since it is our duty to collaborate so that the whole building, joined together, might grow into a holy temple in the Lord (Ephesians 2.21).

Accordingly, we have judged that careful consideration must be given to inquiring, first, about the nature of the good, how especially the human good is put in order, by what law the human good of order is corrupted by sin, and finally what human resources there are for restoring the human good of order. Once we have achieved a firm grasp of these matters, we will understand more deeply and more fruitfully how important to any and all of our contemporary problems is the great gift of God our Father that we have received through our crucified and risen Lord in the Holy Spirit.

1 [The autograph may be found on www.bernardlonergan.com at 25300DTL060. Lonergan's list of footnotes may be found at 25280DOL060. Editors' footnotes are in brackets.]

## Articulus 1: De bono in genere

*Omne bonum est ens.*

Nam ens et bonum convertuntur; sicut ergo omne ens est bonum, ita omne bonum est ens.

*Qui dicit bonum, dicit concretum.*

Nam omne bonum est ens, et omne ens est concretum.

Differentiae enim cuiuscumque entis non addunt super illud ens sed in eo includuntur. Quod autem in se includit omnes suas differentias concretum est. Omne ergo ens concretum est, et ideo pariter omne bonum.

Iterum, ipsa intentio concreti nihil est aliud quam intentio entis. Qui enim concretum intendit, neque diversos rei aspectus explicite cogitat, neque ullatenus ab ipsa rei realitate abstrahit. Pariter qui ens intendit, neque varios aspectus seu differentias explicite cogitat, neque ullatenus a rei realitate praescindit sed eam totam considerat.

*Qui dicit bonum, dicit omnia.*

Nam quodcumque est, ens est. Ens ergo sese extendit ad omnia. Sed ens et bonum convertuntur. Et ideo bonum sese extendit ad omnia.

*Quod Deus est bonus per essentiam, caetera autem per participationem.*[2]

Essentia enim Dei est ipsa entis et boni essentia; sed essentia creaturae non est nisi imperfecta quaedam divinae essentiae imitatio vel participatio; sicut ergo creatura imitatur vel participat divinam essentiam, ita etiam imitatur vel participat essentiam boni.

Iterum, essentia creaturae non est nisi essentia hominis vel equi vel rosae vel alterius cuiusdam speciei; et nulla eiusmodi species est ipsa essentia entis vel boni cum, ea intellecta, multa alia entia et multa alia bona maneant intelligenda. Sed intellecta divina essentia, totum ens et totum bonum in ea intelliguntur; et ideo essentia Dei est essentia entis et boni.

## Article 1: On the good in general

*All good is being.*

'Good' and 'being' are convertible; therefore, as all being is good, so all good is being.

*To speak of the 'good' is to speak of the concrete.*

For all good is being, and all being is concrete.

The differences of any being whatsoever are not additions to that being but are included in it. But that which includes all its differences in itself is concrete. Every being therefore is concrete, and so likewise every good.

Also, to intend what is concrete is nothing other than to intend being. For whoever intends what is concrete neither explicitly thinks of the diverse aspects of the thing nor in any way abstracts from its reality. Similarly, whoever intends a being neither explicitly thinks of its various aspects or differences nor in any way abstracts from the reality of the thing but rather considers it in its totality.

*To speak of the 'good' is to speak of everything.*

Whatever is, is being. 'Being,' therefore, extends to everything. But 'being' and 'good' are convertible; therefore 'good' extends to everything.

*God is good by essence, but all other things are good by participation.*[2]

The essence of God is the very essence of being and of the good. But the essence of a creature is but an imperfect imitation of or participation in the divine essence. Hence, as a creature imitates or participates in the divine essence, so does it imitate or participate in the essence of the good.

Also, the essence of a creature is nothing but the essence of humans or of horse or of rose or of any other species. No such species is the very essence of being or of the good, since even when we have understood the essence of a species many other beings and many other goods remain to be understood. But when the divine essence is understood, all being and all good are understood in it, and so the essence of God is the essence of being and of the good.

2 [In chapter 6 of the present manuscript Lonergan speaks of 'bonum per essentiam,' 'bonum per participationem,' and 'bonum per communicationem.' See below, pp. 646–47.]

*Quod hac in vita imperfecte et analogice bonum intelligimus, concipimus, cognoscimus.*

Nam qualis est intelligentia, talis est conceptio; et qualis est conceptio, talis est cognitio. Cognitio enim nostra est conceptionis affirmatio vel negatio; et conceptio nostra non est nisi intelligentiae expressio.

Sed propria et perfecta cuiusque intelligentia ex perspecta eiusdem essentia habetur; boni autem essentia est ipsa divina essentia; et cum hac in vita nisi imperfecte et analogice divinam essentiam non intelligamus, concipiamus, cognoscamus, sequitur omnino nos hac in vita imperfecte et analogice boni essentiam intelligere, concipere, cognoscere.

*Quod boni creati duplex est consideratio.*

Primo enim, ea quae appetuntur bona dicuntur; et haec sunt bona particularia.

Deinde vero, cum bonum sit concretum, prima illa consideratio omnino insufficiens videtur. Nam frustra esset appetibile sine appetitu; frustra essent appetibile et appetitus sine appetitione; frustra essent appetibile, appetitus, et appetitio sine appetente; frustra essent haec omnia nisi appetens ita appetibile prosequeretur ut id consequi eoque frui posset; neque prosecutio, consecutio, fruitio esse possent nisi praesto essent necessaria media adiunctaque propitia. Quae cum ita sint, si quidem appetibile est bonum, etiam bona suo modo sunt appetitus, appetitio, appetens, prosecutio, media, adiuncta, consecutio, fruitio. Quae quidem omnia non simpliciter multa sunt, sed naturaliter inter se ordinantur ut unum quoddam totum, concretum, dynamicum efformetur. Quod si partes huius totius suo modo bonae esse dicuntur, multo magis ipsum totum ordinatum nominatur bonum. Quam ob causam, praeter appetibilia seu bona particularia, etiam bonum ordinis agnosci oportet.[3]

*Quod tripliciter consideratur bonum ordinis.*

Nam prima est consideratio abstracta; altera est schematica, typica, hypothetica; tertia denique est concreta atque actualis.

*In this life we understand, conceive, and know the good only imperfectly and by way of analogy.*

For as we understand things, so we conceive them; and as we conceive them, so we know them. For our knowing is the affirmation or negation of a conception, and our conception is but the expression of what we have understood.

Now, a proper and perfect understanding of any thing comes from grasping its essence. The essence of the good, however, is the divine essence itself. Since in this life we understand, conceive, and know the divine essence only imperfectly and analogically, it follows that in this life we understand, conceive, and know the essence of the good imperfectly and analogically.

*There are two ways of considering created good.*

First, those things that are desired are called good; these are particular goods.

Secondly, however, since what is good is concrete, this first consideration seems quite inadequate. For objects of desire would be pointless without capacities for desire; and both the object and the capacity would be pointless without the actual desiring; and the objects, capacities, and acts of desire would be pointless apart from a desirer; and these would all be pointless unless the desirer could pursue the desirable so as to attain and enjoy it; and the pursuit, attainment, and enjoyment could not occur without the necessary means and favorable circumstances. This being the case, if indeed the desirable is a good, so too are the capacity, the act, the desirer, the pursuit, the means, the circumstances, the attainment, and the enjoyment also good, each in its own way. All of these are not simply many different things but are naturally related one to the other so as to form one concrete dynamic whole. And if each of the parts of this whole is said to be good in its own way, all the more is the ordered whole itself to be called good. Hence besides objects of desire or particular goods, we must also recognize the good of order.[3]

*There are three ways of considering the good of order.*

The first consideration is abstract, the second is schematic, typical, and hypothetical, and the third is concrete and actual.

3 [For comments on the good similar to what is expressed in this paragraph, see Bernard Lonergan, *Topics in Education*, vol. 10 in Collected Works of Bernard Lonergan, ed. Robert M. Doran and Frederick E. Crowe (Toronto: University of Toronto Press, 1993) 27–28. The fact that these lectures were delivered in the summer of 1959 may add support to the hypothesis stated

Primam ergo et abstractam considerationem iam supra adhibuimus, cum ex ipsa ratione appetibilis ad appetitum, appetitionem, appetens, prosequens, etc., conclusimus.

Altera autem consideratio abstractam praesupponit et eatenus ad concretum procedit quatenus problema concretae realizationis proponit et ad solutionem quandam schematicam, typicam, hypotheticam pervenit. Supra enim non statuimus nisi abstractum quoddam ordinis bonum. Non enim diximus cuiusnam naturae sit appetens, utrum unicum sit an multa, utrum semel an multoties appetant, utrum idem semper sit appetibile an diversa, quanam lege varientur appetibilia, utrum ipsa appetentia aliis appetentibus sint vel appetibilia vel media vel adiuncta, et quaenam quibus, etc. At si quis has quaestiones ponit et ita respondere vult ut possibile sit singula appetentia talibus appetibilibus toties frui quoties convenit, non solum abstractas ordinationes considerare debet, sed ad concretam dispositionem spatialem et temporalem deveniat necesse est. Quot vero felices invenit dispositiones (quae equilibria nominari solent: puta propter disrupta equilibria ultra omnem modum multiplicatos esse cuniculos in Australiam, passeres in Americam invectos), tot sunt huius problematis solutiones schematicae, typicae, hypotheticae. Neque alia essentialiter est consideratio eorum qui de evolutione specierum speculantur sed, facta hypothesi particulari, idem problema modo pleniori ponunt circa omnia, nempe, viventia, super totam terrae faciem, ex temporibus antiquissimis.

Tertia denique est actualis et concreta consideratio quae, praesuppositis tum ordinatione abstracta tum ordinationibus schematicis et hypotheticis, ad illum procedit ordinem quam divina sapientia infallibiliter novit, divina bonitas efficaciter elegit, divina potentia irresistibiliter facit. Et quia bonum est ens et concretum et omnia respicit, per solam hanc tertiam considerationem ad notitiam boni creati pervenitur. Qui enim schematica et hypothetica considerat, non ad ea quae sunt sed ad ea quae forte esse possunt attendit. Qui autem ad sola bona particularia attendit, ipse se magis appetentem quam reflectentem manifestat, cum solam boni partem et non totum et concretum bonum consideret. Qui, caeteris omissis, hoc vel illud totum, concretum, dynamicum ordinis bonum examinat, legitima sane praecisione utitur, modo divinae sapientiae omnia ordinantis, divinae electionis omnia volentis, divinae potentiae mundum ordine unum[4] facientis non obliviscatur. Nam 'finis quidem universi est aliquod bonum

We followed the first, abstract way of considering the good of order in the preceding section, in drawing conclusions from the notion of the object of desire about appetite, desiring, the desirer, the pursuit, and so on.

The second consideration presupposes this abstract consideration and proceeds to the concrete insofar as it sets forth the problem of concrete realization and reaches a schematic, typical, and hypothetical solution. For in our analysis above we established only an abstract good of order. We did not indicate the particular nature of the desirer, whether there was only one desirer or many, whether they desire many times or only once, whether the object of desire is always the same or there are diverse objects, by what law the objects vary, whether the desirers themselves are desirable to others, or are means or circumstances for them, and which are to which, and so forth. But if someone asks these questions and wishes to reply that it is possible for every desirer to enjoy such objects of desire as often as is fitting, one has to consider not only abstract orders but also concrete spatial and temporal arrangements. There are as many schematic, typical, and hypothetical solutions to this problem as there are successful arrangements (which are called equilibria: for instance, because of disturbed equilibria, rabbits introduced to Australia and starlings introduced to America have multiplied beyond measure). So this is essentially the same consideration as is made by those who speculate about the evolution of species; but having made a particular hypothesis, they pose the same problem more fully with regard to all living things over the whole face of the earth and over an extremely long period of time.

The third consideration is actual and concrete. Presupposing both the abstract order and the schematic and hypothetical order of things, it proceeds to that order which divine wisdom infallibly knew, divine goodness efficaciously chose, and divine power irresistibly implements. And, since the good is being and concrete and refers to all things, it is only through this third consideration that we arrive at a knowledge of created good. A schematic and hypothetical consideration looks not to what is but to what might possibly be. On the other hand, those who concern themselves only with particular goods reveal themselves to be desirers rather than reflective thinkers, since they attend to only a part of the good and not the whole concrete good. But those who set other considerations aside to examine this or that whole, concrete, dynamic good of order legitimately prescind,

in the General Editors' Preface regarding the dating of the present manuscript.]

in ipso exsistens, scilicet ordo ipsius universi.'[5] Et 'perfectius participat divinam bonitatem et repraesentat eam totum universum quam alia quaelibet creatura.'[6]

## Articulus II: De bono ordinis humano

### *1 Quale sit bonum ordinis in rebus humanis*

Illud humano generi proprium est ut non solum, sicut caetera viventia, intra ordinis bonum oriatur eoque iugiter fruatur, sed etiam ipsum suum ordinis bonum ratione et voluntate aliquatenus constituat, et constitutum secundum processum quendam historicum perficere studeat. Quod ut summis saltem lineamentis intelligatur, primo, de generali situatione humana quaedam dicenda esse videntur, deinde, de processu quo homines ex alia in aliam situationem transeunt, et tertio denique de altiori illa cultura secundum quam homines omnis regionis omnisque aetatis quodammodo inter se communicare possunt.

Quantum ergo ad generalem situationem attinet, homines invenimus non tam singula bona particularia quaerere quam eorundem seriem quandam et continuam et certam, quippe qui non semel tantum in vita vescantur, tunicas induant, tecto pluvia arceant, igni frigus repellant, sed his omnibus perpetuo fere indigeant. Cum tamen singuli soli haud sibi sufficiant ad totam hanc bonorum seriem comparandam, societates ineunt ut per cooperationem atque collaborationem omnes singulis et securius et facilius optatum bonorum quasi fluvium consequantur. At ipsa haec cooperatio suos exserit fructus. Ex actibus enim repetitis acquiruntur habitus operativi tam apprehensivi quam appetitivi, ut singuli socii propria arte, virtute, scientia perficiantur, et ipsa tota societas propriam indolem in consuetudinibus, legibus, aliisque institutis exprimat. Quod si amare est bonum velle alicui, illi sane mutuo se amant qui ita bono communi incumbant ut omnem fere eorum operationem gubernet, ut ipsos eorum habitus mentis et cordis formet, ut non solum multiplici interdependentia saepe fere inconscia sed etiam usu familiari atque cotidiano eos inter se coniungat.

as long as they do not lose sight of the divine wisdom that orders all things, the divine choice that wills all things, and the divine power that effects one world order.[4] For, 'the end of the universe is a good existing in it, namely, the order of the universe itself.'[5] Again, 'the universe as a whole participates and represents the divine goodness more perfectly than any other creature whatever.'[6]

## Article 2: The human good of order

### *1 The good of order in human affairs*

It is proper to human beings that they not only come into existence within a good of order and constantly enjoy its benefits, as do other living things, but also that to some extent they constitute their own good of order by reason and will and strive through a historical process to improve the order thus constituted. In order to understand this, at least in broad outline, something should be said, first, about the overall human situation, second, about the process by which people go from one situation to another, and third, about that higher culture by means of which people in all places and in every age are able to communicate with one another in some way.

With regard to their overall situation, we find that human beings seek not so much this or that particular good as rather a continuous and secure series of goods, inasmuch as they do not eat or put on clothes or take shelter from the rain or warm themselves by a fire only once in their lifetime, but are constantly in need of these goods. Since, however, individuals by themselves are not capable of acquiring this whole series of goods, they form societies in order that through their mutual collaboration and cooperation they all may have more secure and easy access to a steady stream, so to speak, of these desired goods. Now this cooperation produces benefits of its own. From repeated acts are developed operative habits both of knowing and of willing, so that each member of a society develops his or her special skill or talent or knowledge, and the society as a whole expresses its unique character in its customs, laws, and other institutions. If love means to wish well to another, then surely there is mutual love among all those who are so dedicated to the common good that this common good itself governs virtually all their activity, forms their habits of mind and heart, and unites them

4 Thomas Aquinas, *Summa theologiae*, 1, q. 47, a. 3 c.
5 Ibid. q. 103, a. 2, ad 3m.
6 Ibid. q. 47, a. 1 c.

Eiusmodi igitur invenitur bonum ordinis humanum ut continuam securamque bonorum particularium seriem tamquam finem intendat, per coordinatas semperque repetitas operationes hunc finem assequatur, per habitus institutaque ipsam cooperationem tueatur, per mutuam denique amicitiam vitam communem ornet atque perficiat. Ita enim bonum ordinis domesticum viro, uxori, liberis innumera fere bona particularia parit; quo ordine declinante, dulcia fiunt amara, utilia incommodis replentur, et ipse mutuus amor suspicionibus, querelis, dissidiis, rixis suffocatur. Ita etiam bonum ordinis oeconomicum non in opificum labore, non in materiis abundantibus, non in conducentium sollertia atque audacia residet, sed in his omnibus et simul sumptis et rite ordinatis, ut vigente ordine omnia omnibus fere prospere procedunt et, solo ordine deficiente, communis omnibus imponitur miseria. Ita denique bonum ordinis politicum caetera externa bona tuetur; neque vacillare potest quin omnium dissipationem atque destructionem comminetur.[7]

## 2 *Quemadmodum humanum ordinis bonum proficiat*

Non tamen unum idemque ordinis bonum apud homines cuiusvis loci et aetatis invenitur. Alii enim mensuris aliis alia appetibilia prosequuntur; alii aliter laborem inter se dividunt; aliis aliae sunt consuetudines, leges, instituta, aliae sunt artes et scientiae, aliae magis laudantur virtutes, et cuique est sua religio. Cuius maximae variationis atque diversitatis causa non tam in adiunctis externis reponenda esse videtur quam in ipso interno intellectus profectu.

Exsistit enim motus quidam circularis quo externa et concreta hominis situatio in intellectum agit, intellectus deinde in voluntatem, voluntas denique in ipsam situationem. Qui quidem motus semper uniformis maneret si intellectus nihil umquam perspiceret nisi iam exsistens ordinis bonum. At eiusmodi est mentis humanae irrequietudo ut externa situatio facile inquirentem movet ad novum quidpiam forteque vel commodius vel utilius vel quomodocumque melius inveniendum. Inventionem sequuntur nova consilia; consiliis persuadendi artes accedunt; persuasio consensum evincit;

not only by multiple instances of interdependence, of which they are often largely unaware, but also through the familiar intercourse of daily living.

The human good of order, then, aims at securing a continuous flow of particular goods, maintains it through the repetition of coordinated operations, safeguards this cooperation through customs and institutions, and through mutual friendly relationships enriches and enhances the life of the community. The domestic good of order brings innumerable particular goods to husband, wife, and children. When that order weakens, pleasant ways become irksome, helpful tasks become impositions, and mutual love withers as a result of suspicion, complaining, disagreements, and quarreling. So also, the economic good of order is to be found not in the labors of the workers, not in the abundance of raw materials, not in the shrewdness and daring of entrepreneurs, but in all of these factors taken together and well ordered. When this good order thrives, nearly everyone prospers, and its breakdown is enough to impose suffering on all. So, finally, the political order safeguards all other external goods, and any weakening or wavering on its part threatens the whole order with disarray and eventual collapse.[7]

### 2 *How the human good of order progresses*

The good of order in human societies is not the same everywhere and at all times. Different people have different criteria for determining what is desirable. The division of labor varies from one group to another. Different societies have different customs, laws, and institutions, have different arts and sciences, place different values on various virtues, and each has its own form of religion. The reason for this great variety and diversity is to be found not so much in external circumstances as in the internal factor of intellectual development.

There is a sort of circular movement in which one's external concrete situation influences one's intellect, which in turn influences the will, which acts upon the situation. This movement would continue along the same lines if the intellect never attended to anything except the existing good of order. Such, however, is the restlessness of the human mind that an external situation easily impels it to devise something new or more convenient or

7 [Here Lonergan discusses the good of order in its domestic, economic, and political dimensions. Later (p. 281) he will add 'technology.' The discussion in chapter 7 of *Insight* relates technological, economic, and political dimensions to one another.]

consensus novum agendi, faciendi, cooperandi modum inducit, ut ipsa externa situatio commutetur. Qua commutatione peracta, reincipit circulus, sive quia defectus novi consilii ipsis factis demonstrantur et iam quaeruntur remedia, sive quia nova situatio novas aperit possibilitates, novas inventiones stimulat, et nova melioraque consilia postulat. Neque huic motui circulari atque progressivo intrinsecus quidam imponitur finis, cum ipsa sua natura intellectus dicatur quo sit *omnia* facere et fieri.[8]

Humanum ergo ordinis bonum duplicem praebet aspectum. Nam secundum generalem quandam structuram seu formam unum quodammodo atque constans invenitur, cum semper et ubique continuam certamque bonorum particularium seriem homines quaerant, cum semper et ubique per coordinatas operationes hanc seriem assequantur, cum semper et ubique ipsa haec cooperatio et instituta externa et publica et internos habitus inducat, cum semper et ubique relationes interpersonales ex bonis divisis, ex collaboratione, ex institutis communibus, ex ipsis internis habitibus oriantur. At idem ordinis bonum ita generalem hanc structuram retinet ut tamen intelligentibus et consentientibus sociis levi quodam sed perpetuo fluxu commutetur. Minimae sane videri possunt singulae mutationes. Parvis omnino gressibus perficitur ordo. Sed quo tendit qui festinat, eo saepius pervenit qui perseverat. Neque perseverantia caret genus humanum, quod novae cuique generationi ea omnia tradit atque praecipit quaecumque usu et experientia sunt probata.

Quibus perspectis, non solum rerum humanarum mutabilitatem intelligis sed etiam maximas illas differentias quae in diversis et humanis traditionibus observantur. Cum enim intrinsecum quoddam mutationis principium in ipsa humana natura agnoscatur, cum hoc principium definiatur quo sit omnia facere et fieri, genetice explicari possunt quaecumque maximam civilizationem a cultura prorsus primitiva secernunt. Quod si valet genetica eiusmodi explicatio, statim concludi potest tum quanti momenti sit historica rerum intelligentia tum in quonam consistat humana quae dicitur solidaritas.

Qui enim historice seu genetice res humanas intelligit, non solum generale quoddam perspicit theorema, nempe, bonum ordinis humanum ab ipsis hominibus intelligentibus et consentientibus pedetentim esse evolutum, sed etiam ad elementa atque particularia descendit ut de singulis dicere possit

more useful or better in some way or other. Discovery begets new proposals; these proposals are supported by persuasive rhetoric; persuasion produces agreement, to introduce new ways of doing or making things and new forms of collaborative effort, so that the external situation itself is changed. When this change is complete, the cycle begins again, sometimes because defects appear when the new proposals are put into practice and so remedies have to be found, or sometimes because the altered circumstances themselves reveal new possibilities, stimulate new discoveries, and call for fresh and better proposals. There is no intrinsic reason why this progressive cycle should end, since the mind by its very nature is said to be that which can make and become *all* things.[8]

There are, then, two aspects to the human good of order. In its general structure or form it exhibits a certain uniformity and constancy in that always and everywhere people seek a continuous and secure flow of particular goods, always and everywhere they pursue this series through coordinated operations, always and everywhere their collaboration leads to both external public institutions and interior habits of mind, and always and everywhere interpersonal relations arise from the division of goods, collaborative effort, common institutions, and these interior habits themselves. But the same good of order maintains its general structure, while minute changes are continually taking place as a result of the insights and communal decisions of its members. Individually these changes are all but imperceptible; but, one small step at a time, the social order develops. Perseverance reaches its goal more often than does haste. And perseverance has never been lacking to the human race, which hands on to each new generation what has been proven valuable through experience and practice.

From all this we can appreciate not only the changeableness in human affairs but also the enormous differences that are to be found in various human traditions. Once the intrinsic principle of change that is within human nature itself is acknowledged, and when this principle is understood as 'that which can make and become all things,' then factors that distinguish a high civilization from a culture utterly primitive can be explained genetically. If such genetic explanation is valid, we may readily grasp both the importance of a historical understanding of human affairs and the nature of what is called human solidarity.

One who has a historical or genetic understanding of human affairs not only grasps a general theorem, namely, that the human good of order has

8 [Aristotle, *De Anima*, III, 430a 14–15.]

quibusnam adiunctis sint inventa, quibusnam gressibus perfecta, quibusnam fructibus retenta. Quae sane notitia, quatenus re vera haberi potest, non solum speculativo veritatis valore ornatur sed etiam maxima atque practica utilitate. Cum enim cuilibet, vel parum sapienti, manifestum sit neque omnia esse innovanda neque omnia conservanda, perdifficile tamen et admodum rarum est bene iudicare quaenam vetera quonam periculo derelinquerentur et quaenam nova quibusnam emolumentis introducerentur. Et quamvis eiusmodi quaestiones de futuro sint neque bene aestimentur nisi ab iis qui praesentem rerum statum penitus noverint, non parum tamen confert rei historicae amplitudo, ne more eorum qui agros colant nihil sana et tamen audaci imaginatione concipere possimus, neve cum plebe urbana omne quod diuturno usu probatum est eo ipso spernamus.

Quantum vero solidaritatem humanam respicit, ipsum quod exposuimus humanum ordinis bonum satis manifestat. Ex hoc enim ordinis bono singuli nati atque nutriti sumus. Ex eodem fonte omnia fere didicimus quae ad cultum faciant imaginationis, ad emotionum sobrietatem, sentimentorum vim, artis et scientiae acquisitionem, voluntatis firmitatem, verborum usum, actionis constantiam, modestiam, efficaciam. Quod ipsi exemplis, praeceptis, doctrinis imbibimus, fere idem nostro ingenio nostraque voluntate paulo modificatum, aliis tradimus. Quem processum ipsi nunc ferimus; olim patres, avi, proavi ferebant; ferentque posteri. Neque quidquam aliud esse videtur ipsum humanum ordinis bonum quam magna quaedam atque fidelissima summatio sive integratio eorum omnium quae ingenium humanum aliquando invenit et voluntas humana acceptanda, conservanda, tradenda elegit.

### *3 Quaenam sit quae dicitur cultura superior*

Quod hactenus consideravimus ordinis bonum, cum directe non respiciat nisi domestica, technica, oeconomica, politica,[9] bonum humanum exterius nominari licet. Cum tamen non solo pane vivat homo, aliud et culturale bonum iam investigari oportet.

been gradually built up through the insights and communal decisions of people themselves, but can also descend to particular factors so as to be able to determine the circumstances in which any one item was invented or discovered, by what steps it was developed, for what benefits it was retained. This knowledge, insofar as it is truly possessed, is enriched not only with the value of speculative truth but also with a very great practical usefulness. It is obvious to anyone who has even a modicum of wisdom that not every innovation is desirable and that not everything that exists should be kept unchanged; but it is a rare and difficult thing to judge surely what should be discarded and at what risk, and what innovations are to be admitted and to what advantage. True, these questions have to do with the future and are best pondered by those who have a thorough knowledge of the present state of affairs; still, a certain historical breadth of vision can be very helpful in these matters, lest, like tillers of the soil, we be incapable of conceiving sound yet bold and imaginative ideas, or on the other hand, like city folk, we reject what is traditional for the simple reason that it is so.

As for human solidarity, what we have said about the human good of order has made that sufficiently clear. Each one of us was born in and nurtured from this good of order. From this same source we have learned virtually everything that contributes to the cultivation of imagination, the control of emotions, the power of feelings, the acquisition of skills and knowledge, strength of will, use of language, and constancy, moderation, and effectiveness of action. What we ourselves have learned through example, precept, and teaching we hand on to others, slightly modified perhaps by our own insights and choices. We are now carrying out this process, as our forebears did before us and posterity will do after us. The human good of order seems indeed to be but an immense and carefully preserved summation and integration of all that human ingenuity at any time has discovered and the human will has chosen to adopt, maintain, and hand on.

### 3 *What is meant by 'higher culture'?*

The good of order that we have been considering so far, as it bears directly on household, technology, economics, and politics,[9] may be called the external human good. But since not by bread alone do we live, we must now examine another good, the cultural.

9 [See above, note 7.]

Si enim altiores quaeris humanae actionis radices, quattuor invenis ab ipsa natura indita desideria, nempe, (1) naturale intelligendi desiderium, quod non quiescat donec Deum per divinam essentiam cognoscat,[10] (2) naturale rectitudinis desiderium atque obligationem ut, quaecumque imperet ratio, exsequatur voluntas, (3) naturale felicitatis desiderium quod, quamvis de se indeterminatum sit,[11] determinationem maxime ex superiori hominis natura accipit,[12] et (4) naturale immortalitatis desiderium ut homo non solum hac in vita mortali sed etiam in alia eaque sempiterna numen supremum, rerum omnium principium et finem, cognoscat, laudet, colat. Quibus spiritualibus desideriis accedunt mira illa sentimentorum elevatio humanaeque sensibilitatis plasticitas quae hominem manifestant magis spiritum esse incarnatum quam animal ratione utens.

His ergo indigentiis hacque capacitate permotus, dupliciter homo in finem spiritualem procedere potest. *Aut* enim mysticorum more ex domestico, technico, oeconomico, politico ordinis bono sese retrahit ut, a materialibus conditionibus quam maxime liberatus, immediatum quendam accessum ad Deum quaerat, *aut* per ipsa materialia, corporalia, sensibilia in intelligibilia seu spiritualia pertingere contendit. Ubi primum eligitur, supremus colitur individualismus, non solum quia mysticus a communi hominum vita separatur, sed etiam quia id ipsum ad quod pervenit ne signis quidem exprimi et communicari potest. Ubi vero eligitur alterum, duplex stadium distingui oportet, primitivorum nempe et excultiorum hominum.

Primitivi ergo excultioribus neque ingenio neque aliis naturae donis inferiores inveniuntur: immo primitivi nascimur omnes. Imaginatione sane utuntur, intelligentia, iudicio, libero arbitrio, et signis. Neque minus in bonum spirituale quam in corporale tendunt, cum maxima apud eos observetur religio. Neque spirituale bonum cum corporali confundunt, cum aliter agros et aliter deos colant. Attamen sicut communiter bono ordinis corporali incumbunt, ita communibus ritibus spiritualia bona quaerunt. Sicut communis iis est vita, ita communis fere invenitur eorum cogitatio, deliberatio, electio, quibus proficit bonum humanum. Signis denique utuntur quae ita vitae communi tam ornandae quam ordinandae inserviant,

If you look for the deeper roots of human activity, you will find four desires implanted in us by nature herself: (1) the natural desire to understand, which will not be satisfied until we know God through his essence;[10] (2) the natural desire for rectitude, and the obligation of the will to carry out whatever reason commands; (3) the natural desire for happiness which, however indeterminate in itself,[11] receives its determination principally from our higher nature;[12] and (4) the natural desire for immortality, that we not only in this life but in a never-ending future life might know, praise, and worship a supreme deity as the source and goal of all things. To these spiritual desires there is joined a remarkable elevation of feeling and a plasticity of sensibility, which reveal us to be incarnate spirits more than animals having the use of reason.

Motivated by these needs and these capabilities, we can proceed to our spiritual goal via two routes. *Either*, like the mystics, we can withdraw from the domestic, the technological, the economic, and the political good of order so that, freed from material conditions as much as possible, we might seek immediate access to God. *Or* we can strive to attain the intelligible and the spiritual through the material, corporeal, and sensible. The former route develops a high degree of individualism, not only because mystics separate themselves from human society, but also because what they attain cannot be expressed and communicated even by signs. But where the second route is chosen, one must distinguish the stage of primitive peoples from that of more highly developed peoples.

Primitive peoples are found to be not at all inferior to the more advanced either in intelligence or any other natural gifts; in fact, we are all 'primitive' at birth. They certainly make use of imagination, intelligence, judgment, free will, and signs. They are as intent upon spiritual as upon physical well-being, for they are most careful in religious observances. Nor do they confuse spiritual goods with those of the body: they cultivate their deities quite differently from the way they cultivate their fields. However, just as they apply themselves to the bodily good of order in common, so do they seek spiritual goods in common rites of worship. As their life is communal, so as a rule are their thinking, their deliberation, and their decision-making for the promotion of the human good. Finally, while they use signs both to enrich and to regulate their communal living, they nevertheless are not given to those

10 Thomas Aquinas, *Summa theologiae,* 1, q. 12, a. 1; 1-2, q. 3, a. 8; *Summa contra Gentiles*, 3, cc. 25–63.
11 Thomas Aquinas, *Summa theologiae,* 1-2, q. 1, a. 7.
12 Ibid. q. 2, a. 3.

ut tamen a technicis et reflexis illis abstineant considerationibus quae non solum signis perficiuntur[13] sed etiam quodammodo circa signa versantur.

Qui autem excultiores dicuntur, ita reflexe in ipsa signa intendunt ut grammaticam dicant scientiam quae interiorem signorum ordinem respiciat, rhetoricam quae eorum expendat vim ad alios docendos atque commovendos, logicam quae connexionum necessitatem rationalem examinet, semanticam quae signi ad significatum habitudinem determinet, criticam[14] denique quae altioribus e principiis disputationes semanticas resolvere intendat. Qui maximus et diuturnus labor, quamvis primitivis omnino inutilis videatur, verae cuidam indigentiae humanae respondet. Cuius enim desiderium intellectuale in totum ens fertur nisi per signa technice elaborata neque in rerum naturalium essentias neque in spiritualium cognitionem analogicam clare, distincte, exacte procedere potest. Praeterea, cuius intellectus se habet in genere intelligibilium ut potentia tantum, solus parum proficit; et ideo sine signis technice elaboratis deficit illa inventorum communicatio quae ab aliis et posteris recipi, augeri, tradi possit. Denique tandem, ubi signa non communitati sed intellectui inserviunt, relaxatur communitatis dominium ut non solum novus quidam mundus contemplationi atque investigationi humanae aperiatur sed etiam novum communitatis genus efformetur.

technical observations and reflections that are not only completed[13] by means of signs but are even, in a sense, concerned with those signs.

Those peoples, however, who are said to be culturally more advanced do reflect upon their signs, and so they come to speak of grammar as the science concerning the internal ordering of those signs, rhetoric as the science that distributes their power to teach and persuade others, logic as the science that examines the rational necessity of the links between propositions, semantics as the science that determines the relationship between a sign and what it signifies, and criteriology[14] as the science that attempts to resolve semantic disputes by an appeal to higher principles. This laborious and time-consuming study may seem to primitive people quite useless, but it does respond to a genuine human need. For without a technical elaboration of these signs, one whose intellectual desire reaches out to all being cannot clearly, distinctly, and accurately proceed to probe the essences of natural things or to acquire an analogical knowledge of spiritual realities. Moreover, since the human intellect is only in potency in relation to the order of intelligible things, one will make little progress working in isolation. And thus, without this technical knowledge of signs there will be lacking that communication of discoveries that can be received, developed, and handed on by others and to posterity. Finally, when these signs serve not the community but the understanding, the domination of the community is loosened, so that not only is a whole new world opened up for one's contemplation and investigation, but even a new kind of community takes shape.

13 [Lonergan had written 'perficiuntur,' which he then changed to the active 'perficiunt' by crossing out by hand the last two letters. As it stands, 'quae [sc., considerationes] signis perficiunt' is ungrammatical, 'perficere' being a transitive verb. Possible alternatives would be either (1) 'quae signa perficiunt' or (2) 'quae signis proficiunt.' Both yield good meanings. In favor of the second is that he had used 'proficit' four lines above in the intransitive sense of 'progress,' 'develop,' 'advance'; and see also p. 292 below, where he speaks of mental development going hand in hand with linguistic development: '... haud fieri potest ut alia [sc. mens] sine alia [sc. lingua] multum proficiat'; and p. 298 below, where 'ordo proficiat secundum sapientiam iudicantis et bonitatem eligentis,' 'order grows in accordance with the wisdom of those who make judgments and the goodness of those who make decisions.' In any case, 'proficiunt' is virtually equivalent to 'perficiuntur.' The editors decided to restore 'perficiuntur,' while admitting that 'proficiunt' is an equally acceptable alternative.]

14 [In Scholastic philosophy, criteriology or critical philosophy, also sometimes called epistemology, is that part concerned with the grounds of certitude, the validity of knowledge, and its justification as knowledge.]

Qui enim exteriori ordinis bono occupatur, solus operari non potest sed in multis mentalitati atque arbitrio aliorum sese submittere debet. Qui autem technico signorum usu liberatur, non rerum materialium mordacibus curis[15] retinetur, non 'practicorum' hominum placitis atque decretis huc illuc distrahitur, sed altissimis illis desideriis ducitur quae rerum omnium intelligentiam et voluntatis rectitudinem et idealem quandam hominis felicitatem et spiritus immortalitatem quaerant, cogitent, optent. Per litteras ergo humaniores ad explicitam sui conscientiam pervenit homo. Per scientias puras tam propriam quam aliarum rerum perspicit naturas. Per philosophiam et theologiam mentem elevat tum ut ordinem universi speculetur tum ut universi creatorem cognoscat, laudet, eique serviat. Per historiam denique ita addiscit quid homo vel fuerit vel fecerit, ut clarius distinctiusque perspicere possit quid iam corrigendum, sperandum, faciendum sit.

Quod culturale bonum, cum aliud exterius praeter signa non exigat, facillime ex loco in locum transit et ex antiquissimis temporibus servatur. Cum praeterea ex ipsis altissimis naturae humanae radicibus procedat, stirpis, gentis, traditionis particularismum frangit et in universalem quandam animorum civitatem tendit.[16] Cum totum ens totumque bonum significare possit, interiorem hominis vitam ita auget, locupletat, perficit, ut homo exsistat non quasi pars quaedam vel instrumentum esset exterioris processus biologici, technici, oeconomici, et politici, sed suae dignitatis, libertatis, responsibilitatis conscius et ipsius exterioris processus iudex atque dominus.

Nam, uti superius diximus, exterius ordinis bonum ita hominibus intelligentibus et consentientibus iugiter commutatur ut ex quavis initiali situatione in quamlibet finalem levibus quidem sed perseverantibus gradibus procedatur. Sed ipsa superior cultura maxime in intellectu voluntateque humana residet et ideo in omne consilium omnemque consensum quibus exterius bonum evolvitur et suo iure et superiori quadam potestate influere solet. Quam ob causam, et ipsi materialistae non solum artes practicas et

Whoever is involved with the external good of order cannot operate alone, but in many things has to submit to the thinking and the will of others. But one who has been liberated through the technical use of signs is not held back by gnawing worries[15] about material things or pulled this way and that by the preferences and determinations of so-called practical people, but is drawn by those deeper desires which seek after, contemplate, and pursue an understanding of all things, moral rectitude, ideal human happiness, and spiritual immortality. Through literature and the humanities, we come to explicit self-consciousness. Through the pure sciences, we grasp our own nature and that of other things as well. Through philosophy and theology, we raise our mind to contemplate the order of the universe and to know, praise, and serve its creator. Through history, finally, we learn what humankind has been and has done, that we may grasp more clearly and distinctly what is now to be corrected, hoped for, done.

This cultural good, since it needs nothing external apart from signs, is easily transported from one place to another and well preserved from very ancient times. And since it springs from the deepest roots in human nature, it breaks through the particularism of tribe, race, and tradition and tends towards a universal commonwealth of persons.[16] Since it can express all being and all good, it enlarges, enriches, and develops the interior life, so that a person exists not merely as a cog or tool in some external biological, technological, economic, and political process, but as conscious of human dignity, freedom, and responsibility, the arbiter and master of the external process itself.

For, as we remarked above, the external good of order is continually changing as a result of people's insights and decisions, so that it moves from an initial situation to some final situation by imperceptible but persevering steps. But the higher culture itself resides principally in the human intellect and will, and hence in its own right and by its superior power it influences all those deliberations and agreements by which the external order evolves. That is why even materialists have a high regard not only for practical skills

15 ['mordacibus curis': an echo of a recurring phrase in Augustine: *Confessions* 7.5.7, ML 32, 736–37; 9.1.1, ML 32, 763; *The City of God* 22.22, ML 41, 784. See J.J. O'Donnell's commentary on *Confessions* 9.1.1, http://www.stoa.org/hippo/frames9.html, accessed 1/9/2017).]

16 [In 'Finality, Love, Marriage,' Lonergan called this 'the great republic of culture.' See *Collection*, vol. 4 in Collected Works of Bernard Lonergan, ed. Frederick E. Crowe and Robert M. Doran (Toronto: University of Toronto Press, 1988) 39.]

applicatas quae dicuntur scientias, sed et ipsam scientiam puram doctrinasque psychologicas, oeconomicas, politicas, historicas, maximi faciunt.

Ipsum denique culturale bonum saeculorum decursu proficere ita manifestum est ut tamen gravissimis malis saepius obscuretur. Quare de hac evolutione nihil ante dicendum esse censemus quam de malis tractaverimus.

### Articulus III: De signis

Quanta sit in humana vita signorum vis atque efficacia, facillime ex eo aestimatur quod, signis sublatis, tolluntur omnis hominum cooperatio, omnis traditio, omnis progressus, ut inter homines humanum nihil relinqui videatur. Quaecumque enim modo humano ab aliis accipimus, per signa accipimus; quaecumque exacte cogitamus, per signa quasi figimus atque tenemus; quodcumque agimus, non sola voluntate sed etiam sensibilitate signis excitata, directa, mota perficimus. Imo, ipsam nostram internam experientiam haud ipsi nobis clare manifestamus nisi eam signis exprimimus, obiectificamus, incorporamus; neque solam quae conscia dicitur vitam afficiunt signa sed etiam profundam atque latentem regnare videntur. Quae cum ita sint, haud miraris, ubi de bono quaeritur, ibi etiam de signo tractari, cum boni humani instrumentum tam necessarium quam universale exsistat signum.

Quod vero ad naturam signorum attinet, quattuor elementa seu principia maxime attendenda videntur, nempe, concretionis, conformationis, informationis, et mediationis.

*Concretionis* principium dicimus quod significatio fit et alicui et ab aliquo. Quod superflue dictum videretur nisi tot iam pridem exsisterent signa quae adeo abbreviata, technice elaborata, et multiplici mediatione remota sint (libros puta ab ignotis auctoribus lectoribus pariter ignotis conscriptos), ut facilius notionem quandam platonicam signi per se subsistentis formemus quam realitatem humanae communicationis apprehendamus.

*Conformationis* deinde dicimus principium seu elementum quo ita significans isque cui significatur inter se coniunguntur ut sensibilitas unius ad sensibilitatem alterius conformetur. Quod quidem exigit non solum conditiones illas externas ut alius indigitet et alius aspiciat, alius loquatur et alius audiat, alius tangat et alius tangatur, alius scribat et alius idem legat, sed etiam mutuam plurium affinitatem vel communem quendam finem vel similem internae conscientiae orientationem. Sicut enim canis non cuilibet sed domino ad nutum obedit, sicut amici intimis et vix ab aliis perceptis

and applied sciences, but also for pure science and for psychological, economic, political, and historical learning.

Finally, it is obvious that over the ages cultural development is often overshadowed by great evils. Hence it is best not to treat this development until we have explored evil.

### Article 3: Signs

The power and efficacy of signs in human affairs can readily be measured from the fact that without them all collaborative effort, all tradition, and all progress would disappear, so that nothing properly human would seem to be left among human beings. Whatever we receive from others in a human way we receive through signs. Whatever we have carefully thought out, we nail down, so to speak, and hold on to by means of signs. Whatever we do stems not only from our will but also from a sensibility that is aroused, directed, and moved by signs. Even our own interior experiences become clear to us only when expressed, objectified, and embodied in signs. Nor do signs affect just the life that is called conscious; they seem to dominate also the hidden depths. In the light of all this, it is no wonder that in treating the good we also have to examine the sign, seeing that it is such an indispensable and universal instrument of the human good.

As to the nature of signs, there are four elements or principles to be especially attended to, namely, the principles of concreteness, of conformation, of information, and of mediation.

By the principle of *concreteness* we mean that signification is done both to someone and by someone. Such an assertion might seem superfluous were it not that for a long time there have been so many signs that are so abbreviated, technically elaborated, and removed by multiple mediations (for example, books by unknown authors written for equally unknown readers) that we could easily form some Platonic notion of sign subsisting by itself instead of apprehending the reality of human communication.

Next, by the principle or element of *conformation* we mean that by which the signifier and the one to whom the sign is directed are connected in such a way that the sensibility of one is conformed to that of the other. This requires not only certain external conditions, so that one person signals and another watches, one speaks and another listens, one touches and another is touched, one writes and another reads, but also an affinity between them in various ways or a common purpose or a similar orientation of interior consciousness. Just as dogs obey not anybody but only their masters,

signis inter se communicant, ita etiam patet non omnes auditores iisdem magistris vel omnes lectores iisdem scriptoribus pariter attendere, sed alios aliis libentius, plenius, fructuosius accedere.

Attamen, praeter generale conformationis principium, etiam ad gradum conformationis attendendum est. Alia enim signa nisi ad apprehensionem non ordinantur; alia autem ad sympathiam, compassionem, participationem nos movent. Qui enim uno eodemque modo et folia diurna legeret et morientis matris ultima verba audiret, aut semper gravissimis motibus perturbaretur aut frigidus nimis durusque esse videretur. Nam sicut caetera sensibilia, signa etiam sensus nostros ita afficiunt ut tamen non omnia pariter imaginationem excitent, memoriam stimulent, emotiones evocent, sentimenta commoveant, desideria et timores aliasque animi passiones actuent. Qua de causa, secundum convenientem conformationis gradum, alia signa magis *denotativa* sunt quae vel parum vel nihil nos commoveant, alia autem magis *expressiva* sunt quae, sicut ex intensa significantis experientia procedant, ita tam profunde quam efficaciter totam alterius sensibilitatem penetrent.

Post conformationem, tertium *informationis* diximus esse signorum elementum. Eiusmodi enim est mutua formae et materiae coaptatio ut ubi similes sint formae, similes etiam sint dispositiones materiae, et vicissim ubi similes sint materiae dispositiones, similes etiam sint formae. Iam vero actus intelligendi se habet ad apprehensionem sensitivam sicut forma ad dispositiones materiae; et similiter comparatur actus volendi ad motum appetitus sensitivi. Quam ob causam, cum significans et is cui significatur quoad sensibilitatem gradu convenienti per signa mutuo conformati sint, ipsam hanc sensibilitatis conformationem in partem intellectivam extendit informationis principium. Nam qui ad eadem sensibilia attendunt, idem intelligunt. Qui multa et diversa eodem modo intelligunt ad iudicia similia perveniunt. Qui non solum intelligentia et iudicio sed etiam sensitivis appetitionibus assimilantur, similia eos velle atque eligere vix dubitatur. Per signa ergo denotativa communem quandem evolutionem intellectualem participant homines; per signa vero expressiva ita appetitionibus et electionibus uniuntur ut complurium diceres unam quandam esse animam et cor unum.

Quartum denique erat principium *mediationis*. Primum autem et principale medium est proprium uniuscuiusque corpus, quod non solum instrumentum animae coniunctum exsistit sed etiam hominis pars substantialis.

just as friends communicate by intimate signs that are hardly noticed by others, so it is clear that not all students pay equal attention to the same professors nor do all readers read the same authors with equal avidity, but different people listen to different teachers or read different authors with varying degrees of interest, thoroughness, and profit.

But besides the general principle of conformation there are also degrees of conformation. Some signs are intended merely to communicate knowledge; others move one to sympathy, compassion, participation. One who would read a newspaper and listen to the last words of his or her mother on her deathbed in the very same frame of mind would either be a highly excitable person or else exceedingly cold and unfeeling. Like other perceptible objects, signs affect our senses in different ways, so that not all excite our imagination, stimulate our memory, summon emotions, stir up sentiment, and agitate desires and fears and other passions of the soul to the same degree. Hence, according to the appropriate degree of conformation, some signs are mainly *denotative*, that is, they move us either very little or not at all; others are more *expressive* in that they proceed from an intense experience on the part of the signifier and penetrate the whole sensibility of another as deeply as they do powerfully.

The third element with regard to signs is that of *information*. Matter and form are so well adapted to each other that where there are similar forms there are also similar dispositions of matter, and conversely, where there are similar dispositions of matter there are similar forms. Now the act of understanding is to sensitive apprehension as form to the dispositions of matter; and the act of willing is similarly related to the movement of the sense appetite. Therefore, since the sensibilities of the signifier and the one to whom the sign is directed are conformed to each other in an appropriate degree, the principle of information extends this conformation of sensibility to their intellects. Those who attend to the same sensible objects understand the same things. Those who understand many different things in the same way arrive at similar judgments. Those who share not only the same understanding and judgments but also the same sensitive appetites are virtually certain also to will and to choose similar things. Thus, through denotative signs people share a common intellectual development, and through expressive signs they are so united in their desires and choices that, though many, they could be said to be of one mind and heart.

The fourth principle is that of *mediation*. The first and basic medium is each one's own body, which is not only a conjoined instrument of the soul but also a substantial component of a human being. This is why what is

Quam ob causam, magis immediate quam mediate significari videntur quae vultu, aspectu, tactu, risu vel lacrymis, vocis qualitate vel silentio, gestibus vel immobilitate, non citius exprimantur quam intersubiectiva quadam humanae naturae affinitate communicentur atque participentur. Quod si totum corpus magis intense, vivide, immediate latentem animam manifestat, longe maiorem evolutionem atque specializationem admittunt vocis articulatae usus et ipsarum vocum mediatio sive per nuntios, legatos, histriones, sive per litteras scriptas, missas, conservatas, sive per artes technicas et recentiores. Age vero, et ipsae linguae evolvuntur. Quamvis enim alius sit mentis et alius linguae progressus, haud fieri potest ut alia sine alia multum proficiat, si quidem omne quod exacte cogitetur etiam exacte significetur. Quam ob causam, quasi graduum series in singulis linguis discerni potest prout vocabulis antiquioribus magisque concretis perpetuo accedunt vocabula nova ad nova cogitata tam breviter quam accurate dicenda. Cui sane gradationi quodammodo correspondet audientium et legentium divisio, cum alii nisi voces magis elementares easque picturis illustratas intelligere non valeant, alii autem lingua evolutiori, pleniori, exactiori uti possint.

Secundum quattuor ergo vel principia vel elementa, concretionis nempe, conformationis, informationis, et mediationis, ex ipsa humanae communicationis realitate ad naturam signorum aliqualiter intelligendam processimus. Quibus perspectis, quasi colores per spectrum, ita etiam signa secundum differentias communicationis humanae dividi oportet. Alia enim sunt signa quorum magis conscii sumus et alia quorum vix conscii esse possumus. Alia sunt signa quae solam apprehensionem afficiunt et alia quae in partem appetitivam tam spiritualem quam sensitivam pertingere intendunt. Alia sunt signa quibus persona personae per proprium corpus immediate significat; alia sunt per personas intermedias significata; et alia sunt ita aliis signis mediata ut totam quandam mentis linguaeque evolutionem cognosci oporteat ut verus signorum sensus innotescere possit. Alia sunt signa tam brevia tamque simplicia ut ipsa per se sola significare videantur; et alia sunt quae sensum determinatum non accipiunt nisi per multa et alia signa loco forte et tempore maxime distantia. Alia denique sunt signa quae quilibet fere intelligere valet; et alia non intelliguntur sine praeparatione, initiatione, studio, imo mentis vitaeque conversione.

Dividuntur ergo signa secundum effectum conscium vel magis inconscium, secundum intentionem magis denotativam vel magis expressivam,

signified by facial expression, looks, touch, laughter or tears, tone of voice or silence, gestures or immobility, seems to be signified immediately rather than mediately, so that by reason of a certain intersubjective affinity in human nature it is no sooner expressed than communicated and shared. Now if the whole body manifests the hidden movements of the soul more intensely, vividly, immediately, the use of articulate speech and its mediation, whether by way of messengers, envoys, or actors, or by letters written, sent, and preserved, or by modern technological means, admits of far greater development and specialization. For one thing, languages themselves evolve. Although mental development and linguistic development are not the same thing, one can make very little progress without the other, since everything thought exactly is also expressed exactly. Hence a gradual development in every language can be detected as new words succinctly and accurately expressing new ideas are added to an older and more concrete vocabulary. To this gradual development there is a corresponding division among hearers and readers, for some are able to understand only simpler words, illustrated with pictures, while others can use a language more developed, fuller, more exact.

By way of these four elements or principles, therefore – concreteness, conformation, information, and mediation – we have arrived at some understanding of the nature of signs from the reality of human communication itself. In the light of this we must also divide signs, like colors in the spectrum, according to the differences in human communication. We are more aware of certain signs, less so of others, and there are still others that we are hardly aware of at all. Some signs affect only apprehensive faculties, others affect the appetitive part, spiritual as well as sensitive. There are some signs by which one person immediately communicates to another through their bodily presence to each other, and other signs that are made through personal intermediaries. There are signs that are mediated through other signs, so that one must be acquainted with an entire intellectual and linguistic development in order to know the true meaning of those signs. Some signs are so short and simple as to be self-explanatory. On the other hand, there are signs that cannot be definitively understood except by other signs which may often be quite remote in both time and place. Finally, there are signs that just about anyone can understand, while there are others that are not understood without preparation, initiation, study, and, indeed, a conversion of mind and life.

Signs, therefore, are divided by their effects, which may be more or less conscious; by the intention, which may be more denotative or more

secundum immediationem corporalem vel mediationem quae fit vel per alias personas vel per ipsam signorum evolutionem atque elaborationem, secundum extensionem contextus, et secundum capacitatem accipientis. Tanta enim est signorum vis et eo usque extenditur eorum efficacia quantum valeat spiritus humanus et incarnatus in alium sibi similem influere.

Quae cum ita sint, ad aliud longeque perfectius signorum genus mentem paulisper elevemus. Nam Dei Verbum caro factum sua carne non solum quae humanae naturae sed etiam quae divinae sunt personae manifestat, exprimit, communicat. Quae sane signa, sicut et caetera, elementis concretionis, conformationis, informationis, mediationis ita constant ut tamen a caeteris eminentia significantis differant. Quae per signa intendere et efficere potest spiritus humanus, ea omnia clarius, distinctius, efficacius potest Christus. Quae autem humani spiritus intentionem superant et efficaciam excedunt, intra proportionem iacent divinae personae. Analogice ergo inter se comparantur signa a Christo facta et caetera, neque per easdem normas haec et illa mensurantur. Utrinque invenitur potentia instrumentalis ad totam formandam humanam vitam, inde a latentibus et inconsciis structuris dynamicis usque ad intellectus vim, voluntatis aspirationem, cordis sinceritatem. Utrinque invenitur unitatis instrumentum quo homines tam exterius ordinis bonum perficiunt quam interiorem mentis evolutionem voluntatisque constantiam colunt. Sed humanis signis terrestris efficitur civitas, et mysterio Verbi incarnati inauguratur, crescit, perficitur regnum Dei.

## Articulus IV: De comparatione bonorum

Quaecumque in ipsa sua ratione contradictionem internam non includant, absolute potest facere Deus.

Porro, divina sapientia totum posse divinae potentiae comprehendit; non enim alia et minor est divina sapientia sed una et realiter eadem ac ipsa divina potentia. Proinde sapientis est ordinare. Et ideo dicendum est tot esse ordines rerum seu mundos possibiles quot requirantur ad omnia absolute possibilia ordinanda.

Praeterea, finis creationis est divina bonitas manifestanda, neque infinita sapientia a fine deficere potest. Quilibet ergo mundus possibilis ita sollerter per divinam sapientiam ordinatur ut ab infinita bonitate divina eligi possit ad eandem bonitatem divinam digne manifestandam.

expressive; by bodily immediacy or the mediation realized through other persons or through the development and elaboration of the signs themselves; by the scope of their context; and by the capacity of the receiver. The power of signs, and the range of their efficacy, is as great as the ability of one incarnate human spirit to influence another like oneself.

Having said all this, let us for a moment raise our minds to another and far more perfect kind of sign. The Word of God made flesh by his flesh manifests, expresses, communicates not only what belongs to human nature but also what belongs to the divine person. These signs, like the others, possess the elements of concreteness, conformity, information, and mediation, but of course they differ from those others by reason of the preeminent dignity of the signifier. Whatever the human spirit can intend and bring about through signs, Christ can intend and bring about more clearly, distinctly, and efficaciously; while what surpasses the intention of the human spirit, what exceeds its power, lies within the proportion of a divine person. Therefore, Christ's signs are compared to others analogically, and cannot be measured against the same norms. In both is found an instrumental potency for the total formation of human life, from the dynamic structures, hidden and unconscious, to the power of the intellect, the aspirations of the will, and sincerity of heart. In both is found an instrument of the unity by which people perfect the external good of order and foster the mind's interior development and the will's interior constancy. But human signs build a terrestrial city, while the mystery of the incarnate Word inaugurates, increases, and perfects the kingdom of God.

### Article 4: The comparison of goods

God can absolutely do whatever does not involve an internal contradiction.

Furthermore, divine wisdom embraces all that divine power can do; for God's wisdom is not different from or less than his power; both are one and the same reality. Moreover, it is the function of the wise person to establish order. Therefore, we conclude that there are as many possible orders of reality, or worlds, as are required for the ordering of all absolutely possible realities.

Besides, the end of creation is to manifest divine goodness, and infinite wisdom cannot fall short of attaining its end. Any possible world, therefore, is so sagaciously ordered by divine wisdom that it may be chosen by infinite divine goodness as a worthy manifestation of this same goodness.

Quibus perspectis, statim elucet tribus quasi elementis componi bonum creatum. Primum enim est elementum potentiale, quod in singulis possibilibus cernitur. Alterum est elementum formale, quod in ordinatione sapienti perspicitur. Tertium denique est elementum actuale seu valor, quod in proportione ad finem et ideo in eligibilitate consistit.

Quod autem in omni bono creato invenitur, in bonis humanis adsit necesse est. Nec cuipiam dubium esse potest bona particularia ad elementum potentiale pertinere, bonum ordinis ad elementum formale, bonum denique culturale, quo homo ad veram sapientiam producitur, ad elementum actuale seu ad valorem.

Bona enim particularia, si singula seorsum considerantur, infra proportionem humani appetitus inveniuntur. Nam appetitiones perpetuo recurrunt et ideo, ut bona correspondentia pariter recurrant, systemate quodam dynamico ordinari debent. Quod sane systema bonum ordinis est, quod ad bona particularia comparatur sicut forma artificialis et dynamica ad materialia arte ordinata. Proinde, cum ordines possibiles sint multi neque de ulla re tam acriter tamque vehementer disputent, imo et dimicent, homines quam de ordine quodam nuper invento sive technico sive oeconomico sive politico, tertium quoddam est humani boni elementum quod valores respiciat, quod iudicium sapiens et voluntatem bonam reddere intendat, quod bonum culturale nominetur.

Neque his tribus ratio hierarchica deest. Tanto enim bonum ordinis bonis particularibus maius est quanto certa atque continua bonorum series singulis seorsum bonis praeferenda est. Tanto autem bonum culturale bono ordinis praestat quanto sapiens progressus in ordines semper meliores anteponitur insipienti regressui in mala semper peiora. Sicut enim bonum ordinis facit ut bona particularia continuo recurrant, ita bonum culturale facit ut continuus ordinis fluxus atque mutatio non solum aberrationes evitet sed et in melius semper vertatur.

Cum tamen homo factus sit ad imaginem et similitudinem Dei, ita divinam perfectionem participat ut non solum sit bonum quoddam originatum sed etiam bonum bona originans.[17] Imaginatione enim bona particularia

In light of this it becomes immediately clear that created good is composed of three elements. First, there is the potential element that is found in possibilities taken singly; second, the formal element that is discernible in a wise ordering; third, the actual element, or value, which consists in its proportion to an end and hence its choiceworthiness.

But whatever is found in any created good must necessarily be present in human goods. Clearly, particular goods belong to the potential element, the good of order to the formal element, and cultural good, by which we are led to true wisdom, to the actual element or to value.

If particular goods are considered separately each by itself, they are found to be less than proportionate to human appetite or desire. For desires continually recur, and so in order for the goods corresponding to them likewise to recur, they must be arranged in some dynamic system. This system is of course the good of order, which stands to particular goods as a dynamic artificial form to the materials put in order by design. Accordingly, since there are many possible orders and since there is nothing that human beings argue about, indeed fight about, more bitterly and fiercely than some recently devised technological or economic or political order, there is a third element in the human good, which has to do with values, which aims to make judgment wise and the will good, and which is called the cultural good.

There is a hierarchy among these three. The good of order is as far superior to particular goods as a constant series of these goods is to each one taken separately. Cultural good is as far superior to the good of order as wise progress towards ever better orders is to foolish regression towards evils ever worse. Just as the good of order guarantees the continual recurrence of particular goods, so does cultural good enable the constant fluctuation and change occurring in the order not only to turn away from aberrations but also always to turn towards even better arrangements.

Since we are made in the image and likeness of God, we participate in the divine perfection in such a way that we are not only originated goods but also are ourselves instances of good originating goods.[17] By our imagination

17 [What Lonergan would come to call 'originating values': see his description of 'personal value' in the expanded hierarchy or scale of values presented in Bernard Lonergan, *Method in Theology*, vol. 14 in Collected Works of Bernard Lonergan, ed. Robert M. Doran and John D. Dadosky (Toronto: University of Toronto Press, 2017) 33: 'originator of values in himself and in his milieu.' There is also a parallel structure in the scheme of the human good suggested in *Method in Theology*: particular good, good of order, and terminal value. See Lonergan, *Method in Theology* 48.]

atque sensibilia repraesentat; inquisitione, intelligentia, et conceptione eadem ordinat; reflectione, iudicio, voluntate de imaginatis et ordinatis decernit. Sicut ergo originata bona sunt imaginata, ordinata, et decreta, ita bonum originans, ut quod, est ipse homo, et, ut quo, est actio repraesentandi, ordinandi, decernendi.

Praeterea, cum homo ab homine dependeat, eo usque divinam bonitatem participamus ut non solum bona originata sed etiam originantia producimus. Quatenus enim bonum ordinis externum cognoscimus, volumus, facimus, novam hominum generationem procreatam, nutritam, caeterisque vitae instrumentis donatam efficimus. Quatenus autem bonum culturale conservare atque promovere studemus, (1) imaginationem humanam ita evolutam volumus ut quodcumque bonum intellectu concipiatur etiam signis claris atque exactis imaginatione repraesentari possit, (2) intelligentiam humanam ita arte et scientia perfectam volumus ut sollerter ordinare possit non solum sensibilia bona particularia sed etiam spiritualia bona quae imaginatione tantum per signa repraesentetur, (3) sapientiam denique atque bonitatem humanam tales volumus quales meliorem semper ordinem certo sciant atque efficaciter velint.

Caeteris vero bonis anteponendas esse sapientiam atque bonitatem manifestum est tum propter intrinsecam dignitatem tum propter consectaria. Quo enim sapientiores melioresque sumus, eo perfectius Dei trini imaginem in nobis intus exprimimus: sapientis enim est propter perspectam evidentiam verbum verum dicere, et boni est propter bonum vere affirmatum amorem spirare. Quod si neque sapientia neque bonitate deficimus, caetera bona omnia suo tempore sequentur, cum bona particularia per ordinis progressum continuo augeantur, et ordo proficiat secundum sapientiam iudicantis et bonitatem eligentis. Quam ob causam, docuit nos ipse Dominus: 'Quaerite primum regnum Dei et iustitiam eius, et haec omnia adicientur vobis' (Mt 6.33).

Quod si in singulis propter dignitatem et in omnibus propter consectaria praestant sapientia atque bonitas, praeter ordinem ordinisque profectum qui exterius cernuntur alius quidam est ordo homini interior ut pars sensitiva rationi subdatur et debilis humana ratio summo enti, summo vero, summo bono subordinetur.[18] Si enim regit pars sensitiva, regit animal,

we represent to ourselves particular, sensible goods; by inquiry, insight, and conception we set them in order; by reflection, judgment, and will we make decisions regarding those things that we have imagined and put in order. Therefore, as originated goods are imagined, ordered, and chosen, so the originating good, as that which originates, is we ourselves, and, as that by which we originate, is the action of representing, ordering, and choosing.

Moreover, since human beings are dependent upon one another, our sharing in divine goodness is such that we produce not only originated goods but also originating goods. For insofar as we know and will and bring about the external good of order, we bring into existence a new generation of humanity born and nourished and equipped with all the other requirements for living. Insofar as we strive to maintain and improve cultural good, we want (1) a human imagination developed enough to be able to represent clearly and accurately in signs whatever the intellect conceives as good; (2) a human intelligence endowed with the skills and knowledge by which it can wisely order not only particular sensible goods but also spiritual goods that are represented in the imagination by signs only; (3) a human wisdom and goodness that knows with certainty and effectively wills an even better order.

Wisdom and goodness are obviously to be preferred to all other goods both by reason of their intrinsic dignity and because of their consequences. The wiser and better we are, the more perfectly we express inwardly the image of the triune God: it is the mark of a wise person to utter a true word on the basis of evidence clearly grasped, and of a good person to breathe love on the basis of a good truly affirmed. If we lack neither wisdom nor goodness, all other good things will follow in due course, since particular goods increase with the growth of order, and order grows in accordance with the wisdom of those who make judgments and the goodness of those who make decisions. Hence the Lord himself taught us, 'Strive first for the kingdom of God and his righteousness, and all these things will be given to you as well' (Matthew 6.33).

Now if wisdom and goodness are of supreme worth in each because of their intrinsic excellence and in all because of their beneficial consequences, there is, in addition to the external order and its progressive development, another, an interior order, in which our sensitive part is subordinated to our reason, and weak human reason is in turn subordinated to the supreme being, supreme truth, supreme good.[18] For if the sensitive part of our

18 [At this point Lonergan is moving into the territory marked by what the later scale of values calls personal value and religious value. See ibid.]

non qualecumque sed quod intellectu tamquam instrumento utatur. Si autem ratio a suprema regula ultimoque fine avertitur, iam insipiens facta est; iam verum ordinis bonum iudicat malum, et bonum mere apparens affirmat verum; iam continuum illum ordinis fluxum in bona mere apparentia vertere nititur et brevi, novarum rerum spe elatus, quaecumque vere bona sint destruere conabitur.

Quae cum ita sint, summi cuiusdam pretii est ordo ille interior quo ratio Deo et pars sensitiva rationi subditur. Quod quidem in omni rerum statu verum esset, in praesenti autem magnum fidei mysterium est cum homo naturalibus suis viribus non relinquatur sed supernaturaliter adiutus ad ipsum divinum bonum fruendum destinetur. Quam ob causam, etsi forte disputari possit utrum in ordine quodam alio, hypothetico, et mere naturali, homo inordinatus in se ipso ordinem quendam interiorem producere possit, in actuali tamen rerum statu ex infusis gratiae donis iisque solis ita rectus ordinatusque homo efficitur, ut filius Dei adoptivus constitutus, et Spiritus sancti templum exsistens, accessum personalem ad Deum Patrem habeat.

Quibus perspectis, quanti momenti sint relationes personales facile concluditur. Sicut enim per habitudines quibus persona personis coniungitur maxime solidatur eorum exterius ordinis bonum qui communem atque crescentem bonorum seriem coordinatis operationibus secundum instituta communia et secundum habitus usu cotidiano inductos prosequantur, ita etiam bonum culturale, quod exterius ordinis bonum salvat atque perficit, ultimam suam perfectionem atque efficaciam ex iis habitudinibus habet quibus per gratiam sanctificantem Patri per Filium in Spiritu coniungimur et per gratias actuales imaginem Dei trini, unusquisque suam, in nobis exercemus atque augemus.

### Articulus v: De malo

Malum est quod bono opponitur.

Quia ergo bonum dicit et ens et concretum et omnia, relinquitur malum nullam realitatem positivam habere. Quare non est essentia quaedam mali, et multo minus exsistit malum per essentiam seu summum malum.[19]

being is in control, an animal is in control, and not just any animal but one that uses intelligence as its instrument. And if reason turns away from its supreme norm and ultimate end, it has already become foolish: it judges a true good of order to be bad, and affirms a merely apparent good to be a true good. It tries to divert the ongoing changes in the order towards merely apparent goods and, in short, in its enthusiasm for novelty and revolutionary change, it will attempt to destroy everything that is truly good.

This being so, that interior order in which reason is subject to God and our sensitive part is subject to reason is of the utmost value. What would be true in any state of things is in our present state a great mystery of faith, since we are not left to our natural powers but are given supernatural assistance to attain our destined end, the enjoyment of the divine goodness itself. For this reason, even though one could perhaps debate whether in another, hypothetical, and purely natural order a disordered person could produce in himself a certain interior order, in the actual state of affairs it is by the infused gifts of grace and by these alone that we are set aright and in good order, so that, constituted as adopted children of God and temples of the Holy Spirit, we might have personal access to God the Father.

From all this it can easily be seen how important interpersonal relations are. The various interrelations that bind people together contribute most of all to consolidating the external good of order of those who seek a common and ever-increasing series of goods by their coordinated efforts, through their common institutions, and through the customs they have developed in their daily living. Similarly, the cultural good, which preserves and perfects the external good of order, receives its own perfection and efficacy from those relationships by which, through sanctifying grace, we are united to the Father through the Son in the Holy Spirit, and through actual graces, we exercise and develop within ourselves, each in his or her own way, the image of the triune God.

## Article 5: Evil

Evil is what is opposed to the good.

Therefore, since good denotes being and the concrete and everything, it follows that evil has no positive reality. Hence there is no essence of evil, and much less does there exist what is evil by essence or a supreme evil.[19]

19 Thomas Aquinas, *Summa theologiae*, 1, q. 49, a. 3.

Quia vero bonum dividitur in originans et originatum et bona originata dividuntur in bona particularia, bonum ordinis exterius, et bonum culturale, sequitur malum bono oppositum pariter dividi, ut sint malum originans et mala originata, et ut haec in mala particularia, in malum ordinis, et in malum culturale dividantur.

Praeterea, sicut bonum ordinis importat (1) seriem quandam continuam et certam bonorum particularium, (2) operationes coordinatas, (3) harum expeditionem tum per instituta tum per illam naturam secundam quae habitibus constituitur, et (4) personales amoris relationes, ita malum ordinis pro sua gravitate his omnibus plus minus opponitur. Dicit ergo malum ordinis (1) seriem quandam continuam et certam malorum particularium, (2) defectum tam operationis quam coordinationis, (3) harum impeditionem sive per vitia sive per instituta inepta, et (4) personales relationes quae suspicionibus, querelis, rixis, disidiis, simultatibus, bellis, odiisque signantur.

Ulterius, sicut bonum culturale continuum illum exterioris ordinis fluxum in melius semper dirigit et, quodammodo loci et temporis limitatione liberatum, ita interiorem hominis perfectionem promovet ut singuli, altioribus et spiritualibus indigentiis attendentes, homines veri nominis exsistant et omnes in unam quandam civitatem culturalem convocentur, ita malum culturale pro sua gravitate his omnibus opponitur. Sicut enim sapientia et bonitas ordinem mutabilem in melius, ita insipientia et malitia eundem in peius vertunt. Sicut bonum culturale ex materialibus in spiritualia hominem manuducit, ita malum culturale ex spiritualibus ad materialia hominem revocat. Sicut bonum culturale hominem ita liberare contendit ut, suae dignitatis conscius, determinismos sociales frangat, ita malum culturale in externum et materialem processum hominem retrudit. Sicut bonum culturale animorum unitatem intendit, ita malum culturale vel vi et armis vel indigentiis oeconomicis vel insidiis psychologicis exteriorem uniformitatem imponit.

Quae originata mala, sive particularia sive ordinis sive culturae, ex malo originante procedunt. Quare, cum homo sit bonum originans per imaginationem, per intelligentiam, et per rationalem libertatem, per defectum earundem malum originans efficitur. Nam per defectum imaginationis impeditur repraesentatio bonorum particularium; per defectum intelligentiae impeditur repraesentatorum ordinatio; per defectum libertatis rationalis aut peior ordinatio iudicatur melior aut melior, ut melior agnita, tamen non eligitur.

But since the good is divided into originating good and originated good, and originated goods are divided into particular goods, the external good of order, and cultural good, it follows that evil, as what is opposed to the good, is similarly divided. Thus we have originating evil and originated evil, and the latter is divided into particular evils, the evil of order, and cultural evil.

Moreover, as the good of order implies (1) a continual and secure flow of particular goods, (2) coordinated operations, (3) the facilitation of these operations both through institutions and through that second nature which consists of habits, and (4) loving personal relations, so the evil of order is opposed to all these to a greater or lesser degree according to its gravity. Hence the evil of order denotes (1) a continual and secure series of particular evils, (2) a breakdown in both operation and coordination, (3) a blocking of these through moral shortcomings or inept institutions, and (4) personal relations that are marked by suspicion, quarrels, strife, discord, feuds, war, and hatred.

Furthermore, as cultural good always seeks to channel the constant changes in the external order towards what is better, and, freed in a way from the limitations of time and place, promotes the interior development of persons so that by tending to their higher spiritual needs each may be a true human being and all may come together in one cultural community, so cultural evil in proportion to its gravity is opposed to all of these. As wisdom and goodness change the order for the better, so foolishness and ill-will change the order for the worse. As cultural good leads us from material to spiritual concerns, so cultural evil recalls us from the spiritual to the material. As cultural good strives to liberate human beings so that, being conscious of their dignity, they may free themselves from social determinisms, so cultural evil on the other hand pushes them back into the external material process. As cultural good aims at unity of minds and hearts, so cultural evil imposes on society an outward uniformity either by force or by economic deprivation or by insidious psychological means.

These originated evils, whether particular evils or the evil of order or cultural evil, all proceed from originating evil. Therefore, since persons are originating goods through their imagination, their intelligence, and their rational freedom, failure in the same makes them originating evils. A failure in imagination impedes a true representation of particular goods; a failure in intelligence impedes the proper ordering of what the imagination has represented to it; a failure in rational freedom results either in a worse ordering being judged to be the better, or in the better ordering not being chosen, even when acknowledged to be better.

Deficit autem imaginatio vel (1) inquantum ne sensibilia quidem bona repraesentat quae concreta, sensitiva, et forte diuturna experientia nondum innotuerunt, vel (2) inquantum ad efficacem signorum usum non pervenit ut repraesentari possint tum bona spiritualia tum maiores bonorum particularium series, vel (3) inquantum ordinanti intelligentiae parum inservit, partem forte materiae ordinandae subministrans sed non totam, ut rudes subtiliora in ratione agendi omittant, frivoli et improvidentes nisi de momento praesenti non cogitent, phantastici vivida quidem imaginatione eaque sola ducantur, eccentrici et solitarii ab ea empathia deficiant quae aliorum sentimenta, desideria, timores, gaudia, tristitias quodammodo praesentiat atque exspectet.

Intelligentia deinde deficere potest tum secundum comparationem ad materiam repraesentatam tum secundum comparationem ad rationem iudicantem. Sed quantum ad primum attinet, intellectus nisi per accidens non deficit. Quae enim intelligibilis unitas vel relatio in imaginatis perspicitur, illa sane iisdem imaginatis propria est. Sicut tamen in speculativis alia accidit imaginatione repraesentari et re vera alia sentiri, ita etiam in practicis accidit alia repraesentari et alia de facto evenire. Quod sane accidens ille non excludit qui, primo quodam intelligendi actu contentus, non ulterius inquirat utrum res vel situatio secundum omnes suos aspectus ita se habeat prout imaginatione repraesentata est.[20] Imo, cum practica etiam sint futura, cum futura incerta sint, non solum diuturnior rerum usus requiritur ut pedetentim evolvatur intelligentia practica, sed etiam, hac evolutione peracta, perpetuae manet cuiusdam vigilantiae necessitas ne olim peritissimi iam nunc ineptiores inveniamur.

Quod si deficere potest intelligentia relate ad ea quae imaginatione repraesentantur, longe facilior atque communior est defectus relate ad iudicium praeparandum. Nam sapientis est iudicare. Sapiens autem non est qui hanc tantummodo illamve materiam rite intelligit, et multo minus sapiens est qui nullam materiam perspectam habet. Sed plus quam humana est sapientia quae in omnibus et singulis rebus intellectis fundatur. Et ideo relinquitur eatenus ad sapientiam humanam pertingi quatenus per quandam ipsius intelligentiae intelligentiam summa saltem omnium rerum lineamenta perspiciuntur iisque earum ordo mutuaque interdependentia innotescunt, ut et vana dubia sperni possint et fundata dubia admittantur,

The imagination fails insofar as (1) it fails to represent even sensible goods which are not yet conspicuous from concrete, sensitive, perhaps even lengthy experience; or (2) it has not attained sufficient expertise in the effective use of signs to be able to represent both spiritual goods and the more important series of particular goods; or (3) it serves ordering intelligence poorly by providing it with only a part of the material to be ordered and not the whole, so that the less educated leave out the subtler factors in a plan of action, frivolous and thoughtless people think only of the present moment, visionaries are led by their vivid imagination and it alone, and eccentrics and loners lack the empathy that somehow senses beforehand and anticipates the feelings, desires, fears, joys, and sorrows of others.

Next, intelligence can fail both in relation to the material represented to it and in relation to rational judgment. In the first case, the intellect fails only *per accidens.* For whatever intelligible unity or relation is discerned in the imagined data certainly belongs to those imagined data. But as it can happen in speculative matters that what was represented by the imagination may not be the same as what was actually perceived by the senses, so in practical matters it sometimes happens that what actually turns out is not what had been imagined. Now this accidental occurrence is certainly not going to be prevented by one who, being satisfied with the first act of the intellect, does not ask further whether the thing or situation really is in all its aspects just as it was represented in the imagination.[20] Moreover, since practical matters are in the future and the future is uncertain, not only is considerable experience required for the gradual development of practical intelligence, but even when this development has taken place, we remain in need of a kind of perpetual vigilance lest we find that where once we were experts, now we are clueless.

If intelligence can fail in relation to what is represented to it by the imagination, much more easily and frequently does it fail preparing for judgment. For to judge belongs to the wise. One who correctly understands only this or that particular matter is not wise, however, and much less wise is one who has grasped nothing at all. But the wisdom grounded upon an understanding of each and every thing is beyond us. It remains, therefore, that one attains human wisdom to the extent to which through an understanding of what understanding is one grasps at least the broad lines of all things and by them knows their order and mutual interdependence, so that baseless doubts may be rejected and grounded doubts admitted, insoluble

20 [The first act of the mind is understanding; the second is judgment.]

ut insolubiles quaestiones qua tales agnoscantur et quemadmodum circa solubilia procedendum sit aperiatur. His enim ignotis tamquam navis gubernaculo privata huc illuc fluctuatur ratio neque ad firma certaque pervenit iudicia, cum iudicii criterion seu motivum sit perspecta evidentiae sufficientia, criterion autem sufficientiae non ex singulis rebus seorsum sumptis desumi possit, si quidem omnes tam in entitate quam in bonitate inter se colligentur.

Tertio deficit homo in ipsa sua rationali libertate per quam tum ordines intellectos tum particularia bona intra ordines contenta ad rationem valoris iudicando promovet et eligendo actualitate donat. Quod quidem in homine et intrinsece optimum est et caeterorum iudex atque dominus. In se optimum est ut, intra conscientiam rationalem et vi ipsius rationalis conscientiae, propter perspectam evidentiam affirmetur verum, et propter bonum vere affirmatum spiretur boni amor. Caeterorum iudex atque dominus est, cum bonorum particularium repraesentatio intelligentem ordinationem postulet, et multae ordinationes possibiles, acuta intelligentia inventae, rationalem comparationem, evaluationem, electionem exigant.

Optimi autem pessima est corruptio. Quod enim deficit rationalis conscientia, hoc factum quoddam est. Cur autem deficiat, neque causa proportionata neque vera ratio assignari potest. Malum enim quod rationali conscientiae opponitur irrationale est. Quod irrationale est, eius nulla est vera ratio, secus irrationale non esset. Quod irrationale est, eius nulla est proportionata causa; quod enim in homine, ratione inferius, in actus humanos influit, non plena et proportionata causa actus humani exsistit, sed incompleta et partialis quae complementum rationalis iudicii liberaeque electionis per se exspectet. Cur ergo peccaverunt angeli? Cur Adamus? Non est 'cur.' Imo si fuisset 'cur,' non fuisset peccatum. Nam propter veram rationem rationaliter iudicat et eligit conscientia rationalis; et qui per rationem eamque veram ducitur, ille non peccat. Quod si alia praeter rationalem conscientiam assignaretur causa proportionata, processus non rationalis sed mere naturalis fuisset, ut iterum excludatur peccatum.

At si caeterorum iudex dominusque corrumpatur, corrumpantur caetera necesse est. Imo, ipsa profectus ratio atque vis in vim quandam regressivam atque destructivam convertitur. Ideo enim exterius ordinis bonum ex parvis quibuscumque initiis per meliora semper inventa in maximam civilizationis perfectionem procedit, quod ipsa materialia sunt in potentia intelligibilia. Nam nisi iis potentialis intelligibilitas inesset, nulla esset

problems may be recognized as such, and it may become clear how to proceed with regard to those that can be solved. For unless these things are known, human reason, like a ship without a rudder, is blown this way and that and never arrives at sound and certain judgments, since the criterion or motive of judgment is a grasp of the sufficiency of the evidence, and the criterion of sufficiency cannot be based upon individual things taken separately, since all things are mutually bound together in both their being and their goodness.

Third, we can fail in our rational freedom itself. By rational freedom, we promote to the status of value in judgment both the orders we understand and the particular goods they include, and we give actuality to them in decision. It is rational freedom indeed that is both intrinsically noblest in humankind and judge and master of all else. It is noblest in itself in that, within rational consciousness and by force of rational consciousness itself, the truth is affirmed because the evidence is grasped, and love is spirated on account of the good truly affirmed. It is judge and master of all else, since the imaginative representation of particular goods calls for an intelligent ordering, and the many possible orderings discovered by a keen intelligence require rational comparison, evaluation, and choice.

The corruption of the best, however, is the worst. That rational consciousness fails is simply a fact. As to why it fails, no proportionate cause, no true reason, can be given. For the evil opposed to rational consciousness is irrational. What is irrational has no true reason; otherwise it would not be irrational. What is irrational has no proportionate cause; for that part of us, inferior to our reason, which influences human acts is not the full and proportionate cause of human acts, but rather an incomplete and partial cause that awaits its completion by rational judgment and free choice. Why, then, did the angels sin? Why did Adam? There is no 'why.' On the contrary, if there were a 'why,' it would not be sin. It is on account of a true reason that rational consciousness judges and chooses; and whoever is led by a true reason is not sinning. And should some other proportionate cause besides rational consciousness be assigned, that process would not be rational but merely natural, and so again sin would be excluded.

But if the judge and master of all the others is corrupted, inevitably the others will be corrupted too. Indeed, the very driving force of progress is thus turned into a regressive and destructive force. The reason the external good of order grows from small beginnings through better and better discoveries into a great civilization is that material things are intelligible in potency. If there were in them no potential intelligibility, there would be no

actualis intelligibilitas ab intellectu invenienda, a ratione iudicanda, a voluntate eligenda; quae si non esset, nullatenus bonum ordinis vel exsistere vel augeri posset. Sed, uti nuperrime vidimus, quod deficit conscientia rationalis irrationale est, nullam veram rationem habet, neque causa eius proportionata assignari potest. Quod si irrationalis et absurda est voluntatis electio, pariter irrationalis atque absurda est consequens actio; si irrationalis et absurda est actio, haud minus irrationalis atque absurda est obiectivae situationis mutatio. Iam vero, totalis obiectiva situatio ex parvis et accumulatis mutationibus constituitur. Qua ergo lege ex primitiva penuria ad maximas civitatum divitias proceditur, eadem lege per parva sed accumulata irrationalia ad situationem penitus irrationalem pervenitur. Quatenus vero situatio irrationalis est, quatenus absurda est, eatenus ne potentia quidem intelligibilis est. Scatent problemata, sed desunt solutiones, cum problema ad solutionem comparetur sicut intelligibile potentia ad actu intelligibile. Febrili quadam activitate quaeruntur remedia sed frustra, cum ea tantummodo intellectu inveniri possint quae morbum alium in alium forte peiorem commutent. Maxima sane est vis intellectualis, cum potens sit omnia facere et fieri; tanta tamen non est ut absurdum actu intelligat; et ideo post multa et vana tentamina alii de rebus humanis desperantes in solatium deserti confugiunt; alii alias et novas semper et exquisitiores invehunt doctrinas, ut omnes diversa opinantes circa nullum fere commune consilium consentire possint; alii denique, novarum rerum prophetae, hominem iudicant animal quoddam symbolicum, humanumque ordinis bonum in eo ponunt quod socii maximis et gravissimis poenis perterriti efficiantur dociles, ut dociles facti per vacuam quandam propagandam regantur. Quo tamen in carcere quis custodit custodes? Quonam captivorum gregem ducunt qui non sapientia neque bonitate sed sola potestate emineant?

His igitur perspectis, non solum progressivum sed etiam regressivum esse constat motum illum circularem quo situatio in intelligentiam, intelligentia in voluntatem, voluntas in actionem, actio denique in situationem mutandam agit. Proficit sane exterius ordinis bonum quatenus potentialem situationis intelligibilitatem actuat diligens intellectus. Sed quatenus subrepit absurdum, eatenus amor in odium, virtutes in vitia, instituta in instrumenta nequitiae, coordinatio in pugnam, operatio in inertiam, bonorum profluvium in egestatem, ipsiusque intellectus ad omnia potentia in impotentiam transit. Quam ob causam, magna imperia magna latrocinia nominavit

actual intelligibility to be discovered by the intellect, affirmed by reason, and chosen by the will – in which case no good of order could exist or expand at all. But, as we have just seen, the failure of rational consciousness is irrational, lacks any true reason, nor can any proportionate cause be assigned to it. But if the choice of the will is irrational and absurd, the consequent action is equally irrational and absurd; and if the action is irrational and absurd, the change in the objective situation will be no less irrational and absurd. Now the total objective situation is built up of small accumulated changes. The law by which a city or nation progresses from poverty-stricken beginnings to great affluence is the same law by which the accumulation of minor irrationalities leads ultimately to a thoroughly irrational situation. To the degree to which a situation is irrational and absurd, it is not even potentially intelligible. Problems abound, but solutions are nowhere to be found, since a problem is to its solution as the potentially intelligible is to the actually intelligible. There is a lot of fevered activity to find remedies, but all in vain, since intelligence can find only those things that might exchange one sick situation for another and possibly worse one. The power of the intellect is, of course, very great, since the intellect can make and become all things; but it is not so great as to actually understand the absurd. Hence, after many fruitless efforts, some people, despairing of humanity, take refuge in the desert; others bring in all kinds of novel and far-fetched theories so that, with everyone having a different opinion, no common plan of action can be agreed upon. Others, finally, as prophets of revolution, consider a human being to be a 'symbolic animal,' and for them the human good of order consists in so terrorizing its members with extreme forms of punishment as to render them quite docile and hence able to be swayed by inane propaganda. In such a prison as this, who will guard the guards? Where will those who are in command, not by reason of their wisdom or goodness but by naked power, lead their captive flock?

From all this it is clear that that circular movement by which the external situation influences the intellect which in turn influences the will to act upon and modify the situation can be not only progressive but also regressive. No doubt the external good of order is advanced when keen intelligence actuates the potential intelligibility of a situation. But to the degree to which the absurd creeps in, love is replaced by hatred, virtue by vice, good institutions by instruments of wickedness, cooperation by strife, activity by inertia, abundance by want, and the universal power of the mind by intellectual impotence. This is why St Augustine referred to great empires

S. Augustinus;[21] eandemque ob causam, sicut lapides sursum in aerem proiecti alius alio altius ascendit sed omnes in terram denuo cadunt, ita in rebus humanis alii populi aliis magis bonum ordinis perfecerunt ut tamen singuli suo tempore decadentiam atque disintegrationem subirent.

Neque perturbato ordine externo salvum tutumque consistere potest bonum culturale quod interiorem hominis perfectionem in primis intendit. Haec enim perfectio finis quidem est. Sed qualis quisque est, talis finis videtur ei.[22] Qui ergo in bonitate inaequales sint, alii aliam iudicant interiorem hominis perfectionem; qui autem de fine non consentiant, de mediis aptis dissident ut eadem studia, eaedem scholae, iidem magistri aliis humanitatis et veritatis fontes, aliis autem tristia antiquitatis monumenta esse videantur.

Quae tamen mentium divisio paulo altius consideranda est. Aliud enim est bonum culturale quod naturali desiderio intelligendi, rectitudinis, verae felicitatis, et immortalitatis concipitur atque evolvitur. Aliud autem est bonum culturale quod concretis humanae vitae adiunctis ita accomodatur ut theoria et praxis non toto caelo inter se distant. Illud enim ex altissimis humanae naturae radicibus depromitur ut pulcherrimum quoddam ideale[23] definiatur. Hoc autem usui cotidiano consonum est. Quae quidem duo eo magis inter se distant quo magis concreta humanae vitae adiuncta et cotidianus exsistentium hominum usus inficiuntur absurdo. Quam ob causam, qui bonum culturale et ideale prosequuntur, otiosum finem quaerere videntur cum ideale illud ab exsistentibus hominibus nimis alienum inveniatur. Qui autem bonum culturale concretis vitae adiunctis accommodant, bonum illud detorquent atque corrumpunt cum illud absurdo consonum faciant.

Neve hanc conclusionem miremini. Prima enim alienatio facta est cum intra rationalem conscientiam exortum sit irrationale. Quo admisso, fieri non potest quin cultura et vita, theoria et praxis, ideale et reale ita inter

as larceny on a grand scale.[21] For the same reason, just as when stones are thrown up in the air, some go higher than others but all eventually fall to the ground, so in human affairs some nations may surpass others in achieving the good of order but all in due time decline and crumble.

When the external order is disturbed, cultural good, which aims primarily at interior personal perfection, cannot remain unscathed. This interior development is an end, a goal, but 'as each one is, so does his end seem to him to be.'[22] Hence persons of unequal goodness will judge differently about interior human perfection; but in disagreeing about the end they will disagree about the suitable means to that end, so that the same studies, the same schools, the same teachers that seem fountains of truth and humanity to some seem to others but sad monuments of the past.

The difference between these mentalities merits somewhat deeper consideration. There is one kind of cultural good that is conceived and developed from the natural desire for understanding, rectitude, true happiness, and immortality. There is, however, another kind of cultural good, so accommodated to the concrete conditions of human living that theory and practice are not worlds apart. The first kind is drawn from the deepest roots of human nature so that it is laid down as a beautiful ideal.[23] The second kind harmonizes with daily behavior. The more the concrete circumstances of people's lives and actual everyday activities are infected by the absurd, the farther apart these two cultural goods will be. Hence those who pursue the ideal cultural good seem to be pursuing a useless goal, since that ideal is so far removed from actual human living. But those who adapt cultural good to the concrete conditions of life twist and corrupt that good when they harmonize it with the absurd.

Do not be surprised by this conclusion. The first alienation occurs when the irrational emerges within rational consciousness. Once it is let in, it is inevitable that culture and life, theory and practice, the ideal and the real

21 ['Remota itaque justitia, quid sunt regna nisi magna latrocinia?' Augustine, *De civitate Dei* IV, 4, ML 41, 115.]

22 [Aristotle, *Nicomachean Ethics*, III, 5, 1114b 1. Thomas cites this saying, for example, in *Summa theologiae*, 1, q. 83, a. 1, obj. 5. Lonergan paraphrases in *Early Works on Theological Method 3*, vol. 24 in Collected Works of Bernard Lonergan, trans. Michael G. Shields, ed. Robert M. Doran and H. Daniel Monsour (Toronto: University of Toronto Press, 2013) 42–43: 'What kind of person I am and what kind of world is present to me are correlative.']

23 [Translator's note: 'pulcherrimum quoddam ideale' seems to be Lonergan's rendering of the French expression 'beau idéal' as it is incorrectly, albeit commonly, understood by English speakers as 'a beautiful ideal.']

se opponantur ut alterum alteri alienissimum iudicetur. Tolleretur sane haec alienatio si converteretur vita, reformaretur praxis, transformaretur reale. Sed stante primo irrationali, neque vita convertitur neque praxis reformatur neque reale transformatur. Stante primo irrationali, aliam minusque arduam incedunt homines viam, ut cultura vitae accommodetur, theoria praxi adaptetur, et ipsum ideale quasi mythus vel somnium reputetur.

Prima ergo alienatio, qua ipsa rationalis conscientia contra se dividitur, in aberrationem culturalem abit. Ipsum bonum culturale, quod aptum natum est ad interiorem hominis perfectionem communicandam atque augendam, prava honestis et falsa veris admiscet atque confundit. Non minus quam exterius ordinis bonum, bonum etiam culturale tam legi regressus quam progressus legi subicitur. Ubi tamen ordo exterior, rebus inhaerens, certo loco certoque tempore restringitur, neque deficere potest quin per manifestam inefficaciam, decadentiam, disintegrationem vitia sua omnibus inspicienda exhibeat, culturale bonum, signis inhaerens, non solum omnia loca et tempora pervadere potest sed etiam ita corrumpitur ut corruptionem suam tegat, ita falsa disseminat ut vera reputentur, ita mala spargit ut hominibus minus rationalibus maxime placeant.

Cuius alienationis signa atque consectaria ubique inveniuntur. Qui primi induxerunt idola ad numen supremum repraesentandum, non solum homines sensibilibus immersos ad Deum sed Deum etiam ad homines conducere volebant. Venatores qui animalia quasi deos colebant, agricultores qui deas fertilissimas fingebant, nomades qui corpora caelestia venerabantur, communem diversi voluntatem habuerunt ut religio concretis vitae adiunctis non aliena sed consona atque intellectu facilior videretur. Quod si imperatores multas et diversas gentes in unum regnum subiciebant, sacerdotes singularum gentium deos in unum pantheon adunabant, ut mythologi collectionem genealogiis explicarent. Esto magnos philosophos crisin deorum instituisse. Sed ab ipsis fere initiis multae et oppositae fuerunt philosophiae, neque purissima quaeque et altissima etiam concretis vitae adiunctis maxime consona invenitur; imo, dum Academia ad scepticismum, dum Lycaeum ad empirismum, dum elevatio Plotini ad miras Iamblichi superstitiones quasi humano pondere declinantes vergebant, satis sibi constabant qui partes atomistarum et Epicureorum placita sustinuerunt.

will be so opposed to each other that one will be considered quite alien to the other. True, this alienation would disappear if there were to occur a conversion of life, a reform of practice, and a transformation of reality. But as long as the first irrationality remains, there will be no conversion of life, no reform of practice, no transformation of reality. As long as the first irrationality remains, people will continue to travel along another less arduous road, so that culture is accommodated to life, theory adapted to practice, and that ideal itself is counted as a myth or a dream.

The first alienation, therefore, by which rational consciousness is divided against itself, leads to cultural aberration. Cultural good itself, which is meant to communicate and develop our interior perfection, mixes and confuses the base with the noble and the false with the true. No less than the external good of order, cultural good too is subject to the law of decline as well as the law of progress. But while the external order, inherent in things, is limited to a particular place and time and cannot break down without revealing its flaws for all the world to see in its obvious ineffectiveness, decadence, and disintegration, cultural good, inherent in signs, not only can spread throughout all places and times, but also can be corrupted in such a way as to hide its own corruption, disseminates what is false under the guise of truth, and broadcasts evil in a manner most appealing to less rational people.

The signs and the consequences of this alienation are everywhere. Those who first introduced idols to represent a supreme being wanted not only to lead people immersed in sensible things to God, but also to bring God down to people. Hunters who honored animals as gods, farmers who fashioned images of fertility goddesses, nomads who venerated the heavenly bodies – all these various types had this common intent, that religion should not appear to be apart and aloof from the concrete circumstances of daily life but rather be in close harmony with them and easier to understand. If emperors succeeded in bringing many diverse peoples under one rule, priests brought the gods of every nation together in one pantheon, so that mythologizers explained this collection in terms of genealogies. Granted that the great philosophers instituted a critique of the gods; but almost from the very beginning a host of contradictory philosophies arose, and even the purest and deepest of them are also found to have been largely in tune with the concrete conditions of those times. In fact, while the Academy was degenerating into skepticism, the Lyceum into empiricism, and the lofty thought of Plotinus into the bizarre superstitions of Iamblichus by a typically human downward pull, so to speak, those who subscribed to the notions of the atomists and of the Epicureans remained fairly consistent.

Neque antiqua suggerimus exempla quasi deessent recentiora. Si enim angustiis premimur, non solum propter exteriorem ordinem periclitantem angimur sed etiam propter profundam atque fere universalem animorum alienationem. Nobiscum Protestantes ita religionem positivam et supernaturalem retinent ut tamen illi ecclesiam visibilem et vera auctoritate praeditam reiciant. Nobiscum liberales personalem integritatem, libertatem, responsibilitatem ita laudant ut tamen illi omnem religionis supernaturalis utilitatem vel possibilitatem negent. Nobiscum totalitariani exterioris boni augmentum iustamque distributionem praedicant qui tamen omnem religionem funestam deceptionem et omnem aliorum philosophiam ideologiam iudicent. Quibus profundioribus differentiis accedunt multa et alia undequaque provenientia, ut dividantur primitivi populi et magis exculti, occidentales et orientales, singulae nationes, classes, coetus, imo et homines diversi coloris, neque solum ob actuales difficultates sed etiam propter acerbam praeteriti temporis memoriam futurique iustum terrorem.

Quod ergo intra rationalem conscientiam exoritur irrationale, et hominem ipsum sibi alienum facit et homines inter se et homines a rerum natura. Quae tamen mala, etsi fere innumera atque gravissima, tamen minora sunt. Fecit Deus hominem ad imaginem et similitudinem suam. Fecit hominem rationalem ut, sicut Filius a Patre ut Verbum et sicut Spiritus sanctus a Patre Filioque ut Amor procedunt, etiam homo suam quisque Dei trini imaginem exprimat cum vi conscientiae rationalis verum propter perspectam evidentiam affirmet et boni amorem propter bonum vere affirmatum spiret. Fecit hominem personam ut, sicut divinarum personarum una est tribus communis essentia atque operatio, ita etiam personae humanae communi ordinis et culturae bono fruerentur. Fecit hominem personam Deo similem ut eum diligeret, in filium adoptaret, in vitam aeternam produceret. Ab hac tamen divina intentione recedit qui ita abusus est sua Dei imagine ut et sibi et aliis totique naturae se alienum fecisset. Ab hac divina intentione recedit qui oblatam Patris amicitiam et collatam Filii assimilationem et inhabitantis Spiritus consuetudinem et vitae aeternae spem indeclinabilem noluit. Quod nolle, peccatum est, Dei offensa est, alienatio a Deo est. Sed cui Deus alienus est, ei verum per essentiam alienum est, ei bonum per essentiam alienum est, ei ens per essentiam alienum est. Qui his alienus exsistit, omni vero, omni bono, omni enti alienus reapse est, cum ea quae per participationem dicantur eatenus vera, bona, entia sint quatenus illud participent quod per essentiam verum, bonum, ens sit. Qui tandem denique Deo et sibi et hominibus et reliquae naturae alienus est, qui toti vero, toti bono, toti enti alienus est, quid ei dici potest ab ipsa divina

Nor are we adducing examples from the ancient world as if there were no recent ones. If we are in dire straits today, it is because we are in distress not only from imminent danger to the external order, but also from a profound and virtually universal spiritual alienation. Protestants hold on to positive supernatural religion, as we do, yet reject a visible church endowed with real authority. Liberals extol personal integrity, liberty, responsibility as we do, yet entirely deny the use or even the possibility of supernatural religion. Totalitarians preach with us the increase and just distribution of external goods while condemning all religion as a baneful fraud and all other philosophies as ideology. On top of these profound differences there are a host of others from many different sources: underdeveloped and developed nations, western and eastern peoples, individual states and classes and groups, even people of different color, all divided one against the other not only on account of present grievances but also because of bitter memories of the past and well-founded fears of the future.

The irrationality that emerges within rational consciousness alienates us from ourselves, from others, and from nature. Yet all these evils, however numerous and serious, are relatively minor. God made human beings in his own image and likeness. He endowed us with rationality so that, as the Son proceeds as Word from the Father, and the Holy Spirit proceeds as Love from the Father and the Son, each human being might in his or her own way show forth an image of the triune God by the power of rational consciousness: affirming truth because of evidence grasped, and spirating a love of the good because of goodness truly affirmed. He made us persons so that just as the three divine Persons share a common essence and activity, human persons might enjoy in common the good of order and of culture. He made us persons similar to God so he might love us, adopt us as his children, and bring us to eternal life. Those who so abuse their godlike image as to become alienated from themselves, from others, and from the world of nature withdraw from this plan of God. They withdraw from it in refusing the Father's offer of friendship, assimilation to the Son conferred by grace, the abiding presence of the Spirit, and the sure hope of eternal life. This refusal is sin: it is an offense against God, alienation from God. But the person alienated from God is alienated from the essentially true, alienated from the essentially good, alienated from what is essentially being. And whoever is alienated from these is in very truth estranged from all that is true, all that is good, all that is, since whatever is called true, good, being by participation is so inasmuch as it participates in what is essentially true, good, being. To those, finally, who are totally alienated from God, from

bonitate praeter illud, 'Discedite a me maledicti in ignem aeternum' (Mt 25.41). Discedunt quia accedere noluerunt. Maledicuntur quia mali sunt. Abeunt in poenas aeternas non fallibili iudicio vel inepta lege humana sed divino decreto quod, quamvis intellectum nostrum excedat, divinitus tamen revelatum certo credimus et ex divina sapientia atque bonitate processisse certo scimus.

## Articulus VI: E malis bonum

Sicut bona nexu multiplici inter se colligantur ipsaque mala bono opposita mutuato quodam ordine aliud ex alio procedit, ita e malis in bonum renovari atque restaurari potest mutabilis atque materialis creatura.

Nam in primis ipsa numerica rerum multiplicatio perpetuam quandam renovationem importat. Moriuntur senes iam correctionis incapaces, sed vitiis nondum acquisitis nascuntur parvuli. In singulis praeterea populis ita decidit atque collabitur exterius ordinis bonum ut tamen alius populus minusque corruptus, quasi lampada acciperet, artes ab alio inventas ordinemque ab alio institutum in novam perfectionem adducere possit. Bonum denique culturale ita priori aetate exstingui potest ut denuo sub aliis adiunctis apud alios renascatur; quod nobis notissimum est cum culturalem occidentalem formaverint poetae, geometrici, philosophi graeci, iurisque consulti romani.

At praeter hanc renovationem fere materialem qua ita interit malum ut in alio servetur bonum, etiam verioris nominis exsistunt conversio e malis bonorumque restauratio ut sive in individuo sive in societate sive in processu historico ipsa malorum particularium perpessio ordinem doceat, mala ordinis bonum culturale promoveant, et mala culturalia redemptorem divinitus missum flagitent.

Omnino enim perspicuum est e malis particularibus perpessis addisci ordinem. Nam ea lege vel naturalem vel stabilitum rerum ordinem addiscimus singuli ut, ubi sensus negligentior vel intellectus segnior fuerit, per perpessum dolorem vel damnum cautiores et acutiores in posterum efficiamur. Quod autem singulos singula et particularia docent mala, idem multiplicata et particularia mala docent societatem. Minus enim homines trahit futurae abundantiae spes incerta quam impellit praesens atque

their ownmost selves, from other people, and from nature, who are alienated from all that is true, all that is good, all that is – what can the divine goodness say to them except, 'Depart from me, you accursed, into the eternal fire' (Matthew 25.41)? They depart because they have refused to draw near. They are accursed because they are evil. They go to eternal punishment not because of a fallible pronouncement or some inept human law but by a divine decree which, though beyond our human understanding, we firmly believe to have been revealed by God and which we know for sure issues from divine wisdom and goodness.

**Article 6: From evil, good**

Just as goods are interconnected in various ways and the evils opposed to the good proceed one from the other in a way that mirrors, so to speak, the order among goods, so a creature that is changeable and material can be renewed and restored from evil to good.

First of all, the very multiplication of things makes for ongoing renewal. Old men who are beyond correction die, and children as yet untouched by vice are born. In every people the external good of order declines and falls, but the torch is passed to a new and less corrupt people, to improve upon the skills developed and the order established by the former group. Finally, the cultural good of an earlier age can disappear only to be born again among other peoples and under different circumstances. We are quite familiar with such a process, since our Western culture has its roots in Greek poetry, geometry, and philosophy, and in Roman jurisprudence.

Besides this almost material renewal in which evil disappears while good is preserved elsewhere, there occurs a conversion from evil and a restoration of good in a truer sense, such that in individuals or in society or in the historical process the painful experience of particular evils shows what good order is, the evils of order promote cultural good, and cultural evils call for a heaven-sent redeemer.

It is very obvious that we can learn what the right order is from the suffering of particular evils. This is how each of us learns the natural or the established order of things: when our senses have been inattentive or our minds lazy, the pain or loss we suffer as a result makes us more careful and quick-witted in the future. What as individuals we learn from the experience of individual particular evils, society learns from a multiplicity of particular evils. People are much less strongly motivated by an uncertain hope of

onerosa miseria ut, expertis et probatis consuetudinibus relictis, novam quandam rerum ordinationem invehant, tentent, accipiant.

Quid autem mala faciant ut in individuo interior perfectio vel in societate augeatur bonum culturale, breviter et simpliciter dici non potest. Nam si ea excipias quae universale Dei dominium respiciant, nisi dispositive non influunt caetera in usum rationalis libertatis. Quare ne simillimis quidem ex causis semper exspectandi sunt similes effectus. Neque in rebus humanis, ubi tanta est varietas, facile inveniuntur causae re vera similes. Quae ergo subiungimus exempla magis quid responderi posset innuunt quam firmam certamque legem statuere volunt.

Iam vero corporis animaeque humanae unio substantialis adeo intima est ut malum corpori inflictum novam quandam dispositionem menti voluntatique imprimere soleat. Quod metaphysice dictum etiam psychologice exprimi potest. Quae enim in plantis cernitur 'lex effectus,' vel plenius in consciis valet ut fructuosa operatio eiusdem repetitionem evocet, infructuosa autem appetitionem et nisum diminuat forteque exstinguat.[24] Quam ob causam, praxis ascetica liberationem quandam spiritus producit cum sensitivos appetitus hebetet atque obtundat totiusque conscientiae orientationem in altiora quodammodo dirigat. Quem finem etiam intendunt parentes qui filios castigent, et simul alium quem superius diximus, ut ex perpesso malo stabilitus rerum ordo certius et efficacius addiscatur. Quod si ad poenas legales transimus, non invenimus nisi quandam analogiam. Ubi enim parentes interiorem filii ordinem intendunt ut pars sensitiva rationi subdatur et ipsa ratio erudiatur, auctoritas publica non privato sed publico bono consulit cum malos carcere includat vel capite damnet ut caeteri scilicet tum legem addiscant tum ad legem observandam salutari quodam timore impellantur.[25]

future prosperity than by the burden of present misery to cast aside the old ways sanctioned by custom and embark upon, test, and accept some new order of things.

How evils can work to improve the interior perfection of individuals or the cultural good of societies cannot be stated briefly and simply. If we leave out what concerns God's universal dominion, nothing remains but dispositive influences on the use of rational freedom. Hence not even causes that are very similar can always be expected to produce similar results. And in human affairs, where there is such great variety, it is not easy to find causes that are really similar. The following examples, therefore, merely suggest what might be expected to result; they are not meant to lay down a sure and certain law.

The substantial unity of body and soul is so intimate that evil suffered by the body impresses a new disposition upon the mind and will. What we have just said in metaphysical terms can be expressed psychologically as well. The 'law of effect' that can be seen in plant life is even more valid in conscious beings, so that a successful operation calls for its repetition while lack of success weakens and perhaps even leads to abandoning the effort to continue.[24] It is for this reason that asceticism produces a certain spiritual freedom, by dulling and blunting the sensitive appetites and, so to speak, raising the orientation of one's entire consciousness to nobler aims. This is what parents have in mind in disciplining their children, and at the same time they have the further purpose, noted above, namely, that their children should come to know more surely and effectively the established order through suffering an evil. Moving from this to legal penalties, we find only a certain analogy. Parents seek their child's interior order, the subordination of sense to reason and the education of reason itself, while civil authorities are concerned not with private but with the public good when they imprison or execute evil-doers, in order that others may both learn the law and, out of a salutary fear, be induced to obey it.[25]

24 [Lonergan discusses the developmental 'law of effect' briefly in *Insight* at 491–92, 495.]

25 Whereas both medicinal and retributive punishments seek a good of order, medicinal punishment as such aims at order in an individual, but retributive punishment as such seeks the good order not of an individual but of the community. [Latin: Quare tam medicinales poenae quam vindictivae ordinis quoddam bonum quaerunt; sed medicinales per se individuum ordinant, vindictivae autem per se non individuum sed communitatem.]

Quibus exemplis illud commune est quod particularibus malis non solum moventur individua ad ordinem addiscendum sed etiam ipsa mali perpessione vel eiusdem timore ad bonum efficacius volendum convertuntur. Aliud ergo genus aggredimur si eos consideramus qui ex aegritudine vel mala fortuna resipiscant. Non enim ex particulari quodam malo eoque solo moventur sed potius ex tota vitae ratione collapsa. Nam quod olim omnibus viribus et fere continuo intendebant iam infirmitate corporis vel opum egestate ex inopinato iis subtrahitur. Novum vivendi modum atque rationem excogitare debent neque otium iis deest ut, paulo altius ascendentes, in ipsam humanam conditionem inquirant, sensum finemque huius vitae meditentur, quid sapientia, quid bonitas dictitent et attentius considerent et honestius decernant.

At maius quoddam exemplum remanet. Sicut enim homo particularis super totam suam vitam reflectitur[26] ut eam deinceps sapientius atque honestius ordinet, ita etiam exsistit universalior quaedam reflectio quae ordinem universi inspiciat, quae systematice hominis munus finemque excogitat, quae, principiis exinde inventis, crisi subicit tam interiorem hominis vitam quam exterius ordinis bonum. Quam sane reflectionem usitato nomine philosophiam nuncupamus. Sed sicut nomen ita rem ex Graecis habemus. Et cum ipsa res etiam minus a primitivis quam ab hodierno vulgo sit possessa, quibusnam sub adiunctis ortum sumpserit (quantum fieri potest) dicendum esse videtur.[27]

Primae ergo at magnae civilizationes, quales in Aegypto et Mesopotamia (post annum 4000 a.C.) novimus, secundum flumina Indus (post 3000) et Hoang-ho (post 2000), in Mexico et Peru (post Christum), ita exterius

The common element in these examples is that particular evils not only move individuals to come to know order but also that by the very endurance of evil or fear of it they are turned to a more effective willing of the good. We come, then, to a different kind of experience of evil if we consider those who recover from illness or misfortune. They are moved not by some particular evil but by the total collapse of their reason for living. What they had formerly worked at constantly with all their strength is now suddenly taken from them through physical infirmity or lack of material resources. They are forced to devise a new way of living and a new reason for living, and they have time now to raise their minds to try to understand the human condition, to ponder the meaning and purpose of life, and to consider more carefully and determine more honestly what wisdom and goodness really require.

But there is an even better example. Just as a particular individual reflects[26] on his or her whole life in order to direct it more wisely and virtuously, so there exists a more general reflection which investigates the order of the universe, examines in a systematic way the function and end of human beings, and uses the principles thus discovered to critique both the interior life and the external good of order. We call this reflection by the familiar name of philosophy. We get both the name and the thing itself from the Greeks. And since among primitive people it was an even rarer possession than it is among the masses today, it may be helpful to say something (as much as is possible here) about the conditions and circumstances in which it began.[27]

The first great civilizations, then, those in Egypt and Mesopotamia after 4000 BC, in the valley of the Indus after 3000 BC and of the Huang-ho after 2000 BC, and in Mexico and Peru after Christ, had a highly developed

26 [Translator's note: 'reflectitur' here and 'reflecti' on pages 332 and 334 below are apparently an idiosyncratic use of the passive form to express the intransitive use of the verb 'reflectere,' similar to the middle voice in Greek, which has passive forms; see also note 36 below.]

27 What follows here is more fully outlined in Karl Jaspers, *Vom Ursprung und Ziel der Geschichte* (Munich: R. Piper; Zürich: Artemis-Verlag, 1949 [9th edition, Munich and Zürich: R. Piper, 1988]). [In English, *The Origin and Goal of History*, trans. Michael Bullock (New Haven: Yale University Press, 1953; 4th ed., 1968; reprint ed., Westport, CT: Greenwood Press, 1976.] However, Jaspers fails to look beyond the impotence of philosophy to Christ, the center of human history. [Latin: Quae statim sequuntur plenius exponuntur apud K. Jaspers, *Vom Ursprung und Ziel der Geschichte,* München, 1949, 1950. Qui tamen ultra impotentiam philosophicam in Christum, historiae humanae centrum, conspicere non ausus est.]

ordinis bonum ad magnam deduxerunt perfectionem ut organizatione scriptis regulata uterentur, publica opera maximae utilitatis summa sollertia facienda curarent, exercitibus coactis dominium proprium late extenderent, urbesque magnis aedificiis stylo nobis exotico ornarent. At eo non pervenisse videntur ut mentalitatem quandam mythicam excuterent, ut ultimas explicite ponerent quaestiones, ut ratione duce et personalis libertatis conscii omnia crisi subicerent. Quod tamen brevi quodam temporis intervallo (ab a. 800 ad 200 a.C.) factum est in Sinis, in Indis, inter Graecos, ubi mythus expugnatus est, ubi omnes cuiuscumque fere indolis philosophiae sunt exortae, ubi crisi subiecti sunt dei, religiones, consuetudines, instituta, ubi praedicatae sunt moralitas rationalis et personalis responsabilitas. Quo tempore effloruerunt neque magni imperii tranquillitas neque stabilis et bene organizata prosperitas sed, uti fieri solet inter multas parvioresque civitates statusque, rebus prosperis citius succedebant bella saevique triumphi. Praecessisse ergo videntur primae civilizationes, ut artes atque instituta ab aliis inventa alios pararent qui in rebus incertis altiorem illam reflectionem peragerent superiorisque culturae ea ponerent fundamenta quae hodie usque maximum quoddam haberent momentum.[28]

At eiusdem tendentiae exemplum ipso nostro tempore praebetur. Nam mala ordinis sane patimur qui ex primo quodam et fere universali bello in gravissimam et fere universalem crisin oeconomicam processimus, ex crisi in alterum et fere universale bellum, ex altero denique bello in communem illam insecuritatem atque impotentiam quam experimur omnes. Quae tamen ordinis mala de se neque sapientiam donare neque bonitatem conferre possunt. Eatenus tantum se extendit eorum efficacia ut hominem ad reflectendum disponant, neque ipsa effecta dispositio ambiguitate caret, cum quidquid recipiatur ad modum recipientis recipiatur. Qui iam pridem absurdo decipiuntur illud omnibus viribus faciendum curant ut caetera quaecumque absurdo consona atque accommodata fiant. Qui absurdum undenam sit certo sciunt ita ideale tuentur ut quid boni facere possint parum perspiciant. Qui perplexi at ancipites inter haec extrema haerent tam doctrina quam actione deficiunt. Sed si fructus vel parvus vel nullus

external good of order. They enjoyed an organization based on the art of writing, undertook useful public works with great ingenuity, extended their rule far and wide by means of their armies, and in a style we find exotic furnished their cities with grand public buildings. But apparently they did not reach the point of shaking off their mythic mentality, of explicitly posing ultimate questions, of subjecting everything to critical questioning guided by reason and in full consciousness of personal freedom. This did happen, however, within a rather brief span of time, between 800 and 200 BC in China, in India, and among the Greeks, when myth was routed, when virtually every kind of philosophy sprang up, when the gods were subjected to a critique along with religious beliefs and customs and institutions, and when rational morality and personal responsibility were proclaimed. This was not a period of tranquility guaranteed by great empires, or of stable and well-organized prosperity; rather, as is usually the case where there is a multitude of small cities and states, prosperity would be very quickly followed by wars and savage conquests. It would seem, therefore, that those first civilizations prepared the way, so that the arts and institutions developed by one group of people would equip others during a time of instability and uncertainty to undertake that deeper reflection and so lay the foundations of that higher culture which has been so influential right down to the present time.[28]

Our own times, in fact, provide us with an example of this same progression. We have certainly been suffering from the evils of order, having gone from one world war to a worldwide economic crisis and from that into a second world war, and now into a time of insecurity and powerlessness felt by all. By themselves, of course, these evils of order cannot endow us with wisdom or goodness. Their effectiveness in this respect is limited to disposing us to reflection, and even this disposition is not without ambiguity, since whatever is received is received according to the capacity of the receiver. Those who have for some time been led astray by the absurd do their best to make everything else harmonize and fit with their particular absurdity. Those who do have a sure knowledge of the sources of the absurd are so idealistic that they little realize what good people can actually do. And the bewildered, caught hesitating between these extremes, want for both knowledge and action. But if few or no good results are foreseen,

28 [See also Lonergan's brief discussion of the same historical period, but with a slightly different focus, in *The Triune God: Doctrines,* translated from *De Deo trino: Pars dogmatica* (1964) by Michael G. Shields, vol. 11 in Collected Works of Bernard Lonergan, ed. Robert M. Doran and H. Daniel Monsour (Toronto: University of Toronto Press, 2009) 204–207.]

perspicitur, profunda quaedam peragitur praeparatio. Minus iam audiuntur qui paulo ante audacter annuntiabant progressum humanum esse spontaneum, automaticum, necessarium. E rebus naturalibus in ipsum hominem convertitur attentio ut de homine authentico quaeratur et de multiplici alienatione humana consideretur. Quot fundamentales erant directiones seu orientationes philosophicae, tot remanent; sed maximum illud intercedit discrimen ut ipsae orientationes, quas nuperrime nisi in libris et scholis nemo fere magni fecerit, iam ex ipsa nostra situatione concreta sensum, vitam, realitatem, valorem accipere videantur.

Qui enim ita se impotentes sentiunt ut nihil intendant nisi quam maxime frui bonis immediatis bene intelligunt antiquum illud praeceptum, 'Carpe diem.' Qui de homine authentico loquuntur, in memoriam eos revocant qui olim de homine caelesti, de autanthropo,[29] de sapiente disserebant. Subtilissime nobis exponitur quid significet 'se-esse,'[30] quod tamen antiquitus illo innuebatur praecepto, 'Cognosce te ipsum.' 'Alienatio' et 'absurdum' ita sonum edunt novum ut vetustum dicant peccatum. Neque ipsa mors, e latebris repressae conscientiae nuper liberata, alium praebet aspectum quam inimicum illum atque formidolosum quem supponunt scripta Paulina. Reflectionis ergo contemporanea signa sunt clarissima. Eo usque communibus indigentiis respondent ut in ipsas litteras humaniores haud parvum influant. At alia est reflectio et alia est salus. Sicut enim 'lex paedagogus noster fuit in Christo, ut ex fide iustificemur' (Gal 3.24), ita rationalis conscientia per reflectionem evigilat atque disponitur ut ad perfectiora perduci possit. Sicut autem 'ex operibus legis non iustificabitur omnis caro coram illo. Per legem enim cognitio peccati' (Rom 3.20), ita etiam mala particularia et mala ordinis quae patimur ad reflectionem nos movent; sed ipsa reflectio manifestat nos absurdo esse implicatos quin ex absurdo nos extricet, et multiplicem nostram revelat alienationem quin reconciliationem conferat.

a more profound and thorough preparation is carried out. We hear much less these days from those who used to proclaim confidently that human progress was something spontaneous, automatic, inevitable. Attention is shifting from the physical world to the human world, to inquire about human authenticity and to ponder the manifold alienation of humanity. There are as many basic philosophical directions or orientations as before, but there is this most important difference, that those orientations which until recently virtually no one except in books or schools valued very highly, now as a result of our present situation seem to have come alive and to have taken on new meaning, vitality, reality, and importance.

Those who feel so powerless that they simply aim at getting the most enjoyment from immediate goods understand very well the ancient adage, *Carpe diem.* Those who talk about the 'authentic man' remind us of those who used to speak about the 'heavenly man' [1 Corinthians 15.47], the *autoanthrōpos,*[29] the Sage. Subtle disquisitions on what it means to 'be oneself'[30] remind us of the ancient precept, 'Know thyself.' 'Alienation' and 'absurd' are new ways of saying the old word 'sin.' Even death itself, lately released from the depths of repressed consciousness, looks very much like that dreaded enemy which St Paul wrote about. So these days the signs of reflection are very clear. They address the needs and concerns of society so well that they have had a considerable influence on contemporary literature. Still, reflection is one thing, salvation is another. Just as 'the law was our disciplinarian until Christ came, so that we might be justified by faith' (Galatians 3.24), so by reflection rational consciousness is awakened and disposed to being brought to a higher level. As 'no human being will be justified in his sight by deeds prescribed by the law, for through the law comes knowledge of sin' (Romans 3.20), so our experience of particular evils and evils of order may move us to reflect; but reflection by itself merely makes us aware that we are mired in absurdity without rescuing us from that absurdity, and reveals our manifold alienation without effecting any reconciliation.

29 [Aristotle, *Nicomachean Ethics,* I, 1096b 1.]

30 For example, Karl Jaspers, *Von der Wahrheit,* vol. 1 in *Philosophische Logik* (Munich: R. Piper, 1947) 76–83. [An excerpt in English from these pages, which begins with a four-line introduction by the editors, can be found in Karl Jaspers, *Basic Philosophical Writings: Selections,* edited, translated, with introduction by Edith Ehrlich, Leonard H. Ehrlich, and George B. Pepper (Athens, OH: Ohio University Press, 1986) 153–58. The editors also direct the reader to their Selection 8, titled 'Existence – Existenz' (pp. 62–73) for a further clarifying text from Jaspers.]

## Articulus VII: De impotentia humana[31]

Ita e malis in bonum renovari atque restaurari humanum genus diximus ut mala particularia in bonum ordinis hominem impellent, et mala ordinis in bonum culturale hominem disponant, quin tamen ipse homo mala culturalia evincere possit. Quae sane impotentia quam sit nefasta, perspicuum est; nisi enim eradicantur mala culturalia, insipientia atque malitia manent in disordinationem atque corruptionem hominis interioris, ut ordo exterior perpetuo in peius commutetur, et particularia minuantur bona malaque multiplicentur, donec penitus exstinguatur bonum humanum. Regnat enim peccatum in mortem (Rom 5.21).

Cur autem homo ita sit impotens, quamvis libero polleat arbitrio, quaestio obscurior multis videtur, quam tamen praeterire haud possumus. Nam ipsa humana in bonum impotentia non solum manifestat quaenam sit tenebrarum potestas diabolique potentia sed etiam, cum contraria contrariis curentur, viam indicat quam incessit Dominus et Salvator noster ut nos e malis liberaret et in bonis confirmaret. Quam ob causam, humanae impotentiae quattuor quasi radices exponamus oportet, nempe, et intellectus obscurationem et voluntatis inefficaciam et obiectivam boni difficultatem et ipsam denique a Deo alienationem.[32]

Et in primis nemo non videt quanta efficacia et bonum impediant malumque necessitent ignorantia et error. Voluntatis enim est intellectum sequi et ideo, nisi antecesserit vera boni cognitio, sequi non poterit vere boni volitio. Quod quamvis subiective culpa carere possit, obiective tamen perpetuum quendam malorum fontem constituit; non enim fragilitate vel inconstantia ab ignorante vel errante fit malum, ut sperare possimus eum interdum saltem fragilitatem esse superaturum bonumque facturum, sed ei virtus est atque perfectio ut optimum quod cognoscat faciat, quod tamen optimum bono inferius atque contrarium est.

## Article 7: Human impotence[31]

We have described the renewal and restoration of the human race from evil to good as a progression in which particular evils lead us to consider the good of order, and the evils of order dispose us towards cultural good even while leaving us incapable, by ourselves, of overcoming cultural evils. It is clear how utterly ruinous this impotence is. For unless cultural evils are eradicated, stupidity and wickedness remain to wreak disorder and corruption in our interior life, so that the external order is in constant decline, particular goods decrease and particular evils multiply, until the human good is totally extinguished. For sin reigns in death (Romans 5.21).

Why human beings are so impotent, even though they exercise free will, is a question that many find hard to understand; nevertheless, we cannot ignore it. Human impotence with regard to good not only reveals the power of darkness and the power of the devil but also, since ills are cured by their contraries, points to the way our Lord and Savior followed to deliver us from evil and strengthen us in good. Accordingly, we must examine four roots of human impotence, namely, darkness of intellect, weakness of will, the objective difficulty of the good, and finally alienation from God.[32]

To begin with, everyone sees how effectively ignorance and error hinder the good and make evil inevitable. The will follows the intellect, and therefore, unless there is first a true knowledge of the good, there cannot follow a true willing of the good. Although this may occur without subjective guilt, objectively it constitutes an ongoing source of evil. For evil is not the result of frailty or fickleness on the part of ignorant or mistaken individuals whom we may expect now and again to overcome their defect and do the right thing; rather, for such persons virtue and moral perfection mean doing the best they know how, though their 'best' falls short of the good and is contrary to it.

31 [See also Lonergan's discussion in *Insight* of the 'Conditions of Effective Freedom' (645–47), of 'Moral Impotence' (650–53), of 'The Problem of Liberation' (653–56), and of the fact of evil as 'The Problem' (710–15).]

32 Obviously, we are speaking here of a hypothetical impotence, that is, that which would exist if we did not have the grace of God through Christ. [Latin: Uti patet, de impotentia hypothetica agitur, de ea scilicet quae esset nisi gratiam Dei per Christum haberemus.]

Dixerit tamen quispiam ignorantes atque errantes addiscere posse. At qui addiscere potest, non tamen addiscit nisi vult; neque vult nisi bonum addiscendi cognoscit. Quo facilius ergo addiscendi bonum perspicitur, eo plures et fidelius et ardentius addiscendi labori incumbunt. Florent ergo artes technicae et scientiae naturales, neque eae negliguntur scientiae humanae e quibus sperari potest quoddam bonum hominibus obventurum. At ipsa haec spes ignorantia et erroribus ita coarctatur atque limitatur ut, quo magis studia ad sapientiam gignendam et ad virtutem promovendam accedant, eo pauciores inveniantur qui seriam atque constantem addiscendi voluntatem exhibeant. Neque horum paucorum una est mens unaque sententia. Sed ita in multas et oppositas abeunt partes ut, si solos philosophos adeas, nullum fere videatur verum quod disputari non possit, et nullum fere bonum quod omni dubio maius exsistat.

Neve hanc ignorantiam credas casu accidere, quasi sperare liceret hominem aliquando meliori fortuna esse usurum, ut his de tenebris ipse se eriperet atque liberaret. Quae enim ab omnibus hominibus expedite, firma certitudine, et nullo admixto errore innotescere soleant, non solo interioris lucis criterio iudicantur, sed etiam usu atque experientia constant. Sicut enim primitivi profana et practica quasi ratione duce obeunt, ut tamen sacra mythis commisceant et, quodcumque longius ab immediata experientia iaceat, artibus magicis regere conentur, ita etiam moderni in naturalibus scientiis maxime proficiunt ubi experimenta excogitari atque applicari possint, humanasque excolunt scientias quatenus ad instar naturalis scientiae reduci posse videantur, sed caetera incognoscibilia conclamitant quasi ipsa haec fere ritualis verborum iteratio anxios suos animos quodammodo demulceret.

Cuius rei ratio haud obscura est. Uti enim superius diximus, qui puro intelligendi desiderio verique amore ducantur, ea concludunt quae aliena nimis a concretis vitae adiunctis usuque humano videantur; qui autem ipsi conditioni atque situationi humanae inhaereant, per irrationale illud atque absurdum decipiuntur quod ex conscientia rationali sed deficiente in actiones et per actiones in totam humanam vitam procedat atque penetret. Quos enim fingebat Plato in spelunca ligatos qui nisi umbras numquam vidissent, ipsi sumus peccaminoso huic mundo ita assuefacti ut absurdum censeamus quod consueto absurdo parum conveniat. Quod si pauci quidam e specu elapsi in solis lucem conscendunt, vel quod ipsi vident quodammodo dubitant vel certi aliis vix persuadere possunt. Quae cum ita sint,

Someone may interject here that ignorant and mistaken individuals are capable of learning. Even so, people do not learn unless they want to, and they do not want to unless they know the good of learning. The more readily the good of such learning is perceived, the more numerous will be those who are willing to give themselves faithfully and eagerly to the task. Technical studies and the natural sciences are flourishing, as are those human sciences which it is hoped may be of some benefit to humanity. But this very hope is so narrow and limited as a result of ignorance and error that the closer certain studies come to generating wisdom and fostering virtue, the fewer persons will be found to pursue them seriously and with constancy. And even these few are not all of the same mind or opinion. There are in fact so many diverse schools of thought among them that if you go only to philosophers you will find hardly one truth that is not disputed among them or one good that is acknowledged to be such beyond all doubt.

Do not imagine that such ignorance is accidental, as if one might hope that the lot of humanity will eventually change for the better, so that we may rescue and free ourselves from this darkness. For those things that all people generally come to know expeditiously, with firm certitude, and without any admixture of error are not judged to be true by the sole criterion of their inner light but are also confirmed by experience and in practice. Just as primitive peoples go about their secular practical affairs in a rational way while their religious practices are full of myths, and try to control by magic all that lies beyond their immediate experience, so people today are most adept in the natural sciences where they can do experiments and apply their results, and they cultivate the human sciences insofar as they seem able to be conducted in the manner of the natural sciences, while loudly proclaiming all else to be unknowable, as if this ritual-like refrain might somehow soothe their troubled souls.

The reason for this is not hard to find. As we said above, those who are led by a pure desire to understand and by a love of truth reach conclusions that seem to be too far removed from the concrete circumstances of everyday life and human behavior; but those who are totally caught up in this human situation are led astray by that irrational absurdity which from a consciousness that is rational but deficient leads to action, and through this action pervades and penetrates all aspects of human life. Like Plato's prisoners in the cave who had never seen anything but shadows, we have grown so accustomed to this sinful world that we dismiss as absurd all that is not in tune with its usual absurdity. If some do escape from the cave and climb up to the sunlight, they either doubt what they see or, if they themselves are

solemniter docuit concilium Vaticanum relativam illam divinae revelationis necessitatem 'ut ea, quae in rebus divinis humanae rationi per se impervia non sunt, in praesenti quoque generis humani conditione ab omnibus expedite, firma certitudine et nullo admixto errore cognosci possint' (DB 1786).

*Cui intellectus obscurationi accedit voluntatis inefficacia.*[33] Libero sane pollemus arbitrio. Quod tamen quid sibi velit et quo usque valeat iam perpendendum est.

Et *in primis* dicendum est libertatem humanam ita circa obiecta versari et ita in actibus consistere ut aut velle aut nolle possimus, ut hoc vel illud eligere in nostra potestate ponatur, ut in verum bonum intendamus aut ab hac intentione deficiamus.

At *deinde* addendum est inter nudam volendi potentiam et ipsum secundum volendi actum alios intercedere primos actus,[34] qui facile vel difficile mobiles sint, et dispositiones vel habitus nominentur. Quare per nudam potentiam in illa indifferentia invenimur qua aequaliter ad quodlibet obiectum inclinamur; per actum secundum ita altero obiecto adhaeremus ut alterum reiciamus; sed per dispositionem vel habitum ita ab initiali indifferentia recedimus ut antequam actu secundo velimus iam actu primo ad obiectum determinatum volendum parati simus. Sicut enim in veris omne verum intelligere potest qui intellectum habet, ita in bonis qui voluntatem habet omne bonum velle potest. Sicut etiam in veris qui nudum habet intellectum inquisitione et addiscentia indiget antequam actu intelligat, ita in bonis qui nudam volendi potentiam habet reflectione et persuasione indiget antequam actu velit. Sicut denique in veris qui scientiam acquisiverit, cum brevissima reflectione et sine ulteriori doctrina statim intelligere potest, ita in bonis qui dispositionem vel habitum habet, cum brevissima reflectione et sine ulla persuasione statim velle potest. Quibus in omnibus ita similes sunt intellectus et voluntas ut haec maxime maneat dissimilitudo, quod habitus in intellectu receptus inclinat non voluntatem sed intellectum, sed habitus in voluntate receptus ipsam voluntatem inclinat; et ideo circa usum habitus intellectualis plena manet indifferentia in voluntate, sed circa usum habitus electivi ipse habitus nihil aliud est quam inclinatio in usum sui ipsius.

certain, they have a hard time trying to convince others. No wonder the First Vatican Council solemnly taught the relative necessity of divine revelation, 'in order that those truths concerning God that are in themselves not unattainable by human reason, in the present condition of humanity may be known by all with relative ease, with firm certitude, and without any admixture of error' (DB 1786, [DS 3005, ND 114]).

*In addition to this darkness of intellect there is weakness of will.*[33] Certainly we exercise free will; but just what this means and how important a factor it is must now be considered.

*First,* the fact is that human freedom regards objects and consists in acts in such a way that we can will or not will, that it is in our power to choose this or that, that we either intend a true good or fall short of this intention.

*Next,* however, it must be added that between the bare capacity to will and the second act of actually willing, there are other first acts,[34] some easily and some not so easily changeable, called dispositions or habits. Hence, by the bare capacity to will we are in a state of indifference so that we are inclined equally regarding any object; in the second act of willing we move to one object and reject the other; but a disposition or habit diminishes somewhat our initial indifference, so that before we perform the second act of willing we are by a first act ready to will a particular object. As in the matters of truth whoever has intelligence is capable of understanding every truth, so with regard to good whoever has a will is capable of willing every good. As also with regard to truth those who have bare intelligence need inquiry and learning before they actually understand, so regarding the good those who have the bare capacity to will need reflection and persuasion before they actually will. Finally, just as in the area of truth those who have acquired knowledge can with the briefest reflection and without any further instruction immediately understand, so regarding the good those who have a certain disposition or habit can immediately will with the briefest reflection and without any persuasion. In all this the intellect and will are similar, but there is one great dissimilarity concerning the use of the habits: because a habit received in the intellect predisposes the intellect, not the will, the will remains fully indifferent about the use of an intellectual habit; but because a habit received in the will predisposes the will itself, a habit of choosing is itself nothing other than a predisposition to its own use.

33 See Thomas Aquinas, *De veritate,* q. 24, a. 12; *De malo,* q. 16, a. 5.
34 [The 'other first acts' are habits.]

*Tertio,* non directe sed indirecte dispositiones et habitus efficimus. Directe enim versatur libertas circa obiecta; directe efficit actus secundos; sed ex his secundis actibus reliquuntur in voluntate dispositiones quae in habitus formandos cumulantur atque coalescunt; et ideo indirecte tantum nostras dispositiones et habitus producimus, quatenus per seriem actuum circa obiecta convenientia qualitatem voluntatis pedetentim determinamus.

*Quarto,* eadem in genere est lex tam circa mutationem quam circa acquisitionem dispositionum et habituum. Sicut ergo per seriem actuum acquirimus, ita etiam per seriem actuum quod acquisivimus mutamus.

*Quinto,* qualibet in serie unusquisque actus est actus liber. Neque ullum habemus liberum actum, quasi extra seriem positum, quo libere determinamus omnes liberos actus intra seriem contentos. Si enim hi actus ante determinarentur, iam liberi esse non possent. Quam ob causam, qui bonum facit propositum seriem quandam actuum serio intendit; quae tamen intentio nullatenus aufert libertatem quae singulis actibus competit; et ideo alia est bona intentio et longe alia est eiusdem exsecutio.

*Sexto,* qui serio bonum propositum facit, nihil in sua voluntate ponit quam dispositionem unam. Bonum enim propositum unus est actus; et unus actus non est actuum series; et per solam actuum seriem fortior dispositio vel habitus acquiritur. Quam ob causam, utilissima est bonarum intentionum renovatio, cum intentio semel tantum elicita longe minus voluntatem inclinet quam dispositiones et habitus iam pridem acquisiti.

*Septimo,* qui qualitatem propriae voluntatis mutandam decernit, diuturniori reflectione atque persuasione vehementiori indiget. Non enim vult secundum inclinationem suarum dispositionum atque habituum neque praeter hanc acquisitam inclinationem, sed contra eam. Reflectione ergo indiget ut quod sponte vult non statim velit; et persuasione indiget ut ab eo quod hactenus dilexerit iam abhorrere incipiat, et ut id a quo hactenus abhorruerit iam diligere incipiat. Neque solummodo in bono proposito eliciendo hac reflectione atque persuasione indiget. Nam ipsum bonum propositum nisi unam dispositionem non ponit; et ideo singulis vicibus et reflecti et sibi persuadere debet, donec per actus contrarios et tota acquisita qualitas auferatur et nova atque intenta qualitas inducatur.

*Octavo,* eatenus ergo potest homo dispositiones atque habitus propriae voluntatis mutare quatenus non unum volendi actum elicit sed seriem actuum, quorum unusquisque est actus liber neque ante determinatur quam per diutiorem reflectionem atque vehementiorem persuasionem eliciatur. Quam ob causam, rarius accidit ut quis acquisitas dispositiones atque habitus voluntatis revera mutet. Non enim eiusmodi est humana vita ut,

*Third,* we produce dispositions and habits not directly but indirectly. Freedom directly regards objects; directly it produces second acts; but from these second acts there remain in the will dispositions which come together and coalesce to form habits. Hence we produce our dispositions and habits only indirectly, inasmuch as it is through a series of acts concerning suitable objects that we gradually determine the character of our will.

*Fourth,* in general the same law holds for changing our dispositions and habits as for acquiring them. As we acquire them through a series of acts, so through a series of acts we change what we have acquired.

*Fifth,* in any series each act is a free act. We do not have any free act, performed as if outside the series, by which we determine all the free acts within that series. For if these acts were predetermined they could not be free. Accordingly, one who forms a good intention seriously intends a certain series of acts; but this intention in no way diminishes the freedom of these individual acts, and therefore a good intention is one thing and execution is quite another.

*Sixth,* one who seriously forms a good intention produces in the will only a single disposition. For a good intention is one act, and one act is not a series of acts; and it is only by a series of acts that a stronger disposition or habit is acquired. For this reason, it is most useful to renew one's good intentions, since an intention elicited only once inclines the will much less strongly than long-established dispositions and habits.

*Seventh,* a decision to change the quality of one's will needs longer reflection and stronger persuasion. For, in such a case, one is not following the acquired inclination of one's dispositions and habits, nor willing alongside it, but willing against it. Reflection is needed so that one does not immediately will what he or she spontaneously wants. Persuasion is needed so that one begins to abhor what hitherto was loved, and to love what up to now was abhorred. Furthermore, it is not only in forming a good intention that this reflection and persuasion are needed; for a good intention itself constitutes only one disposition, and so on each successive occasion one has to reflect and persuade oneself, until by repeated contrary acts the former quality of will is entirely removed and the new desired quality is introduced.

*Eighth,* it follows that one can change one's dispositions and habits only inasmuch as one elicits not just one act of willing but a series of acts, each act of which is free and not determined until it is elicited by long reflection and powerful persuasion. Hence it happens very rarely that anyone really does change acquired dispositions and habits of will. For our human life is not such that we can, whenever we want, interrupt the course of events until

quandocumque voluerimus, rerum eventuumque cursum interrumpere possimus donec necessariam nobis reflectionem atque persuasionem peragamus. Neque eiusmodi est constantia humanae mentis ut quod heri optimum videbatur propositum, hodie et cras et deinceps eodem bonitatis splendore effulgeat. Imo, ipsa acquisita atque mutanda voluntatis qualitas contra propositam mutationem nititur, ut menti suggerat tum omnia dubia quae propositum consilium infirment tum omnes difficultates quae ipsam voluntatem deterreant. Partim ergo a bonis propositis deficimus quia in repentinis reflecti nobisque persuadere non possumus, partim quia de vera bonitate consilii propositi atque decreti dubitare incipimus, et partim quia fatigati totum reflectendi atque persuadendi negotium reincipere nolumus. Quae sane frustratio minime impedit quominus toties bonum propositum renovemus quoties recidamus. At aliud est quod absolute fieri potest et aliud quod ipsi nos aliquando facturos serio audacterque speramus. Quod si desperare incipimus, si aliis meliores nos fore dubitamus, minori fiducia et sinceritate minori ipsae boni propositi renovationes fiunt.

*Nono,* in multis deficimus omnes (DB 107). Non ergo uno tantummodo bono proposito ad perfectam vitae rationem procedimus, sed serie bonorum propositorum indigemus quorum unumquodque seriem bonorum actuum exigit. Multi sane a serie serierum bonorum actuum, a serie serierum reflectendi sibique persuadendi laborum, penitus deterrentur. At fortissimus quisque, quamvis imperterritus maneat, non ideo usque in finem perseverabit. Nam bonum, imo optimum, propositum quod seriem bonorum propositorum respicit, omnes singulorum difficultates cumulat, ut etiam hic verissimum illud sit, aliud esse bonum velle et aliud bonum perficere.

*Decimo,* quae superius de obscuratione intellectus quaeque nuperrime de voluntatis inefficacia diximus, summa quadam convenientia mutuo fulciuntur. Ignorantia enim voluntatem suam esse malam ignorat ut eam ab onere bonorum propositorum liberet. Et mala voluntas intellectum ignorantiae suae conscium fieri minime vult, tum quia mala est tum quia intellectus qua ignorans vel bonam voluntatem parum movet. Quam ob causam, etsi sacra eloquia doceant hominis vitam super terram esse militiam, eandem tamen satis pacificam probat ignorantium neque bonum volentium torpor.

we have completed that necessary reflection and persuasion. Nor does the human mind possess such constancy that what seemed yesterday to be ideal, today and tomorrow and later on will still have the same glow of goodness about it. In fact, that acquired quality of will that is to be changed militates against the proposed change, suggesting to the mind all sorts of doubts that weaken the proposal and all kinds of difficulties that deter the will. Therefore, we fall short of our good intentions, partly because in a sudden crisis we are not able to reflect and persuade ourselves, partly because we begin to doubt whether our plan and decision are truly good, and partly because being weary we are reluctant to begin the whole process of reflection and persuasion all over again. True, this frustration does not absolutely prevent us from renewing our good intention each time we backslide; but what is absolutely possible is one thing, and what we ourselves can seriously and boldly hope to accomplish is another. But if we begin to lose hope, if we doubt that we are going to be better than others, we will renew our good intentions with less confidence and sincerity.

*Ninth,* we all fail in many things (DB 107, [DS 229, ND 1905]). Hence, we do not advance towards a perfect way of life by just one good intention; we need a series of good intentions, each one of which requires a series of good actions. Certainly, many people are entirely deterred by a series of series of good acts, a series of series of efforts at reflection and self-persuasion. But even the very strongest among us, though they may remain undaunted, will not on that account persevere to the end. For a good intention, indeed even the very best intention, involving as it does a series of good intentions, accumulates the difficulties of all of them, so that here too it is most true that good will is one thing, performance another.

*Tenth,* the darkness of intellect previously referred to and the weakness of will that we have just now outlined conspire to support each other. Ignorance does not know its will is bad and so frees it of the burden of good intentions. Bad will for its part by no means wants the intellect to become aware of its ignorance, both because it itself is bad and because the intellect precisely as ignorant has little influence upon even a good will. Therefore, although preachers tell us that our life on earth is a warfare, the lassitude of those who do not know and do not will the good shows that it can also be quite peaceful.

*Sed ad tertium transeamus caput,* cum ignorantiae atque inefficaciae accedit obiectiva boni difficultas. Aliud enim est, rebus adhuc integris,[35] bonum potentia in bonum actu reducere; sed aliud longeque difficilius est, cum bonum malis corruptum sit, e malis in bonum restaurandum procedere. Neque cuipiam dubium esse potest non illam sed hanc esse nostram conditionem humanam.

Nam non solum singulis malum est quod obscuratione intellectus voluntatisque inefficacia laborant, sed hoc ipsum in singulis exsistens commune quoddam atque publicum malum facit. Exterius ordinis bonum corrumpit ut bona particularia diminuantur et mala particularia augeantur. Culturale bonum corrumpit, ne sapientia bonum a malo secernat neve bonitas bonum eligat malumque respuat.

Quod si tot tantisque malis premimur, etiam patiamur necesse est. Si enim aliam in membris videmus legem et aliam mente perspicimus (Rom 7.22–23), utramque simul sequi non possumus. Aut enim membrorum legi consentimur[36] ut spiritus patiatur aut spiritus legi consentimur ut membris patiamur. Si aliam in mundo legem obtinere videmus et aliam intellectu et ratione docemur, aut hanc aut illam sequamur necesse est; qui tamen cum mundo gaudet, animam suam perdit; et qui animam salvat, huius saeculi miseriam sustinere debet.

Neve synthesin quaeras ut duobus dominis servire possis (Mt 6.24), ut bono ita fruaris ut tamen malum non patiaris. Lex enim peccati regnumque peccati et ex peccato sunt et in peccatum inclinant (Rom 7.23, 5.20; DB 792). Quia ex peccato sunt, per illud irrationale seu absurdum constituuntur quod ex defectu conscientiae rationalis oritur. In peccatum vero inclinant quia pati nolumus, quia cum peccato commisso synthesin quaerimus, quia cum peccatoribus consociari consentimur.

*Let us proceed now to the third root cause* of our moral impotence, since added to ignorance and ineffectiveness there is the objective difficulty of the good. It is one thing, when things are yet whole,[35] to bring potential good to actual good; but it is another, far more difficult matter, once the good has been corrupted by evils, to move from evils to a restoration of good. And no one can doubt that the latter, not the former, is our human condition.

For darkness of intellect and weakness of will are an evil not only for individuals. This evil existing in individuals becomes a common and public evil. It corrupts the external good of order, so that particular goods become scarce and particular evils multiply. It corrupts cultural good, so that wisdom cannot separate good from evil, and goodness cannot choose the good and reject the evil.

With so many serious evils weighing upon us it is inevitable that we are going to suffer from them. If we perceive one law in our members and another in our mind (Romans 7.22–23), we cannot follow both of them at the same time. We either consent[36] to the law of our members so that the spirit suffers, or we consent to the law of the spirit so that we suffer in our members. If we see that one law holds for the world and yet are taught another law by our intellect and reason, we have to choose to follow either one or the other. Those who rejoice with the world lose their soul; and the ones who would save their soul will have to endure the wretchedness of this world.

And do not seek a synthesis so as to be able to serve two masters (Matthew 6.24), enjoying good things without suffering evil. For the law of sin and the reign of sin originate from sin and predispose us towards sin (Romans 7.23, 5.20; DB 792, [DS 1515, ND 512]). Since they originate in sin they are essentially constituted by that irrational or absurd element which springs from the failure of rational consciousness. They predispose us towards sin

35 [That is, before the fall.]

36 [Translator's note: 'consentimur': here and a few words later Lonergan had written 'consentimus' but changed by hand the final 's' to 'r,' as if it were a deponent or a passive verb with the force of the Greek middle voice, even though previously (e.g. 'consentire,' p. 308, and 'consentiant,' p. 310), he had used the active form 'consentire.' I can find no precedent for a passive or deponent form of this verb or of its opposite 'dissentire' (but see next note), in classical or medieval Latin. This obviously deliberate change is puzzling. I can only conjecture that Lonergan either was assimilating 'consentire' to a closely related verb with a similar meaning, 'assentiri,' which is always deponent, or, more likely, was imitating the Greek middle as he had done with 'reflectitur' and 'reflecti' (see above, p. 321, note 26, and below, p. 373, note 33.).]

Facilis ergo non est via, neque lata, neque plana, neque a multis frequentata, quae in bonum ex malis conducat. Via enim crucis est quam omnibus commendavit Dominus noster: 'Dicebat autem ad omnes: "Si quis vult post me venire, abneget semetipsum et tollat crucem suam cotidie et sequatur me"' (Luke 9.23). Via crucis est, quam amplexus est Dominus noster qui a mundo damnatus est, flagellatus, cruci fixus, occisus, ut de mortuis resurgens nos doceat quemadmodum e malis ad bonum procedere oporteat.

Quod si pati nolueris, specie boni ita decipi poteris ut mala hominibus toleranda quam maxime augeas. Absurdum enim obiectivum, quia factum quoddam est, electionem nostram non tantum poscit sed exigit. Quod si voluntariam malorum perpessionem nolumus, absurdum esse absurdum atque ideo patiendum negamus. Si absurdum qua tale negamus, in facto absurdo intelligibilitatem quaerimus. Si invenire videmur quod quaerebamus, absurdum in mentem admittimus et pedetentim de propria sede intelligibile atque verum detrudimus. Quod his ultimis saeculis nobis evenisse suadetur. Absurdum enim erat ecclesiam Dei corruptionibus esse infectam; quo absurdo decipiebantur qui ecclesiam veram esse invisibilem protestabantur. Absurdum deinceps erat multas quae consequebantur religiones esse bellorum causam; quo absurdo decepiebantur qui omnem religionem supernaturalem esse reiciendam concludebant. Absurdum denique erat singulos ita proprio atque individuali rationis lumini inhaerere ut de omnibus fere dissentirentur[37] et ideo bono communi consulere non possent; quo absurdo decipiebantur qui rationis lumen ideologiarum fontem habebant, universale omnium dominium statui cedebant, homines in servitutem non solum corporalem sed etiam spiritualem reducebant. Qua synthesium succesione ex unitate Catholica in multas religiones, ex religione supernaturali in rationalismum atque liberalismum, ex liberalismo in totalitarianismum processimus. Latam viam atque planam elegimus, iamque totius fere humani boni eversionem atque exitium timemus.[38]

because we shrink from suffering, because we seek a compromise with sin already committed, and because we agree to associate with sinners.

So the way that leads from evil to good is neither easy nor broad nor level nor much traveled. For it is the way of the cross that our Lord recommends to all: 'Then he said to them all, "If any want to become my followers, let them deny themselves and take up their cross daily and follow me"' (Luke 9.23). It is the way of the cross, embraced by our Lord, who was condemned by the world, scourged, nailed to a cross, killed, so that rising from the dead he might teach us how good must come out of evil.

If you shrink from suffering, you can be so deceived by the appearance of good that you add greatly to the evils to be borne by the human race. For objective absurdity, because it is a fact, not only invites but requires our choice. If we refuse to suffer evils willingly, we thereby deny that the absurd is absurd and therefore to be endured. If we deny that the absurd is absurd, we are seeking intelligibility in an absurd fact. If we seem to find what we were seeking, we admit the absurd into our mind and gradually drive the intelligible and the true from its proper throne. Perhaps this is what has been happening to us during these last few centuries. The infection of God's church by corruption was absurd, and this absurdity deceived those who protested that the true church is invisible. From here it was absurd that the many consequent religions were the cause of wars, and this absurdity deceived those who concluded that all supernatural religion was to be rejected. It was absurd, finally, for everyone to hold so fast to his or her own individual light of reason that they disagreed[37] about virtually everything and hence could not agree on what was for the common good. This absurdity deceived those who held the light of reason to be the source of ideologies, turned the universal ownership and control of everything over to the state, and reduced people not only to bodily but even to spiritual servitude. In this succession of syntheses, we have gone from Catholic unity to a multiplicity of religions, from supernatural religion to rationalism and liberalism, and from liberalism to totalitarianism. We have chosen the broad and level road and now we fear the overthrow and destruction of virtually all human good.[38]

37 [Translator's note: 'dissentirentur': see previous note. The one obscure instance of a deponent form of this verb cited by the grammarian Priscianus in the sixth century AD suggests that he may have noted it as an oddity.]

38 [For a similar brief global characterization by Lonergan of the course of Western civilization, at least from the founding of the schools of Charlemagne, see *Insight* 256–66.]

*At quarta manet humanae impotentiae radix* caeteris profundior, cum ideo homo ignorantia intellectus et inefficacia voluntatis et obiectiva boni difficultate laboret quia a Deo aversus atque alienatus est. Qui enim a Deo avertitur non se agnoscit Dei instrumentum, ut in omnibus bonum a Deo intentum invenire quaerat et inventum eligat, sed, quasi prima causa esset, suis viribus fretus illud prosequitur bonum quod propria eius ratio invenerit et propria eius libertas elegerit. Qui vero prima causa non est et tamen agit ac si prima causa esset, propriam impotentiam addiscat necesse est. Cuius ratio non bonum a Deo intentum sed aliud a se inventum vere bonum esse iudicat, suam insipientiam addiscat necesse est. Cuius libera voluntas non bonum per essentiam super omnia diligit sed aliud quoddam per participationem bonum tamquam supremum atque ultimum intendit, propriam malitiam addiscat necesse est. Caeterae enim creaturae, quae irrationales sunt et cogitationis incapaces, a finibus suis non impediuntur quia se Dei esse instrumenta neque sciunt neque volunt. Sed creatura rationalis quae per suum intellectum suamque voluntatem in finem dirigitur atque producitur, non potest suam instrumentalitatem ignorare vel nolle quin circa finem insipiens erret, oboedientiam superbus abiciat, et a fine malus deficiat.

Quare Apostolus: 'Quia cum cognovissent Deum, non sicut Deum glorificaverunt aut gratias egerunt, sed evanuerunt in cogitationibus suis et obscuratum est insipiens cor eorum, dicentes enim se esse sapientes stulti facti sunt ... Et sicut non probaverunt Deum habere in notitia, tradidit illos Deus in reprobum sensum, ut faciant ea quae non conveniunt, repletos omni iniquitate, malitia, fornicatione, avaritia, nequitia, plenos invidia, homicidio, contentione, dolo, malignitate, susurrones, detractores, Deo odibiles, contumeliosos, superbos, elatos, inventores malorum, parentibus non obedientes, insipientes, incompositos, sine affectione, absque foedere, sine misericordia' (Rom 1.21–22, 1.28–31).

Et iterum idem Apostolus: 'Videte enim vocationem vestram, fratres, quia non multi sapientes secundum carnem, non multi potentes, non multi nobiles; sed quae stulta sunt mundi elegit Deus ut confundat sapientes; et infirma mundi elegit Deus ut confundat fortia; et ignobilia mundi et contemptibilia elegit et ea quae non sunt, ut ea quae sunt destrueret; ut non glorietur omnis caro in conspectu eius' (1 Cor 1.26–29).

*But a fourth and deeper root of human impotence* is that we labor under ignorance of intellect, weakness of will, and the objective difficulty of the good because we are turned away and alienated from God. Those turned away from God do not recognize themselves as God's instruments to seek in all things the good intended by God and to choose it when they have found it. Instead, acting as if they were the First Cause, they trust in their own abilities to pursue the good that their own reason has found and their own freedom has chosen. Now those who are not the First Cause but act as if they were need to learn about their own impotence. Those whose reason judges to be good, not that good intended by God but another discovered by themselves, need to learn about their lack of wisdom. Those whose free will does not love above all else that which is good by its very essence but seeks rather something else that is good by participation as its supreme and ultimate good need to learn about their own iniquity. All other creatures, being nonrational and incapable of thought, are not deflected from their end because they neither know nor will themselves to be instruments of God. But rational creatures, directed and led to their end through their own intellect and their own will, cannot ignore or deny that they are instruments without mistaking their end in foolishness, casting off obedience in pride, and forsaking their end in iniquity.

Hence the words of the Apostle Paul: '... for though they knew God, they did not honor him as God or give thanks to him, but they became futile in their thinking, and their senseless minds were darkened. Claiming to be wise, they became fools ... And since they did not see fit to acknowledge God, God gave them up to a debased mind and to things that should not be done. They were filled with every kind of wickedness, evil, covetousness, malice. Full of envy, murder, strife, deceit, craftiness, they are gossips, slanderers, God-haters, insolent, haughty, boastful, inventors of evil, rebellious toward parents, foolish, faithless, heartless, ruthless' (Romans 1.21–22, 1.28–31).

Again Paul writes: 'Consider your own call, brothers and sisters: not many of you were wise by human standards, not many were powerful, not many were of noble birth. But God chose what is foolish in the world to shame the wise; God chose what is weak in the world to shame the strong; God chose what is low and despised in the world, things that are not, to reduce to nothing things that are, so that no one might boast in the presence of God' (1 Corinthians 1.26–29).

Et iterum: 'Scimus autem quoniam diligentibus Deum omnia cooperantur in bonum iis qui secundum propositum vocati sunt sancti' (Rom 8.28).

Quare etiam S. Petrus et S. Iacobus: 'Deus superbis resistit, humilibus autem dat gratiam' (1 Pet 5.5, Jac 4.6, Prov 3.34).

Quorum omnium rationem ultimam ipse Dominus dedit: 'Nemo bonus nisi unus Deus' (Mc 10.18). Unicum enim est bonum per essentiam. Caetera autem bona sunt quatenus divinam bonitatem participant, quatenus divina sapientia ordinantur, quatenus divina bonitate eliguntur. Qui vero a Deo aversus est atque alienatus, non solum ab unico bono recedit sed etiam ita in alia tendit ut haec ab unico boni fonte secernantur. Non enim divina sapientia dirigitur; non divinae electioni obedit; non bona finita approbat et vult quatenus divinam bonitatem participant, sed bona qua mere apparentia et insipiens approbat et superbus vult, ut civilizationem atque culturam absurdo infectam sibi faciat. Quod si arboris malae mali fructus ei displicent, fieri non potest ut, stante eadem aversione atque alienatione a Deo, ipse se de suis malis in bonum restauret. Stante enim hac aversione, non divina sapientia sed sua insipientia dirigitur, non divinae electioni sed alteri cuilibet obedit, non verum bonum sed quodlibet apparens prosequitur.

## Articulus VIII: De peccato originali

Cum alio in tractatu Catholica de peccato originali doctrina exponi soleat, octavus hic articulus brevissimus esse potest et debet.

Caetera ergo mala ex malo culpae et fieri et augeri diximus, neque hominem posse, humanis viribus fretum, haec mala tollere. Cuius impotentiae radicem in eo posuimus quod, stante reatu culpae, ita homo a Deo alienatur et in habitibus operativis malis figitur ut quod absolute facere posset et etiam facere vellet, numquam tamen faciat.

Quod sane non solum demonstrat quantum redemptione indigeat genus humanum sed etiam quaestionem movet cur Deus Pater caelestis conditionem humanam fecerit talem. At ipsa haec conditio non Dei est opus sed hominis. Quaecumque enim de humana impotentia enumeravimus aliud non dicunt quam obscurationem illam intellectus et voluntatis debilitatem

And again: 'We know that all things work together for good for those who love God, who are called according to his purpose' (Romans 8.28).

Hence also St Peter and St James: 'God opposes the proud, but gives grace to the humble' (1 Peter 5.5, James 4.6, Proverbs 3.34).

The ultimate reason for all this is given to us by the Lord himself: 'No one is good but God alone' (Mark 10.18). For there is only one that is good by essence. All other things are good insofar as they participate in the divine goodness, insofar as they are ordered by divine wisdom, insofar as they are chosen by divine goodness. Those who are turned away from God and alienated from him have not only withdrawn from the one Good but also tend towards other things in such a way that these things also are separated from the sole source of good. For they are not guided by divine wisdom, do not heed what God has chosen, do not approve and desire finite goods insofar as they share in the divine goodness, but foolishly approve and proudly choose merely apparent goods and so fashion for themselves a civilization and culture that is infected by the absurd. If they do not like the bad fruit of a rotten tree, it is impossible for them in their present state of aversion and alienation from God to do anything to extricate themselves from their evils and restore themselves to good. As long as this aversion remains they are guided not by divine wisdom but by their own foolishness; they follow not God's will but some other course, they pursue not true good but some apparent good.

### Article 8: Original sin

Since Catholic theology treats elsewhere of original sin, this eighth article can and should be very brief.

We have said that it is to culpable evil [basic sin] that all other evils owe their origin and increase, and that human beings cannot get rid of them by relying on human resources. We have placed the root of this impotence in the fact that so long as culpable evil remains, people are so alienated from God and so fixed in bad operative habits that what absolutely speaking they could do and even would want to do, they can never do.

This fact surely demonstrates our need of redemption; it also raises the question why God our heavenly Father made the human condition to be such. But this condition is not God's work, but ours. All that we have been saying about human impotence points to the darkening of the intellect and the weakening of the will, to the difficulty inherent in good and the

et in bonis difficultatem et ad mala inclinationem, quae ex peccato originali profluxisse credimus. Quia vero haec omnia non solum ex interiori hominis statu provenire vidimus sed etiam per societatem humanam mediari quodammodo et consistere et transmitti, convenientiam quandam perspicere possumus illius decreti divini quod in primo homine quasi in capite genus humanum inter conditionem bonam et quam habemus malam eligere debuit.

inclination to evil, which we believe flow from original sin. And since, as we have seen, all this not only arises from the minds and hearts of individuals but is also somehow mediated and fixed and transmitted through human society, we can see the fittingness of the divine ordinance by which the whole human race, in the person of the first human being as its head, was made to choose between a good human condition and the sad state in which we now find ourselves.

# Caput Alterum: De Iustitia Dei[1]

Qui iustitiam dicit, codices cogitat iurisque consultos, iudices et tribunalia, carceres et custodes, carnifices atque patibula. Sensibilibus enim immersi, eo magis unumquodque verum et reale ducimus quo facilius sensus nostros afficit et efficacius affectum nostrum commovet.

At ipsa haec iustitiae non tam notio quam impressio minime sufficit ubi de Dei iustitia agitur. Quam enim dixit Apostolus multiformem Dei sapientiam (Eph 3.10), eandem divinae iustitiae legem perspici oportet. Neque eam et simplicem et infinitam, quamdiu peregrinamur a Domino, contemplari possumus, sed e rebus creatis secundum analogiam procedere debemus ut imperfectam quandam infinitae perfectionis notionem formemus.

Quem in finem non pariter inserviunt omnes et quaelibet creaturae. Pedetentim ergo hoc capite ita ex rerum ordine, ex conditione humana historica, ex iudicio Dei personali, rationem divinae iustitiae quaerimus, ut ulteriorem eiusdem rationis perfectionem minime excludamus quae tertio capite in Verbo Dei carne facto perspici possit atque debeat.

# 2 The Justice of God[1]

The word 'justice' conjures up thoughts of law codes and lawyers, judges and juries, prisons and prison guards, hangmen and gallows. Because we are immersed in things of sense, the more readily something affects our senses and the more effectively it moves our feelings, the more true and real we consider it to be.

But such a notion, or rather impression, of justice is quite inadequate in dealing with the justice of God. What the Apostle Paul calls 'the wisdom of God in its rich variety' (Ephesians 3.10) must be understood as being at the same time the law of God's justice. In itself it is simple and infinite, but so long as we are 'away from the Lord' [2 Corinthians 5.6] we cannot contemplate it as it is. We must proceed, rather, by analogy from created things to form some imperfect notion of infinite perfection.

Not all created things are equally helpful to us in this endeavor. In this chapter, therefore, we shall proceed step by step from the order of the world, the historical human condition, and God's personal judgment, to seek the meaning of divine justice, but in such a way as to leave room for the further perfection of this meaning, which then in the third chapter we will be able to grasp as we should in the Word of God made flesh.

1 [The autograph may be found on the website www.bernardlonergan.com at 25310DTL060.]

### Articulus IX: De notione divinae iustitiae

Cum hac in vita Deum nisi analogice non cognoscamus, ab humana iustitia ita ordiri oportet ut, iis exclusis quae Deo competere non possint, quid perfectioni divinae conveniat perspiciamus.

Humana ergo iustitia aut commutativa aut legalis aut distributiva aut etiam forte, si quarta distinguitur, socialis est. Nam iustitia quandam ordinis rectitudinem dicit. Per ordinem autem e multis efficitur unum quoddam et totum. Quatenus ergo multa et singula recte inter se ordinantur, commutativa est iustitia; quatenus eadem multa uni et toti recte subordinantur, legalis est iustitia; quatenus unum totumque ad multa et singula recte se habet, distributiva est iustitia; quatenus denique ipse ordo rite proficit, disputata et quarta iustitia socialis est.[2]

Quibus perspectis, cum Deus creaturis neque coordinari neque subordinari possit, neque commutativam neque legalem iustitiam admittit. Quia vero Deus est omnium auctor atque largitor, secundum rectum huius donationis ordinem distributiva iustitia ei attribuitur. Quia denique huius donationis ordo nihil est aliud quam ordo totius universi creati, qui immutatus omnem partialis ordinis profectum in se includit, iustitia quae forte socialis dicitur Deo convenire haud potest.

Iam vero universi ordo multipliciter considerari potest. In ipso enim universo est quasi forma artificialis qua hic mundus est unus;[3] est etiam ordinis bonum et finis universo intrinsecus;[4] est denique illa causarum dispositio seu series quae fatum nominari potest.[5] Et sicut ex facto ordinis ad exsistentiam Dei concludimus,[6] ita ex unitate ordinis ad Dei unicitatem,[7] et ex congruitate ordinis ad iustitiam Dei distributivam.[8] Imo, cum optimum in rebus creatis exsistens sit bonum ordinis universi, fieri non potest ut hic ordo non

## Article 9: The notion of divine justice

In this life we know God only by analogy. Hence it is necessary to start from the notion of human justice and, excluding whatever cannot be applied to God, grasp the justice befitting divine perfection.

Human justice, then, is commutative or legal or distributive or, if one distinguishes a fourth kind, social justice. Justice names a rightness of order, and order brings a multiplicity of things together into a unity and whole. To the extent that many individuals are rightly ordered to one another, there is commutative justice; to the extent that they are duly subordinated to the unity and whole, there is legal justice; to the extent that the unity and whole is correctly related to the many individuals, there is distributive justice; and to the extent that the order itself is rightly progressing, there is social justice – though this fourth is somewhat disputed.[2]

Since God can neither be set in an order with creatures nor be subordinate to them, there is no question of legal or commutative justice being attributed to God. But since God is the source and lavish giver of all things, distributive justice is attributable to him with regard to the right order among his gifts. Finally, since the order among these gifts is simply the order of the whole created universe, an order which without change includes within itself the progress of each partial order, what is called 'social justice' does not apply to God.

The order of the universe can be considered in several ways. It is a kind of artificial form of the universe, by which this world is one;[3] it is also the good of order and intrinsic end of the universe;[4] finally, it is the disposition or seriation of causes that can be referred to as 'fate.'[5] And as we conclude to the existence of God from the fact of order,[6] so we conclude to the uniqueness of God from the unity of this order,[7] and to the distributive justice of God from the congruity of this order.[8] Moreover, since that which

2 [The term 'social justice' would within several years of the composition of this work take on a different significance from that which appears here. It is important not to read back into Lonergan's text a later meaning to this expression. The question here is whether an ontology of justice needs a fourth explanatory category besides commutative, legal, and distributive.]
3 Thomas Aquinas, *Summa theologiae*, 1, q. 47, a. 3.
4 Ibid. q. 103, a. 2, ad 3m.
5 Ibid. q. 116, a. 2, ad 1m; a. 3 c. [See Lonergan, *Grace and Freedom* 85–86.]
6 Ibid. q. 2, a. 3 c.
7 Ibid. q. 11, a. 3.
8 Ibid. q. 21, a. 1.

sit per se et proprie a Deo omnium causa intentus; et ideo menti divinae inest idea ordinis universi, quae caeteras rerum creatarum ideas in sua unitate includit.[9]

Proinde, cum sapientis sit ordinare, cumque divina sapientia sit infinita ut totum posse divinae potentiae comprehendat,[10] non solum idea ordinis huius universi sed etiam ideae omnium ordinum seu mundorum possibilium menti divinae insunt, ut nihil absolute possibile sit[11] quod Deus sapientissime facere non possit.[12] Sed repugnat infinitam sapientiam ita possibilia ordinare ut singulis non tribuat quae iis conveniant; et ideo non solum sapientissimus sed etiam iustissimus est quilibet rerum ordo seu mundus a Deo conceptus.[13]

Praeterea, cum bonum intellectum sit obiectum voluntatis, impossibile est Deum velle nisi quod ratio suae sapientiae habet.[14] Sicut ergo divina sapientia est quasi lex iustitiae, ita consequens divinam sapientiam divina voluntas necessario recta atque iusta est, sive hunc mundum creare eligit sive alium quemlibet sive, cum omnes finiti sint valoris, nullum.

Praeterea, sicut ex ordine universi ad Deum sapientem iusteque eligentem ascendimus, ita etiam ex Deo ad ordinem universi redire possumus. Quatenus ergo ratio ordinis in mente divina res creatas in fines proprios producendas respicit, divina providentia est;[15] quatenus autem per divinam voluntatem atque potentiam exsecutio providentiae habetur, divina gubernatio est.[16] Quatenus ratio ordinis, omnia ordinata intentionaliter continens, comparatur ad ipsas res ordinatas, logica veritas divinae scientiae consideratur; quatenus autem ipsae res ordinatae comparantur ad rationem ordinis in mente divina, ad ontologicam rerum veritatem attenditur.[17] Quatenus ratio ordinis in mente principis consideratur, lex aeterna est;[18] quatenus autem legis aeternae participatio in creaturis consideratur, lex naturalis est.[19] Quatenus singula quae sunt vel eveniunt a divina sapientia

is best in all creation is the good of order of the universe, this order must be per se and properly intended by God, the cause of all things. In the divine mind, therefore, there is the idea of the order of the universe, the idea that contains in its unity the ideas of all other created things.[9]

Accordingly, since putting things in order is the work of the wise, and since divine wisdom, being infinite, extends to all that divine power can effect,[10] there is in the divine mind not only the idea of the order of this universe but also the ideas of all possible orders or worlds, so that there is nothing intrinsically possible[11] that God could not most wisely do.[12] But it is inadmissible that infinite wisdom should order possible realities in such a way as to deny to each one what properly belongs to it; hence any world or order of reality conceived by God is not only most wise but also most just.[13]

Furthermore, since the object of the will is a good apprehended by the intellect, it is quite impossible for God to will anything but what his wisdom approves.[14] Therefore, as the divine wisdom is, so to speak, the law of justice, so the divine will that follows divine wisdom is necessarily right and just, whether it chooses to create this world or some other world, or even, since all are of finite value, none at all.

Besides, as we can reason from the order of the universe to the existence of a God who chooses wisely and justly, so we can return from God to the order of the universe. Therefore, inasmuch as the idea of order in the divine mind regards creatures being led forward to their proper ends, it is divine providence;[15] inasmuch as this providence is carried out by God's will and power, it is divine governance.[16] Inasmuch as the idea of order, containing in an intentional way all things ordered, is related to these ordered things, it is considered to be the logical truth of divine knowledge; inasmuch as the ordered things themselves are related to the idea of order in the divine mind, we have the ontological truth of things.[17] Inasmuch as the idea of order is considered as in the mind of the Creator, it is the eternal law;[18] but inasmuch as participation by creatures in this eternal law is

9 Ibid. q. 15, a. 2.
10 Ibid. q. 25, a. 5.
11 Ibid. q. 25, a. 3.
12 Ibid. q. 25, a. 5, ad 1m.
13 Ibid. q. 25, a. 5.
14 Ibid. q. 21, a. 1, ad 2m.
15 Ibid. q. 22, a. 1.
16 Ibid. q. 103, a. 6.
17 Ibid. q. 21, a. 2.
18 Ibid. 1-2, q. 91, a. 1.

ordinantur, ratio uniuscuiusque cur sit vel fiat assignari potest; quatenus autem totus ordo libere a divina voluntate eligitur, ultima omnium ratio est libera Dei electio.[20]

Quae cum ita sint, Dei iustitia originaliter quidem ad divinam sapientiam pertinet, actualiter autem ad iustam sapientis ordinis electionem, consequenter autem in rebus invenitur creatis quatenus sapienter iusteque ordinantur tum inter se tum ad finem ultimum qui ipse Deus est.

**Articulus x: De iusto rerum ordine**

Cum parum conveniat ita ordinis nomen dictitare ut nihil in mente habeamus quod huic nomini correspondeat, iam quaeramus oportet qualis sit ille iustitiae ordo quem conceperit divina sapientia, elegerit divina voluntas, producat divina potentia.

*In primis* ergo ordinantur omnia inquantum formas habent legesque naturaliter sibi inditas. Nihil enim aliud est lex naturalis quam participatio quaedam legis aeternae unde caeterae quidem res materiales sua sponte in proprium actum finemque procedant, homines autem moveantur non solum ut faciant sed etiam ut quid iis faciendum sit cognoscant et cognitum libere eligant.[21]

Aliud *deinde* magisque concretum est universalis ordinis elementum, quod res ita inter se coniunguntur ut circularis quaedam vel serialis legum complicatio oriatur. Sicut enim abstractas motus leges invenit Newton, magis concretam vero systematis planetaris periodicitatem demonstravit Laplace, ita in omnibus aliud est determinare quid sub debitis conditionibus atque adiunctis *per se fieret,* et longe aliud est schematicam illam rerum coniunctionem seu constellationem invenire unde certis temporum intervallis et impleantur conditiones debitae et *actu fiant* eventus praevisi. Illud enim singulas leges considerat easque abstractas; et cum a concretis rerum adiunctis atque conditionibus praescindat, nisi cognitionem prorsus hypotheticam non praebet. Hoc autem non unam tantum legem considerat sed complurium simul complicationem; neque a rebus praescindit sed eas ita schematice inter se coniungit ut mutua earum dispositio ipsi legum complicationi correspondeat; neque conditiones adiunctaque praetermittit sed

considered, it is natural law.[19] Inasmuch as everything that exists or happens is ordained by divine wisdom, the reason for its being or happening can be assigned; but inasmuch as the whole order is freely chosen by the divine will, the ultimate reason of all things is God's free choice.[20]

Thus, the justice of God in its origin belongs to divine wisdom, in its realization it is the just choice of a wise order, and in its effects it is found in created things inasmuch as they are wisely and justly ordered, both among themselves and in relation to their ultimate end, which is God himself.

**Article 10: The just order of reality**

It would hardly be right to keep speaking of 'order' without explaining what is meant, so now we must ask what is this order of justice which divine wisdom has conceived, divine will has chosen, and divine power causes to be.

*First,* all things are ordered, inasmuch as they have forms and laws that are innate, that is, naturally implanted in them. For the natural law is nothing but a participation in the eternal law whereby the other material things proceed spontaneously to their proper acts and ends, while human beings are moved not only to act but also to know how they ought to act and to freely choose on the basis of this knowledge.[21]

*Second,* there is another and more concrete element in the universal order, namely, the fact that things are so interrelated and interconnected that there results a circular or serial conjunction of laws. Just as Newton discovered the abstract laws of motion but Laplace demonstrated the more concrete periodicity of the planetary system, so it is one thing to determine what *per se should occur* in all things under the proper conditions and circumstances, but quite another to determine that schematic conjunction or constellation as a result of which at certain times the proper conditions will be fulfilled and the events foreseen *will actually occur.* The former case is a consideration of individual abstract laws, and since it prescinds from concrete conditions and circumstances, it affords only a purely hypothetical knowledge. The latter case is a consideration not only of one law taken in isolation but of the interconnection of several laws together. It does not prescind from things, but rather links them together schematically so that

19 Ibid. q. 91, a. 2.
20 Thomas Aquinas, *Summa contra Gentiles,* 3, c. 97, ¶13, §2735.
21 Thomas Aquinas, *Summa theologiae,* 1-2, q. 91, a. 2.

eas ipsa rerum dispositione legumque coniunctione regulat atque dominatur; neque cognitionem mere hypotheticam praebet sed, pro diversitate materiae, vel physice certam vel plus minus probabilem.

Abstracta ergo ordinis elementa considerat physicus in gravium motibus, chimicus in aquis vaporantibus et condensantibus, meteorologicus in directione et velocitate ventorum. Quae tamen omnia simul coniunguntur ubi ad schematicam aquarum circulationem attenditur; nam vaporantibus maribus efformantur nubes; aspirantibus ventis terra nebulis operitur; condensantibus vaporibus descendunt pluviae; fluentibus aquis augentur flumina et replentur maria. Qua in circulatione non alias novasque perspicis leges sed concretam legum applicationem; neque eam consideras applicationem quae ex quolibet universali ad particulare quodlibet procedit, sed certam legum universalium seriem rebus certo ordine dispositis applicas; neque sine fine vel disponuntur res vel leges coniunguntur, cum ex ipsa hac dispositione atque coniunctione exoriatur perpetua quaedam atque viventibus perutilis aquarum circulatio.

Quod vero in periodico planetarum systemate et in aquis circumeuntibus illustravimus ita in omnibus verificatur ut exsistat communis quidam rerum eventuumque cursus qui multo clarius multoque certius omnibus hominibus innotescat quam recentissima legum abstractarum scientia. Nam ipsa hominis vita, sive respirationem consideras, sive motum cordis sive ciborum intussusceptionem sive vigilantiae et somni alternationem sive laborem cotidianum sive prolis generationem atque educationem, ita rhythmo quodam peragitur, ita repetitis actionibus constat, ita rerum circulationibus dependet, ut mundum simili quodam modo ordinatum exigat. Neque ille sufficit ordo qui in abstractis legibus ita ponitur ut a concretis eventibus praescindat, sed alius prorsus qui ita leges inter se complicat et res mutuis habitudinibus disponit ut certus quidam eventuum cursus consequatur.

At *tertius* manet gressus ut ad actualem rerum ordinem perveniatur. Non enim una tantum exsistit legum complicatio schematica, si quidem alia in periodico planetarum systemate et alia in aquis circumeuntibus perspicitur. Neque multae sed inordinatae sunt, cum aliae aliis vel subordinentur vel coordinentur. Nisi enim prius exstitit systema solis et planetarum, haud circumferuntur aquae; nisi circumeunt aquae, non vivunt plantae; sine

their mutual arrangement corresponds to the interaction itself of the laws. Nor does it ignore conditions and circumstances, but by this very arrangement of things and linking of laws regulates and controls them. It does not provide purely hypothetical knowledge, but knowledge that is either physically certain or more or less probable, depending on the nature of the subject matter.

Abstract elements of order are considered by the physicist in the movement of masses, by the chemist in the evaporation and condensation of water, and by the meteorologist in the direction and velocity of wind. But all these elements are brought together in considering the schematic circulation of moisture: clouds are formed from the evaporation of the seas; the wind blows the clouds over the land; the condensing moisture falls as rain; the resulting runoff swells the rivers and replenishes the seas. In this circulation you find no new laws but a concrete application of laws. Nor do you consider the application that proceeds from just any universal to just any particular, but you apply a definite series of universal laws to things arranged in a certain order. Nor are things arranged or laws combined to no end, since it is from this very arrangement and combination that there results that continuous circulation of moisture that is of such vital importance to living things.

The process we have illustrated in the periodicity of the planetary system and in the circulation of moisture is so verified in everything that there is a common flow of things and course of events which is familiar to everyone with much more clarity and certainty than the latest science of abstract laws. For whether you consider your breathing or heartbeat or food intake or the alternation of sleep and wakefulness, or your daily work, or the procreation and education of children, human life follows a certain rhythm, consists of certain repeated actions, and depends upon a continuing round of things so as to require a world that is ordered in a somewhat similar way. But the order of abstract laws, prescinding from concrete events, is not at all sufficient; what is needed is that quite different order which connects laws to one another and arranges things according to their mutual relationships in such a way that some sure course of events ensues.

Now there remains a *third* step to be taken in order to reach the actual order of things. For there exists more than one schematic conjunction of laws, since we find one in the periodicity of the planetary system and another in the circulation of moisture. Nor are these many schemes lacking order among them, since some are subordinated to or coordinated with others. Had the sun and its planetary system not been in existence, the earth's

plantis, tot animalium species esse non possunt; et in singulis animalibus non solum distinguuntur sed mirabiliter etiam inter se coniunguntur atque dependent systemata digestivum, respirativum, vasculare, ossium et musculorum, nervosum, et sensitivum.[22]

Ipsae ergo quas superius distinximus schematicae rerum dispositiones legumque complicationes alio quodam et magis concreto magisque universali ordine comprehenduntur. Qui sane ordo ipsius divinae sapientiae atque providentiae est, quae omnia complectitur secundum omnes singulorum determinationes etiam minimas, quae omnia disponit atque dirigit, quae omnia in fines singulis proprios producit.[23] Quod si vel leges abstractas non omnes perspicimus, si pauca admodum schemata cognoscimus, multo minus universalem hunc ordinem et concretum prorsus et actualem perfecte intelligimus.

At ubi deest cognitio perfecta, adesse potest imperfecta, quae in principiis quibusdam potioribus determinandis iisque modo generico applicandis consistat. Et in primis elucet quantum habeat momentum ipsa divina providentia. Quod enim singulis rebus proprium est, hoc etiam hypotheticum est. Singulis enim proprium est ut, impletis conditionibus debitis, secundum suas naturas operentur. Si ergo implentur conditiones, operantur; sin autem conditiones non implentur, non operantur; neque ulli rei creatae inconditionata conceditur operatio. Quare in omnibus rebus et creatis et conservatis, cum singularum operatio conditionata atque hypothetica sit, nulla invenitur causa per se et proportionata ut res ulla agat. Quod si dicis aliam per aliam iam operantem accipere ut conditiones propriae operationis impleantur, factum sane non ignoras, sed explicationem adhuc omittis. Non enim casu fit ut (1) res aliae ita operentur ut impleantur conditiones sub quibus aliae operari incipiant, (2) omnes res ita iugiter disponantur ut

moisture would not circulate; without this circulation of moisture there would be no plant life, and without plants the many species of animals could not exist. Again, each animal has within itself several systems that are not only distinct from one another but marvelously interrelated and interdependent: the digestive system, the respiratory system, the vascular system, the skeletal system and musculature, the nervous system and the sensory apparatus.[22]

Thus the schematic arrangements of things and conjunctions of laws distinguished above are all encompassed in another more concrete and more universal order. This order, of course, is that of divine wisdom and providence, which embraces all things down to the smallest details, arranges and directs all things, and brings each one to its proper end.[23] But if we do not understand all abstract laws, and if we know only a very few schematic arrangements, much less do we have a perfect understanding of this actual and wholly concrete order of the universe.

However, where perfect knowledge is lacking, imperfect knowledge is possible, a knowledge that consists in determining some of the more important principles and applying them in a generic way. First of all, the importance of divine providence is quite clear. What is proper to individual beings is also hypothetical, for it is proper to individual beings that, with the requisite conditions fulfilled, they operate in accord with their natures. If the conditions are fulfilled, they operate; if not, they do not operate, and no created being is capable of unconditioned operation. Hence in the case of all things created and conserved, since the operations of each are conditioned and hypothetical, there is no cause per se and proportionate that anything actually act. If you assert that one thing already operating fulfils the conditions requisite for the operation of another, you are right about the fact but you still do not have an explanation of that fact. For it is not a matter of chance (1) that some beings operate in such a way as to fulfil the

22 [These paragraphs echo positions Lonergan worked out in greater detail in the early chapters of *Insight* when he discussed classical laws and their abstractness, concrete inferences from classical laws, statistical laws and their distinct mode of abstractness, the complementarity of classical and statistical investigations, schemes of recurrence, etc. On the systems in animals, see the discussion of mediation in 'The Mediation of Christ in Prayer,' in Bernard Lonergan, *Philosophical and Theological Papers 1958–1964*, vol. 6 in Collected Works of Bernard Lonergan, ed. Robert C. Croken, Frederick E. Crowe, and Robert M. Doran (Toronto: University of Toronto Press, 1996) 160–82.]

23 [See Lonergan, *Insight* 686–88.]

nulla aliarum et praemoventium[24] adiutorio privetur, et (3) ex hac perpetua rerum dispositione legumque naturalium complicatione, non solum merum factum actualis operationis resultet sed mirus ille atque beneficus efficiatur ordo quem communem rerum cursum nominemus. Quod si casu non fit, divina providentia facit tum ut singulae res actu agant tum ut omnes ipsum universi ordinem instrumentaliter efficiant.

Porro, ut propius ad rationem divinae iustitiae accedamus, eiusmodi est communis rerum cursus universique ordo ut (1) sit effectus Deo proprius et (2) per causas secundas producatur. Nam Deo proprius est ille effectus quem Deus solus producere potest; sed communis rerum cursus universique ordo proportionem excedit tam singularum quam omnium rerum creatarum et conservatarum; singularum enim excedit quia nulla res creata operationem inconditionatam habet; et omnium excedit cum eatenus in communi effectu ordo perspici possit quatenus iam ante in operaturis ordinatio adfuerit. Sicut enim singulae ab aliis accipiunt ut conditiones operationis propriae impleantur, ita omnes a Deo accipiunt illam dispositionem atque ordinationem unde ordinatus producitur effectus communis.[25]

Neque minus verum est Deum per causas secundas communem rerum cursum universique ordinem producere. Frustra enim crearentur et conservarentur res quae non operarentur. Neque operari possent nisi divina sapientia eas ordinaret atque dirigeret. Neque ordinatae et directae ab eo communi cursu atque ordine deficere possunt quem divina sapientia intendit. Neque aliam altioremque regulam habet sive divina bonitas sive divina iustitia quam ipsa divina sapientia.

conditions under which other beings begin to operate; (2) that all things are constantly so arranged that none of them is deprived of the assistance of others that are already premoving;[24] and (3) that from this constant arrangement of things and the conjunction of laws of nature not only does there result the simple fact of actual operation, but there is produced also that marvelous and beneficent order that we call the common course of events. But if all this does not come about by chance, it is divine providence that sees to it that each individual being actually operates and that all things are instruments in effecting the order of the universe.

Moreover – to move a step closer to the notion of divine justice – this common course of events and order of the universe is (1) an effect proper to God, and (2) produced through secondary causes. That effect is said to be proper to God which only God can produce; but the common course of events and order of the universe exceeds the proportion of created and conserved beings, singly or in whole. It exceeds the proportion of individual creatures because no created being enjoys unconditioned operation. It exceeds the proportion of all of them together, because order could be discerned in their common effect only insofar as there was an ordering already in them prior to their operating. For just as each individual thing receives from others the fulfilment of the conditions requisite for its own operation, so all things taken together receive from God that arrangement and ordering from which a well-ordered common effect follows.[25]

It is no less true that God produces the common course of events and order of the universe through secondary causes. Things would be created and conserved in vain if they did not operate; and they could not operate without an ordering and direction from divine wisdom. Thus ordered and directed, they cannot fail in effecting the common course and order intended by divine wisdom. Nor has divine goodness or justice any higher rule than divine wisdom itself.

24 We are referring to premotion here in the Aristotelian, not Bañezian, sense; see Bernard Lonergan, 'St. Thomas' Theory of Operation' 382–83. [Lonergan's Latin: 'De praemotione agitur sensu non Bañeziano sed Aristotelico; cf. Theol. Stud., iii (1942) 382.' The latter is available now in Lonergan, *Grace and Freedom* 74–75. See also Lonergan, *Insight* 687, where Lonergan distinguishes his position from the positions of Bañez and Molina; and Lonergan, 'On God and Secondary Causes,' *Collection* 53–65.]

25 ['... God controls each event because he controls all, and he controls all because he alone can be the cause of the order of the universe on which every event depends.' Lonergan, *Insight* 687.]

Quae cum ita sint, qualis in genere sit ordo divinae iustitiae aliqualiter dici potest. Nam in primis constat ultimum finem in quem omnia sunt dirigenda esse ipsam divinam bonitatem manifestandam.[26] Deinde, determinatum est medium quo utitur divina sapientia ad hunc finem attingendum, nempe, ipsae rerum naturae atque leges naturales. Tertio, constat divinam sapientiam non usu et experientia addiscere ut ab incepto consilio desistat et alium novumque tentet, sed ab ipsis primis initiis in finem usque omnia uno intuito perspexisse, ordinasse, approbasse. Quarto denique determinatum est quale sit hoc unum consilium, nempe, ita res disponere atque coniungere ut serialia vel circularia operationum schemata resultent, et ita ipsa schemata tum temporum decursu tum simultanea hierarchia ordinare ut communis rerum cursus universique ordo consequatur.

Quae quidem quattuor determinationes quid sibi velint, exemplis et obiectionibus maxime manifestatur. Quaerere ergo solent homines cur tot sint astrorum collectiones nebulosae, cur tam magnae sint distantiae astronomicae, cur tam diuturnae fuerint aetates geologicae, cur tot olim exstiterint viventium species iam exstinctae, cur tam immisericors sit illa oeconomia qua vivens viventi praeda atque cibus sit, cur tot alia eveniant quae humano iudicio graviora, duriora, imo immania esse videantur. Quibus sic fere responderi potest:

(1) haec omnia fieri secundum leges rebus naturaliter inditas; et his uti legibus ad divinam iustitiam pertinere;

(2) materiae abundantiam et temporum diuturnitatem esse indicia signaque legum statisticarum; adeo ergo ineptam effusionem, vanum dispendium, ingenii tarditatem non probare, ut potius Deum demonstrent agere secundum propriam rerum convenientiam;[27]

(3) alia adiuncta aliis viventium speciebus magis convenire; unde iterum constare Deum agere non pro lubitu suae potentiae sed secundum iustitiam suae sapientiae;

From all this we can say at least something about the general nature of divine justice. First of all, it is evident that the ultimate end to which all things are to be directed is the manifestation of the divine goodness.[26] Second, we have determined the means used by divine wisdom to attain this end, namely, the natures of things and natural laws. Third, it is clear that divine wisdom does not learn by experience or by trial and error, embarking on one plan only to abandon it later for another, but rather in a single view has understood, ordered, and approved all things from the very first beginnings of the universe right down to the end. Fourth, we have determined of what kind this one plan is, namely, to arrange and connect things in such a way that serial or circular schemes of operations may result, and to order these schemes both in the course of time and in a simultaneous hierarchy in such a way that the common course of events and order of the universe may ensue.

The best way to clarify what these four determinations mean is by giving examples and answering objections. People ask why there are so many constellations and nebulae, why astronomical distances are so great, why the geological ages have been so long, why so many species of plants and animals are now extinct, why such a ruthless economy makes one living creature the prey and food of another, why so many other things happen that to our human way of thinking seem so very harsh and cruel, even monstrous. To these questions, our general reply is

(1) all of this happens according to laws naturally inherent in things, and to use these laws pertains to divine justice;

(2) the vast amount of matter and the great length of time in the universe are indicators and signs of statistical laws; they do not prove God foolishly prodigal, wasteful, or slow to learn; rather, they show that God acts in accordance with what is appropriate to every creature;[27]

(3) different circumstances are best suited to different species of living things; hence once again it is clear that God acts not by whim or willful display of power but in accordance with the justice of his wisdom;

26 ['The unrestricted act of understanding grasps the total range of possible world orders; each is a consequence and manifestation of divine intelligence and wisdom, of divine reality and truth, of divine goodness and love ...' Ibid. 717.]

27 [See ibid. 146–48 on the significance of the size of the universe and of long intervals of time.]

(4) numquam ergo nos satis mirari posse ordinem universi quem per res infimas et secundum proprietatem earum naturarum producit divina sapientia, secundum illud: 'Deus igitur per suum intellectum omnia movet ad proprios fines';[28]

(5) fieri sane mala, et potuisse Deum, ubi defuerit contradictio, omnia mala impedire; finem tamen universi in quem omnia ordinentur esse non creaturarum bonitatem sed divinam manifestare;[29] et ideo Deum iuste mala permittere, tum ut res creatae secundum veritatem naturae finitae et imperfectae agant, tum ut bonum per participationem atque creatum non sit nisi medium ad bonum per essentiam manifestandum.

Attamen ulterius quaeritur cur Deus homo, cur tot saeculis exspectari debuerit Salvator, cur ad populum hebraicum advenerit, cur tam lenta sit fidei propagatio, cur tot factae sint haereses, apostasiae, et revelatae veritatis calumniae, cur inter ipsos fideles tot sint peccatores, tot tepidi, cur inter ipsos ferventes tam saepe impediatur fructus bonae voluntatis per errores vel tarditatem mentis. Quibus omnibus eadem est generalis responsio, ad divinam nempe iustitiam pertinere ut Deus agat per causas secundas et secundum convenientiam ipsarum naturarum. Quapropter Deus ipse factus est homo ut sit causa secunda et proportionata ad omnia instaurando (Eph 1.10) novaque facienda (2 Cor 5.17), 'quoniam quidem per hominem mors et per hominem resurrectio mortuorum' (1 Cor 15.21). Quod si 'in propria venit, et sui eum non receperunt' (Io 1.11), quamvis

(4) we can never, therefore, cease to wonder at the order of the universe which God in his wisdom brings about through lowly creatures in accordance with their respective natures: 'By his intellect God moves all things to their appropriate ends;'[28]

(5) certainly evils exist, and God could have prevented all evils, at least where this would not have involved a contradiction; nevertheless, the purpose of the universe, to which everything is directed, is to manifest not the goodness of creatures but the goodness of God;[29] with justice, therefore, does God permit evil to occur, so that creatures may act in accordance with the truth of their limited and imperfect natures, and also in order that created good, good by participation, may be only a means towards the manifestation of what is good by essence.

As to further questions, about why God became human, why so many ages had to wait for the Savior, why he came to the Jewish people, why the spread of the faith is so slow, why there have been so many heresies, apostasies, and calumnies against revealed truth, why among the faithful there are so many sinners, why so many are lax and lukewarm, why even among the devout the efforts of good will are so often frustrated through error and stupidity: to all of these questions there is the same general answer, namely, that it is the way of God's justice to act through secondary causes and in accordance with their natures. This is why God himself became human, that he might be a secondary and proportionate cause in restoring all things (Ephesians 1.10) and making all things new (2 Corinthians 5.17); 'since death came through a human being, the resurrection of the dead has also come through a

28 Thomas Aquinas, *De substantiis separatis*, c. 15; see Bernard Lonergan, 'St. Thomas' Theory of Operation' 391 [*Grace and Freedom* 82. Note that in the original article, in the footnote referring to *De substantiis separatis* (footnote 76), Lonergan gave the reference as '*De Subst. Sep.*, 13, Mand. 1, 121.' In the corresponding footnote in *Grace and Freedom* (numbered in that work as footnote 79) the reference is given as '*De substantiis separatis*, c. 14, § 129.' The reference given here to c. 15 follows the chapter divisions of *De substantiis separatis* as they appear in the online *Corpus Thomisticum*. For the online version of *De substantiis separatis* in *Corpus Thomisticum* and the chapter divisions it follows, see http://www.corpusthomisticum.org/ots.html.]

29 ['... every tendency and force, every movement and change, every desire and striving is designed to bring about the order of the universe in the manner in which in fact they contribute to it; and since the order of the universe itself has been shown to be because of the perfection and excellence of the primary being and good, so all that is for the order of the universe is headed ultimately to the perfection and excellence that is its primary source and ground.' Lonergan, *Insight* 688.]

sui tot prophetis tantisque signis eruditi tam ardenter eum exspectavissent, haud fructuosior fuisset primus ille adventus si ante temporum plenitudinem (Gal 4.4) accidisset vel sine lege quae paedagogus noster fuit in Christo (Gal 3.24). Neque Dominus in tempore hoc restituit regnum Israel (Act 1.6) quod subitaneo incursu et manifesta potestate omnia sibi subiceret, sed granum sinapis seminavit (Mt 13.31) quod lentius crescere videretur, tum quia fructus interiores ephemeridibus non narrantur, tum quia per causas secundas, per homines, annuntiatur regnum atque propagatur. Quae sane omnia longiori disquisitione essent exponenda nisi praesens intentio ad illud restringeretur, qualis scilicet in genere sit ordo divinae iustitiae.

## Articulus xi: De ordine iustitiae historico

Quae in genere de ordine divinae iustitiae diximus immediatam admittunt applicationem ad ea quae homines magis respiciant; et ipsam hanc applicationem iam ante praeparavimus cum primo capite de bonis et malis disseruerimus.

Nam tria in ordine divinae iustitiae distinximus: (1) rerum nempe naturae legesque naturales; (2) schemata operationum vel serialia vel circularia quae ex rerum dispositione et legum complicatione resultant; (3) ipse ordo divinae sapientiae, iustitiae, providentiae, quae ita seriem atque hierarchiam schematum excogitat atque ordinat ut sequatur communis rerum cursus ordoque universi.

Tria pariter in bonis humanis distinximus: (1) bona particularia; (2) bonum ordinis externum; et (3) bonum culturale. Sed bonum particulare sequitur operationem cuiusdam legis naturalis; bonum ordinis externum est quoddam schema seriale vel circulare; et bonum culturale diffusionem respicit illius interioris ordinis et perfectionis qua homo per rationem et voluntatem sibi providet et ipsam divinam providentiam quodammodo participat.[30] Praeterea, sicut divina providentia in rebus seriem et hierarchiam schematum efficit, ita in hominibus bonum culturale dirigit atque in melius commutat bonum ordinis externum; et sicut schemata faciunt ut res naturales iugiter secundum proprias leges operentur, ita bonum ordinis externum bonorum particularium profluvium quoddam comparat.

human being' (1 Corinthians 15.21). But if 'he came to what was his own, and his own people did not accept him' (John 1.11), even though 'his own' had been taught by so many prophets and were given such striking miracles and were eagerly awaiting him, that first coming of his would not have been more successful had he come before the fullness of time (Galatians 4.4) and in the absence of the law which was 'our disciplinarian until Christ came' (Galatians 3.24). Nor did the Lord at that time restore a kingdom of Israel (Acts 1.6) that would suddenly and with manifest power bring all things under its sway; he preferred rather to sow a grain of mustard seed (Matthew 13.31), which seems to grow slowly because interior fruit is ignored by the news media and also because the kingdom is proclaimed and propagated through secondary causes, namely, human beings. This entire subject calls for a longer treatment, but our present purpose is limited to determining the general nature of the order of divine justice.

**Article 11: The historical order of justice**

What we have said in general about the order of divine justice has immediate application to human affairs. We already prepared the way for this application when in the first chapter we dealt at length with the question of good and evil.

We have distinguished three elements in the order of divine justice: (1) the natures of things and natural laws; (2) schemes of operations, whether serial or circular, which result from the arrangement of things and the conjunction of laws; (3) the order itself of divine wisdom, justice, and providence, which so devises and arranges this series and hierarchy of schemes that the common course of events and the order of the universe ensues.

We also distinguished three levels in the human good: (1) particular goods, (2) the external good of order, and (3) cultural good. Now a particular good follows the operation of some law of nature; the external good of order is a serial or circular scheme; and cultural good has to do with the spread of that interior order and perfection by which human beings through reason and will provide for themselves and so in some way participate in divine providence.[30] Furthermore, just as divine providence puts into effect a series and hierarchy of schemes in things, so in human affairs it directs the cultural good and improves the external good of order; and just as these schemes make natural beings operate with constancy according to the laws of their nature, so the external good of order provides a continuous flow of particular goods.

30 Thomas Aquinas, *Summa theologiae*, 1-2, q. 91, a. 2.

Bonis tamen humanis opponuntur mala, nempe, (1) mala particularia, (2) mala ordinis externi, et (3) mala culturalia; quae quidem ex oppositis bonis ordinem quendam mutuant. Nam ex malis particularibus conducuntur homines in bonum ordinis exterius quaerendum atque perficiendum; ex malis ordinis conducuntur ad bonum culturale inveniendum atque evolvendum; et ex ipsis malis culturalibus, tamquam ex culpa felici, ad Redemptorem flagitandum atque exspectandum moveri debent. Maximum enim malum est quod interiorem hominis ordinem corrumpit et in culturae decadentia sese manifestat; nam radicem suam habet in illa alienatione a Deo quae moralem impotentiam inducit, obscurationem nempe intellectus et voluntatis infirmitatem et obiectivam quandam boni graviorem difficultatem; quibus vicissim corrumpitur bonum ordinis externum, unde et bona particularia iugiter minuuntur et mala particularia in dies augentur.

Quae bonorum malorumque oppositio atque interdependentia clarissime manifestant divinae iustitiae ordinem. Cum enim Deus per causas secundas et secundum convenientiam earum naturarum operetur, etiam hominis liberum arbitrium adhibet tamquam medium suo modo suaque proprietate usurpandum, secundum illud: 'Deus ab initio constituit hominem et reliquit illum in manu consilii sui' (Eccli 15.14). Quia vero liberum arbitrium in malum declinare potest, ita divina sapientia tam mala quam bona ordinavit ut non solum e bonis bonum sequatur sed etiam e malis ad bonum addiscendum et perficiendum homo revocetur. Quia autem finis ultimus est ipsa divina bonitas manifestanda, ita omnia bona omniaque mala ordinavit Deus ut ex humili submissione sequantur omnia bona, secundum illud: 'Quaerite ergo primum regnum Dei et iustitiam eius, et haec omnia adicientur vobis' (Mt 6.33), sed ex superbia et alienatione sequantur omnia mala, secundum illud: 'ut non glorietur omnis caro in conspectu eius' (1 Cor 1.29).

Dixerit tamen quispiam haec omnia adeo esse generalia ut intimum quendam et magis fundamentalem iustitiae aspectum minime tangant. Quod quam verum sit, proxime dicemus. Sed antequam ad profundiora atque subtiliora procedamus, oportet omnino ut clare et distincte perspiciamus quam iustus sit etiam erga personas ille rerum humanarum ordo quem conceperit divina sapientia et elegerit divina bonitas.

Nam etsi hac in vita persona humana ita ingenti quodam historiae processu includatur ut nisi ipsius processus pars quaedam eaque minima non esse videatur, nullo modo tamen dici potest hoc aliter fieri quam secundum convenientiam humanae naturae. Quatenus enim homo et physicus et chimicus et biologicus et sensitivus est, fieri non potest quin moveatur sicut et

Opposed to these human goods are human evils, namely, (1) particular evils, (2) evils of the external order, and (3) cultural evils. These evils borrow their order, so to speak, from their opposite goods. Particular evils lead human beings to examine and improve the external good of order; the evils of the external order lead them to discover and develop cultural good; and cultural evils, as by a 'happy fault,' ought to move them to beg hope for a Redeemer. The greatest evil is that which corrupts the interior order of human beings and manifests itself in the decline of culture; for it is rooted in that alienation from God that leads to moral impotence, namely, the darkness of intellect and weakness of will, and a greater objective difficulty in choosing the good. These in turn corrupt the external good of order, and as a result particular goods are diminished and particular evils grow greater day by day.

The opposition and interdependence among goods and evils manifest most clearly the order of divine justice. Since God works through secondary causes in accordance with their respective natures, he makes use of our free will as a means to be used in the manner proper to it: 'It was he who created humankind in the beginning, and he left them in the power of their own free choice' (Sirach 15.14). But because free will can decline towards evil, divine wisdom has arranged both evils and goods in such a way that not only does good result from good but also that we ourselves might be recalled from evil to discover and implement the good. However, since the ultimate end is to manifest the divine goodness, God has so arranged all goods and evils that all good things result from humble submission: 'Strive first for the kingdom of God and his righteousness, and all these things will be given to you as well' (Matthew 6.33), but all evils spring from pride and alienation, 'so that no one might boast in the presence of God' (1 Corinthians 1.29).

One may object that all this is so general as to scarcely touch upon the basic and most fundamental aspect of justice. True enough, as we shall soon see. But before going deeper and with greater subtlety into the question, we must clearly grasp how just, even regarding persons, is that order in human affairs which divine wisdom has conceived and divine goodness chosen.

Even though in this life the human person is situated within so vast a historical process as to seem but a tiny part of that process, nevertheless one absolutely cannot say that this is otherwise than what is fitting to human nature. A human being, as physical, chemical, biological, and sensitive, must necessarily move like other material bodies, undergo changes like

alia gravia, alteretur sicut et alia mixta vel composita, nutriatur, crescat, moriatur sicut et alia viventia, sentiat atque appetat sicut et alia animalia. Quod si conceditur, omnino fatendum est hominem his in omnibus vi ipsius suae naturae ad materialem rerum processum pertinere. Imo, si ad ipsum hominis intellectum attendis, qui in genere intelligibilium non est nisi potentia quae se habet ad omnes formas intelligibiles sicut materia prima ad omnes formas sensibiles, sane aut hominem ponis intra processum historicum atque culturalem, aut omnes homines ad perpetuam atque inevitabilem primitivorum mentalitatem redigis. Quod si hoc non placet, illud eligis et iterum hominem agnoscis tamquam partem processus universalis. Age vero, illud ipsum quod in homine maxime personale est, quo vi conscientiae suae rationalis et verum iudicat et bonum amat, quamvis ratione actuum actionumque prorsus immanens sit, nihilominus ratione obiectorum circa aliud non versatur quam ipsum huius mundi processum eiusdemque principium atque finem. Quam ob causam, si forte mysticos excipias, nihil homini hac in vita adeo est privatum, individuale, incommunicabile, ut relationem non dicat eamque essentialem ad externum et historicum rerum processum. Neve queraris relationes humanas et interpersonales esse omissas, cum ad bonum ordinis pertineant non solum bonorum particularium series, et coordinatae operationes, et habitus interiores, et exteriores consuetudines legesque, sed etiam relationes interpersonales quae tum ex illis omnibus resultent tum in illa iugiter influant. Quod si totus homo secundum corpus, vitam, sensitivitatem, intellectum, rationalitatem, relationesque personales ad processum quendam historicum vi ipsius suae naturae pertineat, fateamur oportet tam iuste quam sapienter eum includi intra talem processum et ipsius processus subdi legibus atque ordini.

### Articulus XII: De ordine iustitiae personali

Ita hac in vita exsistit homo ut aliam in vitam ex-sistat. Ita historico iustitiae ordini subditur ut alium in ordinem assumatur. Iuste quidem et secundum convenientiam suae naturae includitur homo intra processum huius mundi. Sed ita mundo includitur ut vi suae naturae per mortem mundo eripiatur. Atque eripitur ut iudicetur. Atque iudicatur ut praemietur vel puniatur. Quamdiu hac in vita versatur, obiectivo quodam et fere impersonali processu contineri videtur. Sed ideo hic versatur ut alibi qualis ipse fuerit iudicet alius. Ex-sistimus enim ut personae ante illud tribunal sistamus quo de

other chemical mixtures and compounds, feed, grow, and die like other living things, sense and desire like other animals. But if so, it must be admitted that in all these respects humans by their very nature belong to the material process of things. Moreover, if you attend to human intelligence – which is, in the genus of intelligible beings, only a potency related to all intelligible forms just as prime matter is to all sensible forms – you must either place humans within the historical and cultural process or else reduce them all, perpetually and without escape, to the primitive mentality. If you do not like this latter alternative, you opt for the former and once again acknowledge humans to be part of the universal process. In fact, that very element in them which is most personal, that by which through rational consciousness they judge what is true and love what is good, even though by reason of its acts and activity it is entirely immanent, nevertheless by reason of its objects it is totally engaged in the ongoing process of this world and its beginning and end. That is why, with the possible exception of the mystics, nothing in human life is so private or individual or incommunicable as not to be related, and related essentially, to the external historical process. And do not complain that we have said nothing about interpersonal human relations, since to the good of order belong not only series of particular goods, coordinated operations, interior habits, and external customs and laws, but interpersonal relations as well, which result from all these others and in turn are constantly influencing them. So if the whole person – body, life, senses, intelligence, rationality, and personal relations – belongs by nature to a historical process, we must conclude that his or her inclusion within this process and subordination to its laws and order is as just as it is wise.

### Article 12: The personal order of justice

We as human exist in this life in order to 'ex-sist' in another life. We are subordinate to the historical order of justice so as to be taken up into another order. Our insertion within the process of this world is indeed just and in conformity with our nature; but we are so inserted into this world that, in virtue of our nature, we will be taken from it by death. We are taken to be judged. We are judged to be rewarded or punished. As long as we live here on earth, we seem to be contained within an objective and almost impersonal process. But in fact we live here below so that elsewhere another

nostra personalitate a persona iudicemur sortemque sempiternam unusquisque suam accipiamus.

Quae quidem iustitia prorsus personalis, quantum humanae naturae conveniat, expendendum est. Per actus enim humanos non solum pergit obiectivus processus historicus, non solum fiunt actiones bonae malaeque, non solum perpetuo quodam fluxu commutatur situatio conditioque humana, sed etiam fiunt, imo se faciunt, homines bonos vel malos. Si enim actus quem ratione voluntateque pono, in situationem humanam commutandam modica sua mensura influit, multo magis sane multoque intimius influit idem actus in me commutandum. Si ipsa situatio conditioque humana per actus humanos vel olim vel nuper factos constituitur, quanto magis ipsi actus quos ipse sciens et prudens pono in me constituendum cumulantur atque coalescunt. Neque hoc in processu intimiori sum ipse ego tantummodo is qui efficior, sed etiam idem sum ego qui iugiter efficio. Nam si liberum actum perpendis, recte dicis eum determinari neque ab adiunctis externis, neque a statu animae sensitivo, neque ab obiecto finiti valoris, neque a fine in quem multis et diversis viis proceditur. Quod si hic actus a caeteris omnibus relinquitur indeterminatus, undenam actualem suam determinationem accipit? Sane a mea voluntate tamquam a principio quo. Sane a me ipso tamquam a principio quod. Sicut enim sensus non sentit sed homo per sensum, sicut intellectus non intelligit sed homo per intellectum, ita etiam voluntas non vult sed homo per voluntatem. Liber ergo ego propriis meis actibus libere me efficio atque me constituo.

Quatenus ergo ipse me liberis meis actibus efficio atque constituo, eatenus opus meum sum. Neque tale sum opus meum quales sunt litterae in aquis conscriptae vel figurae in arena extructae, ut quidquid voluero quandocumque voluero statim fieri possim, neque quod antea fecerim nullatenus vel adiuvet vel impediat quod postea fieri velim. Sed quamdiu hac in vita conversor, mutari potest mea voluntas, sive extrinsece per mutatam cognitionem vel per mutatam corporis dispositionem, sive intrinsece per divinam gratiam interius in ipsa voluntate operantem.[31] Post autem hunc vitae[32] statum, secundum sapientissimam Dei ordinationem, mutationis causae iam tolluntur, et qualis moriens fuerim, talis in aeternum manebo.

will judge the quality of that life. We 'ex-sist' to stand as persons before that judgment seat where our personhood will be judged by a person, and each one will receive his or her eternal lot.

Let us carefully weigh how well suited this thoroughly personal justice is to our human nature. Not only is the objective historical process carried on through human acts, not only do good and bad actions occur, not only is the human situation and condition changed in a seemingly perpetual flow, but we ourselves become, or rather make ourselves, good or evil. If an act which I posit by reason and will effects some change, however slight, in the human situation, how much more, and more intimately, will the same act effect a change in me. If the human situation and condition itself is constituted by human acts ancient and new, how much more will those acts which I posit with knowledge and practical reason gather and coalesce to constitute me. And in this more intimate process I am not only the one who is being formed, I am also the same one who is continually doing the forming. For if you think about a free act, you will rightly conclude that it is not determined by external circumstances, nor by the sensitive state of the soul, nor by an object of finite value, nor by an end approached in many different ways. Now if this act is left indeterminate by everything else, whence does it get its actual determination? Surely from my will as the principle-by-which, and surely from myself as the principle-which. For just as it is not the sense that senses but the person who senses through the senses, and as it is not the intellect that understands but the person through the intellect, so also it is not the will that wills but the person through the will. In my freedom, therefore, I by my own actions freely fashion and constitute myself.

To the extent to which by my free acts I fashion and constitute myself, I am my own handiwork. But my own handiwork is not like something written in water or a figure molded in sand, such that I can make myself instantly into whatever I want whenever I want, as if what I have done till now could in no way either help or hinder what I should later like to become. But as long as I am in this life my will can change, either from without by a change in my knowledge or my physical condition, or from within by divine grace operating interiorly in the will itself.[31] At the end of this present state of life,[32] however, in accordance with the most wise determination of God the agents of change are removed, and as I was at death, so shall I be forever.

31 Thomas Aquinas, *De malo*, q. 16, a. 5.
32 [Lonergan wrote 'viae,' not 'vitae,' but the meaning seems to dictate 'vitae.']

Quot vero inter homines intercedant differentiae, quamque variae sint, enumerari videtur neque possibile neque ad nostrum finem utile. Nam ad duas classes essentiales reducuntur omnia illa opera quae faciunt homines quatenus ipsi se faciunt. Aut enim boni sunt, aut mali. Aut dictanti rationi rationales consentiuntur[33] aut irrationales non consentiuntur. Quod si rationales consentiuntur, opus intelligibile se faciunt, tum quia intelligibile est creaturam rationalem rationi consentiri, tum quia creatura rationalis, rationi consentiens, ipsa se facit partem intelligibilem intra ordinem a sapientia divina institutum. Sin autem irrationales non consentiuntur, opus non-intelligibile se faciunt, tum quia non-intelligibile est creaturam rationalem rationi non consentiri, tum quia creatura rationalis, rationi non consentiens, ipsa se subducit ab ordine intelligibili quo divina sapientia omnia ordinat tam inter se quam ad finem ultimum.

Per actus meos liberos ergo non solum sum opus meum, non solum sum opus meum per se duraturum, sed etiam sum aut opus intelligibile, ordinatum, ordini universi integratum, aut opus non-intelligibile, inordinatum, ordini universi subtractum. Si me intelligibilem facio, sub lege intelligibili atque universali ex-sisto particularis; si ordinatum me facio, pars mea sensitiva rationi subditur, et ipsa mea ratio Deo subditur; si me ordini universi integro, intelligibiliter coniungor et Deo et hominibus et caeteris creaturis. Si me non-intelligibilem facio, extra legem intelligibilem atque universalem ex-sisto exceptio, neque exceptio rationabilis sed irrationalis, neque explicanda sed absurda. Si inordinatum me facio, neque ratio mea Deo subditur, neque pars mea sensitiva rationi subditur. Si me ordini universi subtraho, non-intelligibiliter alienum me facio tum Deo tum ipse mihi tum hominibus tum caeteris creaturis.

Quod opus sive intelligibile sive absurdum per se durat. Qua in duratione perspicitur meriti et demeriti, praemii et poenae fundamentum. Nam duratio operis intelligibilis fundat operis inclusionem intra ordinem rerum intelligibilem; et duratio operis absurdi fundat operis exclusionem extra ordinem rerum intelligibilem. Si fundatur inclusio intra ordinem, fundatur

It would not serve our purpose here to go through all the many differences there are among human beings, even if that were possible. But all the works that we produce when we fashion ourselves can be reduced to two essential classes: good or evil. We either rationally consent[33] to the dictates of reason, or irrationally refuse to consent to them. If we rationally consent, we make of ourselves an intelligible work, both because it is intelligible for rational creatures to consent to reason, and because rational creatures by consenting to reason make themselves to be intelligible parts within the order established by divine wisdom. But if irrationally we withhold consent, we make of ourselves a nonintelligible work, both because it is nonintelligible for rational creatures to withhold consent to reason, and because rational creatures by withholding such consent withdraw themselves from the intelligible order by which divine wisdom orders all things to one another and to their ultimate end.

As a result of my free acts, therefore, I am not only my own handiwork, not only my work that of itself is destined to perdure, but I am also a work that is either intelligible, well-ordered, and integrated with the order of the universe, or one that is nonintelligible, disordered, and withdrawn from the order of the universe. If I make myself intelligible, I ex-sist as a particular instance under an intelligible and universal law; if I make myself well-ordered, then my sensitive part is subjected to reason and my reason itself is subjected to God. If I am integrated into the order of the universe, then I am intelligibly linked to God and the rest of humanity and all other creatures. If I render myself nonintelligible, I ex-sist as an exception outside the intelligible and universal law, an exception that is not reasonable but irrational, inexplicable, and absurd. If I render myself disordered, my reason is not subjected to God, nor is my sensitive part subjected to reason. If I withdraw myself from the order of the universe, I unintelligibly alienate myself from God, from myself, from others, and from all the rest of creation.

This work, whether intelligible or absurd, perdures by itself. This quality of durability grounds merit and demerit, reward and punishment. For the durability of an intelligible work is the basis of its inclusion within the intelligible order of reality; and the durability of an absurd work is the basis of its exclusion from the intelligible order of reality. Inclusion within the

33 [In this and the next two sentences Lonergan first typed the active forms 'consentiunt' and 'consentire,' which he subsequently changed with his pen to the passive forms 'consentiuntur' and 'consentiri' respectively. See p. 337, note 36.]

fruitio ordinis secundum omnia bona quibus Deus hominem ordinat; si fundatur exclusio extra ordinem, fundatur exclusio ab omnibus bonis quibus Deus hominem ordinat. Sicut enim in naturalibus operatur Deus secundum convenientiam naturae, ita etiam in voluntariis operatur Deus secundum convenientiam ipsius operis quod singuli ipsi se libere faciunt. Si quis ergo ordinem vult, ordine fruitur: en meriti et praemii fundamentum. Si quis autem ordinem non vult, extra ordinem ipse se detrudit: en fundamentum demeriti et poenae.

Quam ob causam, in ipsis rebus humanis clarissime distinguuntur iustitia historica et iustitia positiva. Per illam enim ex operibus obiective bonis sequuntur bona et ex operibus obiective malis sequuntur mala; neque subiectiva operantis conscientia consectaria obiectiva mutat. Non enim magis patiuntur neque minus qui hodie dominio communistico subiciuntur, sive inculpabiliter deceptus sive mala fide opera sua conscripsit Karl Marx. Sed iustitia positiva ad personalem responsabilitatem attendit. Non tantum materialem actum eiusque consequentias expendit sed, quantum fieri potest, formale formalis actus considerat. Inter malitiam et infirmitatem distinguit, inter deceptionem inculpabilem et culpabilem, inter circumstantias quae voluntarium sive augent sive minuunt. Personas qua personas secernit ut eluceat quis vero apertus et bono fidelis intra societatem personarum retineri possit, et quis vero bonoque adeo alienus factus sit ut verae bonaeque societatis incapacem se reddiderit. In multis sane imperfecta inveniuntur tribunalia humana. Quid vero intendant leges, iudices, sententiae, castigationes, carceres, patibula, manifestum est. Nam praeter obiectivam illam iustitiam quae processu historico evolvitur, exsistit alia iustitia secundum quam personae a personis iudicantur utrum cum personis consociare possint. Neve dicas leges poenasque humanas non exsistere nisi utilitatis causa ut mali scilicet vel re-educentur vel saltem a malis operibus deterreantur. Nefas enim est malum facere ut eveniat bonum. Et malum est personam iuribus personae privari et, quasi merum instrumentum esset, poenas dare propter utilitatem quandam consequentem. Nisi enim malefactores per propriam nequitiam personarum iuribus sese indignos esse demonstrant, nisi ipsi retributionis fundamentum ponunt reatumque culpae et poenae induunt, iniuste subiciuntur medicinali castigationi et iniuste efficiuntur tristia poenarum exempla ad alios deterrendos.

Quod si in rebus humanis necessario agnoscitur personas se facere vel dignos vel indignos humanae societatis, certitudine fidei constat de iusto

order in turn is the basis for enjoying the order in accord with all the goods to which God orders humanity; exclusion from this order is the basis for exclusion from all those same goods. Just as in natural things God operates in accordance with their natures, so also in beings with free will God operates in accordance with the work which we each freely make of ourselves. If we will order, we enjoy the fruits of order: this is the basis of merit and reward. If we do not will order, we thrust ourselves outside the order, and this is the basis of demerit and punishment.

It is for this reason that in human affairs there is a very clear distinction between historical justice and positive justice. In the former, good results follow from works that are objectively good, and evil results follow from works that are objectively bad; the subjective conscience of the doer does not affect the objective results. Those who today find themselves under the yoke of communism do not suffer any more or any less whether Karl Marx wrote his books in bad faith or was inculpably deceived. But positive justice looks to personal responsibility. It considers not only a material act and its consequences, but also, as much as possible, the formal element of a formal act. It distinguishes between malice and weakness, between culpable and inculpable deception, and between circumstances which either increase or diminish the voluntariness of an act. It separates persons as persons to reveal those who are open to the truth and faithful to the good and are thus acceptable within human society, and those who have become so alienated from truth and goodness as to have rendered themselves unfit for a true and good society. It is true that in many ways human systems of justice are imperfect. Nevertheless, the purpose of laws, judges, sentences, punishments, prisons, and gallows is quite obvious. For besides that objective justice which unfolds in the historical process, there is another justice in accord with which persons are judged by persons as to their fitness for a society of persons. It must not be said that human laws and penalties have only a utilitarian purpose, namely, to re-educate wrongdoers or at least deter wrongdoing. For it is absolutely wrong to do evil for a good purpose. And it is an evil to deprive people of their rights as persons and, as if they were mere instruments, punish them for the purpose of obtaining some useful result. Unless wrongdoers demonstrate by their wickedness that they are unworthy of their personal rights, unless they lay the foundation of retribution and take on the liability of fault and punishment, it would be unjust to inflict medicinal punishment upon them and unjust also to make of them an example to deter others.

But if in human affairs we are bound to acknowledge that persons make themselves worthy or unworthy of human society, the certitude of faith

iudicio 'Dei qui reddet unicuique secundum opera eius' (Rom 2.6). 'Omnes enim nos manifestari oportet ante tribunal Christi, ut referat unusquisque propria corporis, prout gessit sive bonum sive malum' (2 Cor 5.10). Cuius iudicii haec summa brevis est: 'Amen dico vobis, quamdiu fecistis uni ex his fratribus meis minimis, mihi fecistis' (Mt 25.40). Et: 'Amen dico vobis, quamdiu non fecistis uni de minoribus his, nec mihi fecistis' (Mt 25.45).

Quod tamen iudicium, etsi a persona de personis exercetur, etiam consectarium quoddam naturale exprimit. Uti enim testatur S. Ioannes: 'Non enim misit Deus Filium suum in mundum ut iudicet mundum sed ut salvetur mundus per ipsum. Qui credit in eum, non iudicatur; qui autem non credit, iam iudicatus est, quia non credit in nomine unigeniti Filii Dei. Hoc est autem iudicium, quia lux venit in mundum et dilexerunt homines magis tenebras quam lucem; erant enim opera eorum mala. Omnis enim qui male agit odit lucem et non venit ad lucem, ut non arguantur opera eius; qui autem facit veritatem venit ad lucem, ut manifestentur opera eius, quia in Deo sunt facta' (Io 3.17–21). Et iterum: 'Ego lux in mundum veni ut omnis qui credit in me in tenebris non maneat. Et si quis audierit verba mea et non custodierit, ego non iudico eum; non enim veni ut iudicem mundum sed ut salvificem mundum. Qui spernit me et non accipit verba mea, habet qui iudicet eum. Sermo quem locutus sum, ille iudicabit eum in novissimo die' (Io 12.46–48). Qui sane sermo (λόγος) etiam verbum erat de quo dicitur: 'Erat lux vera quae illuminat omnem hominem venientem in hunc mundum. In mundo erat, et mundus per ipsum factus est, et mundus eum non cognovit' (Io 1.9–10). Neve tardiores credatis aliter S. Matthaeum et aliter S. Ioannem iudicium Domini concepisse. Quam enim societatem facit caritas, eam prius cognoscit lux illa intellectualis atque increata, cuius participatio quaedem creata est lumen intellectus nostri tum naturale tum fidei tum gloriae.

Quod si ratio consectarii naturalis in divina iustitia personaliter exercita non deest, neque divina sapientia ita obiectivum historiae processum dirigit ut de personis non curet. Nam totum fere Vetus Testamentum specialem divinam providentiam circa populum Israeliticum manifestat, et ipse Dominus in Novo docet: 'Si autem faenum agri, quod hodie est et cras in clibanum mittitur, Deus sic vestit, quanto magis vos modicae fidei? Nolite ergo solliciti esse dicentes, "Quid manducabimus aut quid bibemus aut quo

establishes the just judgment of God, who 'will repay according to each one's deeds' (Romans 2.6). 'For all of us must appear before the judgment seat of Christ, so that each may receive recompense for what has been done in the body, whether good or evil' (2 Corinthians 5.10). This judgment of the Lord can be summed up as follows: 'Truly I tell you, just as you did it to one of the least of these who are members of my family, you did it to me' (Matthew 25.40), and 'just as you did not do it to one of the least of these, you did not do it to me' (Matthew 25.45).

This judgment, however, although rendered upon persons by a person, also expresses a sort of natural consequence. As we read in John's Gospel, 'God did not send the Son into the world to condemn the world, but in order that the world might be saved through him. Those who believe in him are not condemned; but those who do not believe are condemned already, because they have not believed in the name of the only Son of God. And this is the judgment, that the light has come into the world, and people loved darkness rather than light because their deeds were evil. For all who do evil hate the light and do not come to the light, so that their deeds may not be exposed. But those who do what is true come to the light, so that it may be clearly seen that their deeds have been done in God' (John 3.17–21). And again: 'I have come as light into the world, so that everyone who believes in me should not remain in the darkness. I do not judge anyone who hears my words and does not keep them, for I came not to judge the world, but to save the world. The one who rejects me and does not receive my word has a judge; on the last day the word that I have spoken will serve as judge' (John 12.46–48). Surely this word (λόγος) is also the Word of whom it is said he was 'the true light, which enlightens everyone who comes into the world. He was in the world, and the world came into being through him; yet the world did not know him' (John 1.9–10). And do not think for a moment that Matthew and John had different ways of understanding the judgment of the Lord. For the society that love creates is first known by that uncreated intellectual light of which our natural intellectual light, as well as the light of faith and the light of glory, is a created participation.

While the aspect of natural consequence is present in divine justice carried out in a personal way, divine wisdom does not direct the objective historical process without care for persons. Virtually the whole of the Old Testament manifests the special providence of God for the people of Israel; and in the New Testament the Lord himself tells us, 'But if God so clothes the grass of the field, which is alive today and tomorrow is thrown into the oven, will he not much more clothe you – you of little faith? Therefore, do

operiemur?" Haec enim omnia gentes inquirunt. Scit enim Pater vester quia his indigetis' (Mt 6.30–32). Imo, ad commercium personale nos invitat per ipsa nostra desideria: 'Petite, et dabitur vobis; quaerite, et invenietis; pulsate, et aperietur. Omnis enim qui petit accipit, et qui quaerit invenit, et pulsanti aperietur vobis. Aut quis est ex vobis homo, quem si petierit filius suus panem, numquid lapidem porriget ei? Aut si piscem petierit, numquid serpentem porriget ei? Si ergo vos, cum sitis mali, nostis bona data dare filiis vestris, quanto magis Pater vester qui in caelis est dabit bona petentibus se?' (Mt 7.7–11).

Quam ob causam, quamvis valde inter se distare nobis videantur et processus obiectivus et personale iudicium, nulla tamen inter haec ex parte Dei datur distinctio (cum persona divina realiter eadem sit ac ipsum intelligere), neque aliud ex parte nostra habetur distinctionis fundamentum nisi quod hac in vita secundum convenientiam nostrae naturae nostrorumque actuum versamur ut in vita futura quales ipsi nos fecerimus tales boni vel mali maneamus.

**Articulus XIII: De iusta Dei voluntate**

Quod hoc rerum ordine sumus atque regimur, ex libera Dei electione est. Quae sane electio iustissima est, tum quia in infinitam bonitatem tamquam in finem tendit, tum quia ex infinita bonitate ipsius divinae voluntatis procedit, tum quia infinitam Dei sapientiam sequitur.

Quaerentibus autem utrum Deus res aliter ordinare potuisset, modo desit contradictio interna, omnino affirmandum est. Quodcumque enim contradictione caret, absolute potest Deus facere. Quodcumque absolute potest facere, etiam sapientissime potest facere, cum divina sapientia totum posse divinae potentiae comprehendat.[34] Neque perfectior divinae voluntatis datur regula quam infinita Dei sapientia.

Si tamen quaeritur cur Deus alium ordinem non elegerit, ad mysterium divinae voluntatis acceditur, ubi iam non inquirendum sed obediendum est. Qui enim omnes ordines suo intellectu non comprehendit, alium cum alio comparare non potest; qui alium ordinem cum alio comparare non potest, cur alius alteri posthabeatur dicere nequit. Sed nullus theologus

not worry, saying, "What will we eat?" or "What will we drink?" or "What will we wear?" For it is the Gentiles who strive for all these things; and indeed your heavenly Father knows that you need all these things' (Matthew 6.30–32). Indeed, he invites us to enter into friendly personal relations with him by means of these very desires of ours: 'Ask, and it will be given you; search, and you will find; knock, and the door will be opened for you. For everyone who asks receives, and everyone who searches finds, and for everyone who knocks, the door will be opened. Is there anyone among you who, if your child asks for bread, will give a stone? Or if the child asks for a fish, will give a snake? If you then, who are evil, know how to give good gifts to your children, how much more will your Father in heaven give good things to those who ask him!' (Matthew 7.7–11).

Accordingly, although it may seem to us that there is a vast difference between the objective process and personal judgment, there is no distinction between them on the part of God (since a divine person is not really distinct from understanding itself). Nor on our part is there a basis for this distinction except the fact that we live this life in a manner befitting our nature and our acts, so that as we have made ourselves, good or evil, so shall we remain in the life to come.

### Article 13: The just will of God

It is by God's free choice that we are part of and subject to this order of reality. This choice is surely most just, since it is directed towards infinite goodness as its goal, since it proceeds from the infinite goodness of the divine will itself, and since it follows upon the infinite wisdom of God.

To the question whether God could have instituted another order of reality, so long as no internal contradiction is involved, the answer is wholly affirmative. God can do absolutely anything that does not involve an internal contradiction. Whatever he can do absolutely, he can do most wisely, since the divine wisdom extends to all that divine power is capable of.[34] There is no higher rule for the divine will than the infinite wisdom of God.

If, however, one asks why God chose this order and not some other, then we are up against the mystery of the divine will, where we are not to inquire but to submit. One whose understanding does not comprehend all orders is incapable of comparing one with another; and one who is incapable of comparing one order with another cannot say why one order should be preferred

34 Thomas Aquinas, *Summa theologiae*, 1, q. 25, a. 5 c.

omnes ordines rerum possibiles suo intellectu comprehendit. Imo, ne Christus homo quidem hanc omniscientiam habuisse docetur.[35] Et ideo prorsus inepta est haec comparativa quaestio.

Praeterea, uti monuit S. Augustinus, etiam si Deus aliter fecessit, nostrae tamen insipientiae ipse alius ordo non placeret.[36] Pariter enim ex divina sapientia divinaque bonitate procederet ordo alius, sed 'sicut exaltantur caeli a terra, sic exaltatae sunt viae meae a viis vestris, et cogitationes meae a cogitationibus vestris' (Is 55.9).

Quapropter, divinae electioni simpliciter obediendum est. Sicut enim Christus non alium mundum expetivit sed in omnibus voluntatem suam voluntati Patris subiecit,[37] factus obediens usque ad mortem, mortem autem crucis (Phil 2.8),[38] ita et nos hunc actualem rerum ordinem nobis a Deo Patre praeceptum habemus. Praecipere enim nihil est aliud quam per rationem et voluntatem movere.[39] Et Deus per suam sapientiam atque electionem, sicut omnia creat et conservat, ita omnia movet.[40] Cui motioni in omnibus obediendum est, a rebus naturalibus quidem secundum formas sibi inditas, a rationalibus autem creaturis secundum quod hunc rerum ordinem et vere intelligunt et diligentes sequuntur.

Sed ulterius circa divinam voluntatem nonnulla recolenda videntur ne anthropomorphice eam concipiamus. Et in primis unica est Dei volitio. Sicut enim Deus et se et omnia alia cognoscit unico intelligendi actu, ita etiam Deus et se et omnia alia vult unica volitione. Praeterea, sicut ordinata intelligit, ita etiam ordinata vult.

Unde statim concluditur quod Deus non vult hoc quia vult illud, sed vult hoc esse propter illud.[41] Excluditur primum quia in Deo non sunt multae volitiones quarum alia alterius causa sit. Affirmatur secundum quia Deus vult et hoc et illud et ordinem huius ad illud per unicam illam volitionem qua et se et alia omnia ordinata vult.

to another. But no theologian's understanding comprehends all possible orders of reality. Indeed, not even the human Christ is said to have had such omniscience.[35] Therefore, this question of comparison is utterly silly.

Besides, as St Augustine admonished, even if God had created something else, that other order too would have failed to satisfy our foolishness.[36] For any other order would equally proceed from divine wisdom and divine goodness; but 'as the heavens are higher than the earth, so are my ways higher than your ways, and my thoughts higher than your thoughts' (Isaiah 55.9).

Hence our duty is simply to submit to God's choice. Just as Christ himself did not ask for another world but in all things submitted his will to his Father's,[37] 'and became obedient to the point of death – even death on the cross' (Philippians 2.8),[38] so we also accept this present order of reality as a command given to us by God our Father. To command is to move a person through reason and will.[39] Just as God creates and conserves all things by his wisdom and choice, so also does he move all things.[40] All must yield to this motion, natural beings according to the forms they have been given and rational creatures accordingly as they truly understand and lovingly follow this order of reality.

There are, however, some further points to recall concerning the divine will in order to avoid conceiving it anthropomorphically. First of all, God has but one act of willing. As God knows both himself and all other things in one single act of understanding, so he wills both himself and all else in one single volitional act. Again, as he understands all things in their order, so does he will them in this order.

From this it immediately follows that God does not will *B* because he wills *A*, but wills that *B* should be because of *A*.[41] The former is ruled out because in God there are not several acts of will of which one is the cause of another; the second is affirmed because God wills *A* and *B* and the order between them in that one single volitional act in which he wills himself and all other things in their ordered relationships.

35 Ibid. 3, q. 10, a. 2. [See also Lonergan, *The Incarnate Word* 688–91.]
36 [Lonergan has in mind Augustine, *De agone Christiano*, c. XI, 12; ML 40, 297. See above, p. 201.]
37 Thomas Aquinas, *Summa theologiae*, 3, q. 20, a. 1.
38 Ibid. q. 47, a. 2.
39 Ibid. 2-2, q. 104, a. 1 c.
40 Ibid. a. 4 c.
41 Ibid. 1, q. 19, a. 5. [See above, p. 159.]

Concluditur praeterea hanc unicam Dei volitionem a nulla creatura causari sed omnis et cuiuscumque entis finiti causam exsistere. Non enim movetur Deus sed movet, et non efficitur sed efficit.

Quibus perspectis, si in rigore sermonis loqueris, semper dices Deum velle satisfactionem Christi esse propter peccata, et peccatorum remissionem esse propter satisfactionem, et praemia esse propter bona merita, et poenas esse propter peccata. Non autem dices Deum velle satisfactionem quia peccata odit, vel Deum velle peccata remittere quia satisfactio eum placavit, vel Deum velle praemiare quia bona merita ei placuerunt, vel Deum velle punire quia peccata eum offendunt. Illa enim affirmant unam multorum et ordinatorum volitionem. Haec autem et multas divinas volitiones supponunt et interdum creaturam ponunt causam et divinam volitionem effectum.

Neve rigorem sermonis in praesenti quaestione parvi momenti iudicaveris. Cum enim praecipue contra dogma redemptionis obiciatur quod anthropomorphicum sit, huic calumniae ansam praebere non debet theologus Catholicus.

At alia et gravior est quaestio, cum Deum dixerimus omnia quaecumque hoc in mundo contineantur et sua sapientia ordinare et sua voluntate eligere. Nam hoc in mundo sunt mala culpae, mala poenae, et mala naturalis defectus. Numquid Deus mala velit?

Et in primis dicendum est nullam voluntatem ne diaboli quidem directe in malum tendere. Obiectum enim voluntatis est bonum, et ideo nemo directe malum vult. Indirecta autem malorum volitio haberi potest quatenus quis bonum quoddam vult cui coniungitur malum. Et ita indirecte Deus vult tum mala naturalis defectus tum mala poenae, quatenus directe vult tum bonum naturalis ordinis cui consequuntur mala naturalis defectus, tum bonum iustitiae personalis cui consequuntur mala poenae. Quae quidem indirecta volitio est bona, uti exemplis facile constat.

Puta vehiculum aereum certis in adiunctis in terram esse casurum nisi suspenditur lex gravitatis. Et certa illa adiuncta oriuntur nisi vel eadem vel aliae suspenduntur leges. Quaero ergo utrum melius suspendantur leges naturales, quibus totus ordo rerum naturalis constat, an melius cadat vehiculum in terram, ut homines cautiores esse et prudentiores addiscant. Sane hoc. Hoc enim malum particulare est ex quo profluat bonum; illud autem bonum ordinis impediret ex quo profluvium bonorum particularium

We further conclude that this one act of the divine will is not caused by any creature, but is rather the cause of each and every finite being. God is not moved: he moves; he is not caused: he causes.

Strictly speaking, therefore, you will always say that God wills the satisfaction made by Christ to be because of sin, wills the forgiveness of sins to be because of this satisfaction, wills reward to be on account of merit, and wills punishment to be on account of sin. You will not say that God wills Christ's satisfaction because he hates sin, or that he wills the forgiveness of sins because this satisfaction has placated him, or that he wills reward because meritorious deeds have pleased him, or that he wills punishment because sins have offended him. The former set of statements affirms the single act in which God wills many interrelated things; the latter supposes a multiplicity of volitional acts on the part of God and sometimes makes a created thing the cause and the divine will the effect.

One must not consider this strictness in speaking to be of little importance in the matter at hand. When the main objection to the dogma of the redemption is that it is anthropomorphic, no Catholic theologian should give any sort of handle to this calumny.

But another and more serious question arises when we say that God in his wisdom orders and in his will chooses all things that are contained in this world. For in this world there are evils: culpable evil, the evil of punishment, and the evil of defects in nature. Does God, then, will evil?

In dealing with this question, the first point that must be made is that no will, not even that of the devil, directly intends evil. The object of the will is the good, and therefore no one directly wills evil. There can, however, be an indirect willing of evil in that one may will a good to which an evil is connected. It is in this sense that God can be said to will indirectly both the evil of natural defects and the evil of punishment, in that he directly wills both the good of the order of nature, of which the evil of natural defects is a consequence, and also the good of personal justice, of which the evil of punishment is a consequence. This indirect volition on the part of God is itself good, as the following examples will easily demonstrate.

Imagine an airplane that under definite circumstances will fall to earth unless the law of gravity is suspended. And those circumstances arise, unless that law or others are suspended. Which is better: to suspend the laws of nature, by which the whole order of the universe is constituted, or to let the plane fall to the ground, so that people learn to be more careful? Surely the latter. The latter is a particular evil, from which good might flow; but the former would obstruct the good of order, from which we have the flow of

habetur. Instas tamen. Nonne potuit Deus ita hunc mundum ordinare ut nulla evenirent mala particularia et tamen nullae leges naturales suspenderentur? Potuit utique, nam haec internam contradictionem non dicunt. Cur ergo non fecerit? Cui quaestioni iam superius responsum est; nam etiamsi Deus alium ordinem elegisset, etiam ille alius ordo nostrae insipientiae non placuisset. Quod scimus, hoc in ordine invenitur quem infinita sapientia ordinavit et infinita bonitas elegit. Cui electioni nobis simpliciter obediendum est.

Et similiter in poenas aeternas quidam esset damnandus nisi Deus ordinem suae sapientiae suspenderet, et post mortem gratiam operantem concederet quae malam voluntatem malamque personam faceret bonam. Volendo ergo ordinem suae sapientiae atque iustitiae, hunc hominem damnandum indirecte vult Deus. Quae quidem volitio bona est, cum melius bonum sit bonum ordinis ex quo tota liberi arbitrii gravitas totumque eius momentum profluant quam bonum hoc particulare quod converteretur qui finaliter impoenitens fuerit. Iterum forte instas. Nonne potuit Deus ita res ordinare ut nemo sit finaliter impoenitens? Potuit utique, cum hoc contradictionem internam non dicat. Cur ergo non fecerit? Cui quaestioni iam superius responsum est. Imo, iam nobis adorandum est mysterium divinae voluntatis, secundum illud: 'O altitudo divitiarum sapientiae et scientiae Dei, quam incomprehensibilia sunt iudicia eius et investigabiles viae eius!' (Rom 11.33).

Quod si Deus indirecte vult malum naturalis defectus et malum poenae, nullo tamen modo vult malum culpae.[42] Non enim directe vult, quia nemo malum directe vult. Neque indirecte vult, quia indirecta mali volitio habetur quatenus quis bonum vult cui connectitur malum. Sed malum culpae bono non connectitur sed opponitur totaliter. Non enim est ens sed entis privatio, neque privatio intelligibilis sed irrationalis et nonintelligibilis. Iam vero omnis connexio quendam ordinem intelligibilem dicit; et quodcumque ordinem intelligibilem ad ens habet, illud eatenus intelligibile est. Malum culpae ergo nullam connexionem cum ente habet, et ideo nullam connexionem cum bono habet. Neque ergo directe neque indirecte vult Deus malum culpae.

Dices tamen: qui nimis probat nihil probat; sed nimis probat qui omne peccatum facit impossibile. Et argumentum propositum excludit volitionem mali culpae indirectam non solum a Deo sed etiam a peccatore.

particular goods. But, you will say, couldn't God have ordered things in such a way that no particular evils would happen and yet no laws of nature would be suspended? Yes, he could have, since this does not involve an internal contradiction. Why then did he not do so? We answered this question above: even if God had created something else, that order too would not have satisfied our foolishness. All that we know is found in this order which infinite wisdom has ordered and infinite goodness chosen. Ours is but to submit to that choice.

The same could be said in the case of someone who would be condemned to eternal punishment, unless God suspended the order of his wisdom and granted, after death, an operative grace making the evil will and evil person good. By willing the order of his wisdom and justice, God indirectly wills this person's damnation. For God so to will is good, since the good of order, from which flow the whole weight and consequence of free will, is a better good than would be this particular good, that a person impenitent to the last should be converted. Again, you will object, could God not have arranged matters in such a way that no one would be impenitent to the last? Certainly he could have, since this would involve no internal contradiction. Why, then, did he not do so? The answer is the same as that given above. All we can do is adore the mystery of the divine will: 'O the depth of the riches and wisdom and knowledge of God! How unsearchable are his judgments and how inscrutable his ways!' (Romans 11.33).

If, however, it is true that God indirectly wills the evil of natural defects and the evil of punishment, in no way does he will culpable evil.[42] He does not will it directly, because no one directly wills evil. Nor does he will it indirectly, because indirect willing of evil entails the willing of a good to which an evil is connected. But culpable evil is not connected to any good; rather, it is totally opposed to good. It is not a being, but is the privation of being; nor is it an intelligible privation, but is irrational and nonintelligible. Now any connection implies a certain intelligible order; and whatever has an intelligible order to being is to that extent intelligible. Culpable evil, therefore, has no connection with being and so no connection with good. Neither directly nor indirectly, then, does God will culpable evil.

But, you may object: to prove too much is to prove nothing; yet to render all sin impossible is to prove too much, and the argument advanced above rules out the indirect willing of culpable evil not only by God but even by a sinner.

42 Ibid. a. 9.

Respondetur: argumentum propositum excludit indirectam volitionem mali culpae ab omni cuius intellectus non obscuratur et cuius voluntas irrationaliter non agit. Quod autem peccatoris intellectus non obscuratur eiusque voluntas irrationaliter non agit, supponit obiciens sed manifeste probare non potest.

Instas vero peccata fieri non posse si Deus ea nullo modo vult. Efficax enim est divina voluntas ut quodcumque velit fiat et quodcumque non velit non fiat.

Respondetur quod 'Deus ... neque vult mala fieri neque vult mala non fieri, sed vult permittere mala fieri. Et hoc est bonum.'[43] Neve leviter iudices hoc merum esse effugium, nam, uti postea dicetur, praeter ens et non-ens est irrationalis privatio entis, praeter bonum et non-bonum est malum culpae, praeter verum et non-verum est ontologica peccati falsitas.

Instatur tamen malum culpae manifeste connexionem habere intelligibilem cum libertate finita atque defectibili.

Respondetur verum esse hominem *posse peccare* quia liber atque defectibilis sit, sed negatur hominem ideo *actu peccare* quia liber atque defectibilis sit.

Instatur saltem inter peccatum et redemptionem intercedere connexionem intelligibilem.

Respondetur (1) nexum intelligibilem intercedere inter divinam peccati permissionem et redemptionem, et (2) tam permissionem quam redemptionem respicere peccatum ut factum, secundum quod 'Deus est adeo potens quod etiam potest bene facere de malis.'[44] Sed negatur permissio esse causa peccati, vel peccatum esse causa permissionis; et similiter non peccatum sed divina bonitas est causa redemptionis.

Videtur tamen quod, si malum culpae sit malum prorsus, bonum esse non potest permittere malum culpae.

Respondetur quod bonum est ut sint creaturae rationales vere liberae, bonum est 'ut non glorietur omnis caro in conspectu eius' [1 Cor 1.29], et bonum est e malitia peccatorum efficere bonitatem redemptionis. Quas ob causas, etsi permissio peccati ex peccato bonitatem non habeat, tamen non desunt aliae rationes unde bonitas eius perspici possit. Quantum autem attinet electionem inter permittere et non permittere malum culpae, uti

To this objection we reply as follows: that argument holds that the indirect willing of culpable evil is impossible for anyone whose intellect is not darkened and whose will does not act irrationally. The objection supposes that the sinner's mind is not darkened and his will does not act irrationally, which obviously cannot be proven.

You may further object: if God in no way wills sin, then sin is impossible; for such is the efficacy of the divine will that whatever God wills is done and whatever he does not will is not done.

To this objection we reply: 'God ... neither wills that evil be done nor wills that evil not be done, but wills to permit evil to be done; and this will is good.'[43] And do not dismiss this as a mere evasion; for, as we shall see, besides being and non-being there is the irrational privation of being, besides good and not good there is culpable evil, and besides the true and the not true there is the ontological falsity of sin.

A still further objection: culpable evil obviously has some intelligible connection with a freedom that is limited and easily fails.

To this we reply that while it is true that we *can sin* because we are free and easily fail, we deny that we *actually do sin* because we are free and easily fail.

Again, the objector goes on: at least between sin and redemption there must be some intelligible connection.

To this we reply as follows: (1) there is an intelligible connection between God's permission of sin and redemption, and (2) both permission and redemption regard sin as a fact, and so we say, 'God's power is such that he can even draw good out of evil.'[44] But we deny that the permission is the cause of the sin, or that sin is the cause of the permission; and likewise it is not sin but God's goodness that is the cause of redemption.

But still, it seems that if culpable evil is utterly evil, it cannot be good to permit it.

Our response to this further objection is that it is good for there to be rational creatures that are truly free; it is good 'that no one might boast in the presence of God' [1 Corinthians 1.29], and it is good to bring the goodness of redemption out of the wickedness of sinners. Hence, even though the permission of sin does not derive its goodness from sin, there are a number of other reasons for seeing goodness in it. But as to a choice between

43 Ibid. ad 3m.

44 Ibid. q. 48, a. 2, ad 3m. See St Augustine: 'God judged it better to draw good out of evils than not to allow evils to exist.' *Enchiridion* 27, ML 40, 245.

superius dictum est, non iam datur locus inquisitionis sed obedientiae atque adorationis.

Obicitur tamen ex alio capite contra ea quae de unica et incausata divina volitione dicta sunt, quod magis ens supremum et hellenisticum sapiunt quam Deum Christianorum. Et in primis quod re vera tollitur divina orationis exauditio.

Respondetur quod tollitur anthropomorphica huius exauditionis conceptio sed minime tollitur eiusdem realitas, cum Deus faciat tum ut obsecremus tum ut impetremus propter obsecrationem.

Instatur nullum re vera dari nexum causalem inter orationem et effectum. Non enim hic ex illa procedit, sed utrumque ex divina sapientia rerumque ordine.

Respondetur alium esse nexum causalem qui scientiis humanis cognosci potest et alium esse nexum qui secundum intentionem divinae providentiae re vera adest. Si enim Deus et orationem et orationis exauditionem praevidit atque praeparavit, scientiae humanae utriusque seorsum causas determinare possunt. Sed neque affirmare neque negare possunt utrum Deus res ita disposuerit *quia* effectum propter orationem esse voluerit; neque determinare possunt utrum, si homo non orasset, res ita disponerentur ut effectus haberetur vel non haberetur. Fidelis autem divinis eloquiis eruditus effectum esse propter orationem secundum intentionem divinae providentiae certo cognoscit.

Instatur quod si unicus actus est divina volitio, uno eodemque actu Deus et bonos amat et peccata odit, irascitur contra peccatores, et per satisfactionem Christi placatur. Quae divina indifferentia realis sensui Christiano omnino repugnat.

Respondetur quod obiciens non satis distinguit inter id quod est verum et reale et, alia ex parte, ea quae in analysi metaphysica ponuntur tamquam constitutiva vel conditiones eius quod verum et reale est.

Primo ergo, verum et reale est Deum et bonos amare et peccata odio habere et contra peccatores irasci et per satisfactionem placari. Quod omnino retinendum est ab omnibus, sive metaphysicam analysin capere possint sive non.

Deinde, proprie dici potest Deus amare et odio habere quia hi actus possunt esse proprie dicti etiamsi in sola voluntate spirituali exsistant. Sed analogice tantum dicitur Deus irasci vel placari, quia hi actus proprie dicti important motum sensitivae partis vel huius motus sedationem. Vere ergo et realiter irascitur Deus inquantum poenas peccatoribus praeparat; sed

permitting and not permitting culpable evil, as we have already said it is no longer a matter for inquiry but rather for submission and adoration.

An objection from a different angle can be brought against what we have said about God's unique, uncaused volition, namely that this smacks of the Hellenistic notion of a supreme being rather than that of the Christian God – especially because it really takes away divine answer to prayer.

Our reply to this is that what is ruled out is an anthropomorphic conception of answer to prayer, not the reality of it, since God brings it about both that we pray and that we obtain an answer because of our prayer.

But, the objector continues, there is really no causal nexus between the prayer and the effect, since the effect does not proceed from the prayer, but both proceed from the divine wisdom and the order of reality.

To this further objection we say that there is one sort of causal nexus that can be known by human sciences and another that is really present according to the intention of divine providence. For if God has foreseen and prepared for both our prayer and its answer, human sciences can determine separately the causes of each. But they can neither affirm nor deny that God so arranged matters *because* he willed that the effect should occur on account of prayer; nor can they determine whether, if a person had not prayed, the same result would have occurred. But a believer who is well versed in the word of God knows with certainty that what happened was the result of prayer in accordance with the intention of God's providence.

A final objection: if God has but one single act of willing, then in one and the same act he both loves the virtuous and hates sin, is angry with sinners and placated by Christ's sacrifice; such real divine indifference is utterly repugnant to Christian sensibility.

To this objection we reply that the objector has not sufficiently distinguished between what is true and real and, on the other hand, what elements in a metaphysical analysis are required as constitutive of or conditions for what is true and real.

First of all, then, it is true and real that God loves the virtuous and hates sin, that he is angry with sinners and placated by satisfaction. Everyone must hold fast to these truths, whether they are capable of metaphysical analysis or not.

Second, to love and to hate may be properly predicated of God, since these acts can be properly said to exist even in a purely spiritual will. But to be angry or placated can be predicated of God only by analogy, since properly speaking these acts refer to a stirring up of the sensual element, or a quieting of this movement. Therefore, God really and truly is angry in that

analogice tantum irascitur quia partem sensitivam non habet quae commoveatur; et vere et realiter placatur Deus inquantum peccatorum remissionem praeparat; sed analogice tantum placatur quia partem sensitivam non habet quae commoveri et sedari possit.

Tertio, constituitur amor divinus erga bonos per actum infinitum, et ideo summe verus atque realis est; constituitur odium divinum per actum infinitum, et ideo summe verus atque realis est; constituuntur denique per actum infinitum tam ira quam placatio divina, et ideo summe verae et reales sunt. Sicut enim sufficit actus infinitus intelligendi ad bonos et peccatores cognoscendos, ita sufficit actus infinitus volendi ad illos amandos et hos ad poenas destinandos.

Quarto, quae contingenter de Deo vere et realiter dicuntur, praecise inquantum contingentia sunt, terminum ad extra convenientem, non per modum constitutivi sed per modum conditionis, exigunt.[45] Totus enim amor divinus per actum infinitum constituitur; sed enuntiabile verum et contingens adaequationem in re non habet per solum actum necessarium; et ideo per modum conditionis exigitur terminus ad extra conveniens atque contingens qui est effectus divini amoris. Similiter, odium divinum constituitur per actum infinitum, sed verum enuntiabile et contingens terminum contingentem exigit, qui quidem terminus est peccatum quod fieri permisit Deus.

Quinto, quamvis creatura in Deum agere non possit sive physice sive moraliter, tamen sub Deo vere et realiter agere potest ut Deo placeat vel displiceat, ut Deus irascatur vel placetur. Non potest in Deum agere, quia non potest causare actum infinitum sive essendi sive cognoscendi sive volendi. Potest tamen agere ut Deo placeat vel displiceat, ut Deus irascatur vel placetur, quia potest terminos causare qui non exsistant quin Deus vere et realiter amet, oderit, irascatur, placetur.

Quibus perspectis, tum omnia et singula salvantur quae a fidelibus vel simplicissimis creduntur, tum omnis prorsus anthropomorphismus excluditur.

he prepares punishment for sinners; but he is only analogously angry, since he has no sensual element to be moved. He really and truly is placated in that he prepares the forgiveness of sin; but he is only analogously placated, since he has no sensual part in his being to be aroused and allayed.

Third, God's love for the virtuous is constituted by infinite act, and therefore is supremely true and real; divine hatred is likewise constituted by infinite act, and so is supremely true and real; and both divine anger and the placating of it are constituted by infinite act and are therefore supremely true and real. For just as God's infinite act of understanding suffices for him to know both the virtuous and sinners, so his infinite act of willing suffices for him to love the former and destine the latter for punishment.

Fourth, whatever truths are predicated of God contingently, precisely inasmuch as they are contingent, require an appropriate external term, not as a constitutive element but as a condition.[45] The totality of God's love is constituted by infinite act; but a true contingent predication does not adequately correspond to reality solely by this necessary act; it therefore requires as a condition an appropriate contingent external term which is the effect of God's love. Likewise, God's hatred is constituted by infinite act; but a true contingent predication requires a contingent term, and this is the sin which God permitted to occur.

Fifth, although no creature can act upon God either physically or morally, creatures can, by his leave, really and truly please or displease God, and anger or placate him. A creature cannot act upon God, since it cannot cause an infinite act of being or of knowing or of willing. But it can act to please or displease God and anger or placate him because it can cause terms which could not exist without God really and truly loving or hating, or being angry or placated.

The foregoing explanation preserves all that even the simple faithful believe, while at the same time eliminating every trace of anthropomorphism.

45 [See Bernard Lonergan, *The Ontological and Psychological Constitution of Christ*, vol. 7 in Collected Works of Bernard Lonergan, trans. Michael G. Shields, ed. Frederick E. Crowe and Robert M. Doran (Toronto: University of Toronto Press, 2002) 94–99; Lonergan, *The Triune God: Systematics* 438–43.]

## Articulus XIV: De voluntarismo affinibusque erroribus

Duplex esse videtur voluntarismus: alius magis conscius atque apertus qui voluntatis amorisque celebret laudes; alius magis inconscius atque tectus qui, cum praecipue in ratione intelligibilitatis parum perspecta consistat, partes voluntatis consequenter exaggeret. Illum satis innocentem sentimentis suis relinquimus; hunc autem perniciosum, cum divinam iustitiam obscuret, dissolvendam censemus. Quapropter quattuor[46] brevissimis capitulis de voluntarismo tecto atque latente agendum est.

### *(a) Divinam voluntatem sequi intellectum*

Cum Deus libere mundum crearit, voluntarie eum creasse fatendum est. Sed bonum intellectum est obiectum voluntatis. Ergo 'impossibile est Deum velle nisi quod ratio suae sapientiae habet.'[47] 'Dicere autem quod ex simplici voluntate dependeat iustitia, est dicere quod divina voluntas non procedit secundum ordinem sapientiae, quod est blasphemum.'[48]

### *(b) Ordinem sapientiae divinae non in omnibus necessarium esse*

Etsi enim in multis cernatur necessitas sive ex fine sive ex agente sive etiam aliis modis,[49] non tamen in omnibus a Deo ordinatis invenitur necessitas. Quod maxime patet in iis quae redemptionem respiciant, ubi tota fere res in gratuitis Dei donis liberisque hominum actibus consistat. In quibus tamen non minus invenitur intelligibilis ordinatio divinae sapientiae quam in aliis et necessariis.

Non enim idem dicit intelligibile quod necessarium, sed latius patet illud, cum intelligibile dividatur in necessarium et possibile. Ita, necessarium est bis bina esse quattuor, sed quamvis necessarium non sit, tamen positive intelligibile est accelerationem gravitatis esse constantem. Iterum, positive

## Article 14: Voluntarism and related errors

Voluntarism would seem to be of two kinds, one that is more conscious and open, singing the praises of the will and of love, and another more unconscious and hidden. Since the latter consists mainly in largely ignoring intelligibility, it exaggerates accordingly the role of the will. The former kind is relatively harmless, and we leave it to its own sentiments; but the latter is pernicious and must be refuted utterly, since it obscures the meaning of divine justice. We shall deal with this hidden, latent form of voluntarism in the following four[46] brief sections.

*(a) The divine will follows the intellect*

Since God created the world freely, we must admit that he created it voluntarily, that is, by his will. But the object of the will is good understood as such; therefore 'it is impossible for God to will anything that is not in his wisdom.'[47] 'To assert that justice depends on the will alone is to say that the divine will does not proceed according to the order of wisdom, which is blasphemy.'[48]

*(b) Not everything in the order of divine wisdom is necessary.*

Although in many things one may discern the element of necessity arising either from the end or from the agent or in some other manner,[49] nevertheless necessity is not found in everything ordered by God. This fact is most obvious in matters having to do with redemption, which consists almost entirely in God's free gifts and our free acts. In these, however, the intelligible ordination of divine wisdom is just as clear as in other, necessary matters.

The intelligible and the necessary are not synonymous. The former has a wider extension, since the intelligible is divided into the necessary and the possible. Thus it is necessary that two times two equals four. On the other hand, that the acceleration of gravity be constant is not necessary, even

46 [Lonergan wrote 'quinque,' 'five,' but there are only four, as indicated by 'a,' 'b,' 'c,' and 'd.' Section (d), a rather lengthy section, seems to go right to the end of this article.]
47 Thomas Aquinas, *Summa theologiae,* 1, q. 21, a. 1, ad 2m.
48 Thomas Aquinas, *De veritate,* q. 23, a. 6.
49 Thomas Aquinas, *Summa contra Gentiles,* 2, c. 30.

intelligibile est hanc constantem accelerationem considerari secundum geometriam Euclideanam, sed etiam positive intelligibile est eam considerari secundum aliam geometriam.

Quibus perspectis, vehementer eos errare censemus qui divinum intellectum in necessariis, in caeteris aut divinam voluntatem primas habere partes asserant. Verum sane dicerent, si omne intelligibile etiam necessarium esset; cum tamen aliud intelligibile praeter necessarium exsistat, ex parum perspecta intelligibilitatis ratione in voluntarismum erronee declinant.

### *(c) Possibile et conveniens non stricte demonstrari*

Sicut duplex est intelligibile, ita etiam duplex est probandi genus. Quod enim necessarium est argumentis necessariis demonstratur. Quod autem possibile est nisi ex indiciis undique collectis, cumulatis, contextis non probatur. Iterum, quod necessarium est contradictorii possibilitatem excludit; quod vero possibile est non possibilitatem contradictorii sed factum contradictorium vel certo vel probabiliter negat.

Quae cum ita sint, parum admodum proficit qui ita duplex intelligibile agnoscat ut tamen nisi unum non sciat probandi modum. Gloriari sane solent de proprio rigore scientifico qui vanam otiosamque iudicent speculationem quodcumque vel ipsis sensibus non constet vel necessario ex necessariis non concludatur. Quorum tamen rigor potius mortis esse videtur quam rigor scientificus. Nam omnes scientiae sive naturales sive humanae non necessarium investigant sed possibile quod de facto exsistit. Neque ipsa oeconomia salutis necessaria est, sed possibilis et de facto exsistens. Imo ipsa suprema mysteria divina, quamvis quoad se necessaria sint, tamen eorum necessitas minime a nobis perspicitur (DB 1816), quamvis aliqua eorum intelligentia et analogica et imperfecta hac in vita a nobis haberi possit.

Quaesiverit tamen quispiam quemadmodum discerni possit inter vanas otiosasque speculationes et veram etsi contingentem intelligibilitatis cognitionem. Cui nulla brevis facilisque responsio dari potest. Deus enim uno intuitu eoque aeterno omnia intelligit. Angelus a primo suae exsistentiae instante omnia quae intra suam proportionem naturalem iaceant statim intelligere potest. Sed homo non est in genere intelligibilium nisi ut potentia, et ideo ei laborandum est ut eius intelligentia, scientia, sapientia

though it is positively intelligible. Again, it is positively intelligible for this constant acceleration to be considered according to Euclidean geometry, but it is also positively intelligible that it be considered according to some other geometry.

Accordingly, we strongly reject as erroneous the opinion of those who hold that in necessary things the divine intellect has the primacy while in other matters the divine will plays the leading role. They would be right if every intelligible were also necessary; but since the intelligible is broader than the necessary, they fall into the error of voluntarism through an insufficient grasp of the meaning of intelligibility.

*(c) The possible and the fitting are not strictly demonstrated.*

As the intelligible is of two kinds, so there are two kinds of proof. What is necessary is demonstrated by necessary arguments. What is possible, on the other hand, is proven only by collecting, accumulating, and connecting pieces of evidence from various sources. Again, what is necessary excludes the very possibility of its contradictory; whereas what is possible does not negate the possibility of its contradictory, but with either certainty or probability negates the fact of its contradictory.

This being the case, those are not going to get very far who acknowledge two kinds of intelligible but know only one manner of proof. They boast about their scientific rigor and at the same time dismiss as empty and idle speculation whatever is not verified by the senses or is not a necessary conclusion from necessary premises. This is not scientific rigor; it is more like *rigor mortis.* All the sciences, both the natural and the human sciences, investigate not the necessary but the possible that de facto exists. Nor is the economy of salvation itself a necessary reality, but a possible reality that de facto exists. Indeed, even the supreme mysteries of God, albeit necessary *quoad se,* are not at all grasped by us in their necessity (DB 1816, [DS 3041, ND 137]), even though in this life we can have some analogical and imperfect understanding of them.

Someone may have wondered how we can distinguish between idle speculation and a true, albeit contingent, knowledge of intelligibility. There is no short and simple answer to this. God understands all things in one eternal act of knowing. Angels from the very first moment of their existence understand everything that falls within the proportion of their natures. But in the genus of intelligible being, human beings are but potency, and therefore our lot is laboriously to develop our understanding, knowledge, and

pedetentim proficiat. Quod si intelligentiae augmentum non quaerit sed ab ipsis initiis demonstrationes postulat, experimentum saeculi decimi quarti ipse in se repetet. Nam quo minus quaeritur rerum intelligentia, eo minor habetur intelligentia; quo minor habetur, eo pauciores nexus ab eo perspici possunt; quo pauciores perspiciuntur, eo rariores fiunt certitudines; quo rariores sunt certitudines, eo magis ad scepticimsum acceditur. Bene noverant rigorem scientificum Scotus et Ockham; sed post pauca decennia advenit Nicolaus de Ultricuria, cui tantus erat rigor ut nihil fere ei evidenter certum supererat (DB 553–70).

E contra, quo magis augetur intelligentia, eo plures atque exactiores exprimuntur conceptus universales, qui clarius vel necessario vel possibiliter et convenienter inter se ligentur, unde numerosiores deducantur conclusiones sive cum certitudine sive cum probabilitate. Quod intelligentiae scientiaeque augmentum pedetentim in sapientiam conducit, quae omnia et inter se et ad finem ultimum ordinet, unde tam de singulis quam de omnibus fieri potest iudicium clarius, exactius, tutius. Neque sine sapientia de divina sapientia vel de divina iustitia iudicari potest. Imo, cum nulla sapientia finita divinae sapientiae proportionetur, quo sapientior est theologus eo etiam promptius atque libentius suae sapientiae iudicium illi magisterio submittit cui Deus assistit.

*(d) Alium intelligentiae et alium sapientiae esse ordinem*

Divinae iustitiae ordinem esse diximus, quem originaliter concipit divina sapientia, actualiter eligit divina voluntas, in tempore facit divina potentia, et ipsis in rebus cernitur. Quod tamen fieri non posse videtur. In illo enim ordine aut includuntur peccata aut non; sed si includuntur, Deus est auctor peccati; et si non includuntur, dominium Dei non est universale.

Cuius dilemmatis solutio in eo est quod (1) alius intelligentiae et alius sapientiae est ordo cum hic sed non ille includat non-intelligibilia, et (2) aliter intelligibilia et aliter non-intelligibilia comparantur ad divinam sapientiam, divinam electionem, et divinam actionem.

Intelligibile ergo dicimus id ipsum quod intelligendo aut innotescit (intelligibile actu) aut innotescere potest (intelligibile potentia). Quod forte aliis clarum et aliis obscurum videtur. Quibus autem clarum est, ab iisdem

wisdom little by little. If, however, we seek not an increase in understanding but instead demand proofs from the very beginning, we shall be repeating the experience of the fourteenth century. The less we seek an understanding of reality, the less understanding there will be; the less understanding there is, the fewer connections will we be able to grasp; the fewer connections we grasp, the rarer will our certitudes be; and the rarer certitudes are, the closer we approach to skepticism. Scotus and Ockham were well acquainted with scientific rigor; but a few decades later Nicholas of Autrecourt arrived on the scene, who was so rigorous that he was left with virtually nothing that was obviously certain (DB 553–70, [DS 1028–49]).

On the other hand, the more understanding increases, the more frequently and accurately are universal concepts expressed and the more clearly are they linked together, either necessarily or possibly and fittingly, and thus the more numerous are the conclusions that can be deduced either with certitude or with probability. This increase in understanding and knowledge gradually leads to that wisdom which sets all things in order both among themselves and in relation to their ultimate end, as a result of which judgments about each thing and all things can be made with greater clarity, precision, and surety. Without wisdom no judgment can be made concerning divine wisdom or divine justice. In fact, since no finite wisdom is proportionate to divine wisdom, the wiser a theologian is the more readily and gladly will he submit the judgment of his own wisdom to that teaching authority which is assisted by God.

*(d) The order of understanding is not the same as the order of wisdom.*

We have said that the order of divine justice is that which was originally conceived by divine wisdom, actually chosen by the divine will, produced in time by divine power, and discerned in created things. And yet, this seems to be impossible. For in this order, sins are either included or not; if they are, then God is the author of sin; if not, God's dominion is not universal.

The solution to this dilemma is to be found in the fact that (1) the order of understanding is different from the order of wisdom, since the latter includes the nonintelligible while the former does not; and (2) intelligibles and nonintelligibles are differently related to the wisdom, the choice, and the action of God.

The intelligible is that which either is known by understanding (intelligible in act) or can be known by understanding (intelligible in potency). This will perhaps seem clear to some and obscure to others. Those to whom

exercetur intelligendi actus; quibus vero obscurum est, ab iisdem non exercetur intelligendi actus; et cum eadem in omnibus sit claritatis vel obscuritatis ratio, quilibet in se ipso experiri potest quinam sit intelligendi actus, ille scilicet quem in claris experiatur et in obscuris non experiatur. Quod si quis ad hanc experientiam sedulo attendit eamque ab omnibus aliis secernit, claram acquiret intelligentiae et intelligibilis notitiam. Sin autem ad alia confugit, sive ad sensibilia sive ad imaginata sive ad conceptus sive ad iudicia sive ad ratiocinia, certo certius semper ei obscurum erit quid per nomina intelligentiae et intelligibilis vel significetur vel significari possit. Inquirendo enim in actum intelligendi tendimus. Intelligendo elucet intelligibile, quod sensibilibus vel imaginatis additur. Postquam intelleximus, incipit possibilitas concipiendi, definiendi, iudicandi, ratiocinandi. Sed totius processus nodus, clavis, centrum est ipse intelligendi actus, qui ultra sensibilia et imaginata procedit, sed conceptus, universalia, nexum inter conceptus, iudicia, ratiocinia antecedit atque fundat.

Quod si claram quandam intelligentiae et intelligibilis notitiam acquisiverimus, ulterius poterimus procedere. Non enim omnia pariter sunt intelligibilia, cum alia in se ipsis intelligantur, alia autem non in se sed in alio, et alia utrumque modum coniungant. Quae ergo dicitur forma, si proprie adhibetur nomen, in se ipsa est intelligibilis. Materia vero conditionesque materiae non in se sed in forma intelliguntur. Essentia rei materialis, cum non solum formam sed etiam materiam saltem communem includat, ita habet quod in alio intelligitur ut tamen etiam aliud illud habet in quo intelligatur. Quaecumque proinde contingenter vel exsistunt vel eveniunt, non in se sed in causis extrinsecis efficienti et finali intelliguntur. Ipse Deus denique, in quo nulla est materia nullaque contingentia, totus est in se intelligibilis.

Sed praeter ea quae vel in se vel in alio intelligi possunt, etiam concipi potest quod neque in se neque in alio ne potentia quidem intelligibile est. Neque tantummodo concipi potest non-intelligibile sed etiam illud esse affirmari potest. Nam eiusmodi est formale formalis peccati, seu illa irrationalis rationalitatis privatio quae in peccato formali invenitur. Quamvis enim intelligi possit ipsa peccandi actio quatenus entitatem quandam atque bonitatem habeat, sane nullo modo vere intelligi potest sive in se sive in alio ipse rationalitatis defectus irrationalis. Si enim vere intelligeretur,

it is clear are performing an act of understanding; those to whom it is obscure are not performing an act of understanding. And since the meaning of clarity and obscurity is common to all, anyone can determine from their own experience what an act of understanding is, namely, that act which is experienced in matters that are clear and is not experienced in matters that are obscure. If we carefully attend to this experience and distinguish it from all other experiences, we shall acquire a clear knowledge of both understanding and the intelligible. But if we resort to other matters, whether to sense impressions, or to the products of the imagination, or to concepts, or to judgments, or to reasonings, most certainly will we be forever in the dark about what is meant or can be meant by understanding and the intelligible. For by asking questions we move towards an act of understanding; in the act of understanding the intelligible shines forth, which is added to the data of sense and of the imagination. Once we have understood, the way is open to the possibility of conceiving, defining, judging, reasoning. But the pivotal point, the key and center of this whole process, is the act of understanding, which goes beyond the data of the senses and the imagination, but precedes and grounds concepts, universals, the connections between concepts, judgments, and reasonings.

If we have acquired a clear knowledge of understanding and the intelligible, we can proceed further. Not all things are equally intelligible, since some are intelligible in themselves, some are intelligible not in themselves but in something else, and still others are both. That which is called 'form,' in the proper sense of the term, is intelligible in itself. But matter and the conditions of matter are not understood in themselves but in form. The essence of a material thing, since it includes not only form but also matter, at least common matter, has that which is understood (matter) in another in such a way that it also has that other in which it is understood (form). Again, contingent existence or occurrence is understood, not in itself, but in extrinsic causes, efficient and final. Finally, God, in whom there is no matter and no contingency, is totally intelligible in himself.

But besides those things which can be understood either in themselves or in another, there can also be conceived what is intelligible neither in itself nor in another, even potentially. Indeed, not only can this nonintelligible be conceived, it can even be affirmed to be. For such is the formal element of formal sin, that is, the irrational privation of rationality which is found in formal sin. Although the action of sinning itself can be understood, inasmuch as it has some being and goodness, the irrational defect of rationality itself can certainly not be truly understood in any way, either in itself or in

irrationalis non esset, sed intellectam rationem intrinsecam vel extrinsecam eamque veram haberet.

Quibus perspectis, alium elucet esse ordinem intelligentiae et alium ordinem sapientiae. Intelligentia enim intelligibilia ordinat; sed sapientia ordinat non solum intelligibilia sed etiam non-intelligibilia. Non ordinat intelligentia nisi intelligibilia, cum tota sit in intelligendo sive quae in se sive quae in alio intelligibilia sint. Etiam non-intelligibilia ordinat sapientia, cum latius pateat sua attentio suaque virtus. Attendit enim sapiens ad omnia quaecumque de facto sunt, etiamsi esse non debeant, etiamsi intelligi non possint. Neque ordo sapientiae non-intelligibilia praetermittit quasi non essent quae tamen sunt, sed ita ea agnoscit ut ipsa eorum non-intelligibilitate maiorem esse sapientiam demonstret.

Quae cum ita sint, resolvitur dilemma quod superius propositum est. Nam intra ordinem quem excogitat divina sapientia, eligit divina voluntas, facit divina potentia, includuntur quidem peccata, non tamen quasi intelligibilia essent sed uti sunt non-intelligibilia. Neque eodem modo se habet divina sapientia vel electio vel actio tam ad non-intelligibilia quam ad intelligibilia.

Divina enim sapientia intelligibilia ordinat tamquam ea quae intentioni suae atque ordinationi concordant, sed non-intelligibilia ordinat tum inquantum antecedenter ea fieri districte prohibet gravissimasque poenas minatur, tum inquantum concomitanter ea ut de facto evenientia agnoscit, tum inquantum consequenter etiam de tantis malis bonum efficit. Similiter, divina electio bona directe vult, mala naturalis defectus et poenae indirecte vult, sed mala culpae non-intelligibilia nullo modo vult. Denique, divina actio est causa prima omnium quaecumque sunt; et ideo omnia entia in Deum agentem reducuntur et omnia non-entia in Deum non agentem reducuntur, sed non-intelligibilia sive in Deum agentem sive in Deum non agentem reduci non possunt; si enim reducerentur, essent intelligibilia in alio, quae tamen neque in se neque in alio intelligibilia sunt.

Quod si Deus ea fieri permittit quae omnino prohibeat neque ullo modo velit vel faciat, sane peccatorum auctor ipse non est. Cum tamen ab aeterno hunc rerum ordinem actualem et cognoverit et elegerit, neque quicquam eveniat praeter hunc ordinem, prorsus universale manet divinum dominium.

something else. If it were truly understood, it would not be irrational, but would have an understood reason, intrinsic or extrinsic, and a true reason at that.

From all this it is clear that the order of understanding is not the same as the order of wisdom. Understanding puts intelligibles in order; wisdom, though, orders not only intelligibles but also nonintelligibles. Understanding orders only what is intelligible, since its entire function is to understand what is intelligible either in itself or in something else. But wisdom orders even the nonintelligible, since its scope and power extend further. It looks to all that actually is, even if it ought not to be, even if it cannot be understood. Nor does the order of wisdom overlook nonintelligibles as if they were not when in fact they are, but acknowledges them so as to show that wisdom is greater than their very lack of intelligibility.

All this provides a solution to the dilemma posed above. Within the order devised by divine wisdom, chosen by the divine will, and executed by divine power, sins are indeed included, not, however, as if they were intelligible, but as they are: nonintelligible. Nor are God's wisdom, choice, and action related in the same way to nonintelligibles as they are to intelligibles.

Divine wisdom orders intelligibles as harmonious with its intention and ordination; but nonintelligibles it orders antecedently, concomitantly, and consequently. Antecedently to them, divine wisdom strictly forbids their occurrence and threatens dire punishments. Concomitantly with them, it acknowledges the fact of their occurrence. Consequently to them, it brings about good, even from such great evils. Similarly, divine choice wills the good directly and the evils of natural defects and of punishment indirectly, but wills nonintelligible culpable evils in no way whatsoever. Finally, God's action is the first cause of all that is; therefore, all beings are reduced to God acting and all non-beings are reduced to God not acting, but nonintelligibles cannot be reduced either to God acting or God not acting. If they were so reduced, they would be intelligible in another; but, in fact, they are intelligible neither in themselves nor in anything else.

If God simply permits the occurrence of what he utterly forbids and would in no way will or create, he is surely not the author of sin. Since, however, he knew and chose this actual order of reality from all eternity, and nothing happens outside this order, God's dominion remains entirely universal.

## Articulus xv: Praecedentium recapitulatio

Divinae iustitiae originem legemque diximus esse divinam sapientiam; exercitium autem esse liberam Dei electionem; effectum denique esse universi creati ordinem concretum et actualem secundum omnes suas determinationes.

Cum ergo divina sapientia nostrum intellectum longe excedat, in primis rationem *mysterii* divinae iustitiae vindicavimus. Quodcumque agit Deus, hoc iustum est; sed quemadmodum iustum sit, nisi imperfecte atque analogice intelligere non possumus. Quam ob causam Apostolus ad Romanos, postquam capitulo nono ad undecimum reiectionem populi Israeletici consideravit, divinae iustitiae mysterium admirans atque adorans exclamavit: 'O altitudo divitiarum sapientiae et scientiae Dei, quam incomprehensibilia sunt iudicia eius et investigabiles viae eius! "Quis enim cognovit sensum (νοῦν) Domini? Aut quis consiliarius eius fuit? Aut quis prior dedit illi et retribuetur ei?" Quoniam ex ipso et per ipsum et in ipso (εἰς αὐτὸν) sunt omnia: ipsi gloria in saecula. Amen' (Rom 11.33–36).

Quam mysterii rationem in iis praecipue attendere debemus, ubi actualis ordo cum alio et possibili ordine comparatur. Alios enim ordines fere nescimus nisi quod possibiles sunt, quod multi sunt, quod infinita sapientia ordinantur in divinam bonitatem manifestandam, quod infinita Dei bonitate eligi possunt, quod omnes simul sumpti includunt quodcumque internam contradictionem non dicat. Quae sane brevissima notitia minime sufficit ad comparationem instituendam, multoque minus ad actualem divinam electionem iudicandam. Quae ergo aliter fuisse potuerunt, cum non sint facta, nobis inquirendum non est sed, prout res fert, vel sanctitas divinae voluntatis adoranda vel ipsi divinae determinationi a nobis obediendum est.

Sed ex ratione mysterii et aliud concluditur. Qui enim legem divinae iustitiae in divina sapientia ponit, in ignoto eam ponit ut postea possit tum mysterium agnoscere tum in intelligentia, scientia, et sapientia proficere. Qui autem a definitionibus determinatis et divisionibus et regulis iustitiae incipit, quamvis valde scientificus esse videatur, magis tamen in arena quam in lapide domum suam fundat. Nam determinatae definitiones, divisiones, regulae e rebus humanis sumuntur et nisi analogice ad Deum applicari non possunt. Sed vix fieri potest ut tam lector quam auctor ad multiplicem analogiam semper attendat, unde haud ab omnibus evitatur omnis anthropomorphismus. Quod vero gravius est, ex insufficientia cuiuslibet analogiae

**Article 15: Recapitulation of the foregoing**

We have said that the origin and law of divine justice is divine wisdom, that its exercise is God's free choice, and finally that its effect is the actual concrete order of the universe in all its determinations.

Since the wisdom of God far exceeds our understanding, we have first of all established the character of *mystery* in divine justice. Whatever God does is just; but we can only imperfectly and analogically understand how it is just. And so St Paul in his Epistle to the Romans, after having treated the rejection of the people of Israel in chapters 9 to 11, marveling at the mystery of divine justice and adoring it, exclaims: 'O the depth of the riches and wisdom and knowledge of God! How unsearchable are his judgments and how inscrutable his ways! "For who has known the mind (νοῦν) of the Lord? Or who has been his counselor? Or who has given a gift to him, to receive a gift in return?" For from him and through him and to him (εἰς αὐτὸν) are all things. To him be the glory forever! Amen' (Romans 11.33–36).

In all of this we must keep in mind the character of mystery, especially when comparisons are made between the actual order of things and some other possible order. We know almost nothing of other orders, apart from the fact that they are possible, that they are many, that they are ordered by divine wisdom for the manifestation of the divine goodness, that they can be chosen by God's infinite goodness, and that all of them together include everything that does not involve an internal contradiction. Surely this scanty knowledge hardly suffices to set up such a comparison, much less to make a judgment upon the actual choice that God has made. There is no point in asking about what might have been, since that has not happened; ours is simply, as the occasion requires, to adore the holiness of God's will or obey what he has determined.

This character of mystery leads to another conclusion. To locate the law of divine justice in divine wisdom is to locate it in what is unknown, so that subsequently one can both acknowledge the mystery and at the same time advance in understanding, knowledge, and wisdom. But to take established definitions and divisions and rules of justice as one's starting point, though it may seem to be very scientific to do so, is nevertheless to build one's house on sand rather than on a rock. For established definitions, divisions, and rules are all taken from human affairs and can be applied to God only by analogy. It is practically impossible for either the reader or the author to pay constant attention to multiple analogies, and as a result

oritur; nam inter creatorem et creaturam non potest tanta similitudo notari quin inter eos maior sit dissimilitudo notanda (DB 432); et ideo, sicut ex similitudine species determinatae scientiae haberi potest, ita ex maiori dissimilitudine tanta exsurgit difficultatum multitudo tantaque penuria solutionum ut systema fortiter audacterque inceptum ante labefactetur atque collabatur quam perfici possit.

Deinde, cum divina sapientia totum universi creati ordinem ad determinationes etiam minimas elaboratum divinae voluntati exhibeat, cumque hunc ordinem tam exacte determinatum et eligat divina voluntas et exsequatur divina potentia, modo prorsus concreto atque actuali divinam iustitiam concepimus. Qua ex conceptione, varia sequuntur emolumenta.

Nam *in primis* amovetur periculum ne confundentur iustitia divina prout est actuque exercetur et eadem divina iustitia prout a nobis imperfecte et analogice consideratur atque cognoscitur; nam aliud manifeste est id quod fit secundum omnes suas determinationes, et longe aliud est idem ipsum quod fit secundum determinationes ad quas attendimus quasque plus minus intelligimus et maiori vel minori probabilitate vel certitudine cognoscimus.

*Deinde,* amovetur periculum ne umquam arbitremur nos totam divinae iustitiae rationem perspexisse, vel in rebus quae parviores esse appareant vel in magno mysterio nostrae redemptionis.

*Tertio,* accedit quod addiscere possumus qualis sit divinae iustitiae ordo non solum ex iure usuque tribunalium humanae iustitiae sed etiam ex ipso divino agendi modo qui tum in rebus naturalibus tum in tota historia humana tum in sacris eloquiis nostrae contemplationi atque admirationi exhibetur; nam 'ordo universi, qui apparet tam in rebus naturalibus quam in rebus voluntariis, demonstrat Dei iustitiam.'[50]

*Quarto,* qualis sit haec Dei iustitia concreta atque actualis, cum in multis necessitatem non habeat sed aliter fuisse potuerit, non solum stricte dictis demonstrationibus sed etiam argumentis convenientiae et sapientium iudicio determinandum est.

*Quinto,* denique, quanti sit momenti ad querelas calumniasque haereticorum praecavendas, ut omnis vel species anthropomorphismi evitetur, neminem non videre autumno qui libros eorum perlegerit finesque perspexerit. Quam ob causam, hac in re ad prima principia theologica recurrimus,

some anthropomorphism is unavoidable. But a more serious flaw arises from the inadequacy of all analogy, for however great the similarity may be between creator and creature, the dissimilarity between them is much greater (DB 432, [DS 806, ND 320]); and therefore, as the similarity can give the appearance of determinate knowledge, so this greater dissimilarity gives rise to such a profusion of problems and such a dearth of solutions that the whole systematic endeavor so bravely and boldly begun totters and falls before it can reach completion.

Next, since divine wisdom presents to the divine will the whole order of the created universe down to its least details, and since the divine will chooses and divine power implements this order with all its details, we have conceived divine justice in a totally concrete and actual way. This way of conceiving it has several advantages.

*First,* it averts the danger of confusing divine justice as it is and is actually exercised with the same divine justice as imperfectly and analogically considered and known by us. For there is plainly a great difference between what is made, with all its determinations, and the same reality with the determinations we happen to notice, more or less understand, and know with greater or less probability or certainty.

*Second,* it averts the danger of ever thinking that we have grasped the full meaning of divine justice, whether in matters which seem unimportant or in the great mystery of our redemption.

*Third,* there is the fact that we can learn about the nature of the order of divine justice not only from the laws and practices of human systems of justice but also from God's way of working which we contemplate and marvel at in nature, in human history, and in sacred scripture; for 'the order of the universe, which is manifest in nature as well as in matters of free will, displays the justice of God.'[50]

*Fourth,* because of the fact that in many areas it does not possess necessity but could have been otherwise, the nature of this concrete actual justice of God must be determined not only by demonstratrions in the strict sense but also by arguments from fittingness and the judgment of the wise.

*Fifth,* finally, I am sure that no one who has read the writings of heretics and grasped their aims will fail to realize how important it is, in guarding against their complaints and calumnies, to avoid even the semblance of anthropomorphism. That is why in dealing with this question we have had

50 Thomas Aquinas, *Summa theologiae,* 1, q. 21, a. 1 c.

nempe, ad Dei simplicitatem atque immutabilitatem notamque scholasticis distinctionem inter *entitative* atque *terminative*.[51]

Fatendum tamen est numquam fieri potuisse ut ordo universi concretus atque actualis tamquam ordo ipsius divinae iustitiae haberetur nisi accedisset distinctio superius elaborata inter ordinem intelligentiae et ordinem sapientiae. Cum enim sapientiae sit non solum intelligibilia ordinare sed etiam ea quae ab intelligibilitate deficiant, omnia prorsus, ne peccatis quidem exceptis, sub ordine divinae iustitiae inveniri non solum potuimus asserere sed et debuimus. Sicut enim iuste bonos bonis praemiat Deus et malos malis punit, ita etiam iuste homines peccare permittit atque a peccatis redemit. Nam 'universa quae condidit Deus providentia sua tuetur atque gubernat, attingens a fine usque ad finem fortiter et disponens omnia suaviter' (DB 1784; Sap 8.1).

Quibus perspectis, iam oportet magis particulariter de divina iustitia determinare et, in primis, quemadmodum discernatur inter divinam iustitiam et alia ex parte divinam bonitatem, divinam liberalitatem, divinam misericordiam. Quae quidem distinctio, cum tripliciter sumi possit, non raro confusionem gignit. Divina enim bonitas vel iustitia vel liberalitas vel misericordia aut (1) sumitur in sua radice intra ipsum Deum, aut (2) sumitur secundum comparationem effectuum creatorum inter se, aut (3) sumitur secundum habitudinem ipsius Dei ad creaturas.

Primo modo, bonus est Deus quia libere et de nihilo ens et bonum et creat et diffundit; iustus est Deus quia ordinem rerum ab infinita sapientia determinatum eligit; liberalis est Deus quia divina sapientia res ordinat non in divinam utilitatem sed in divinam bonitatem manifestandam; et misericors est Deus quia longe praestat ordinatio in divinam bonitatem ordinationi in quamlibet bonitatem creatam.[52]

Altero modo, effectus creati et inter se ordinati comparantur ut proportionati vel non proportionati; et cum omnes ex Deo sint, illi secundum iustitiam, hi autem secundum liberalitatem vel misericordiam procedere dicuntur. Ita benedictio Abrahae promissa secundum iustitiam Iudaeis et secundum misericordiam Gentibus concessa est.[53] Ita remissio peccatorum peccatori conceditur secundum misericordiam sed Christo superabundanter satisfacienti secundum iustitiam. Ita corona gloriae bonis meritis

recourse to theological first principles, namely, the simplicity and immutability of God and the distinction, familiar to Scholastics, between 'entitatively' and 'terminatively.'[51]

We must admit, however, that the concrete actual order of the universe could never have been regarded as the order of divine justice without bringing in the distinction made above between the order of understanding and the order of wisdom. For since it belongs to wisdom to order not only what is intelligible but even what lacks intelligibility, we have been able to assert, as indeed we must, that absolutely everything, including sin, falls under the order of divine justice. Just as God justly rewards the good with good and punishes the wicked with evil, so also with justice he permits people to sin and redeems them from sin. Everything that God created he preserves and directs by his providence 'from one end of the earth to the other, ordering all things for good' (DB 1784, [DS 3003, ND 413]; Wisdom 8.1).

With these points well understood, we must now go on to determine more particularly the meaning of divine justice and, to begin with, to see how to distinguish between divine justice on the one hand and divine goodness, divine generosity, and divine mercy on the other. This distinction, since it can be taken in three different ways, frequently gives rise to confusion. For God's goodness or justice or generosity or mercy can be taken either (1) in their root in God himself, or (2) according to the comparison of created effects among themselves, or (3) according to the relationship of God to creatures.

According to the first way, God is good because he freely and from nothing creates and diffuses being and good; God is just because he chooses the order of reality determined by infinite wisdom; God is generous because divine wisdom does not order things for God's advantage but to manifest divine goodness; and God is merciful because ordination to divine goodness far excels ordination to any created goodness.[52]

According to the second way, effects created and ordered among themselves are related to one another as proportionate or not proportionate; and since all come from God, the former are said to issue forth according to justice, and the latter according to God's generosity or his mercy. Thus the blessing promised to Abraham was conferred upon the Jews according to justice but upon the Gentiles according to mercy.[53] So also the remission

51 [See the discussion of contingent predication, p. 391 above.]
52 Thomas Aquinas, *Summa theologiae*, 1, q. 21, aa. 1, 3, 4; q. 44, a. 4.
53 Ibid. q. 21, a. 4, ad 2m; see Romans 15.8–9.

secundum iustitiam datur, sed ipsa bona merita ex divina liberalitate procedunt. Ita peccatorum castigatio ex iustitia est, sed castigatio citra condignum ex misericordia est.[54]

Tertio denique modo, consideratur habitudo Dei ad creaturas; et cum omnis habitudo fundamentum habeat, alia non est haec tertia consideratio ac prima vel altera. Cum prima enim coincidit si Deus ipse sumitur ut fundamentum relationis; cum altera coincidit si effectus creati et inter se ordinati fundamentum praebent; neque novum aliquid ex utriusque coniunctione habetur, nisi forte subintrat fallacia.

Quae tamen fallacia non adeo rara est. Qui enim de iusta habitudine inter Deum et creaturam quaerit, eo ipso Deum et creaturam quasi ex aequo ponit; unde et quaerit non solum quid Deo a creatura sed etiam quid creaturae a Deo debeatur; neque solum profert quaestionem sed etiam rationem invenit, nempe, exigentiam finis. Iam vero, uti patet, finis exigit id quod ad finem est, unde valent argumenta ex necessitate finis petita. Sed quod ad finem est ne cogitatur quidem nisi ex suppositione finis. Et ideo semper primo ponitur finis libere a Deo electus et deinde ea quae ad finem sunt et nisi propter finem non eliguntur, ut dicta finis exigentia simpliciter auferatur. Verum sane est Deum homini dare omnia quae ad hominem tamquam finem ordinantur; verum praeterea est Deum homini dare omnia quae ei conveniant ut ad finem pertingat; quod tamen Deus facit non quia homini quidquam debet sed quia ipse ordinem suae iustitiae tam in homine quam in aliis rebus adimplet. Deus ergo ad hominem se habet ut bonus et iustus et liberalis et misericors; sed ita se habet propter nomen suum et non propter debitum erga hominem.[55]

Denique tandem, uti postea constabit, specialis quaedam ratio divinae iustitiae in cruce Domini nostri conspicitur; quam tamen suo loco (cap. IV) convenientius exponi videtur.

of sins is granted to the sinner according to mercy but to Christ, superabundantly making satisfaction, according to justice. So also is the crown of glory given for merits according to justice, but the merits themselves flow from divine generosity. Likewise, chastisement for sin is a matter of justice, but a chastisement short of condign is due to God's mercy.[54]

The third way considers the relationship of God to creatures. Because every relation has a base, this third consideration is not another one over and above the first two. It coincides with the first, if God himself is taken as the base of the relation; it coincides with the second, if created effects mutually interrelated provide the base; and no new factor enters in from the conjunction of these two – unless it happens that a fallacy creeps in.

But such a fallacy is not all that rare. One who asks about a just relationship between God and a creature by this very question places God and a creature on what amounts to an equal footing. Hence one goes on to ask not only what is due to God from a creature but also what is due to a creature from God; and not only is this question asked, but even a reason is found for it, namely, the requirement from an end. Now of course an end requires whatever is a means to it, and so arguments drawn from what is needed for an end are valid. But the means to an end cannot even be thought of except on the supposition of an end. What comes first, therefore, is an end freely chosen by God, and then the means to the end chosen solely for the end; thus the so-called requirement from the end simply disappears. Certainly it is true that God gives us everything that is ordered to us as to an end, and it is also true that God gives us everything befitting us for the attainment of our end; yet God does this not because he owes anything to us, but because he fulfils the order of his justice in human beings as in all other creatures. In his relationship to us, therefore, God is good and just and generous and merciful; but he is all these things for his Name's sake, not because of anything he owes to us.[55]

Finally, as will be shown, a special aspect of divine justice appears in the cross of our Lord; but it seems more fitting to defer an explanation of this to chapter 4.

54 Thomas Aquinas, *Summa theologiae*, 1, q. 21, a. 4, ad 1m.
55 Ibid. a. 1, ad 3m; see Thomas Aquinas, *Summa contra Gentiles*, 2, c. 29, §§ 1058–62.

# Caput Tertium: De Christo Mortuo et Resurrecto[1]

Aliam christianae fidei doctrinam neque clarius neque plenius exposuerunt Novi Testamenti auctores quam ipsum redemptionis dogma. Quam ob causam, ea in primis colligere atque recitare visum est quae in primariis revelationis fontibus traduntur. Sex ergo quae sequuntur articulis de morte Christi (XVI), de pretii solutione (XVII), de sacrificio Novi Testamenti (XVIII), de obedientia meritoria (XIX), de vicaria passione (XX), et de virtute resurrectionis (XXI), non alia fere continentur quam quae in scripturis leguntur.

## Articulus XVI: De morte Christi[2]

*Causae proximae.* Secundum narrationem evangelicam mortem Christi effecerunt proditor Iudas (Mc 14.21, 14.43), summi sacerdotes (Mc 14.55–64), turba Hierosolymitana a pontificibus concitata (Mc 15.11–14), milites (Mc 15.16, 15.21–24), et si consentientes addis (Rom 1.32), praetereuntes et blasphemantes (Mc 15.29–31).

# 3 The Death and Resurrection of Christ[1]

No Christian doctrine has received a clearer or fuller treatment in the New Testament than the dogma of the redemption. Accordingly, it seems best to collect and set forth first of all what primary sources of revelation teach on this matter. The next six articles, therefore – on the death of Christ (article 16), the payment of the price (article 17), the sacrifice of the new covenant (article 18), meritorious obedience (article 19), vicarious suffering (article 20), and the power of the resurrection (article 21) – will simply express what is to be found in scripture.

**Article 16: The death of Christ[2]**

*Proximate causes.* According to the gospel narratives, the death of Christ was brought about by: Judas his betrayer (Mark 14.21, 14.43), the chief priests (Mark 14.55–64), the Jerusalem mob stirred up by the priests (Mark 15.11–14), the soldiers (Mark 15.16, 15.21–24), and, if one adds those who showed their approval (Romans 1.32), the passers-by who jeered at him (Mark 15.29–31).

1 [The autograph may be found on the website www.bernardlonergan.com at 25320DTL060.]
2 [This section, up to 'Distinctions,' is very similar to what is found in thesis 15, preliminary note 1, above, pp. 16–19.]

*Altiora principia.* Quartum evangelium non solum Iudaeorum oppositionem continuo manifestat[3] sed etiam ea exhibet principia quae hanc oppositionem communi rerum humanarum cursu fere necessariam fuisse suadent.

Christus enim Dei verbum erat lux vera quae illuminat omnem hominem (Io 1.9), erat lux mundi (Io 8.12), in hoc natus est et ad hoc venit in mundum ut testimonium perhiberet veritati (Io 18.37), et testimonium quidem perhibuit, Ioanne Baptista maius, testimonium nempe Dei Patris, scripturarum, Moysis (Io 5.36–46). At dilexerunt homines magis tenebras quam lucem; erant enim eorum mala opera. Omnis enim qui male agit odit lucem et non venit ad lucem, ut non arguantur opera eius; qui autem facit veritatem venit ad lucem ut manifestentur opera eius quia in Deo facta sunt (Io 3.19–21; cf. 7.7). Quam ob causam Iesus Iudaeis dicebat: 'Sermo meus non capit in vobis' (Io 8.37); et oppositionem delineavit inter Deum et diabolum, veritatem et mendacium, fidem et homicidium (Io 8.37–47). Proinde, etsi nemo ad Christum venire possit nisi Pater traxerit, docuerit, dederit (Io 6.44–45, 6.65), culpabiliter (Io 9.41) tamen et maiori peccato (Io 19.11) erant Iudaei fidei incapaces oculis quippe excaecatis et corde indurato (Io 12.39–40).

*Intentio divina.* At ulterius docet Novum Testamentum Christum 'definito consilio et praescientia Dei traditum' (Ac 2.23); neque alia fecisse Herodem et Pontium Pilatum cum gentibus et populis Israel quam quae manus Dei Deique consilium decreverunt fieri (Ac 4.28); immo oportuisse Christum pati (Lc 24.26, 24.46) secundum scripturas (1 Cor 15.3, Ac 3.18).

Quibus accedunt quae de mandato Patris narrantur (Io 10.18), propriae passionis et mortis praedictiones a Christo factae (Mc 9.12, 9.31, 10.33–34), voluntaria eiusdem passionis et mortis acceptatio (Mc 14.36, Mt 26.39), et ab apostolis celebrata Christi obedientia (Rom 5.19, Phil 2.8, Heb 5.8, 10.5–7).

*Higher principles.* The fourth gospel not only continually points out the opposition of the Jewish leaders[3] but presents those principles that lead one to think this opposition was all but inevitable in the ordinary course of human affairs.

For Christ the Word of God was the true light who enlightens everyone (John 1.9), was the light of the world (John 8.12), was born for this and for this he came into the world, to give testimony to the truth (John 18.37), and he did give this testimony, a testimony greater than that of John the Baptist, that is, the testimony of God the Father, of the scriptures, and of Moses (John 5.36–46). But people loved darkness more than light; for their deeds were evil. Everyone who does evil hates the light and does not come to the light lest his deeds be exposed; but those who do what is true come to the light so that it may be plainly seen that what they do is done in God (John 3.19–21; see also 7.7). That is why Jesus said to the Jewish leaders, 'There is no place in you for my word' (John 8.37), and described the opposition between God and the devil, between truth and lies, between faith and murder (John 8.37–47). Furthermore, although no one can come to Christ unless the Father draws him, teaches him, and grants him the grace (John 6.44–45, 6.65), yet those Jewish leaders were culpably (John 9.41) and with greater guilt (John 19.11) incapable of faith whose eyes were blinded and whose hearts were hardened (John 12.39–40).

*God's intention.* But the New Testament further teaches that Christ was 'delivered up according to the definite plan and foreknowledge of God' (Acts 2.23). It tells us that Herod and Pontius Pilate, along with the Gentiles and the peoples of Israel, did nothing other than what God in his power and wisdom had predetermined should happen (Acts 4.28), and in fact that Christ had to suffer (Luke 24.26, 24.46) in accordance with the scriptures (1 Corinthians 15.3, Acts 3.18).

To this there is added mention of the command of the Father (John 10.18), Christ's own predictions about his passion and death (Mark 9.12, 9.31, 10.33–34), his willing acceptance of his passion and death (Mark 14.36, Matthew 26.39), and his obedience so often praised by the apostles (Romans 5.19, Philippians 2.8, Hebrews 5.8, 10.5–7).

3 John 5.16–18, 6.52–53, 6.60, 6.66, 6.70, 7.12–13, 7.20, 7.31–32, 7.45–49, 7.51–52, 8.48–59, 9.16, 9.22, 9.30–34, 10.19–21, 10.31, 10.39, 11.46–53, 11.56, 12.19, 12.42–43.

*Distinctiones.* Quibus perspectis, quotupliciter mors Christi considerari possit, distinguendum est.

Consistit ergo mors Christi ut naturalis seu physica in separatione animae a corpore. Sed idem actus, motus, eventus ut ab agente procedens dicitur actio, et ut in recipiente productus dicitur passio. Physice ergo mors Christi erat et actio Iudaeorum a Iudaeis procedens et passio Christi in Christo producta.[4]

Proinde, unumquodque ad genus morum accedit quatenus est voluntarium. Sed alia et alia voluntate voluntaria erat mors Christi, cum gravissimo peccato mortem hanc effecerint Iudaei, et summa virtute eandem pertulerit Christus. Moraliter ergo spectata, mors Christi ut actio Iudaeorum erat nequissima, sed ut passio Christi erat excellentissima.

Unde et similes distinctiones fieri oportet circa divinam intentionem. Malum enim culpae Deus nullo modo vult sed tantum permittit;[5] et ideo formale formalis peccati eorum qui Christum oderunt atque occiderunt neque directe neque indirecte voluit Deus. Malum autem naturalis defectus et malum poenae vult Deus, non quidem directe cum obiectum voluntatis sit bonum, sed indirecte inquantum bonum ordinis universi intendit atque curat; et ideo mala Christo inflicta, quatenus peccati consectaria erant, nisi indirecte non voluit Deus. E contra, bonam sanctamque voluntatem directe vult Deus, et secundum hoc Deus directe voluit illam passionis et mortis acceptationem quam Christus obediens peregit. Praeterea, bonae sunt actiones quae secundum praecepta evangelica fiunt; sed evangelium reprobat legem talionis, inimicorum dilectionem praecipit (Mt 5.38–48), et malorum perpessionem propter iustitiam summopere laudat (Mt 5.10–12); quare S. Petrus passionem mortemque Domini nobis sequendum exemplum proponit (1 Pet 2.19–24); et ideo totam Christi passionem eiusque mortem, quatenus a voluntate Christi mitis et humilis processit, directe voluit Deus.

*Distinctions.* With all this in mind, we must distinguish the various ways in which the death of Christ can be considered.

As a natural or physical event, the death of Christ consists in the separation of the soul from the body. But this same act or motion or event considered as proceeding from an agent is regarded as an action, and considered as produced in the recipient is regarded as a passion. Considered physically, therefore, the death of Christ was both an action of the Jewish leaders as proceeding from them, and a passion of Christ as an effect produced in him.[4]

Again, inasmuch as an act is voluntary it comes into the area of morality. But the death of Christ was willed differently by different wills, since it was the gravest of sins on the part of the Jewish leaders who wished to kill him, and yet it was borne with supreme virtue by Christ. Considered morally, therefore, the death of Christ as an action of the Jewish leaders was utterly reprehensible, but as a passion of Christ a most excellent thing.

Similar distinctions must be made, therefore, concerning God's intention. God in no way wills culpable evil, but merely permits it;[5] therefore neither directly nor indirectly did God will the formal element of the formal sin of those who hated and killed Christ. God does will the evil of natural defects and the evil of punishment, not directly, of course, since the object of the will is good, but indirectly inasmuch as he intends and cares for the good of universal order. The evils inflicted upon Christ, therefore, insofar as they were the consequences of sin, were not willed by God except indirectly. On the other hand, God does directly will a good and holy will, and so God directly willed the acceptance of suffering and death on the part of the obedient Christ. Moreover, actions that are in accordance with the precepts of the gospels are virtuous. Now the gospel rejects the law of retaliation, commands love of one's enemies (Matthew 5.38–48), and praises the suffering of evil for the sake of justice (Matthew 5.10–12); hence St Peter proposes the sufferings and death of Christ as examples for us to follow (1 Peter 2.19–24). The whole of Christ's passion and death, therefore, inasmuch as it proceeded from the gentle and humble Christ, was directly willed by God.

4 Thomas Aquinas, *Summa theologiae,* 1-2, q. 20, a. 6, ad 2m; Peter Lombard, *Sententiae,* 3, d. 20, cc. 5–7.

5 Thomas Aquinas, *Summa theologiae,* 1, q. 19, a. 9.

*Effectus immanentes.* Epistola ad Hebraeos conveniens fuisse affirmat Deum perfecisse Christum per passiones (Heb 2.10). Quam vero intendit perfectionem, forte declarat postea affirmans 'cum [etsi] esset Filius Dei, didicit ex iis quae passus est obedientiam et consummatus [perfectus] factus est omnibus obtemperantibus sibi causa salutis aeternae' (Heb 5.8–9). S. Paulus praeterea ad Philippenses docet exaltationem Christi esse propter humiliationem eius qui formam servi acceperat et obediens erat factus usque ad mortem, mortem autem crucis (Phil 2.7–11, Heb 2.9). Et similiter omnia quae Dominum a dextris virtutis sedentem respiciunt, tamquam finem mortis et resurrectionis exhibet: 'In hoc enim Christus mortuus est et resurrexit, ut et mortuorum et vivorum dominetur' (Rom 14.9).

*Effectus universalis.* Praecipue vero docet scriptura Christum mortuum esse pro peccatis nostris (1 Cor 15.3, 1 Pet 3.18), pro impiis (Rom 5.6), pro omnibus (2 Cor 5.15, Heb 2.9) et singulis (Rom 14.15, 1 Cor 8.11, Gal 2.20), pro nobis (Rom 5.8, 1 Thess 5.10); in morte Christi nos baptizari (Rom 6.3), Eucharistiam mortem Domini annuntiare (1 Cor 11.26); quam praeterea mortem fuisse in redemptionem praevaricationum (Heb 9.15); ut filios Dei, qui erant dispersi, congregaret in unum (Io 11.51–52) ut et qui vivunt, iam non sibi vivant sed ei qui pro ipsis mortuus est et resurrexit (2 Cor 5.15); ut sive vigilemus sive dormiamus simul cum illo vivamus (1 Thess 5.10); ut nos offerret[6] Deo (1 Pet 3.18); in reconciliationem universalem (2 Cor 5.19, Rom 5.10, Eph 2.16, Col 1.20–22); ut per mortem destrueret eum qui habebat mortis imperium, id est diabolum, et liberaret eos qui timore mortis per totam vitam obnoxii erant servituti (Heb 2.14). Quibus accedunt omnia quae de sanguine et cruce Domini dicuntur, de eius sacrificio, de eius dilectione, suique traditione.

*Immanent effects.* The Epistle to the Hebrews states that it was fitting that God made Christ perfect through his sufferings (Hebrews 2.10). The sort of perfection that is meant is perhaps made clear in a later passage where it is stated that 'although he was a Son, he learned obedience through what he suffered; and having been made perfect, he became the source of eternal salvation for all who obey him' (Hebrews 5.8–9). Again, St Paul in his letter to the Philippians teaches that Christ's exaltation was due to his self-abasement in assuming the condition of a slave and becoming obedient unto death, even death on a cross (Philippians 2.7–11, Hebrews 2.9). In a similar vein he presents as the purpose of Christ's death and resurrection all that refers to him as Lord sitting at the right hand of God's power: 'For to this end Christ died and lived again, so that he might be Lord of both the dead and the living' (Romans 14.9).

*Universal effect.* Scripture teaches above all that Christ died for our sins (1 Corinthians 15.3, 1 Peter 3.18), on behalf of sinners (Romans 5.6), for all (2 Corinthians 5.15, Hebrews 2.9), for each one (Romans 14.15, 1 Corinthians 8.11, Galatians 2.20), for us (Romans 5.8, 1 Thessalonians 5.10); that we were baptized into the death of Christ (Romans 6.3), that the Eucharist proclaims the death of the Lord (1 Corinthians 11.26), a death undergone for redemption from transgressions (Hebrews 9.15); that he died in order to gather together the scattered children of God (John 11.51–52), and so that all who live should live no longer for themselves but for him who died and was raised to life for them (2 Corinthians 5.15); that he died so that, awake or asleep, we might live with him (1 Thessalonians 5.10); in order to offer[6] us to God (1 Peter 3.18), to bring about a universal reconciliation (2 Corinthians 5.19, Romans 5.10, Ephesians 2.16, Colossians 1.20–22), and to destroy by his death him who had power over death, that is, the devil, and set free all those who had been held in slavery all their lives by the fear of death (Hebrews 2.14). To all this we may add everything that scripture says about the blood and the cross of the Lord, about his sacrifice, his love, and his self-surrender.

6 [Reading of the Vulgate; Greek, προσαγάγῃ, conduct, lead to, bring (NRSV)].

## Articulus XVII: De pretii solutione[7]

Voces in versione Vulgata adhibitae, redimere, redemptio, diversis vocibus graecis correspondent quarum aliae transactionem quandam commercialem proprie significant, aliae autem connexum quidem sed longe generaliorem sensum eumque interdum remotum habent.

Ter significatur quod a piis Iudaeis exspectabatur divinum liberationis beneficium: Lc 1.68, 2.38 (λύτρωσις), 24.21 (λυτροῦσθαι). Quibus addi potest Moyses (λυτρωτής), Act 7.35.

Quater agitur secundum contextum de peccatorum remissione accepta vel intenta: Eph 1.7, Col 1.14, Heb 9.15 (ἀπολύτρωσις), Tit 2.14 (λυτροῦσθαι).

Quater, ut videtur,[8] intenditur completa illa redemptio ultimo die peragenda: Lc 21.28, Rom 8.23, Eph 1.14, 4.30 (ἀπολύτρωσις).

Semel ipse Christus redemptio dicitur (1 Cor 1.30), semel idem aeternam redemptionem invenisse (Heb 9.12), semel denique connectitur redemptio cum gratia et gratuita iustificatione et brevi post cum propitiatorio per fidem in sanguine Christi (Rom 3.24–25); in quibus bis adhibetur vox ἀπολύτρωσις, semel autem λύτρωσις (Heb 9.12).

Remanent tamen loca nunc examinanda quae medium quoddam adhibitum vel pretium solutum significant.

1 'Nam et Filius hominis non venit ut ministraretur ei sed ut ministraret et daret animam suam redemptionem pro multis' (δοῦναι τὴν ψυχὴν αὐτοῦ λύτρον ἀντί πολλῶν). Ita Mc 10.45 et Mt 20.28, in quibus idem praeterea est contextus, nempe, petitio pro filiis Zebedaei, indignatio duodecim, praeceptum Domini ut, inter discipulos, maiores sint ministri et primi sint servi (cf. 1 Pet 5.3), quod exemplo ipsius Filii hominis confirmatur.

'Dare animam suam' semitismus videtur, uti 'ponere animam suam' apud Io 10.11, 10.15, 10.17.

## Article 17: The payment of the price[7]

The words *redimere, redemptio,* used in the Latin Vulgate, correspond to various Greek words, some of which refer strictly to a commercial transaction, while others have such a reference but in a much more general and sometimes remote sense.

In three instances, it means the divine blessing of liberation expected by devout Jews: Luke 1.68, 2.38 (λύτρωσις), 24.21 (λυτροῦσθαι). To this may be added Moses as λυτρωτής [redeemer], Acts 7.35.

In four cases the context has to do with the remission of sins, received or intended: Ephesians 1.7, Colossians 1.14, Hebrews 9.15 (ἀπολύτρωσις), Titus 2.14 (λυτροῦσθαι).

Four occurrences, it seems,[8] refer to the redemption to be accomplished on the last day: Luke 21.28, Romans 8.23, Ephesians 1.14, 4.30 (ἀπολύτρωσις).

Christ himself is spoken of once as 'redemption' (1 Corinthians 1.30), once as having won an eternal redemption (Hebrews 9.12), and in one passage redemption is connected with grace and gratuitous justification and immediately afterwards with atonement made through faith in the blood of Christ (Romans 3.24–25); in these passages the word ἀπολύτρωσις is used twice, and λύτρωσις is used once (Hebrews 9.12).

Let us now examine those passages which speak of a means that is used or a price paid.

1 'For the Son of man came not to be served but to serve, and to give his life a ransom for many' (δοῦναι τὴν ψυχὴν αὐτοῦ λύτρον ἀντί πολλῶν). Thus in Mark 10.45 and Matthew 20.28, in which, moreover, the context is the same, namely, the request made on behalf of the sons of Zebedee and the indignation of the twelve, the Lord's instruction that the greater among his disciples should be servants of the rest, and the first among them should be the slave of all (see 1 Peter 5.3), is confirmed by the example of the Son of man himself.

'To give one's life' would seem to be a Semitism, as 'to lay down one's life' in John 10.11, 10.15, 10.17.

7 [This section parallels, though usually not verbatim, thesis 15, preliminary note 3, 'The Meaning of the Word "Redemption" in the New Testament.']

8 Daniel a Conchas, 'Redemptio acquisitionis ...' 14–29, 81–91, 154–69. [At the equivalent place in thesis 15 we find 'four or five times.' See above, p. 29.]

'Redemptio' hoc in loco dicit medium quoddam liberationis.[9]

Praepositio adhibita non ὑπέρ sed ἀντί; sensus possibilis ex usu NT illustratur sequentibus: (1) *loco alterius*, regnare pro patre suo, Mt 2.22; (2) *retributio*, oculum pro oculo, malum pro malo, Mt 5.38, Rom 12.17, 1 Thess 5.15, 1 Pet 3.9; (3) *substitutio*, pro pisce dare serpentem, Lc 11.11; (4) *electio*, proposito gaudio, sustinuit crucem, Heb 12.2; (5) *in utilitatem*, dare staterem ex ore piscis sumptum pro me et te, Mt 17.27.

'Pro multis' recolit Is 53.11: 'iustificabit ipse iustus servus meus *multos* et iniquitates eorum ipse portabit.'

Conferendum videtur verbum Domini: 'Quid enim prodest homini si mundum universum lucretur, animae vero suae detrimentum patiatur? Aut quam dabit homo commutationem (ἀντάλλαγμα) pro anima sua?' (Mt 16.26, Mc 8.37). Et illud S. Pauli: 'Omnia detrimentum feci et arbitror ut stercora, ut Christum lucrifaciam' (Phil 3.8).

2 '... homo Christus Iesus, qui dedit redemptionem semet ipsum pro omnibus' (ὁ δοὺς ἑαυτὸν ἀντίλυτρον ὑπέρ πάντων'). Ita S. Paulus (1 Tim 2.5–6), ubi universalem Christi mediationem praedicat et fere repetit ipsa verba Domini.

3 '... non corruptibilibus auro vel argento redempti estis ... sed pretioso sanguine quasi agni immaculati Christi et incontaminati ...' Ubi de sanguine tamquam liberationis instrumento loquitur S. Petrus (1 Pet 1.18–19).

4 Accedunt varia loca ubi adhibentur voces τιμή, ἀγοράζειν, ἐξαγοράζειν.[10] Ita Corinthii pretio empti esse dicuntur, ut corpora sua non sua sed Christi sint, ut ipsi non sui sed Spiritus sancti sint (1 Cor 6.15–20), ut qui liberi vocati sint, servi hominum fieri nolint, cum servi sint Christi (1 Cor 7.22–23). Dicitur praeterea Christus nos coemisse de maledicto legis (Gal 3.13) et eos qui sub lege erant coemisse (Gal 4.5). Reprobat S. Petrus eos qui 'eum qui emit eos Dominum negant' (2 Pet 2.1). In Apocalypsi emptio fit

'Redemption' in this passage indicates a means of liberation.[9]

The preposition used is not ὑπέρ but ἀντί; the possible meanings it can have in the New Testament are illustrated by the following instances: (1) *in the place of another,* as in Matthew 2.22, to reign in place of his father; (2) *retribution,* an eye for an eye, evil for evil (Matthew 5.38, Romans 12.17, 1 Thessalonians 5.15, 1 Peter 3.9); (3) *substitution,* as in Luke 11.11, to give a snake instead of a fish; (4) *choice,* as in Hebrews 12.2, For the sake of the joy he endured the cross; (5) *for a purpose,* as in Matthew 17.27, to give the coin to them for me and for you.

'For many' recalls Isaiah 53.11, 'The righteous one, my servant, shall make *many* righteous, and he shall bear their iniquities.'

A comparable expression seems to be that saying of the Lord, 'For what will it profit them if they gain the whole world but forfeit their life? Or what will they give in return (ἀντάλλαγμα) for their life?' (Matthew 16.26, Mark 8.37). See also St Paul, 'I have suffered the loss of all things, and I regard them as rubbish, in order that I may gain Christ' (Philippians 3.8).

2 '... Christ Jesus, himself human, who gave himself a ransom for all' (ὁ δοὺς ἑαυτὸν ἀντίλυτρον ὑπέρ πάντων'): so writes Paul (1 Timothy 2.5–6), where he proclaims the universal mediation of Christ and practically repeats the words of the Lord.

3 '... you were ransomed ... not with perishable things like silver or gold, but with the precious blood of Christ, like that of a lamb without defect of blemish.' Here Peter (1 Peter 1.18–19) speaks of blood as the instrument of liberation.

4 There are also a number of places where the words τιμή, ἀγοράζειν, and ἐξαγοράζειν are used.[10] Thus the Corinthians are said to have been bought at a price, so that their bodies are not their own but belong to Christ and so that they themselves are not their own but belong to the Holy Spirit (1 Corinthians 6.15–20); and similarly freed persons who have been called [by the Lord] must not be the slaves of other human beings, since they are now slaves of Christ (1 Corinthians 7.22–23). Again, Christ is said to have redeemed us from the curse of the Law (Galatians 3.13), to have redeemed

9 Stanislas Lyonnet, *Theologia biblica Novi Testamenti: De peccato et redemptione* (Rome: Pontifical Biblical Institute, 1956; mimeographed notes) 163; see 145–71. [See above, p. 27, where this work is compared to another, two-volume publication by Lyonnet, also entitled *De peccato et redemptione.*]

10 Ibid. 171–83. [Lonergan has a note to the effect that [Daniel a Conchas,] 'Redemptio acquisitionis,' seems to be 'recentior,' which the editors take to mean 'quite recent.' The published date for a Conchas's article is 1952.]

Deo in sanguine Christi ex omni tribu, populo, et natione (Apoc 5.9), 144,000 de terra (14.3), virginum (14.4).

5 Neque aliena sunt loca ubi affirmatur Dominus se dedisse pro peccatis nostris (Gal 1.4), se dedisse pro nobis ut nos redimeret ab omni iniquitate (Tit 2.14), se tradidisse pro me (Gal 2.20), pro nobis (Eph 5.2), pro ecclesia (Eph 5.25), vel traditum esse propter delicta nostra (Rom 4.25), pro nobis omnibus (Rom 8.32).

Quibus perpensis, sequentia ex doctrina NT concluduntur:

(1) Distinguendum est inter redemptionem ut finem et redemptionem ut medium. Redemptio *ut finis* est status ille quo liberamur a potestate tenebrarum, a peccatis, a poenis, a timore mortis, quo repromissionem accipimus, Deo reconciliamur, iustificamur, inhabitationem Spiritus et filiorum adoptionem habemus, spe salvati sumus, cum fiducia ad Deum accedere possumus, resurrectionem carnis, vitam cum Christo, gloriae coronam vel adhuc exspectamus vel quandoque possidebimus. Redemptio autem *ut medium* dicit id quo hic status oritur et producitur, non solum causalitate sed etiam et praecipue sub illa conditione Christo onerosa, quae erat mors crucis. Potuit enim Dei Verbum de caelis nos salvare; potuit Verbum caro factum praeter passionem et mortem nos salvare; sed de facto passione et morte nos salvos fecit.[11]

(2) Iis suppositis quae superius de morte Christi collegimus et nuperrime de solutione pretii recitavimus, satis docent Christum, ex divino decreto de actuali rerum ordine, sub onerosa conditione 'dandi animam suam' salutem omnium hominum esse operatum. Metaphorica sane fuit illa pretii solutio, quippe quae non corruptibilibus auro vel argento peracta est; at realis quaedam operatio et quasi commutatio per pretii solutionem

those who were subjects of the Law (Galatians 4.5). Peter rebukes those who 'deny the Master who bought them' (2 Peter 2.1). The Book of Revelation speaks of those bought for God by the blood of Christ from every tribe and people and nation (5.9), of the 144,000 bought from the earth (14.3), virgins (14.4).

5 Related passages are those which speak of the Lord having given himself for our sins (Galatians 1.4), and to redeem us from all wickedness (Titus 2.14); having given himself up for me (Galatians 2.20), for us (Ephesians 5.2), for the church (Ephesians 5.25), for our sins (Romans 4.25), and for us all (Romans 8.32).

Once all this is weighed, the following conclusions may be drawn from the teaching of the New Testament:

(1) A distinction must be made between redemption as an end and redemption as a means. Redemption *as an end* is that state in which we are freed from the power of darkness, from sin, from punishment, from the fear of death, in which we receive the promise, are reconciled to God, are justified, enjoy the indwelling of the Holy Spirit and adoptive filiation, are saved in hope, are able to approach God with confidence, and have the resurrection of the flesh, life with Christ, and the crown of glory in hope or, one day, full possession. Redemption *as a means* refers to that process by which this state begins and is brought about, not only by causality but also and especially under that condition most burdensome to Christ, namely, death on the cross. The Word of God could have saved us without coming down from heaven; the incarnate Word could have saved us without undergoing suffering and death; but in actual fact it was through his passion and death that he did save us.[11]

(2) On the basis of the texts we adduced above concerning the death of Christ and those we have just now listed regarding the payment of a price, it seems quite clear that Christ, by divine decree concerning the actual order of things, wrought the salvation of all humankind under the burdensome condition of 'giving his life.' 'Paying the price' is a metaphor, no doubt, since the price was not paid in perishable gold or silver; but by payment of a price a real action and, as it were, an exchange is signified,

11 Thomas Aquinas, *Summa theologiae*, 3, q. 46, a. 2. [On redemption as end and as means, see above, p. 29, where Lonergan refers to redemption as end and redemption as mediation.]

significatur, cum realis fuerit mors Christi, realis sit nostra salus, et haec cum illa asseratur connexa.

(3) Sensus fundamentalis illustrari videtur optime ex illis verbis Domini: 'Aut quam dabit homo commutationem pro anima sua?' Si de vita terrestri agitur, nihil mere terrestre non daretur pro ipsa sua vita. Si de vita aeterna agitur, nihil est quod pro ea non sit dandum. Christus vitam suam terrestrem dedit pro vita aeterna omnium.

(4) Quod si quaeritur cuinam solutum sit pretium, nimis premi videtur metaphora. Saltem dicendum est opinionem aliquando diffusam Christum diabolo pretium solvisse, iam pridem censeri obsoletam.

(5) At ulterius quaeri potest curnam Deus pretium nostrae salutis exegerit. Sed quamvis certissimum sit adesse rationem prorsus sufficientem eamque iustissimam, certum etiam est nos non posse eam intelligere nisi imperfecte et analogice. Quare, quamvis haec intelligentia forte fructuosior sit quam reliqua intelligentia theologica, prudentius tamen procedit qui primo clare determinet quid sit intelligendum ut postea aliquam intelligentiam assequi nitatur.

### Articulus XVIII: De sacrificio Novi Testamenti[12]

In sacrificiis distinguuntur (1) *effectus*: peccatorum remissio, sanctificatio, accessus ad Deum cum fiducia; (2) *effectum recipiens*: populus pro quo fit oblatio; (3) *agens*: sacerdos, pontifex; (4) *patiens*: hostia, victima; (5) *actio*: oblatio victimae a sacerdote; et (6) *fundamentum*: foedus, testamentum, quo constituitur sancta illa societas in qua assumuntur sacerdotes de populo ut sacrificia pro populo offerant Deo.

Caeteris fundamentis praestat foedus seu testamentum divinitus institutum. Quod tamen foedus Deus per Moysen cum populo Israelitico in sanguine (Exod 24.8, Heb 9.19–21) inivit, veterandum praedixit Ieremias novumque annuntiavit, quo omnes intime Deum Deique leges scirent, quo 'ero eis in Deum et ipsi erunt mihi in populum,' quo 'propitius ero iniquitatibus eorum, et peccatorum eorum iam non recordabor' (Heb 8.8–12, Ier 31.31–34). Quod promissum atque novum testamentum initum est et

inasmuch as the death of Christ was real, our salvation is real, and a connection between them is affirmed.

(3) The basic meaning would seem to be very well illustrated in that saying of the Lord, 'What will they give in return for their life?' [Matthew 16.26, Mark 8.37]. If it is earthly life that is at stake, there is nothing on earth that anyone would not give for one's life. If it is a matter of eternal life, there is nothing whatsoever that should not be given for it. Christ gave his earthly life in exchange for the eternal life of all.

(4) If one asks to whom the price was paid, that would seem to be pushing the metaphor too far. But at least we may mention here that the once rather widespread opinion that Christ paid the price to the devil has for a long time now been deemed obsolete.

(5) A further question may be asked, however, as to why God required a price for our salvation. Although it is most certain that there is an utterly sufficient reason for this, one that is most just, it is also quite certain that we can understand it only imperfectly and by analogy. Therefore, although such an understanding might be more fruitful than any other theological understanding, it would be more prudent to determine first just what is to be understood, so that subsequently one might try to arrive at some understanding of it.

### Article 18: The sacrifice of the new covenant[12]

In sacrifices the following elements may be distinguished: (1) the *effect*: the forgiveness of sins, sanctification, access to God with confidence; (2) the *recipient of the effect*: the people for whom the sacrifice was offered; (3) the *agent*: the high priest; (4) the *patient*: the victim; (5) the *action*: offering of the victim by the priest; and (6) the *foundation*: the compact or covenant by which is constituted that holy society in which priests are taken from among the people to offer sacrifices to God for the people.

A divinely instituted compact or covenant is superior to all other foundations. That the Mosaic covenant forged in blood (Exodus 24.8, Hebrews 9.19–21) between God and the people of Israel would become old was predicted by Jeremiah, who foretold a new covenant in which all people would inwardly know God and the laws of God, in which 'I will be their God, and

12 [This section parallels, often verbatim, thesis 15, part 5, pp. 52–59 above.]

sancitum in sanguine Christi qui pro multis effundetur in remissionem peccatorum (Mc 14.24, Mt 26.28, Lc 22.20, 1 Cor 11.25). Quam ob causam dicitur Dominus melioris et novi testamenti sponsor atque mediator (Heb 7.22. 8.6, 9.15, 12.24).[13]

Quantum autem veteri novum praestet testamentum fere tota ad Hebraeos epistola exponit, comparatis (1) mediatoribus Moyse (cf. Gal 3.19–20) et Filio, (2) sacerdotiis Levi et Melchisedech, (3) sacrificiis ad emundationem carnis et sacrificio ad emundationem conscientiae.

(1) Fidelis quidem erat Moyses, sed sicut famulus in domo Dei; fidelis autem est Christus sicut Filius in domo sua quae sumus nos (3.2–6). Ipse enim Filius, splendor gloriae et figura substantiae divinae, heres constitutus universorum per quem fecit et saecula (1.2–3), cui omnia subiecta (1.13, 2.8), participavit carni et sanguini (2.14) per omnia nobis assimilatus absque peccato (2.17, 4.15). Nam ut misericors fieret et fidelis pontifex ad Deum (2.17, 4.15, 5.2), passionibus eum perfici decuit (2.10), et passus est et tentatus per omnia pro similitudine (2.18, 4.15), unde et ex iis quae passus est didicit obedientiam et perfectus factus est omnibus obtemperantibus sibi causa salutis aeternae (5.8–9).

(2) Deinde, postquam secerdotium secundum Melchisedech sacerdotio Levitico superius demonstratum est (7.1–14), introducitur sacerdos secundum similitudinem Melchisedech 'qui non secundum legem mandati carnalis factus est, sed secundum virtutem vitae insolubilis' (7.16). Qui quidem divino iuramento sacerdos constituitur (5.4–6, 7.17, 7.21), dum Levitici sine iuramento erant (7.20). Hic sempiternum habet sacerdotium et in aeternum manet (7.24, 7.3), sed illi quia moriebantur multi erant (7.23). Hic innocens, sanctus, impollutus, segregatus a peccatoribus ex excelsior caelis factus (7.26), sed illi pro propriis delictis offerre debebant (5.3, 7.27). Hic semel in ipsum caelum per suam hostiam apparuit (9.24–26), sed illi saepe in tabernaculum manufactum introierunt (9.6–7, 9.25). Hic Filius in aeternum perfectus (7.28), sed lex nihil ad perfectum adduxit (7.11, 7.18–19).

they shall be my people,' and 'I will be merciful toward their iniquities, and I will remember their sins no more' (Hebrews 8. 8–12, Jeremiah 31.31–34). This new and promised covenant was established and ratified in the blood of Christ shed for many for the forgiveness of sins (Mark 14.24, Matthew 26.28, Luke 22.20, 1 Corinthians 11.25). Hence the Lord is said to be the guarantor and mediator of a new and better covenant (Hebrews 7.22, 8.6, 9.15, 12.24).[13]

Almost the whole Letter to the Hebrews expounds the superiority of this new covenant over the old, comparing (1) the mediators, Moses (see Galatians 3.19–20) and the Son, (2) the priesthoods of Levi and Melchizedek, and (3) the sacrifices for the purification of the flesh and the sacrifice for the purification of conscience. Thus:

(1) Moses was indeed faithful, but as a servant in the household of God; Christ was faithful as Son in his own house, which house we are (3.2–6). For the Son himself, the radiance of God's glory and the imprint of God's very being, the heir of all things, through whom he made the ages (1.2–3), to whom all things are subject (1.13, 2.8), shared in our flesh and blood (2.14), and is like us in all things but sin (2.17, 4.15). That he might be a merciful and faithful high priest before God (2.17, 4.15, 5.2), it was fitting that he be made perfect through suffering (2.10), and so he suffered and was tested in every way that we are (2.18, 4.15), whereby through what he suffered he learned obedience, and having thus been made perfect he became for all who obey him the source of eternal salvation (5.8–9).

(2) Next, after the priesthood according to Melchizedek was shown to be superior to the Levitical (7.1–14), a priest like Melchizedek is introduced, 'one who has become a priest, not through a legal requirement concerning physical descent, but through the power of an indestructible life' (7.16). He was constituted priest by a divine oath (5.4–6, 7.17, 7.21), while the Levites were priests without an oath (7.20). He has an everlasting priesthood and abides forever (7.24, 7.3), whereas they, because they died, were many in number (7.23). He was innocent, holy, undefiled, separated from sinners, and raised above the heavens (7.26), while they had to offer sacrifices for their own sins (5.3, 7.27). He appeared once for all in heaven itself through his sacrifice (9.24–26), but they had to go many times into a tabernacle made by human hands (9.6–7, 9.25). He is the Son made perfect forever (7.28), whereas the law brought nothing to perfection (7.11, 7.18–19).

13 See Ceslaus Spicq, 'Médiation – IV: Dans Le Nouveau Testament,' DBS V, 1020–83.

(3) Denique, sacrificia legis nisi umbram non habebant futurorum bonorum (10.1), nisi emundationem carnis non efficiebant (9.10, 9.13), non poterant iuxta conscientiam perfectum facere servientem (9.9, 10.1–2), neque peccata auferre (10.4, 10.11). Quibus reprobatis, ipse Filius corpore sibi aptato venit ad faciendam voluntatem Dei (10.5–7), in qua voluntate sanctificati sumus per oblationem corporis Iesu Christi semel (10.10, 7.27). Cuius sanguis emundat conscientiam nostram ab operibus mortuis ad serviendum Deo viventi (9.14), tollit praevaricationes quae erant sub priori testamento (9.15). Christus enim semel in consummatione saeculorum ad destitutionem peccati per hostiam suam apparuit (9.26); semel oblatus est ad multorum exhaurienda peccata (9.28); unam pro peccatis offerens hostiam in sempiternum sedet in dextera Dei (10.12), una enim oblatione consummavit in aeternum sanctificatos (10.14). Impletum ergo est verbum propheticum: 'Et peccatorum et iniquitatum eorum iam non recordabor amplius. Ubi autem horum remissio, iam non est oblatio pro peccato' (10.17–18).

Christus ergo novi testamenti factus est sponsor, mediator, sacerdos, et hostia; per suum sanguinem sanctificavit populum (13.12) et purgationem peccatorum effecit (1.3).

Quod in caeteris scriptis NT brevius indicatur. Etenim pascha nostrum immolatus est Christus (1 Cor 5.7; cf. Io 1.29, Act 8.32, Is 53.7, 1 Pet 1.19, 1 Io 3.5). Christus factus est sanctificatio nostra (1 Cor 1.30; cf. Heb 2.3,13.12). Christus dilexit nos et tradidit semet ipsum pro nobis oblationem et hostiam Deo in odorem suavitatis (Eph 5.2, Ps 39.7). Missus est propitiatio pro peccatis nostris et pro peccatis totius mundi (1 Io 2.2, 4.10). Eum proposuit Deus propitiatorium per fidem in sanguine eius (Rom 3.25).[14]

Quibus accedunt quae de efficacia sanguinis Christi affirmantur. In eo enim iustificamur (Rom 5.9); per eum habemus redemptionem, remissionem peccatorum nostrorum (Eph 1.7, Col 1.14), pacificationem (Col 1.20). In eo Christus nos redemit Deo (Apoc 5.9) et lavit nos a peccatis nostris (Apoc 1.5, 7.14). In eo qui erant longe facti sunt prope (Eph 2.13). Sanguis Iesu Christi emundat nos ab omni peccato (1 Io 1.7); eius aspersio

(3) Finally, the sacrifices of the law were merely a shadow of the good things to come (10.1), effected only a purification of the flesh (9.10, 9.13), and could neither perfect the conscience of the worshiper (9.9, 10.1–2) nor take away sin (10.4, 10.11). Rejecting these, the Son himself came with a body fitted to him to do God's will (10.5–7), and by this will we are sanctified through the offering of the body of Jesus Christ once for all (10.10, 7.27). His blood purifies our conscience from dead works to serve the living God (9.14), and takes away the transgressions under the former covenant (9.15). Christ has appeared once for all at the end of the age to remove sin by the sacrifice of himself (9.26); he has been offered once to bear the sins of many (9.28); having offered for all time a single sacrifice for sins, he sat down at the right hand of God (10.12) for by a single offering he has perfected for all time those who are sanctified (10.14). Thus was fulfilled the word of the prophet: '"I will remember their sins and their lawless deeds no more." Where there is forgiveness of these, there is no longer any offering for sin' (10.17–18).

Christ, therefore, has been made the guarantor, mediator, priest, and victim of the new covenant; he sanctified the people through his own blood (13.12) and effected the purification of sins (1.3).

All this is more briefly indicated in other passages in the New Testament. Christ our paschal lamb is sacrificed (1 Corinthians 5.7; see John 1.29, Acts 8.32, Isaiah 53.7, 1 Peter 1.19, 1 John 3.5). He has become our sanctification (1 Corinthians 1.30; see Hebrews 2.3, 13.12). Christ loved us and gave himself up for us, a fragrant offering and sacrifice to God (Ephesians 5.2, Psalm 39.7 [EVV 40.6]). He was sent to be the atoning sacrifice for our sins and for the sins of the whole world (1 John 2.2, 4.10). God put him forward to be the sacrifice of atonement that would win reconciliation by his blood, effective through faith (Romans 3.25).[14]

To this we may add those statements which attest to the efficacy of the blood of Christ. In it we are justified (Romans 5.9), and through it we have redemption, the forgiveness of our sins (Ephesians 1.7, Colossians 1.14), and peace (Colossians 1.20). In his blood Christ redeemed us for God (Revelation 5.9) and washed us clean from our sins (Revelation 1.5, 7.14). In it those who were far apart have been brought close (Ephesians 2.13).

14 Lyonnet, *Theologia biblica Novi Testamenti: De peccato et redemptione* 184–235 [pp. 184–209, Art. 4: 'Notio expiationis'; pp. 209–35, Art. 5: 'De munere sanguinis in expiatione']. See Hebrews 2.17, 8.12, 9.5–14. It is theologically clear and certain that a creature cannot act upon an unmovable mover.

melius loquitur quam sanguis Abel (Heb 12.24; cf. 1 Pet 1.2); eo adquiritur ecclesia (Act 20.28); propter eum habetur victoria (Apoc 12.11).

### Articulus XIX: De obedientia meritoria[15]

Missio Filii a Deo Patre in opus nostrae salutis (Gal 4.4–5, Rom 8.3–4) tum ipsam Filii personam respicit tum actus eius humanos. Quatenus ipsam personam respicit, missio dicit aeternam personae processionem a Patre, addito ad extra termino conveniente.[16] Quatenus autem actus humanos a Filio perficiendos respicit, illam dependentiam dicit quam obedientiam nominamus. Sicut enim praecipere est alium per rationem et voluntatem movere,[17] ita obedire est ab alio per rationem et voluntatem moveri.[18]

Ita Christus affirmat se habere a Patre tum alia mandata (Io 15.10), tum mandatum quid dicat et loquatur (Io 12.49), tum denique mandatum ponendi animam suam et iterum sumendi eam (Io 10.17–18). Quibus mandatis respondent facta. Testatus enim est Christus se docere non suam doctrinam sed eius qui eum misit (Io 7.16–18, 8.28, 14.24), se de caelo descendisse ut faceret non voluntatem suam sed eius qui eum misit (Io 6.38), se quaerere non voluntatem suam sed eius qui eum misit (Io 5.30), suum cibum esse ut faceret voluntatem eius qui eum misit et opus eius perficeret (Io 4.34), se semper facere quae placita sunt Patri (Io 8.29), se mandata Patris servare et in dilectione Patris manere (Io 15.10). Quare in articulo mortis dixit: 'Consummatum est' (Io 19.30).

The blood of Jesus Christ cleanses us from all sin (1 John 1.7); the sprinkling of it speaks a better word than the blood of Abel (Hebrews 12.24; see 1 Peter 1.2). By it he acquired the church (Acts 20.28), and through it victory is won (Revelation 12.11).

### Article 19: Meritorious obedience[15]

The mission, the sending of the Son by God the Father for the work of our salvation (Galatians 4.4–5, Romans 8.3–4), regards both the person of the Son and his human acts. Inasmuch as it regards his person, the mission refers to the eternal procession of the person from the Father, with the added appropriate external term.[16] Inasmuch as it regards the human acts to be performed by the Son, it refers to that dependence that we call obedience. For just as to command is to move another through reason and will,[17] so to obey is to be moved by another through reason and will.[18]

Thus Christ states that he has other commands from the Father (John 15.10), the command about what he should say and speak (John 12.49), and finally the command to lay down his life and take it up again (John 10.17–18). His deeds correspond to these commands. For Christ testified that he taught not his own doctrine but that of him who sent him (John 7.16–18, 8.28, 14.24), that he came down from heaven not to do his own will but the will of him who sent him (John 6.38), that he sought not his own will but that of him who sent him (John 5.30), that his food was to do the will of him who sent him and to complete his work (John 4.34), that he always did what was pleasing to the Father (John 8.29), and that he observed the Father's commands and remained in the Father's love (John 15.10). And so at the moment of his death he could say, 'It is finished' (John 19.30).

15 [This section parallels, often verbatim, thesis 15, part 6, above, pp. 58–65.]
16 Lonergan, *Divinarum personarum* 206–12 [=*De Deo trino: Pars systematica* 226–32, and *The Triune God: Systematics* 454–67.]
17 Thomas Aquinas, *Summa theologiae,* 2-2, q. 104, a. 1.
18 Ibid. 3, q. 47, a. 2, ad 1m: 'This is not to be understood in the sense that [Christ] first waited to hear [the Father's command] and needed to learn from it; rather, he clearly proceeded voluntarily, thus removing any suspicion of opposition to the Father.' See ibid. a. 3 c.: 'He [the Father] inspired him with the willingness to suffer for us.'

Obedientiam Christi in passione et morte acceptanda memorant tum alia evangelia (Mc 14.36 et loc. par.) tum S. Paulus (Phil 2.8) qui etiam obedientiae meritum innuit (Rom 5.19), si quidem non per ipsam unius obeditionem iusti constituuntur multi nisi inquantum obeditio est opus praemio dignum.

Secundum epistolam ad Hebraeos Christus mundum ingrediens agnovit tum sacrificia veteris legis esse reprobata tum corpus sibi esse aptatum, dixitque 'Ecce venio. In capite libri scriptum est de me: ut faciam, Deus, voluntatem tuam' (Heb 10.5–7);[19] quibus paulo post additur, 'in qua voluntate sanctificati sumus per oblationem corporis Iesu Christi semel' (Heb 10.10). Sed et praeterea legimus decuisse Deum Patrem passionibus Filium perficere (Heb 2.10), ipsumque Filium ex iis quae passus est obedientiam didicisse et, cum ad perfectionem pertegisset, factum esse omnibus obtemperantibus sibi causam salutis aeternae (Heb 5.8–9).

Quaenam autem sit illa ex passionibus orta perfectio et obedientiae addiscentia, forte sic declarari potest. Sicut ipse homo non solum anima sed etiam corpore constituitur, ita etiam actus humanus plenus atque perfectus non solum actu interiori intellectus et voluntatis sed etiam actu exteriori sensibili et corporali componitur, et ipsa denique obedientia non solum intellectus et voluntatis obsequium sed etiam corporis exsecutionem complectitur. Iam vero cum in nobis spiritus quidem promptus sit, caro autem infirma (Mc 14.38), omnino manifestum est quantum intercedat inter velle et perficere, quantoque perfectior sit ipse interior voluntatis actus cum non solum velimus bonum facere sed etiam ita velimus ut faciamus.

Quam quidem difficultatem auget quidem lapsa nostra natura humana sed fundat potius ipsa differentia inter proportionem partis intellectivae et proportionem partis sensitivae. Quatenus enim intellectuales sumus, in totum ens totumque bonum naturaliter tendimus; quatenus autem sensitivi sumus, in ea obiecta tendimus quae sensibus sensitivisque appetitibus proportionantur; et ideo, etiam praecisione facta a corruptione nostrae

Both the other gospels (Mark 14.36; *loc. par.*) and St Paul (Philippians 2.8) note Christ's obedience in accepting his passion and death. Paul also suggests the merit of this obedience (Romans 5.19), since many would not have been made just by the obedience of this one human being except insofar as this obedience was deserving of a reward.

According to the Letter to the Hebrews, Christ, on coming into the world, recognized that the sacrifices of the old law were unacceptable and that a body had been prepared for him, and declared, 'Behold, I have come! At the top of the scroll it has been written of me that I should do your will, O God' (Hebrews 10.5–7);[19] and shortly after are the words, 'It is by God's will that we have been sanctified through the offering of the body of Jesus Christ once for all' (Hebrews 10.10). But we also read that it was fitting for God the Father to perfect the Son through suffering (Hebrews 2.10), and for the Son himself to have learned obedience from what he suffered, and once he had been made perfect, to become for all who obey him the source of eternal salvation (Hebrews 5.8–9).

What this perfection arising from suffering and learning through obedience might mean can perhaps be explained in the following way. Just as a human being is made up not only of a soul but of a body as well, so a full and complete human act comprises not only the interior acts of intellect and will but also the exterior sensible and bodily acts. Obedience, then, would include not only submission of intellect and will but external bodily execution as well. Now since in us the spirit is willing but the flesh is weak (Mark 14.38), it is all too obvious how great a distance there is between willing and performing, and how much more perfect is that interior act of will when we are not only willing to do a good deed but also will in such a way that we do it.

This difficulty, although aggravated by our fallen human nature, is rooted in the divergence between the proportion of the intellectual part and the proportion of the sensitive part of our makeup. As intellectual beings, we naturally tend to all being and all good; as sensitive beings, we tend towards those objects that are proportionate to our senses and sense appetites. Hence, even prescinding from the corruption of our nature, it is no

19 [NRSV: '… when Christ came into the world, he said, "Sacrifices and offerings you have not desired, but a body you have prepared for me; in burnt offerings and sin offerings you have taken no pleasure. Then I said, 'See, God, I have come to do your will, O God' (in the scroll of the book it is written of me)."']

naturae, non parvae virtutis est corpore perficere quaecumque approbat intellectus et optat voluntas intellectum sequens.

Iam vero Dei Verbum, caro factum (Io 1.14), ita corpus sibi aptatum habuit (Heb 10.5), ita carni et sanguini communicavit et participavit (Heb 2.14), ut fratribus per omnia similaretur (Heb 2.17) tentatus per omnia pro similitudine absque peccato (Heb 4.15). Cumque inter opera supernaturalia opus supremum non solum mente sed etiam corpore perfecturus fuerit, mirari non possumus quam narrant evangelia coartationem (Lc 12.50), quam animae conturbationem (Io 12.27), quod desiderium (Lc 22.15), quem pavorem, quod taedium, quam tristitiam usque ad mortem (Mc 14.34).

Quae cum ita sint,[20] dicendum videtur ideo Christum passionibus esse consummatum seu perfectum (Heb 2.10) et ideo ex iis quae passus est obedientiam didicisse (Heb 5.8) quod actus exterior interioribus actibus eo plus perfectionis addit quo magis opus intellectu et voluntate intentum proportionem sensibilitatis et corporis excedit.

Quam Christi obedientiam usque ad mortem, mortem autem crucis, et liberam fuisse et meritoriam dubitari non potest. Nam ipse suam libertatem affirmat (Io 10.17–18) seque posse a Patre impetrare sui liberationem e manibus Iudaeorum (Mt 26.53). Cumque opus excellentissimum peregerit viator, sane praemio dignum fuit. Quod innuit Apostolus docens Christum propter humilitatem et obedientiam esse exaltatum (Phil 2.9); quod pariter insinuat epistola ad Hebraeos cum Iesum affirmet propter passionem mortis gloria et honore coronatum (Heb 2.9); quod vidimus in eo contentum quod per unius obeditionem iusti constituuntur multi (Rom 5.19); quod docet concilium Tridentinum, causam nempe meritoriam nostrae iustificationis esse suam sanctissimam passionem in ligno crucis (DB 799).[21]

small act of virtue to perform externally with our bodies what the intellect judges as good and the will, following the intellect, chooses.

Now, the Word of God made flesh (John 1.14) had a body prepared for him (Hebrews 10.5) and took part in flesh and blood (Hebrews 2.14), so that he was like his brethren in every way (Hebrews 2.17) and was tested like us in every respect, yet without sin (Hebrews 4.15). And since among his supernatural works he was about to perform his supreme work not only with his mind but also with his body, it is no wonder that the gospels relate his anguish (Luke 12.50), his troubled soul (John 12.27), his longing (Luke 22.15), his fear, his weariness, his sorrow even unto death (Mark 14.34).

Accordingly,[20] it would seem that the reason why Christ is said to have been made perfect through suffering (Hebrews 2.10) and to have learned obedience by what he suffered (Hebrews 5.8) is that an external action adds to interior acts as much further perfection as a work intended by intellect and will exceeds the proportion of the sensibility and the body.

There is no doubt that this obedience of Christ unto death, the death of the cross, was free and meritorious. He himself affirms his freedom (John 10.17–18), and states that he can ask the Father to free him from the hands of the Jews (Matthew 26.53). When a person in this life has performed a most excellent action, he is surely worthy of a reward. St Paul suggests this in teaching that Christ was raised up on account of his lowliness and obedience (Philippians 2.9); and Hebrews implies the same thing when it speaks of Jesus being crowned with glory and honor on account of the death that he suffered (Hebrews 2.9). The same idea is to be found in the statement that through the obedience of one man, many are made just (Romans 5.19), a point confirmed by the teaching of the Council of Trent that the meritorious cause of our justification was his holy suffering on the wood of the cross (DB 799, [DS 1528–29, ND 1923]).[21]

20 [From this point to the end of the section, the discussion differs significantly from the corresponding treatment in thesis 15.]

21 See DB 790, [DS 1513, ND 510]: 'If anyone asserts that this sin of Adam … is taken away by any other remedy than through the merits of the unique mediator, our Lord Jesus Christ, who has reconciled us with the Father in his own blood …: let him be anathema.'

## Articulus xx: De vicaria passione[22]

Vicarium intelligimus qui quodammodo vice alterius vel agit vel patitur.

Vicarium sensu activo fuisse Christum dubitari non potest. Non enim nos sed ille pro nobis pretium nostrae redemptionis solvit. Neque nos sed ille pro nobis sacrificium Deo Patri obtulit. Neque nos sed ille pro nobis meritorie obedivit.

Quibus tamen in omnibus aspectus activus a passivo disiungi non potest. Nam non solum Christus pretium solvit sed etiam 'dare animam suam' erat pretium solvendum. Non solum ipse sacerdos sacrificium obtulit sed etiam hostia erat offerenda. Non solum Deo Patri obedivit, sed ipsa haec obedientia mortis acceptatio fuit.

Quapropter haud fieri potuit ut Christus ita vicarius vice nostra egerit ut non etiam vicarius vice nostra sit passus. Cum ergo tam saepe in sacris litteris repetatur vel 'pro nobis' vel 'pro nostris peccatis,' intelligit sensus fidelium non solum Christum egisse ut peccata nostra auferantur sed etiam eum ideo esse passum quia nos peccavimus.

Quae cum ita sint, de vicaria Christi passione inquirimus, non ut Christum ita egisse et fecisse probemus ut peccata tollerentur, sed ut Christum passum esse et mortuum demonstremus quia contra Deum ab hominibus peccatum est, peccatur, et peccabitur.

Quae quidem quaestio ponitur non tam de nudo facto quam de nexu causali. Facta supra vidimus, Christum scilicet pretium solvisse, sacrificium obtulisse, meritorie obedivisse. Nunc vero causam quaerimus, non quidem finalem quae in aperto est, sed antecedentem et moventem propter quam non aliud fuerit pretium quam 'dare animam suam,' neque alia fuerit sacrificii hostia quam corpus suum datum et sanguis suus effusus, neque alia fuerit obedientia quam acerbissimae in cruce mortis acceptatio.

Praeterea, antecedentem hanc atque moventem causam quaerimus secundum divinam intentionem. Potuit enim Christus passionem mortemque declinare (Mt 26.53). Voluisset calicem transferri, nisi aliam scivisset esse Patris voluntatem (Mc 14.36). Sed oportebat eum pati (Lc 24.26, 24.46). Definito consilio et praescientia Dei traditus est (Act 2.23, 4.28). Secundum

**Article 20: Vicarious suffering**[22]

We understand by 'vicarious' someone who acts or suffers in the stead of another.

Christ was undoubtedly vicarious in the active sense. For we did not pay the price of our redemption, but he did for us. We did not offer sacrifice to God the Father, but he did for us. We did not merit by obedience, but he did for us.

In all of these things it is not possible to separate the active aspect from the passive. Christ not only paid the price, but the price to be paid was 'to give his life'. He was not only the sacrificing priest but also the sacrificial victim. He not only obeyed the Father, but this very obedience consisted in the acceptance of death.

Thus it was impossible for Christ to act vicariously in our stead without by the same token suffering vicariously in our place. When, therefore, the words 'for us' or 'for our sins' are so often repeated in scripture, the sense of the faithful understands them in the sense that Christ not only acted to take away our sins but also that he suffered precisely because we sinned.

Accordingly, our inquiry into the vicarious suffering of Christ has as its purpose, not to prove that Christ acted in such a way that sins were taken away, but to show that he suffered and died because of past, present, and future sins against God on the part of human beings.

The question we pose regards not so much the mere facts as the causal link. The facts we have already noted, namely, that Christ paid the price, offered sacrifice, and obeyed meritoriously. Now we investigate the cause, not the final cause, which is obvious, but rather the antecedent moving cause because of which there was no other price to be paid except 'to give his life,' no other sacrificial victim than his body given and his blood poured out, and no other act of obedience than the acceptance of a most painful death on the cross.

Moreover, we are seeking this antecedent moving cause as it was in accordance with the intention of God. Christ could have refused to suffer and die (Matthew 26.53). He would have wanted the cup to be taken away from him except that he knew that the Father had willed otherwise (Mark 14.36). It was necessary for him to suffer (Luke 24.26, 24.46). It was by the deliberate intention and foreknowledge of God that he was handed over (Acts 2.23, 4.28). His death was in accordance with the scriptures (1 Corinthians

22 [This article is loosely parallel to thesis 15, part 4, above, pp. 44–53.]

scripturas mortuus est (1 Cor 15.3, Act 3.18). Deus Pater proprio suo Filio non pepercit sed pro nobis omnibus tradidit illum (Rom 8.32).

Quod si passio morsque Christi secundum divinam intentionem facta est, sane sine ratione non est facta. Quam rationem quaerimus et dicimus Christum ad nos redimendos, non in nubibus caeli et sedentem a dextris virtutis venisse, sed in carne passibili atque passura propter peccata. Ideo ergo Christus pro nobis vicarius non solum egit et fecit sed etiam passus et mortuus est, quia non solum vitam aeternam nobis communicandam habuit sed etiam peccata auferenda et peccatores Deo Patri reconciliandos.

Neque Christianum quemquam hoc dubitare posse censemus, cum tam saepe in sacris scripturis non actio Christi sed passio, non vita Christi sed mors, pro nobis et pro nostris peccatis esse dicatur. Pro omnibus enim mortuus est Christus (2 Cor 5.15, Heb 2.9), pro singulis (Rom 14.15, 1 Cor 8.11), pro impiis (Rom 5.6), pro nobis (Rom 5.8, 1 Thess 5.10) et pro nostris peccatis (1 Cor 15.3, 1 Pet 3.18). Unde et dicitur dedisse animam suam redemptionem pro multis (Mc 10.45, Mt 20.28) et pro omnibus (1Tim 2.6) seque dedisse pro nobis (Tit 2.14) et pro nostris peccatis (Gal 1.4), seque tradidisse pro nobis (Eph 5.2) et pro ecclesia (Eph 5.25) et pro me (Gal 2.20), et traditum esse pro nobis omnibus (Rom 8.32) et propter delicta nostra (Rom 4.25).

Quibus quamvis sufficiant accedit quod praetermittere non oportet. Nam apud Isaiam 53.4–12 narratur de quodam iusto (9cd, 11c) atque tacente (7d), qui propter iniquitates alienas (5abc, 7a, 8d, 11d, 12e) divina voluntate (6c, 10a) vulneratur, atteritur, conteritur, laborat, ponit animam suam, tradidit in mortem animam suam (5ab, 10ab, 11a, 12c) unde fructum duraturum meretur multorumque iustificationem (10cd, 11bc, 12ab). Qui quidem locus, etsi in multis et subtilioribus quaestionibus exegetas iam pridem occupet,[23] quoad sensum tamen generalem nostraeque intentioni sufficientem omnino clarus est. Praeterea, etsi non omnia de morte Domini fuerint semper intellecta (Mt 8.17, 10.6), in ipso tamen Novo Testamento locus uti messianicus habetur (Act 8.32–36) et de morte Domini intelligitur non solum brevioribus allusionibus (Mc 15.28, Lc 22.37, 23.34, Rom 4.25) sed

15.3, Acts 3.18). God the Father did not spare his own Son but gave him up for us all (Romans 8.32).

Now if the passion and death of Christ occurred according to the divine intention, it surely was not without reason. This is the reason we seek, and we say Christ came to redeem us, not on clouds of glory and sitting at the right hand of the Power, but in flesh that could suffer and would suffer on account of sin. And this, then, is why Christ did not only act vicariously for us, but also suffered and died vicariously for us: he not only had eternal life to impart to us, but also the task of taking away our sins and reconciling sinners with God the Father.

This is something that we feel no Christian can doubt, since in so many scriptural passages it is not the action of Christ but his passion, not the life of Christ but his death, that is said to be for us and for our sins. Christ died for all (2 Corinthians 5.15, Hebrews 2.9), for each (Romans 14.15, 1 Corinthians 8.11), for the ungodly (Romans 5.6), for us (Romans 5.8, 1 Thessalonians 5.10), and for our sins (1 Corinthians 15.3, 1 Peter 3.18). Hence he is said to have given his life as a ransom for many (Mark 10.45, Matthew 20.28) and for all (1 Timothy 2.6), to have given himself for us (Titus 2.14) and for our sins (Galatians 1.4), and to have handed himself over for us (Ephesians 5.2) and for the church (Ephesians 5.25) and for me (Galatians 2.20); and that he was handed over for us all (Romans 8.32) and because of our sins (Romans 4.25).

However sufficient all this may be, we may add the following, which ought not to go unmentioned. In Isaiah 53.4–12 reference is made to a certain just (9cd, 11c) and silent one (7d) who, on account of the iniquity of others (5abc, 7a, 8d, 11d, 12e), and by the divine will (6c, 10a), is wounded, bruised, crushed, burdened, lays down his life, and surrenders himself to death (5ab, 10ab, 11a, 12c), whereby he merits lasting fruit and justification for many (10cd, 11bc, 12ab). The sense of this passage, although it has long been a source of many difficulties for exegetes,[23] is in general quite clear and sufficient for our present purpose. Besides, even though many aspects of the death of Christ were not always understood (Matthew 8.17, 10.6), this passage in Isaiah was looked upon as a messianic passage in the New Testament itself (Acts 8.32–36) and understood as referring to the

23 Henri Cazelles, 'Les poèmes du serviteur: leur place, leur structure, leur théologie,' *Recherches de Science Religieuse* 43 (1955) 5–55; David M. Stanley, 'The Theme of the Servant of Yahweh in Primitive Christian Soteriology, and Its Transposition by St. Paul,' *Catholic Biblical Quarterly* 16 (1954) 385–425.

etiam longiori sermone (1 Pet 2.22–25). Imo vix dubitatur ipsum Iesum hunc locum de se intellexisse, et cum Filium hominis passurum, moriturum, resurrecturum praedixerit (Mc 9.12, 9.31, 10.33–34, 10.45), et cum mortem declinare potuerit et noluerit (Mt 26.53–54), et cum se mori oportuisse explicaverit (Lc 24.26, 24.46). Denique tandem constat traditionem Catholicam hunc locum de morte Domini et sponte et constanter interpretatam esse.

Caeterum, nec desunt scripturae loca quae speciali modo et nostra peccata et Dominum nostrum patientem atque morientem coniungant. Nam 'peccata nostra ipse pertulit in corpore suo super lignum … cuius livore sanati estis' (1 Pet 2.24); et 'traditus est propter delicta nostra' (Rom 4.25); et 'Deus Filium suum mittens in similitudinem carnis peccati et de peccato damnavit peccatum in carne' (Rom 8.3); et 'eum qui non noverat peccatum pro nobis peccatum fecit' (2 Cor 5.21);[24] et 'Christus nos redemit de maledicto legis factus pro nobis maledictum, quia scriptum est: "Maledictus omnis qui pendet in ligno"' (Gal 3.13, Deut 21.23); quibus accedunt quae de agno, sane symbolo passivitatis, dicuntur (1 Pet 1.19, Io 1.29, Apoc 7.14, 12.11).

**Articulus XXI: De virtute resurrectionis**[25]

Iam distinximus redemptionem ut medium et redemptionem ut finem. Et finis quidem erat omnia instaurare in Christo (Eph 1.10), medium autem pretii solutio, victimae a sacerdote oblatio, meritoria obedientia, passio morsque vicaria. Cum tamen regnum, quo omnia instaurantur atque reconciliantur (Col 1.8), filios Dei, qui erant dispersi, in unum congreget (Io 11.52), ideoque per paenitentiam atque fidem propagetur (Mc 1.15, Act 2.37–38), non tam per medium quam per mediatorem efficitur, neque tam in morte Christi constituitur quam in Christo mortuo atque resurrecto.[26]

death of the Lord not only in brief allusions (Mark 15.28, Luke 22.37, 23.34, Romans 4.25) but even in a longer passage (1 Peter 2.22–25). Indeed, Jesus must doubtless have understood it as referring to himself when he foretold the suffering, death, and resurrection of the Son of man (Mark 9.12, 9.31, 10.33–34, 10.45), when he could have refused death but would not (Matthew 26.53–54), and when he explained that it was necessary for him to die (Luke 24.26, 24.46). Finally, Catholic tradition has spontaneously and at all times understood this passage as referring to the death of the Lord.

Besides, there are a number of other scriptural passages which in a special way link our sins with the passion and death of the Lord. Thus: 'He himself bore our sins in his body on the cross ... by his wounds you have been healed' (1 Peter 2.24); he 'was handed over to death for our trespasses' (Romans 4.25); God 'by sending his own Son in the likeness of sinful flesh ... condemned sin in the flesh' (Romans 8.3); 'for our sake he made him to be sin who knew no sin' (2 Corinthians 5.21);[24] and, 'Christ redeemed us from the curse of the law by becoming a curse for us – for it is written, "Cursed is everyone who is hangs on a tree"' (Galatians 3.13, Deuteronomy 21.23). To all this may be added several references to the lamb, an obvious symbol of passivity (1 Peter 1.19, John 1.29, Revelation 7.14, 12.11).

### Article 21: The power of the resurrection[25]

We have made a distinction between redemption as means and redemption as end. As end, it was to restore all things in Christ (Ephesians 1.10); as means, it meant the payment of the price, the offering of the victim by the priest, meritorious obedience, and vicarious passion and death. However, since the kingdom is one in which all things are restored and reconciled (Colossians 1.18) and scattered children of God are gathered into one (John 11.52), and which is therefore propagated through repentance and faith (Mark 1.15, Acts 2.37–38), it is brought about by a mediator more than by a means and is established upon the death and resurrection of Christ rather than upon the fact of his death alone.[26]

24 Stanislaus Lyonnet, *Exegesis epistulae secundae ad Corinthios* 256–66.
25 [This section has some parallels to thesis 15, part 7, above, pp. 64–75.]
26 Durrwell, *La résurrection de Jésus*; Stanislas Lyonnet, 'La valeur sotériologique de la résurrection du Christ selon saint Paul,' *Gregorianum* 38 (1958) 295–318. [In the autograph, Lonergan just had 'S. Lyonnet, *Gregorianum*.' But in a roughly parallel text in *De Verbo incarnato*, found above on p. 69, after

Christus enim, mortificatus quidem carne vivificatus autem spiritu (1 Pet 3.18), non iam cognoscitur secundum carnem (2 Cor 5.16) cum factus sit spiritus vivificans (1 Cor 15.45, Io 6.62–63) et Filius Dei in virtute secundum spiritum sanctificationis ex resurrectione mortuorum (Rom 1.4, Act 13.33). Nam 'traditus est propter delicta nostra et resurrexit propter iustificationem nostram' (Rom 4.25). Quare 'si Christus non resurrexit, vana est fides vestra; adhuc enim estis in peccatis vestris' (1 Cor 15.17). Quod sane non ita intelligendum est quasi non sufficeret mors Christi ad peccata tollenda; sed ideo asseritur ut praeter medium nostrae salutis in mentem reducatur eiusdem mediator.[27] Sicut enim peccatum non est impersonalis quidam actus humanus malus sed Dei offensa, ita etiam per personam Filii mediatorem Deo Patri reconciliamur.

Quam ob causam, non in sola cruce moriens erat Christus noster sacerdos, sed factus est pontifex in aeternum (Heb 6.20, 7.28), melius sortitus ministerium (Heb 8.6), consedens in dextera sedis magnitudinis in caelis, sanctorum minister et tabernaculi veri quod fixit Dominus et non homo (Heb 8.1–2). 'Non enim in manufacta sancta Iesus introivit exemplaria verorum, sed in ipsum caelum, ut appareat nunc vultui Dei pro nobis' (Heb 9.24); unde et facit 'sanguinis aspersionem melius loquentem quam Abel' (Heb 12.24, Gen 4.10, 1 Pet 1.2); nam qui per aeternum spiritum semetipsum obtulit immaculatum Deo et aeternam redemptionem invenit, eius sanguis emundabit conscientiam nostram ab operibus mortuis ad serviendum Deo viventi (Heb 9.14, 9.12). Vivit enim (Heb 7.8) et sacerdos est non secundum legem mandati carnalis sed secundum virtutem vitae insolubilis

Having been put to death in the body but raised to life in the spirit (1 Peter 3.18), Christ is no longer known in the flesh (2 Corinthians 5.16), for he has become a life-giving spirit (1 Corinthians 15.45, John 6.62–63) and appointed the Son of God in power through the spirit of holiness by reason of his resurrection from the dead (Romans 1.4, Acts 13.33). For 'he was handed over to death for our trespasses and was raised for our justification' (Romans 4.25). Hence it follows that 'if Christ has not been raised, your faith is futile and you are still in your sins' (1 Corinthians 15.17). Of course, this is not to be understood in the sense that the death of Christ was insufficient to take away sin; rather, these things are said to bring to mind not only the means but also the mediator of our salvation.[27] Just as sin is not merely some impersonal human misdeed but an offense against God, so it is through the person of the Son as mediator that we are reconciled to God the Father.

This is why Christ is not only our priest in his death on the cross but has been made High Priest forever (Hebrews 6.20, 7.28), has been allotted a far higher ministry (Hebrews 8.6), sits at the right hand of the throne of majesty in the heavens, is the minister of the sanctuary and of the true tent which the Lord and not any mortal has set up (Hebrews 8.1–2). 'For Christ did not enter a sanctuary made by human hands, a mere copy of the true one, but he entered into heaven itself, now to appear in the presence of God on our behalf' (Hebrews 9.24). Hence the sprinkling of his blood speaks a better word than the blood of Abel (Hebrews 12.24, Genesis 4.10, 1 Peter 1.2); for the blood of him who offered himself as the perfect sacrifice to God through the eternal Spirit and won an eternal redemption for us will purify our conscience from dead works to serve the living God (Hebrews 9.14, 9.12). He still lives (Hebrews 7.8) and is a priest not by virtue of a law about physical descent, but by the power of an indestructible life (Hebrews 7.16) and 'he holds his priesthood permanently, because he

---

giving the Durrwell reference, he had '"Christus victor mortis," *Gregorianum* 39, 1958,' which is a series of articles by various authors on the resurrection. Presumably, therefore, Lonergan had in mind here the article in the series by Lyonnet.] Christopher R. North, *The Suffering Servant in Deutero-Isaiah: An Historical and Critical Study*, corrected ed. (Oxford: Oxford University Press, 1950). [Lonergan gave the reference for North's book as *The Servant Songs in Deutero-Isaiah* (Lund, 1951). But see above, p. 49, note 14.]

27 1 Timothy 2.5, Hebrews 8.6, 9.15, 12.24; see also 7.22. Spicq, 'Médiation – IV: Dans Le Nouveau Testament,' DBS V, 1020–83.

(Heb 7.16), et 'eo quod maneat in aeternum, sempiternum habet sacerdotium' (Heb 7.24) quo 'proximamus ad Deum' (Heb 7.19).

Imo, semper vivit ad interpellandum pro nobis (Heb 7.25) Christus Iesus qui mortuus est, immo qui resurrexit, qui est ad dexteram Dei, qui etiam interpellat pro nobis (Rom 8.34, cf. 1 Io 2.1). Quid autem interpellet narrare videtur S. Ioannes in illa oratione in qua dixit Iesus: 'Et iam non sum in mundo' et 'cum essem cum eis, ego servabam eos' (Io 17.11–12). Quo in loco, postquam pro se (Io 17.1–5) et pro apostolis (vv. 6–19) oravit, etiam eos memorat 'qui credituri sunt per verbum eorum in me' (v.20). Pro quibus orat 'ut unum sint, sicut tu, Pater, in me et ego in te, ut et ipsi in nobis unum sint' (vv. 21–22). Affirmat se iis illam claritatem dedisse quam Pater ipsi Christo dedit (v. 22); Patrem eos diligere sicut et Christum diligit (vv. 23, 26). Orat 'ut ubi sum ego et illi sint mecum, ut videant claritatem meam quam dedisti mihi, quia dilexisti me ante constitutionem mundi' (v. 24; cf. v. 5). Neque dubitari potest Christum, sicut se ipsum sanctum seu sacrum pro apostolis fecit, ita etiam se sacrum fecisse pro credituris (v. 19) quos etiam Deo offert (1 Pet 3.18; cf. 2.5).

Accedit quod ante glorificationem Iesu non est datus Spiritus (Io 7:39); 'si enim non abiero, Paraclitus non veniet ad vos; si autem abiero, mittam eum ad vos' (Io 16.7). Iam vero tam in Spiritu Dei nostri quam in nomine Domini Iesu Christi abluti, sanctificati, iustificati sumus (1 Cor 6.11); renascimur enim ex aqua et Spiritu sancto (Io 3.5) per lavacrum regenerationis et renovationis Spiritus sancti (Tit 3.5); et ideo filii adoptionis facti sumus quia misit Deus Spiritum Filii sui in corda nostra clamantem: 'Abba,' 'Pater' (Gal 4.6, Rom 8.15);[28] et per donum Spiritus sancti a Domino resurrecto factum accepta est potestas clavium (Io 20.22–23).

Quibus perspectis, quia 'consummatus factus est omnibus obtemperantibus sibi causa salutis aeternae, appellatus a Deo pontifex iuxta ordinem Melchisedech' (Heb 5.9–10), dicendum esse videtur non per solam mortem sed per mortem et resurrectionem causam salutis esse factam, qui non solum pro peccatis nostris mortuus est sed etiam resurrexit ut spiritus vivificans sit et sacerdos in aeternum, semper pro nobis interpellans, et Spiritum Patris nobis immittens et nos in caelo secum desiderans. Praeterea, cum

continues forever' (Hebrews 7.24), 'through which we approach God' (Hebrews 7.19).

Indeed he lives forever to intercede on our behalf (Hebrews 7.25) – Christ Jesus, who died but rose again, who sits at the right hand of God and who pleads for us (Romans 8.34; see 1 John 2.1). The fourth gospel seems to indicate the content of this pleading in the prayer in which Jesus says, 'I am no longer in the world,' and, 'While I was with them, I protected them' (John 17.11–12). In this same passage, after he prays for himself (vv. 1–5) and for the apostles (vv. 6–19), he goes on to mention 'those who will believe in me through their word' (v. 20). For these he prays 'that they may all be one. As you, Father, are in me and I am in you, may they also be in us' (vv. 21–22). He declares that he has given them the glory that the Father gave to him (v. 22); that the Father loves them just as he loves Christ (vv. 23, 26). He prays that they 'may be with me where I am, to see my glory, which you have given me because you loved me before the foundation of the world' (v. 24; see v. 5). There is no doubt that Christ, just as he sanctified or consecrated himself for the sake of his apostles, so also he consecrated himself for those who would come to believe in him (v. 19), those whom he offers to God (1 Peter 3.18; see 2.5).

Again, before Jesus' glorification the Spirit was not given (John 7.39): 'If I do not go away, the Advocate will not come to you; but if I go, I will send him to you' (John 16.7). In fact, we are washed clean, sanctified and justified in the Spirit of God as well as in the name of the Lord Jesus Christ (1 Corinthians 6.11); we are born again of water and the Holy Spirit (John 3.5) in the regenerative and restorative waters of the Holy Spirit (Titus 3.5). This is why we have become children by adoption: because God has sent into our hearts the Spirit of his Son crying out, 'Abba, Father!' (Galatians 4.6; Romans 8.15);[28] and by the gift of the Holy Spirit, the power of the keys was received from the risen Lord (John 20.22–23).

In view of all this, it seems it must be said that because 'having been made perfect, he became the source of eternal salvation for all who obey him, having been designated by God a high priest according to the order of Melchizedek' (Hebrews 5.9–10), he became the cause of our salvation not by his death alone but by his death and resurrection; that he not only died but also rose again for our sins to be a life-giving spirit, a priest forever, interceding for us always, imparting to us the Spirit of his Father and wanting

28 Silvero Zedda, *L'adozione a figli di Dio e lo Spirito santo: storia dell'interpretazione e teologia mistica di Gal. 4, 6* (Rome: Pontifical Biblical Institute, 1952.)

addatur 'causa omnibus obtemperantibus sibi,' causalitatis modus innui videtur. Nam a Patre persona mittitur Filius persona ad nos personas in opus reconciliationis, ut dilectio qua Filium proprium dilexit etiam nobis detur, ipse nempe Spiritus, qui est Amor a Patre Filioque procedens. Sicut enim in baptismo Christi et declaratur dilectio Patris erga Filium et eadem dilectio sub forma columbae apparuit, ita etiam in baptismo nostro dilectio Patris erga Filium propter Filium in filios adoptionis extenditur ut per donum Spiritus sancti clament 'Abba,' 'Pater'; quod quidem donum increatum cum creato gratiae dono et peccatorum remissione nectitur, uti alibi explicari solet.

us to be with him in heaven. Besides, the phrase 'the source [αἴτιος, 'cause'] of salvation for all who obey him' seems to indicate causality. For from the person of the Father there is sent the person of the Son to us persons in the work of reconciliation, so that the very same love with which the Father loves his own Son is given to us, that is, the Holy Spirit, who is Love proceeding from Father and Son. Just as at Christ's baptism the Father proclaimed his love for his Son, a love visibly symbolized in the form of a dove, so also in our baptism the Father's love for his Son is extended to his adopted children because of that Son, so that by the gift of the Spirit the sanctified cry out, 'Abba, Father!' This uncreated gift is bound up with the created gift of grace and the forgiveness of sins, as is explained in another treatise.

# Caput Quartum: De Cruce Christi[1]

Alias christianae fidei doctrinas saepius contingit quoad ipsum factum in Novo Testamento explicite contineri sed quoad pleniorem facti intelligentiam nisi a Patribus et theologis non explicite proponi. Sed nostrae redemptionis dogma, sicut abundantius in verbo Dei inspirato exponitur, ita etiam ea lege declaratur ut quemadmodum sit intelligendum haud dubitari possit. Crux enim Christi non solum factum quoddam est sed etiam praeceptum atque exemplum; Christo crucifixo conformari eique consociari debemus; neque aliud principium in tota nostrae salutis oeconomia altius iacet quam malorum in bonum transformatio. Quam ob causam, prius de ratione, lege, mysterio, iustitia crucis agendum esse duximus quam alias et theologicas quaestiones adgrederemur.

### Articulus XXII: De ratione crucis

Ratio crucis est mali in bonum transformatio, secundum illud 'Noli vinci a malo, sed vince in bono malum' (Rom 12.21). Dicit ergo (1) malum vincendum, (2) victoriam voluntariam, et (3) bonum e malo per victoriam ortum. Consideratur autem haec ratio tripliciter: nam prima est *analytica* consideratio quae ipsam rationem examinat; altera est *generalis* consideratio quae eandem rationem in tota vita christiana perspicit atque observat;

# 4 The Cross of Christ[1]

It is often the case with other doctrines of the Christian faith that their factual basis is usually contained explicitly in the New Testament while a fuller understanding of the facts is to be found explicitly only in the writings of the Fathers and the theologians. But as the dogma of our redemption is found most abundantly in the inspired word of God, so also by the same token it is so clearly presented there that the way it is to be understood is beyond doubt. For the cross of Christ is not only a fact but also a precept and an example: we are to be conformed to and associated with Christ crucified. In the whole economy of our salvation there is no higher principle than the transformation of evil into good. For this reason we have judged it best to treat the meaning, the law, the mystery, and the justice of the cross before going on to address other theological questions.

**Article 22: The meaning of the cross**

The meaning of the cross is the transformation of evil into good: 'Do not be overcome by evil, but overcome evil with good' (Romans 12.21). This implies (1) evil to be conquered, (2) a victory of the will, and (3) good that emerges from evil through this victory. Now this meaning can be considered in three ways: the first is an *analytic* consideration, which examines this meaning itself; the second is a *general* consideration, which grasps and

1 [The autograph may be found on the website www.bernardlonergan.com at 25330DTL060.]

tertia est *specialis* consideratio quae in Christo crucifixo Dei sapientiam contemplatur (1 Cor 1.23–24). Quare, analytice de ipsa crucis ratione agemus, generaliter de lege crucis quae vitam christianam informat, et specialiter de mysterio crucis quo salus nostra peracta est.

Circa ipsum malum vincendum, distingui oportet inter malum culpae et consequens malum poenae. Malum enim culpae est defectus rationalitatis intra ipsam rationalem conscientiam creaturae rationalis. Malum autem poenae includit omne malum consequens sive intra ipsum peccatorem, sive in actione eius exteriori, sive in situatione humana in peius mutata, sive in retributione iusta propter culpam inflicta. Quare in rebus humanis sufficienter dividitur malum in malum culpae et malum poenae,[2] si quidem mala quae ex causis naturalibus proveniunt quasi per accidens res humanas afficere reputantur.

Iam vero malum poenae non solum ex malo culpae oritur sed etiam vehementer in malum culpae inclinat. Nam conscientia rationalis est imago Dei intra hominem, et participata similitudo lucis increatae, et personalis habitudo ad lucem illam personalem quae omnem hominem illuminat. Qui ergo a propria rationalitate deficit et contra se ipse peccat quatenus participatam suam lucem facit tenebras, et contra Deum suum peccat quatenus a Deo illuminante et in vitam divinam invitante recedit ut a Deo separatus in tenebris habitet atque in umbra mortis. Attamen si 'lumen quod in te est tenebrae sunt' (Mt 6.23), non tamen simpliciter tenebrae sunt ut ulterioris peccati incapacitas oriatur, sed potius oculum internum faciunt nequam ut et verum bonum non cogitetur et vere malum facillime multiplicetur. Iterum, si bona conscientia te Deo coniungit, sollicitus es quae Domini sunt quomodo placeas Deo (1 Cor 7.32); sed si mala conscientia te a Deo seiungit, vivis alienatus et inimicus sensu in operibus malis (Col 1.21), spem non habens et sine Deo in hoc mundo (Eph 2.12).

observes this same meaning in the whole of Christian life; and the third is a *special* consideration, which contemplates the wisdom of God in Christ crucified (1 Corinthians 1.23–24). We shall deal, therefore, in an analytic way with the very meaning of the cross [the present article], in a general way with the law of the cross as it informs Christian life [article 23], and in a special way with the mystery of the cross by which our salvation was accomplished [article 24].

First, with regard to evil to be conquered, we must distinguish between culpable evil and the consequent evil of punishment. Culpable evil is the absence of rationality within the rational consciousness of a rational creature. The evil of punishment includes every evil consequence, whether within sinners themselves, or in their external actions, or in a change for the worse in the human situation, or in just retribution imposed because of fault. The division, therefore, of evil in human affairs between culpable evil and the evil of punishment is sufficient,[2] since the evils that result from natural causes are considered as affecting humanity only *per accidens*, as it were.

The evil of punishment not only results from culpable evil but also strongly predisposes one to culpable evil. For rational consciousness is the image of God in us, a likeness by participation of uncreated light, and a personal orientation towards that personal light which enlightens every human being. Those who fail in their own rationality sin both against themselves by turning their participated light into darkness, and against their God by withdrawing from the God who gives them light and invites them into divine life, so that instead they dwell apart from God in darkness and in the shadow of death. Nevertheless, if 'the light in you is darkness' (Matthew 6.23), it is still not unrelieved darkness, in which case further sin would be impossible; rather it is a darkness that renders the inner eye of the mind evil, so that no thought is given to what is truly good, and the truly evil is readily multiplied. Again, if a good conscience unites you to God, you care about the Lord's affairs and are concerned about how to please God (1 Corinthians 7.32); but if a bad conscience separates you from God, you live as strangers and enemies [of God] in the way you think and in the evil things you do (see Colossians 1.21), having no hope and without God in the world (Ephesians 2.12).

2 Thomas Aquinas, *Summa theologiae*, 1, q. 48, a. 5.

Neque minus exteriora quam interiora peccati consectaria in peccatum inclinat. Si enim 'lumen quod in te est tenebrae sunt, ipsae tenebrae quantae erunt?' (Mt 6.23). Interior enim rationalitatis defectus in exteriori actione et in effectibus actionis sese repetit atque extendit. Ex quo fit ut in situatione peccatis corrupta cum personis peccato corruptis vivendum sit quatenus vivimus et collaborandum sit quatenus collaboramus. Quae sane vita atque collaboratio esse non potest nisi regnum peccati secundum quandam peccati legem, nisi mira quaedam supervenerit lux, nisi facta erit nova creatura, nisi data erit Dei iustitia.

Quod malum culpae et poenae secundum rationem crucis per victoriam voluntariam est vincendum. Haec ergo victoria non in eo est quod delentur peccatores ut nullum iam remaneat culpae vel poenae malum. Neque haec victoria in eo est quod suspenduntur leges naturales, psychologicae, sociales, religiosae, historicae, quibus ex privato et individuali malo culpae per innumera poenae mala premimur atque urgemur in mala culpae multiplicanda. Sed manentibus malo culpae et malo poenae, vincitur malum in bono per victoriam voluntariam.

At quomodo vincitur malum? Contraria contrariis curantur. Sicut oritur malum culpae per defectum conscientiae rationalis atque per aversionem a Deo, ita vincitur malum culpae per conversionem ad Deum et per restaurationem rationalis conscientiae. Sicut malum poenae in malum culpae inclinat quia tam interius quam exterius bonum reddit difficilius, ita vincitur malum poenae quatenus bonum, etiam iusto difficilius, efficitur. Praeterea, sicut multiplicatur malum culpae quatenus ex malo culpae malum poenae oritur et, donec vincatur, malum culpae repetitur, ita ipsa haec multiplicatio vincitur quatenus malum poenae per difficilius bonum patienter absorbetur.

Haec ergo victoria voluntaria non ipsam iustitiam respicit sed inter peccatores possibilitatem iustitiae. Ipsa enim humana iustitia reddit 'cuique suum' et 'ad aequalitatem.' Sed peccatum humanum sibi rapit quod alterius est, neque secundum mensuram rapit sed quantum potest. Peracto ergo peccato, statum qui ante peccatum erat quaerunt iusta tribunalia et iusta bella. Peracto peccato, ipsa iustitia aliud non intendit quam ut e rapientibus rapta eripiantur et iustis dominis restaurentur. Sed alia est haec iustitia victrix et alia est ratio crucis. Crucis victoriam reportant non iudices neque belli duces sed mites et humiles corde. Crucis victoria per legem 'meum alteri' vincit legem raptoris 'alterius mihi.' Crucis victoria per mensuram

The exterior consequences of sin, no less than its interior effects, predispose one towards further sin. For 'if the light in you is darkness, how great is the darkness!' (Matthew 6.23). An interior defect of rationality reproduces and prolongs itself in exterior action and the effects of action. Hence if one is to live and collaborate in a situation corrupted by sin, one must live and collaborate with persons corrupted by sin. Such living and collaborating can only be the reign of sin governed by a certain law of sin – unless some marvelous light shall have made its appearance, a new creation been established, the justice of God been given.

In accord with the meaning of the cross, culpable evil and the evil of punishment are to be conquered through a victory of the will. This victory is not a matter of destroying sinners so that no culpable evil or evil of punishment remains. Nor does this victory involve the suspension of natural, psychological, social, religious, or historical laws, by which, from culpable evils that are private and individual, we are oppressed by countless evils of punishment, and incited to multiply culpable evils. Rather, while culpable evil and the evil of punishment remain, evil is conquered by good through the victory of the will.

But how is evil conquered? Things are cured by their contraries. Just as culpable evil arises through a defect in rational consciousness and through turning away from God, so it is conquered through conversion to God and the restoration of rational consciousness. Just as the evil of punishment predisposes to culpable evil by making both interior and exterior good more difficult, so the evil of punishment is conquered inasmuch as the good, which is more difficult for the virtuous too, is done. Moreover, just as culpable evil is multiplied inasmuch as the evil of punishment arises from culpable evil and, until it is conquered, culpable evil keeps recurring, so this multiplication itself is conquered to the extent to which the evil of punishment is patiently absorbed by a more difficult good.

This victory of the will, therefore, does not regard justice itself but the possibility of justice among sinners. Human justice renders 'to each his own' and 'in equal measure.' But human sin seizes what belongs to another, and not up to a certain measure either, but takes as much as it can. After the sin has been committed, just tribunals or just wars seek to restore the state of affairs to what it was before the sin was committed. After the sin has been committed, justice itself seeks nothing but to plunder the plunderers of their plunder and restore it to the rightful owners. This conquering justice is one thing, however, and the meaning of the cross is quite another. Those who win the victory of the cross are not judges or military leaders but the

suae superabundantiae vincit avaritiam raptoris insatiabilem. Et similiter res se habet circa alias virtutes sicut et se habet circa iustitiam.

Tertio, considerandum est bonum e malo per victoriam ortum, quod quidem duplex est. Nam ipsa victoria in se maxime confert tum ad perfectionem vincentis tum ad situationem humanam in melius mutandam. Quibus accedit divina providentia quae facit ut diligentibus Deum omnia cooperentur in bonum (Rom 8.28); ex hac enim dilectione fit ut, sive bonum sive malum accipimus, vel aliud bonum vel maximum crucis bonum habeamus. Et Deus 'modicum passos ipse perficiet' (1 Pet 5.10) secundum mensuram suam bonam et confertam et coagitatam et supereffluentem (Lc 6.38).

### Articulus XXIII: De lege crucis

Lex crucis est ratio crucis prout ad novum testamentum pertinet.[3] Pertinet autem per modum praecepti, per modum exempli, conformationis, et consociationis, et per modum oeconomiae.

Praeceptum multipliciter declaratur. 'Audistis quia dictum est: Oculum pro oculo, et dentem pro dente. Ego autem dico vobis non resistere malo; sed si quis te percusserit in dexteram maxillam tuam, praebe illi et alteram; et ei qui vult tecum iudicio contendere et tunicam tuam tollere, dimitte ei et pallium; et quicumque te angariaverit mille passus, vade cum illo et alia duo. Qui petit a te, da ei; et volenti mutuari a te ne avertaris. Audistis quia dictum est: Diliges proximum tuum et odio habebis inimicum tuum. Ego autem dico vobis: Diligite inimicos vestros, benefacite his qui oderunt vos, ut sitis filii Patris vestri qui in caelis est, qui solem suum oriri facit super bonos et malos, et pluit super iustos et iniustos. Si enim diligitis eos qui vos diligunt, quem mercedem habebitis? Nonne et publicani hoc faciunt? Et si salutaveritis fratres vestros tantum, quid amplius facitis? Nonne et ethnici hoc faciunt? Estote ergo perfecti sicut et Pater vester caelestis perfectus est' (Mt 5.38–48).

gentle and humble of heart. The victory of the cross by its law, 'mine for the other,' conquers the law of the plunderer, 'the other's for me.' The victory of the cross by the measure of its own superabundance conquers the insatiable greed of the plunderer. And what we have said here in connection with the virtue of justice can be similarly applied to the other virtues as well.

Third, let us consider the good, which is indeed twofold, that arises from evil through this victory. For the victory itself greatly contributes both to the perfection of the one who wins it and to a change for the better in the human situation. To these, there is added divine providence, which makes all things work together unto good for those who love God (Romans 8.28); and from this love it comes to be that, whether good or evil comes our way, we shall have either another good, or the highest good, the good of the cross. And after you have suffered a little while, God himself will perfect you (1 Peter 5.10) with his 'good measure, pressed down, shaken together, running over' (Luke 6.38).

### Article 23: The law of the cross

The law of the cross is the meaning of the cross as it pertains to the new covenant.[3] It pertains to the new covenant by way of precept, by way of example, conformation, and association, and by way of the economy of salvation.

The precept is proclaimed in many ways. 'You have heard that it was said, "An eye for an eye, and a tooth for a tooth." But I say to you, Do not resist an evildoer. But if anyone strikes you on the right cheek, turn the other also; and if anyone wants to sue you and take your coat, give your cloak as well; and if anyone forces you to go one mile, go also the second mile. Give to everyone who begs from you, and do not refuse anyone who wants to borrow from you. You have heard that it was said, "You shall love your neighbor and hate your enemy." But I say to you, Love your enemies and pray for those who persecute you, so that you may be children of your Father in heaven; for he makes his sun rise on the evil and on the good, and sends rain on the righteous and on the unrighteous. For if you love those who love you, what reward do you have? Do not even the tax collectors do the same? And if you greet only your brothers and sisters, what more are you doing than others? Do not even the Gentiles do the same? Be perfect, therefore, as your heavenly Father is perfect' (Matthew 5.38–48).

3 [And so to the whole of Christian life; see above, p. 451.]

Iterum: 'Et convocata turba cum discipulis suis dixit eis: Si quis vult me sequi, deneget semetipsum et tollat crucem suam et sequatur me. Qui enim voluerit animam suam salvam facere, perdet eam; qui autem perdiderit animam suam propter me et evangelium, salvam faciet eam' (Mc 8.34–35).

Iterum: 'Amen, amen, dico vobis, nisi granum frumenti cadens in terram mortuum fuerit, ipsum solum manet; si autem mortuum fuerit, multum fructum affert. Qui amat animam suam perdet eam; et qui odit animam suam in hoc mundo, in vitam aeternam custodit eam' (Io 12.24–25).

Deinde per modum et praecepti et exempli: 'Iesus autem vocans eos ait illis: Scitis quia hi qui videntur principiari gentibus dominantur eis, et principes eorum potestatem habent ipsorum. Non ita est autem in vobis, sed quicumque voluerit fieri maior erit omnium minister, et quicumque voluerit in vobis primus esse erit omnium servus. Nam et Filius hominis non venit ut ministraretur ei sed ut ministraret et daret animam suam redemptionem pro multis' (Mc 10.42–45, Mt 20.25–28; cf. 1 Pet 5.3: 'neque ut dominantes in cleris').

Iterum per modum et praecepti et exempli: 'Haec est enim gratia, si propter Dei conscientiam sustinet quis tristitias, patiens iniuste. Quae enim est gloria si peccantes et colaphizati suffertis? Sed si bene facientes patienter sustinetis, haec est gratia apud Deum. In hoc enim vocati estis, quia et Christus passus est pro vobis, vobis relinquens exemplum ut sequamini vestigia eius. Qui peccatum non fecit, nec inventus est dolus in ore eius; qui cum malediceretur non maledicebat; cum pateretur non comminabatur; tradebat autem se iudicanti se iniuste.[4] Qui peccata nostra ipse pertulit in corpore suo super lignum ut peccatis mortui, iustitiae vivamus; cuius livore sanati estis' (1 Pet 2.19–24).

Iterum per modum praecepti et exempli, cum S. Paulus Philippenses exhortatus sit ut 'in humilitate superiores sibi invicem' arbitrentur (Phil 2.3), eius attulit exemplum qui semet ipsum exinanivit formam servi accipiens, et semet ipsum humiliavit factus obediens usque ad mortem crucis (Phil 2.3, 2.7–8).

Again: 'He called the crowd with his disciples, and said to them, "If any want to become my followers, let them deny themselves and take up their cross and follow me. For those who want to save their life will lose it, and those who lose their life for my sake, and the sake of the gospel, will save it' (Mark 8.34–35).

Again: 'Very truly, I tell you, unless a grain of wheat falls into the earth and dies, it remains just a single grain; but if it dies, it bears much fruit. Those who love their life lose it, and those who hate their life in this world will keep it for eternal life' (John 12.24–25).

Next, by way of both precept and example: 'Jesus called [the twelve] and said to them, "You know that among the Gentiles those whom they recognize as their rulers lord it over them, and their great ones are tyrants over them. But it is not so among you; but whoever wishes to become great among you must be your servant, and whoever wishes to be first among you must be slave of all. For the Son of man came not to be served but to serve, and to give his life a ransom for many' (Mark 10.42–45, Matthew 20.25–28; see also 1 Peter 5.3: 'Do not lord it over those in your charge').

Again by way of both precept and example: 'For it is a credit to you if, being aware of God, you endure pain while suffering unjustly. If you endure when you are beaten for doing wrong, what credit is that? But if you endure when you do right and suffer for it, you have God's approval. For to this you have been called, because Christ also suffered for you, leaving you an example, so that you should follow in his steps. "He committed no sin, and no deceit was found in his mouth." When he was abused, he did not return abuse; when he suffered, he did not threaten, but he entrusted himself to the one who judges justly.[4] He himself bore our sins in his body on the cross, so that, free from sins, we might live for righteousness; by his wounds you have been healed' (1 Peter 2.19–24).

Once again by way of precept and example, when St Paul exhorted the Philippians, 'in humility regard others as better than yourselves,' he adduced the example of Christ who 'emptied himself, taking the form of a slave … and humbled himself and became obedient to the point of death – even death on a cross' (Philippians 2.3, 2.7–8).

4 [In fact, Lonergan's Latin follows the Vulgate translation, which means 'handed himself over to the one who judges unjustly.' Both readings are represented in the manuscript tradition, but the translation here follows the reading preferred by the best critical editions.]

Ulterius, per modum conformationis et consociationis. Sicut enim Dominus noster secundum mandatum Patris sui posuit animam suam ut iterum sumeret eam (Io 10.17–18), ita nos compatimur ut conglorificemur (Rom 8.17). Quare, socii passionum eius configuramur morti eius si quomodo occurramus ad resurrectionem quae est ex mortuis (Phil 3.10–11). Et communicantes Christi passionibus nunc quidem gaudemus ut in revelatione gloriae eius exultemus (1 Pet 4.13). Quia enim mundus, sicut magistrum, ita discipulos odio habet (Io 17.14), dixit Paulus minister: 'Gaudeo in passionibus pro vobis et adimpleo ea quae desunt passionum Christi in carne mea pro corpore eius quod est ecclesia' (Col 1.24). Quos enim praescivit Deus, eos praedestinavit conformes fieri imaginis Filii sui, ut sit ipse primogenitus in multis fratribus (Rom 8.29). Sed vix dici potest quantum in Novo Testamento inculcatur dilectio Christi crucifixi, eius imitatio, ad eum conformatio, cum eo consociatio.[5]

Denique tandem ratio crucis in novo testamento legem facit ipsius oeconomiae. Non is enim erat mundi salvator quem exspectabant vel ipsi discipuli (Lc 24.21, Act 1.6), neque rationem crucis ante intellexerunt (Act 5.41) quam virtutem supervenientis Spiritus sancti accepissent (Act 1.8). Sapientia enim huius mundi erat quae salutem per deletionem status anterioris voluit, et illum iustitiae regnum his in terris exspectabat quod nullam iniustitiam a iustis patienter tolerandam haberet. Sed ipsa Dei virtus Deique sapientia in Christo crucifixo agnoscenda est; quamvis enim Iudaeis scandalum sit et Gentibus stultitia, attamen stultum Dei sapientius est hominibus et infirmum Dei fortius est hominibus (1 Cor 1.23–25). Quod vero ab homine animali agnosci non potest sed a solo spiritali, qui per Spiritum sanctum sensum Christi accepit (1 Cor 2.12–16, Io 8.37, 8.47).

Quantum autem totam nostrae salutis oeconomiam penetret ratio crucis, ex ipsa ratione crucis declaratur.

Furthermore, the law of the cross pertains to the new covenant by way of conformation to Christ and association with him. Just as our Lord on the command of his Father laid down his life so as to take it up again (John 10.17–18), so we suffer with him to be glorified with him (Romans 8.17). Thus, as companions in his sufferings, we become patterned upon his death, if in that way we may hope to attain to resurrection from the dead (Philippians 3.10–11). We find joy in sharing Christ's sufferings in this life because we shall experience a much greater joy when his glory is revealed (1 Peter 4.13). Because the world, having hated the Master, likewise hates his disciples (John 17.14), Paul, his minister, says, 'I am now rejoicing in my sufferings for your sake, and in my flesh I am completing what is lacking in Christ's afflictions for the sake of his body, that is, the church' (Colossians 1.24). For 'those whom he foreknew he also predestined to be conformed to the image of his Son, in order that he might be the firstborn of many children' (Romans 8.29). The New Testament passages that teach love for Christ crucified, imitation of him, conformation to him, and association with him are almost too numerous to mention.[5]

Finally, the meaning of the cross in the new covenant constitutes the law governing the economy of salvation. The Savior of the world was not the sort of savior expected even by his disciples (Luke 24.21, Acts 1.6), nor did they understand the meaning of the cross (Acts 5.41) until the Holy Spirit came down upon them with power (Acts 1.8). It was the wisdom of this world that wanted salvation through the annihilation of the previous state, and that was looking for a reign of justice in this world that would have no injustices to be patiently born by the just. But God's very power and God's wisdom are to be acknowledged in Christ crucified; for though a stumbling-block for Jews and foolishness to the Gentiles, yet the folly of God is wiser than human wisdom and the weakness of God is stronger than human strength (1 Corinthians 1.23–25). This, of course, cannot be grasped by the unspiritual person, but only by the spiritual person, who has received the mind of Christ through the Holy Spirit (1 Corinthians 2.12–16, John 8.37, 8.47).

How far the meaning of the cross should penetrate the whole economy of our salvation is clear from the very meaning of the cross itself.

5 For example, Romans 8.35–39, 12.2, 13.13–14, 1 Corinthians 15.49, 2 Corinthians 4.7–14, 5.14–15, Galatians 2.19–20, 3.26–28, 4.19, Ephesians 4.22–24, Philippians 3.20–21, Colossians 3.9–11.

Haec enim ratio malum vincendum praesupponit. Sed 'per unum hominem peccatum in hunc mundum intravit, et per peccatum mors, et ita in omnes homines mors pertransiit' (Rom 5.12); proinde 'regnavit peccatum in mortem' (Rom 5.21) et illa quidem amplitudine atque efficacia quam descripsit Apostolus (Romans 1.18–3.20, 7.4–25).

Porro, malum per victoriam voluntariam vincitur. Quae quidem victoria in primis est Christi, qui a se ipso posuit animam suam (Io 10.18) ut per mortem destrueret eum qui habebat mortis imperium, id est diabolum (Heb 2.14); ut sicut regnavit peccatum in mortem, ita et gratia regnet per iustitiam in vitam aeternam (Rom 5.21). Nam 'per hominem mors et per hominem resurrectio mortuorum, et sicut in Adam omnes moriuntur, ita in Christo omnes vivificabuntur' (1 Cor 15.21–22).

Quam voluntariam Christi victoriam imitamur et sacramentaliter et moraliter et physice. Sacramentaliter quatenus 'consepulti enim sumus cum illo per baptismum in mortem' (Rom 6.4, Col 2.12). Moraliter autem quatenus 'servi estis eius cui obeditis, sive peccati ad mortem sive obeditionis ad iustitiam' (Rom 6.16), quia 'prudentia carnis mors est, prudentia autem spiritus vita et pax' (Rom 8.6), et ideo 'si enim secundum carnem vixeritis, moriemini; si autem spiritu facta carnis mortificaveritis, vivetis' (Rom 8.13); sicut enim Christus est 'mortificatus quidem carne, vivificatus autem spiritu' (1 Pet 3.18), ita etiam 'peccata nostra ipse pertulit in corpore suo super lignum ut peccatis mortui, iustitiae vivamus' (1 Pet 2.24); et 'si unus pro omnibus mortuus est, ergo omnes mortui sunt, et pro omnibus mortuus est Christus ut et qui vivunt iam non sibi vivant sed ei qui pro ipsis mortuus est et resurrexit' (2 Cor 5.14–15; cf. Rom 14.7–9, Col 2.20; passim).[6] Sacramentali denique et morali victoriae succedit victoria physica, si quidem 'nostra conversatio in caelis est, unde etiam exspectamus Dominum nostrum Iesum Christum, qui reformabit corpus humilitatis nostrae configuratum corpori claritatis suae, secundum operationem qua etiam possit subicere sibi omnia' (Phil 3.20–21).

This meaning presupposes evil to be conquered. But 'sin came into the world through one man, and death came through sin, and so death spread to all' (Romans 5.12); just so, 'sin reigned in death' (Romans 5.21), and the scope and virulence of its reign is described by St Paul (Romans 1.18–3.20, 7.4–25).

Furthermore, evil is conquered by a victory of the will. This victory belongs first of all to Christ, who of his own accord laid down his life (John 10.18) that through death he might destroy the one who wielded the power of death, that is, the devil (Hebrews 2.14), so that just as sin reigned in death, now grace reigns through righteousness unto eternal life (Romans 5.21). For 'since death came through a human being, the resurrection of the dead has also come through a human being, for as all die in Adam, so all will be made alive in Christ' (1 Corinthians 15.21–22).

We imitate this victory of will on the part of Christ sacramentally, morally, and physically. We imitate it sacramentally in that 'we have been buried with him by baptism into death' (Romans 6.4, Colossians 2.12). We imitate it morally inasmuch as 'you are slaves of the one whom you obey, either of sin, which leads to death, or of obedience, which leads to righteousness' (Romans 6.16); for 'to set the mind on the flesh is death, but to set the mind on the Spirit is life and peace' (Romans 8.6). Therefore, 'if you live according to the flesh, you will die; but if by the Spirit you put to death the deeds of the body, you will live' (Romans 8.13). As Christ himself 'was put to death in the flesh, but made alive in the spirit' (1 Peter 3.18), he also 'bore our sins in his body on the cross, so that, free from sins, we might live for righteousness' (1 Peter 2.24); and if 'one has died for all, therefore all have died; – and he died for all, so that those who live might live no longer for themselves, but for him who died and was raised for them' (2 Corinthians 5.14–15; see also Romans 14.7–9; Colossians 2.20; passim).[6] Finally, physical victory follows upon sacramental and moral victory, since 'our citizenship is in heaven, and it is from there that we are expecting a Savior, the Lord Jesus Christ. He will transform the body of our humiliation that it may be conformed to the body of his glory, by the power that also enables him to make all things subject to himself' (Philippians 3.20–21).

6 [Presumably 'passim' refers to the New Testament. The theme of dying to self and living for Christ, or of moral participation in Christ's cross, is found throughout the New Testament, just as above Lonergan mentioned that the New Testament passages regarding imitation, conformation, and association are almost too numerous to mention.]

Tertium denique secundum rationem crucis est bonum victoriam consequens. 'Sed sicut scriptum est: Quod oculus non vidit, nec auris audivit, nec in cor hominis ascendit, quae praeparavit Deus iis qui diligunt illum' (1 Cor 2.9). Et tamen ex fructibus bonae arboris et malae ratiocinantes (Mt 7.17–18), aliquam huius rei intelligentiam consequi possumus (DB 1796).

Nam nostris temporibus inimici crucis Christi (Phil 3.18) ipsam crucis rationem impugnant. Dixit quidem Caiphas, pontifex anni illius: 'Vos nescitis quidquam nec cogitatis quia expedit vobis ut unus moriatur pro populo et non tota gens pereat' (Io 11.49–50). At Nietzsche non infirmum practici hominis argumentum protulit ex eo quod expedit, sed ipsam Dei sapientiam in Christo crucifixo manifestatam irrisit, quasi ratio crucis servorum mentem exprimeret qui propriam ignaviam virtutem nominare vellent. Iterum, cum Dominus professus sit se in hoc natum esse et in hoc in mundum venisse ut testimonium perhiberet veritati, respondit Pilatus, 'Quid est veritas?' (Io 18.37–38). At fortius respondit Marx dictam veritatem esse ideologiam ideo excogitatam ne plebs propria iura vindicaret. Ex quo factum est ut novum nostrorum temporum evangelium non dilectionem proximi sed odium, neque crucem sed revolutionem praedicet. Quos autem fructus haec profert arbor, in bellis immanibus et integris nationibus ad servitutem redactis conspicere possumus. Reiecta enim Christi lege, ad illud imperii atque dominii genus quodammodo redimus, quod ante Christum vigebat et martyrum sanguis vicit.

Bonae autem arboris fructus in primis in ipso Domino nostro resurrecto videmus qui est primitiae dormientium (1 Cor 15.20). Absorpta enim est mors in victoriam (1 Cor 15.54). Quod brevissimo temporis intervallo in se ipso transfigurato manifestavit Christus homo (Mc 9.2–10, 2 Pet 1.16–18), hoc corpus claritatis suae iam pridem sacerdos in aeternum habet. Cuius tamen claritatis causa interna non defuit, cum Christus homo apud Iordanem eandem vocem paternam audierit, 'Tu es Filius meus dilectus, in te complacui' (Mc 1.11, 9.7). Cum enim dilectio ad personam terminetur, eadem dilectione Deus Pater Filium Deum et Filium hominem diligit; quae quidem dilectio est ipse Spiritus sanctus seu Amor procedens, in baptismo

Third, finally, according to the meaning of the cross, good follows upon victory. 'As it is written, "What no eye has seen, nor ear heard, nor the human heart conceived, what God has prepared for those who love him"' (1 Corinthians 2.9). Nevertheless, by thinking about the fruits of the good tree and those of the bad tree (Matthew 7.17–18), we can arrive at some understanding of this matter (DB 1796, [DS 3016, ND 132]).

In our days the enemies of the cross of Christ (Philippians 3.18) attack the very idea of the cross. Caiaphas, the high priest that year, had pointed out, 'You know nothing at all! You do not understand that it is better for you to have one man die for the people than to have the whole nation destroyed' (John 11.49–50). Nietzsche, however, ignoring the practical man's weak argument from expediency, ridiculed the very idea of divine wisdom being manifested in Christ crucified, on the grounds that the meaning of the cross expresses a servile mentality that prefers to call its own cowardice virtue. Again, when the Lord declared that he was born and had come into the world to give testimony to the truth, Pilate replied, 'What is truth?' (John 18.37–38). But Marx's response was much stronger, saying that the truth in question was an ideology devised to keep the common people from claiming their rights. And so our age has a new gospel that preaches not the love but the hatred of one's neighbor, not the cross but revolution. The fruits of this tree are very obvious: widespread wars and whole nations reduced to servitude. Rejecting the law of Christ, we have in some sense gone back to those forms of despotism and domination that flourished before the time of Christ and were conquered by the blood of martyrs.

The fruits of the good tree, however, are to be seen first of all in the risen Lord himself, who is 'the first-fruits of those who have died' (1 Corinthians 15.20). Death is swallowed up in victory (1 Corinthians 15.54). The glory with which the man Christ Jesus was for a brief moment transfigured (Mark 9.2–10, 2 Peter 1.16–18) now shines forth from the body of the eternal high priest. The internal source of this glorification was not lacking, since the human Christ had heard by the river Jordan the voice of his Father declaring, 'You are my Son, the Beloved; with you I am well pleased' (Mark 1.11, 9.7). For since love is directed towards a person, God the Father loves the Son as God and the Son as a human being with the same love. And this love is none other than the Holy Spirit, Proceeding Love, symbolized at the

sub specie columbae figuratus (Mc 1.10), in monte autem per obumbrantem nubem intellectus (Mc 9.7).[7]

Iam vero 'quos praescivit, et praedestinavit conformes fieri imaginis Filii sui, ut sit ipse primogenitus in multis fratribus' (Rom 8.29). Quare Filius Patri de credituris dixit: 'Dilexisti eos sicut et me dilexisti;' et iterum, 'ut dilectio qua dilexisti me in ipsis sit' (Io 17.23, 17.26). Quae quidem dilectio dat adoptionem filiorum et donum increatum Spiritus sancti et creatum gratiae donum; quibus conducimur in vitam aeternam et in societatem civium caelestium per Christum Dominum nostrum. Consepulti enim cum Christo per baptismum in mortem (Rom 6.4), paternae dilectionis gratiam accipimus. Quod si compati debemus ut conglorificemur, non tamen 'condignae sunt passiones huius temporis ad futuram gloriam quae revelabitur in nobis' (Rom 8.17–18).

## Articulus XXIV: De mysterio crucis

Quod genus humanum secundum rationem crucis a peccatis redimitur, haud mysterium est. Qui enim peccat, difficilius sibi reddit bonum facere, et ideo malum in primis vincendum habet, et deinde voluntariam super malum victoriam, et tertio bonum ex victoria consequens. Quod autem Dei Filius ita carni et sanguini communicavit (Heb 2.14) ut ipse secundum rationem crucis genus humanum in vitam divinam redimeret, hoc magnum mysterium est in Christo et ecclesia (Eph 5.32; cf. 1 Cor 6.15–17), temporibus aeternis tacitum, nunc secundum praeceptum aeterni Dei ad obeditionem fidei patefactum et in cunctis gentibus cognitum (Rom 16.25–26); quod manifestum est in carne, iustificatum est in spiritu, apparuit angelis, praedicatum est in gentibus, creditum est in mundo, assumptum est in gloria (1 Tim 3.16).

baptism by the figure of a dove (Mark 1.10), and on Mount Tabor by the cloud overshadowing their intellects (Mark 9.7).[7]

'For those whom he foreknew he also predestined to be conformed to the image of his Son, in order that he might be the firstborn of many children' (Romans 8.29). For this reason, the Son said to his Father concerning those who would come to believe in him, 'You have loved them even as you have loved me'; and again, 'that the love with which you have loved me may be in them' (John 17.23, 17.26). This is the love that grants adoptive filiation and the uncreated gift of the Holy Spirit and the created gift of grace, by all of which we are led to eternal life and into the company of the saints through Christ our Lord. Having been buried with him by baptism into death (Romans 6.4), we have received the free gift of the Father's love. And if we have to suffer so as to share his glory, yet 'the sufferings of this present time are not worth comparing with the glory about to be revealed to us' (Romans 8.17–18).

## Article 24: The mystery of the cross

The fact that the human race is redeemed from sin in accord with the meaning of the cross is hardly a mystery. For those who sin make it more difficult for themselves to do good, and so first there is evil to be conquered, then the victory of will over evil, and thirdly the good that results from this victory. But the fact that the Son of God shared so completely in our flesh and blood (Hebrews 2.14) that he redeemed the human race into the life of God in accord with the meaning of the cross – this is indeed a great mystery, a mystery in Christ and in the church (Ephesians 5.32; see 1 Corinthians 6.15–17), a mystery kept secret for endless ages, but now disclosed by command of the eternal God for the obedience of faith, and made known in all nations (Romans 16.25–26), a mystery 'revealed in the flesh, vindicated in the spirit, seen by angels, proclaimed among Gentiles, believed in throughout the world, taken up in glory' (1 Timothy 3.16).

7 See Thomas Aquinas, *Summa theologiae,* 3, q. 45, a. 4, ad 2m; Lonergan, *Divinarum personarum* 215–39 [*De Deo trino: Pars systematica* 235–59; *The Triune God: Systematics* 472–521; see also Bernard Lonergan, 'Mystical Body of Christ,' in *Shorter Papers*, vol. 20 in Collected Works of Bernard Lonergan, ed. Robert C. Croken, Robert M. Doran, and H. Daniel Monsour (Toronto: University of Toronto Press, 2007) 107.].

Quod quidem mysterium est 'instaurare omnia in Christo' (Eph 1.9–10), et temporalem esse caecitatem in Israel (Rom 11.25–32), et 'gentes esse coheredes et concorporales et comparticipes promissionis eius' (Eph 3.6), et 'Christus in vobis, spes gloriae, quem nos annuntiamus' (Col 1.27–28), 'in quo habemus fiduciam et accessum in confidentia per fidem eius' (Eph 3.12; cf. Rom 5.1–2).

Quod regni mysterium ab excaecatis non agnoscitur (Mc 4.11–12, Is 6.9–10, Io 12.40, Act 26.28), sicut crucis mysterium mundanae sapientiae opponitur (1 Cor 1.23–25), et Dei sapientia quam in mysterio loquimur (1 Cor 2.7) a Deo per Spiritum suum nobis revelatur (1 Cor 2.10–16).

Quo in mysterio perspiciuntur Dei sapientia, voluntas, caritas, misericordia, atque iustitia. Nam Christus crucifixus est Dei sapientia (1 Cor 1.23–24); Christus factus est nobis sapientia a Deo (1 Cor 1.30); hanc Dei sapientiam loquebatur Paulus in mysterio (1 Cor 2.7); per mysterii praedicationem innotescit multiformis sapientia Dei (Eph 3.10); et in Christo Iesu sunt omnes thesauri sapientiae et scientiae absconditi (Col 2.2).

Idem proinde mysterium est 'sacramentum voluntatis suae' (Eph 1.9), qua voluntate Deus Pater prior dilexit nos (1 Io 4.9; cf. Rom 5.8, 8.32) et, cum essemus mortui peccatis, propter nimiam caritatem suam qua dilexit nos, dives in misericordia (Eph 2.4–5) erat in Christo mundum reconcilians sibi (2 Cor 5.19), et Christum proponens propitiationem ad ostensionem iustitiae suae, ut sit ipse iustus et iustificans eum qui est ex fide Iesu Christi (Rom 3.25–26).

Quod Dei consilium liberrimum fuisse constat, tum ex caritate et misericordia Dei Patris erga inimicos (Rom 5.8–10), tum ex libertate ipsius Christi (Io 10.17–18, Mt 26.53), tum ex consensu Patrum et theologorum.[8]

This mystery is 'to gather up all things in Christ' (Ephesians 1.9–10), that there be a temporary blindness in Israel (Romans 11.25–32), that 'the Gentiles have become fellow heirs, members of the same body, and sharers in the promise' (Ephesians 3.6), and that 'Christ [is] in you, the hope of glory, ... he whom we proclaim' (Colossians 1.27–28), 'in whom we have access to God in boldness and confidence through faith in him' (Ephesians 3.12; see Romans 5.1–2).

This mystery of the kingdom is not recognized by those who have been blinded (Mark 4.11–12, Isaiah 6.9–10, John 12.40, Acts 26.28), just as the mystery of the cross is opposed to the wisdom of the world (1 Corinthians 1.23–25), and the wisdom of God which we utter in secret (1 Corinthians 2.7.) is revealed to us by God through his Spirit (1 Corinthians 2.10–16).

In this mystery we may discern the wisdom, the will, the love, the mercy, and the justice of God. For Christ crucified is the wisdom of God (1 Corinthians 1.23–24); God has made Christ to be our wisdom (1 Corinthians 1.30); this is the wisdom of God that Paul speaks in secret (1 Corinthians 2.7); through the preaching of this mystery the manifold wisdom of God is made known (Ephesians 3.10); and in Christ Jesus are hidden all the treasures of wisdom and knowledge (Colossians 2.2).

This same mystery is 'the mystery of his will' (Ephesians 1.9), the will by which God the Father first loved us (1 John 4.9; see Romans 5.8, 8.32); and when we were dead through our sins, on account of the great love with which he loved us, God, rich in mercy (Ephesians 2.4–5), was in Christ reconciling the world to himself (2 Corinthians 5.19), appointing Christ to be a sacrifice of atonement so as to make his justice known: to show positively that he is just and that he justifies everyone who believes in Jesus Christ (Romans 3.25–26).

That this plan of God was a totally free choice is most certain, from the love and mercy of God the Father towards his enemies (Romans 5.8–10), from the freedom of Christ himself (John 10.17–18, Matthew 26.53), and from the consensus of the Fathers and theologians.[8]

8 Adhémar d'Alès, *De Verbo incarnato* 343. [The thesis d'Alès is arguing is: '*Redemptio generis humani nulla absoluta necessitate requirebatur, sed fuit purum divinae gratiae beneficium.*' See also Lonergan's discussion of Christ's freedom, *The Incarnate Word* 726–61.]

Quo sensu autem rationem mysterii in cruce Domini nostri agnoscere debeamus, paulo fusius declarandum esse videtur. Nam vi vocis in scripturis adhibitae, concludi non potest nisi secretum Dei consilium.[9] Praeterea, quamvis concilium Vaticanum ad doctrinam de mysteriis declarandam citationes ex contextu paulino (1 Cor 2.7–10) desumpserit, eas tamen modo generali de gratia et veritate quae per Iesum Christum facta est intellexit (DB 1795).

Constat tamen mysteria stricte dicta in nostra redemptione contineri, Patrem nempe misericordem, Filium incarnatum, Spiritum sanctificantem, finem absolute supernaturalem, et media ad finem suo modo proportionata.

Constat praeterea in opere nostrae redemptionis revelari Deum esse talem qualem naturaliter cognoscere non possumus. Etsi enim naturale rationis lumen demonstrare possit Deum esse sapientem, liberum, diligentem, misericordem, iustum, haec tamen omnia nisi ex analogia creaturarum non concludit. Quare ex Filio Dei incarnato, mortuo, resurrecto aliam longeque altiorem analogiam accipimus ad ipsum Deum cognoscendum prout in se est. Novam hanc divinae sapientiae notitiam celebrat S. Paulus (1 Cor 1.18–2.16, 3.18–19, Rom 11.33, 16.27). Novam hanc divinae misericordiae et caritatis notitiam admirati sunt non solum Novi Testamenti auctores sed etiam tota traditio Catholica. Quanta autem sit Dei libertas, nunc scimus ex eo quod libere homo factus est et libere obediens factus est usque ad mortem crucis. Qualis denique sit Dei iustitia, iam non solum ex analogia tribunalium et carcerum et patibulorum sed etiam ex Filio proprio crucifixo concludimus.

Sed praeter sensum theologicum, quo de mysteriis stricte dictis loquimur, alius est sensus quo de mysteriis vitae Christi vel de mysteriis coronae BMV loqui solemus. Et ita ipsum sensibile corpus Domini patiens, moriens, resurgens dicitur mysterium per quod ex sensibilibus ad intelligibilia et spiritualia et divina manuducimur. Qui quidem huius nominis sensus cum anteriori annectitur, cum Verbum caro factum sit Deus factus sensibilis, ut

We should perhaps explain a bit more fully in what sense we are to discern the meaning of mystery in the cross of the Lord. From the use of the word μυστήριον in scripture alone we could conclude only to its meaning as 'the hidden plan of God.'[9] Moreover, although the [First] Vatican Council quoted citations from a Pauline context (1 Corinthians 2.7–10) to illustrate its teaching on mysteries, it understood those citations in a general sense as referring to the grace and truth that come through Jesus Christ (DB 1795, [DS 3015, ND 131]).

There is nevertheless general agreement that the work of our redemption does involve mysteries in the strict sense of the word, namely, the merciful Father, the incarnate Son, the sanctifying Spirit, our absolutely supernatural end, and the means proportionate to that end.

There is likewise general agreement that in the work of our redemption God is revealed to be such as we could never know by our natural knowledge. Even if the natural light of reason can demonstrate that God is wise, free, loving, merciful, just, we draw these conclusions only by way of analogy from creatures. But from the Son's incarnation, death, and resurrection we receive another and much loftier analogy for coming to know God as he is in himself. St Paul often acclaims this new knowledge of God's wisdom (1 Corinthians 1.18–2.16, 3.18–19, Romans 11.33, 16.27). Both the authors of the New Testament and the whole Catholic tradition have marveled at this new awareness of divine mercy and love. How great is the sovereign freedom of God we now know from the fact that freely the Son became man and freely became obedient even to death on the cross. We know what God's justice is like, no longer only on the analogy of law courts and prisons and gallows, but also from the crucifixion of his own Son.

In addition to the theological meaning of the term by which we speak of mysteries in the strict sense, there is another sense in which we speak of the mysteries of the life of Christ or the mysteries of the Rosary of the Blessed Virgin Mary. In this way too the sensible body of the Lord, suffering, dying, and rising, can be called a mystery, since by it we are led from sensible things to those that are intelligible and spiritual and divine. Indeed, this

9 See D. Deden, 'Le "mystère" paulinien,' *Ephemerides theologicae Lovanienses* 13 (1936) 405–42; E. Vogt, '"Mysteria" in textibus Qumrān,' *Biblica* 37 (1956) 247–57; K. Prümm, 'Zur Phänomenologie des paulinischen Mysterion und dessen seelischer Aufnahme. Eine Übersicht,' *Biblica* 37 (1956) 135–61; K. Prümm, 'Mystères,' DBS VI, cols. 1–225. [The part of Prümm's article that discusses 'Le mystère dans la Bible' extends from col. 175 to col. 225.]

per propriam carnem manifestet mentem suam humanam atque cor suum humanum, per haec vero nobis ipsam suam divinitatem interpretetur.

Accedit proinde et alius sensus his ex extremo oppositus quo mysterium iniquitatis iam operari dicitur (2 Thess 2.7). Qui quidem sensus, nisi exacte consideratur, maximam difficultatem atque confusionem inferre solet. Nam praeter intelligibile quod proportionatum obiectum nostri intellectus in statu praesentis vitae constituit,[10] et praeter divinum intelligibile quod intellectum creatum excedit neque hac in vita nisi imperfecte et analogice intelligere non valemus (DB 1796), etiam datur irrationale, absurdum, non-intelligibile quod peccato ideo inest quia dictamini rectae rationis opponitur. Quod quidem irrationale et non-intelligibile multos decipit, quippe qui illud sicut et alia intelligere studeant. Sed sicut concipitur irrationale et non-intelligibile per negationem rationalitatis et intelligibilitatis, ita etiam circa idem non est aliud intelligendum nisi hoc quod irrationale qua tale et non-intelligibile qua tale non intelliguntur.

Praeterea, in mysterio crucis non solum coniunguntur mysteria divina quae nostrum intellectum excedunt quia nimis sunt intelligibilia, et non-intelligibilia peccata quae obiective ab intelligibilitate deficiunt, sed inter divinam excellentiam et peccati miseriam intercedit aliud valde ambiguum, quod maxime in morte conspicitur.

Nam in primis mors habet rationem poenae. Scriptum est enim 'in quocumque die comederis ex eo, morte morieris' (Gen 2.17, 3.19); et 'invidia autem diaboli mors introivit in orbem terrarum' (Sap 2.24); et 'per unum hominem peccatum in hunc mundum intravit, et per peccatum mors' (Rom 5.12); et 'finis illorum mors est' et 'stipendia peccati mors' (Rom 6.21, 6.23). Quae quidem omnia eam Dei iustitiam dicunt secundum quam ex peccato sequuntur retributio atque poena.

latter sense of the word is connected to the former, since the Word-made-flesh is God made sensible, so that through his own body he manifests his human mind and his human heart, and it is through these that he interprets his divinity for us.

Completely opposed to this is another sense of mystery, 'the mystery of iniquity already at work' (2 Thessalonians 2.7). If this meaning is not carefully considered it can create a great deal of difficulty and confusion. For in addition to the intelligible that constitutes the proportionate object of our intellect in this life,[10] and in addition also to the divine intelligible that exceeds the scope of a created intellect and hence is knowable to us in this life only imperfectly and by analogy (DB 1796, [DS 3016, ND 132]), there is also the irrational, the absurd, the nonintelligible which is that property of sin as being contrary to the dictates of right reason. This irrational and nonintelligible leads many astray, those, namely, who try to understand it as they would anything else. But just as the irrational and nonintelligible are conceived by way of a negation of rationality and intelligibility, so there is nothing about them to be understood except the fact that the irrational as such and the nonintelligible as such simply are not understood.

Moreover, in the mystery of the cross we find not only the divine mysteries, which by reason of their over-intelligibility exceed the scope of our intellects, together with nonintelligible sins, which objectively lack all intelligibility, but also another aspect, highly ambiguous, lying between the excellence of God and the wretchedness of sin, which is to be found especially in death.

First of all, death has the meaning of a punishment. We read in scripture, 'In the day that you eat of it [the tree of the knowledge of good and evil] you shall die' (Genesis 2.17, 3.19); 'through the devil's envy death entered the world' (Wisdom 2.24); 'sin came into the world through one man, and death came through sin' (Romans 5.12); 'the end of those things is death,' and 'the wages of sin is death' (Romans 6.21, 6.23). All of these passages speak of the justice of God in accordance with which retribution and punishment follow upon sin.

10 ['... in the *Pars prima* one reads that the proper object of human intellect is the *quidditas rei materialis.* This proper object is also the proportionate object of our intellects, their first object, their *primo et per se cognitum,* their object according to the state of the present life.' Lonergan, *Verbum* 168.]

Sed e contra mors etiam medium est. Nam 'ipse similiter participavit eisdem [carni et sanguini] ut per mortem destrueret eum qui habebat mortis imperium, id est diabolum' (Heb 2.14); et propter mortem crucis Deus Iesum exaltavit (Phil 2.9); et gloria et honore eum coronavit (Heb 2.9); et 'reconciliati sumus Deo per mortem Filii eius' (Rom 5.10); et 'mori lucrum' (Phil 1.21); et 'cum autem mortale hoc induerit immortalitatem, tunc fiet sermo qui scriptus est: Absorpta est mors in victoria' (1 Cor 15.54–55). Quae quidem omnia non Dei iram (Rom 1.18–32) atque infligendam poenam (Rom 2.4–9) dicunt sed illam salutis oeconomiam qua Deus Pater 'eripuit nos de potestate tenebrarum et transtulit in regnum Filii dilectionis suae' (Col. 1.13; cf. Eph 2.4–6).

Quod vero mors et poena peccati et salutis medium est, per aequivocum quendam eiusdem vocabuli usum minime explicatur. Nam ex ipsa crucis ratione constat ipsum malum quod ex peccato procedit per victoriam voluntariam in bonum esse transformandum. Poena ergo est mors inquantum ex peccato oritur (Rom 5.12); poena pariter est mors inquantum ad peccatum inclinat eos qui 'timore mortis per totam vitam obnoxii erant servituti' (Heb 2.15); at ipsa haec poena in medium salutis transformatur secundum divinam crucis sapientiam quae iudicavit non vetus malum delendum esse novumque bonum creandum secundum placita eschatologica et iudaica, sed ipsum vetus malum per hominem in bonum esse transmutandum. Nam 'per hominem mors et per hominem resurrectio mortuorum; et sicut in Adam omnes moriuntur, ita et in Christo omnes vivificabuntur' (1 Cor 15.21–22)

Quae cum ita sint, quo crucis mysterium et ordinatius dicatur et facilius retineatur, quinque enumerandi videntur eius modi seu aspectus, videlicet (1) symbolicus, (2) intellectualis, (3) voluntarius, (4) providentialis, et (5) divinus.

Imprimis ergo crux Domini est symbolum. Ipsum enim Christi crucifixi sensibile corpus sanguisque effusus et interiores actus mentis cordisque Christi repraesentant atque exprimunt nostrosque sensus sentimentaque percellunt, unde fructum spiritualem in aperitione oculorum voluntatisque affectibus percipimus. Quatenus ergo symbolum est, crux Christi (1) ratione sui in nostram sensibilitatem eamque totam agit, (2) ratione coniunctionis inter partem nostram sensitivam et intellectivam, ulterius agit in nostrum

On the other hand, death is also a means. For 'he himself likewise shared the same things [flesh and blood], so that through death he might destroy the one who has the power of death, that is, the devil' (Hebrews 2.14); and because of his death on the cross, God raised Jesus on high (Philippians 2.9) and crowned him with glory and honor (Hebrews 2.9); and 'we were reconciled to God through the death of his Son' (Romans 5.10); and 'dying is gain' (Philippians 1.21), and 'when this mortal body puts on immortality, then the saying that is written will be fulfilled: "Death has been swallowed up in victory"' (1 Corinthians 15.54–55). All of these passages speak not of the wrath of God (Romans 1.18–32) and of punishment to be meted out (Romans 2.4–9), but rather of that economy of salvation by which God the Father 'has rescued us from the power of darkness and transferred us into the kingdom of his beloved Son' (Colossians 1.13; see Ephesians 2.4–6).

That death is both the penalty for sin and the means of salvation cannot be explained by an equivocal use of the same word. From the meaning of the cross it is clear that the evil that flows from sin is to be transformed into good through the victory of the will. Death, therefore, is a penalty inasmuch as it results from sin (Romans 5.12); it is likewise a penalty inasmuch as it predisposes towards sin those 'who all their lives were held in slavery by the fear of death' (Hebrews 2.15). But this very penalty has been transformed into the means of salvation through the divine wisdom of the cross, which deemed it better not to wipe out past evil and create a totally new good, to the satisfaction of eschatological and Jewish expectations, but rather that the past evil itself should be transformed, through a human being, into good. 'For since death came through a human being, the resurrection of the dead has also come through a human being; for as all die in Adam, so all will be made alive in Christ' (1 Corinthians 15.21–22).

Accordingly, in order that the mystery of the cross may be presented in a more orderly way and be more easily remembered, we shall list five modes or aspects of it: symbolic, intellectual, volitional, providential, and divine.

First, the cross of the Lord is a symbol. The sensible body and poured-out blood of Christ crucified represent and express outwardly the interior acts of his mind and heart; they forcefully strike our senses and deeply move our emotions, so that we receive spiritual benefit from the very act of gazing at the crucifix and from the affections of our will. As a symbol, therefore, the cross of Christ (1) in and of itself acts upon the whole of our sensibility, (2) by reason of the intimate union between the sensitive and intellectual parts

intellectum atque voluntatem, et (3) ratione divinae gratiae intellectum illuminantis et voluntatem inspirantis, eos fructus producere solet propter quos contemplatio Christi patientis et morientis schola sanctitatis habetur.

Deinde, crux Christi dicit rationem quandam intelligibilem. Non ea enim est nostra redemptio quae mala antecedentia simpliciter delet et nova bona pro malis substituit, sed in eo consistit quod mala ex peccato provenientia per voluntariam victoriam in bona nova transformantur. Quae quidem crucis ratio tam in ipso praeeunte Christo (Mc 10.45, 1 Pet 2.19–24) quam in nobis subsequentibus (Mc 8.34, Mt 5.38–48) conspicitur. Et ipsa haec ratio, quamvis in se intelligibilis quidam sit rerum ordo a divina sapientia conceptus, attamen a nobis dupliciter non intelligitur. Nam quatenus peccatum praesupponit, non-intelligibile atque irrationale praesupponit quod obiective ab intelligibilitate deficit. Quatenus autem ipsam Dei sapientiam, caritatem, misericordiam, iustitiam revelat atque in ipsum Deum conducit, infinitam respicit intelligibilitatem quae a nobis hac in vita nisi imperfecte et analogice intelligere non possumus.

Tertio, crux Christi ex voluntate diversitatem accipit. Physice enim crucifixio Christi est una, sed moraliter dualitatem habet, cum alius alium crucifigat.[11] Quatenus ergo Christi crucifixio voluntaria erat voluntate Pilati et pontificum et turbae, gravissimum erat peccatum. Quatenus autem eadem Christi crucifixio voluntaria erat voluntate Christi acceptantis, opus erat perfectissimum.

Ideo ergo ratio crucis dicit mali in bonum transformationem, quia illud quod physice unum est duplicem moralitatem habere potest secundum diversas voluntates eorum qui crucem aliis imponunt et qui crucem ab aliis impositam patienter sustinent. Quapropter qui Dominum audit, proximum diligit; qui Dominum imitatur, crucem sustinet; qui aliis autem crucem imponit, a diabolo decipitur, cum non Christum sed Pilatum sequatur.

Quarto, accedit aspectus divinae intentionis atque consilii, qui differentiam facit inter crucem Christi et crucem ab aliis Christi sequacibus sustentam.[12] Quamvis enim in utraque eadem cernatur generalis crucis ratio, aliter tamen de duce et aliter de milite ratiocinandum est. Eadem in utraque

of our nature has a further effect upon our mind and will, and (3) by reason of divine grace enlightening our mind and inspiring our will produces those fruits of the spirit whereby the contemplation of the suffering and dying Christ is considered to be a school of holiness.

Second, the cross of Christ expresses some intelligible meaning. Our redemption is not a matter of utterly wiping out previous evils and putting new goods in their place, but consists rather in transforming the evils that result from sin into new goods through a victory of the will. This meaning of the cross is to be grasped both in Christ, who leads the way (Mark 10.45, 1 Peter 2.19–24), and in us his followers (Mark 8.34, Matthew 5.38–48). And although this meaning is intelligible in itself as being an order of reality conceived by divine wisdom, we fail in our understanding of it in two ways. For inasmuch as it presupposes sin, it presupposes the nonintelligible and irrational, which objectively falls short of intelligibility; and inasmuch as it manifests the wisdom, love, mercy, and justice of God and leads us to him, it involves that infinite intelligibility which in this life we can understand only imperfectly and by analogy.

Third, the cross of Christ admits a difference by reason of will. Physically the crucifixion was one reality but morally it was two, since one person was crucified and others did the crucifying.[11] As willed by Pilate and the priests and the crowd, the crucifixion of Christ was a most heinous sin; but as willed by an accepting Christ, it was a most excellent deed.

The cross, therefore, denotes transformation of evil into good because that which is physically one can have a twofold morality according to the different wills of those who lay the cross on others and those who patiently bear the cross laid upon them. Accordingly, the one who listens to the Lord loves his neighbor, and the one who imitates the Lord shoulders his cross; but one who lays a cross upon others is deceived by the devil, since he follows not Christ but Pilate.

Fourth, there is the further aspect of God's intention and plan, which creates a difference between the cross of Christ and the cross borne by his followers.[12] Although the same general meaning of the cross is discerned in both instances, we ought to think differently of the general than of the

11 Thomas Aquinas, *Summa theologiae*, 1-2, q. 20, a. 6, ad 2m.
12 Pope Leo the Great, *Sermones* 64, 3 [ML 54, 359–60]; Franks, *A History of the Doctrine of the Work of Christ*, vol. 1, 138.

cernitur generalis ratio, si quidem ipse Dominus affirmavit suam mortem esse exemplum disponibilitatis christianae (Mc 10.42–45) et S. Petrus passionem Domini exemplum nobis propositum docuit ut sequamur vestigia eius (1 Pet 2.19–24). At generica haec identitas differentiam specificam minime impedit, cum Dominus noster per suam crucem non pro suis sed pro alienis peccatis satisfecerit, non sibi soli sed generi humano resurrectionem meruerit, se pro aliis victimam obtulerit, pro multis pretium suam vitam dederit. Quare, quamvis malum sit vincendum per victoriam voluntariam tam a nobis quam a Christo, secundum intentionem divinam et propter dignitatem Filii Dei ipsa Christi victoria alterius victoriae omnis et causa exsistit et exemplar et motivum.

Quinto, denique, crux Christi est Dei revelatio. Nam longe altius Deum cognoscit qui Dei sapientiam Deique bonitatem concipit non ex analogia caeterarum creaturarum sed ex Christo homine eoque pro nobis mortuo atque resurrecto.

Accedit quod in divino hoc crucis aspectu iterantur quodammodo omnes aspectus huc usque enumerati, si quidem ab aeterno Deus totam crucis rationem concrete applicatam et sua sapientia concepit et sua bonitate elegit. At quamvis haec iteratio in aliis specialem difficultatem non faciat, novam tamen fallaciae occasionem iis praebere solet qui non-intelligibilitatem peccati omnino intelligendam esse ducant. Quod si paulo melius sapis, malum culpae dicis falsitatem ontologicam atque obiectivam,[13] idque in divinam sapientiam reducis non ordinantem sed prohibentem et praecognoscentem, in divinam autem voluntatem nullo modo volentem sed tantummodo permittentem.[14] Quantum autem ad malum naturalis defectus et malum poenae, quae Deus non directe sed indirecte vult,[15] aspectum distinguis antecedentem et consequentem. Quia enim Deus vult ordinem universi, posito uno malo, vi ipsius ordinis sequitur malum aliud. Quia autem Deus etiam de malis bonum educere vult, ortis malis conceditur etiam malorum remedium usque ad impaenitentiam finalem.[16]

soldier. The same general meaning is discerned in both because the Lord himself declared his death to be an example of Christian self-donation (Mark 10.42–45) and Peter sets the passion of the Lord before us as an example for us to follow in his steps (1 Peter 2.19–24). But this generic identity still allows for specific differences, since our Lord by his cross satisfied not for his own sins but for those of others, won resurrection not for himself alone but for the whole human race, offered himself as a victim on behalf of others, and gave his life as a ransom for many. Therefore, although evil is to be conquered by a victory of the will both on the part of Christ and on our part, in accordance with the divine intention and because of the exalted dignity of the Son of God, Christ's victory stands as the cause and exemplar and motive of every other such victory.

Fifth, finally, the cross of Christ is a revelation of God. One who grasps the wisdom and goodness of God not by analogy from creatures but from the human Christ Jesus and his death and resurrection on our behalf has a far more profound knowledge of God.

Here we may add that this divine aspect of the cross recapitulates, in a way, all the aspects mentioned above, since from eternity God in his wisdom conceived and in his goodness chose the whole concrete application of the meaning of the cross. Although this recapitulation does not in itself present any special difficulty, it does tend to lead astray those who think that the nonintelligibility of sin is something to be understood. But one who is a little wiser will affirm that culpable evil is ontological and objective falsity;[13] it reduces to divine wisdom, not as ordering, but as forbidding and foreseeing; and to divine will, not as willing it in any way whatever, but only as permitting.[14] In the matter of the evil of natural defects and the evil of punishment, which God wills only indirectly,[15] one must distinguish between an antecedent and a consequent aspect. Because God wills the order of the universe, given one evil, another follows in virtue of this order. But because God also wills to draw good out of evil, where there are evils there is also provided an antidote to these evils – all the way until final impenitence.[16]

13 Thomas Aquinas, *Summa theologiae*, 1, q. 17, a. 1. See above, chapter 1, article 5, and chapter 2, article 12.
14 Ibid. q. 19, a. 9, ad 3m.
15 Ibid.
16 Ibid. q. 48, a. 2, ad 3m.

## Articulus XXV: De iustitia crucis

Circa iustitiam crucis duo sunt consideranda: primo breviter recolenda sunt generalia principia circa divinam iustitiam; deinde haec principia rationi crucis sunt applicanda.

Et quantum ad generalia principia attinet, quia non erit impossibile apud Deum omne verbum (Lc 1.37), absolute potest Deus facere quodcumque internam contradictionem non implicat.[17] Deinde, quia sapientia Dei multiformis est (Eph 3.10), ita totum posse divinae potentiae comprehendit ut quodcumque Deus absolute potest facere, etiam sapientissime in divinam bonitatem manifestandam ordinare possit.[18] Tertio, quia ideo recta atque iusta est Dei voluntas quod quemlibet rerum ordinem ab infinita sapientia determinatum eligit exsequendum;[19] constat Deum summa rectitudine summaque iustitia facere posse quodcumque absolute potest facere. Quae cum ita sint, actualem rerum ordinem concludes et maxime convenientem esse quia divina sapientia eum ordinavit, et maxime iustum esse quia divina electio divinam sapientiam secuta est, et maxime liberum esse quia pari sapientia infinita et pari bonitate infinita potest Deus facere quodcumque absolute potest facere. Cui conclusioni aliam prudenter adiungis, nempe, theologum infinitam Dei sapientiam non habere et ideo eum illos alios rerum ordines pariter convenientes pariterque iustos quales sint dicere non posse. Quapropter quaerentibus utrum Deus aliter nos salvos facere potuisset, semper brevissime cum S. Augustino respondendum est: 'Poterat omnino; sed si aliter faceret, similiter vestrae stultitiae displiceret.'[20]

Deinde, cum principia nuperrime tradita tam actuali rerum ordini quam cuilibet ordini possibili conveniant, facillima est eorum applicatio. Quaecumque enim facta sunt, consilio divino facta sunt et liberrimo et sapientissimo et convenientissimo et rectissimo et iustissimo. Praeterea, uti supra habitum est, Deus per Christum hominem secundum rationem, legem, mysterium crucis nostram salutem operatus est. Quaecumque ergo ad hanc rationem, legem, mysterium pertinent, summa Dei sapientia, bonitate, libertate, et iustitia sunt a Deo facta.

## Article 25: The justice of the cross

Concerning the justice of the cross there are two points to be considered: first, a brief review of the general principles of divine justice; secondly, the application of these principles to the meaning of the cross.

As to general principles, since with God all things are possible (Luke 1.37), absolutely speaking God can do anything that does not involve an internal contradiction.[17] Again, since God's wisdom is manifold (Ephesians 3.10), it comprehends the entire range of the divine power, so that whatever God absolutely can do, he can also most wisely direct to the manifestation of divine goodness.[18] Third, God's will is right and just for this reason, that any order of reality it chooses to bring about has been determined by infinite wisdom;[19] hence it is clear that whatever God can do absolutely, he can do with the utmost rectitude and justice. From this we conclude that the actual order of things is most fitting because ordained by divine wisdom, most just because God's choice follows his wisdom, and most free because whatever God can do absolutely, he can do with an equally infinite wisdom and an equally infinite goodness. Here it might be prudent to add that theologians are not endowed with God's infinite wisdom and hence cannot say anything about the nature of those other equally fitting and just orders of reality. That is why when asked whether God could have saved us in some other way, we should answer very briefly with St Augustine, 'Of course he could have; but if he had, your foolishness would be just as unhappy.'[20]

Second, the application of these principles presents little difficulty, since they underlie every possible order as well as the actual order of things. Whatever is done is done in accordance with the supremely free, wise, fitting, right, and just divine plan. Besides, as we have already noted, God has wrought our salvation through the mediation of the human Christ Jesus by way of the meaning, law, and mystery of the cross. All that pertains, therefore, to this meaning, law, and mystery has been done by God with God's supreme wisdom, goodness, freedom, and justice.

17 Ibid. q. 25, a. 3.
18 Ibid. a. 5.
19 Ibid. q. 21, a. 1, ad 2m.
20 Augustine, *De agone Christiano* XI, 12; ML 40, 297.

Quod magis particulariter declarari potest si singula considerantur elementa quae in ratione, lege, mysterio crucis continentur. Quorum primum est ipsa divina intentio salvifica atque activitas; alterum est ratio atque lex crucis secundum quam evolvitur haec activitas; tertium est mediatoris interventio per quem activitas salvifica procedit; quartum est ipsum mediatorem secundum rationem crucis opus suum peragere; quintum denique est ea divinae bonitatis manifestatio quae mala fieri permittit ut de malis efficiat bonum.

Primum ergo elementum est ipsa divina intentio atque salvifica activitas quae bona deperdita restaurat et promissionem Abrahae factam (Act 3.25, Gal 3.8, 3.16–18, 3.29, 4.21–31) fideliter (Rom 4.20–21) adimplet. Quam salvificam activitatem nominavit S. Paulus Dei iustitiam (Rom 3.21–22, 3.25–26; cf. 3.20; Ps 142.2)[21] eamque Dei irae contraponit. In malis enim innumeris peccatum consequentibus revelatur ira Dei (Rom 1.18–3.20); sed iustitia Dei iusti et iustificantis manifestatur atque ostenditur per Christum a Deo propositum propitiatorium proprio sanguine aspersum, quo credentibus conceditur gratuita iustificatio, ut non glorietur omnis caro in conspectu eius (Rom 3.21–28, 1 Cor 1.29–31).

Alterum deinde elementum est decretum ut genus humanum secundum rationem crucis salvum fiat. Supposita enim divina intentione salvifica atque humano bono per malum culpae corrupto, *aut* bonum malo corruptum deletur et novum creatur bonum, *aut* vetus malum sine homine cooperante in bonum commutatur, *aut* malum in bonum per voluntariam hominis victoriam commutatur. Sed hoc tertium, in quo ratio crucis conspicitur, caeteris viis convenientius est. Si enim vetus et corruptum deletur et novum creatur bonum, non redimitur vetus sed deperditur. Neque restauratur bonum humanum mala voluntate corruptum nisi mala hominis voluntas redditur bona. Neque convenienter mala voluntas in bonam convertatur nisi ipsa voluntas suae in bonum conversioni consentit. Neque sufficienter bona facta est voluntas nisi mala malitiae suae consectaria per victoriam voluntariam in bonum commutare possit atque ita velit ut perficiat.

This will become clearer if we consider each of the elements that are contained in the meaning, law, and mystery of the cross. The first of these is God's salvific intention and activity; the second is the meaning and the law of the cross according to which this activity unfolds; the third is the intervention of the mediator through whom this salvific activity is carried out; the fourth is the fact that this mediator accomplished his work according to the meaning of the cross; the fifth, finally, is that manifestation of divine goodness which permits evils to happen so that good may be drawn out of them.

The first element, then, is God's intention and salvific activity to restore goods lost and fulfil his promise to Abraham (Acts 3.25, Galatians 3.8, 3.16–18, 3.29, 4.21–31) faithfully (Romans 4.20–21). Paul called this salvific activity the justice of God (Romans 3.21–22, 3.25–26; see 3.20; Psalm 142.2 [EVV],[21] and he makes it a counterpoint to the wrath of God. For God's wrath is revealed in the innumerable evils that result from sin (Romans 1.18–3.20), while the justice of a just and justifying God is made known and displayed in Christ, whom God appointed as a propitiatory sacrifice by the sprinkling of his own blood, through which the free gift of justification is granted to those who believe, so that the human race may have nothing to boast about before God (Romans 3.21–28, 1 Corinthians 1.29–31).

The second element is the decree to save the human race according to the meaning of the cross. Supposing God's salvific intention and the corruption of the human good by culpable evil, three possibilities follow: *either* to destroy the good corrupted by evil and create a completely new good in its place, *or* to transform the former evil into good without human cooperation, *or* to transform evil into good through a victory of the human will. Now this third alternative, which embodies the meaning of the cross, is more fitting than the first two. For if the former corrupted good is destroyed and a new one created, the former good is not redeemed but is utterly lost. Nor is there any restoration of the human good corrupted by an evil will unless human wills themselves are rendered good. And it is not fitting that an evil will should be converted to good without the will's consent to its conversion. Nor is the will made sufficiently good unless the evil consequences of its malice can be transformed into good through a victory of the will, and it wills to carry this out.

21 Lyonnet, *De peccato et redemptione* 242–49. See also the series of articles by Lyonnet in *Verbum Domini* 25 (1947).

Et hanc Dei iustitiam intellexerunt Patres qui diabolum non potentia sed iustitia vincendum fuisse dictitabant:

> Non autem diabolus potentia Dei sed iustitia superandus fuit. Nam quid Omnipotente potentius? Aut cuius creaturae potestas potestati Creatoris comparari potest? Sed cum diabolus vitio perversitatis suae factus sit amator potentiae et desertor oppugnatorque iustitiae; sic enim et homines eum tanto magis imitantur quanto magis neglecta vel etiam perosa iustitia potentiae student, eiusque vel adeptione laetantur vel inflammantur cupiditate: placuit Deo ut propter eruendum hominem de diaboli potestate non potentia diabolus sed iustitia vinceretur; atque ita homines imitantes Christum iustitia quaererent diabolum vincere non potentia … Hoc ergo tempore quo differtur potentia populi Dei, non repellet Dominus plebem suam et haereditatem suam non derelinquet; quantalibet acerba et indigna ipsa humilis atque infirma patiatur, quoadusque iustitia, quam nunc habet infirmitas piorum, convertatur in iudicium, hoc est, iudicandi accipiat potestatem: quod iustis in fine servatur, cum praecedentem iustitiam ordine suo fuerit potentia subsecuta … Optandum est itaque ut potestas nunc detur, sed contra vitia propter quae vincenda potentes nolunt esse homines et volunt propter vincendos homines; utquid hoc, nisi ut vere victi falso vincant nec sint veritate sed opinione victores? Velit homo prudens esse, velit fortis, velit temperans, velit iustus, atque ut haec veraciter possit, potentiam plane optet atque appetat ut potens sit in se ipso et miro modo adversus se ipsum pro se ipso. Caetera vero quae bene vult et tamen non potest, sicut est immortalitas et vera ac plena felicitas, desiderare non cesset et patienter exspectet.[22]

Cur ergo non potentia sed iustitia superandus est diabolus? Quia potentia et dominium et potestas, quamvis in se non sint mala, illusio tamen sunt et error diaboli et gentium. Quia inter Christi sequaces maior est minister

The Fathers of the Church understood this justice of God very well, insisting that the devil had to be conquered not by power but by justice.

> The devil had to be overcome not by the power but by the justice of God. After all, what is mightier than the Almighty? And what creaturely power is comparable to the power of the Creator? Just as the devil through his perversity has become a lover of power and a fugitive from and opponent of justice, so do human beings imitate him to the extent to which they neglect or even detest justice and strive for power instead, being inflamed with a desire for it and exulting in its possession. Hence God chose to rescue us from the power of the devil not by conquest of force but of justice; and so we imitate Christ in seeking to conquer the devil by justice rather than by power … During these times, therefore, when the power of God's people is deferred, the Lord will not reject his people or abandon his inheritance. Whatever afflictions and outrages this lowly and weak people may have to suffer, the time will come when justice, which the weakness of the devout faithful now possesses, will be turned to judgment, that is, will receive the power to judge. This power is being kept for the just until the last days, when it will succeed the prior justice in due course … At the present time, therefore, power is most desirable, power, that is, against sin and vice. Against these, however, men are not interested in having power, but are very desirous of having power to put down their fellow men. So what can be said, except that the victors are falsely so considered and are really the vanquished: they are victorious not in truth but in the eyes of men. Let man desire prudence, fortitude, temperance, and justice; and so that he might truly be able to possess these virtues, let him wholeheartedly desire and seek power over himself, a power that is paradoxically both against himself and for his good. As for other things that he may laudably desire and yet cannot get for himself, such as immortality and the fullness of true happiness, let him not cease to desire them, but await them patiently.[22]

Why, then, do we say that the devil must be overcome by justice rather than by power? Because power and dominion and might, although not evil in themselves, are an illusion and the error of the devil and of the nations.

22 Augustine, *De Trinitate* XIII, xiii, 17; ML 42, 1026–27.

et primus est omnium servus, sicut et Filius hominis non venit ut ministraretur ei sed ut ministraret et dare animam suam redemptionem pro multis (Mc 10.42–45).

Tertium autem elementum erat ut activitas salvifica per mediatorem fieret, ipsum, scilicet, proprium Dei Filium. Iam vero regnum Dei *aut* simul per omnes conversos incipit, *aut* per quosdam simul conversos qui caeteros ad conversionem induceret, *aut* per unum quendam totius oeconomiae fundamentum atque caput. Et tertium caeteris convenientius fuisse constat. Nam omnes homines non sunt simul sed successivis generationibus oriuntur atque moriuntur; neque salvatur communis rerum cursus ordoque a divina sapientia constitutus si omnes qui uno tempore vivunt homines simul e multis et diversis malis in unum verumque bonum miraculoso quodam interventu divino efficaciter convertuntur. Praeterea, assignari haud potest ratio cur omissis aliis quidam primo in bonum convertantur et potestatem alios convertendi accipiant; quod si ratio deest, a convenientia deficit etiam altera via. Remanet ergo ut per unum hominem incipiat regnum Dei, et eo convenientius hic unus seligitur quo magis in se ipso rationem habeat cur caeteri[23] in regnum per eum conducantur. Quae quidem ratio facillime in Filio Dei conspicitur. Nam 'qui etiam proprio Filio suo non pepercit sed pro nobis omnibus tradidit illum, quo modo non etiam cum illo omnia nobis donabit?' (Rom 8.32). Dato ergo Filio, dari debent omnia. Sicut autem prorsus sufficiens est ratio quae in Filio Dei invenitur, ita etiam quodammodo necessaria est. Qui enim in adoptionem filiorum praedestinantur, tamquam filii essent diliguntur. Neque alia est ratio cur peccatores tamquam filii diligantur nisi [quia] Filio consociantur atque conformantur, 'ut dilectio qua dilexisti me in ipsis sit,' secundum illud 'dilexisti eos sicut et me dilexisti' (Io 17.26, 17.23). Quapropter et illud patristicum retinemus, Filium Dei hominem esse factum ut homines suam divinitatem participent.[24]

With the followers of Christ, the greater among them is a servant and the first among them is the slave of all, just as the Son of man himself came not to be served but to serve and give his life as a ransom for many (Mark 10.42–45).

The third element we mentioned was the fact that the work of salvation was carried out through a mediator, namely, God's own Son. The kingdom of God could be inaugurated *either* all at once through the conversion of all, *or* through some converted believers who in turn would convert all the others, *or* through one individual as the foundation and head of the whole economy of salvation. This third alternative was clearly more appropriate than the others. After all, human beings are not all in existence at the same time, but are born and die as one generation succeeds another. Nor would the common course of events and the order established by divine wisdom be maintained if all the people living at one given time were by some miraculous divine intervention successfully converted from a multitude of evils to the one true good. Again, there can be no reason why some should be left out and others first be converted to good and receive the power to convert the rest; and if no such reason exists, the second alternative also is inappropriate. It remains therefore for the kingdom of God to be inaugurated by one human being, and the most suitable person to be selected would be the one of whom it makes more sense that others[23] would be brought into the kingdom through him. Such a qualification is most easily to be seen in the Son of God. For 'he who did not withhold his own Son, but gave him up for all of us, will he not with him also give us everything else?' (Romans 8.32). Having given his Son, what can he refuse? And as this qualification in the Son is sufficient, it is also in a way necessary. For those who are predestined for adoption as children are loved as if they were children. There is no other reason why sinners should be loved as children unless they are associated with the Son and conformed to him, 'so that the love with which you have loved me may be in them,' since you 'have loved them even as you have loved me' (John 17.26, 17.23). Thus we fully agree with the saying of the Fathers, that the Son of God became man that we might share in his divinity.[24]

23 [Lonergan had 'caeteri' (nominative) but changed it to 'caeteros' (accusative). The editors have restored 'caeteri.']

24 Augustine, *Enarrationes in Psalmos,* Sermo 16, 6: ML 37, 1546: 'We should not become sharers in his divinity if he were not a sharer in our mortality.'

Quartum vero elementum erat ut mediator, etsi Filius Dei esset, secundum rationem crucis in salutem nos perduceret. Cuius rei quanta sit convenientia vix dici potest. Eatenus enim convenienter Deus Pater eadem dilectione ac proprium suum Filium etiam nos diligit, quatenus ex Filio et nobis efficitur unum. Eatenus ex Filio et nobis efficitur unum quatenus et Filius nobis assimilatur atque coniungitur et nos Filio assimilamur atque coniungimur.[25] Quae duplex assimilatio atque coniunctio quam convenientissime quamque efficacissime per ipsum Filium mediatorem facta est quatenus ipse secundum rationem crucis in salutem nos perducit.

Et prima quidem assimilatio atque coniunctio quae est Filii ad nos, per incarnationem et Incarnati dilectionem facta est. 'Quia ergo pueri communicaverunt carni et sanguini, et ipse similiter participavit eisdem' (Heb 2.14) 'per omnia fratribus' assimilatus (Heb 2.17). Verbum ergo caro factum est (Io 1.14), neque caelestem quandam carnem sibi assumpsit[26] sed ex muliere (Gal 4.4), ex semine David secundum carnem (Rom 1.3), ex Israelitis cognatis meis secundum carnem (Rom 9.3–4) formam servi accepit (Phil 2.7) et similitudinem carnis peccati (Rom 8.3). Corpus peccati quodammodo habuit ut in ipso crucifixo corpus peccati destrui posset (Rom 6.6), ut in sua carne damnari posset peccatum (Rom 8.3), ut peccatum pro nobis fieri posset (2 Cor 5.21). Sub dominio mortis quodammodo erat ut semel peccato mortuus non iam sub mortis dominio esset (Rom 6.9–11). Sub lege factus est (Gal 4.4) ut maledictionem legis subire et ideo benedictio Abrahae fieri posset (Gal 3.13–14). Eam carnis infirmitatem habuit ut ex ea crucifigi potuerit (2 Cor 13.4), et carne mortificari sed spiritu vivificari (1 Pet 3.18), et salutem impetrare (Heb 5.7) et aeternam invenire redemptionem (Heb 9.12), et secundo sine peccato esse appariturus (Heb 9.28). Eam assumpsit humanitatem ut per passionem eum perfici et consummari decuerit (Heb 2.10) et ex iis quae pateretur obedientiam addiscere potuerit (Heb 5.8), si quidem 'qui sanctificat et qui sanctificantur ex uno omnes' (Heb 2.11).[27]

The fourth element we mentioned was that the mediator, Son of God though he was, brings us to salvation according to the meaning of the cross. It is hard to put into words just how fitting this is. It is fitting for the Father to love us with the same love with which he loves his Son, to the extent that we and the Son are made one. But we and the Son are made one inasmuch as the Son is assimilated and joined to us and we in turn are assimilated and joined to the Son.[25] This twofold assimilation and union has been most fittingly and effectively accomplished by the Son as mediator in bringing us to salvation according to the meaning of the cross.

The first assimilation and union, of the Son to us, has been effected through the incarnation and the love of the Incarnate Word. 'Since, therefore, the children share flesh and blood, he himself likewise shared the same things' (Hebrews 2.14) and became 'like his brothers and sisters in every respect' (Hebrews 2.17). So the Word was made flesh (John 1.14), not by taking on some celestial flesh,[26] but flesh from a woman (Galatians 4.4), from the seed of David according to the flesh (Romans 1.3), and from 'my kindred according to the flesh,' the Israelites (Romans 9.3–4), taking the form of a slave (Philippians 2.7) and the likeness of sinful flesh (Romans 8.3). He had, in some way, the sinful body, that in its crucifixion the sinful body might be destroyed (Romans 6.6), that in his own flesh he might condemn sin (Romans 8.3), and that he might become sin for our sake (2 Corinthians 5.21). He was in some sense under the power of death so that having once died to sin, he might no longer be in death's power (Romans 6.9–11). He was born under the law (Galatians 4.4) so that he might be under the curse of the law and thus the blessing promised to Abraham might be fulfilled (Galatians 3.13–14). He had the weakness of the flesh so that from it he could be crucified (2 Corinthians 13.4), that in the body he could be put to death and raised to life in the spirit (1 Peter 3.18), obtain salvation (Hebrews 5.7) and win an eternal redemption (Hebrews 9.12), and he will appear a second time, having nothing any more to do with sin (Hebrews 9.28). It was fitting that he took to himself a human nature so as to be able to be perfected through suffering (Hebrews 2.10) and to learn obedience in the school of suffering (Hebrews 5.8), since 'the one who sanctifies and those who are sanctified all have one origin' (Hebrews 2.11).[27]

25 Ibid. Sermo 171, 3; ML 38, 934.
26 Augustine, *De Trinitate*, XIII, 18, 23; ML 42, 1032.
27 [Lonergan had a marginal note after 'uno': 'ex eadem stirpe ? Abrahae' ('from the same stock ? that of Abraham); clearly, the translation in NRSV has a different interpretation: '... all have one Father.']

Cui assimilationi in natura et stirpe et conditione sorteque humana accessit illa coniunctio, imo quasi identificatio, quam facit dilectio. Amicus enim amicum apprehendit ut 'alterum se' inquantum scilicet vult ei bonum sicut et sibi ipsi. Et inde est quod amicus dicitur esse *alter ipse*;[28] et Augustinus dicit in IV *Confessionum*: 'Bene quidam dixit de amico suo, dimidium animae meae.'[29] Quanta autem qualisque fuerit dilectio Christi erga nos, et ipse sicut factis ita etiam verbis testatus est, dicens: 'Maiorem hac dilectionem nemo habet ut animam suam ponat quis pro amicis suis' (Io 15.13). Sed quam intima, quam tenera, fuerit fortissima illa dilectio testatus est S. Paulus, quasi per transennam dicens: 'Viri, diligite uxores vestras sicut et Christus dilexit ecclesiam et se ipsum tradidit pro ea, ut illam sanctificaret mundans lavacro aquae in verbo vitae, ut exhiberet ipse sibi gloriosam ecclesiam non habentem maculam aut rugam aut aliquid huiusmodi sed ut sit sancta et immaculata. Ita et viri debent diligere uxores suas ut corpora sua. Qui suam uxorem diligit se ipsum diligit. Nemo enim umquam carnem suam odio habuit, sed nutrit et fovet eam, sicut et Christus ecclesiam, quia membra sumus corporis eius' (Eph 5.25–30; cf. 1 Cor 6.15–17).

Quod si inter virum et uxorem, inter amicos, omnia mea sunt tua et omnia tua sunt mea (cf. Io 17.10), quomodo fieri potuit ut nostram crucem suam non faceret Christus? Quinimmo, ita suam fecit ut eam esse nostram obliviscamur, eamque Christi esse dicere soleamus. At peccatoris est secundum rationem crucis in amicitiam divinam pervenire. Sed Christus peccatum non fecit (1 Pet 2.22) neque noverat (2 Cor 5.21) sed tentatus per omnia pro similitudine absque peccato (Heb 4.15); pontifex sanctus, innocens, impollutus, segregatus a peccatoribus sine necessitate offerendi pro propriis delictis (Heb 7.26–27), agnum immaculatum et incontaminatum (1 Pet 1.19) se ipsum Deo obtulit. Crucem ergo quae sua non erat suam fecit. Nos enim novit stultos et tardos corde ad credendum (Lc 24.25). Nos etiam novit magis exemplo quam praecepto esse docendos. Sed et illud novit: 'Ego si exaltatus fuero a terra, omnia traham ad me ipsum' (Io 12.32). Quam ob causam, non solum assimilationem atque coniunctionem sui ad nos effecit, sed modo maxime efficaci ad assimilationem et coniunctionem cum ipso nos invitavit.

In addition to this assimilation to our human nature and race, condition, and lot, there is that union, indeed a quasi-identification, that love brings about. A friend regards his friend as a 'second self' in that he wants the same good things for his friend as he does for himself. So it is that a friend is said to be one's 'other self';[28] and Augustine in the *Confessions* exclaims, 'Well has someone called his friend "half my soul."'[29] As to the greatness and excellence of Christ's love for us, he himself has given ample testimony by his deeds and also in his words: 'No one has greater love than this, to lay down one's life for one's friends' (John 15.13). But how intimate, how tender was that most powerful love is attested by St Paul, who says, as if in passing: 'Husbands, love your wives, just as Christ loved the church and gave himself up for her, in order to make her holy by cleansing her with the washing of water by the word, so as to present the church to himself in splendor, without a spot or wrinkle or anything of the kind – yes, so that she may be holy and without blemish. In the same way, husbands should love their wives as they do their own bodies. He who loves his wife loves himself. For no one ever hates his own body, but nourishes and tenderly cares for it, just as Christ does for the church, because we are members of his body' (Ephesians 5.25–30; see 1 Corinthians 6.15–17).

Now if between husband and wife, between friends, 'all mine are yours, and yours are mine' (see John 17.10), how could it be otherwise than that Christ should make our cross his own? So thoroughly did he do so, in fact, that we forget it is our cross and usually refer simply to 'the cross of Christ.' But in point of fact it is through the mystery of the cross that sinners are to come into friendship with God. Christ, however, was sinless (1 Peter 2.22) and a stranger to sin (2 Corinthians 5.21), tempted in every way as we are, though without sin (Hebrews 4.15); he was a holy priest, innocent, undefiled, sinless, without need of an offering for his own sins (Hebrews 7.26–27), who offered himself to God as a pure and spotless lamb (1 Peter 1.19). A cross, then, that was not his, he made his own. He knew that we are foolish and slow of heart to believe (Luke 24.25). He knew well that we are taught more effectively by example than by precept. And this also he knew, that 'I, when I am lifted up from the earth, will draw all people to myself' (John 12.32). For this reason, then, he not only assimilated and united himself to us, but in a most compelling manner invited us into assimilation and union with himself.

28 Aristotle, *Nicomachean Ethics*, IX, 1166a 31; see also 1171b 33.
29 Augustine, *Confessions*, IV, 6; ML 32, 698. See Thomas Aquinas, *Summa theologiae*, 1-2, q. 28, a. 1 c. [See above, p. 243, note 10.]

Age vero. Ipsa crucis acceptatio non tota crucis ratio est quippe quae malum culpae et consequens malum poenae praesupponat, neque tantummodo humanam super malum victoriam dicat sed etiam ad optimi Patris (Mt 7.11) larga dona conducat. Quam ergo crucem principes sacerdotum et Iudas proditor et turba urbana et Pilatus et milites Christo imposuerunt, ea obedientia acceptavit Christus ut et suam resurrectionem et gloriam (Phil 2.9, Heb 2.9) et nostram iustificationem (Rom 5.19) meritus sit. Eam passionem vicariam quam Christus subiit vicariam satisfactionem habuit Deus Pater pro nobis nostrisque peccatis (DB 799, 904). Eam crucis mortem sacrificium voluit Deus Pater a sacerdote aeterno oblatum. Illud dare animam suam pretium iudicavit solutum ut a potestate tenebrarum erepti (Col 1.13) populus acquisitionis (1 Pet 2.9) atque acceptabilis efficeremur.

Quibus peractis, ut symbolo utar antiquo, de latere Christi nata est ecclesia. Cum enim ex amore nostri nostram crucem acceptaverit Christus homo, quantum fieri potuit tantum fecit ut ipse se nobis assimilaret atque coniungeret; iterum, quantum fieri potuit per modum meriti, satisfactionis, sacrificii, redemptionis, atque humanae tractionis, tantum fecit ut nos ei assimilari atque coniungi consentiremur;[30] iam ergo in causa atque virtute exsistebat illa Capitis membrorumque unitas quae est ecclesia; propter quam unitatem Deus Pater dilectionem suam erga proprium Filium in membra Filio unita extendit ut filiorum adoptionem largiatur et Spiritum Filii sui in corda eorum mittat clamantem: 'Abba,' 'Pater' (Gal 4.5–6).

Quintum denique fuit elementum quod, hoc in rerum ordine per divinam sapientiam constituto, ea est divinae bonitatis manifestatio quae mala fieri permittit ut de malis efficiatur bonum. Quamvis enim Deus nullatenus sit auctor mali culpae quod divinae sapientiae per ontologicam et obiectivam suam falsitatem[31] opponitur, quod prohibet Deus neque directe neque indirecte vult,[32] idem tamen malum culpae et praecognoscit Deus et permittit quod nisi permisisset esset nullum prorsus. Praeterea, cum ipse Deus sit bonus, etiam haec Dei permissio bona est.[33] Quam Dei bonitatem ea lege agnoscere possumus quod bonitatem nobis analogice notam transcendentes, et ipsum bonum per essentiam dicentes, et solum Deum bonum

Note, however, that this acceptance of the cross itself does not exhaust the entire meaning of the cross, which presupposes culpable evil and the consequent evil of punishment, and does not only signify a human victory over evil but also opens the way to receiving the lavish gifts of a most excellent Father (Matthew 7.11). The cross laid upon him by the chief priests, Judas the traitor, the city mob, Pilate, and the soldiers, Christ accepted with such perfect obedience that he merited both his own glorious resurrection (Philippians 2.8–9, Hebrews 2.9) and our justification (Romans 5.19). Christ's vicarious suffering was accepted by God the Father as vicarious satisfaction for us and our sins (DB 799, 904, [DS 1529, 1690–91, ND 1932, 1631–32]). His death on the cross the Father willed to accept as a sacrifice offered by the eternal Priest. He judged the giving of his life to be the price of rescuing us from the power of darkness (Colossians 1.13) that we might be made acceptable to him, his very own people (1 Peter 2.9).

When this was all done, the church, according to the ancient symbolism, was born from the side of Christ. When out of love for us the human Christ accepted our cross, he did all he could to assimilate and unite himself to us; again, by way of merit, satisfaction, sacrifice, redemption, and drawing all people to himself, he did his utmost for our consent[30] to be assimilated and united to him. That unity of head and members which is the church already existed in its cause and virtually; and on account of this unity God the Father extended his love for his own Son to those members united to the Son, to bestow upon them adoptive filiation and to send the Spirit of his Son into their hearts crying, 'Abba, Father!' (Galatians 4.5–6).

The fifth element we mentioned was that in this present order of reality, established as it is by divine wisdom, there is manifested a divine goodness that permits evils to occur so that good may be made of them. Although God is in no way the author of culpable evil, which in its ontological and objective falsity[31] is opposed to divine wisdom and which God forbids and neither directly nor indirectly wills,[32] at the same time God both foreknows and permits culpable evil, which would not be at all were it not permitted. Furthermore, since God is good, this permission on his part is also good.[33] This goodness of God we can acknowledge in this law: that transcending the goodness analogically known to us, and declaring God good by essence,

30 [On 'consentiremur' see above, p. 373, note 33.]
31 Thomas Aquinas, *Summa theologiae*, 1, q. 17, a. 1.
32 Ibid. q. 19, a. 9.
33 Ibid. ad 3m.

confitentes (Mc 10.18) solumque Deum sapientem (Rom 16.27), vere theologi efficimur simulque adoratores in spiritu et veritate (Io 4.23–24). Cui gressui primo accedit alter: 'Neque enim omnipotens Deus ... rerum cui summa potestas, cum summe bonus sit, ullo modo sineret mali aliquid esse in operibus suis nisi usque adeo esset omnipotens et bonus ut bene faceret et de malo.'[34] Cui altero gressui addendus est tertius. Nam non aliter Deus e malis facit bonum quam secundum rationem, legem, mysterium, iustitiam crucis; neque ipse Deus aliis ita hanc voluntariam mali in bonum transmutationem imponit ut ipse, in omnibus primatum tenens, prius non faciat quod ab aliis in suam gloriam poscat.

and confessing that God alone is good (Mark 10.18) and God alone is wise (Romans 16.27), we are made true theologians and, at the same time, worshipers in spirit and in truth (John 4.23–24). To this first step is added a second: 'God, the all-powerful ruler of all things, being supremely good, would in no way allow any evil in his works were he not so omnipotent and good as to draw good even out of evil.'[34] And to this second step, a third is to be added. In no other way does God draw good out of evil than according to the meaning, the law, the mystery, and the justice of the cross. Nor does God himself lay this voluntary transformation of evil into good upon others without himself, holding first place in all things [see Colossians 1.18], being first to do what he asks of others for the sake of his glory.

34 Augustine, *Enchiridion*, XI; ML 40, 236. See Thomas Aquinas, *Summa theologiae*, 1, q. 48, a. 2, ad 3m.

# Caput Quintum: De Satisfactione Christi[1]

Cum doctrina de satisfactione Christi elementa alia ex scripturis et traditione ducat, alia autem ex speculatione S. Anselmi cur Deus homo, primo ipsam quaestionem dividimus (art. XXVI), et deinde Anselmianae disiunctionis intelligentiam quaerimus, quonam scilicet sensu dicatur aut satisfactio aut poena. Quem in finem, primo negamus absolute fieri non potuisse ut tertium praeter satisfactionem et poenam daretur (art. XXVII), deinde pariter negamus ita intelligendam esse satisfactionem ut ab ea per se omnis ratio poenae excludatur (art. XXVIII et XXIX), tertio denique negamus ipsas peccatorum poenas simpliciter dictas esse in Christum innocentem translatas (art. XXX). Quibus stabilitis, determinatur satisfactionem Christi esse intelligendam secundum analogiam satisfactionis sacramentalis (art. XXXI), Christum hominem de nostris peccatis doluisse (art. XXXII) et in expressionem huius doloris passionem mortemque suam acceptasse ut haec passio haecque mors satisfactionis rationem haberent (art. XXXIII) et quidem superabundantis (art. XXXIV).

### Articulus XXVI: Dividitur quaestio

Latinum nomen *satisfactio,* verbumque *satisfacere,* sensum acceperunt (1) ex usu communi, (2) ex usu iuridico, (3) ex usu theologico circa sacramentum

# 5 The Satisfaction Made by Christ[1]

Since the doctrine of Christ's satisfaction draws some of its elements from scripture and tradition and others from St Anselm's speculation about why God became human, we shall first divide the question itself (article 26), and then seek to understand the Anselmian disjunction 'either satisfaction or punishment.' To this end, we first of all deny the absolute impossibility of a third member besides satisfaction and punishment (article 27), next we likewise deny that satisfaction has to be understood in such a way as to exclude per se any notion of punishment (articles 28 and 29), and thirdly we deny that the punishments of sinners, as such, have been transferred to the sinless Christ (article 30). Having established these premises, we go on to determine that Christ's satisfaction is to be understood according to the analogy of sacramental satisfaction (article 31), that the human Christ grieved for our sins (article 32), and that as an expression of this sorrow he accepted his passion and death so that this passion and this death might have the meaning of satisfaction (article 33) and indeed of superabundant satisfaction (article 34).

**Article 26: Division of the question**

The noun 'satisfaction' and its corresponding verb 'satisfy' get their meaning (1) from common usage, (2) from juridical usage, (3) from theological

1 [The autograph may be found on the website www.bernardlonergan.com at 25340DTL060.]

paenitentiae, et (4) ex usu theologico circa redemptionem a Domino nostro peractam.

Communis usus multiplex fuit, sed de praesenti citari sufficit illud: 'Pilatus autem volens populo *satisfacere* dimisit illis Barabbam et tradidit Iesum flagellis caesum ut crucifigeretur' (Mc 15.15).

Iuridicus usus fundamentalis distinguit debiti solutionem atque satisfactionem: solvit qui modo praescripto procedit; satisfacit qui creditore libere consentiente alia quadem via debitum exstinguit.

In sacramento paenitentiae tres actus ipsius paenitentis quasi materiam ipsius sacramenti faciunt, contritio scilicet, confessio, atque satisfactio (DB 896, 904).

Denique ipse Christus pro nobis nostrisque peccatis satisfecisse affirmatur (DB 799, 904). Quo sensu autem Christus satisfecerit, cum non sit una omnium sententia, breviter dici non potest. Et in primis distinguendum esse videtur inter sensus magis dogmaticos et sensus magis speculativos.

Secundum sensum magis dogmaticum satisfactio Christi dicit vel (1) ipsam redemptionem, vel (2) vicariam Christi passionem, vel (3) pretium per vicariam passionem solutum, vel (4) placationem Dei pro peccatis per vicariam passionem, vel (5) meritum Christi vicaria passione adeptum unde tollitur omnis reatus et culpae et poenae.

Quod si dogmatice satisfactio Christi ita intelligitur, quaestio iam soluta est. Superius enim capite tertio probavimus (1) redemptionem ut medium a Domino nostro peractam, (2) Christum secundum divinam intentionem pro nobis nostrisque peccatis esse passum atque mortuum, (3) hanc Christi mortem cuiusdam pretii solutionem fuisse, (4) hanc eandem mortem fuisse sacrificium quod efficaciter peccata tollit et accessum ad Deum cum fiducia praebet, id quod Deum placatum demonstrat, et (5) obedientiam Christi usque ad mortem meruisse nostram iustificationem, quae quidem in baptismate omnem reatum culpae et poenae tollit.

At res tam breviter tamque faciliter expedire non possumus.[2] Nam S. Anselmus, qui primus fere de satisfactione Christi tractavit, non dogmaticum sed speculativum intendebat finem. Rationem enim quaerebat cur

usage regarding the sacrament of penance, and (4) from theological usage regarding the redemption accomplished by our Lord.

The common uses of the word are many, but for our present purpose it may suffice to cite this example: 'Pilate, wishing to *satisfy* the crowd, released Barabbas for them; and after flogging Jesus, he handed him over to be crucified' (Mark 15.15).

The fundamental juridical usage distinguishes between the payment of a debt and satisfaction. Payment is made according to the prescribed procedure; satisfaction is given when the creditor freely agrees that the debt may be extinguished in some other way.

In the sacrament of penance three acts on the part of the penitent make up the matter of the sacrament, namely, contrition, confession, and satisfaction (DB 896, 904, [DS 1673–75, 1689–92, ND 1620–21, 1630–33]).

Finally, Christ himself is said to have satisfied for our sins on our behalf (DB 799, 904, [DS 1529, 1690–91, ND 647, 1631–32]). What this means, since there are several opinions about it, cannot be briefly stated. And first we must make a distinction between the more dogmatic and the more speculative meanings.

In the more dogmatic sense of the word, the satisfaction offered by Christ means either (1) the redemption itself, or (2) the vicarious passion of Christ, or (3) the price paid by his vicarious passion, or (4) the appeasement of God for sins through his vicarious passion, or (5) the merit of Christ gained by his vicarious passion as a result of which all liability of fault and punishment is taken away.

If Christ's satisfaction is understood dogmatically, the question is already answered. In chapter 3 above we demonstrated (1) that the redemption as means to an end was carried out by our Lord, (2) that Christ in accordance with God's intention suffered and died for us and for our sins, (3) that his death was the payment of a certain price, (4) that this same death was a sacrifice that efficaciously takes away sins and provides confident access to God, which shows that God has been appeased, and (5) that Christ's obedience unto death merited our justification, which in fact in baptism takes away all liability of fault and punishment.

But we cannot dispatch this matter quite so quickly and easily.[2] St Anselm, who was virtually the first to treat of Christ's satisfaction, had a speculative rather than dogmatic interest in mind. He asked for the reason why God

2 [The remainder of this article parallels, sometimes verbatim, thesis 16, preliminary note 1, above, pp. 106–11.]

Deus homo. Neque ei placuit theoria recapitulationis ex S. Irenaeo per S. Augustinum tradita, quae potius picturam quam rationem praestaret. Neque ei placuit theoria demonstrati amoris divini, cum multis et aliis modis posset Deus suum amorem nobis demonstrare. Neque ei placuit theoria redemptionis ex potestate diaboli, cum Deus diabolo nihil deberet sed eius omnipotens Dominus esset.[3] Invenienda ergo erat ratio, quam nominavit S. Anselmus necessariam, cur Deus homo; et quamvis interdum argumentis convenientiae usus sit,[4] quamvis inter necessitatem cogentem et non cogentem distinxerit,[5] hoc tamen argumentum simpliciter urget: 'Necesse est ergo ut aut ablatus honor solvatur aut poena sequatur. Alioquin aut sibi Deus iustus non erit aut ad utrumque impotens erit; quod nefas est vel cogitare.'[6] Qua in necessitate fundatur reliqua theoria, merum nempe hominem omnia prorsus Deo debere ideoque satisfactionem simpliciter supererogatoriam peragere non posse,[7] Deum-hominem mori non debere et ideo moriendo satisfacere posse,[8] hanc Dei-hominis satisfactionem omnibus prorsus peccatis maiorem exsistere, et omnium peccatorum remissionem merere.[9]

Quare[10] in conceptione Anselmiana duplex elementum distinguendum esse videtur. Materialiter enim satisfactio est opus bonum, simpliciter indebitum, in honorem Dei factum, pro omnibus peccatis compensans, et omnium peccatorum remissionem merens; quod quidem opus erat Deum-hominum dare animam suam. Formaliter vero satisfactio erat ratio illa necessaria cur Deus homo, quae vel insufficientiam aliarum theoriarum compleret vel fundamentum solidum iis praeberet.

became man. He was not content with the theory of recapitulation St Augustine handed on from St Irenaeus, which presents a picture rather than a reason. Nor was he content with the theory about the demonstration of God's love, since God could have demonstrated his love for us in many other ways. He was not content with the theory of ransom from the power of the devil, since God owed the devil nothing and was his omnipotent Lord.[3] A reason had to be found, which Anselm called a necessary reason, why God became man; and although he sometimes used arguments of fittingness[4] and distinguished between compelling and non-compelling necessity,[5] nevertheless he simply advanced this argument: 'It is therefore necessary either for the honor that has been removed to be repaid or else for punishment to result. Otherwise, either God would not be just towards himself, or else he would be powerless to do the one or the other: heinous things, these, even to think about.'[6] Upon this necessity Anselm grounds the rest of his theory, namely, that a mere human being owes absolutely everything to God and hence cannot make satisfaction that is simply supererogatory,[7] but that a God-man is not obliged to die, and therefore in dying can give satisfaction,[8] and that such satisfaction on the part of the God-man is greater than all sins whatsoever and merits the forgiveness of all sins.[9]

Thus,[10] it seems that two elements should be distinguished in this conception of Anselm's. Materially considered, satisfaction is some good work, absolutely non-obligatory, done in honor of God as compensation for all sins and meriting the remission of all sins; and this work was in fact that of the God-man giving his life. Formally considered, satisfaction was the necessary reason for God becoming man, which would make up for the inadequacies in other theories or provide them with a solid foundation.

3 Anselm, *Cur Deus homo*, book 1, cc. 3–9, Schmitt [see above, p. 87, note 7] 50–64.
4 Ibid. book 1, c. 12; book 2, c. 11 [Schmitt 69–71, 109–12].
5 Ibid. book 2, c. 17 [Schmitt 122–26].
6 Ibid. book 1, c. 13; Schmitt 71, lines 24–26.
7 Anselm, *Cur Deus homo*, book 1, cc. 19–24 [Schmitt 84–94].
8 Ibid. book 2, c. 11 [Schmitt 109–12].
9 Ibid. book 2, cc. 14–15, 19 [Schmitt 113–16, 129–31].
10 [At this point the present article departs from the parallel in thesis 16, preliminary note 1. That note here introduces the problem of the theorem of the supernatural, without which Anselm could not formulate his question precisely; it goes on to distinguish the question of satisfaction from the question of the purpose of the incarnation. The present article introduces the same issues by its distinction between the material and formal components of Anselm's theory.]

Iam vero omnis theoria graviori hac difficultate laborat quod ex ipsa theoria ulteriores oriuntur quaestiones. Cui legi theoria Anselmiana exceptionem non fecit. Quaeritur enim qua necessitate mortuus sit Christus et qua necessitate propter eius mortem concedatur peccatorum remissio. Quaeritur deinde utrum mors Christi rationem poenae habuerit et qua iustitia haec poena a Christo sit sumpta. Quaeritur tertio in quonam praecise consistat satisfactio Christi, utrum fuerit superabundans, quemadmodum vicaria esse potuerit, quemadmodum per vicariam satisfactionem reliquiae peccatorum tollantur et rerum ordo restauretur. Quaeritur quarto utrum totum Christi opus deduci oporteat ex ratione Anselmiana necessaria, an alia via ad intelligentiam theologicam procedendum sit.

### Articulus XXVII: De ratione necessitatis[11]

Cum breviter resumatur theoria Anselmiana per disiunctionem, aut satisfactio aut poena, primo quaeri solet utrum tertium dari posset, ut neque satisfactio praeberetur neque poena daretur.

Quod si de actuali rerum ordine intelligitur, negative respondetur. Nam de facto pro nostris peccatis satisfecit Christus (DB 799, 904), neque in alio aliquo datur salus (Act 4.12), neque per aliud remedium tollitur peccatum originale quam per meritum unius mediatoris Domini nostri Iesu Christi (DB 790).

Si autem quaeritur utrum Deus potuisset aliter nos salvos facere quam per mortem Christi, sententia affirmativa est communis et certa.[12]

Now, every theory labors under this rather grave difficulty, namely, that the theory itself gives rise to further questions. Anselm's theory is no exception to this law. The question arises, why was it necessary for Christ to die, and why did his death necessarily call for the remission of sins? Second, was the death of Christ in some way a punishment, and if so by what sort of justice was this punishment taken on by Christ? Third, in what precisely does Christ's satisfaction consist? Was it superabundant? How could it have been vicarious, and how does vicarious satisfaction remove the residual damage of sin and restore the order of reality? Fourth, must the whole work of Christ be deduced from Anselm's necessary reason, or is there some other way to come to a theological understanding of this matter?

**Article 27: The notion of necessity**[11]

Since the Anselmian theory can be summed up in the disjunction 'either satisfaction or punishment,' first we must ask whether there might be a third possibility, so that neither satisfaction would be given nor a penalty paid.

If this question is asked with regard to the actual order of reality, the answer is no. For in fact Christ did satisfy for our sins (DB 799, 904, [DS 1529, 1690–91, ND 647, 1631–32]), and in no one else is salvation given (Acts 4.12); nor is original sin taken away through any other remedy than the merits of the one mediator, our Lord Jesus Christ (DB 790, [DS 1513, ND 510]).

If, however, the question is asked whether God could have saved us in some other way than through the death of Christ, an affirmative answer is common and certain.[12]

11 [This article runs parellel to thesis 16, preliminary note 2, above, pp. 110–13.]

12 See d'Alès, *De Verbo incarnato* 342. This was the opinion of Augustine, *De Trinitate*, XIII, X, 13; ML 42, 1024; *De agone Christiano*, XI, 12; ML 40, 297; of Peter Lombard, [*Sententiae*], 3, d. 20, c. 1; of the *Summa fratris Alexandri* (Quaracchi: Collegium S. Bonaventurae, 1924–48), book 3, tract. 1, q. 1, c. 4, in vol. IV/1, 14–17, at 16 [the later parts of the *Summa fratris Alexandri* are usually attributed to John of Rupella]; of Thomas Aquinas, *Summa theologiae*, 3, q. 46, aa. 1–2; of Duns Scotus, *In 3 Sententiarum*, d. 20, ques. unica; of Suárez, *Commentaria ac disputationes in tertiam partem D. Thomae*, in *Opera omnia*, vol. XVII, q. 1, a. 2; disp. 4, sect 2, no. 2, 51–52, at 51; and of theologians generally. In fact, they interpret Anselm in this sense, as, for example, Suárez's benign interpretation, ibid. 52. [Lonergan had this in his Latin text: 'Quam tenent S. Augustinus (*De Trin.* XIII, X, 13, ML 42, 1024; *De Agone Christiano* XI, 12, ML 40, 297), Petrus Lombardus (3 d. 20, c. 1), *Summa Alexandrina* (Lib. 3, tr. 1, q. 1, c. 4; Ad claras aquas: Tom. IV, p.16), S. Thomas (*Sum. theol.*, III, 46, 1 et 2), Scotus (*In III Sent.*, d.20), Suárez (*In Sum. theol.*, III, q. 1, a. 2; disp. 4, sect. 2, §2; Breton 17, 51), et theologi communiter. Imo in hunc sensum S. Anselmum interpretantur, uti benigne Suárez (ibid. 52).']

Ratio autem est Deum posse facere quidquid contradictionem internam non dicit, tam sapienter quam bene,[13] neque ulla iustitiae lege Deum teneri ad satisfactionem exigendam.[14]

Praeterea, non solum potuisset Deus omnia peccata gratis condonare, sed etiam si satisfactionem voluisset, suffecisset una minima Christi passio. Quod quidem contineri videtur in eo quod affirmat S. Thomas: 'Secundum sufficientiam una minima passio Christi suffecit ad redimendum genus humanum ab omnibus peccatis.'[15] Et idem docet Clemens VI (DB 550), et communiter theologi ubi de superabundante Christi satisfactione agunt. Si enim actualis satisfactio Christi superabundat, alia et minor suffecisset.

Sed et ulterius quaerunt theologi cur Christus tantum subierit dolorem. Et respondit S. Thomas: 'Christus voluit genus humanum a peccatis liberare non sola potestate sed etiam iustitia. Et ideo non solum attendit quantam virtutem dolor eius haberet ex divinitate unita: sed etiam quantum dolor eius sufficeret secundum naturam humanam ad tantam satisfactionem.'[16] Quod quidem secundum convenientiam intellexit S. Thomas,[17] sed posteriores theologi, qui aliam methodum vel voluntaristicam vel hypotheticam adhibuerunt, aut simpliciter ad beneplacitum divinae acceptationis recurrebant, aut subtilissimas inveniebant distinctiones ut demonstrarent Christum ex condigno et secundum rigorem iustitiae satisfecisse.

## Articulus XXVIII: De ratione poenae[18]

Circa eandem disiunctionem, aut satisfactio aut poena, ulterius quaeritur utrum re vera sensus sit, aut poena a Christo danda aut poena a peccatoribus danda.

Iam vero Christus mortuus est, et secundum scripturam mors est poena peccati, uti constat ex Gen 2.17, 3.19, Sap 2.24, Rom 5.12, 6.23.

The reason for this is that God can do anything that does not involve an internal contradiction, can do it both wisely and well,[13] and is bound by no law of justice to require satisfaction.[14]

Besides, not only could God have gratuitously pardoned all sins, but even had he wanted satisfaction, the slightest suffering on the part of Christ would have sufficed. This seems to be part of St Thomas's affirmation that 'so far as sufficiency is concerned, the slightest suffering of Christ would have sufficed to redeem the human race from all its sins.'[15] The same doctrine is taught by Pope Clement VI (DB 550, [DS 1025]) and by all theologians generally in treating of the superabundant satisfaction made by Christ. For if the actual satisfaction of Christ is superabundant, then another and lesser would have sufficed.

But theologians ask the further question, why Christ suffered such great pain. Thomas's reply is that 'Christ willed to free the human race from sins not only by power but also by justice. He therefore not only considered the value his sorrow would have by virtue of union with the Godhead, but also how much, according to his human nature, it would avail for so great a satisfaction.'[16] Thomas understood this in terms of fittingness,[17] but later theologians, employing other, voluntaristic or hypothetical methods, either simply had recourse to a divine decree of acceptance, or concocted supersubtle distinctions to show that Christ gave condign satisfaction in accordance with the full rigor of justice.

### Article 28: The notion of punishment[18]

Concerning the same disjunction, 'either satisfaction or punishment,' the further question may be asked whether the real sense of it is 'either punishment borne by Christ or punishment borne by sinners.'

Christ did die, and according to scripture death is a punishment for sin, as is clear from Genesis 2.17, 3.19, Wisdom 2.24, Romans 5.12, 6.23.

13 Thomas Aquinas, *Summa theologiae,* 1, q. 25, aa. 3 and 5.
14 Ibid. 3, q. 46, a. 2, ad 3m.
15 Ibid. a. 5, ad 3m.
16 Ibid. a. 6, ad 6m; see also previous note.
17 Ibid. a. 5, ad 3m.
18 [This article draws from various parts of thesis 16, including the discussion of opinions, preliminary note 3, and preliminary note 9. There are some verbatim parallels but, obviously, there is a significant reorganization of the order.]

Unde S. Augustinus, peccati poenam intelligens mortem, de Christo affirmavit: 'Suscipiendo poenam et non suscipiendo culpam, et culpam delevit et poenam.'[19] Et similiter alii Patres.

Pariter Petrus Lombardus: 'Peccata enim nostra, id est poenam peccatorum nostrorum, dicitur in corpore suo super lignum portasse (1 Pet 2.24), quia per ipsius poenam quam in cruce tulit omnis poena temporalis quae pro peccato converso debetur, in baptismo penitus relaxatur, ut nulla a baptizato exigatur, et in paenitentia minoratur.'[20]

Proinde *Summa fratris Alexandri*, qui totus est in S. Anselmo citando, exponendo, defendendo, non tam de opere bono et morte Christi locutus esse videtur quam de poena et de passone Christi. Distinxit poenam duplicem, aliam reatum separationis a Deo, aliam exercitium virtutis ad meritum et praemium.[21] Passionem Christi maxime habuit poenalem quatenus et naturae contrariam et voluntati sensualitatis.[22] Quam passionem duxit de convenientia divinae iustitiae 'ut numquam peccatum dimittatur sine poena.'

> Aut ergo peccatum ordinatur de destricta iustitia, ut puniatur aeternitaliter, aut de iustitia cum misericordia, ut puniatur temporaliter. Et sic passio est de iustitia, quia non poterat reatus solvi per purum hominem, secundum quod probat Anselmus. Homo enim non poterat reddere sed debebat; Deus poterat sed non debebat; oportuit ergo quod solveret homo Deus: homo qui deberet, Deus qui posset.[23]

Ad obiectionem, 'Innocentem condemnare non est iustum,' primo cum S. Anselmo respondit Christum voluntarie mortem subiisse, et volenti nullam inferri iniuriam. Deinde vero de suo addit Deum de potentia absoluta sine iniustitia innocentem punire posse secundum Rom 9.21; et praeterea, cum Deus mala ordinet, ideo etiam innocentem iuste punire posse ut

Hence St Augustine, understanding death as a punishment for sin, declares in the case of Christ, 'By accepting our punishment and not our fault, he wiped away both fault and punishment.'[19] Other Fathers of the Church expressed similar opinions.

Peter Lombard: 'He is said to have carried our sins, that is, the punishment for our sins, in his body on the cross (1 Peter 2.24), because by reason of the punishment he bore on the cross all temporal punishment due to sin is thoroughly loosed in baptism, so that none is required of the baptized, and reduced in the sacrament of penance.'[20]

Again, the *Summa fratris Alexandri*, which is entirely devoted to quoting, explaining, and defending St Anselm, seems to speak not so much about the good work and the death of Christ as about his punishment and passion. The author distinguished two kinds of punishment, the debt of separation from God and the exercise of virtue to obtain merit and reward.[21] He held Christ's passion to be the most punitive because it was contrary to nature and to sensual desire.[22] He also regarded this suffering to be appropriate to divine justice, 'that no sin might be forgiven without punishment.'

> Sin either falls under strict justice and so is punished eternally, or falls under justice tempered with mercy, and so is punished temporally. Thus the passion is a matter of justice, since the debt could not be paid by a mere mortal, as Anselm proves. Human beings owed the debt of sin but could not pay it; God could pay it but did not owe it. Hence it was necessary that the God-man make the payment: man who owed it and God who could pay it.[23]

To the objection that it is unjust to condemn an innocent person, the author first answers with Anselm that Christ went willingly to his death, and no injustice is done to one who wills it. But then he adds an argument of his own to the effect that God in his absolute power can without injustice punish an innocent person, according to Romans 9.21; besides, since God sets evil in order, he may therefore also justly punish even an innocent person

19 *Sermo* 171, 3; ML 38, 934.
20 Peter Lombard, *Sententiae*, 3, d. 19, c. 7.
21 *Summa fratris Alexandri* Tomus IV/1, Liber III, tract. 1, q. 4, mem. 3, cap. 2 (p. 68, at 45).
22 Ibid. tract 4, q. 3, a. 3 (p. 193, at 140).
23 Ibid. tract. 5, q. 1, mem. 4, cap. 1, a. 1 c. (p. 212, at 152).

bonum inde eliciat; hoc modo punitum esse Iob pro bono proprio, et Christum pro bono alieno.[24]

Quem loquendi modum etiam alibi adhibuit. Pater enim Filium et Filius semet ipsum tradidit 'ad hoc ut poenam sustineret pro liberatione humani generis.' Quod tradere erat malum ex genere et malum absolute; sed bonum erat ex fine.[25]

S. Thomas mala in rebus humanis sufficienter divisa duxit per culpam et poenam.[26] Poenam tripliciter divisit. *Poena simpliciter* est propter culpam sive originalem sive actualem, et 'sic solum unusquisque pro peccato suo punitur.'[27] *Poena medicinalis* est malum secundum quid, ut 'homo patiatur detrimentum in minori bono ut augeatur in maiori: sicut cum patitur detrimentum pecuniae propter sanitatem corporis, vel in utroque horum propter salutem animae et gloriam Dei.'[28] Et 'nihil prohibet talibus poenis aliquem puniri pro peccato alterius, vel a Deo, vel ab homine: utpote filios pro patribus, et subditos pro dominis, inquantum sunt quaedam res eorum.'[29] *Poena satisfactoria* denique voluntarie assumitur: 'quia contingit eos qui differunt in reatu poenae, esse unum secundum voluntatem unione amoris, inde est quod interdum aliquis qui non peccavit, poenam voluntarius pro alio portat.'[30] Et eiusmodi fuit poena satisfactoria Christi.[31]

Praeterea, S. Thomas saevitiam habuit poenam sumere praeter culpam eius qui punitur, et crudelitatem censuit poenam sumere ultra culpam eius qui punitur.[32]

Statum quaestionis non parum mutavit novatorum saec. XVI doctrina. Negata enim satisfactione sacramentali (DB 922–25), sublata etiam est haec analogia ad satisfactionem Christi intelligendam. Introducta autem fide

in order to bring about good; in this way Job was punished for his own good and Christ was punished for the good of others.[24]

The author speaks this way elsewhere as well: the Father handed over his Son and the Son handed himself over 'to suffer punishment for the liberation of the human race.' This act of handing over was evil from its genus and evil absolutely; but it was good on account of its end.[25]

St Thomas held that in human affairs the twofold division of evil into culpable evil and punishment is complete,[26] and that there are three kinds of punishment. *Simple punishment* is punishment for sin, whether original or personal, according to which 'each person is punished only for his or her own sin.'[27] *Medicinal punishment* is a qualified evil, 'when a person suffers a loss in a lesser good so as to receive a greater good, as, for example, when one suffers a monetary loss for the sake of the health of one's body, or suffers a loss of both money and health for the sake of one's spiritual good and the glory of God.'[28] In this case, 'there is nothing against one person's being punished for another's sin whether by God or by man; as, for example, when children suffer on account of their fathers, or subjects because of their lords, since in a way they belong to them.'[29] Finally, *satisfactory punishment* is undergone willingly: 'since it can happen that those who have unequal liability to punishment are of one will through their union in love, so that sometimes one who has not sinned willingly bears the punishment in the stead of the other.'[30] Christ's satisfactory punishment was of this kind.[31]

Aquinas also maintained that to inflict punishment upon a person without any regard to his fault or innocence is brutality, while to punish one beyond what his fault deserves is cruelty.[32]

The state of the question was greatly altered with the teaching of the sixteenth-century reformers. Once sacramental satisfaction was denied (DB 922–25, [DS 1712–15, ND 1652–55]), this analogy for understanding Christ's satisfaction was also destroyed. Once fiduciary faith and the imputation to us

24 See ibid. a. 1 (p. 212, at 151).
25 Ibid. mem. 6, cap. 2 (p. 225, at 162).
26 Thomas Aquinas, *Summa theologiae,* 1, q. 48, a. 5.
27 Ibid. 1-2, q. 87, a. 8 c.
28 Ibid. a. 7 c.
29 Ibid. a. 8 c.; 2-2, q. 108, a. 4.
30 Ibid. 1-2, q. 87, a. 7 c.
31 Ibid. ad 3m; see also 3, q. 48, a. 2, ad 1m.
32 Ibid. 2-2, q. 159, a. 2.

fiduciali et iustitia Christi nobis imputata, aperta etiam est via ad nostram iniustitiam Christo quodammodo imputandam.

Secundum Melanchthon Christus fuit victima ad iram divinam placandam; debuit tantam iram tantis in doloribus ita sustinere ut iustitiam divinam simul laudaret; his laudibus omissis, punitio Christi non fuisset Dei placatio; neque potuisset merus homo tantos perferre dolores et simul Deum laudare.[33]

Secundum Calvinum caro humana pretium fuit quod divinae iustitiae satisfaceret; caro Christi debitum a nobis contractum solvit; in ordine actuali Deus iustus gratiam non confert nisi expiatio iram divinam placat; neque suffecit ipsa Christi mors, sed et anima eius ad inferos descendit ut divinae vindictae sentiret severitatem et damnatorum subiret tormenta.[34]

E contra F. Socinus (1539–1604), qui ita antiquum renovavit adoptionismum ut SS. Trinitatem, Verbi Dei incarnationem, et divinam B.V.M. maternitatem negaret, etiam argumenta undique coacervavit ex scripturis, ex nominalium theologia, et ex iurisprudentia ad duplicem hanc probandam thesin, neque factam esse a Christo pro nobis nostrisque peccatis satisfactionem, neque ullam a Deo Patre esse requisitam in remissionem peccatorum.[35]

Unde et alius theologus iurisque peritus, H. Grotius (1583–1645), Iacobi Arminii sequax, novam invexit theoriam. Redemptionem enim habuit amnestiam quandem generalem ea conditione concessam ut Christus pro nostris peccatis puniretur. Ne enim homines propter gratuitam prorsus peccatorum remissionem et parvi peccatum facerent et levius peccarent, necessariam fuisse duxit insigne quoddam exemplum atque divinae iustitiae demonstrationem quae quidem fuit Christi non afflictio sed punitio. Cuius punitionis iustitiam tam ex scripturis quam ex principiis iuris defendit; et quamvis punitionem iustam esse non posse nisi propter delictum admiserit, negavit tamen eius iniustitiam, saltem in casu Dei et Christi, qui innocentem pro nocentibus puniret.[36]

of Christ's righteousness were introduced, the way was also opened to somehow imputing our unrighteousness to Christ.

According to Melanchthon, Christ was a victim for placating the wrath of God; he had to bear this great wrath in such great suffering while simultaneously praising the justice of God. Without this praise, Christ's punishment would not have placated God, and no mere human being could have suffered such pain while praising God at the same time.[33]

For Calvin, human flesh was the price that would satisfy divine justice. The flesh of Christ paid the debt contracted by us; in the present order, a just God does not confer grace unless expiation has placated the divine wrath. Nor was Christ's death itself sufficient, but his soul also descended into hell in order to experience the severity of divine retribution and undergo the torments of the damned.[34]

On the other hand, Fausto Sozzini (1539–1604), who revived the ancient heresy of adoptionism, thus denying the Trinity, the incarnation of the Word of God, and the divine maternity of the Blessed Virgin Mary, also compiled arguments from scripture, from nominalist theologians, and from jurisprudence to prove his twofold thesis, namely, that Christ did not give satisfaction for us and for our sins, and that none indeed was required by God the Father for the remission of sins.[35]

Proceeding from this, another theologian and jurist, Hugo Grotius (1583–1645), a follower of Jacob Arminius, came up with a new theory. He regarded the redemption as a sort of general amnesty granted on the condition that Christ was punished for our sins. For lest the utter gratuitousness of such a redemption might lead people to make light of sin and be casual about sinning, a conspicuous example and an open demonstration of divine justice had been necessary, and this in fact was the passion of Christ, not as mere suffering and pain, but as punishment. He defended the justice of this punishment from both scripture and the principles of law; and although he admitted that to punish where there is no offense could not be justified, still he denied that there was any injustice, at least in the case of God and Christ, in an innocent person's being punished in place of the guilty.[36]

33 Franks, *A History of the Doctrine of the Work of Christ*, vol. 1, 412–13.
34 Ibid. 427–28, 431, 434–35.
35 Ibid. vol. 2, 13–33; see DB 993 [DS 1880, ND 648].
36 Franks, *A History of the Doctrine of the Work of Christ*, vol. 2, 57–67.

Denique apud Lutheranum Quenstedt (1617–1688) 'orthodoxam' Protestantium opinionem plene evolutam invenies. Deum enim per ipsam divinam iustitiam teneri docuit, ut solutionem totius debiti ex peccatis contracti exigeret; quo pretio non soluto, Deum peccata remittere absolute non potuisse. Christus ergo tam pro omnibus peccatis quam pro omnibus poenis satisfecit, qui voluntarie totum nostrum debitum suscepit, sibique imputatum habuit, et secundum rigorem iustitiae exsolvit, cum ipsa inferni tormenta (non tamen in inferno neque aeternaliter) subierit.[37]

Quibus perspectis, Anselmiana disiunctio, aut sublatus honor solvatur aut poena sequatur, de medio tolli videtur. Nam ex una parte Sociniani, liberales, modernistae ipsam Christi satisfactionem negant; sed ex alia parte tam Catholici quam Protestantes de poena Christi loquuntur.

Ex quo factum est ut J. Rivière, hac in re eruditissimus, Anselmianum quaestionis statum renovandum esse censeret. Distinxit ergo (1) castigationem, (2) expiationem, et (3) reparationem ut, prioribus exclusis, tertium satisfactionis modum amplecteretur.[38]

Castigationem fuisse satisfactionem Christi ideo negavit (1) quia nemo umquam docuit Christum invitum pro nostris peccatis satisfecisse, (2) quia S. Thomas neminem praeter ipsum peccatorem poena stricte dicta puniri affirmavit,[39] et (3) quia extremum huius opinionis consectarium (Christum scilicet poenis inferni punitum esse) a consultoribus Tridentinae synodi, a Maldonato, a Suárezio, a S. Francisco Salesio, a S. Bellarmino reprobatum est.[40]

Expiationem (quae in libera mali perpessione consistit) pariter negandam esse reputavit (1) quia malum non potest esse obiectum directum et primarium, imo finis quidam principalis, divinae voluntatis, (2) quia hunc in sensum interpretandos iudicavit S. Bonaventuram, Suárezium, S. Bellarmino, (3) quia recentior de solidaritate theoria non melius hanc difficultatem amovet quam antiquior et iuridica opinio, (4) quia expiatio magis ad consequentem poenam attendit quam ad antecedentem et fundamentalem

Finally, you will find the 'orthodox' Protestant opinion fully developed by the Lutheran Johannes Andreas Quenstedt (1617–1688). He taught that God, by reason of divine justice itself, was bound to require full payment of the debt contracted because of sin, and that if the price was not paid, he absolutely could not forgive sins. Accordingly, Christ made satisfaction for all sins as well as for all punishments by voluntarily assuming our entire debt and having it imputed to himself, and discharged it in accord with strict justice, since he suffered the torments of hell – not in hell itself, however, nor eternally.[37]

In view of the above opinions, it would seem that Anselm's disjunction that 'either God's honor be restored, or punishment be carried out' cannot be maintained. For there are on the one hand Socinians, liberals, and modernists who deny Christ's satisfaction, and on the other hand both Catholics and Protestants who speak about the punishment of Christ.

For this reason Jacques Rivière, a foremost authority on this question, felt that the Anselmian statement of the question needed to be revised. He distinguished therefore between (1) chastisement, (2) expiation, and (3) reparation; rejecting the first two, he opted for the third mode of satisfaction.[38]

He rejected chastisement as the mode of Christ's atonement on the grounds (1) that no one ever taught that Christ unwillingly gave satisfaction for our sins, (2) that St Thomas held that none but the guilty person himself could strictly speaking be punished,[39] and (3) that the ultimate conclusion that this opinion leads to, namely that Christ was punished with the pains of hell, was utterly rejected by the theological consultants at the Council of Trent, by Maldonatus, by Suárez, by St Francis de Sales, and by St Robert Bellarmine.[40]

Expiation, which consists in freely submitting to evil, he likewise rejected (1) because evil cannot be the direct and primary object, let alone a principal end, of the divine will; (2) because he judged that Bonaventure, Bellarmine, and Suárez were to be interpreted in this sense; (3) because the more recent theory of solidarity [between Christ and humanity] did not solve the difficulty any better than the older juridical opinion; (4) because expiation looks rather to the consequent penalty than to the prior and

37 Ibid. 81–94.
38 Rivière, 'Rédemption' 1969–70.
39 Thomas Aquinas, *Summa theologiae,* 1-2, q. 87, a. 8.
40 Rivière, 'Rédemption' 1973.

culpam, et (5) quia expiatio affinitatem quandam habet cum castigatione atque saepius in conclusiones nimis similes conduxit.[41]

Reparationem denique intellexit secundum definitionem S. Thomae: 'Ille proprie satisfacit pro offensa qui exhibet offenso id quod aeque vel magis diligit quam oderit offensam.'[42] Quod autem exhibuit Christus erat summa sanctitas quae quam perfectissime Deo offenso honorem sublatum reddidit. Accessit sane expiatio per passionem Christi; at ipsa mali perpessio non erat nisi elementum de facto, subordinatum, secundarium, superficiale; unde potius dicendum est Christum in doloribus quam per dolores satisfecisse.[43]

Quam sententiam ita non pauci sunt secuti ut alii eam parum tutam iudicaverint. His non placet reparationis systema quatenus negat Christum per dolores pro peccatis satisfecisse; quare et urgent non merum quoddam accidens fuisse ipsam corporalem atque sensibilem Christi passionem. Sed alii aliter procedunt et, cum omnium sententias recitare haud possimus, sufficit forte doctrinam a B. Xiberto propositam citare:

> Viam qua sacrificio Christi inest ordo ad redemptionem, signate nominamus expiationem poenalem. Acerbitas dolorum quos passus est coniungitur cum opere redemptivo non tantum incidenter sed ex divina ordinatione; influit in redemptionem non tantum indirecte, puta occasionem praebendo exercendae caritatis, sed directe operando in destructionem peccati.[44]
>
> Expiationem poenalem numerandam esse inter essentialia elementa sacrificii crucis etiam dogmatice certum videtur, quia traditio ecclesiastica illam quam maxime extollere consuevit, et quidem evangelicae narrationi inhaerens. Expiationem consulto negligere temerarium videtur.[45]

basic fault; and (5) because the notion of expiation is quite close to that of chastisement and has often led to conclusions that are all too similar.[41]

Finally, he understood the notion of reparation according to the definition of Aquinas: 'One properly gives satisfaction for an offense who presents something the offended one loves equally, or even more than he detested the offense.'[42] What Christ presented was that supreme holiness which in the most perfect way possible restored to God the honor taken away by sin. True, there was the added element of expiation in the sufferings of Christ; but that painful submission to evil was but a de facto element, subordinate, secondary, and superficial. Hence it is more correct to say that Christ offered satisfaction in his sufferings than by his sufferings.[43]

Although quite a few theologians have followed this opinion, others have felt it to be rather unsafe. These latter dislike the system of reparation inasmuch as it denies that Christ satisfied for sins by his sufferings. They therefore insist that the painful bodily suffering of Christ was no merely incidental element. Others take a different tack, and while we cannot possibly mention them all, it may suffice to quote the opinion of Bartholomaeo Xiberta on this point:

> The way in which Christ's sacrifice was redemptive is properly referred to as penal expiation. The painfulness of what he suffered is linked to his redemptive work not just incidentally but by divine ordination. It had a bearing on the redemption not just indirectly, as if it were, for example, simply the occasion for performing an act of charity, but worked directly towards the destruction of sin.[44]
>
> That penal expiation must be numbered among the essential elements of the sacrifice of the cross seems dogmatically certain, since the tradition of the Church, following closely the gospel narratives, has constantly mentioned it with highest praise. To deliberately ignore such expiation seems rash and temerarious.[45]

41 Ibid. 1974–75.
42 Thomas Aquinas, *Summa theologiae*, 3, q. 48, a. 2 c.
43 Rivière, 'Rédemption' 1972.
44 Xiberta, *Tractatus de Verbo incarnato*, vol. 2, 551–52.
45 Ibid. 553.

Iterum ergo pro disiunctione Anselmiana, aut satisfactio aut poena, iam ponitur alia, aut expiatio poenalis aut poena.[46]

**Articulus XXIX: De poena Christi**

Quidquid sit de aliis linguis, Latinum nomen *poena* ab opere Christi vix separari potest. Uti enim vidimus, et scriptura dicit mortem esse poenam, et S. Augustinus mortem Christi poenam nominat, et etiamsi S. Anselmus de satisfactione loqui maluerit, Petrus Lombardus, *Summa fratris Alexandri*, et S. Thomas nomen *poena* reintroducunt. Verum sane est S. Thomam ita satisfactionem proprie dictam concepisse ut habitudinem intrinsecam ad perpessionem mali non haberet;[47] sed idem S. Thomas non solum de poenis satisfactoriis locutus est[48] sed etiam de dolore qui sufficeret secundum humanam naturam ad tantam satisfactionem.[49] Quapropter etsi concedamus theoriam sibi cohaerentem ita excogitari posse ut satisfactio mali perpessionem per se non includat, credimus tamen theoriam eiusmodi ad nostram materiam parum facere, cum constet Christum Deo volente pro nobis nostrisque peccatis esse passum atque mortuum.

Quod si hoc elementum in sententia J. Rivière corrigendum ducimus, aliud elementum omnino laudandum iudicamus, scilicet, tum Deum directe malum non velle, tum passionem mortemque Christi non bonum simpliciter, non boni carentiam, sed boni privationem fuisse eamque acerbissimam et gravissimam. Iam vero Deus satisfactionem Christi directe voluit, et ideo satisfactio Christi cum perpessione mali simpliciter identificari non potest. Hac ratione motus illam expiationem poenalem reiecit J. Rivière quae in mali perpessione consistat.[50]

So again in place of Anselm's disjunction, 'either satisfaction or punishment,' we have another one, 'either penal expiation or punishment.'[46]

**Article 29: The punishment of Christ**

Whatever may be true of other languages, in Latin the word *poena* can hardly be separated from Christ's work. As we have seen, scripture refers to death as a punishment, and Augustine calls Christ's death a punishment; and even though Anselm preferred to speak of 'satisfaction,' Peter Lombard, the *Summa fratris Alexandri*, and Aquinas reintroduced the word *poena*. While it is true that Aquinas understood satisfaction in the proper sense as not having an intrinsic connection with enduring evil,[47] at the same time he speaks not only of 'satisfactory punishment'[48] but also of the sorrow that would be sufficient according to human nature to render satisfaction.[49] Granted that one could develop a coherent theory according to which satisfaction would not of itself include enduring evil, nevertheless in our opinion such a theory would contribute little to the present discussion, since it is universally acknowledged that Christ, in accordance with God's will, suffered and died for us and for our sins.

While we feel that this element in Rivière's opinion warrants correction, at the same time we must wholeheartedly approve of another element in it, namely, that God does not directly will evil, and that Christ's passion and death was not a good pure and simple, nor merely a lack of good, but a privation of good and indeed a privation of the most painful and severe kind. God did directly will Christ's satisfaction, and therefore the satisfaction given by Christ cannot simply be identified with the endurance of evil. For this reason Rivière rejected the notion of penal expiation which consists in enduring evil.[50]

46 See Pesch, *Das Sühneleiden unseres göttlichen Erlösers*; A. d'Alès, *Revue du clergé français*, 15 Nov. 1919, t. 100, pp. 294–99 [see above, p. 101, note 12]; Rivière, *Le dogme de la Rédemption dans la théologie contemporaine* 147–60; Solano, 'El sentido de la muerte redentora de Nuestro Señor Jesucristo y algunas corrientes modernas' 399–414; Solano, 'Actualidades cristológico-soteriológicas' 43–69; de San Pablo, 'Irenismo en soteriologia' 455–503; de San Pablo, 'El Doctor Juan Rivière, Teólogo de la Redención,' *Revista Española de Teología* 14 (1954) 79–103.

47 Thomas Aquinas, *Summa theologiae* 3, q. 48, a. 2.

48 Ibid. 1-2, q. 87, a. 7, ad 3m.

49 Ibid. 3, q. 46, a. 6, ad 6m.

50 Rivière, 'Rédemption' 1970, 1973.

Dices tamen haec tria inter se conciliari non posse, nempe, (1) Christum patiendo satisfecisse, (2) Deum satisfactionem Christi directe voluisse, et (3) Deum passionem Christi directe non voluisse.

Sed optime inter se conciliantur, et quidem dupliciter: uno modo omnibus accommodato, secundum modum loquendi quem adhibuerunt scriptura et Patres; alio modo magis scholastico, qui ultimas problematis radices revelat.

Secundum primum modum distinguuntur partes diaboli eiusque servorum, partes Christi hominis, et partes Dei Patris. Et clarissime partes diaboli memorat scriptura: nam 'haec est hora vestra (pontificum) et potestas tenebrarum' (Lc 22.53); et 'vos ex patre diabolo estis et desideria patris vestri vultis facere. Ille homicida erat ab initio' (Io 8.44); et 'nunc princeps huius mundi eicitur foras' (Io 12.31) et 'iudicatus est' (Io 16.11) et tamen 'venit' (Io 14.30) 'cum diabolus iam mississet in cor ut traderet eum Iudas Simonis Iscariotae' (Io 13.2).

Neque partes diaboli a Patribus tacentur. Quaesivit enim S. Augustinus utrum ex Rom 5.10 concludendum sit Deum Patrem contra nos iratum esse sed Filium amicum et placatum. Respondit autem quod ex Rom 8.32 pariter concludendum esse Patrem esse placatum et amicum sed Filium invitum. In Eph 1.4 invenit Patrem nos diligentem et eligentem, et in Gal 2.20 Filium nos diligentem et pro nobis se tradentem. Quibus perpectis de peccato originali et de partibus diaboli disserere incepit.[51]

Neque has diaboli partes omisit S. Thomas, qui eo fortius affirmare potuit passionem mortemque Christo inflictam non sacrificium fuisse sed maleficium atque peccatum gravissimum.[52]

Sed praeter partes diaboli etiam adfuerunt partes Christi hominis, qui potestatem habuit ponendi animam suam et iterum sumendi eam (Io 10.17–18), qui si voluisset utique a Patre impetrare potuisset plusquam duodecim legiones angelorum (Mt 26.53), qui se a Patre derelictum esse confessus est (Mt 27.46) sed minime dixit irrisionem, flagellationem, crucem sibi a suo Patre esse inflictam.

The objection may be raised that these three elements are incompatible, namely (1) Christ made satisfaction by suffering, (2) God directly willed Christ's satisfaction, (3) God did not directly will Christ's passion.

But in fact it can be shown that these three are quite compatible, and in two ways: in the first way, accessible to all, according to the manner of speaking presented by scripture and the Fathers, and in another, more Scholastic manner, which gets to the ultimate roots of the problem.

According to the first way, we distinguish the parts played by the devil and his minions, by the man Christ Jesus, and by God the Father. Scripture clearly speaks of the part played by the devil: 'this is your (the priests') hour, and the power of darkness' (Luke 22.53); 'You are from your father the devil, and you choose to do your father's desires. He was a murderer from the beginning' (John 8.44); and, 'now the ruler of this world will be driven out' (John 12.31) and 'condemned' (John 16.11) and yet he 'is coming' (John 14.30), 'since the devil had already put it into the heart of Judas son of Simon Iscariot to betray him' (John 13.2).

The Fathers also speak about the role of the devil here. Augustine wondered whether from Romans 5.10 we are to conclude that God the Father was angry with us while the Son was friendly and well disposed. His answer was that on the contrary one could equally conclude from Romans 8.32 that the Father was friendly and well disposed, but the Son was reluctant. In Ephesians 1.4 he finds the Father loving us and choosing us, and in Galatians 2.20 the Son loving us and giving himself up for us. From here Augustine goes on to discuss original sin and the part played by the devil.[51]

Nor did St Thomas overlook the devil's role, for by reason of it he was able to assert all the more strongly that the passion and death inflicted upon Christ was not a sacrifice but an atrocity and a most grave sin.[52]

But besides the devil's role there was also the human Christ's, who had the power to lay down his life and take it up again (John 10.17–18), who, had he so wished, could have obtained from the Father more than twelve legions of angels (Matthew 26.53), who admitted his abandonment by the Father (Matthew 27.46) but never in the least indicated that the ridicule heaped upon him and the scourging and crucifixion he suffered were being inflicted upon him by his Father.

51 Augustine, *De Trinitate*, XIII, xi–xii, 15–16; ML 42, 1025–26.

52 Thomas Aquinas, *Summa theologiae*, 3, q. 46, a. 3, ad 3m; q. 48, a. 4, ad 2m, 3m; q. 49, a. 2 c., ad 1m; q. 48, a. 3, ad 3m; q. 47, a. 4, ad 2m.

Tertio aderant partes Dei Patris et, quamvis non desint intellectu difficilia, omnino manifestum est quid primo loco posuerit scriptura quae Deum Patrem toties ideo laudavit quia 'hunc Iesum resuscitavit Deus, cuius nos omnes testes sumus. Dextera igitur Dei exaltatus, et promissione Spiritus sancti accepta a Patre, effudit hunc quem vos videtis et auditis. Non enim David ascendit in caelum; dixit autem ipse: "Dixit Dominus Domino meo: sede a dextris meis, donec ponam inimicos tuos scabellum pedum tuorum." Certissime sciat ergo omnis domus Israel, quia et Dominum eum et Christum fecit Deus hunc Iesum, quem vos crucifixistis' (Act 2.32–36).

Aliae ergo sunt partes diaboli passionem mortemque infligentis; aliae sunt partes Christi passionem mortemque voluntarie subeuntis; et tertiae sunt partes Dei Patris dilectum Filium resuscitantis atque exaltantis.

Neque difficile in istis tribus est perspicere rationem, legem, mysterium, iustitiam crucis. Haec enim et malum praesupponit, et malum per victoriam voluntariam victum dicit, et in bonum superabundans a Deo Patre collatum conducit.

Praeterea, per rationem crucis eadem tria in unum conflantur. Quamvis enim inter se maxime sint diversae partes diaboli et partes Christi et partes Dei Patris, in tribus simul sumptis una est crucis ratio, quae et malum vincendum praesupponit, et ipsum hoc malum in bonum transformat, et per malum in bonum transformatum eo pervenit ut sciat quid sit illud, 'Diligentibus Deum omnia cooperantur in bonum' (Rom 8.28).

Quae trium unitas non solum in Christiana intelligentia et ratione invenitur sed etiam in ipsa reali Christi carne, in qua potestas tenebrarum suum sacrilegium perfecit, in qua ipse Christus patiens et moriens victoriam suam reportavit, in qua resurrecta atque exaltata medium nostrae salutis Deus Pater constituit.

At vocem Bosonis[53] obicientis audire videor, hanc pulchram quandam esse picturam sed ultimam rei rationem non attingere. Cur enim Deus omnium Dominus omnipotens ita cum diabolo tractare dignatus est? Cur proprio suo Filio non pepercit sed pro nobis omnibus tradidit illum?

Third, there is the part played by God the Father. Although this is not without some points that are difficult to grasp, it is very clear what is put in the first place by scripture, lavish in its praise of God the Father because 'This Jesus God raised up, and of that all of us are witnesses. Being therefore exalted at the right hand of God, and having received from the Father the promise of the Holy Spirit, he has poured out this that you both see and hear. For David did not ascend into the heavens, but he himself says, "The Lord said to my Lord, Sit at my right hand until I make your enemies your footstool." Therefore let the entire house of Israel know with certainty that God has made both Lord and Messiah this Jesus whom you crucified' (Acts 2.32–36).

So we have the role of the devil perpetrating Jesus' passion and death, the very different role of Christ willingly submitting to his passion and death, and thirdly the unique role of God the Father resurrecting and exalting his beloved Son.

It is not difficult to discern in these three roles the meaning, the law, the mystery, the justice of the cross. For the cross presupposes evil, it includes the notion of the triumph of the will over evil, and it leads to superabundant good conferred by God the Father.

Besides, these three roles converge into one through the meaning of the cross. However divergent the roles of the devil, of Christ, and of God the Father are among themselves, the three come together in the single meaning of the cross, which presupposes evil to be conquered, transforms that evil into good, and through evil transformed into good brings us to know the meaning of the text, 'all things work together for good for those who love God' (Romans 8.28).

The unity of these three aspects is to be found not only in Christian understanding and reason but also in the real flesh of Christ upon which the power of darkness perpetrated its sacrilege, that flesh in which the suffering and dying Christ won his victory and in which, now resurrected and exalted, God the Father has established the means of our salvation.

But here it seems to me I hear Boso[53] objecting that this is all a pretty picture, to be sure, but it doesn't really get down to the ultimate meaning of the matter. Why would God the all-powerful Lord of all things condescend to have such dealings with the devil? Why did he not spare his own Son but instead hand him over on behalf of us all?

53 [The protagonist in dialogue with Anselm in *Cur Deus homo.*]

Ultimam ergo rei rationem iam dixerat S. Augustinus: 'Melius enim iudicavit [Deus] de malis bene facere quam nulla mala esse permittere.'[54]

Posita autem divina mali permissione, non sequitur et tamen habetur malum. Non enim ordinat divina sapientia ut mala culpae fiant; et tamen ea fieri et prohibet et praevidit, et ulterius facit ut de iis fiat bonum. Neque malum culpae aut directe aut indirecte vult Deus; quod tamen fieri permittit. Stat ergo dominium Dei et absolutum et universale quin tamen Deus ullatenus sit peccati vel causa vel auctor. Neve obicias hoc intelligi non posse, sed potius illud intellige quod peccatum est irrationale, non-intelligibile, absurdum et ideo non in Deum reducendum quasi intelligibile esset (cf. art. XIV). Quod si neque hoc intelligis, illud saltem crede: 'Perditio tua, Israel, ex te est; tantummodo ex me auxilium tuum.'[55]

Proinde, cum malum culpae et vere sit, et a Deo non sit, et nisi Deo permittente non fiat, illud iam habemus quod in dicta pictura per diabolum repraesentatur et sub nomine diaboli quodammodo latet. Non ergo est quaerendum cur Deus omnipotens Dominus ita cum diabolo tractare dignatus sit, sed illud potius est humiliter acceptandum quod Deus solus sapiens (Rom 16.27) malum culpae esse permisit.

Quibus perspectis, ad disiunctionem Augustinianam reverte. Duo enim posuit S. Augustinus: aut nulla mala esse permittere aut de malis bene facere. Illud nobis melius forte videtur; sed hoc Deus melius iudicavit ut, scilicet, et mala fieri permittatur et ex malis bonum efficiatur. Posita ergo mali permissione, non remanet nisi ut de permisso malo bonum fiat. Sed quomodo fit? Quo alio modo quam per rationem, legem, mysterium, iustitiam crucis?

Deus ergo non pepercit proprio Filio suo, inquantum peccata permisit et daemonum et Adami et Iudae proditoris et summorum sacerdotum et Pontii Pilati. Deus ergo tradidit proprium Filium suum inquantum eum non protexit a passione et morte sed persequentibus expositum dereliquit.[56] Et pro nobis omnibus Deus proprium Filium tradidit quatenus secundum rationem, legem, mysterium, iustitiam crucis ab aeterno constituit 'per eum reconciliare omnia in ipsum' (Col 1.20).

The ultimate meaning of the matter has already been given by St Augustine: '[God] judged it better to draw good things out of evil than to permit no evils to exist.'[54]

Evil does not result from the divine permission of evil, and yet it happens. Divine wisdom did not ordain that culpable evils should occur; nevertheless it both forbade and foresaw them, and further arranged for good to be drawn out of them. Neither directly nor indirectly does God will culpable evil – but he does permit it to occur. Thus God's absolute and universal dominion remains intact, without God being in any way the cause or author of sin. Do not say that this makes no sense; rather, try to understand that sin is irrational, nonintelligible, absurd, and therefore not to be reduced to God as if it were intelligible (see article 14). But if you do not understand this, at least believe 'Your downfall, O Israel, is all your own doing; your only help is in me' [Hosea 13.9].[55]

Accordingly, since culpable evil truly is, and is not from God, and occurs only by his permission, we now know what is represented by the devil in the picture painted above, and in a way lies hidden under the name of 'devil.' Ours is not to ask why God the omnipotent Lord should condescend to have such dealings with the devil, but rather to accept humbly the fact that God who alone is wise (Romans 16.27) permits culpable evil to happen.

With this in mind, let us go back to Augustine's disjunction. Augustine stated a twofold proposition: either permit no evils to be, or draw good out of evils. To our way of thinking, perhaps, the former seems the better choice; but God preferred the latter, that is, to permit evils to occur and bring good out of them. Once this permission of evil was granted, it remained only to draw good from the evil permitted. But how? How else than through the meaning, the law, the mystery, the justice of the cross?

Thus, God did not spare his own Son, inasmuch as he permitted the sins of the fallen angels, of Adam, of Judas, of the high priests, and of Pontius Pilate. He therefore handed over his own Son inasmuch as he did not shield him from his passion and death but left him defenseless to his persecutors.[56] He handed over his own Son on behalf of us all inasmuch as he decided from all eternity 'through him ... to reconcile to himself all things' (Colossians 1.20) according to the meaning, the law, the mystery, the justice of the cross.

54 Augustine, *Enchiridion* 27, ML 40, 245.
55 Thomas Aquinas, *Summa theologiae*, 1, q. 23, a. 3, arg. 2m and ad 2m.
56 Ibid. 3, q. 47, a. 3.

Quae sane eo non perveniunt ut rationem satisfactionis Christi explicent; sed hanc utilitatem eamque haud parvam habent ut et falsas opiniones amoveant et solidum praebeant fundamentum ad veritatem determinandam. Quod quidem statim perspici potest si ad rationem poenae redimus.

Aderat ergo in passione et morte Christi ratio poenae quia (1) passio et mors de se sunt mala et (2) haec mala ex peccato processerunt. Passio enim et mors Christi non fuerunt vel bonum simpliciter, vel mera boni carentia, sed boni privatio eaque gravissima; et boni privatio est ipsa mali ratio. Praeterea, hoc malum ex peccato processit: historice enim processit ex peccatis Iudae, sacerdotum, Pilati; et secundum ipsam divinam intentionem ideo Deus haec peccata et consequentes actiones permisit quia secundum rationem crucis per victoriam proprii sui Filii sacerdotis et victimae nos redimere decrevit.

Quod si generica poenae ratio est malum ex peccato proveniens, tot sunt poenarum species quot sunt nexus secundum multiformem Dei sapientiam (Eph 3.10) quibus malum ex peccato sequatur. Et cum divina sapientia sit lex divinae iustitiae,[57] omnes hae poenarum species sunt iustae secundum ipsam Dei sapientiam atque iustitiam.

Est ergo poena simpliciter, quae ipsi peccatori ex proprio peccato provenit sive originali sive actuali.[58] Et quamvis maxime inter se different poena aeterna,[59] poena purgatoria (DB 840), poena limbi parvulorum (DB 493a), poena satisfactoria paenitentium quorum remissa est culpa sed non poena universa (DB 904–905), et poena publica vel privata pro vero delicto inflicta,[60] tamen omnes hae poenae eatenus similes sunt quatenus ex proprio peccato ipsi peccatori adveniunt. Neque ulla eiusmodi poena in Christo

All this, of course, does not fully explain what is meant by Christ's satisfaction, but it does serve the useful purpose of clearing away false opinions and laying a firm foundation for determining the truth of the matter. This we can determine right now by turning to examine the notion of punishment.

The meaning of punishment was involved in the passion and death of Christ because (1) passion and death are evils in themselves, and (2) these evils result from sin. Christ's passion and death were not a good pure and simple, nor merely a lack of good, but a privation of good, and indeed a most grievous one; and the privation of good is the very meaning of evil. Moreover, this evil resulted from sin: historically it resulted from the sin of Judas, of the priests, of Pilate; and it was in accordance with his divine intention that God permitted these sins and their consequent actions because he had decided to redeem us according to the meaning of the cross through the victory of his own Son as both priest and victim.

Now if the generic meaning of punishment is evil that results from sin, there will be as many kinds of punishment as there are connections, in accordance with God's manifold wisdom (Ephesians 3.10), by which evil is consequent upon sin. And since divine wisdom is the law of divine justice,[57] it follows that all these kinds of punishment are just according to the very wisdom and justice of God.

First of all, then, there is simple punishment, which comes to the sinner by reason of his own sin, whether original or actual.[58] Although there is a great deal of difference between eternal punishment,[59] purgatorial punishment (DB 840, [DS 1580]), the punishment of limbo (DB 493a, [DS 926]), the satisfactory punishments of penitents whose sin is fully remitted but not all of their punishment (DB 904–905, [DS 1689–92, ND 1630–33]), and the punishment inflicted either publicly or privately upon one convicted of a crime,[60] still they all have this in common, that they are brought upon the

57 Ibid. 1, q. 21, a. 1, ad 2m.
58 Ibid. 1-2, q. 87, a. 7, aa. 7 and 8.
59 Matthew 25.41, 10.28, 5.29–30.
60 Solano, 'Actualidades cristológico-soteriológicas' 57–58. [On limbo as the afterlife condition of those who die in original sin without being assigned to hell, see the International Theological Commission's document, 'The Hope of Salvation for Infants Who Die Without Being Baptized,' January 19, 2007, http://www.vatican.va/roman_curia/congregations/cfaith/cti_documents/rc_con_cfaith_doc_20070419_un-baptised-infants_en.html. 'The conclusion of this study is that there are theological and liturgical reasons to hope that infants who die without baptism may be saved and brought into eternal happiness, even if there is not an explicit teaching on this question found in Revelation.']

esse potuit. Nam in Christo nullum fuit peccatum uti abundanter et saepissime testatur scriptura (2 Cor 5.21, 1 Pet 1.19, 2.22, Heb 4.15, 7.26–27).

Est etiam poena medicinalis 'non solum sanativa peccati praeteriti sed etiam praeservativa a peccato futuro et promotiva in aliquod bonum; et secundum hoc aliquis interdum punitur sine culpa, non tamen sine causa.'[61] Cum tamen inter theologos constet Christum fuisse impeccabilem, pariter constat eum sui causa tali medicina non indiguisse ut a futuro peccato praeservaretur. Et ideo poena Christi non potuit esse poena medicinalis eo sensu quo superius haec poena a S. Thoma exposita est.

Est denique poena pure satisfactoria. Quae in eo invenitur qui neque peccavit neque peccare potuit. Et quia non peccavit, differt a poena simpliciter. Quia vero peccare non potuit, differt a poena medicinali. Quia denique ex alienis peccatis processit et in ea auferenda tendit, ad tertiam quandam atque propriam pertinet speciem. Cuius quidem ratio non legitur in tractatu iuris de delictis et poenis, neque ad illam paternam prudentiam reducitur quae proprium filium castigat, sed in mysterio crucis collocatur prout Christus crucifixus est Dei sapientia (1 Cor 1.23–24).

Quae quidem poena, in mysterio posita, et inflicta est, et accepta, et praemiata, et permissa, et inspirata, et intenta.

Quatenus vero inflicta est, iniusta erat (1 Pet 2.19–23).

Quatenus autem accepta est, etiam transformata est. Quod enim erat sacrilegium occidentium, etiam morientis factum est sacrificium.[62]

Quatenus proinde praemiata est, factus est Christus homo omnibus obtemperantibus sibi causa salutis aeternae (Heb 5.9).

Quatenus denique ipse Deus ab aeterno et inflictionem permisit et acceptationem inspiravit et praemiationem intendit,[63] habetur illud divinae sapientiae consilium secundum quod 'melius enim iudicavit [Deus] de malis bene facere quam nulla mala esse permittere.' Quod quidem consilium

sinner because of his or her sin. None of these kinds of punishment is applicable to Christ, whose sinlessness is so abundantly and frequently attested in scripture (2 Corinthians 5.21, 1 Peter 1.19, 2.22, Hebrews 4.15, 7.26–27).

There is also medicinal punishment, 'not only healing the past sin, but also preserving from future sin, or conducing to some good, and in this way a person is sometimes punished without fault, yet not without cause.'[61] Since, though, theologians all agree that Christ was incapable of sinning, it is likewise common doctrine that there was in him no cause for such medicine to preserve him from future sin. Christ's punishment, therefore, could not have been medicinal in the sense explained above by St Thomas.

Finally, there is punishment that is purely satisfactory. This is the punishment of him who neither sinned nor could sin. Because he did not sin, it differs from simple punishment. Because he was incapable of sin, it differs from medicinal punishment. Because, finally, it proceeded from the sins of others and aims to take them away, it belongs to a third species of punishment, proper to Christ. We do not find it defined in legal treatments of crime and punishment, nor does it come down to the prudence of parents chastising their children; it is to be gathered, rather, from the mystery of the cross: Christ crucified, the wisdom of God (1 Corinthians 1.23–24).

This punishment, then, affirmed in mystery, was inflicted, accepted, and rewarded, permitted, inspired, and intended.

In the measure it was inflicted, it was unjust (1 Peter 2.19–23).

In the measure it was accepted, it was also transformed. For what was a sacrilege on the part of those who put Christ to death became a sacrifice on the part of him who died.[62]

In the measure it was rewarded, the human Christ was made the source of eternal salvation for all who obey him (Hebrews 5.9).

In the measure, finally, that God himself in his eternal decree permitted this punishment to be inflicted and inspired its acceptance and intended its reward,[63] we can discern that plan of divine wisdom according to which '[God] judged it better to draw good things out of evil than to permit no evils to exist.' This plan was carried out according to the meaning, the law,

61 Thomas Aquinas, *Summa theologiae*, 2-2, q. 108, a. 4; 1-2, q. 87, aa. 7 and 8; 1 Corinthians 9.27.
62 Thomas Aquinas, *Summa theologiae*, 3, q. 48, a. 3, ad 3m.
63 Ibid. q. 47, a. 3.

erat secundum rationem, legem, mysterium, et iustitiam crucis, secundum quam Christus crucifixus agnoscitur esse Dei sapientia (1 Cor 1.23–24).

Quae tamen nisi generale rei schema non determinant. Restat enim dicendum quemadmodum satisfactoria fuerit poena Christi. Sed antequam ipsam hanc quaestionem adgrediamur, excludenda videtur veterum Protestantium sententia quae Christum quodammodo condemnatum atque castigatum voluit.

**Articulus XXX: De poenis in Christum translatis**

Iam ad initium nostrae inquisitionis iterum redeundum est, ut alius et quartus aspectus Anselmianae disiunctionis consideretur. Diximus enim illam disiunctionem, aut satisfactio aut poena, eo sensu esse veram ut hoc in rerum ordine aut Christus pro peccatis satisfaciat aut ipsi peccatores poenas dent (Act 4.12; DB 790). Negavimus vero eandem disiunctionem ita esse veram ut absoluta Dei potentia tertium membrum, gratuita nempe peccatorum condonatio, dari non possit (cf. art. XXVII), vel ut omnis ratio poenae a morte Christi sit excludenda (cf. art. XXIX). Remanet tamen demonstrandum aliam prorsus rationem poenae in morte Christi inveniri et aliam in ipsis peccatoribus qui Christo salutis causae (Heb 5.9) non obtemperent. Satisfactio enim Christi, etsi poenae nomen habeat, secundum divinam crucis sapientiam atque iustitiam redditur; sed poenae simpliciter quae peccatoribus ipsis infliguntur secundum sapientiam et iustitiam divini iudicis solvuntur. Quae cum ita sint, alio et quarto modo eoque vero redit disiunctio, aut satisfactio aut poena, ut in actuali rerum ordine illud valeat, aut iustitia crucis aut iustitia iudicis.

Attamen, ut haec disiunctio stabiliatur, contra eos (cf. art. XXVIII) agendum est qui crucis iustitiam praetermittunt et Christum arbitrantur secundum iustitiam iudicis poenas stricte dictas dedisse. Quorum sane error iam radicitus expugnatus est, cum Christum secundum divinam crucis sapientiam atque iustitiam esse passum, mortuum, et resurrectum superius demonstraverimus (cap. III). At quamvis, sublata erroris radice, per se eiusdem consectaria etiam tollantur, efficacius tamen procedit qui singula consectaria examinet atque refutet.

*Primum* ergo sit argumentum quod iustus iudex non bis de eodem delicto poenas sumit. Si ergo Christus poenas stricte dictas pro omnibus peccatis iam dedisset, nemo alius ad poenas dandas iam teneretur. Evacuatur ergo

the mystery, and the justice of the cross, by reason of which Christ crucified is acknowledged to be the wisdom of God (1 Corinthians 1.23–24)

This, however, is but a general outline of the question. We must now determine more precisely how Christ's punishment was satisfactory. But before doing so we had better reject the opinion of the early Protestant theologians who held that Christ was in some way condemned and chastised.

### Article 30: Transference of punishment to Christ

We must now go back to the beginning of our inquiry to consider a fourth aspect of Anselm's disjunction. We said that that disjunction, 'either satisfaction or punishment,' is true in this sense, that in the present order of things either Christ satisfies for sins or the sinners themselves are punished (Acts 4.12; DB 790, [DS 1513, ND 510]). We said, however, that the same disjunction is not true in the sense of excluding a third possibility, namely, the gratuitous pardon for sin by God's absolute power (see article 27), or in the sense that all notion of punishment whatsoever is to be excluded from the death of Christ (see article 29). Now we must go on to show that there is one kind of punishment connected with the death of Christ and quite a different one for those sinners who do not obey Christ, the source of salvation (Hebrews 5.9). For Christ's satisfaction, although it may be referred to as punishment, is made according to the divine wisdom and justice of the cross; but simple punishment, punishment as such, is imposed upon sinners themselves according to the wisdom and justice of a divine judge. And so the disjunction, 'either satisfaction or punishment,' comes back in a fourth form, the correct one, namely that in the actual order of reality this is the operative disjunction, 'either the justice of the cross or the justice of a judge.'

To establish this disjunction, we have to argue against those who, ignoring the justice of the cross, hold that Christ received punishment in the strict sense of the term according to the justice of a judge (see article 28). We struck the root of this error when we demonstrated in chapter 3 that Christ suffered, died, and was raised up in accordance with divine wisdom and justice. But although the destruction of the roots of the error entails the rejection of its consequences, nevertheless it will be more effective if we scrutinize and refute each consequence separately.

Let our *first* argument be as follows. A just judge does not punish twice for the same offense. If Christ had already been punished in the strict sense for all sins, no one else would any longer be liable for punishment for them.

infernus. Evacuatur purgatorium. Neve quis dicat mala huius mundi rationem poenae habere.

Dices tamen etsi Christus sufficienter pro omnibus delictis poenas dederit, non ideo omnibus pariter meritum Christi esse applicatum.

Instatur meritum Christi certo iis applicatur quorum peccata in sacramento paenitentiae remittuntur. Saltem ergo eorum omnis poena remittitur; quod tamen haereticum est, et contra novatores saec. XVI anathematizatum (DB 904, 905, 922–25).

*Alterum* deinde sit argumentum quod poena stricte dicta, peccato mortali contracta, est aeterna poena damni et sensus. Si ergo Christus poenas pro peccatis debitas dedit, hanc poenam dedit. Quod manifeste falsum est, cum iam pridem exaltatus ad dexteram Patris sedet.

Dices tamen cum Calvino aliisque eiusdem mentis Protestantibus satis fuisse Christum ad breve tempus hanc poenam subiisse.

Respondetur sic derelinqui opinionem quae asserit Christum eam dedisse poenam quae pro peccatis debetur; et etiam sic non pertingi ad veritatem cum sine serio fundamento asseritur Christus poenam infernalem dedisse.

*Tertium* est argumentum quod contra doctrinam novi testamenti asseritur ira Dei Patris contra suum Filium intenta.

Nam Deus qui infert iram non est iniquus (Rom 3.5) sed reddet unicuique secundum opera eius (Rom 2.5). Christus autem peccatum non fecit (1 Pet 2.22) neque noverat (2 Cor 5.21), absque peccato (Heb 4.15, 7.26–27), immaculatus (1 Pet 1.19); et iustus pro iniustis (1 Pet 3.18) iniuste iudicatus est (1 Pet 2.23). Non ergo erat natura filius irae (Eph 2.3) sed Filius dilectionis (Col 1.13); neque erat vas irae aptum in interitum (Rom 9.22) neque positus in iram qui nos ab ira eripuit, adquisivit, salvos fecit (1 Thess 1.10, 5.9, Rom 5.9). Lex quidem iram operatur (Rom 4.15) sed Filius dedit nobis non legem sed gratiam et veritatem (Io 1.17) eosque qui sub lege erant redemit (Gal 4.5). Est praeterea ira Dei super omnem iniquitatem[64] et iniustitiam (Rom 1.18; cf. Apoc. 11.18, 14.10, 16.19); sed eadem ira est in eos qui in Christum non credunt (Io 3.36, Rom 2.8, Eph 5.6, Col 3.6) vel evangelium impediunt (1 Thess 2.16). Est denique ira

Hell would be empty. Purgatory would be empty. One could not say that the evils of this world meet the definition of punishment.

You may object that even though Christ was punished sufficiently for all transgressions, it does not follow that his merits are applied equally to all.

Furthermore, you may say, Christ's merits are certainly applied to those whose sins are forgiven in the sacrament of penance. At least, then, in their case all liability to punishment is remitted. But this is heretical, and was condemned against the sixteenth-century reformers (DB 904, 905, 922–25, [DS 1689–91, 1692, 1722–15, ND 1630–32, 1633]).

Our *second* argument: punishment in the strict sense for mortal sin is the everlasting pain of loss and pain of sense. If Christ was duly punished for sin, this was his punishment. But this is obviously false, since he is now exalted at the right hand of the Father.

You may object, along with Calvin and like-minded Protestants, that it would have been enough for Christ to undergo such punishment for a very short time.

We reply that this objection in fact abandons the opinion that Christ suffered the punishment that is due to sin; and moreover, to assert without any serious grounds that Christ suffered the pains of hell does not contribute towards determining the truth of the matter.

Our *third* argument: it is contrary to the teaching of the New Testament to state that the anger of God the Father was directed against his Son.

For God, though angry, is not unjust (Romans 3.5), but renders to each according to his or her deeds (Romans 2.5). Christ, however, did not sin (1 Peter 2.22), knew no sin (2 Corinthians 5.21), was without sin (Hebrews 4.15, 7.26–27), was spotless (1 Peter 1.19); and just though he was, on behalf of the unjust (1 Peter 3.18) he was unjustly condemned (1 Peter 2.23). He was not by nature a child of wrath (Ephesians 2.3), but the Son that God loves (Colossians 1.13). Nor was he an object of God's anger, fit only to be destroyed (Romans 9.22), nor was he subject to wrath who rescued us from wrath and won salvation for us (1 Thessalonians 1.10, 5.9, Romans 5.9). The law brings wrath (Romans 4.15), but the Son has come to bring us not the law but grace and truth (John 1.17) and to redeem those who were under the law (Galatians 4.5). Besides, God's anger is directed against all iniquity[64] and injustice (Romans 1.18; see also Revelation 11.18, 14.10, 16.19); but this same anger is directed at those who do not believe in Christ (John 3.36, Romans 2.8, Ephesians 5.6, Colossians 3.6) or who hinder the

64 [Vulgate, *impietatem*, 'impiety.']

ventura (Mt 3.7, Lc 21.23) quae tamen non solius Dei est sed etiam Agni (Apoc. 6.16–17; cf. 14.15–20, 19.15).[65]

*Quartum* sit argumentum quod ii qui in Christo patiente et moriente iustitiam crucis nolunt et iustitiam iudicis volunt, iniuriam faciunt Deo Patri, ipsi Christo, exemplo Christi, et praecepto Christi.

Iniuriam faciunt Deo Patri. Pilatus enim, cum Christum condemnaturus esset, 'accepta aqua, lavit manus coram populo dicens: "Innocens ego sum a sanguine iusti huius"' (Mt 27.24). At opinio quam impugnamus vult eundem Christum secundum eandem iudicis iustitiam ad easdem poenas a Deo Patre esse destinatum.

Ulterius, secundum hanc opinionem, quamvis Christus repudiarit legem talionis et praedicarit sapientiam crucis, Deus Pater hanc sapientiam ignorasse videtur et illam legem esse secutus.

Quae quidem iniuria Deo Patri fit circa ipsum maximum actum suae dilectionis erga nos. Ipse enim prior dilexit nos (1 Io 4.9) et dives in misericordia propter nimiam caritatem qua dilexit nos cum essemus mortui peccatis (Eph 2.4–5) erat in Christo mundum reconcilians sibi (2 Cor 5.19) et commendavit caritatem suam in nobis (Rom 5.8) et, cum proprium Filium pro nobis traderet, 'quo modo non etiam cum illo omnia nobis donavit?' (Rom 8.32).

Neque innocua est haec iniuria Deo Patri facta, uti ex doctrina sociniana, liberali, modernistica patet, quae mavult nostram redemptionem negare quam hanc opinionem de Deo Patre admittere.

Dices tamen Christum in se fuisse innocentem sed, quatenus cum iniquis reputatus est (Mc 15.28), iram Dei Patris subiisse.

Respondetur Christum cum iniquis esse reputatum, distinguitur: a Pilato et pontificibus et turba, conceditur; a Deo Patre, negatur.

Deinde illam Dei Patris iram contra Christum intentam aut veram fuisse aut fictam. Si ira vera erat, tunc ficta erat dilectio erga Filium dilectionis suae. Si ira ficta erat, cur ficta factis admiscentur? Non enim ficta erat passio

preaching of the Good News (1 Thessalonians 2.16). There is also the wrath that is to come (Matthew 3.7, Luke 21.23), which is the wrath not only of God but also of the Lamb (Revelation 6.16–17; see also 14.15–20, 19.15).[65]

Our *fourth* argument: those who see in the passion and death of Christ the justice of a judge and not the justice of the cross do an injustice to God the Father, to Christ himself, and to Christ's example and precept.

They do an injustice to the Father. As Pilate was about to condemn Christ to death, 'he took water and washed his hands in front of the crowd, saying, "I am innocent of the blood of this just man"' (Matthew 27.24). But the opinion we are refuting would have this same Christ marked out according t the same justice of a judge for the same punishment by God the Father.

Furthermore, according to this opinion, even though Christ himself repudiated the law of retaliation and preached the wisdom of the cross, God the Father would seem to have ignored this wisdom and followed that discredited law instead.

In fact, this injustice to God the Father touches upon his greatest act of love towards us. He first loved us (1 John 4.9) and being rich in mercy, because of his superabundant love for us when we were dead through our sins (Ephesians 2.4–5) he was in Christ reconciling the world to himself (2 Corinthians 5.19); he thus proved his love for us (Romans 5.8), and since he handed over his Son on behalf of us all, 'how could he refuse to give us all things besides?' (Romans 8.32).

Again, this injustice to the Father has done considerable damage, as is clear from the doctrines of the Socinians, the liberals, and the modernists, who prefer to deny our redemption altogether rather than to accept this opinion of God the Father.

You may object that Christ, though innocent in himself, nevertheless inasmuch as he was ranked among criminals (Mark 15.28) incurred the anger of God the Father.

To this we reply that Christ was ranked among criminals by Pilate and the high priests and the mob, but not by his Father.

Next, this alleged anger of God the Father towards Christ was either real or else it was fictitious. If it was real, then his love for 'the Son whom he loved' was a pretense. But if his anger was fictitious, why mix fiction with

65 On this passage, see also [the commentary on the Book of Revelation by] A. Gelin, in *La Sainte Bible: texte Latin et traduction française d'après les textes originaux, avec un commentaire exégétique et théologique, commencée sous la direction de Louis Pirot, continuée sous la direction de Albert Clamer*, vol. 12 (Paris: Letouzey & Ané, 1946) 615–66, 639–40, 654–55.

Christi, neque ficta erat mors Christi, neque pro peccatis fictis passus et mortuus est.

Primo, ergo, arguitur hanc imputationis opinionem non sibi consistere, cum ficta et facta commisceat. Non enim ficta erat passio vel mors Domini nostri. Neque ficta erat innocentia Domini, impeccantia, imo impeccabilitas. Quod si his tam veris tamque realibus imputationem quandam addis, confusionem potius propriae mentis introducis, quam rei realitate qualitercumque attingis. Dicis propter aliena sed imputata peccata Christum a iusto iudice condemnari; at simul cognoscis iustum iudicem scivisse Christum prorsus innocentem esse et ideo re vera Deum Patrem Filium proprium non condemnasse. Quia fictione laborat peccatorum imputatio, fictione pariter laborat ipsa condemnatio. Dicis Christum poenas stricte dictas dedisse, sed simul cognoscis Christum innocentem neque re vera esse condemnatum neque aliam quam vicariam pro aliis satisfactionem praebuisse. Non minus ergo quam imputatio et condemnatio, etiam fictione laborant poenae quae tamen stricte dictae affirmantur. Dicis iram Dei contra peccatores per imputationem esse conversam in iram contra Christum; et tamen cognoscis Christum innocentem, Dei Patris Filium dilectum; fictam ergo Dei iram addis fictae imputationi, fictae condemnationi, fictis poenis stricte dictis. At realis erat mors Christi, realis erat eius passio. Ludere videris, qui haec realissima per fictionem explicare coneris. Potius ergo 'in omnibus exhibeamus nosmet ipsos sicut Dei ministros … in caritate non ficta, in verbo veritatis' (2 Cor 6.4, 6.6–7). Nisi enim ficta caritas non augetur, ubi a verbo veritatis receditur.[66]

Deinde, iniuria fit ipsi Christo. Qui enim 'dilexit ecclesiam et se ipsum tradidit pro ea, ut illam sanctificaret mundans lavacro aquae in verbo vitae, ut exhiberet sibi gloriosam ecclesiam non habentem maculam aut rugam

fact? The passion of Christ was no fiction, his death was no fiction, and the sins, for which he suffered and died, were no fiction.

Our first argument, then, against this opinion imputing guilt to an innocent Christ is its inconsistency, in that it mixes fact and fiction. The passion and death of our Lord were not fictitious. Neither were the innocence and sinlessness, indeed impeccability, of Christ. But if to these very true and real facts you add an imputation of guilt, you only confuse your own mind rather than attain in whatever way you can the reality of the matter. You maintain that Christ was condemned by a just judge for sins that were not his but were simply imputed to him; but at the same time you know that this just judge was aware that Christ was entirely innocent, and therefore that in reality God the Father did not condemn his Son. Because this imputation of sins is a fiction, so also is his condemnation. You hold that Christ was punished in the strict sense, and yet at the same time you know that he was innocent, that he was not really condemned, that he only offered vicarious satisfaction for others. Therefore this punishment in the strict sense is no less a fiction than the imputation and condemnation. You say the wrath of God against sinners was turned upon Christ by imputation, yet you know Christ was innocent, the beloved Son of the Father; so on top of fictitious imputation and fictitious condemnation and fictitious punishment you add a fictitious wrath of God. But Christ's death was real, and his suffering was real. You seem to be playing games, trying to explain realities by means of fictions. No, let us rather "in all things show that we are God's servants … by a love free of pretense, by a word of truth" (2 Corinthians 6.4, 6.6–7). For only a fictitious love can flourish when we depart from the word of truth.[66]

Second, the opinion [that sees the justice of a judge rather than of the cross] is unjust towards Christ. He who 'loved the church and gave himself up for her, in order to make her holy by cleansing her with the washing of

66 [This paragraph, which occupies an entire page (see www.bernardlonergan.com at 25260DTL060), seems to have been intended for this place in the argument (none of the pages is numbered). At some point, however, and for an unknown reason, this leaf was separated from the others in the autograph, or was not added to them. The verso features a handwritten draft of article-headings for the present chapter. In the autograph, the preceding paragraph introducing the 'fact and fiction' motif was originally followed by quotations from Augustine and Aquinas explaining that the wrath of God is not a passion but a metaphor for God's retributive justice. These, however, trail off at the end of the page and are crossed out, and it seems most likely the present prolongation of the 'fact and fiction' argument was intended to replace them.]

aut aliquid huiusmodi, sed ut sit sancta et immaculata' (Eph 5.25–27), idem ipse cogitatur, non uti erat secundus Adam et caput corporis sui quod est ecclesia, sed uti non erat primus Adam, caput omnium peccatorum, et secundum iustitiam iudicis debitas luens poenas.

Tertio, iniuria fit exemplo Christi. Christus enim nobis exemplum dedit ut patienter toleremus poenas non iuste sed iniuste inflictas (1 Pet 2.19–24). Sed secundum opinionem quam impugnamus, Christus dedit poenas iuste inflictas secundum iustissimam Dei voluntatem.

Quarto, iniuria fit praecepto Christi. Praecepit enim Christus sapientiam et iustitiam crucis (Mt 5.38–48, Mc 8.34, 10.42–45, Io 15.12–13). Sed si in ipso Christo crucifixo perspicienda est sapientia et iustitia non crucis sed iudicis, quis se super Magistrum constituet et praecepto crucis obtemperabit?

*Quintum* denique inde petitur argumentum quod aliud est peccatum vel delictum condemnare et aliud est personam condemnare. Omnes enim proprio utimur iure cum peccata vel delicta condemnemus; at soli iudices legitime constituti personas propter delicta ad poenas simpliciter dictas condemnant.

Praeterea, illud maxime intercedit inter condemnationem peccati et condemnationem personae, quod non illa sed haec statum interpersonalem mutat. Peccati enim condemnatio nihil aliud est quam peccati detestatio. Sed personae condemnatio super detestationem peccati addit praemissam minorem atque explicitam conclusionem ut dicamus hanc personam et peccasse et castigandam esse.

Quare, sicut de peccatis, ita etiam de poenis simpliciter dictis pariter ratiocinandum est. Sicut enim peccatum non tantummodo actus humanus malus est sed etiam Dei offensa, ita etiam poena simpliciter dicta non tantummodo est iusta quaedam boni privatio sed etiam personae dedecus. Quod quidem in rebus humanis omnino clarum est: multi enim duriorem agunt vitam quam ii qui in carceribus retinentur; et tamen melior est illorum sors, quia condemnationis dedecore non dishonorantur. Imo inter ipsos condemnatos, quamvis alii aliis graviores dent poenas, una tamen est poena in omnibus aequalis eaque gravissima quod iuste condemnati sunt.

Quibus perspectis, in Christo crucifixo summam quandam peccati condemnationem conspici minime negamus. Imo, hoc ipsum asseremus cum de satisfactione Christi agamus, nempe, tam Deum Patrem quam ipsum

water by the word, so as to present the church to himself in splendor, without a spot or wrinkle or anything of the kind – yes, so that she may be holy and without blemish' (Ephesians 5.25–27) – he is thought of, by this opinion, not as he really was, the second Adam and head of his body, the church, but rather as the first Adam, which he was not, the head of all sinners, paying the due penalty for sin in accordance with the justice of a judge.

Third, it does an injustice to the example of Christ. For Christ gave us an example of patiently accepting punishment even when inflicted unjustly (1 Peter 2.19–24). But according to the opinion we are rejecting, Christ was justly punished according to the just will of God.

Fourth, it does an injustice to Christ's precept. Christ taught the wisdom and justice of the cross (Matthew 5.38–48, Mark 8.34, 10.42–45, John 15.12–13). But if Christ himself exemplified not the wisdom and justice of the cross but that of a judge, who would ever place himself above the Master and obey the precept of the cross?

Our *fifth* objection is that to condemn a sin or a fault is one thing, but to condemn a person is quite another. We all have a right to condemn sins or faults; but only legitimately constituted judicial authority has the right to exact punishment from persons for their offenses.

Furthermore, the most important difference between the condemnation of a sin and the condemnation of a person is that the latter alters a person's status in society while the former does not. To condemn sin is to express one's detestation of sin. But to condemn a person is to add to the detestation of this sin the minor premise and explicit conclusion that this person both sinned and should be chastised.

This reasoning concerning sin applies likewise to simple punishment. As a sin is not only an evil human act but also an offense against God, so also punishment simply so called is not only the just privation of a good but also a disgrace to the person punished. This is evident in ordinary human experience, where many people have a harder life than the inmates of prisons; and yet their lot is preferable, since they are not dishonored by the disgrace of condemnation. Even among convicts, in fact, although some may have more severe sentences than others, there is one penalty, and a severe one at that, which they share equally, the fact that they have been justly condemned.

We do not by any means deny that in Christ crucified we see an extreme condemnation of sin. In fact, when we treat of Christ's satisfaction we shall stress this point, to wit, both God the Father and Christ himself expressed

Christum per mortem crucis supremam peccati detestationem expressisse, et quidem secundum iudicium et Dei et Christi iustissimum.

Quamvis tamen peccatum in carne Christi damnatum esse (Rom 8.3) affirmemus, negamus prorsus ipsum Christum secundum iustitiam iudicis ad poenas simpliciter dictas esse condemnatum. Non enim condemnatur ipse Christus quin secunda persona SS. Trinitatis condemnetur. Neque sine blasphemia ponitur intra ipsam SS. Trinitatem quod alia divina persona aliam condemnavit.

Neque mitior sed potius gravior redditur haec opinio quod divina persona personam divinam condemnasse dicitur propter peccata non sua sed aliena. Hoc enim, quod additur, ipsam condemnationem secundum iustitiam iudicis non tollit sed divinum iudicem esse iniustum insinuat.

## Articulus XXXI: De analogia sacramentali

Iam pridem illud venamur, quid sit satisfactio. Et primo distinximus ipsa elementa scripturistica et speculationem Anselmianam (art. XXVI). Deinde, disiunctionem examinavimus, aut nempe satisfactio aut poena, utrum tertium dari posset (art. XXVII), utrum ipsa satisfactio sit quodammodo poena (art. XXVIII et XXIX), utrum sit poena secundum iustitiam crucis an secundum iustitiam iudicis (art. XXX).

Unde tria habemus: satisfactionem Christi non absolute necessariam esse; satisfactionem Christi non ita esse opus bonum in honorem Dei factum ut de se ipsam sensibilem et corporalem Christi passionem et mortem non dicat; et satisfactionem Christi non eo sensu esse poenam vel poenalem expiationem ut propter aliena delicta secundum iustitiam iudicis Deus Pater eam a Christo requisiverit.

Quibus determinatis, reliqua via iam lata et plana facta esse videtur. Docet enim synodus Tridentina:

> ... Dominus noster Iesus Christus, qui, cum essemus inimici, propter nimiam caritatem qua dilexit nos, sua sanctissima passione in ligno crucis nobis iustificationem meruit et pro nobis Deo Patri satisfecit (DB 799).

by his death on the cross the supreme detestation of sin, according, moreover, to the most just judgment of God and Christ.

Although we shall maintain that in the flesh of Christ sin has been condemned (Romans 8.3), we utterly deny that Christ himself was sentenced to simple punishment in accordance with the justice of a judge. For to condemn Christ is to condemn the second person of the Trinity, and to have one person of the Trinity condemning another is blasphemous.

This erroneous opinion is not mitigated but rather made worse by saying that one divine person has condemned another not for his own sins but for the sins of others. Such an added nuance does not do away with condemnation according to the justice of a judge, but rather insinuates that a divine judge is unjust.

### Article 31: The sacramental analogy

We have spent considerable time now trying to determine just what is meant by satisfaction. First we distinguished the scriptural elements from Anselm's speculative efforts (article 26). Next we examined the disjunction, 'either satisfaction or punishment,' to determine whether there might be a third possibility (article 27), whether satisfaction itself might in some sense be considered a punishment (articles 28 and 29), and whether it would be a punishment according to the justice of the cross or the justice of a judge (article 30).

Accordingly, we make these three assertions: (1) the satisfaction offered by Christ was not absolutely necessary; (2) this satisfaction was not in such a way excellent in itself and done for the honor of God that it did not include Christ's painful passion and death; and (3) this satisfaction was not a punishment or a punitive expiation in the sense that God the Father required it of Christ for the sins of others in accordance with the justice of a judge.

Having established these points, the rest of the way in our inquiry seems quite easy. For this is what the Council of Trent teaches:

> Our Lord Jesus Christ, out of his immense love for us, when we were God's enemies, merited justification for us by his most holy passion and cross, and made satisfaction to God the Father on our behalf (DB 799, [DS 1529, ND 647]).

Et alibi addit:

> ... dum satisfaciendo patimur pro peccatis, Christo Iesu qui pro nostris peccatis satisfecit ... conformes efficimur ... (DB 904).

Unde concludimus satisfactionem Christi secundum analogiam satisfactionis sacramentalis esse intelligendam.

Quam conclusionem comprobat traditio theologica. Nam antequam S. Anselmus de satisfactione Christi disserere inceperit, iam pridem exsistebat eiusdem nominis ecclesiasticus usus de satisfactione paenitentis.[67] Ipse deinde S. Anselmus, uti inter eruditos constare videtur, non aliunde sed ex ipso usu ecclesiastico suam inspirationem desumpsit.[68] Petrus Lombardus, qui influxum quendem maximum in posteriores theologos exercuit, quamvis opinionis Anselmianae nullam mentionem fecerit, clare tamen nexum posuit inter poenam Christi et poenae vel relaxationem in baptizatis vel in paenitentibus minorationem.[69] *Summa fratris Alexandri* ita doctrinae Anselmianae inhaeret ut etiam de passione Christi ut poena et non solum de morte Christi ut satisfactione loquatur. S. Thomas non solum poenam simpliciter, poenam medicinalem, et poenam satisfactoriam distinxit,[70] sed etiam de ipsa Christi satisfactione tractans, postquam in corpore articuli posuit satisfactionem proprie consistere in opere quod magis placet, in solutione tamen ad primum [argumentum] transit ad analogiam sacramentalem;[71] et paulo ante dixerat, 'et ideo [Christus] non solum attendit quantam virtutem dolor eius haberet ex divinitate unita: sed etiam quantum dolor eius sufficeret secundum naturam humanam ad tantam satisfactionem.'[72]

Eandem conclusionem comprobat theologia sacramentalis. Sicut enim in morte Christi baptizamur (Rom 6.3) mortemque Domini per Eucharistiam annuntiamus donec veniat (1 Cor 11.26), ita omnia sacramenta mortem

And elsewhere the Council adds:

> As we suffer something in making satisfaction for sin, we become like Christ who satisfied for our sins (DB 904, [DS 1690, ND 1631]).

From this we conclude that the satisfaction given by Christ is to be understood according to the analogy of sacramental satisfaction.

Theological tradition confirms this conclusion. For some time before Anselm began to discuss the satisfaction given by Christ, the church had been using the same word in reference to the satisfaction made by penitents.[67] Anselm himself, as the scholars seem to have settled, drew his inspiration from none other than this ecclesiastical usage.[68] Although he does not mention Anselm's opinion, Peter Lombard, who had a great influence on later theologians, quite clearly connected the punishment of Christ with the loosing of punishment for the baptized and its mitigation for penitents.[69] The *Summa fratris Alexandri* follows Anselm in speaking also of the passion of Christ as punishment and not only of his death as satisfaction. St Thomas not only distinguished the three kinds of punishment, simply punitive, medicinal, and satisfactory,[70] but also, in treating the satisfaction given by Christ, having pointed out in the body of the article that satisfaction properly speaking consists in a work more pleasing [to the offended person than the offense was displeasing], nevertheless in the response to the first objection goes on to the sacramental analogy;[71] and just prior to that he had stated, 'He therefore not only considered the value his sorrow would have by virtue of union with the Godhead, but also how much, according to his human nature, it would avail for so great a satisfaction.'[72]

Sacramental theology also confirms this conclusion. As we are baptized into the death of Christ (Romans 6.3) and in the Eucharist proclaim the death of the Lord until he comes (1 Corinthians 11.26), so do all the

67 Paul Galtier, 'Satisfaction,' DTC XIV (27) cols. 1129–1210.
68 Rivière, 'Rédemption' 1943; d'Alès, *De Verbo incarnato* 321.
69 Peter Lombard, *Sententiae*, 3, d. 19, c. 7.
70 Thomas Aquinas, *Summa theologiae*, 1-2, q. 87, a. 8; see also a. 7.
71 Ibid. 3, q. 48, a. 2 c. and ad 1m.
72 Ibid. q. 46, a. 6, ad 6m.

Domini significant,[73] eiusdemque virtute agunt.[74] Eatenus enim effectum passionis Christi consequimur quatenus ei configuramur; et ideo 'oportet quod illi qui post baptismum peccant, configurentur Christo patienti per aliquod poenalitatis vel passionis quam in seipsis sustineant. Quae tamen multo minor sufficit quam esset condigna peccato, cooperante satisfactione Christi.'[75] Quibus clare docetur configuratio, et ideo analogia, inter satisfactionem Christi et paenitentis satisfactionem.

Eandem conclusionem tertio comprobat argumentum quod praecedentibus articulis elaboravimus. Qui enim notionem satisfactionis ex analogia iuris quaerunt, aliter satisfactionem non concipiunt quam secundum iustitiam iudicis; sed satisfactio Christi non fuit secundum iustitiam iudicis sed secundum iustitiam crucis; et ideo conceptio satisfactionis ex iure petita admitti non debet. Qui autem secundum theoriam reparationis ita premunt illam satisfactionis definitionem quae opus bonum et magis Deo placens ponit, ut ipsa sensibilis et corporalis passio Christi 'un élément de fait,' 'un trait secondaire et superficiel'[76] reputetur, theoriam elaborare videntur quae parum confert ad vicariam Christi passionem (art. XX) intelligendam. Exclusis autem et conceptione iuridica et reparationis theoria, non manet alia satisfactionis notio et traditionalis et theologica praeter eam quae ex analogia satisfactionis sacramentalis petitur.

Quae cum ita sint, etiam perspicuum est non univoce dici sed analogice Christum et paenitentes satisfacere. Non enim pro suis peccatis sed pro alienis satisfecit Christus, neque secundum iustitiam iudicis sed secundum iustitiam crucis. Paenitens autem pro suis peccatis satisfacit, quorum remissionem per actum iudicialem absolutionis (DB 919) habet quoad culpam sed non quoad universam poenam (DB 922–25); ideoque satisfactio ei imponitur secundum potestatem clavium non 'tantum ad novae vitae custodiam et infirmitatis medicamentum sed etiam ad praeteritorum peccatorum vindictam et castigationem' (DB 905). Sed in Christo numquam fuit vetus et peccaminosa vita ut nova custodiatur, neque aderat infirmitas quae medicamento indiguit, neque aderant praeterita peccata quoad culpam

sacraments signify the death of the Lord[73] and are efficacious by its power.[74] We obtain the effects of Christ's passion insofar as we are conformed to Christ in his sufferings. That is why 'it is necessary that those who commit sin after their baptism be conformed to the suffering Christ by some form of punishment or suffering endured by themselves. Yet, by the cooperation of Christ's satisfaction, much lighter penalty suffices than if it were proportionate to the sin.'[75] All of this clearly indicates the conformity, and hence the analogy, between the satisfaction given by Christ and that given by a penitent.

A third confirmation of this conclusion is provided by the argument developed in the previous articles. Those who try to base the notion of satisfaction upon a juridical analogy will necessarily conceive it according to the justice of a judge. But Christ's satisfaction was not according to the justice of a judge but according to the justice of the cross, and hence we should not accept a concept of satisfaction taken from jurisprudence. On the other hand, those who according to a theory of reparation lay such emphasis upon the definition of satisfaction as a good work more pleasing to God that they reduce the physical sufferings of Christ to 'un *élément* de fait,' 'un trait secondaire et superficiel,'[76] would seem to be expounding a theory which contributes little to understanding the vicarious suffering of Christ (article 20). If, then, both the juridical concept of satisfaction and the theory of reparation are eliminated, we are left with that notion of satisfaction, both traditional and theological, which is based upon the analogy with sacramental satisfaction.

From what we have said, it is obvious as well that satisfaction is predicated of Christ and of penitents not univocally but analogously. Christ offered satisfaction not for his own sins but for the sins of others, and not according to the justice of a judge but according to the justice of the cross. Penitents, however, satisfy for sins of their own, which by a judicial act of absolution (DB 919, [DS 1709, ND 1649]) are remitted as to guilt but not as to the entire punishment due to them (DB 922–25, [DS 1712–15, ND 1652–55]). For this reason the duty of satisfaction is imposed upon a penitent according to the power of the keys 'not only as a safeguard for their renewed spiritual life and a healing of weakness but also as retribution and chastisement for their past sins' (DB 905, [DS 1692, ND 1633]). But Christ never had a sinful past

73 Ibid. q. 60, a. 3.
74 Ibid. q. 62, a. 5.
75 Ibid. q. 49, a. 3, ad 2m.
76 Rivière, 'Rédemption' 1973.

remissa sed non quoad universam poenam ut secundum vindictam castigaretur. Et ideo non habetur satisfactionis univocitas sed analogia.

## Articulus XXXII: De dolore Christi

Quamvis satisfactio ita in actu exteriori consistat ut alius pro alio satisfacere possit,[77] non tamen sine principio interiori fit, quod in primis fuit dolor Christi pro peccatis nostris. De quo dolore haec habet S. Thomas:

> Doloris autem interioris causa fuit, primo quidem, omnia peccata humani generis, pro quibus satisfaciebat patiendo: unde ea quasi sibi adscribit, dicens in Psalmo 21.2: 'Verba delictorum meorum.' Secundo, specialiter casus Iudaeorum et aliorum in eius mortem delinquentium: et praecipue discipulorum qui scandalum passi fuerant in Christi passione.[78]

> Sed secundum rei veritatem, tristitia aliqua laudabilis est, ut Augustinus probat in XIV *De civ. Dei*[79] quando scilicet procedit ex sancto amore, ut puta cum aliquis tristatur de peccatis propriis vel alienis. Assumitur etiam ut utilis ad finem satisfactionis pro peccato: secundum illud 2 Cor 7.10: 'Quae secundum Deum est tristitia paenitentiam in salutem stabilem operatur.' Et ideo Christus, ut satisfaceret pro peccatis omnium hominum, assumpsit tristitiam maximam quantitate absoluta, non tamen excedentem regulam rationis.[80]

> Christus non solum doluit pro amissione vitae corporalis propriae: sed etiam pro peccatis omnium aliorum. Qui dolor in Christo excessit omnem dolorem cuiuslibet contriti. Tum quia ex maiori sapientia et caritate processit, ex quibus dolor contritionis augetur. Tum etiam quia pro omnium peccatis simul doluit: secundum illud Is 53.4: 'Vere dolores nostros ipse tulit.'[81]

life in need of renewal, nor moral weakness in need of healing, nor past sins whose guilt was remitted but not all their punishment and which therefore required retributive chastisement. Here, therefore, 'satisfaction' is an analogous, not a univocal, term.

**Article 32: The sorrow of Christ**

While it is true that satisfaction consists in an exterior act in such a way that one person can make satisfaction on behalf of another,[77] nonetheless it springs from an interior principle; this principle was the sorrow Christ had for our sins. Thomas says about this sorrow:

> The cause of his interior sorrow was, first, all the sins of the human race, for which he gave satisfaction by suffering. Hence he applied to himself, as it were, 'the words of my sins' (Psalm 21.1 [EVV 22.1]). Then there was the special case of the Jews and others who were responsible for his death – especially his own disciples, who were shocked at his passion.[78]
>
> But in fact there is a type of sadness that is praiseworthy, as Augustine shows in Book XIV of *The City of God*,[79] that is, when sadness stems from a holy love, as, for example, when a person is saddened by his own or another's sins. Sadness can also be of help towards satisfying for sin, for 'godly grief produces a repentance that leads to salvation' (2 Corinthians 7.10). Christ, then, to satisfy for the sins of all humankind, experienced the most profound sadness, in absolute terms, though not as much as to go beyond the bounds of reason.[80]
>
> Christ grieved not only on account of the loss of his bodily life but also for the sins of all others. This sorrow of his surpassed any sorrow ever felt by a repentant sinner, first because it proceeded from a greater wisdom and love, by which the sorrow of contrition is intensified, and second, because he grieved for all sins at once. As Isaiah said (53.4), 'Surely he has borne our sorrows.'[81]

77 Thomas Aquinas, *Summa theologiae,* 3, q. 48, a. 2, ad 1m.
78 Ibid. q. 46, a. 6 c.
79 Augustine, *De civitate Dei* XIV, cc. 8–9; ML 41, 411–413.
80 Thomas Aquinas, *Summa theologiae,* 3, q. 46, a. 6, ad 2m.
81 Ibid. ad 4m.

> Christus voluit genus humanum a peccatis liberare non sola potestate sed etiam iustitia. Et ideo non solum attendit quantam virtutem dolor eius haberet ex divinitate unita: sed etiam quantum eius dolor sufficeret secundum naturam humanam ad tantam satisfactionem.[82]

Quem interiorem dolorem non solum ex auctoritate S. Thomae statuimus sed etiam ratione theologica probamus.

Non enim alia erat intentio vel volitio Filii hominis ac Dei Patris (Mc 14.36; DB 291). Sed secundum divinam intentionem atque volitionem Christus pro omnibus peccatis generis humani passus et mortuus est (art. XX). Ergo etiam secundum intentionem et volitionem Filii hominis ipse pro omnibus peccatis passus et mortuus est.

Quod si haec erat eius intentio atque volitio, etiam ideo suam passionem et mortem accepit ut sit pro peccatis; quod quidem non faceret nisi ipsa peccata considerando, detestando, de iis dolendo, utque ea tolleret sibi proponendo.

Et certissime Christus peccata detestatus est. Visione enim immediata divinam bonitatem cognovit, et ideo malitiam peccati profundius intellexit quam vel potuisset quilibet alius viator. Praeterea, sicut summa caritate Patrem dilexit, ita etiam summa detestatione offensam Patris oderat.

Proinde quam maxime pro nostris peccatis doluit. Quo enim perfectior est dilectio Dei, eo perfectior est dilectio proximi (1 Io 3.10, 4.20). Sed Christus homo et perfectissime Deum dilexit, et propter assumptam naturam humanam genus humanum sibi proximum habuit. Maximam ergo dilectionem erga homines habuit, uti ipse testatus est, 'Maiorem hac dilectionem nemo habet ut animam suam ponat quis pro amicis suis' (Io 15.13).

Sed haec Christi dilectio erga nos minime impedivit quominus et summopere peccata detestaretur et verissime nos tot tantisque peccatis infectos esse cognosceret.

Mediator ergo positus erat inter (1) Deum Patrem super omnia a se dilectum et (2) nos Deo Patri inimicos sed sibi et natura et dilectione coniunctos.

> Christ willed to free the human race from sins not only by an exercise of power but also in accordance with justice. He therefore not only considered the value his sorrow would have by virtue of his own divine nature, but also how far his sorrow would go according to his human nature towards giving such satisfaction as was called for by sin.[82]

But we wish not only to ground this interior sorrow on the authority of St Thomas, but also to prove it by theological reasoning.

The intention and will of the Son of man was not different from his Father's (Mark 14.36; DB 291, [DS 556, ND 635]). But it was in accordance with the divine intention and will that Christ should suffer and die for all the sins of the human race (article 20). Therefore it was in accordance with the Son of man's own intention and will to suffer and die for all sins.

Now if this was his intention and will, he also accepted his passion and death as something to be undergone for sins; but he could not do this except by considering sins themselves, by detesting them, grieving for them, and resolving to take them away.

Certainly Christ detested sin. He had immediate vision of the divine goodness, and so he had a more profound understanding of sin than any other human being could have in this life. Besides, he loved the Father with the utmost charity, and so hated an offense against the Father with the utmost detestation.

Furthermore, our sins were for him the cause of the greatest possible sorrow. The more perfect is one's love of God, the more perfect is his love of neighbor (1 John 3.10, 4.20). But the human Christ both loved God perfectly and, on account of his assumed human nature, held the human race as his neighbor. Therefore he loved human beings with the greatest love, as he himself testified: 'no one has greater love than this, to lay down one's life for one's friends' (John 15.13).

But this love of Christ for us in no way prevented him from utterly detesting our sins and most accurately knowing how greatly we have been infected by sin.

He was therefore a mediator placed between (1) God the Father whom he loved above all else and (2) us, God the Father's enemies yet joined to himself by both nature and love.

82 Ibid. ad 6m.

Iam vero ipsa haec boni dilecti cum malo gravissimo coniunctio exsistit doloris origo, fons, causa.[83] Quam maxime ergo doluit Christus pro nobis de nostris peccatis; et ideo de eo intelliguntur verba: 'Attendite et videte si est dolor sicut dolor meus' (Thren 1.12), et ipse dixit: 'Tristis est anima mea usque ad mortem' (Mc 14.34).

Ex hac ergo dilectione, peccati detestatione, et de nostris peccatis dolore, sequebatur firmissimum propositum tollendi peccata mundi. Quo enim magis malum detestamus et magis de malo dolemus, eo firmius nobis proponimus ut malum illud auferamus. Et sicut in Christo maxima fuit dilectio erga Patrem et erga nos, et maxima fuit peccati detestatio, et maximus de nostris peccatis dolor, ita etiam, uti ipse eventus probat, firmissimum fuit propositum tollendi peccata mundi.

Quae cum ita sint, sicut satisfactio paenitentis ex contritione procedit quae 'animi dolor ac detestatio est de peccato cum proposito non peccandi de caetero' (DB 897), ita secundum similitudinem quandam satisfactio Christi ex detestatione peccati, ex dolore de nostris peccatis, ex proposito denique firmissimo peccata auferendi processit.

### Articulus XXXIII: De satisfactione Christi

Quam superius (art. XXXII) in Christo fuisse conclusimus dilectionem Dei Patris et nostri, peccati detestationem, de nostris peccatis dolorem, peccataque omnia auferendi et praecavendi firmissimum propositum, brevitatis causa uno vocabulo nominari licet actum interiorem.

Qui interior actus tripliciter in Christo exerceri potuit.

Primo modo, per scientiam Dei immediatam vel per se infusam et per voluntatem consequentem; et sic semper exerceri potuit, cum scientia Dei immediata et scientia per se infusa sine cooperatione sensibilitatis exerceantur.

Altero modo, per scientiam acquisitam et sensibilitatem interiorem. Qui quidem modus primum minime excludit sed ei addi potest; attamen semper exerceri non potuit, tum quia sensibilitatem evolutam supponit et scientiam acquisitam, tum quia sensibilitas circa unum obiectum operans ad aliud parum attendere potest.

It was precisely this juxtaposition of the good he loved with the greatest of evils that was the root, source, and cause of his sorrow.[83] His grief for us and for our sins was the greatest sorrow possible, and therefore we understand of him the words, 'Look and see if there is any sorrow like my sorrow' (Lamentations 1.12), and, as he said of himself, 'My soul is sorrowful to the point of death' (Mark 14.34).

Out of his great love, his detestation for sin, and his sorrow for our sins he formed the firm resolve to take away the sins of the world. The more we detest evil and the more we grieve over it, the more firmly do we determine to get rid of it. As Christ had the greatest possible love for the Father and for us, the greatest possible detestation for sin, and the greatest possible sorrow for our sins, so also, as the event proved, he had the most resolute determination to take away the sins of the world.

Thus, just as the satisfaction given by a penitent follows contrition, which is an 'interior sorrow and detestation for sin together with the resolve to sin no more' (DB 897, [DS 1676, ND 1622]), so in a similar way Christ's satisfaction stemmed from his detestation of sin, his sorrow for our sins, and his firm resolve to take away sin.

**Article 33: The satisfaction made by Christ**

The conclusion we have reached in the previous article, namely, that Christ loved God the Father and us, that he had a detestation for sin and sorrow for our sins together with a firm resolve to take away sin and prevent future sin, may for the sake of brevity be referred to as an interior act.

This interior act could have been exercised by Christ in three ways:

First, through his immediate or per se infused knowledge of God and his consequent will. In this way he could have exercised this interior act at all times, since immediate knowledge of God and per se infused knowledge do not depend upon sentient operations for their exercise.

Second, through his acquired knowledge and interior sensibility. This way does not in any way exclude the first, but can be added to it. However, it could not have been exercised at all times, because it presupposes a developed human sensibility and acquired knowledge, and also because when the senses are engaged upon one object they can give little attention to another.

83 Ibid. 1-2, q. 35, a. 1.

Tertio modo, ulterius per sensibilitatem exteriorem motusque corporales. Et hic modus priores supponit atque includit, cum actum non hominis sed humanum consideremus;[84] sed quo vehementior fit hic exterior actus, eo etiam rarior esse potest; puta, hominem posse suum dolorem verbis saepissime exprimere, lacrymis rarius, gravissimis paenitentiis rarissime, et mortem crucis subeundo semel tantum.

Quibus perspectis, cum supra interiorem doloris actum consideraverimus (art. XXXII), iam quaeri oportet quid tertius modus super primum et secundum addat.

Primo, ergo, actus tertio modo exercitus magis est completus in ratione actus humani. Sicut enim ipsa anima hominis per se et naturaliter est forma corporis organici, ita etiam actus humani intellectus et voluntatis per se et naturaliter informant, dirigunt, regunt non solum interiorem sensibilitatem sed etiam exteriorem et ipsos motus corporales. Quapropter hominem fere mortuum aestimaremus qui numquam corpus suum ullo modo moveret.

Praeterea, quod interius tantummodo agimus, illud et absconditum et prorsus privatum est; quod autem exterius agimus, iam per se manifestum atque publicum est. Sed homo naturaliter est, non monas quaedam Leibniziana, sed animal politicum seu sociale; et ideo sicut alius homo ex alio generationem accipit, ita etiam nihil fere notatu dignum facit quin multipliciter cooperatio humana et praesupponatur et usurpetur.

Praeterea, ipsi accedentes corporales motus dupliciter effectus ulteriores producunt: primo modo, secundum virtutem naturalem, et sic corpore nostro alia corpora tangimus, movemus, alteramus; alio modo, secundum virtutem intentionalem, et sic tum omnia opera artis producimus tum aliis significamus quid ipsi interius sentiamus, intelligamus, velimus.

Praeterea, uti supra habitum est (art. III), maxime dividuntur haec signa in denotativa et expressiva, quorum illa faciunt ut alii percipiant et intelligant, haec autem eo usque pertingunt ut alii non solum percipiant intelligantque sed etiam commoveantur et modo correspondente agere velint.

Third, it could be further exercised through the exterior senses and bodily movements. This third way presupposes and includes the first two, since what is involved here is a formally human act, *actus humanus*, not an action of a human being, *actus hominis*.[84] The more intense this exterior act is, the rarer it is likely to be; a person, for example, may quite often express his sorrow in words, less often by tears, very rarely by severe penitential acts, and only once by submitting to death on a cross.

Since we have considered the interior act of sorrow in the previous article, let us now look at what this third way adds to the first and second.

First, then, an act performed in the third way is more complete as a human act. As the human soul is per se the natural substantial form of an organic body, so also the human acts of intellect and will per se and naturally inform, direct, and control not only one's interior sensibility but also the external senses and outward bodily movements. For this reason we should regard as practically dead one who never moves his or her body in any way.

Again, whatever we do in a purely interior manner remains totally hidden and private; what we do outwardly, on the other hand, becomes manifest in itself and public. But a human person by nature is not a Leibnizian monad but a political and social animal; hence, just as one person is begotten from another, so also one does very little that is noteworthy without presupposing and making use of the cooperation and contribution of many others.

Moreover, those added bodily movements themselves give rise to further effects in two ways: first, by their natural power, as when by our body we touch, move, or alter other bodies; secondly, by intentional power, as when we produce works of art, or when we signify to others what we interiorly feel, understand, will.

Besides, as we mentioned previously in article 3, these signs are principally divided into denotative and expressive. The denonative cause others to perceive and understand, while the expressive not only get others to perceive and understand, but also rouse them to appropriate action.

84 [The following note appeared in *The Incarnate Word*, p. 729: 'The distinction here is between (1) acts (such as seeing) that are a human being's acts yet are not, for that reason alone, specifically human acts, and (2) acts that are both those of a human being and also specifically human, particularly acts involving moral agency. See Thomas Aquinas, *Summa theologiae*, 1-2, q. 1, a. 3.']

Denique, ubi de signis expressivis agitur, inter ipsam expressionem et consequentem communicationem caute distinguendum est. Ipsa enim expressio perficitur inquantum interiori actui accedunt illi motus corporales qui ad interiorem exprimendum apti nati sunt. Sed non ante incipit communicatio quam, expressione peracta, ita tangitur cor alterius ut ipse intus percipiat, sentiat, intelligat, velit quod per expressionem intendebatur. Ita ad communicationem pertinet quod ipsi hodie experimur dum Dominum nostrum in cruce fixum contemplamur; sed quod hodie nobis communicatur, ab ipso Domino abhinc fere viginti saecula in suo corpore expressum est.

His igitur praemissis quaeruntur quattuor: (1) utrum convenerit Dominum nostrum interiorem suum doloris actum tertio et exteriori modo exercere; (2) utrum convenerit eum hunc in finem passionem suam atque mortem acceptare; (3) utrum ita accepta passio et mors fuerit passio sua vicaria; et (4) utrum ita intellecta passio vicaria fuerit satisfactio vicaria.

*Ad primam* [quaestionem] ergo dicimus convenisse Dominum nostrum tertio et exteriori modo interiorem suum dolorem exercere.

Nam operatio humana et completa non solum secundum partem intellectivam et interiorem sensibilitatem exercetur sed etiam secundum exteriorem sensibilitatem motusque corporales. Sicut ergo Dei Verbum totam naturam humanam assumpsit, ita etiam conveniebat eum operari non tantum per modum animae separatae vel tantum per sensibilitatem interiorem sed secundum totum hominem; et hoc eo magis quod sacrae litterae signate corporis assumptionem affirment, v.g., 'Verbum caro factum est' (Io 1.14) et carni et sanguini similiter participavit (Heb 2.14) et 'corpus autem aptasti mihi' (Heb 10.5).

Praeterea, actus interior est absconditus et privatus, sed actus tertio modo exercitus est manifestus atque publicus. Sed interior Christi dolor pro nobis peccatoribus erat, et de nostris peccatis, et in bonum nostrum libere a nobis accipiendum; et ideo maxime conveniebat Christum hunc dolorem exercere non tantum primo vel secundo modo sed maxime modo tertio, manifesto, publico. Non enim corpus in caelis collocatum assumpsit Dei Verbum, sed his in terris factum ex muliere (Gal 4.4) ex semine David (Rom 1.3) ut in nobis habitaret (Io 1.14). Quod ergo cum nobis exsistens Emmanuel pro nobis fecit ut nos similiter faceremus, actu publico et sociali eum facere conveniebat.

Finally, in discussing expressive signs one should carefully distinguish between the expression itself and the consequent communication. The expression is achieved when the interior act is complemented by those bodily movements that are apt for expressing it. But communication begins only when the completed expression touches the heart of another to inwardly perceive, feel, understand, desire what was intended by the expression. So it is that what we experience within ourselves today as we contemplate our Lord, nailed to the cross, is an instance of communication; but what is communicated to us today was expressed bodily by the Lord nearly twenty centuries ago.

Having laid down these premises, we ask these four questions: (1) Was it fitting for the Lord to exercise his interior act of sorrow outwardly according to this third way? (2) Was it fitting for him to accept his passion and death for this purpose? (3) Was this passion and death as accepted by him vicarious suffering? (4) Was his vicarious suffering, so understood, vicarious satisfaction?

*In response to the first question*: It was fitting for our Lord to exercise his interior act of sorrow outwardly according to this third way.

Complete human operations are performed not only in the intellectual part of a person and one's interior sensibility but also in one's exterior senses and bodily movements. Since, therefore, the divine Word assumed human nature in its totality, it was entirely fitting for him to operate not only in the manner of a separated soul or only through his interior sensibility, but through the whole human being – especially since scripture lays such stress on his assumption of a body, as in 'the Word became flesh' (John 1.14) and likewise shared in the same flesh and blood (Hebrews 2.14), and 'a body you have prepared for me' (Hebrews 10.5).

Furthermore, an interior act is hidden and private, whereas an act performed according to the third way is open and public. Now Christ's interior sorrow was for us sinners and on account of our sins, and for our good, to be freely accepted by us. For this reason it was most fitting that Christ should exercise this sorrow not only in the first or second way but also and especially in the open and public third way. It was no celestial body that the Word of God took to himself but an earthly one, born of a woman (Galatians 4.4), of the seed of David (Romans 1.3), to live among us (John 1.14). Hence it was fitting that Emmanuel existing with us should express by a public and social action that which he was doing for our benefit so that we might do likewise.

*Ad alteram* autem quaestionem dicimus convenisse Dominum nostrum suam passionem et mortem acceptare in expressionem interioris sui doloris.

Quo enim magis ad profundiora humani spiritus acceditur, eo minus apta fiunt nomina verbaque et caetera usitata et communia signa ad veram adaequatamque interioris mentis expressionem. Quod si in aliis hominibus verificatur, multo magis ibi agnoscendum est, ubi agitur de dilectione Christi hominis erga Patrem suum et erga nos, de eius detestatione peccatorum, de eius dolore pro nostris peccatis, de eius proposito nos redimendi. Quae quidem omnia tanta et talia erant ut, nisi per supremum quod facere potest homo, vel innui, multo minus exprimi, non poterant. Quam ob causam ipse dixit tantam esse suam dilectionem quanta maior non esset, ut pro amicis animam poneret (Io 15.13), et tantam esse suam interiorem tristitiam ut usque ad mortem tristis esset (Mc 14.34).

Praeterea, quod hodie fidelibus communicatur, illud olim a Christo expressum est.

Sed hodie fideles Christum crucifixum contemplantes, commoti atque conversi intelligunt quantum Christus homo et Patrem et nos dilexerit, quantum peccata detestatus sit, quantum pro nostris peccatis doluerit, quanta firmitate ad nos redimendos egerit.

Et praeter sensum fidelium opinaretur qui eos tali contemplatione errare diceret, quasi aliud Christus intendisset et aliud fideles intelligerent.

Sed quod vere nunc communicatur et olim intendebatur, illud olim per passionem et mortem Christus expressit.

*Ad tertiam* quaestionem dicimus passionem et mortem in expressionem interioris doloris a Christo acceptam vicariae passionis habere rationem.

Nam vicaria Christi passio (art. xx) in eo est quod secundum divinam intentionem pro nobis et pro nostris peccatis passus et mortuus est Christus, ut scilicet pateretur et moreretur non solum ad peccata tollenda sed etiam propter peccata commissa, secundum illud: 'Peccata nostra ipse pertulit in corpore suo super lignum' (1 Pet 2.24).

Quod quidem (cf. art. xx) actionem quandam ex peccatis nostris in corpus Christi importat.

Quae actio non physica sed intentionalis fuit. Nam propter omnia peccata etiam tunc futura passus et mortuus est Christus. Et peccata tunc futura nisi intentionaliter agere non poterant.

Quae actio intentionalis fuit mediante intellectu et voluntate non Dei Patris sed Christi hominis. Nam Deus Pater non potest esse instrumentum

*In response to the second question*: It was fitting for our Lord to accept his passion and death as an expression of his interior sorrow.

The more deeply one plumbs the depths of the human spirit, the more difficult it is to find words and other commonly used signs to give correct and adequate expression to one's interior mind and heart. And if this is true of others, how much more should we grant it of Christ, when we consider his human love for his Father and for us, his detestation of sin, his sorrow for our sins, and his resolve to redeem us. So immense and so excellent were these interior realities that they could not even be intimated, let alone expressed, save by the greatest deed a human being can do. Wherefore he himself called his love the greatest of all loves, to lay down his life for his friends (John 15.13), and his great interior sorrow a sorrow even unto death (Mark 14.34).

Moreover, what is communicated to believers today is what Christ expressed long ago.

But the faithful today, contemplating Christ crucified, moved and converted, understand how great was Christ's love for his Father and for us, how intense his detestation of sin, how deep his sorrow for our sins, and how resolutely he acted to redeem us.

It would be contrary to the *sensus fidelium* to say that such contemplation is false and erroneous, as if Christ had meant one thing and the faithful understood something else.

Rather, what is communicated truly today and was meant long ago is precisely what Christ expressed by his passion and death.

*In response to the third question*: The passion and death accepted by Christ as an expression of his interior sorrow is rightly understood as vicarious suffering in the proper sense of the word.

The vicarious suffering of Christ (see article 20) consists in this, that according to God's intention Christ suffered and died for us and because of our sins, so that his suffering and death was not only for the purpose of taking away sins, but was also because of sins: 'He himself bore our sins in his body on the cross' (1 Peter 2.24).

This implies (see article 20) some action from our sins upon the body of Christ.

Such action was not physical but intentional, for Christ suffered and died because of all sins, including those that were then in the future, and future sins could have exerted only an intentional influence upon him.

This intentional action was mediated through the intellect and will, not of God the Father but of the human Christ. For God the Father cannot be

quoddam intermedium quod motum movet, sed motor immobilis exsistit. Neque alius praeter Deum nisi Christus homo omnia actualia peccata cognovit ut per eum in Christum agerent peccata.

Relinquitur ergo ut omnia peccata eatenus passionem et mortem Christi causaverint quatenus ipse Christus passionem et mortem acceptavit in expressionem interioris sui doloris. Quod quidem nihil est aliud quam hoc, quod passio morsque Christi rationem vicariae passionis habent quatenus in expressionem doloris interioris acceptae sunt.

*Ad quartam* quaestionem dicimus vicariam Christi passionem, in expressionem interioris doloris acceptam, vicariae satisfactionis rationem habere.

Nam dolor ille interior erat vicarius, nempe, ex dilectione nostri et de nostris peccatis quia Deum Patrem Christo dilectissimum offendebant.

Et passio morsque, in expressionem huius doloris vicarii acceptae, manifeste habent rationem satisfactionis, si quidem satisfactio est opus poenale susceptum ex detestatione peccati, ex dolore de peccatis, ex proposito auferendi peccata eaque praecavendi.

Praeterea, haec satisfactio vicaria erat, tum ratione motivi quia propter peccata aliena suscepta est, tum ratione agentis quia quod in capite actum est pro toto corpore fit (cf. art. XLI), tum ratione effectus quia satisfactio Christi in baptizatis tollit omnem reatum culpae et poenae, et in paenitentibus purgat peccatorum reliquias.[85]

**Articulus XXXIV: De satisfactione superabundante**

Superabundasse Christi satisfactionem, sicut docent theologi,[86] ita etiam Clemens VI, cum doctrinam de indulgentiis fundaret, hisce verbis vivide expressit: '... sanguine ... quem in ara crucis innocens immolatus non guttam sanguinis modicam, *quae tamen propter unionem ad Verbum pro redemptione totius humani generis suffecisset*, sed copiose velut quoddam profluvium noscitur effudisse' (DB 550).

an intermediate instrument that transmits a movement communicated to him, for he exists as the unmovable mover. And apart from God, no one but the human Christ knew all actual sins, so that it was through his intellect and will that sins acted upon him.

We conclude, then, that all sins caused Christ's passion and death inasmuch as he accepted his passion and death to express his interior sorrow. This simply means that the passion and death of Christ are rightly understood as vicarious suffering, inasmuch as they were accepted to express his interior sorrow.

*In response to the fourth question:* This vicarious suffering of Christ, accepted as an expression of his interior sorrow, is rightly understood as vicarious satisfaction.

Christ's interior sorrow was vicarious, that is, it proceeded from his love for us and with regard to our sins which offended God the Father whom he so greatly loved.

His passion and death, accepted as an expression of this vicarious sorrow, clearly fulfils the definition of satisfaction, since satisfaction is a penal work undertaken out of detestation for sin, sorrow for sin, and the intention of wiping away sins and guarding against them.

Moreover, this satisfaction was vicarious, by reason of its motive, having been undertaken on account of the sins of others, by reason of its agent, since what is done in the head is done on behalf of the whole body (see article 41), and by reason of its effect, since the satisfaction given by Christ takes away all guilt and liability for punishment in the case of the baptized, and purges penitents of the residue of sin.[85]

## Article 34: Superabundant satisfaction

That Christ superabundantly atoned for our sins, the common doctrine among theologians,[86] was also given expression in these vivid words of Pope Clement VI when [in 1343] he was laying the doctrinal foundations for indulgences: '... by his blood ... which the innocent victim on the altar of the cross is known to have shed, not just in a little drop, *which on account of his union with the Word would have been enough to redeem the whole human race,* but in an abundant outpouring' (DB 550, [DS 1025, ND 643]).

85 Thomas Aquinas, *Summa contra Gentiles,* 3, c. 158.
86 Thomas Aquinas, *Summa theologiae,* 3, q. 48, a. 2; q. 46, a. 5, ad 3m.

Quam doctrinam facile ad scripturam reducitur. Nam satisfactio Christi non ex parte delicti sed ex parte gratiae se habuit, et 'ubi autem abundavit delictum, superabundavit gratia' (Rom 5.20); quare sicut aliae gratiae ita etiam satisfactio Christi superabundavit.

Quemadmodum autem haec satisfactio superabundaverit, sequentibus fere declaratur.

Primo, enim, subiectum satisfaciens, tam psychologicum quam ontologicum, erat Dei Verbum (DB 124), unus de sancta Trinitate (DB 222), Dominus gloriae (1 Cor 2.8).

Deinde, actus interior unde processit haec satisfactio et cuius pars fuit formalis, talis erat qualis personae divinae convenit quae in natura assumpta operatur. Iam vero divinae personae ea debebantur quae proportionem excedant cuiuslibet subiecti creati et ipsius assumptae naturae, nempe, visio Dei immediata et perfecta Filii erga Patrem dilectio. Qua ex visione quaque ex dilectione proportionate processerunt et peccati detestatio et de peccatis nostris dolor et nos redimendi propositum firmum. Quibus in omnibus ipsam absolutae supernaturalitatis rationem in prima sua radice perspicis, in persona videlicet divina quae in natura assumpta operatur secundum ea quae divinae personae debentur.

Tertio, actus exterior interiori actui eas corporales alterationes addidit quae ad actum interiorem comparantur sicut proprium corpus ad propriam animam. Sicut enim in sensibilibus perspicitur intelligibile, ita etiam actus interior exteriorem informat; et sicut Christus homo interiorem suum actum in passione morteque expressit, ita fideles in hac passione hacque morte contemplantur divinae personae humiliationem, obedientiam, dilectionem, peccati detestationem, pro peccatis dolorem, liberum firmissimumque propositum, et supremam patientiam.

Quarto, quod ex persona divina tamquam subiecto processit, quod secundum convenientiam divinae personae interius in Christo homine actum est, quod proportionate in actu exteriori expressum est, hoc totum positive atque directe in obsequium atque honorem Dei Patris oblatum est. In obsequium quidem cum egerit Christus tam ex obedientia quam ex caritate; praeceptum enim quod a Patre habuit erat opus caritatis pro nobis exercendum; quod praeceptum ex dilectione Patris obediens implevit.[87] In honorem autem, tum quia omne opus bonum in Deo factum in honorem

The scriptural basis of this doctrine is easy to establish. Christ's satisfaction is not to be measured in relation to sin but in terms of grace, and 'where sin increased, grace abounded all the more' (Romans 5.20); hence like other graces, satisfaction by Christ also was superabundant.

In what follows we shall set forth the ways in which this satisfaction was superabundant.

First of all, then, the ontological and psychological subject making satisfaction was the Word of God (DB 124, [DS 263, ND 606/12]), one of the Persons of the Trinity (DB 222, [DS 432, ND 620/10]), the Lord of glory (1 Corinthians 2.8).

Second, the interior act from which this satisfaction issued and which was its formal element was such as befitted a divine person operating in an assumed nature. Now, to a divine person are due those things that exceed the proportion of any created subject and even of an assumed nature, namely, the immediate vision of God and the perfect love of the Son for the Father. From this vision and this love there proceeded in a commensurate manner his detestation of sin, his sorrow for our sins, and his firm resolve to redeem us. In all of these can be seen the formality of absolute supernaturality in its primary root, that is, in a divine person operating in an assumed nature in accordance with all that is due to a divine person.

Third, the exterior act added to the interior act those bodily changes that are to the interior act as a body is to its proper soul. As the intelligible is grasped in the sensible, so does the interior act inform the exterior; and just as the human Christ expressed his interior act in his passion and death, so the faithful contemplate in this passion and death the humiliation, obedience, and love of a divine person, his detestation of sin, his sorrow for our sins, his free but firm resolve, and his supreme patience.

Fourth, what proceeded from the divine person as subject, whatever interior acts took place in the human Christ that befitted his divine person, and all that was proportionately expressed in his exterior acts – all this was positively and directly offered to the service and honor of God the Father. To his service, since Christ acted out of obedience as well as love, for the command he had from his Father was to perform a deed of love for us, and this command he obediently fulfilled out of his love for the Father.[87] And to God the Father's honor, both because any good work done for God redounds to his

87 Ibid. q. 47, a. 2, ad 3m.

Dei cedit, tum praecipue quia satisfactio Christi quam maxime peccatis opponebatur quae unice contra honorem Dei faciunt.

Quinto, longe ergo excessit excellentia satisfactionis Christi super nequitiam omnium peccatorum. Quamvis enim peccatum infinitatem quandam habeat ratione Dei quem offendit, tamen non est nisi actus merae creaturae, neque creatae naturae proportionem excedit, neque ontologice aliud est quam debitae entitatis privatio, neque directe et propter se eligi potest. Satisfactio autem Christi infinitatem habuit tum ratione personae Patris cui oblata est, tum ratione personae Filii a quo oblata est; quibus accedit quod interior Christi actus et positiva realitas fuit, et directe et propter se electa, et secundum proportionem personae divinae in natura assumpta operantis; quae quidem proportio iterum observatur in ipso actu exteriori secundum quod forma ad materiam propriam atque dispositam proportionata esse dicitur.

Sexto, quamvis satisfactio Christi super delicta superabundaverit, non tamen ultra intentionem divinam, neque ultra obedientiam a Christo homine Patri debitam, neque ultra modum operandi divinae personae competentem superabundasse dicenda est.

Non ultra divinam intentionem; nam[88] quodcumque fit secundum totam suam realitatem procedit tamquam a prima causa ex scientia Dei infallibili et ex voluntate Dei efficaci et ex actione Dei irresistibili.

Praeterea, non magis quam Deus Pater, Christus homo peccata detestatus est; neque ultra miseriam nostri status de nostro statu doluit; sed secundum veritatem immediatae visionis Dei et secundum perfectionem dilectionis quam habuit erga Patrem et erga nos, iuste de peccato iudicavit et iustum hoc iudicium proportionate expressit.

Neque ultra debitam obedientiam egit Christus. Qui enim humiliavit semet ipsum formam servi accipiens, non sibi arripuit ut novum et melius consilium de ordine universi vel de salute hominum excogitaret quam quod ab aeterno concepisset divina sapientia et elegisset divina bonitas.

honor, and particularly since Christ's work of satisfaction was the most opposed to sin, which is singularly contrary to the honor of God.

Fifth, the excellence of Christ's satisfaction is far greater than the heinousness of all sins combined. Although sin does have a certain note of infinity about it by reason of the infinite God whom it offends, it nevertheless remains the act of a mere creature, and it does not exceed the proportion of a created nature. Ontologically it is nothing but a privation of due being, and cannot be directly chosen for its own sake. Christ's work of satisfaction, on the other hand, has its infinity both from the person of the Father to whom it was offered and from the person of the Son who offered it. In addition to this is the fact that Christ's interior act was a positive reality, was directly chosen for its own sake, and was exercised in a manner proportionate to a divine person operating in an assumed nature. This proportion is to be found in the external act as well, in accordance with the principle that form is said to be proportionate to its proper and proportionately disposed matter.

Sixth, although the satisfaction offered by Christ far outweighed the sins for which it was offered, still it must not be said to have been superabundant beyond the divine intention, or beyond the obedience the human Christ owed the Father, or beyond the mode of operation suitable to a divine person.

It did not go beyond God's intention. For[88] whatever happens proceeds, in its total reality, from the infallible knowledge, the efficacious will, and the irresistible action of God as from its first cause.

Besides, the human Christ did not detest sins more than God the Father did; nor, in grieving over the human condition, did he exaggerate its wretchedness and misery. Rather, in keeping with the truth of his immediate vision of God and the perfection of his love both for the Father and for us, he judged sin justly and expressed this just judgment in due proportion.

Also, Christ did not act beyond the due bounds of obedience. The one who humbled himself to take the form of a slave did not grasp to himself the conception of some new and better plan for the order of the universe or the salvation of the human race than that which had been conceived by divine wisdom and chosen by divine goodness from all eternity.

88 [Reading 'nam' for an obviously erroneous 'non' in the manuscript.]

Neque egit Christus ultra modum divinae personae competentem. Nam divina persona realiter identificatur cum ipsa infinita bonitate Dei; et sicut Christus qua Deus ultra hanc bonitatem agere non potest, ita Christus qua homo ultra hanc bonitatem supernaturaliter participatam agere non potuit.

Septimo, quamvis Christus superabundanter pro omnibus totius mundi peccatis satisfecerit, minime sequitur nos non debere pro nostris peccatis satisfacere. Nam satisfactio Christi et satisfactio nostra non univoce sed analogice dicuntur; et ideo peracta satisfactione in Capite, remanet peragenda satisfactio in membris. Quod quidem quemadmodum intelligendum sit, postea declarabitur cum de effectibus redemptionis agatur.

Nor did he act beyond the manner suitable to a divine person. For a divine person is really identical with the infinite goodness of God; and just as Christ as God cannot act beyond this goodness, neither could Christ as human act beyond this goodness in which he supernaturally participates.

Seventh, although Christ superabundantly atoned for the sins of all the world, it by no means follows that we are relieved of the duty of offering satisfaction for our sins. For Christ's satisfaction and our satisfaction are not understood in a univocal but in an analogous fashion; hence while satisfaction has been made by the Head, there still remains satisfaction to be made by the members. How this is to be understood will be explained when we discuss the effects of the redemption.

# Caput Sextum[1]

**Articulus XXXV: De opere Christi**

Quam pii Iudaei sperabant exspectabantque redemptionem (Lc 2.38, 24.21) lumen erat ad revelationem gentium et gloria plebis suae (Lc 2.32), cum benedictus Dominus Deus Israel per viscera misericordiae suae secundum testamentum suum et iusiurandum Abrahae factum visitaret redemptionemque faceret plebis suae ut, de manu inimicorum liberati, sine timore Deo servirent in sanctitate et iustitia coram ipso omnibus diebus suis (Lc 1.68–78).

Quae ergo capite III de pretio soluto, de sacrificio novi testamenti, de meritoria obedientia passioneque vicaria recitavimus, nisi redemptionem ut medium vel potius principium non dicunt. Nam praeter redemptionem iam habitam, remissionem peccatorum in sanguine Christi (Eph 1.7, Col 1.14), aeterna etiam est redemptio, iam ab ipso Christo homine inventa (Heb 9.12), quae ultimis diebus appropinquabit (Lc 21.28), corporis

# 6 [The Effects of the Redemption][1]

## Article 35: The work of Christ

The redemption hoped for and awaited by devout Jews (Luke 2.38, 24.21) was a light for revelation to the Gentiles and the glory of his people (Luke 2.32), because the blessed Lord God of Israel in his tender mercy and in accordance with his covenant and his oath to Abraham visited and redeemed his people, so that, delivered from the hands of their enemies, they might without fear serve God in holiness and righteousness in his presence all their days (Luke 1.68–79).

What we said in chapter 3 about the price paid, the sacrifice of the new covenant, and Christ's meritorious obedience and vicarious suffering refers only to redemption as a means, or better, as a principle. For besides redemption as already achieved, the remission of sins through the blood of Christ (Ephesians 1.7, Colossians 1.14), there is also the eternal redemption, already reached by the human being Christ (Hebrews 9.12), which in

1 [The autograph may be found on the website www.bernardlonergan.com at 25460DTL060. The autograph typescript begins with article 35 and no chapter heading or title. Taking his cue from the last words of the previous chapter, Frederick Crowe (*Christ and History* [Toronto: University of Toronto Press, 2015] 109) has suggested the title given here. Note, however, that the verso of our leaf on 'facta et ficta' (25260DTL060, see above, p. 533, note 66) includes a handwritten list of articles for chapter 5, extending two articles beyond the present fifth chapter to include an article 'de satisfactionis effectu' and another 'de synthesi theologica.' It seems, then, that Lonergan did not originally conceive a sixth chapter.]

nostri redemptio (Rom 8.23). Quem in diem redemptionis Spiritu sancto iam signati sumus atque acquisiti (Eph 4.30, 1.13–14, 1 Thess 5.9). Secundum finem ergo exspectamus beatam spem et adventum gloriae magni Dei et Salvatoris nostri qui, secundum medium seu principium, dedit semet ipsum pro nobis, ut nos redimeret ab omni iniquitate, et mundaret sibi populum acceptabilem, sectatorem bonorum operum (Tit 2.14). Quamvis ergo iustificati gratis per gratiam Dei simus, per redemptionem quae est in Christo Iesu (Rom 3.24), minime tamen nos comprehendisse arbitramur sed ad destinatum persequimur, ad bravium supernae vocationis Dei in Christo Iesu (Phil 3.13–14), qui factus est nobis sapientia a Deo et iustitia et sanctificatio et redemptio (1 Cor 1.30).

Sive ergo ipsam vocem redemptionis respicimus, sive ratiocinamur parum cognosci vel medium neglecto fine vel causam praetermisso effectu, et latius et plenius iam oportet opus Domini considcrari. Quapropter, ea articulis sequentibus relinquentes quae ad intelligentiam rei faciant, statim ex scripturis non nulla colligenda ducimus, quae inquisitionis fundamentum praebent et obiectum intelligendum manifestant, nempe, (1) regnum Dei (2) salutemque in Christo positam, unde (3) a peccatis et (4) a lege cultuque Iudaico liberati, (5) ad Deum fidelem iustumque (6) cum fiducia accessum habemus, si quidem (7) per actus personales (8) Christo populoque Dei incorporamur.

Qui ergo Novum Testametum legit, in primis finem Christi regnum Dei esse intelligit. Uti enim narrat S. Marcus: 'Postquam autem traditus est Ioannes, venit Iesus in Galilaeam praedicans evangelium regni Dei et dicens: Quoniam impletum est tempus, et appropinquavit regnum Dei; paenitemini et credite evangelio' (Mc 1.14–15, Gal 4.4, 3.23–25, Rom 3.26, Eph 1.10). Cuius regni mysterium apostolis datum est (Mc 4.11); ipsum sponte sua crescit et maturescit (Mc 4.26–29) donec in virtute veniat (Mc 9.1). Tunc iusti fulgebunt sicut sol (Mt 13.43) et Dominus vinum bibet novum (Mc 14.25). Quod futurum regnum nunc a piis exspectatum (Mc 15.43) neque a sapientibus longinquum (Mc 12.34), difficile divitibus (Mc 10.23) et parvulis accommodatum (Mc 10.14), melius intras luscus quam duos habens oculos in gehennam ignis mitteris (Mc 9.47). Non enim de hoc mundo est (Io 18.36), neque intratur nisi per multas tribulationes (Act 14.22), neque in esca et potu sed in iustitia et pace consistit (Rom 14.17), neque in verbo est sed in virtute (1 Cor 4.20), neque ab iniquis possidetur (1 Cor 6.9), neque

these last days will draw near (Luke 21.28), the redemption of our bodies (Romans 8.23). For this day of redemption we are already stamped with the seal of the Holy Spirit, and acquired for God (Ephesians 4.30, 1.13–14, 1 Thessalonians 5.9). In terms of the end, therefore, we await the blessed hope and glorious coming of our great God and Savior, who, as the medium or principle, gave himself up for us, to redeem us from all iniquity and cleanse for himself an acceptable people zealous for good works (Titus 2.14). Therefore, although we have been gratuitously justified by God's grace through the redemption that is in Christ Jesus (Romans 3.24), we do not at all consider that we have wholly won salvation, but we press on to our goal, the heavenly prize to which we are called by God in Christ Jesus (Philippians 3.13–14), who has become for us wisdom from God and righteousness and sanctification and redemption (1 Corinthians 1.30).

If, therefore, we consider the word 'redemption' itself, or if we reflect that in neglecting the end we have a poor knowledge of the means, or that ignoring the effect we have a poor knowledge of its cause, we must now undertake a broader and fuller survey of the work of the Lord. Accordingly, leaving the work of understanding this matter for subsequent articles, we think it best at this point to collect a number of scriptural passages that will provide a foundation for our inquiry and throw light on what we seek to understand: (1) the kingdom of God and (2) salvation in Christ, whereby (3) being freed from sins and (4) from the Judaic Law and worship, we have access to (5) God who is faithful and just (6) with confidence, since (7) through personal acts (8) we are incorporated into Christ and the people of God.

The reader of the New Testament understands that Christ's end or purpose is first and foremost the kingdom of God. In the words of Mark, 'Now after John was arrested, Jesus came to Galilee, proclaiming the good news of God, and saying, The time is fulfilled, and the kingdom of God has come near; repent, and believe in the good news' (Mark 1.14–15; see Galatians 4.4, 3.23–25, Romans 3.26, Ephesians 1.10). The mystery of this kingdom has been given to the apostles (Mark 4.11); it grows and matures of its own accord (Mark 4.26–29) until it comes in power (Mark 9.1). Then will the just shine like the sun (Matthew 13.43) and the Lord drink the new wine (Mark 14.25). This future kingdom is now awaited by the devout (Mark 15.43) and is not far from the wise (Mark 12.34); it is difficult of attainment for the rich (Mark 10.23), yet well adapted to little ones (Mark 10.14), and it is better for one to enter it with only one eye than to go into Gehenna with two eyes (Mark 9.47). For this kingdom is not of this world (John 18.36), nor does one enter it without many tribulations (Acts 14.22); it

a carne et sanguine (1 Cor 15.50). Regnum enim et gloria Dei est (1 Thess 2.12), et Domini nostri aeternum regnum (2 Pet 1.11) pro quo patimur ut digni in eo habeamur (2 Thess 1.5).

Quod in regnum pervenire salus est, et ideo nomen, Iesus, ei datum est (Mt 1.21) per quem solum salvi fieri possumus (Act 4.12). Venit enim ut mundum salvificet (Io 3.17, 12.47), et quod perierat (Lc 19.10), et peccatores (1 Tim 1.15). Omnis autem qui invocaverit nomen Domini salvus erit (Act 2.21, Rom 10.13), per gratiam Domini nostri Iesu Christi (Act 15.11, Eph 2.5–8), in sanguine eius (Rom 5.9) et in vita ipsius (Rom 5.10), et in spe (Rom 8.24). Salvus fit per ostium Christum (Io 10.9), per evangelium (Rom 1.16), per stultitiam praedicationis (1 Cor 1.21), per confessionem in ore et in corde fidem (Rom 10.9), per perseverantiam usque in finem (Mt 10.22), per perditionem animae suae in hoc mundo (Mt 16.25), ut perveniat in regnum Christi caeleste (2 Tim 4.18).

Per quod regnum quamque salutem liberamur a peccatis (Eph 1.7, Col 1.14), ab omni iniquitate (Tit 2.14), ab omni opere malo (2 Tim 4.18, Mt 6.13), de potestate tenebrarum (Col 1.13), a timore mortis (Heb 2.15), de tentatione (2 Pet 2.9), de corpore mortis huius (Rom 7.24), a lege peccati et mortis (Rom 8.2), ab ipso corpore (Rom 8.23), et ab ira ventura (1 Thess 1.9–10, Rom 5.9). Tam enim Iudaei quam Graeci (Rom 1.18–3.20) eramus peccatores (Rom 5.8), inimici (Rom 5.10), peccatis mortui (Eph 2.5), facientes desideria carnis (Eph 2.3, 1 Cor 6.9–11), alienati (Col 1.21).

Quod si gentes concedis spem non habentes et sine Deo in hoc mundo (Eph 2.12), Iudaeis tamen adfuisse forte dicis legem divinitus institutam atque cultum. At lex, quamvis in se bona fuerit (Rom 7.14, 7.22–23), tamen iustificare non potuit (Rom 3.20, Gal 2.21); non enim dedit nisi cognitionem peccati (Rom 3.20) ut abundaret delictum (Rom 5.20); et ideo omnes sequaces sub maledicto posuit (Gal 3.10; cf. Iac 2.10; Act 15.10). Quare qui sub lege erant (Gal 4.5) de maledicto legis redimuntur (Gal 3.13). Impossibile enim erat sanguine taurorum et hircorum auferri peccata (Heb 10.4), et multo minus secundum conscientiam perfectum effici

consists not in eating and drinking but in righteousness and peace (Romans 14.17), depends not on words but on power (1 Corinthians 4.20), and is possessed neither by the wicked (1 Corinthians 6.9) nor by flesh and blood (1 Corinthians 15.50). For the kingdom is the glory of God (1 Thessalonians 2.12) and the eternal kingdom of our Lord (2 Peter 1.11) for which we suffer in order to be found worthy of it (2 Thessalonians 1.5).

To enter into this kingdom is what salvation means, and for that reason the name Jesus was given to him (Matthew 1.21) through whom alone (Acts 4.12) we can be saved. For he came to save the world (John 3.17, 12.47), to save what was lost (Luke 19.10), to save sinners (1 Timothy 1.15). All who call upon the name of the Lord will be saved (Acts 2.21, Romans 10.13), through the grace of our Lord Jesus Christ (Acts 15.11, Ephesians 2.5–8), in his blood (Romans 5.9) and in his life (Romans 5.10), and in hope (Romans 8.24). One reaches salvation through the gate which is Christ (John 10.9), through the gospel (Romans 1.16), through the foolishness of its proclamation (1 Corinthians 1.21), through confession with one's lips and faith in one's heart (Romans 10.9), through perseverance to the end (Matthew 10.22), through losing one's life in this world (Matthew 16.25) so as to arrive in the celestial kingdom of Christ (2 Timothy 4.18).

Through this kingdom and this salvation we are set free from our sins (Ephesians 1.7, Colossians 1.14), from all iniquity (Titus 2.14), from every evil deed (2 Timothy 4.18, Matthew 6.13), from the power of darkness (Colossians 1.13), from the fear of death (Hebrews 2.15), from being put to the test (2 Peter 2.9), from the body of this death (Romans 7.24), from the law of sin and death (Romans 8.2), from the body itself (Romans 8.23), and from the wrath to come (1 Thessalonians 1.9–10, Romans 5.9). Jews as well as Greeks (Romans 1.18–3.20), we were all sinners (Romans 5.8), enemies [of God] (Romans 5.10), dead through sin (Ephesians 2.5), behaving according to the desires of the flesh (Ephesians 2.3, 1 Corinthians 6.9–11), estranged (Colossians 1.21).

But if you grant that the Gentiles were without hope and without God in this world (Ephesians 2.12), you perhaps may say that the Jews nevertheless did have a divinely instituted law and worship. But the law, though good in itself (Romans 7.14, 7.22–23), was nevertheless unable to justify (Romans 3.20, Galatians 2.21); for it gave only a knowledge of sin (Romans 3.20), so that sin abounded (Romans 5.20), and therefore put all its followers under a curse (Galatians 3.10; see James 2.10; Acts 15.10). Hence those who were under the law (Galatians 4.5) are redeemed from the curse of the law (Galatians 3.13). For it was impossible for sins to be taken away by the blood

servientem (Heb 9.9); sed sanguis Christi emundabit conscientiam nostram ad serviendum Deo viventi (Heb 9.14).

Fidelis enim est Deus (Heb 10.23; cf. 11.11; 12.26) et quaecumque promisit potens est facere (Rom 4.21), et ideo in Christo Iesu habetur benedictio Abrahae repromissa (Act 2.39, 3.25, 13.23, 13.32, 26.6, Gal 3.14–22, 3.29, 4.23, 2 Cor 1.20, 6.16–18, 7.1, Rom 4.13–20, 9.5–8, 15.8, Eph 2.12, 3.6, Heb 4.1, 6.12–20, 7.6, 8.6, 9.15, 10.23, 10.36–37, 11.9, 11.13–17). Etiam habetur promissus Spiritus sanctus (Io 14.26, 15.26, 16.13, Lc 24.49, Act 1.4, 2.17–18, 2.33, Eph 1.13); et post hoc haereditatis pignus habebitur *parousia* Domini (2 Pet 3.9–10), vita aeterna (1 Io 2.25, 2 Tim 1.1, Tit 1.2), corona vitae (Iac 1.12), regnum (Iac 2.5), consortium divinae naturae (2 Pet 1.4), novi caeli novaque terra (2 Pet 3.13).

Iustus pariter est Deus et iustificans eum qui est ex fide Iesu Christi, quem proposuit propitiationem per fidem in sanguine eius, ad ostensionem iustitiae suae in hoc tempore (Rom 3.25–26). Iustificati ergo ex fide pacem habemus ad Deum per Dominum nostrum Iesum Christum, per quem et habemus accessum per fidem in gratiam istam in qua stamus, et gloriamur in spe gloriae filiorum Dei (Rom 5.1–2). Non enim iis solis quibus facta est repromissio, sed iis etiam qui a longe sunt (Act 2.39), qui quaerunt Deum si forte attrectent eum aut inveniant (Act 17.27), dantur fiducia et accessus in confidentia per Christum Iesum (Eph 3.12). Quamvis enim ambulaverint in vanitate sensus sui, tenebris obscuratum habentes intellectum, alienati a vita Dei per ignorantiam quae erat in illis propter caecitatem cordis (Eph 4.17–19), nunc autem reconciliati in corpore carnis eius per mortem exhibentur sancti, immaculati, irreprehensibiles (Col 1.22; cf. Eph 2.11–21). Fiduciam ergo habeamus (1 Io 3.21, 4.17, 5.14); appropinquemus Deo et appropinquabit nobis (Iac 4.8); nam introducta est melior spes per quam appropinquamus ad Deum (Heb 7.19). Adeamus cum fiducia ad thronum gratiae (Heb 4.16); salvare enim in perpetuum potest Christus accedentes per semetipsum ad Deum, semper vivens ad interpellandum pro nobis (Heb 7.25); habentes itaque fiduciam accedamus cum vero corde in plenitudine fidei (Heb 10.19, 10.22) ad Sion montem, et civitatem Dei viventis, Hierusalem caelestem, et multorum millium angelorum frequentiam, et iudicem omnium Deum, et testamenti novi mediatorem Iesum (Heb 12.22–24); si tamen gustastis quoniam dulcis est Dominus. Ad quem accedentes lapidem vivum ab hominibus reprobatum, a Deo autem

of bulls and goats (Hebrews 10.4), much less for the conscience of the worshiper to be made perfect (Hebrews 9.9); but the blood of Christ will purify our conscience to serve the living God (Hebrews 9.14).

For God is faithful (Hebrews 10.23; see also 11.11, 12.26), and whatever he has promised he is capable of doing (Romans 4.21), and therefore in Christ Jesus the blessing promised Abraham is realized (Acts 2.39, 3.25, 13.23, 13.32, 26.6, Galatians 3.14–22, 3.29, 4.23, 2 Corinthians 1.20, 6.16–18, 7.1, Romans 4.13–20, 9.5–8, 15.8, Ephesians 2.12, 3.6, Hebrews 4.1, 6.12–20, 7.6, 8.6, 9.15, 10.23, 10.36–37, 11.9, 11.13–17). There is now also the promised Holy Spirit (John 14.26, 15.26, 16.13, Luke 24.49, Acts 1.4, 2.17–18, 2.33, Ephesians 1.13); and after this pledge of inheritance there will be the *parousia* of the Lord (2 Peter 3.9–10), eternal life (1 John 2.25, 2 Timothy 1.1, Titus 1.2), the crown of life (James 1.12), the kingdom (James 2.5), a sharing in the divine nature (2 Peter 1.4), new heavens and a new earth (2 Peter 3.13).

Likewise, God is just and the justifier of one who has faith in Jesus Christ, whom he has put forward as a sacrifice of atonement through faith in his blood, to display his justice at this time (Romans 3.25–26). Thus justified by faith, we are at peace with God through our Lord Jesus Christ, through whom we have access through faith to the grace in which we now stand, and we boast in our hope for the glory of the children of God (Romans 5.1–2). For all this is not only for those to whom the promise was made, it is also for those who were far away (Acts 2.39), who are searching for God hoping if perhaps they may reach out to him and find him (Acts 17.27), who are given trust and confident access to him through Christ Jesus (Ephesians 3.12). For although they once lived in the futility of their minds, darkened in their understanding and alienated from the life of God through the ignorance resulting from their blindness of heart (Ephesians 4.17–19), now, however, being reconciled in Christ's fleshly body through death, they are presented holy and blameless and irreproachable (Colossians 1.22; see Ephesians 2.11–21). Let us then have trust (1 John 3.21, 4.17, 5.14); let us draw near to God and he will draw near to us (James 4.8); for there is now the introduction of a better hope through which we approach God (Hebrews 7.19). Let us come with confidence before the throne of grace (Hebrews 4.16); for Christ is able for all time to save those who approach God through him, since he lives forever interceding on our behalf (Hebrews 7.25); having such confidence, then, let us go with a heart that is true and in the fullness of faith (Hebrews 10.19, 10.22) to Mount Zion, the city of the living God, the heavenly Jerusalem with its throng of many thousands of

electum et honorificatum, et ipsi tamquam lapides vivi superaedificamini, domus spiritalis, sacerdotium sanctum offerre spiritales hostias acceptabiles Deo per Iesum Christum (1 Pet 2.3–6).

Per Christum enim adoptionem filiorum accipimus et Spiritum sanctum habemus in corda nostra missum et clamantem: Abba, Pater (Gal 4.5–6, Rom 8.15–16); Filium proprium pro nobis habemus traditum et ideo cum illo etiam omnia sunt nobis donata (Rom 8.32); quod tamen fit non ex sanguinibus neque ex voluntate carnis neque ex voluntate viri sed ex Deo (Io 1.13) in paenitentibus et evangelium credentibus (Mc 1.15). Quam ob causam praedicatur paenitentia (Act 2.38, 3.19, 5.31, 11.18, 17.30, 20.21, 26.20) et exigitur fides (Rom 10.9, 1.16–17, 3.22, 3.25, 3.27–28, 3.30, 5.1–2, 9.30).

At quamvis sine personali paenitentia et fide Christo non adnumeremur adulti, multi tamen unum corpus sumus in Christo, singuli autem alter alterius membra (Rom 12.5, 1 Cor 12.12–31), et invicem diligamus oportet sicut Christus dilexit nos (Io 15.12, 1 Cor 13). Quod enim dicitur *pleroma* et corpus Christi, idem ecclesia est (Col 1.18, 1.25),[2] populus adquisitionis (Deut 7.6–10, 14.2, 26.18–19, 1 Pet 2.9, Act 20.28, Eph 1.14, 1 Thess 5.9, Mal 3.17, Is 43.20–21), populus acceptabilis (Tit 2.14, Exod 19.5–6, Ps 78.13), aliquando non populus, nunc autem populus Dei, qui non consecuti misericordiam, nunc autem misericordiam consecuti (1 Pet 2.10, Rom 9.25–26, 2 Cor 6.16–18, Heb 8.8–12, Osee 1.6–9, 2.1, 2.23).

**Articulus XXXVI: De agente per intellectum**

In genere causae ponitur quod influit esse in aliud; in genere autem effectus invenitur quod in esse ab alio dependet; et ideo sicut correlativa sunt causa et effectus, ita pariter correlativa sunt influere et dependere.

angels, to God who is the judge of all, and Jesus, the mediator of the new covenant (Hebrews 12.22–24) – if indeed you have tasted the goodness of the Lord. Coming to him, a living stone, rejected by human beings but chosen and honored by God, we ourselves like living stones are built up into a spiritual house, a holy priesthood to offer spiritual sacrifices acceptable to God through Jesus Christ (1 Peter 2.3–6).

Through Christ we receive the adoption of children and have the Holy Spirit sent into hearts crying out, 'Abba, Father' (Galatians 4.5–6, Romans 8.15–16); God gave his own Son up for us, and so all other things have been given to us along with him (Romans 8.32); this has come about not of blood or of the will of the flesh or the will of man, but by God (John 1.13) for those who are repentant and believe the gospel (Mark 1.15). For this reason repentance is preached (Acts 2.38, 3.19, 5.31, 11.18, 17.30, 20.21, 26.20) and faith is required (Romans 10.9, 1.16–17, 3.22, 3.25, 3.27–28, 3.30, 5.1–2, 9.30).

Although without personal repentance and faith we are not reckoned to be adults in Christ, nevertheless, many as we are, we are one body in Christ, members of one another (Romans 12.5, 1 Corinthians 12.12–31), and ought to love one another as Christ has loved us (John 15.12, 1 Corinthians 13). For what is called the *pleroma* and the body of Christ is also the church (Colossians 1.18–25),[2] the people God has acquired as his own (Deuteronomy 7.6–10, 14.2, 26.18–19, 1 Peter 2.9, Acts 20.28, Ephesians 1.14, 1 Thessalonians 5.9, Malachi 3.17, Isaiah 43.20–21), an acceptable people (Titus 2.14, Exodus 19.5–6, Psalm 78.13 [EVV 79.13]), at one time no people, but now the people of God, who once had not obtained mercy but now have (1 Peter 2.10, Romans 9.25–26, 2 Corinthians 6.16–18, Hebrews 8.8–12, Hosea 1.6–9, 2.1, 2.23).

### Article 36: Agents acting through intellect

In the category of cause is placed whatever exerts an influence upon another as to its being; in the category of effect is found whatever depends upon another as to its being. Thus just as cause and effect are correlative, so also are to influence and to depend.

2 Jacques Dupont, *Gnosis: la connaissance religieuse dans les Épitres de Saint Paul* (Bruges and Paris: Desclée de Brouwer, 1949) 420–76. [Lonergan did not explicitly mention this title by Dupont, but the information he does give, which includes numerals for the page range, and the content of these pages from this work, confirm that this is the book he had in mind.]

Qui influxus vel dependentia non sensibilis est sed intelligibilis. Quare influxum causalem nescit qui boves aratrum trahentes imaginatur nitentes atque anhelantes; et eundem influxum cognoscit verum et realem qui in aratro moto intelligibilem dependentiae relationem vere affirmat.

Neve intelligibile cum necessario confundas, cum multa sint intelligibilia quae tamen aliter esse possunt. Non enim necessario lex gravitationis est acceleratio uniformis, et pariter intelligibilis in gravibus esset acceleratio uniformiter crescens. Neque necessario homines intelligunt et inter se consentiunt, sed intelligibile est quod intelligunt et rationabile est quod consentiunt; qua in intelligentia atque consensu fundatur omnis cooperatio humana, imo fere tota proprie humana causalitas.

Neve dicas minus veram esse causalitatem non necessariam. Non enim ideo habetur causalitas quia habetur necessitas; sed necessaria dependentia ideo est causalis quia intelligibilis est.

Proinde, influendi seu dependendi triplex distinguitur modus. Causa enim intrinseca influit ut *quo*; finalis ut *cuius gratia*; agens ut *a quo*. V.g., anima intellectiva est *quo* primo vivimus, sentimus, intelligimus, vel, aliis verbis, vivimus, sentimus, intelligimus *per* animam intellectivam. Iterum, remissio peccatorum est *cuius gratia* satisfecit Christus, vel, aliis verbis, Christus satisfecit *propter* remissionem peccatorum. Denique, liber *ab* auctore componitur, vel, auctor est *a quo* componitur liber.

Agens subdividitur in agens per naturam et agens per intellectum. Quae quidem inter se differunt tum secundum principium agendi tum secundum modum intendendi tum secundum limitationem in causando.

Differunt secundum principium agendi. Nam agens per naturam agit secundum formam vel naturaliter inditam vel naturaliter acquisitam; ita equus equum generat et homo hominem. Sed agens per intellectum agit secundum formam intentionalem; et ita sartor facit vestes, et coquus prandia parat.

Differunt deinde secundum modum quo effectum intendunt. Agens enim per naturam, debitis conditionibus impletis, effectum suum exserit; non tamen ipsas conditiones cogitat et eas implendas curat; sed hanc impletionem a reliqua natura exspectat. Agens autem per intellectum ipsam

Such influence or dependence is not sensible but intelligible. Therefore, one who has a picture of oxen huffing and puffing as they strain at pulling a plow does not know what causal influence is; but one who truly affirms that there is an intelligible relation of dependence in the plow as moved does know this influence in its true reality.

Also, do not confuse the intelligible with the necessary, since many things are intelligible which nevertheless can be otherwise than they are. It is not a matter of necessity that the law of gravity is uniform acceleration, and a uniformly increasing acceleration of heavy objects would be equally intelligible. Nor is it a matter of necessity that human beings understand and agree with one another, but it is intelligible that they understand, and reasonable that they agree. This understanding and agreement is the foundation of all human cooperation – in fact, virtually the whole of what is properly human causality.

Do not say, either, that non-necessary causality is less true. Causality is not a result of necessity; but necessary dependence is causal because it is intelligible.

We can distinguish three modes of influence and dependence. An intrinsic cause influences as that *by reason of which*; a final cause influences as that *for the sake of which*; an agent influences as that *by (or from) which.* For example, the intellective soul is that *by reason of which* in the first instance we live, sense, and understand; in other words, we live, sense, and understand *through* our intellective soul. Again, the forgiveness of sins is that *for the sake of which* Christ made satisfaction; or, in other words, Christ made satisfaction *for* the forgiveness of sins. Finally, a book is written *by* its author; that is, the author is that *by whom* the book is written.

Agents are subdivided into agents acting through nature and agents acting through intellect. These differ according to their principle of action, according to their mode of intending, and according to their limitation in causing.

They differ according to their principle of action. An agent acting through nature acts in accordance with a form that is either innate or naturally acquired; thus a horse generates a horse, and a human generates a human. But an agent acting through intellect acts in accordance with an intentional form; in this way a tailor makes clothes, and a cook prepares a meal.

Second, they differ according to the way in which they intend their effect. An agent that acts through nature, once the requisite conditions are fulfilled, produces its effect; yet it does not think about those conditions or see to their fulfilment, but awaits their fulfilment from the rest of nature. An

actualitatem effectus intendit, et ideo non solum causas adhibendas sed etiam conditiones implendas curat; inutile enim, imo stupidum iudicat causas adhibere et conditiones negligere.

Differunt denique secundum limitationem suae actionis. Limitatur enim agens per naturam ad eos effectus qui formae naturaliter inditae vel acquisitae proportionantur; limitatur praeterea quia conditiones suae actionis a reliqua natura implendas exspectare debet; limitatur denique secundum conditiones spatii et temporis, ut fortius in propinquiora influat et, sicut ipsae suae actiones, ita etiam actionum effectus alter alteri succedant. Agens autem per intellectum non limitatur nisi inquantum a plena et perfecta intellectus ratione deficit. Quapropter Deus plena et perfecta intellectualitate gaudens invenitur omnipotens. Nos autem ab intellectualitate plena deficientes invenimur limitati, tum ratione ipsius intellectus quia multa non intelligimus, tum ratione voluntatis malae quae in bonum intelligibile non tendit, tum ratione animae corpori coniunctae quae, nisi corpore mediante, in alia influere non potest.

Sed quamvis in multis inveniamur limitati, non eadem tamen est limitatio nostra ac limitatio agentis per naturam. Nisi per corpus in alia non influimus; sed per corpus agimus non solum secundum virtutem eius naturalem sed etiam secundum virtutem intentionalem. Corpus nostrum spatio et tempore limitatur; sed causalitas nostra extenditur ad omne cuius conditiones spatiales et temporales intelligimus et sive directe sive indirecte quantalibet complexitate regere possumus. Nihil efficimus nisi conditiones implentur; sed ipsi ipsas conditiones cogitamus et eas implendas sive directe sive indirecte curamus. Neque ideo minus causae verae et reales sumus quia virtute intentionali per multitudinem mediorum et mediante aliorum libero consensu agimus, sed eo magis causae primae et perfectae assimilamur quae, quaecumque intelligit, facere potest, quae omnes conditiones effectus intenti per se vel per alia vel etiam per alios et liberos implet, quae adeo spatio vel tempore non limitatur ut ipsa, sicut caetera, etiam spatium et tempus faciat.

agent acting through intellect, however, intends the very actuality of the effect and therefore takes care not only to apply the causes but also to fulfil the conditions. Such an agent judges it futile, indeed stupid, to apply the causes while ignoring the conditions.

Finally, they differ according to the limitation of their causal action. That which acts through nature is limited to those effects that are proportionate to its innate or acquired form; it is further limited because it has to wait for the rest of nature to fulfil the requisite conditions for its action; and it is limited by the conditions of space and time, so that it exerts a stronger influence on those objects that are closer to it, and, just as its actions themselves, so also the effects of its actions follow one after another. But an agent acting through intellect is limited only insofar as it falls short of the full perfection of intellect. For this reason, God, who enjoys complete and perfect intellectuality, is omnipotent. We, however, who fall short of full intellectuality, come up against limits, by reason of our intellect itself, because there is much we do not understand; by reason of a bad will that does not tend towards intelligible good; and by reason of the fact that our soul is united to a body and can exert its influence upon other things only through the mediation of that body.

But although we are limited in many respects, our limitation is not the same as the limitation of an agent that acts through nature. We exert a causal influence on other things only through our body, but through our body we act not only according to its natural power but also through intentional power. Our body is limited by space and time, but our causality extends to everything whose spatial and temporal conditions we understand and are able, directly or indirectly, to control with whatever degree of complexity. We effect nothing unless the conditions are fulfilled, but we ourselves know what the conditions are and directly or indirectly see to their fulfilment. Nor does the fact that we act by intentional power through a multitude of means and are dependent upon the free consent of other persons mean that our causality is less genuine and real; rather, by that very fact we have a greater resemblance to the first and perfect cause, which can do whatever it understands, which fulfils all the conditions of the intended effect by itself or through others, even through others who are free, and which is so far from being limited by space or time that it is the creator of space and time along with everything else.

## Articulus XXXVII: De agente sociali

Omnia fere quae facimus per alios vel propter alios agimus. Aedificia non construimus et domos inhabitamus. Agros non colimus, cibos non paramus, et tamen manducamus et bibimus. Non nemus neque contexímus, et tamen vestimur. Libros legimus ab ignotis conscriptos et scientias addiscimus ad ignotos docendos. Exsistit enim, uti primo capite dictum est, magnum quoddam ordinis bonum tum exterius tum culturale; unde ab aliis ea accipimus quibus indigemus, et aliis ea paramus quibus ipsi indigent.

Quod vitae humanae factum praecipuum in eo fundatur, quod agentia per intellectum sumus et ideo non solum causae proportionatae sed etiam, quantum possumus, causae actuales. Causae quidem proportionatae sumus inquantum formas intelligibiles mente tenemus ad effectus similes producendos; et ita sartores ad vestes contexendas, coqui ad prandia paranda, architecti ad aedificia construenda, et universim artifices ad opera artis conficienda proportionantur. Qui tamen omnes qua tales agenti per naturam assimilantur, inquantum singuli seorsum non intendunt ipsam effectus actualitatem sed potius ut, debitis conditionibus aliunde impletis, effectus producatur. Quapropter praeter causas mere proportionatas etiam causae actuales considerandae sunt, quae et causas proportionatas adhibendas et omnes conditiones implendas curant. Nisi enim hae actuales causae agnoscuntur, possunt sane sartores vestes contexere sed actu non contexunt, et possunt coqui prandia parare quae tamen non parant, et possunt architecti aedificia construere quae actu non construunt, et possunt universim artifices opera artis conficere sed ea non conficiunt.

Quaenam ergo sunt hae actuales causae? In genere sunt qui ipsam effectus actualitatem efficaciter volunt. Quae volitio efficax interdum in uno homine seorsum sumpto inveniri potest, ut sartor sibi vestem contexat et coquus sibi prandium paret. Haec tamen exempla magis exceptionem quam regulam dicunt. Sartor enim lanam et linum et filum et implementa ab aliis accipit; neque sibi sed aliis praecipue vestes contexit. Coquus cibos et culinam ab aliis accipit, et aliis praecipue prandia parat. Et ideo communiter actualis causa, ut actu contexatur vestis vel actu paretur prandium, non in uno homine seorsum sumpto invenitur, sed in multis simul idem quoddam commune intelligentibus et volentibus.

## Article 37: Social agents

Virtually everything we do is done through others or for others. We ourselves do not build the houses we live in. We are not farmers or cooks, and still we eat and drink. We do not spin or weave cloth, yet we wear clothes. We read books written by persons we do not know, and we learn sciences in order to teach persons unknown to us. There does indeed exist, as we said in the first chapter, a great good of order both external and cultural; thus we get from others what we ourselves need, and we provide others with what they need.

This salient feature of human life is based upon the fact that we are agents acting through intellect and therefore are not only proportionate causes but also, as much as we can be, actual causes. We are proportionate causes inasmuch as we have in our minds intelligible forms for the purpose of producing the corresponding effects; thus tailors are proportionate to making clothes, cooks to preparing meals, architects to building buildings, and, in general, artisans to producing their respective artifacts. Yet all of them as such are like agents acting through nature in that individually they do not intend the actuality of what they effect but intend rather that the effect be produced upon the fulfilment of the requisite conditions from elsewhere. Therefore, we must consider not only causes that are merely proportionate but also actual causes that see to both the use of the proportionate causes and the fulfilment of all the conditions. For unless these actual causes are acknowledged, tailors may certainly be able to make clothes but not actually make them, cooks may be able to prepare meals but not actually do so, architects may be able to build buildings but not actually build them, and, in general, artisans may be able to produce their respective artifacts but without actually doing so.

What, then, are these actual causes? In general they are those who effectively will the actuality of the effect. This effective willing sometimes can be present in one person alone, as when a tailor makes a garment for himself and a cook cooks herself a meal. But these examples are the exception, not the rule. The tailor gets his wool and linen and thread and the tools of his trade from other people; and he makes clothes mainly for others, not for himself. The cook gets her provisions and the kitchen itself from others, and it is mainly for others that she prepares meals. And so generally speaking the actual cause of a garment being made and a meal being prepared is to be found not in one isolated individual but in several together who have the same common understanding and will.

Cur autem communius fit ut causa actualis non in uno homine quam in multis quodammodo consociatis inveniatur, facile perspicitur. Causae proportionatae sumus secundum formam intentionalem mente conceptam. Sed causae actuales sumus quia intendimus, *quantum possumus*, ipsam effectus actualitatem. Iam vero et plura et maiora possumus cum aliis consociati quam singuli soli. Et ideo singuli secundum proprias quasdam formas intentionales operamur per modum causarum proportionatarum, et omnes circa commune ordinis bonum consentimus ut causae actuales simus et effectus actu producamus.

In eo ergo *fundatur* agens sociale, quod agens per intellectum non solum proportionem ad proprium effectum habet sed etiam conditiones suae operationis considerat et eas implendas curat. Per illud autem *actuatur* agens sociale, quod multa per intellectum agentia intelligunt et volunt alia aliis conditiones actualis operationis implere. Quae quidem actuatio, quoties evenit, etiam actuatio est communis ordinis boni sive exterioris sive culturalis.

Age vero! Hoc ipsum quod multi ita consociantur ut idem intelligere et circa idem consentire possunt, iam aliquod ordinis bonum est. Et ideo ordinis bono ante indigent homines quam vel actuando idem bonum conservant vel mutando idem bonum sive perficiunt sive corrumpunt. Quod si perspicitur, ab agente sociali ad agens historicum transitur. Agens enim per intellectum fit agens sociale, inquantum cum aliis per bonum ordinis ante stabilitum coniungitur; et quamvis stabilitum ordinis bonum vel conservare vel mutare possit, hoc tamen non facit nisi secundum sapientiam et prudentiam et mutuam bonam voluntatem, quas per praevium ordinis bonum iam ante acquisivit. Singula praeterea agentia socialia singulis occasionibus libere eligunt utrum iam exsistens ordinis bonum conservandum sit vel mutandum; sed parum refert quid singuli seorsum sentiant nisi etiam circa unum quoddam commune consilium conveniant; quod tamen non faciunt nisi per iam ante exsistens ordinis bonum. Socialia ergo agentia ita res futuras libere determinant ut ipsa haec eorum determinatio, quatenus communis est atque efficax, quam maxime a praeterito dependeat. Sub conditionibus enim historicis agentia fiunt socialia, et sub conditionibus historicis libertatem suam exercent; et quamvis libertas unius hominis seorsum sumpti limitationes habeat easque graves (cf. art. VII), longe graviores sunt limitationes collectivae illius libertatis quae a liberis eligentibus non exercetur nisi quatenus bono quodam ordinis praeexsistente

It is easy to see why an actual cause is more commonly to be found in many persons linked together in some way rather than in one person alone. We are proportionate causes by reason of an intentional form conceived in the mind. But we are actual causes because we intend, *insofar as we are able,* the actuality of the effect. Now, we can do many more and greater things linked with others than by ourselves alone. And therefore individually each of us operates in accordance with our own particular intentional forms as proportionate causes, and all together agree on a common good of order so that we are then actual causes and actually produce the desired effects.

Social agency, then, is *founded upon* the fact that those who act through intellect not only are proportionate to their proper effect but also consider the conditions for their operation and see to their fulfilment. Social agents, however, are *actuated* through the fact that many agents acting through intellect understand and will that different persons fulfil different conditions for actual operation. This actuation indeed, as often as it occurs, is also the actuation of the common good of order, external or cultural.

Well now! The very fact that many are linked together so as to be able to have a common understanding and agreement about the same thing is already a good of order. Hence human beings need a good of order before they either actuate this same good and so preserve it or change it for better or for worse. But if this is grasped, then we pass from the social agent to the historical agent. For agents acting through intellect become social agents inasmuch as they are linked with others through a previously established good of order; and although they can preserve or change this established good of order, they do not do so except in accordance with the wisdom and prudence and mutual good will that they have acquired through the previous good of order. Individual social agents, moreover, freely choose on individual occasions whether the already existing good of order should be preserved or changed; but it matters little what each one taken separately thinks unless there is some common agreement on a particular proposal, and such agreement is reached only through the previously existing good of order. Social agents, therefore, freely determine the future in such a way that this very determination on their part, to the extent that it is common and effective, depends very greatly upon the past. For agents become social agents under historical conditions, and exercise their freedom under historical conditions; and although the freedom of one person alone has limitations, and serious ones at that (see article 7), far more serious are the limitations of that collective freedom which those who have free choice do not exercise except insofar as they are linked together in a preexisting good

coniunguntur, ut idem eodem fere modo intelligentes atque iudicantes circa commune consilium efficaciter consentire possint.

## Articulus XXXVIII: De agente historico

Agens dicimus historicum quod ordinis bonum vel exterius vel culturale causat.

Plus vel minus historicum est agens prout effectus eius diutius vel brevius permanet.

Totale vel partiale est agens historicum prout partem vel totum boni ordinis producit.

Per se vel per accidens agit prout effectus oritur secundum vel praeter eius intentionem.

Proportionata vel actualis causa exsistit prout ideam ordinis (partialem vel totalem) concipit manifestatque vel conceptam et manifestatam in usum atque efficaciam deducit.

Originaria vel conservativa est causa prout prima ideam concipit vel efficacem reddit vel iam conceptam propagat vel iam efficacem protegit.

Destructiva vel restaurativa est causa quae ordinis bonum vel in peius commutat vel iam declinans in pristinum reducit vigorem.

Agens historicum simpliciter primum est Deus, qui omnia prorsus secundum omnes eorum determinationes per suam sapientiam ordinat infallibiliter et ordinata eligit efficaciter et electa facit irresistibiliter. Quae tamen infallibilitas, efficacia, irresistibilitas necessitatem rebus non imponit.

Verum sane est quod, si Deus hoc aliquid esse scit, necessario hoc est vel, si Deus hoc aliquid esse vult, necessario est vel, si Deus hoc aliquid esse facit, necessario est. At haec ipsa necessitas non absoluta sed conditionata est, sicut in eo quod Socrates dum sedet necessario sedet.

Quod enim Deus hoc aliquid esse scit vel vult vel facit, non necessarium est sed contingens. Quia contingens est, adaequationem veritatis non in solo Deo simplici et necessario habet, sed etiam extra Deum terminum quendam contingentem exigit. Qui quidem terminus nihil est aliud quam ipsum hoc aliquid. Non ergo prius verum est quod Deus hoc aliquid esse

of order, so that by understanding and judging the same things in roughly the same way, they are able to come to an effective agreement on a common plan of action.

**Article 38: Historical agents**

By historical agents we mean those persons who cause either the external or the cultural good of order.

Historical agents are of greater or lesser historical importance according to whether their influence lasts a longer or a shorter time.

Historical agents are partial or total according to whether they produce part or the whole of a good of order.

Historical agents act per se or *per accidens* according to whether their effect is produced according to or beyond their intention.

The historical agent is a proportionate or an actual cause, depending on whether the agent conceives and expresses the (partial or total) idea of an order, or actually puts the conceived and expressed idea into effective practice.

The historical agent is an originating or a conserving cause, depending on whether he or she was the first to conceive an idea or render it effective or, on the other hand, propagates an already conceived idea or safeguards one that is already effective.

The historical agent is a destructive or restorative cause, depending on whether he or she changes the good of order for the worse or restores a declining good of order to its pristine vigor.

The absolutely first historical agent is God, who through his wisdom infallibly orders all things whatsoever with all their determinations, efficaciously chooses what he has ordered, and irresistibly effects what he has chosen. Nevertheless, this infallibility, efficacy, and irresistibility do not impose necessity upon things.

It is certainly true that if God knows something to be, it necessarily is, that if he wills something to be, it necessarily is, and that if he causes something to be, it necessarily is. But this necessity is not absolute but conditioned – as, for example, while Socrates is seated he is necessarily seated.

For the fact that God knows or wills or causes something to exist is itself not necessary but contingent. Because it is contingent, its correspondence to truth lies not in God alone, who is simple and necessary, but also requires some contingent term outside of God; this term is nothing other than the thing itself. Therefore, that God knows, wills, or causes a thing to exist is not

scit vel vult vel facit, quam iam exsistat per modum termini sciti, electi, facti ipsum hoc aliquid. Quare, in antecedente includitur tamquam iam exsistens hoc aliquid, et ideo in consequente concluditur necessario hoc aliquid esse non necessitate absoluta sed necessitate conditionata.[3]

Neve aeternitatis ignorantiam manifestes obiciendo quod ab aeterno Deus scit et ab aeterno vult sed in tempore fit terminus. Non enim apud Deum datur momentorum successio sed omnia divina momenta unum et idem et simul sunt. Quare si nunc datur terminus, nunc Deus scit et vult; et si nunc Deus scit et vult, ab aeterno scit et vult.

Neve simultaneum veritatis signum cum priori naturae vel causalitatis signo confundas. Natura et causalitate praecedit scientia divina et praecedit volitio divina et praecedit actio divina. Non enim Deus scit vel vult vel facit quia datur terminus, sed datur terminus quia Deus scit et vult et facit. Sed haec vera propositio, Deum hoc aliquid esse scire, velle, facere, et haec alia vera propositio, hoc aliquid esse, in veritate sunt simultaneae; neutra enim earum adaequationem veritatis habet sine hoc aliquo iam exsistente. Quae cum ita sint, et salvatur prioritas divini dominii absoluti, et excluditur omnis possibilitas concludendi quod divinum dominium rebus necessitatem imponit. Nisi enim per veras propositiones fieri non possunt conclusiones.

Neve tandem denique elegantissimam hanc doctrinam thomisticam cum opinione banneziana confundas. Quae enim superius de divino dominio probavimus, de solo Deo valent; neque ullo modo attribui possunt mirae et merae illi creaturae, scilicet praedeterminationi physicae quae, si doctrinam thomisticam intelligis, superfluit prorsus.[4]

Agens ergo historicum simpliciter primum atque simpliciter absolutum est Deus.

Agentia vero historica et ministerialia sunt homines. Illud enim est divinae sapientiae consilium ut omnia gubernet et in fines suos producat per causas secundas et secundum convenientiam naturarum earum (cf. art. x et xi). Quod ergo ordinat divina sapientia eligitque divina bonitas, hoc per homines intelligentes, iudicantes, consentientes fit. Quia ergo Deus agens

true prior to the existence of that thing itself, as the term known, chosen, and caused. Hence, in the antecedent [i.e., in God's knowledge, will, power], this particular thing is included as something now existing, and so in the consequent the conclusion is that it necessarily exists, not by an absolute but by a conditioned necessity.[3]

Now, please do not reveal your ignorance about eternity by raising the objection that God knows and wills something from all eternity while the term comes into existence in time. For in God there is no succession of moments, but all divine moments are one and the same and simultaneous. Therefore, if a term is in existence now, God knows and wills it now; and if God knows and wills something now, he knows and wills it from all eternity.

Again, do not confuse this simultaneity in truth with priority in nature or in causality. God's knowing and willing and acting are both naturally and causally prior. God does not know or will or cause because there exists a term, but the term exists because God knows and wills and causes. But this true proposition, 'God knows, wills, and causes this thing to exist,' and this second true proposition, 'This thing exists,' are simultaneous in truth: neither of them has the correspondence of truth unless this particular thing is now in existence. This being the case, the priority of God's absolute dominion is safeguarded, and there is no possible ground for concluding that God's dominion imposes necessity upon things; for conclusions can be derived only from true propositions.

Finally, do not confuse this truly elegant doctrine of St Thomas with the Bannezian opinion. The statements we have made above concerning God's dominion apply to God alone; they can in no way be attributed to that marvelous little creature called 'physical predetermination,' which, if one understands the Thomist doctrine, is quite superfluous.[4]

The absolutely first historical agent in every respect, then, is God.

But human beings are ministerial historical agents. It is the plan of divine wisdom to govern all things in such a way as to bring them to the attainment of their ends through secondary causes and in accordance with their respective natures (see articles 10 and 11). Therefore, what divine wisdom has ordered and divine goodness has chosen comes into existence through human beings who understand, judge, and consent. Since, then, God is the

3 [See, for instance, Lonergan, *Insight*, 684–85.]
4 See our remarks about the authorship of sin in article 14.

principale est, homo non est nisi instrumentale; quia autem homo instrumentum est quod per intellectum agit, ministeriale dicitur.

In agente ministeriali tamen distingui oportet inter ea quae facit virtute agentis principalis et ea quae facit propria virtute. Sicut enim simplex miles in bello haec et illa munera, eaque parva, virtute propria perficit, sed virtute ducis ad hostem vincendum suam partem confert, ita etiam in rebus humanis et historicis singuli proprios in vita fines propria virtute intendimus, sed virtute Dei ad finem divinum attingendum partem nostram conferimus.

Quo usque vero singuli agentia historica simus, nisi per multas et cumulatas distinctiones non declaratur. Singuli sane sumus agentia per intellectum et socialia, si quidem intelligimus, eligimus, neque per nos solos solis nobis operamur. Neque agentia socialia esse possumus quin in ordinis bonum vel exterius vel culturale vel utrumque influamus; non enim actu exsistit ordinis bonum nisi inquantum agentia socialia actu hoc bonum usurpant; et ideo omnis actio humana sub conditionibus socialibus peracta iam exsistens ordinis bonum vel conservat vel corrumpit vel perficit. Quod tamen non demonstrat nos esse agentia historica nisi valde partialia.

Praeterea, si solummodo particularia bona intendimus cum socialiter agamus, in bonum ordinis influimus quidem sed praeter nostram intentionem et ideo per accidens tantum. Sed circa hoc, secundum plus et minus dici videntur per se et per accidens. Non enim ita bonum particulare prosequuntur homines ut ordinis bonum, quo bonum particulare attingunt, nullatenus apprehendant et apprehensum nullatenus velint. At vaga, indistincta, confusa esse solet haec apprehensio, si multitudinem hominum respicis, et ideo potius implicita quam explicita est ipsa consequens volitio.

Ad agentia historica per se, proportionata, et partialia ascendimus, cum ad eos attendamus qui ultra bona particularia ad bonum ordinis (quo omnia fere bona particularia fiunt) elevant mentem, ut partem quandam boni ordinis cogitent et iudicent et de ea colloquantur, disputent, legant, scribant.

Ultra agentia proportionata ad actualia procedimus, cum eos consideremus qui vel legitima auctoritate, vel vi et armis, vel artibus psychologicis, vel ratione et persuasione, vel pluribus simul modis, conceptum et manifestatum consilium in usum atque efficaciam deducunt, vel alicubi deductum in alia loca extendunt, vel extensum conservant, vel conservatum perficiunt, vel perfectum corrumpunt, vel corruptum restaurant.

principal agent, we are only instrumental agents; but because we are instruments that act through intellect, we are called ministerial agents.

In a ministerial agent we must distinguish between what one does by virtue of the principal agent and what one does on one's own. Just as in a war a private soldier carries out his duties, minor as they are, by his own power, but through the power of the general does his bit to defeat the enemy, so in human history we each pursue our aims in life through our own power while by God's power we do our part in attaining God's purpose.

To what extent each of us is a historical agent can only be determined through a number of cumulative distinctions. Each one is, of course, an agent acting through intellect and a social agent, since we understand and choose and do not operate by ourselves alone or for ourselves alone. Nor can we be social agents without having some influence upon either the external or the cultural good of order or both; for the good of order exists in actuality only inasmuch as social agents actually play their part in it, and thus every human action done under social conditions either preserves or corrupts or improves the existing good of order. But this does not show that we are historical agents, except only very partially.

Besides, if we aim at only particular goods when we act socially, we still influence the social order but do so beyond our intention, and so only *per accidens.* But in this matter, it seems that we must speak of influence as being more or less per se or *per accidens.* For people do not pursue a particular good without some awareness of the good of order through which they obtain the particular good or without in some way willing what they have apprehended. But this apprehension of the good of order is generally vague, indistinct, and confused on the part of most human beings, and so the consequent willing of the good of order is more implicit than explicit.

We advance to a consideration of per se, proportionate, and partial historical agents when we turn our attention to those who raise their minds beyond particular goods to the good of order (through which virtually all particular goods come into being), so that they think about and make judgments about some part of the good of order, and talk about it, argue about it, read about it, and write about it.

We proceed beyond proportionate agents to actual agents, when we consider those who, by legitimate authority, or force of arms, or psychological techniques, or reason and persuasion, or in several ways at once, effectively implement a plan that was conceived and made known, or who extend to other places a plan implemented elsewhere, or preserve it when thus extended, or improve it when preserved, or corrupt it when improved, or restore it when corrupted.

Sed ipsa actualia agentia plus vel minus historica esse possunt. Magis enim historica reputantur agentia originaria quam conservativa, et inter ipsa originaria ea magis historica sunt quae aliquod ordinis elementum incipiunt quod sive per se sive per sua consequentia modo permanenti in omnem fere subsequentem actionem socialem influit. Quam ob causam, maxime historica reputantur ea agentia quae homines ex primitiva cultura in civilizationem urbanam deduxerunt, et deinde quae hanc civilizationem reflectione philosophica et scientifica ulterius perfecerunt. Maximus autem inter omnia agentia historica est Verbum caro factum, hominum Salvator, quem iam considerari oportet.

### Articulus XXXIX: De Christo agente[5]

Christus agit tum ut Deus tum ut homo. Ut Deus, idem facit quod Pater et Spiritus sanctus; nam quorum una est essentia, eorum una est operatio. Ut homo autem tum his in terris durante vita sua mortali egit tum ad dexteram Patris sedens in caelis agere pergit.

Dupliciter ergo agentis duplex est agendi principium, divinum et humanum, ut aliter ut Deus agat et aliter ut homo. Et aliqua facit ut Deus quae ut homo non fecit, si quidem homo hominem non creavit. Alia autem facit tum ut Deus tum ut homo, ut duae sint operationes inter se ordinatae sed unus sit effectus productus.

Quae duarum operationum ordinatio per divinum mandatum et obedientiam humanam habetur. Praecipere enim est per rationem et voluntatem alium movere; obedire autem est secundum rationem et voluntatem alterius moveri.[6] Praecipit ergo Deus quatenus sua bonitate ea eligit quae sua sapientia ordinat. Obedit autem Christus homo quatenus in obiecto secundario visionis suae beatae actualem rerum ordinem apprehendit et eundem ordinem exsequendum vult.

Quae Christi obedientia veri nominis erat.[7] Quamvis enim praeceptum explicite expressum non exspectaverit neque audiverit, Patris tamen voluntatem novit et Patris bonitati sese confidit. Nam eiusmodi non erat Christi

But these actual agents can be more or less historical. Originating agents are considered to be more historical than conserving agents, and among the originating agents themselves those are more historical who initiate some element of order which by itself or because of its consequences has a lasting influence upon virtually all subsequent social action. This is why those agents are considered to be the most historical who brought humanity from a primitive state to that of a cultured civilization, and then further improved that civilization through philosophical and scientific thought. The greatest of all historical agents, however, is the Word made flesh, the Savior of humankind, whom we must now proceed to consider.

### Article 39: Christ as agent[5]

Christ acts both as God and as man. As God, he does the same as the Father and the Holy Spirit, since those who possess one and the same essence have the same operation. But he acted as a human being during his mortal life on earth and continues so to act seated at the right hand of the Father in heaven.

He who acts in two different ways has two principles of action, divine and human, so that as God he acts in one way and as human in another. As God he does some things that he did not do as human, since it was not a human who created humans. But other things he does both as God and as human, in such a way that there are two operations ordered to each other, but one effect produced.

This ordering of the two operations takes place through divine command and human obedience. To command is to move another through reason and will; but to obey is to be moved in accordance with the reason and will of another.[6] Thus God commands inasmuch as in his goodness he chooses what his wisdom ordains. But the human Christ obeys inasmuch as he apprehends the actual order of reality in the secondary object of his beatific vision and wills this same order to be carried out.

The obedience of Christ was true and genuine obedience.[7] Although he did not wait for or hear a command explicitly issued, nevertheless he knew the Father's will and entrusted himself to the Father's goodness. Christ's

5 [The discussion of Christ's human freedom here parallels a longer discussion in Lonergan, *The Incarnate Word* 734–61.]
6 Thomas Aquinas, *Summa theologiae*, 2-2, q. 104, a. 1 c.
7 Ibid. 3, q. 47, a. 2, ad 1m.

scientia humana ut omnes rerum ordines possibiles penitus cognosceret;[8] quos ignorans, iudicare non potuit utrum melius esset hunc rerum ordinem eligere in quo tot et tanta passurus erat; sed quod ipse ex inspectis et comparatis omnibus possibilibus ignoravit, propter perspectam Patris bonitatem ex caritate et obedientia accepit.[9]

Libera praeterea erat haec Christi obedientia; nam meritoria erat (DB 790, 799), neque datur meritum sine libertate etiam in statu naturae lapsae (DB 1094) et ideo multo minus in natura Christi non lapsa.

Quae autem in contrarium obici solent, quamvis ea sane includant quae hac in vita intelligere non valemus, minime tamen sunt argumenta stringentia sed omnia systematice solvuntur.

Nam nihil in primis concludi potest ex eo quod Christus impeccabilis fuit; Deus enim impeccabilis est et nihilominus liber; et ideo quamvis in Christo non fuerit libertas contrarietatis, erat libertas specificationis et contradictionis.[10]

Neque quidquam recte concluditur ex ipso divino praecepto. Hoc enim praeceptum erat ordinatio divinae sapientiae et electio divinae voluntatis, si quidem praecipere est per rationem et voluntatem movere.[11] Sed uti supra diximus (art. XXXVIII), divina scientia et electio necessitatem non inducunt nisi conditionatam; et conditionata necessitas libertatem non tollit, secus ne Deus quidem liber esset.

Unde concludes divinum praeceptum in signo veritatis simultaneo fuisse cum ipsa Christi obedientia, quamvis ipsam obedientiam praecesserit natura et causalitate et praecepto. Quam ob causam, potuit Christus impeccabilis rogare Patrem suum atque impetrare duodecim legiones angelorum (Mt 26.53).

human knowledge was not one that gave him a thorough knowledge of all possible orders of reality.[8] Being ignorant of them, he was not able to judge whether it was better to choose this order of reality in which he was destined to suffer so grievously; but what he himself was unable to know by considering and comparing all possibilities, he accepted out of love and obedience because of his intimate knowledge of the goodness of the Father.[9]

Christ's obedience was, moreover, free; for it was meritorious (DB 790, 799, [DS 1513, 1529, ND 510, 1932]), and even in the state of fallen nature there is no merit without freedom (DB 1094, [DS 2003, ND 1989/3]), which would be all the more true in the case of Christ's unfallen nature.

As to the usual objections against this, while they certainly include things that we cannot understand in this life, nevertheless they are not stringent arguments, but are all solved in a systematic way.

First of all, nothing can be concluded from the fact of Christ's impeccability. God is impeccable and nonetheless free, and therefore although there was no freedom of contrariety in Christ, there was freedom of specification and contradiction.[10]

Nor can any conclusions be correctly drawn from the divine command itself. This command was an ordination of the divine wisdom and the decision of the divine will, since to command is to move through reason and will.[11] But as we said above (article 38), God's knowledge and decision impose only conditioned necessity; and conditioned necessity does not take away freedom, for otherwise not even God would be free.

Hence our conclusion is that the divine command was true simultaneously with Christ's obedience, although it was prior to that obedience in nature and in causality and in precept. This is why Christ, though impeccable, could have asked for and received from his Father twelve legions of angels (Matthew 26.53).

8 Ibid. q. 10, a. 2.
9 Ibid. q. 47, a. 2, ad 3m.
10 [The human Christ, that is, was free to determine how he would act (freedom of specification), and free to decide whether to act or not (freedom of contradiction, or exercise), but was not free to act contrary to the will of the Father, that is, to sin (freedom of contrariety).]
11 Thomas Aquinas, *Summa theologiae*, 2-2, q. 104, a. 1 c.

Neque quidquam recte concluditur ex eo quod Christus divinum praeceptum per visionem beatam praecognovit. Sicut enim ipsa divina scientia et voluntas necessitatem absolutam non inducit, ita alia et humana scientia quae in divina fundatur necessitatem absolutam non inducit.[12]

Neque haec in Christo cognitio voluntatem Christi necessitavit. Nam primo, uti supra dictum est, cognitio in mente humana, sicut et divina, in signo veritatis simultaneo erat cum ipsa Christi obedientia. Et praeterea haec obiectio praesupponit voluntatem Christi impeccabilem fuisse invitam vel negligentem vel tardiorem. Sicut enim in Christo ex visa divina essentia sequebatur cognitio omnium actualium, ita etiam in eius voluntate promptissima ex dilectione Dei Patris superabundavit libere volitio obediendi. Et ideo voluntas Christi impeccabilis semper prius Patri obedire voluit quam ex scientia rerum specificationem suae obedientiae expetivit.

Dices tamen hanc Christi obedientiam a nostra veri nominis obedientia valde differre.

Respondetur autem obicientem non considerare quid intercedat inter obedientiam voluntatis peccatricis et obedientiam voluntatis impeccabilis. Peccatrix enim voluntas se ipsam primum agens esse ducit a se ipsa pro sua libertate absoluta determinandum; cui voluntati primo innotescit preceptum, et deinde ab ea quaeruntur effugia, et tertio denique tandem per divinam gratiam ei conceditur magna illa conversio per quam ipsa se submittit atque Deo se subordinat. Sed voluntas impeccabilis iam conversa atque subordinata est, et ipsa sua Dei dilectio minime impeditur quominus statim in volitionem obediendi superabundaret. Quare in voluntate impeccabili non primo habetur praeceptum et deinde reluctantia et tertio submissio, sed primo habetur obediendi volitio et secundo habetur specificationis expetitio et tertio habetur expetitae specificationis acceptio.

Proinde, quia libere obedivit Christus, instrumentum ministeriale fuit ad ea omnia peragenda quae per divinam sapientiam ordinata et per divinam bonitatem electa erant. Quia autem instrumentum fuit Christus, distinguendum est inter ea quae fiebant per virtutem suam humanam qua talem et ea quae fiebant per eandem virtutem quatenus divinitatis instrumentum. Quae quidem distinctio fundatur in proportione virtutis ad effectum. Quia ergo Christus homo erat agens per intellectum, imperando egit. Sed secundum naturam humanam qua talem non immediate motum imperavit nisi in proprio corpore, neque plus per hunc motum corporalem produxit

Nor can any correct conclusion be drawn from the fact that through his beatific vision Christ had prior knowledge of God's command. Just as God's knowledge and will do not entail absolute necessity, neither does any human knowledge that is grounded upon God's knowledge.[12]

Further, this knowledge in Christ did not necessitate his will. First of all, as we said above, knowledge in his human mind, as in the divine mind, was simultaneous in truth with his obedience. And besides, this objection supposes Christ's impeccable will to have been reluctant or negligent or sluggish. But just as Christ's knowledge of all actual reality was a consequence of his vision of the divine essence, so also in his most ready will there was a superabundance of his willingness and readiness to obey freely because of his great love for the Father. Hence the impeccable will of Christ was always ready to obey the Father before seeking a specification of his obedience from his knowledge of things.

Still, you may object that this obedience of Christ is very different from any true obedience on our part.

Our answer is that this objection overlooks the difference between the obedience of a sinful will and that of an impeccable will. A sinful will considers itself as the primary agent to be determined by itself in accordance with its absolute freedom. First it receives knowledge of a precept, then looks for an escape, and finally by the grace of God is granted a great conversion as a result of which it submits and subordinates itself to God. But an impeccable will is already converted and subordinate to God, and this love of God that it has is not hindered in the least from immediately overflowing into a willingness to obey. Hence in an impeccable will there is no movement from, first, a precept then to reluctance and finally to submission, but rather there is first the willingness to obey, then the seeking of specification, and finally the acceptance of the specification sought.

Accordingly, because Christ freely obeyed, he was a ministerial instrument for carrying out all that was ordained by divine wisdom and chosen by divine goodness. Because he was an instrument, however, we must distinguish between what he did through his human power as such and what he did through that same power as an instrument of divinity. This distinction is based upon the proportion between a power and its effect. Because the man Christ was an agent acting through intellect, he acted by commanding. But according to his human nature as such, he commanded movement only in his own body, and through such bodily movement did no more than

12 Ibid. 2-2, q. 171, a. 6, ad 3m.

quam motus corporis virtute naturali vel intentionali producere potest. Quatenus autem natura Christi humana erat coniunctum divinitatis instrumentum, efficacia imperii non limitabatur ad proprium corpus movendum, sed ulterius sese extendebat ut daemoniis, ventis et mari, aegrotantibus ipsisque demortuis efficaciter imperaret. Quinimo, non ita hanc imperandi efficaciam habuit Christus homo ut eam per alios exercere non potuerit; sed etiam per alios eam exercet, uti perspicitur, tum in thaumaturgis qui in nomine Christi miracula patrant, tum in sacramentorum ministris qui signa a Christo instituta ponunt quae gratiam causant.

Quibus praemissis circa actionem Christi in genere, iam particulariter considerari oportet de Christo exemplari, de Christo capite, de Christo agente historico, et de Christo mediatore.

### Articulus XL: De Christo exemplari

Exemplar dupliciter intelligi potest. Primo enim modo exemplar est quod inspicit agens cum per intellectum operetur; et sic Christus nobis est causa exemplaris cum eum imitemur. Alio autem modo exemplar est secundum quandam oeconomiam seu rerum ordinationem ut, quod in exemplari factum sit, etiam in caeteris fiat necesse sit; et sic Christus per modum exemplaris nostram salutem operatus est.[13]

Ad cuius intelligentiam tria sunt consideranda, nempe, ipsum principium oeconomiae, determinatio principii in Christo vel a Christo peracta, et applicatio determinationis in nobis accepta. Ipsum enim principium ex Deo ordinante et eligente est. Principii autem determinatio per vitam Christi efficitur. Quibus positis, tamquam conclusio ex praemissis, sequitur quid in Christianis efficiendum sit atque efficiatur.

Primo ergo, quantum ad ipsum principium, ex scripturis manifestum est Deum praescitos praedestinasse conformes fieri imaginis Filii sui, ut sit ipse primogenitus in multis fratribus (Rom 8.29). Sicut enim Christus est imago Dei (2 Cor 4.4, Col 1.15), ita iubemur renovari spiritu mentis et induere novum hominem qui secundum Deum creatus est in iustitia et sanctitate veritatis (Eph 4.23–24, Col 3.10, Rom 12.2); quod quidem nihil est aliud quam induere Dominum Iesum Christum (Rom 13.14; cf. Gal 3.27, 4.19) ut gloriam Domini speculantes in eandem imaginem transformemur a claritate in claritatem tamquam a Domino Spiritu (2 Cor 3.18); de caelis enim

a bodily movement can do by its natural or intentional power. But inasmuch as Christ's human nature was an instrument conjoined to divinity, the efficacy of his command was not limited to moving his own body, but extended to effectively commanding demons, the winds and the waves, the sick, and even the dead. More than that, this efficacy of Christ's power to command could be exercised through others, as may be grasped in the wonder-workers performing miracles in the name of Christ, and in the ministers of the sacraments who enact signs instituted by Christ which cause grace.

With these preliminary remarks concerning the action of Christ in general, we must now consider in particular Christ as exemplar, Christ as head, Christ as a historical agent, and Christ as mediator.

### Article 40: Christ the exemplar

'Exemplar' can be understood in two ways. First, an exemplar is what an agent examines when operating through intellect; in this sense Christ is an exemplary cause for us when we imitate him. In the second way, an exemplar pertains to a certain economy or ordering of things so that what is done in the exemplar should be done in others. It is in this way that Christ has wrought our salvation as our exemplar.[13]

To understand this, three things must be considered: the principle itself of the economy, the determination of the principle in Christ or accomplished by Christ, and the application received in us of this determination. The principle itself comes from God's ordination and decision, but the determination of the principle is effected through the life of Christ. Hence there follows, as a conclusion from its premises, that which ought to be effected and is effected in Christians.

First, then, as to the principle itself, it is clear from scripture that those whom God foreknew he also predestined to be conformed to the image of his Son, in order that he might be the firstborn of many children (Romans 8.29). Just as Christ is the image of God (2 Corinthians 4.4, Colossians 1.15), so we are bidden to be renewed in our attitude of mind and to clothe ourselves with the new human being created according to the likeness of God in the righteousness and holiness of truth (Ephesians 4.23–24, Colossians 3.10, Romans 12.2), which is none other than to put on the Lord Jesus Christ (Romans 13.14; see also Galatians 3.27, 4.19), so that gazing

13 Ibid. 3, q. 56, a. 1, ad 3m; q. 49, a. 2, ad 2m.

exspectamus salvatorem Dominum Iesum Christum qui reformabit corpus humilitatis nostrae conformatum corpori claritatis suae (Phil 3.20–21).

Quae quidem scripturae loca plus dicunt quam intentum principium; sed ipsum principium manifeste continent, nempe, secundum praesentem oeconomiam salutis Christum esse exemplar et ideo, quod in Christo fit, in salvandis pariter fieri oportere.

Iam vero ipse Christus ut homo, cum omnia actualia noverit,[14] etiam hoc principium novit et eiusdem consectaria intellexit. Quo principio cognito atque intellecto, fieri non potuit ut Christus homo quidquam circa se ipsum determinaret quin idem circa suos determinaret. Non enim exemplar consideramus iam factum, neque iners, sed ratione et libertate gaudens atque utens, et ita se determinans ut eo ipso determinet quid in aliis fieri oporteat.

Praeterea, quod de ipso exemplari verum est, multo magis de Deo verum est qui Christum hominem ideo creavit et omnem Christi actionem ideo direxit atque gubernavit ut in omnibus exemplar convenientissimum esset.

Quare, ut rem exemplis confirmemus, cum Deus Pater Christum etiam hominem dilexerit tamquam Filium suum naturalem, sequebatur Deum Patrem simili dilectione nos diligere, secundum illud, 'Dilexisti eos sicut et me dilexisti' (Io 17.23, 17.26). Sed dilectio Patris erga Filium proprium est ipse Amor procedens, seu Spiritus sanctus,[15] uti in baptismo Christi manifestum est (Mc 1.10–11). Cum ergo secundum principium exemplaritatis eadem dilectio specialissima ad nos terminetur,[16] gratiam sanctificantem accipimus et filii adoptivi constituimur et donum increatum Spiritus sancti inhabitantis habemus. Quod quidem primo fit in nobis cum baptizati Christo baptizato assimilemur.

Praeterea, Christus homo erat persona divina in natura humana operans, et ideo operatio Christi hominis ratione naturae humanae (seu principii-quo) humana esse debuit, sed ratione personae divinae (seu principii-quod) ad divina quodammodo pertingere debuit. Et ideo in Christo non solum ponuntur potentiae et habitus humani sed etiam habitus et actus absolute

upon the glory of the Lord we may be transformed into that same image, going from one degree of glory to another, as from the Lord, the Spirit (2 Corinthians 3.18); for from heaven we are expecting a Savior, the Lord Jesus Christ, who will transform these wretched bodies of ours into copies of his glorious body (Philippians 3.20–21).

These scriptures go beyond stating the principle we have in mind; but they obviously do contain this principle, namely, that in this present economy of salvation Christ is the exemplar, and accordingly what is done in Christ ought to be done likewise in those who are to be saved.

Now the human Christ himself, knowing all actual reality,[14] knew this principle also and understood its consequences. Knowing and understanding this principle, then, it was impossible for the human Christ to determine anything with regard to himself without determining the same with regard to us. For the exemplar we are considering is not one already made or inert, but one who possesses and uses reason and free will, and so in determining himself determines what ought to be done in others.

Moreover, what is true concerning the exemplar himself is all the more true concerning God, who created Christ as man and directed and governed all Christ's activity in such a way that he might be a most fitting and appropriate exemplar in all things.

Therefore, to confirm this by examples, since God the Father also loved Christ as man as his natural Son, it followed that God the Father also loves us with a similar love: 'You have loved them as you have loved me' (John 17.23, 17.26). But the love of the Father for his own Son is proceeding Love itself, the Holy Spirit,[15] as was made clear at Christ's baptism (Mark 1.10–11). When, therefore, according to this principle of exemplarity this same very special love terminates in us,[16] we receive sanctifying grace, are made children by adoption, and have the uncreated gift of the Holy Spirit dwelling within us. This takes place in us first when at our baptism we are assimilated to the baptized Christ.

Moreover, Christ as man was a divine person operating in a human nature, and therefore the operation of the human Christ by reason of his human nature (the principle-by-which) was necessarily human, but by reason of his divine person (the principle-which) belonged to the divine in some way. Therefore in Christ there are said to be not only human powers and habits

14 Ibid. 3, q. 10, a. 2.
15 Ibid. 1, q. 37, a. 2.
16 Ibid. 1-2, q. 110, a. 1.

supernaturales, ut operatio eius humana personae divinae conveniret. Quod cum in Christo homine factum sit, etiam in Christianis fieri oportet secundum principium exemplaritatis. Quare etiam operatio nostra Christiana ad modum personae divinae in natura inferiori operantis esse debet; et ideo simul cum gratia sanctificante etiam virtutes infusas accipimus et Spiritus sancti dona et, prout occasio fert, ipsas Spiritus sancti motiones quibus mens illuminatur et voluntas inspiratur.

Praeterea, Christus homo passus et mortuus et resuscitatus sedet ad dexteram Patris. Quare, secundum principium exemplaritatis, nos oportet adimplere quae desunt passionum Christi (Col 1.24) et compati ut conglorificemur (Rom 8.17); praeterea, 'Quoniam si unus pro omnibus mortuus est, ergo omnes mortui sunt, et pro omnibus mortuus est Christus ut et qui vivunt non iam sibi vivant sed ei qui pro ipsis mortuus est et resurrexit' (2 Cor 5.14–15; cf. 1 Io 3.16); quare 'Mortui enim estis, et vita vestra est abscondita cum Christo in Deo. Cum Christus apparuerit, vita vestra, tunc et vos apparebitis cum ipso in gloria' (Col 3.3–4); nam Deus 'dives est in misericordia, propter nimiam caritatem suam qua dilexit nos, et cum essemus mortui peccatis, convivificavit nos in Christo cuius gratia estis salvati, et conresuscitavit et consedere facit in caelestibus in Christo Iesu' (Eph 2.4–6); quae quidem resurrectio atque consessio, sicut spiritalis est, ita etiam in corpore perficitur; nam 'si Spiritus eius qui suscitavit Iesum a mortuis habitat in vobis, qui suscitavit Iesum Christum a mortuis vivificabit et mortalia corpora vestra propter inhabitantem Spiritum eius in vobis' (Rom 8.11).

Quod vero ex principalibus actibus Christi illustravimus, non minus de caeteris valet. In omnibus enim est eadem lex huius oeconomiae secundum quam praesciti praedestinantur conformes fieri imaginis Filii sui.[17]

Obiecerit tamen quispiam haec potius modum loquendi exponere quam veram et realem causalitatem demonstrare.

Respondetur duplicem esse causalitatem: aliam mere apparentem, v.g., quae in bobus aratrum trahentibus eatenus cognoscitur quatenus ipsum boum nisum imaginamur; aliam autem veram et realem, quae in iisdem bobus cognoscitur quatenus motus aratri a bobus dependere et intelligitur et vere affirmatur. Iam vero in Christo exemplari illa causalitas mere

but also habits and acts that are absolutely supernatural, so that his human operation was in keeping with his divine person. Since this was the case with Christ as human, it also should be so in Christians according to the principle of exemplarity. Therefore, our operations as Christians also ought to be according to the pattern of a divine person operating in a lower nature; and therefore along with sanctifying grace we also receive infused virtues, the gifts of the Holy Spirit, and, as circumstances warrant, movements of the Holy Spirit by which our minds are enlightened and our wills inspired.

Further, the human Christ, having suffered and died and risen, sits at the right hand of the Father. Therefore, according to the principle of exemplarity, it behooves us to complete what is lacking in the sufferings of Christ (Colossians 1.24) and to suffer with him in order to be glorified with him (Romans 8.17). Besides, 'one has died for all; therefore all have died. And Christ died for all, so that those who live might live no longer for themselves, but for him who died and was raised for them' (2 Corinthians 5.14–15; see also 1 John 3.16); therefore, 'you have died, and your life is hidden with Christ in God. When Christ who is your life is revealed, then you also will be revealed with him in glory' (Colossians 3.3–4). For God, 'who is rich in mercy, out of the great love with which he loved us even when we were dead through our trespasses, made us alive together with Christ – by grace you have been saved – and raised us up with him and seated us with him in the heavenly places in Christ Jesus' (Ephesians 2.4–6). This raising up and sitting with Christ, as it is spiritual, so also it is completed in the body; for 'if the Spirit of him who raised Jesus from the dead dwells in you, he who raised Jesus Christ from the dead will give life to your mortal bodies also through his Spirit that dwells in you' (Romans 8.11).

What we have illustrated from the principal acts of Christ holds no less for his other acts. For in all things there is the same law of this present dispensation by reason of which those who are foreknown are predestined to become conformed to the image of the Son.[17]

Yet one may object that this is rather an explanation of a way of speaking than a proof of real causality.

To this we would reply that there are two ways of considering causality: one that is merely apparent, as in the case of the oxen pulling a plow, in which causality is known only inasmuch as the effort of the oxen is imagined; then there is the other causality that is real and true, which is known in those same oxen inasmuch as the movement of the plow is understood

17 See Augustine, *Enchiridion*, 53; ML 40, 257.

apparens non habetur, sed haec vera et realis et ab intelligentibus perspicitur et a rationalibus vere affirmatur. Et hoc ad nostrum propositum sufficit prorsus.

### Articulus XLI: De Christo capite

Ea in viventibus est organorum interdependentia atque cohaesio ut quod in uno perficitur quodammodo tam pro toto quam pro reliquis perficiatur. Ita inter membra humana solus oculus videt; non tamen sibi soli videt oculus sed pariter toti corpori et singulis reliquis membris quae, quamvis ipsa non videant, tamen minime caeca sunt, cum per oculum quodammodo videant.

Quae quidem interdependentia confundi non debet cum efficientia causali. Si caecus manu ducitur, habetur efficientia causalis. Sed longe aliud est hoc caeci adiutorium extrinsecum ac miraculosa visionis restauratio. Per adiutorium extrinsecum diriguntur pedes caeci ne in foveam cadant; sed per visionem restauratam liberantur pedes ab indigentia directionis extrinsecae, cum ipsi iam per oculos naturaliter coniunctos quodammodo videant.

Iam vero multi unum corpus sumus in Christo et singuli alter alterius membra (Rom 12.5, 1 Cor 12.12–31). Cuius corporis membrum principale seu caput est Christus (Col 1.18). Et ideo quod in Christo perficitur, hoc iam in toto et pro toto perficitur.

Quapropter rationem capitis *propriam* a ratione exemplaris et a ratione causae efficientis sedulo distinguas. Quod ut clarius fiat, exemplo sit Christi satisfactio. Quia ergo Christus pro peccatis satisfecit, exemplar est eius quod in membris ideo fieri oportet. Praeterea, ipsa Christi satisfactio diversis modis est causa efficiens ut ipsi satisfacere velimus et actu satisfaciamus. Neque quidquam prohibet quominus etiam haec exemplaritas et efficientia Christo capiti attribuantur, modo non excludatur tertium quod *propriam* capitis rationem dicit, nempe, per ipsam Christi satisfactionem nos iam satisfecisse. Sicut enim vidente oculo videt corpus, et manducante ore manducat corpus, et ambulantibus pedibus ambulat corpus, ita etiam satisfaciente Christo satisfecit corpus, et merente Christo meret corpus, et sacrum faciente Christo sacrum facit corpus, et intercedente Christo intercedit corpus. Sicut enim oculus non sibi praecipue sed corpori videt, sicut os non sibi praecipue sed corpori manducat, sicut pedes non sibi praecipue sed corpori ambulant, ita etiam Christus non pro se sed pro nobis satisfecit, non

and truly affirmed to be dependent upon them. Now in Christ the exemplar there is no merely apparent causality, but only this real and true causality that is grasped by those who understand, and truly affirmed by those who are rational. And this is quite sufficient for our purpose.

### Article 41: Christ the head

In living things the various organs are so interdependent and mutually coherent that what is done in one is in some way done for the whole and all the other parts as well. Among all our organs it is only the eye that sees; yet it does not see only for its own sake but equally for the body as a whole and for each of the other members, which, although they themselves do not see, yet are by no means blind, since, in a way, they see through the eyes.

This interdependence ought not to be confused with efficient causality. If a blind man is led by the hand, that is efficient causality. But such external assistance given to a blind person is vastly different from a miraculous restoration of one's sight. Through external assistance the feet of a blind man are directed lest he fall into a ditch, while through the restoration of his sight his feet are freed from the need for such external help, since now they see, in a way, through the eyes to which they are naturally conjoined.

Now we, many as we are, are one body in Christ and members of one another (Romans 12.5, 1 Corinthians 12.12–31). The principal member, the head, of this body is Christ (Colossians 1.18). Therefore, what is done in Christ is now done in and for the whole body.

Hence you should carefully distinguish what is *proper* to the head alone from his exemplarity and efficient causality. To illustrate this, let us take Christ's satisfaction as an example. Because Christ has made satisfaction for sins, his satisfaction is the exemplar of what ought to be done in his members. Furthermore, Christ's satisfaction itself, in various ways, is an efficient cause of our willing to make satisfaction and of our act of making satisfaction. And there is nothing to prevent us from attributing this exemplarity and efficient causality to Christ the head as long as we do not exclude that third aspect that is *proper* to the head alone, namely, that through Christ's satisfaction we have already made satisfaction. Just as when the eye sees, the body sees, and when the mouth eats, the body eats, and when the feet walk, the body walks, so also in Christ's satisfaction the body has made satisfaction, and in Christ's meriting the body merits, and in Christ's sacrifice the body offers sacrifice, and in Christ's intercession the body makes intercession. And just as the eye does not see primarily for its own sake but for the

pro se praecipue sed pro nobis meruit, non pro se sed pro nobis sacrificium obtulit, non pro se sed pro nobis interpellat semper vivens sacerdos (cf. Heb 7.24–25)

Quod quidem per similitudinem ab ipsis scripturis propositam declaravimus. Et circa ipsum factum iam satis supra dictum est ubi de sacrificio novi testamenti (art. XVIII) egimus, de obedientia meritoria (art. XIX), de passione vicaria (art. XX), et de satisfactione Christi (cap. V). Quantum autem ad rei intelligentiam attinet, non nulla addenda videntur tum ad erroris exclusionem tum ad imperfectam quandam et analogicam mysterii apprehensionem.

Primo, ergo, nostra cum Christo unio non ita est exaggeranda ut substantialis evadat. Quare, Christus homo secundum communicationem idiomatum habet attributa divina, sed ex his attributis stricte divinis nullum nobis competit (cf. DB 2290). Similiter, nos peccare possumus et peccamus, sed Christus neque peccavit neque peccare potuit.

Deinde, opus Christi pro nobis non ita concipi debet ut omne opus nostrum excludatur. Quamvis ergo Christus pro nobis satisfecerit, tamen paenitentes pro se satisfacere debent (DB 904, 905, 922, 924). Quamvis Christus pro nobis meruerit, ipsi etiam meremus (DB 809, 843). Quamvis Christus pro nobis sacrificium semel obtulerit, tamen sacrificium missae vere propitiatorium est (DB 940, 950). Quamvis Christus semper vivat ad interpellandum pro nobis, ipsi tamen orare debemus.

Tertio, exclusa unione exaggerata, pariter excludenda est exaggerata distinctio quae vel Pelagianismum renovaret vel saltem redemptionem ut medium negaret. Sine Christo ergo nihil facere possumus (Io 15.5) et per gratiam Christi omnia facimus quae, sicut oportet, facimus (DB 176–181). Ipse enim 'perfectus factus est omnibus obtemperantibus sibi causa salutis aeternae' (Heb 5.9); 'neque est in alio aliquo salus; nec enim aliud nomen est sub caelo datum hominibus in quo oporteat nos salvos fieri' (Act 4.12; cf. DB 790). At quamvis requiratur, non tamen sufficit Pelagianismum excludere et Christum tamquam nostrae salutis causam agnoscere. Verum est Christum esse causam efficientem ut nos opera salutaria ponamus; sed causa efficiens esse potuit Christus homo si carne caelesti incarnatus esset et semper in caelis mansisset. Verum est Christum esse exemplar vitae

sake of the body, and the mouth eats not primarily for itself but for the body, and the feet walk not primarily for themselves but for the body, so also Christ made satisfaction not for himself but for us, merited not primarily for himself but for us, offered sacrifice not for himself but for us, and intercedes not for himself but for us as an ever living priest (see Hebrews 7.24–25).

We have illustrated this notion by way of a comparison taken from scripture. As to the fact itself, enough has been said above in dealing with the sacrifice of the new covenant (article 18), meritorious obedience (article 19), vicarious suffering (article 20), and Christ's satisfaction (chapter 5). As to understanding the matter, however, it would seem worthwhile to add a few points in order both to obviate error and to acquire a certain imperfect and analogical understanding of the mystery.

First, then, our union with Christ is not to be so greatly exaggerated as to turn it into a substantial union. Hence, although the human Christ, according to the *communicatio idiomatum*, possesses divine attributes, none of these strictly divine attributes belongs to us (see DB 2290, [DS 3814–15, ND 1996–97]). Likewise, we can and do sin, but Christ neither sinned nor could sin.

Next, Christ's work on our behalf should not be understood as entirely excluding work on our part. Therefore, although Christ made satisfaction for us, penitents ought to make satisfaction for themselves (DB 904, 905, 922, 924, [DS 1689–91, 1692, 1712, 1714, ND 1630–32, 1633, 1652, 1654]). Although Christ merited for us, we ourselves also merit (DB 809, 843, [DS 1545–47, 1583, ND 1946–47, 1983]). Although Christ offered sacrifice once for us, nevertheless the sacrifice of the Mass is truly propitiatory (DB 940, 950, [DS 1743, 1753, ND 1548, 1557]). Although Christ lives for ever to intercede for us, we also ought to pray.

Third, having ruled out an exaggerated union, we must similarly rule out an exaggerated distinction that would either revive Pelagianism or at least deny the redemption as means. Without Christ, then, we can do nothing (John 15.5) and through the grace of Christ we do all that we ought to do (DB 176–81, [DS 373–78, ND 1915–20]). For, 'having been made perfect, he became the source of eternal salvation for all who obey him' (Hebrews 5.9); and 'there is salvation in no one else, for there is no other name under heaven given among mortals by which we must be saved' (Acts 4.12; see DB 790, [DS 1513, ND 510]). But although necessary, it is not sufficient to exclude Pelagianism and recognize Christ as the cause of our salvation. It is true that Christ is the efficient cause of our performance of salutary works; but the human Christ could have been an efficient cause even had he

Christianae; et verum praeterea est eum non potuisse eodem modo esse exemplar ac est nisi his in terris degisset et passus mortuusque esset; sed verum non est totum Christi opus pro nobis ad rationem efficientis et exemplaris reduci, cum plus dicat redemptio ut medium, seu, uti quandoque nominatur, redemptio obiectiva. Nam operatio Christi capitis, quamvis ad membra extendi iisque applicari debeat, quamvis similem quandam operationem in membris exigat atque producat, tamen iam in se considerata quodammodo pro membris et membrorum est.

Quae cum ita sint, de ipsa quaestionis exsistentia actum est, scilicet, Christum non sibi sed pro nobis satisfecisse, non sibi praecipue sed pro nobis meruisse, non sibi sed pro nobis sacrificium obtulisse, non sibi sed pro nobis semper interpellare. Quae propria capitis ratio quemadmodum intelligi oporteat, iam aliqua determinavimus quae breviter hic repetenda esse videntur.

Quarto, ergo, haec propria capitis ratio non rationalistice est intelligenda. Non ergo amovenda est omnis Christi consideratio ut solo rationis lumine rationibus necessaribus rem demonstremus.

Quinto, secluso rationalismo, semirationalismus non est admittendus ut, supposito redemptionis mysterio divinitus revelato, iam ad demonstrationes procedatur. Divina enim mysteria suapte natura intellectum creatum excedunt, et ideo non est quaerenda nisi imperfecta quaedam atque analogica eorum intelligentia (DB 1796).

Sexto, neque sufficit generica quaedam rationalismi et semirationalismi exclusio sed etiam formae particulares eorundem errorum sunt reiciendae. Sicut enim superius vidimus, absolute fieri potuit ut Deus sapienter et iuste omnia peccata sine satisfactione Christi vicaria condonaret (art. XXVII). Quod tamen non de sola satisfactione sed pariter de merito, de sacrificio, et de intercessione Christi valet. Omnino enim generalis est S. Augustini et S. Thomae doctrina Deum nos aliter salvos facere potuisse quam per mortem Christi. Quos doctores cum reliquis theologis non sequeris si affirmas mortem Christi non propter satisfactionem sed propter meritum vel propter sacrificium absolute necessariam fuisse.

Septimo, perspecto errore rationalistico, non ideo in errorem ex extremo oppositum confugiendum est. Quamvis enim necessarium non fuerit Christum pro nobis mori, non ideo ex sola Dei voluntate res ita facta est.

been incarnated in celestial flesh and remained forever in heaven. It is true that Christ is the exemplar of Christian life, and it is true also that he could not have been an exemplar in the same way as he is had he not lived on this earth and suffered and died; but it is not true that Christ's entire work on our behalf is reduced to the category of efficient and exemplar causality, since redemption as a means, or, as it is sometime called, objective redemption, means more than that. For the operation of Christ as head, although it should be extended and applied to his members and although it requires and produces a similar operation in the members, still now, considered in itself, is in some sense for the members and of the members.

This being said, we have finished with the question of fact, namely, that Christ made satisfaction not for himself but for us, primarily merited not for himself but for us, offered sacrifice not for himself but for us, and intercedes not for himself but for us. As to how the proper meaning of the head is to be understood, we have already settled upon a few points that would seem to bear repetition briefly here.

Fourth, therefore, this meaning that is proper to the head is not to be understood in a rationalistic way. We must not, then, set aside every consideration of Christ in order to demonstrate the matter from necessary reasons by the light of reason alone.

Fifth, having ruled out rationalism, we ought also to reject the semi-rationalism that grants the divinely revealed mystery of redemption and then proceeds to demonstrations. The mysteries of God by their very nature exceed the created intellect, and so we may seek only an imperfect and analogical understanding of them (DB 1796, [DS 3016, ND 132]).

Sixth, a generic exclusion of rationalism and semi-rationalism is not enough, but even the particular forms of these errors should be rejected. As we saw above, God in his wisdom and justice could, absolutely speaking, have forgiven all sins without Christ's vicarious satisfaction (article 27). And this holds not only for satisfaction but equally for the merit, sacrifice, and intercession of Christ. The teaching of St Augustine and St Thomas that God could have saved us in some way other than through Christ's death is completely general. You are no follower of these Doctors of the Church and other theologians if you hold that his death, if not absolutely necessary for satisfaction, was still absolutely necessary for merit or for sacrifice.

Seventh, having grasped the error of rationalism, you must not fly to the opposite extreme. Although it was not necessary that Christ should die for us, it does not follow that that event happened because of God's will alone.

Voluntas enim Dei divinam sapientiam tamquam legem suae iustitiae sequitur,[18] et si Aquinatem audis eique consentis, blasphemum ducis opinari divinam voluntatem non procedere secundum ordinem sapientiae.[19] Quapropter, quamvis ex libera prorsus electione divina dependeat actualis ordinis exsistentia, ipsi tamen ordines inter quos eligit divina voluntas, per divinam sapientiam determinantur.

Octavo, ordo ergo divinae sapientiae in Christo capite, mortuo et resurrecto, perspici debet. Quam quidem intelligentiam, imperfectam, analogicam, fructuosissimam, ratio fide illustrata sedulo, pie, sobrie quaerit (DB 1796). Proinde, cum divina sapientia effectus necessarios ex causis necessariis fieri ordinet et effectus contingentes ex causis contingentibus, non solum ad nexus necessarios attendendum est sed etiam ad contingentes. Quare non parvus est error eorum qui solas rationes necessarias velint et convenientes respuant, cum ipsam divinam sapientiam parvi faciant et aliam sibi statuant, cum ipsam nostram redemptionem intelligere non studeant, sed eas tantummodo necessarias rationes quae in nostra redemptione illustrari possint.

Quae cum ita sint, non eos sequimur theologos qui toti occupantur ut ex hypothesi condignae satisfactionis vel alia qualibet hypothesi conclusiones necessarias deducant, sed methodum amplectimur S. Thomae qui concretum opus Christi consideravit et quotquot in eo inveniuntur rationes sive necessitatis sive convenientiae quantum potuit enumeravit. Quam methodum facile perspicis tum in longiore articulorum serie[20] tum in uno solo articulo eoque eximio.[21]

Quibus praemissis ad errores sive doctrinales sive methodologicos excludendos, iam ad propriam capitis rationem intelligendam, quantum fieri potest, procedi oportet.

Et primum quoddam intelligentiae elementum ex similitudine habetur quam proponit ipsa scriptura. Sicut enim corporis membra non sibi solis sed toti corpori operantur, ita et Christus non sibi sed pro nobis satisfecit, non sibi praecipue sed pro nobis meruit, non sibi sed pro nobis sacrificium obtulit, non sibi sed pro nobis semper ad interpellandum vivit.

God's will follows the divine wisdom as the norm of his justice,[18] and if you listen to and agree with Aquinas, you will consider as blasphemous the opinion that God's will does not proceed according to the order of his wisdom.[19] Therefore, although the existence of the actual order depends upon God's utterly free choice, the orders themselves among which the divine will chooses are determined by divine wisdom.

Eighth, therefore, we ought to grasp the order of divine wisdom in Christ the head, who died and rose. This understanding, imperfect and analogical yet most fruitful, reason illumined by faith seeks diligently, piously, and soberly (DB 1796, [DS 3016, ND 132]). Accordingly, since divine wisdom ordains that necessary effects result from necessary causes and contingent effects from contingent causes, we must attend not only to necessary connections but also to contingent ones. Thus it is no small error on the part of those who want to have only necessary reasons and scorn reasons of fittingness, since they pay little heed to divine wisdom itself and set up another wisdom for themselves, since they are not interested in understanding our redemption itself, but only those necessary reasons that can be exemplified in our redemption.

This being the case, we do not follow those theologians who are entirely preoccupied with deducing necessary conclusions from a hypothesis of condign satisfaction or any other hypothesis; rather we subscribe to the method of St Thomas, who considered the concrete work of Christ and put down as many reasons for it as he could, whether reasons of necessity or of fittingness. This method can be easily seen both in a lengthy series of articles[20] and in a single outstanding article.[21]

Having ruled out in these preliminary remarks errors both doctrinal and methodological, we must proceed now to understand, as far as we can, that intelligibility that is proper to the head.

The first element in this intelligibility is derived from the comparison found in scripture. Just as the members of a body work not for themselves alone but for the body as a whole, so also Christ made satisfaction not for himself but for us, merited not primarily for himself but for us, offered sacrifice not for himself but for us, and lives for ever to intercede not for himself but for us.

18 Thomas Aquinas, *Summa theologiae*, 1, q. 21, a. 1, ad 2m.
19 Thomas Aquinas, *De veritate*, q. 23, a. 6 c.
20 Thomas Aquinas, *Summa theologiae*, 3, qq. 46–56.
21 Ibid. q. 1, a. 2.

Alterum deinde habetur intelligentiae elementum ex eo quod unio est effectus amoris. Amicus enim est alter ipse, et 'dimidium animae suae.'[22] Quod si ex amicis fit unum, iam ipsi quodammodo possumus quod per amicos possumus. Quam rationem tetigit Apostolus dicens: 'Viri debent diligere uxores suas ut corpora sua. Qui suam uxorem diligit, se ipsum diligit' (Eph 5.28). Sed paulo ante dixerat: 'Viri, diligite uxores vestras sicut et Christus ecclesiam' (Eph 5.25); sicut et postea comparavit unionem matrimonialem cum unione Christi et ecclesiae (Eph 5.31–32). Et similiter S. Thomas satisfactionem Christi pro nobis explicavit non solum quia Christus est caput membrorum sed etiam quia duo homines unum in caritate esse possunt.[23]

Tertium etiam intelligentiae elementum habetur ex ipsa natura humana. Quia enim homines sunt agentia per intellectum, ad omnia quodammodo proportionantur quae intelligunt et volunt; quia autem anima intellectiva corpori coniungitur, in alia agere non valet nisi mediante corpore. Quare homines secundum proportionem potentiae intellectualis maxima opera intendere possunt et solent, sed secundum limitationem corporalem singuli per alios consentientes et in commune bonum agentes effectum proprium attingunt. Quod quidem perspicimus non solum in coquis, sartoribus, opificibus, legislatoribus deputatis, iudicibus, scientiarum peritis, sed etiam in sacerdotibus sacrificia pro populo offerentibus. Quam ob causam, omnino conveniens fuit humanae naturae ut, sicut in caetera bona, ita etiam in salutem per alium pervenirent.

Quartum praeterea intelligentiae elementum ex ipsis hominum peccatis habetur. Quamvis enim singuli individualiter peccant, peccatis tamen corrumpitur non solum individualis homo sed etiam ipsa socialis et historica hominum situatio, ut impotentia quadam morali teneatur non solum individualis peccator sed etiam ipsa peccatorum societas, uti superius articulis v ad VIII declaratum est. Quod si propter peccata aliorum ipsi in peccatum quodammodo ferimur, conveniens fuit ut per opus bonum alterius in salutem restauremur. Quam ob causam dicitur, 'Eratis enim sicut oves errantes' (1 Pet 2.25), et 'Percutiam pastorem et dispergentur oves gregis' (Mt 26.31), et 'Ego sum bonus pastor: bonus pastor animam suam dat pro ovibus suis' (Io 10.11), et 'Iesus erat moriturus … ut filios Dei qui erant dispersi congregaret in unum' (Io 11.51–52), et 'Quos dedisti mihi, custodivi; et nemo ex eis periit nisi filius perditionis' (Io 17.12).

The second element in this intelligibility is drawn from the fact that the effect of love is union. A friend is a second self and half of one's soul.[22] Now if friends are somehow one, then, in a sense, we can do whatever we are able to do through our friends. St Paul touched upon this point in Ephesians 5.28: 'Husbands should love their wives as they do their own bodies. He who loves his wife loves himself.' A little earlier (v. 25) he had said, 'Husbands, love your wives, just as Christ loved the Church,' and later (vv. 31–32) he compared marital union to the union between Christ and the church. In a similar way, St Thomas explained Christ's satisfaction on our behalf not only on the grounds that Christ is the head of his members but also that two persons can be one through love.[23]

The third element in this intelligibility is taken from human nature itself. Since human beings are agents operating through intellect, they are in some way proportionate to all they understand and will. But since our intellective soul is united with a body, it cannot act upon other things except through the medium of the body. In proportion to our intellectual powers, therefore, we are able to intend, and usually do intend, to do great things, but on account of physical limitations, individuals achieve their own objectives in concert with others and in working for the common good. We grasp this not only in the case of cooks, tailors, workmen, elected legislators, judges, and scientists, but also in the case of priests offering sacrifice on behalf of the people. Thus it was entirely in keeping with human nature that, as we realized other goods through another, so should we arrive at salvation.

The fourth element in this intelligibility is found in the sins of human beings. Although sins are committed by people individually, nevertheless they corrupt not only the individual person but also the social and historical human situation, so that not only is the individual sinner but also the community of sinners itself held back by a certain moral impotence, as we have shown above in articles 5 to 8. Now if we are, in a sense, drawn into sin because of the sins of others, it was fitting that we be restored to spiritual health through the good work of another. Hence we read, 'You were going astray like sheep' (1 Peter 2.25), and 'I will strike the shepherd, and the sheep of the flock will be scattered' (Matthew 26.31), and 'I am the good shepherd. The good shepherd lays down his life for the sheep' (John 10.11), and 'Jesus was about to die ... to gather into one the dispersed children of God' (John 11.51–52), and 'I protected ... those whom you have given me ... and not one of them was lost except the son of perdition' (John 17.12).

22 Ibid. 1-2, q. 28, a. 1; q. 109, a. 4, ad 2m.
23 Ibid. 3, q. 48, a. 2, ad 1m.

Quintum proinde intelligentiae elementum ex peccato originali habetur. Quod expresse docuit Apostolus (Rom 5.12–21, 1 Cor 15.21–22).

Sextum denique intelligentiae elementum ex ipsa persona reconciliatoris atque redemptoris habetur. Sicut enim ita per alios agimus ut non vestes a coquis et a sartoribus prandia petamus, sed in singulis rebus suae artis peritissimum quemque adimus, ita etiam in sacris fieri convenit. At nemo alius inter homines convenientius nos ad Deum reducere posset quam divina persona homo factus; nemo alius inter homines et divinam bonitatem et peccati detestabilitatem plenius cognoscere posset quam homo visione Dei immediata fruens; nemo alius inter homines Deum Patrem caeterosque homines propter Patrem tantum diligere posset quantum Filius proprius homo factus; nemo alius inter homines vel tam perfectam obedientiam, vel tantum de peccatis dolorem, vel tantam in sacro faciendo reverentiam praestare posset quam Christus homo. Per Christum ergo Dominum nostrum Filium Patris proprium conveniebat ut propter nos acquiratur obedientiae meritum, pro nobis peragatur de peccatis satisfactio, pro nobis offeratur sacrificium propitiatorium.

Quod si haec per modum unius perspiciuntur, ex analogia rerum humanarum, intelligentia quaedam imperfecta habetur huius magni mysterii quo Dei Filius homo factus modo humano partes capitis, amici, vicarii, sacerdotis, pastoris pro nobis egit.

## Articulus XLII: De Christo agente historico

Christus homo, ut caput, pro membris suis meruit, satisfecit, sacrificium obtulit, intercedit. Sed praeterea fecit facitque Christus ut de filiis irae fiant membra sua quibus applicantur meritum suum, et satisfactionis liberatio, et sacrificii fructus, et intercessionis beneficium.

Iterum, Christus homo, ut exemplar, ea in se ipso perfecit quae ideo in membris pariter perficienda sunt. Sed praeterea fecit facitque Christus ut actu in membris fiant quae propter exemplar in membris fieri debeant.

Remanet ergo, cum et exemplar et propriam capitis rationem consideraverimus, ut ulterius ad illam Christi actionem seu efficientiam attendamus qua fiant atque perficiantur membra corporis atque plenitudinis suae. Quae quidem actio duplex est. Nam alia est quae nunc de caelis ab eo

The fifth element in our understanding comes from original sin, according to the express teaching of St Paul (Romans 5.12–21, 1 Corinthians 15.21–22).

The sixth and final element is derived from the very person of the reconciler and redeemer. Just as in dealing with others we do not ask cooks to make a suit of clothes or tailors to prepare a meal, but go to those who are most skilled in their particular art or trade, so too it is fitting in matters sacred. But among human beings, none could be better suited to bring us back to God than a divine person made human; none could know both the goodness of God and the hatefulness of sin better than one who enjoys the immediate vision of God; no other person could love God the Father and all other human beings for the Father's sake as much as God's own Son become human; no other among human beings could have so perfect an obedience, so great a sorrow for sins, so deep a reverence in offering sacrifice as the human Christ. Therefore it was fitting that Christ our Lord, the Father's own Son, was the one to acquire the merit of obedience for us, to make satisfaction for sins on our behalf, and to offer for us the sacrifice of atonement.

In grasping all this in one synthetic act of understanding through an analogy with human affairs, we have some imperfect understanding of this great mystery in which the incarnate Son of God, acting in a human way and on our behalf, has performed the role of head, friend, vicar, priest, and shepherd for our sake.

### Article 42: Christ the historical agent

The human Christ, as head, merited, made satisfaction, offered sacrifice, and intercedes on behalf of his members. But in addition, Christ made and makes the children of wrath become his members, to whom are applied his merit, the liberation of his satisfaction, the fruit of his sacrifice, and the benefit of his intercession.

Again, the human Christ, as exemplar, has accomplished in himself what ought, for that reason, to be equally accomplished in his members. But in addition, Christ made and makes actually happen in the members what, because of the exemplar, ought to happen in them.

Having considered both the role of Christ as exemplar and the intelligibility proper to him as head, it remains for us to attend to the action or efficient causality of Christ, whereby we become and are perfected as members of his body and of his fullness. This action is twofold. One is that which

exercetur qui ad dexteram Patris sedet semper vivens ad interpellandum pro nobis, uti in sequenti articulo dicetur. Et alia est quae ante viginti saecula olim in Palaestina peracta est, sed modo historico omnibus diebus usque ad consummationem [saeculi] iugiter et influxit et influet.

Qualis autem sit actio Christi historica, ex duobus maxime elucet, nempe, et ex *effectu* qui producitur et ex *modo* quo producitur. Quae quidem duo, quamvis simul dici non possint, ita intime inter se connectuntur ut per modum unius apprehendi atque iudicari debeant. Quam tamen activitatem syntheticam ipsi lectoris intelligentiae necessario relinquimus.

Circa effectum tria distingui oportet, nempe, (1) effectum totius actionis historicae, (2) effectum directe intentum a Christo agente historico, et (3) effectum indirecte ab eodem intentum.

Totius actionis historicae effectus est totum ordinis bonum humanum tum exterius tum culturale, et praeteritum et praesens et futurum. Quod ordinis bonum complectitur (1) bonorum particularium omnis generis profluvium quoddam fere continuum, (2) operationes humanas quibus haec particularia bona oriuntur, (3) interiores habitus et quasi exteriora hominum instituta, mores, consuetudines unde et fiunt et coordinantur operationes, et (4) ipsos denique homines relationibus interpersonalibus coniunctos, qui secundum habitus et instituta operantur et bonis ita ortis fruuntur.

Qui totus effectus, tamquam pars ordinis universi, a Deo ut primo agente producitur secundum ordinem suae sapientiae atque iustitiae. Sed uti supra habitum est, alius quodammodo est ordo divinae iustitiae historicus et alius est ordo divinae iustitiae personalis (cf. art. XI et XII). Hac enim in vita, quamvis personae simus, sub conditionibus tamen materialibus, socialibus, historicis ita versamur ut quod singulis contingat non ex solo merito vel demerito personali determinetur. Sed alia etiam et futura est vita in qua secundum iustum Christi hominis iudicium singulis reddetur pro propriis suis operibus (2 Cor 5.10, Mt 25.31–46). Quae futura vita, quamvis extra campum historicum iaceat, qualis tamen singulis futura sit, intra campum historicum determinatur.

Quae cum ita sint, distingui oportet totum effectum historicum (1) secundum se et (2) secundum ordinem ad vitam futuram atque caelestem. Iam vero ordinatur homo ad hanc futuram vitam, primo quidem secundum divinam intentionem, deinde autem secundum huius intentionis effectum in se receptum, sanctificantem nempe gratiam et infusas virtutes et Spiritus sancti tum dona tum motiones. Quae actualis atque proxima ordinatio, nisi

he now exercises in heaven, seated at the right hand of the Father and living forever to intercede for us, as will be discussed in the next article. The other is the action finished twenty centuries ago in Palestine, but which has never ceased to have its historical influence in every age, and will continue to do so always, to the end of time.

The nature of this historical action of Christ is manifest especially in two ways, namely, from the *effect* it has and from the *way* in which it has this effect. These two, although they cannot be said at once, are so closely connected that they can be apprehended and judged as one. This work of synthesis, however, we necessarily leave to the intelligence of the reader.

Concerning the effect of Christ's action, three things should be distinguished: (1) the effect of his total historical action, (2) the effect directly intended by Christ as a historical agent, and (3) the effect indirectly intended by him.

The effect of his total historical action is the total human good of order both external and cultural, past, present, and future. This good of order comprises (1) a virtually continuous flow of particular goods of every kind, (2) human operations by which these goods are produced, (3) interior habits and external human institutions, behaviors, and customs whereby these operations are performed and coordinated, and (4) human beings themselves linked through their interpersonal relationships, who operate in accordance with these habits and institutions and enjoy the resulting goods.

This total effect, as part of the order of the universe, is produced by God as first agent in accordance with the order of his wisdom and justice. But as mentioned above, the historical order of divine justice is somewhat different from the personal order of divine justice (see articles 11 and 12). For in this life, though we are persons, we are so caught up under material, social, and historical conditions that what happens to each one of us is not determined solely by our own merit or demerit. But there is another, a future life, in which each one of us is recompensed for our own works in accordance with the just judgment of the human Christ (2 Corinthians 5.10, Matthew 25.31–46). This future life lies outside the field of history; but what it will be like for each person is determined within the field of history.

Accordingly, we must distinguish this total effect in history (1) as it is in itself, and (2) according to its ordination to the future life in heaven. We are destined to this future life, first, according to God's intention, and secondly, according to the effect of this intention as received in us, that is, sanctifying grace, the infused virtues, and the gifts and movements of the Holy Spirit. Unless we receive this actual and proximate ordination, we are

recipitur, disordinatus est homo neque solum relate ad vitam futuram sed etiam ad praesentem vitam. Uti enim supra habitum est (art. v ad viii), nisi homo per Dei gratiam in Deum ordinatur, ita in bonum ordinis huius vitae tendit atque operatur ut tamen citius tardius interiori sua disordinatione in mala innumera declinet malisque vincatur. Quapropter, totus effectus historicus secundum se eatenus est bonus quatenus in vitam futuram atque caelestem ordinatur; et ideo qui directe intendit hanc rectam ordinationem efficere, eo ipso indirecte intendit totius effectus historici profectum, secundum illud: 'Quaerite primum regnum Dei et iustitiam eius et haec omnia adicientur vobis' (Mt 6.33).

Quibus perspectis, facile discernitur quinam sit effectus historicus directe a Christo intentus et quinam sit effectus indirecte intentus. Directe enim actio Christi eo tendit ut vita humana et terrestris in vitam futuram atque caelestem ordinetur. Cum tamen ipsa haec ordinatio ita hominem e malis liberet eumque in verum bonum convertat ut ipsum humanum ordinis bonum secundum se maxime proficiat, ipse hic profectus indirecte a Christo agente historico intendatur necesse est.

Sequitur Christum esse agens historicum ratione effectus ab eo intenti. Historicum enim est agens quod bonum ordinis vel exterius vel culturale causat (art. xxxviii). Sed bonum culturale imprimis respicit naturale desiderium videndi Deum per essentiam, naturale desiderium rectitudinis moralis, naturale desiderium beatitudinis et immortalitatis (art. ii); quae quidem omnia eatenus attinguntur quatenus producitur effectus directe a Christo intentus. Praeterea, cum caetera bona humana a recta ordinatione interiori dependeant, cumque ipsa haec recta ordinatio sine directo Christi agentis effectu non habeatur, constat omnia bona humana vel directe vel indirecte a Christo agente dependere.

Praeterea, Christus est agens maxime historicum. Nam plus vel minus historicum est agens prout effectus eius diutius vel brevius permanet. Sed effectus a Christo intentus manet usque in consummationem saeculi.

Praeterea, Christus est agens historicum et totale, non quia totum bonum humanum et historicum directe intendat vel directe in id influat, sed quia ita in principale directe influit ut reliquum bonum, impedimentis remotis, ideo florescat.

Praeterea, Christus est agens historicum per se, nam per visionem Dei immediatam in obiecto secundario omnia actualia cognovit, et ideo totus effectus historicus ab eo productus non praeter sed secundum intentionem eius oritur.

disordered, and not in relation to the future life only, but also in relation to this present life. As we said above (articles 5 to 8), those who are not ordered towards God by God's grace tend towards and work for the good of order in this life, but in such a way that on account of their interior disorder they gradually, or not so gradually, get involved in a host of evils and are overwhelmed by them. This total historical effect, considered in itself, is good to the extent that it is ordered to the future life in heaven; and therefore one who directly intends to effect this right ordering by that very fact indirectly intends the advancement of the total historical effect, in accordance with the words of Scripture, 'Seek first the kingdom of God and his righteousness and all these things will come to you as well' (Matthew 6.33).

From all this one can easily see what is the historical effect directly intended by Christ and what is the effect indirectly intended by him. Christ's action is directly aimed at ordering human life on earth to the future life in heaven. Since, however, this ordering liberates us from evils and turns us towards true good with the result that the human good of order in itself is greatly improved, this improvement itself is necessarily intended indirectly by Christ as historical agent.

It follows that Christ is a historical agent by reason of the effect intended by him. A historical agent is one who has an effect upon the external or the cultural good of order (article 38). But cultural good above all has to do with the natural desire to see God in his essence, the natural desire for moral rectitude, and the natural desire for beatitude and immortality (article 2); and all these are attained to the extent that the effect directly intended by Christ is actually realized. Besides, since all other human goods depend upon this right interior ordering, and since this right ordering is had only through the direct effect of Christ's work, it is clear that all human goods directly or indirectly depend upon Christ as agent.

Besides, Christ is the most historical of agents. For an agent is more or less historical depending upon the duration of his effect; but the effect intended by Christ perdures to the end of the world.

Again, Christ is a total historical agent, not because he directly intends the totality of human good in history or directly influences it, but because he has a direct influence on the principal good, so that, when obstacles are removed, all other goods flourish.

Also, Christ is a historical agent per se, for through his immediate vision of God he knows all actual reality as the secondary object of that vision, and thus the total effect in history produced by him comes about not apart from but according to his intention.

Praeterea, Christus est agens historicum restaurativum. Nam effectus directe ab eo intentus est restauratio illius imaginis Dei in homine secundum quam homo creatus est in iustitia et sanctitate veritatis (Eph 4.24). Qua imagine restaurata, liberatur homo a potestate tenebrarum (Col 1.13) ut caetera bona augeantur atque proficiant.

Sed ulterius considerandum est Christum fuisse agens historicum non solum ratione effectus intenti, quem de caelis producere potuisset, sed etiam ratione modi agendi.[24]

Nam omnis actio socialis vel historica quoddam ordinis bonum iam stabilitum praesupponit. Quod in actione Christi perspicitur, quae diuturnam populi Iudaici praeparationem praesupponit, exspectatione messianica utitur, directe in Iudaeos exercetur, et per haereditatem Iudaeorum culturalem libris sacris contentam declaratur tum ab ipso Christo tum a primaevis Christianis. Quapropter, 'lex paedagogus noster fuit in Christo' (Gal 3.24). Praeterea, ea temporis plenitudine (Gal 4.4, Mc 1.15, Eph 1.10) advenit Christus, cum gentes non solum ad culturam superiorem pervenissent sed etiam humanam impotentiam didicisse possent (Rom 1.18–32); et ideo quamvis inventio culturae superioris eo sensu axis quaedam historica dici possit[25] quia ideam boni modo conscio atque reflexo evolvat, manet tamen adventus Christi centrum historiae humanae axisque praecipua, cum per Christum Dominum nostrum eumque solum ita bonum velimus ut etiam faciamus.[26]

Praeterea, omnis actio socialis et historica per alios quodammodo intelligentes atque consentientes est. Quod in actione Christi perspicuum est cuius regnum propagatur per evangelium, per fidem, per paenitentiam; quod evangelium non praedicatur nisi missione, successione, traditione apostolica; quae fides non habetur nisi ex auditu; quae paenitentia per baptismum Christi in remissionem peccatorum et donum Spiritus sancti fructificat.

Praeterea, Christus non quolibet modo per alios intelligentes atque consentientes agit sed tamquam per membra sua. Sicut enim Christus tamquam caput pro nobis meruit, satisfecit, sacrificium obtulit, ita etiam nos tamquam propria Christi membra opus Christi historicum portamus. Nostra enim

Still further, Christ is a restorative historical agent. The effect directly intended by him is the restoration of the image of God in us according to which we were created in true righteousness and holiness (Ephesians 4.24). With this image restored, we are set free from the power of darkness (Colossians 1.13), so that all other good things may increase and prosper.

But we must go on now to consider that Christ was a historical agent not only by reason of his intended effect, which he could have produced from heaven, but also by reason of his way of operating.[24]

All social or historical action presupposes a certain good of order already established. This is clearly evident in the case of Christ's action, which presupposes the lengthy preparation of the Jewish people, uses their expectation of a messiah, is directed towards the Jews, and is explained by both Christ himself and the early Christians in terms of the Jewish cultural heritage contained in the scriptures. Therefore, 'the law was our disciplinarian until Christ came' (Galatians 3.24). Besides, Christ came in the fullness of time (Galatians 4.4, Mark 1.15, Ephesians 1.10), when the Gentiles had not only attained a high level of culture but also were able to have learned about human impotence (Romans 1.18–32). Therefore, although the emergence of a superior culture could be described as an axial period in history[25] in the sense that there developed an idea of the good in a conscious and reflective way, nevertheless the coming of Christ remains the central event of human history and its principal axis, since it is through Christ our Lord and him alone that we not only will what is good but also do it.[26]

Moreover, all social and historical action is carried out through others who in some way understand and agree. This is clear with regard to the work of Christ, whose kingdom is propagated through the gospel, through faith, and through repentance. But the gospel is preached through the apostolic mission, succession, and tradition; faith comes through hearing; and repentance bears fruit through the baptism of Christ for the remission of sins and the gift of the Holy Spirit.

Again, Christ works through others who understand and agree, not in just any way, but as through his members. Just as Christ as head merited, made satisfaction, and offered sacrifice for us, so also we, as Christ's own members, carry on the historical work of Christ. For our bodies are not our

24 [This is the transition anticipated above, from the effect Christ has to the way he has this effect. See p. 611.]

25 [A reference to Karl Jaspers; see above, p. 321 and note 27.]

26 Thomas Aquinas, *Summa theologiae*, 1-2, q. 111, a. 2.

corpora non nostra sed Christi sunt (1 Cor 6.15–17); et ipsi pretio empti Christi sumus servi (1 Cor 7.22–23); neque nobis vivimus sed ei qui pro nobis mortuus est et resurrexit (2 Cor 5.15, Gal 2.20); sive ergo vivimus sive morimur, Domini sumus (Rom 14.8); quare 'mihi vivere Christus est et mori lucrum' (Phil 1.21); 'qui nunc gaudeo in passionibus pro vobis et adimpleo ea quae desunt passionum Christi in carne mea pro corpore eius, quod est ecclesia, cuius factus sum ego minister secundum dispensationem Dei, quae data est mihi in vos, ut impleam verbum Dei: mysterium quod absconditum fuit a saeculis et generationibus, nunc autem manifestatum est sanctis eius, quibus voluit Deus notas facere divitias gloriae sacramenti huius in gentibus, quod est Christus in vobis, spes gloriae, quem nos annuntiamus, corripientes omnem hominem et docentes omnem hominem in omni sapientia, ut exhibeamus omnem hominem perfectum in Christo Iesu, in quo et laboro, certando secundum operationem eius, quam operatur in me in virtute' (Col 1.24–29).

Praeterea, Christus socialiter et historice agit per membra sua, non qua individua seorsum sumpta, sed qua socialiter, historice, et spiritualiter unum corpus sunt. Multi enim unum corpus sumus in Christo, et singuli alter alterius membra (Rom 12.5). Divisiones gratiarum, ministrationum, operationum sunt, sed non ideo est schisma in corpore; nam patiente uno membro, compatiuntur omnia, et gloriante uno, gloriantur omnia (1 Cor 12). 'Eratis illo in tempore sine Christo, alienati a conversatione Israel et hospites testamentorum promissionis, spem non habentes et sine Deo in hoc mundo. Nunc autem in Christo Iesu vos, qui aliquando eratis longe, facti estis prope in sanguine Christi. Ipse enim est pax nostra, qui fecit utraque unum et medium parietem maceriae solvens inimicitias, in carne sua legem mandatorum decretis evacuans, ut duos condat in semet ipso in unum novum hominem faciens pacem et reconciliet ambos in uno corpore Deo per crucem interficiens inimicitias in semet ipso. Et veniens evangelizavit pacem vobis qui longe fuistis et pacem eis qui prope; quoniam per ipsum habemus accessum ambo in uno Spiritu ad Patrem. Ergo iam non estis hospites et advenae, sed estis cives sanctorum et domestici Dei, superaedificati super fundamentum apostolorum et prophetarum, ipso summo angulari lapide Christo Iesu; in quo omnis aedificatio constructa crescit in templum sanctum in Domino, in quo et vos coaedificamini in habitaculum Dei in Spiritu' (Eph 2.12–22).

own but Christ's (1 Corinthians 6.15–17); we are Christ's slaves bought at a price (1 Corinthians 7.22–23); we live not for ourselves but for him who died and rose for us (2 Corinthians 5.15, Galatians 2.20); whether, therefore, we live or die, we are the Lord's (Romans 14.8); hence, 'for to me, living is Christ and dying is gain' (Philippians 1.21); and, 'I am now rejoicing in my sufferings for your sake, and in my flesh I am completing what is lacking in Christ's afflictions for the sake of his body, that is, the church. I became its servant according to God's commission that was given to me for you, to make the word of God fully known, the mystery that has been hidden throughout the ages and generations but has now been revealed to his saints. To them God chose to make known how great among the Gentiles are the riches of the glory of this mystery, which is Christ in you, the hope of glory. It is he whom we proclaim, warning everyone and teaching everyone in all wisdom, so that we may present everyone mature in Christ. For this I toil and struggle with all the energy that he powerfully inspires within me' (Colossians 1.24–29).

Furthermore, Christ works socially and historically through his members, not as isolated individuals but as one body socially, historically, and spiritually. For we, though many, are one body in Christ and members of one another (Romans 12.5). There are varieties of gifts, of services, and of activities, but there is not on that account any division within the body; for, if one member suffers, all suffer together with it; if one member is honored, all rejoice together with it (1 Corinthians 12). 'You were at that time without Christ, being aliens from the commonwealth of Israel, and strangers to the covenants of promise, having no hope and without God in the world. But now in Christ Jesus you who once were far off have been brought near by the blood of Christ. For he is our peace; in his flesh, he has made both groups into one and has broken down the dividing wall, that is, the hostility between us. He has abolished the law with its commandments and ordinances, that he might create in himself one new humanity in place of the two, thus making peace, and might reconcile both groups to God in one body through the cross, thus putting to death that hostility in himself. So he came and proclaimed peace to you who were far off and peace to those who were near; for through him both of us have access in one Spirit to the Father. So then you are no longer strangers and aliens, but citizens with the saints and also members of the household of God, built upon the foundation of the apostles and prophets, with Christ Jesus himself as the cornerstone. In him the whole structure grows into a holy temple in the Lord; in whom you also are built together spiritually into a dwelling place for God' (Ephesians 2.12–22).

Praeterea, actio Christi, quamvis socialiter et historice medietur, et personalis est et humanis personis accommodatur. Verbum enim caro factum est ut personis humanis fiat signum divinae personae expressivum (cf. art. III). Cum enim humana cognitio a sensu incipiat, Dei Verbum factum est sensibile. Cum sensibile in notitiam intelligibilis et spiritualis veritatis conducat, tota Christi vita terrestris, omnis eius actio, omnia eius verba eo conspirant ut quod in carne manifestatum est in spiritu suscipiatur. Cum denique alia signa mere denotativa sint et alia expressiva, maxime sane expressivum est signum seu mysterium Christi, qui dilexit me et tradidit semet ipsum pro me (Gal 2.20). Quare a S. Thoma dicitur Christus egisse per modum provocantis ad amorem.[27] Et S. Augustinus: 'Quae autem maior est causa adventus Domini, nisi ut ostenderet Deus dilectionem suam in nobis, commendans eam vehementer? ... Nulla est enim maior ad amorem invitatio quam praevenire amando; et nimis durus est animus qui dilectionem, si nolebat impendere, nolit rependere ... Si ergo maxime propterea Christus advenit, ut cognosceret homo quantum cum diligat Deus; et ideo cognosceret ut in eius dilectionem a quo prior dilectus est inardesceret ... manifestum est ... totam Legem et Prophetas in illis duobus pendere praeceptis dilectionis Dei et proximi ...'[28] Unde et ipse Dominus docuit: 'Ego si exaltatus fuero, omnia traham ad me ipsum' (Io 12.32).

Praeterea, eo usque se extendit actio Christi historica ut mediante suo corpore, quod est ecclesia, non solum mentes hominum instruat et corda ad Cor suum trahat sed etiam ipsam interioris hominis renovationem efficiat atque augeat. Septem enim sunt novae legis sacramenta, quae ex opere operato gratiam conferunt (DB 844, 851); et sicut ipsa sacramenta Christi institutione ortum ducunt, sicut a ministrantibus Christi membris conferuntur, ita virtutem ad gratiam conferendam habent ex illa Christi potentia cuius imperium ad proprium suum atque physicum corpus movendum non limitatur.

Denique tandem, ut caetera omittamus quae actionem Christi historicam declarare et illustrare possint, recoli oportet distinctionem iam ante positam (art. XXXIX) inter ea quae facit Christus virtute sua humana et ea quae facit prout instrumentum est divinitatis. Nam virtus humana Christi per actionem socialem atque historicam effectum directe vel indirecte intentum producit contingentem contingenter; sed eadem virtus humana, prout

In addition, Christ's action, although mediated socially and historically, is personal and is adapted to human persons. For the Word became flesh in order to be for human persons an expressive sign of a divine person (see article 3). Since human knowledge begins from the senses, the Word of God became sensible. Since sense knowledge leads to knowledge of intelligible and spiritual truth, the whole of Christ's life on earth, every action of his, every word, all work together so that what is made known in the flesh may be received in the spirit. Finally, since some signs are merely denotative and others are expressive, surely the sign or mystery of Christ, who loved me and gave himself up for me (Galatians 2.20), is the most expressive of all. For this reason St Thomas said that Christ acted to challenge us to love.[27] And as St Augustine put it, 'What greater reason was there for the coming of the Lord than that God make manifest his love for us, commending it most strongly? ... For there is no more pressing invitation to love than to show love first; and that heart is hard indeed which, if reluctant to love, still refuses to requite love ... It was for this reason above all that Christ came, that we might know how much God loves us, and that we might know this so as to become inflamed with love for him who loved us first ... it is clear ... that the whole of the law and the prophets depends upon the two commandments of love of God and of the neighbor.'[28] Hence the Lord himself said, 'And I, when I am lifted up from the earth, will draw all to myself' (John 12.32).

Again, Christ's historical action, mediated through his body the church, extends not only to instructing our minds and drawing our hearts to his Heart, but also to bringing about and deepening the renewal of our interior life. There are seven sacraments of the new law, conferring grace *ex opere operato* (DB 844, 851, [DS 1601, 1608; ND 1311, 1318]); and just as these sacraments trace their origin to Christ and are conferred by ministers who are members of Christ, so they have the power to confer grace from that power of Christ whose command is not limited to moving his own physical body.

Finally – leaving aside other points that could elucidate and illustrate Christ's historical work – we ought to recall here the distinction we made in article 39 between what Christ does by his human power and what he does as an instrument of divinity. Christ's human power exercised by him as a historical social agent produces a directly or indirectly intended effect that is contingent, and does so contingently; but this same human power, exercised

27 Thomas Aquinas, *Summa theologiae*, 3, q. 49, a. 1 c.
28 Augustine, *De catechizandis rudibus*, IV, nos. 7–8; ML 40, 314–15.

est divinitatis instrumentum, illud efficit quod fieri Deus infallibiliter scit, efficaciter vult, irresistibiliter facit. Praeterea, sicut Christus visione Dei immediata actualia omnia noverat et totum suum effectum intendebat, ita etiam noverat et obediens volebat se esse instrumentum illius divinae intentionis quae infallibiliter, efficaciter, irresistibiliter operatur.

**Articulus XLIII: De mediatore caelesti**

Unus enim Deus, unus et mediator Dei et hominum, homo Christus Iesus, qui dedit semet ipsum redemptionem pro multis (1 Tim 2.5–6). Qui melioris testamenti sponsor (Heb 7.22) et melioris novique [testamenti] mediator (Heb 8.6, 9.15, 12.24), non solum his in terris pro nobis mortuus est sed etiam resurrectus semper vivit ad interpellandum pro nobis (Heb 7.25, Rom 8.34, 1 Io 2.1).

Sempiternum enim habens sacerdotium (Heb 7.24), consedit in dextera sedis magnitudinis in caelis, sanctorum minister et tabernaculi veri quod fixit Deus et non homo (Heb 8.1–2); qui ita unam pro peccatis obtulit hostiam et una oblatione consummavit in aeternum sanctificatos (Heb 10.12, 10.14), ut in ipsum caelum introierit, ubi apparet nunc vultui Dei pro nobis (Heb 9.24) agnus tamquam occisus (Apoc 5.6–12, 13.8).

Quae caelestis mediatio, intercessio, aeternaque peracti sacrificii exhibitio non umbram sed imaginem (cf. Heb 10.1) in mysterio eucharistico habet, ubi una eademque est hostia, idem nunc offerens sacerdotum ministerio, et cruentae oblationis fructus per incruentam uberrime percipiuntur (DB 940) ab iis qui mensae Domini participes fiunt (DB 939; 1 Cor 10.21). Qua participatione totum Christi mysterium renovatur, si quidem 'qui manducat me, et ipse vivet propter me' (Io 6.57) tamquam palmes in vite (Io 15.5), et ideo omnes et singuli qui Christiano nomine censentur in hoc unitatis signo, in hoc vinculo caritatis, in hoc concordiae symbolo (DB 882), multi unum corpus sunt in Christo (Rom 12.5).

Quamvis ergo longe a Deo esse possimus (Act 2.39, Eph 2.13, 2.17), non longe a nobis est Deus (Act 17.27) ad quem habemus accessum per fidem (Rom 5.2, Eph 3.12), ad quem appropinquamus (Iac 4.8, Heb 7.19),

as an instrument of divinity, effects that which God infallibly knows, efficaciously wills, and irresistibly causes to be done. Besides, just as Christ in his immediate vision of God knew all actual reality and intended his total effect, so also he knew that he was, and obediently willed to be, an instrument of that divine intention that works infallibly, efficaciously, irresistibly.

**Article 43: The mediator in heaven**

There is one God, and there is one mediator between God and humankind, himself human, Christ Jesus, who gave himself as a ransom for all (1 Timothy 2.5–6). As the guarantor of a better covenant (Hebrews 7.22) and mediator of this new and better covenant (Hebrews 8.6, 9.15, 12.24), not only did he die for our sake when on this earth, but also, having risen, he lives for ever to intercede on our behalf (Hebrews 7.25, Romans 8.34, 1 John 2.1).

He maintains his priesthood for ever (Hebrews 7.24), sits at the right hand of the throne of Majesty in the heavens, a minister of the sanctuary and of the true tent that God, and not any mortal, has set up (Hebrews 8.1–2); he offered one sacrifice for sins and by this single offering perfected for all time those who are sanctified (Hebrews 10.12, 10.14), so that he entered into heaven itself, where he shows himself now in the presence of God on our behalf (Hebrews 9.24), as the Lamb that was slain (Revelation 5.6–12, 13.8).

This celestial mediation, intercession, and eternal display of the completed sacrifice finds in the eucharistic mystery, not its shadow, but its image (see Hebrews 10.1), in which there is one and the same victim making the same offering now through the ministry of priests, and where the fruits of the bloody oblation are obtained in the greatest abundance through this unbloody oblation (DB 940, [DS 1743, ND 1548]) by those who partake in the table of the Lord (DB 939, [DS 1742, ND 1547]; 1 Corinthians 10.21). By this participation the whole mystery of Christ is renewed, since 'whoever eats me will live because of me' (John 6.57), like branches on the vine (John 15.5), and therefore each and every one who goes by the name of Christian, in this sign of unity, this bond of love, this symbol of concord (DB 882, [DS 1649, ND 1524]), many as they are, are one body in Christ (Romans 12.5).

Therefore, though we can be far from God (Acts 2.39, Ephesians 2.13, 2.17), God is not far from us (Acts 17.27), to whom we have access through faith (Romans 5.2, Ephesians 3.12), to whom we draw near (James 4.8, Hebrews 7.19), to whom we come (Hebrews 4.16), whom we approach

adimus (Heb 4.16), accedimus (Heb 7.25, 10.22, 12.22) utique cum illa fiducia quam etiam S. Ioannes adeo commendavit (1 Io 3.21, 4.17, 5.14).

Quae appropinquatio, aditus, accessus cum fiducia, metaphora spatiali declarat quam etiam nominant litterae sacrae reconciliationem. Sicut enim uxor, si a viro discesserit, aut innupta manere tenetur aut viro suo reconciliari (1 Cor 7.11), ita etiam eodem reconciliationis nomine declaratur missio Christi, per quem omnia reconciliantur in Deum (Col 1.20) et inter se (Col 1.22, Eph 2.16). Transierunt enim vetera et nova facta sunt omnia 'ex Deo qui nos reconciliavit sibi per Christum et dedit nobis ministerium reconciliationis. Quoniam quidem Deus erat in Christo mundum reconcilians sibi, non reputans illis delicta ipsorum, et posuit in nobis verbum reconciliationis. Pro Christo ergo legatione fungimur, tamquam Deo exhortante per nos. Obsecramus pro Christo, reconciliamini Deo' (2 Cor 5.18–20). Et iterum: 'Si enim, cum inimici essemus, reconciliati sumus Deo per mortem Filii eius, multo magis reconciliati salvi erimus in vita ipsius. Non solum autem, sed et gloriamur in Deo per Dominum nostrum Iesum Christum, per quem reconciliationem accepimus' (Rom 5.10–11).

Quae reconciliatio, sicut a Patre per Filium ad nos procedit, ita in Spiritu perficitur, qui pignus est haereditatis (Eph 1.14), quem effudit Christus Dominus dextera Patris exaltatus (Act 2.33), qui non venisset nisi abiisset Iesus (Io 15.7), qui in corda nostra missus clamat, 'Abba, Pater' (Gal 4.6, Rom 8.15), qui nobis aperit mysteria Dei (1 Cor 2.10–16, Io 16.13), qui locutus est per prophetas (Act 1.16, 4.25, 28.25), qui cum apostolis testificat et iudicat (Act 5.32, 15.28), qui episcopos ponit regere ecclesiam Dei (Act 20.28).

Qua reconciliatione comprehenditur totum Christi opus. Sicut enim bonum ordinis humanum ita bonorum particularium profluvium dicit et operationes coordinatas et habitus interiores exterioraque instituta, ut tamen haec omnia relationibus interpersonalibus concreta quadam synthesi et colligantur et vivificantur, ita etiam regnum Dei, seu ecclesia, seu corpus *plērōma*que Christi.[29] Hoc enim regnum, hoc corpus, supernaturale

(Hebrews 7.25, 10.22, 12.22), and do so indeed with that confidence which St John also strongly commended (1 John 3.21, 4.17, 5.14).

This drawing near, this approach and confident access, expresses in a spatial metaphor what scripture also refers to as reconciliation. Just as a wife, if she separates from her husband, should either remain unmarried or else be reconciled to him (1 Corinthians 7.11), so also the same term, reconciliation, is used to express the mission of Christ, through whom all are reconciled to God (Colossians 1.20) and to one another (Colossians 1.22, Ephesians 2.16). For the old order has passed away and everything is made new, and this 'from God, who reconciled us to himself through Christ, and has given us the ministry of reconciliation; that is, in Christ God was reconciling the world to himself, not counting their trespasses against them, and entrusting the message of reconciliation to us. So we are ambassadors for Christ, since God is making his appeal through us; we entreat you on behalf of Christ, be reconciled to God' (2 Corinthians 5.18–20). And again: 'For if, while we were enemies, we were reconciled to God through the death of his Son, much more surely, having been reconciled, will we be saved by his life. But more than that, we even boast in God through our Lord Jesus Christ, through whom we have now received reconciliation' (Romans 5.10–11).

This reconciliation, coming to us as it does from the Father through the Son, is accomplished in the Holy Spirit, the pledge of our inheritance (Ephesians 1.14), whom Christ the Lord, exalted to the right hand of the Father, has poured forth (Acts 2.33), who would not have come had Jesus not gone (John 16.7), who is sent into our hearts crying, 'Abba, Father' (Galatians 4.6, Romans 8.15), who opens up to us the mysteries of God (1 Corinthians 2.10–16, John 16.13), who spoke through the prophets (Acts 1.16, 4.25, 28.25), who testifies and judges together with the Apostles (Acts 5.32, 15.28), and who appoints bishops to govern the Church of God (Acts 20.28).

The entire work of Christ is contained in this reconciliation. Just as the human good of order refers to the steady stream of particular goods, coordinated operations, and interior habits and external institutions as all being closely knit together and vivified in a concrete synthesis through interpersonal relationships, so also is the kingdom of God, the church, Christ's body and *plērōma*.[29] For this kingdom, this body, is a supernatural good of order

29 [At this point Lonergan still identified the kingdom of God with the church. See also Lonergan, *The Triune God: Systematics* 495. Vatican II was to change his view on this matter. See *Early Works on Theological Method 1*, vol. 22 in Collected Works of Bernard Lonergan, ed. Robert M. Doran and Robert C. Croken (Toronto: University of Toronto Press, 2010) 555–56.]

quoddam ordinis bonum est in quo inveniuntur et bona particularia gratiae et gloriae, et operationes quibus omnia facimus in nomine Domini Iesu Christi (Col 3.17), et virtutes infusae donaque Spiritus sancti et institutiones omnes ecclesiae; quod tamen totum relationibus interpersonalibus continetur, si quidem huic corpori inesse hocque regnum participare nihil est aliud quam quod saepissime nominat S. Paulus 'in Christo' esse et 'in Spiritu.' Nam inter nos reconciliati a Christo (Eph 2.16), ut patiente vel gaudente uno omnes patiamur vel gaudeamus (1 Cor 12.26), per Christum habemus accessum in uno Spiritu ad Patrem (Eph 2.18). Et quia Christum proprium Dei Filium mediatorem atque reconciliatorem habemus, diligimur a Patre sicut et proprius eius Filius (Io 17.23, 17.26) dilectione procedente quae est ipse Spiritus sanctus.[30]

**Articulus XLIV: De fine Incarnationis**

Finem incarnationis nostram esse redemptionem constat multipliciter. Venit enim Filius hominis non ut ministraretur ei sed ut ministraret et daret animam suam redemptionem pro multis (Mc 10.45); missus pariter est Filius ut eos qui sub lege erant redimeret ut adoptionem filiorum reciperemus (Gal 4.4–5); unde in symbolo dicitur Filius incarnatus propter nos homines et propter nostram salutem.

Sed contrarium esse videtur quod Christus est caput in omnibus primatum tenens (Col 1.18); sed quod caput est et in omnibus primatum habet non ad finem est sed potius ipse finis.

Praeterea, omnia vestra sunt, vos autem Christi, Christus autem Dei (1 Cor 3.22–23). Sed alicuius esse dicitur quod ad ipsum ordinatur, sicut servus est domini, liber autem est sui causa.[31] Quia ergo Christi sumus, in Christum ordinamur tamquam in finem, et non e converso.

In quorum intelligentiam considerandum est dupliciter dici aliquid ad finem esse; unde et duplex distinguitur finis, primarius et secundarius; unde denique duplex est modus quo finis eligitur vel diligitur.

in which are found the particular goods of grace and glory, the operations by which we do everything in the name of our Lord Jesus Christ (Colossians 3.17), the infused virtues and gifts of the Holy Spirit, and all the institutions of the church. All of this is held together through interpersonal relationships, since to be in this body and a member of this kingdom is nothing other than what St Paul so often calls being 'in Christ' or 'in the Spirit.' For having been reconciled to one another by Christ (Ephesians 2.16), so that when one suffers or rejoices all suffer and rejoice (1 Corinthians 12.26), we have access to the Father through Christ in one Spirit (Ephesians 2.18). And because we have Christ, God's own Son, as our mediator and reconciler, we are loved by the Father as he loves his own Son (John 17.23, 17.26), with that proceeding Love which is the Holy Spirit.[30]

**Article 44: The purpose of the incarnation**

It is quite clear in many ways that the purpose of the incarnation is to redeem us. 'The Son of man came not to be served but to serve and give his life as a ransom for many' (Mark 10.45); likewise the Son was sent 'to redeem those who were subject to the Law that we might receive adoptive filiation' (Galatians 4.4–5). Hence in the Nicene Creed the Son is said to have become incarnate 'for us and for our salvation.'

But the fact that Christ is head and has first place in everything (Colossians 1.18) seems to be contrary to this. His being head and having first place in everything seems to be, not for the sake of the end, but rather the end itself.

Besides, 'all belong to you, and you belong to Christ, and Christ belongs to God' (1 Corinthians 3.22–23). But what is said to belong to another is for that other, as a slave is for his master, whereas a free man exists for his own sake.[31] Therefore, since we belong to Christ, we are ordered to him as our end, not the other way around.

To understand this, we must note that a thing can be said to be ordered to an end in two ways; hence we distinguish two ends, a primary and a secondary, and so there are two ways in which an end is chosen or loved.

30 Thomas Aquinas, *Summa theologiae*, 1, q. 37, a. 2.
31 Ibid. 1, q. 21, a. 1, ad 3m.

Nam quod ad finem est, relative bonum est. Sed aliud est relative bonum quatenus utile est ut finis fiat vel acquiratur; aliud autem est relative bonum quatenus ipsam finis bonitatem participat vel communicat.

Porro, quod primo modo est bonum relative, nisi medium non est; non enim ad finem refertur nisi quatenus finis vel fit vel acquiritur; et ideo fine vel facto vel acquisito, derelinquitur. Quod autem altero modo est bonum relative, quia ipsam finis bonitatem quodammodo habet, pariter etiam ipsam finis rationem quodammodo possidet; et ideo non medium est sed secundarius finis.

Ulterius, alia est volitio medii et alia est volitio finis secundarii. Quamvis enim utrumque relative sit bonum, quamvis utrumque non eligatur nisi quatenus ad aliud referatur, tamen medium non diligitur sed tantummodo in ordine ad aliud eligitur, sed finis secundarius diligi potest et diligitur ex superabundantia dilectionis erga finem primarium.

Praeterea, ipse finis secundarius ex multis partibus inter se ordinatis constare potest; et ipsa haec ordinatio aliam partem ad aliam vel superordinari vel coordinari vel subordinari potest; quare, qui finem secundarium ordinate vult, etiam partes eius vult et quidem eius partes eo ordine vult quo inter se ordinantur.

Iam vero unus est finis simpliciter primarius et super omnia propter se diligendus, ipsa nempe divina bonitas quae per essentiam bona est.

Alius autem est finis secundarius qui omnes res creatas inter se debite ordinatas includit. Quem secundarium finem qui modo debito diligit, ex superabundante dilectione erga finem primarium diligit, et omnes eius partes eo ordine diligit quo divina sapientia divinaque bonitate ordinantur.

Praeterea, hic finis secundarius etiam dicitur gloria Dei externa, vel ordo universi, qui est optimum in rebus creatis et perfectius participat divinam bonitatem et repraesentat eam quam alia quaelibet creatura.[32]

Praeterea, idem finis secundarius secundum sacra eloquia est corpus Christi, caput et membra, secundum quod in Christo omnia instaurantur atque reconciliantur sive quae in terris sive quae in caelis sunt in ipso (Eph 1.10, Col 1.20).

That which exists for an end is relatively good. But some things are relatively good insofar as they are useful for the production or the attainment of an end; others, however, are relatively good inasmuch as they participate or communicate the goodness of the end.

Thus, what is relatively good in the first way is just a means; it is not related to the end except insofar as the end is either produced or attained, and therefore once the end is produced or attained, it is relinquished. But what is relatively good in the second way, because it possesses in some way the very goodness of the end, also has something of the very formality of the end; and so it is not just a means, but a secondary end.

Furthermore, willing the means is one thing, willing the secondary end is another. Although both are relatively good, and although both are chosen only as being related to something else, nevertheless a means is not loved but only chosen with a view to that other, whereas a secondary end can be loved and is loved out of superabundant love for the primary end.

Also, a secondary end itself can consist of many interrelated parts, and this ordering can be a superordination or a coordination or a subordination of one part to another. Therefore, one who in an ordered way wills a secondary end also wills its parts and indeed wills them in the way in which they are ordered to one another.

Now there is only one end that is absolutely primary and to be loved above all else for its own sake, namely the divine goodness, which is good by reason of its very essence.

There is, however, another, a secondary end which includes all created things in their due order to one another. One who duly loves this secondary end loves it out of superabundant love for the primary end, and loves all its parts in the order assigned to them by divine wisdom and goodness.

Moreover, this secondary end is also called the external glory of God, or the order of the universe, which is the most excellent thing in all creation and shares more perfectly in the divine goodness and more perfectly reflects it than any other creature whatsoever.[32]

Besides, according to sacred scripture this same secondary end is the body of Christ, head and members, as all things in heaven and on earth are gathered together and reconciled in him (Ephesians 1.10, Colossians 1.20).

32 Ibid. 1, q. 15, a. 2; q. 47, a. 1.

Christus ergo Deus et homo voluntate et divina et humana tum Deum super omnia diligit tamquam finem primarium tum propter divinam bonitatem et ex superabundante dilectione erga eam etiam diligit finem secundarium, gloriam Dei externam, Christique corpus, caput et membra.

Attamen voluntas Christi divina realiter identificatur cum fine primario; et ideo Christus secundum voluntatem suam divinam ipse se super omnia diligit, alia autem propter se et ex condescendentia suae bonitatis. Sed voluntas Christi humana realiter identificatur cum fine secundario, neque humanitas Christi creata est totus hic finis sed pars quaedam eius; et ideo voluntas Christi humana se diligit, non super omnia neque propter se, sed ex superabuntante dilectione erga divinam bonitatem et tamquam partem quandam secundarii finis. Quare quod in divina Christi voluntate est condescendentia bonitatis, in humana eiusdem voluntate est obedientia atque sui subordinatio.

Quibus praemissis, solvitur quaestio. Eadem enim bona eodem modo inter se ordinata vult et diligit Christus qua Deus et qua homo; sed aliud bonum est Christus qua Deus et aliud Christus qua homo. Tam Christus qua Deus quam Christus qua homo vult et diligit totum Christi corpus, caput et membra, tamquam finem secundarium in gloriam Dei. Diligendo corpus, eo ipso diligit et caput et membra, et quidem sicut diligit membra propter corpus ita etiam diligit caput propter corpus; nam pars est propter totum. Ulterius, sicut diligit et caput et membra tamquam corporis partes, ita etiam eas vult rite et debite inter se ordinatas; et ideo vult membra capiti subordinata.

Quatenus ergo dicitur Christus in omnibus primatum tenens, agitur de subordinatione membrorum ad caput. Et similiter ubi dicitur omnia vestra esse et vos Christi et Christus Dei, agitur de subordinatione aliarum rerum ad membra, et membrorum ad caput, et capitis ad Deum.

Quatenus autem dicitur Christus venisse ut ministraret et daret animam suam et redimeret [nos] ut adoptionem filiorum acciperemus, distinguendum videtur inter personam venientem et naturam assumptam. Veniens enim persona ex condescendentia divinae bonitatis agit, sed natura assumpta ex obedientia. Veniens persona ordinatur ad missionem Spiritus sancti, quae tamen ordinatio rationem finis transcendit et ipsum ordinem trinitarium Deo intraneum manifestat. Sed natura assumpta subordinatur ad gloriam Dei externam et ad ordinem universi et ad totum Christi corpus sicut pars ad totum; et cum haec subordinatio ad totum in bonum

Christ, therefore, God and human, with his divine will and his human will, loves God above all things as primary end, and out of his superabundant love for the divine goodness also loves the secondary end, which is God's external glory and the body of Christ, head and members.

But Christ's divine will is really identical with the primary end, and therefore Christ with his divine will loves himself above all things, while he loves other things for his own sake and from the condescension of his goodness. But Christ's human will is really identical with the secondary end, and the created humanity of Christ is not the whole of this end but a part thereof; hence Christ's human will loves itself, not above all else nor for its own sake, but out of his superabundant love for the divine goodness and as a part of the secondary end. Therefore, that which in Christ's divine will is the condescension of his goodness, in his human will is obedience and subordination.

With these considerations, our question is answered. Christ as God and as human wills and loves good things in the same way as ordered among themselves. But Christ as God is one good and Christ as human is another. Christ as God as well as Christ as human wills and loves the whole body of Christ, head and members, as the secondary end for the glory of God. In loving his body, he loves both head and members, and indeed just as he loves the members for the sake of the body so also he loves the head for the sake of the body; for the part is for the sake of the whole. More than that, as he loves both head and members as parts of the body, so also does he will them as properly and duly ordered among themselves; therefore, he wills the members as subordinate to the head.

In speaking of Christ as having the first place in everything, we are referring to the subordination of the members to the head. Similarly, in saying that all things belong to you and you belong to Christ and Christ belongs to God, we are referring to the subordination of all other things to the members, the members to the head, and the head to God.

However, in speaking of Christ as having come to serve and to give his life and redeem us that we might receive adoptive filiation, a distinction seems necessary between the person who came and the nature he assumed. The person who came acts out of the condescending goodness of God, while the nature assumed acts out of obedience. The person who came is ordered to the mission of the Holy Spirit, an ordination that transcends the notion of end and manifests the trinitarian order within God. But the assumed nature is subordinate to God's external glory, to the order of the universe, and to the whole body of Christ as a part is to the whole; and since this subordination

membrorum redundet, ideo propter nos et propter nostram salutem datur Christi anima et effuditur eius sanguis.

Quod sane non sine obscuritate est, cum divina persona in natura humana subsistens divisim consideretur secundum personam et secundum naturam assumptam. Quae tamen obscuritas ad mysterium deputanda videtur, cum ex eo proveniat quod simul et infinitam personam et naturam finitam cogitare non possumus.

## Articulus XLV: Cur Deus homo

Qui *cur* quaerit, causam quaerit; causa autem vel intrinseca est vel extrinseca; et extrinseca est vel agens vel finis. Sed de causa Christi intrinseca agitur ubi de eiusdem constitutione ontologica.[33] Causa autem extrinseca et agens est Deus trinus ad extra operans. Causa denique finalis, uti nuperrime diximus, in primariam et secundariam dividitur, ut primaria sit ipsa divina bonitas, secundaria autem gloria Dei externa et ordo universi et corpus Christi secundum quod omnia in Christo instaurantur atque reconciliantur.

Quibus tamen praemissis atque suppositis, ulterius circa finem quaeri potest cur requiratur persona divina neque alia sufficeret finita hunc in finem assequendum; et ideo quamvis etiam nunc de fine sit quaestio, tamen non generaliter quaeritur de fine incarnationis sed magis particulariter cur Deus homo.

Respondetur ergo ideo Dei Filium esse hominem factum *ut amicitia divina inimicis ordinate communicetur.*

Est autem *amicitia* mutuus amor benevolentiae in communicatione cuiusdam boni. *Amare* autem est velle bonum alicui. Amor *benevolentiae* est velle bonum alteri. *Mutuus* denique amor benevolentiae habetur cum plures commune quoddam bonum singuli aliis velint.[34]

*Divina* proinde amicitia est mutuus benevolentiae amor circa ipsum bonum per essentiam. Quae quidem amicitia divinis personis propria est, secundum quod Pater et Filius et Spiritus sanctus et necessario et ab aeterno bonum divinum Patri et Filio et Spiritui sancto volunt.

extends to the whole body for the good of the members, therefore Christ gives his life and sheds his blood 'for us and for our salvation.'

To be sure, there is some obscurity in this, since in the case of the divine person subsisting in a human nature, the person and the assumed nature are considered separately. And it seems we shall have to be content with mystery here, the result of our inability to think about an infinite person and a finite nature at the same time.

**Article 45: Why did God become man?**

To ask *why* is to ask about a cause. Now causes are either intrinsic or extrinsic, and extrinsic causes are the agent and the end. The intrinsic causes of Christ are dealt with in the treatise on his ontological constitution.[33] His extrinsic cause, as agent, is the triune God operating *ad extra.* Final causes are divided into primary and secondary, as we have just said, so that the primary end is the divine goodness itself, and the secondary end is the external glory of God, the order of the universe, and the body of Christ wherein all things are gathered together and reconciled in him.

With these points being presupposed, we may ask this further question about the end or purpose, namely, why a divine person was required to accomplish this end, why a finite person would not have sufficed. And although this question is still a question about the end, it is not a question about the purpose of the incarnation in general, but more particularly the question is, 'Why did God become man?'

The answer is that the Son of God became man *for the orderly communication of God's friendship to his enemies.*

*Friendship* is mutual benevolent love in the sharing of some good. *To love* is to will good to someone. The love of *benevolence* is to will good to another. Finally, *mutual* love of benevolence is had when several persons will some common good, each one willing it to the others.[34]

*Divine* friendship is mutual love of benevolence with respect to that which is good by its very essence. This friendship is proper to the divine persons alone, in which the Father and the Son and the Holy Spirit necessarily and eternally will divine good to the Father and to the Son and to the Holy Spirit.

33 [See Lonergan, *The Ontological and Psychological Constitution of Christ.*]
34 Thomas Aquinas, *Summa theologiae,* 2-2, q. 23, a. 1; 1, q. 20, a. 1, ad 3m.

*Communicatur* autem haec amicitia creaturis intellectualibus et contingenter et ex tempore: primo quidem modo, in spe, secundum quod Spiritum sanctum inhabitantem habent pignus hereditatis; alio autem modo, in patria, secundum quod in gratia confirmati visione Dei immediata gaudebunt.

Deo autem *inimici* sunt peccatores, peccato mortali maculati sive originali sive etiam actuali, qui ideo reatum habent non solum culpae sed etiam poenae, tum futurae et aeternae tum etiam huius vitae; unde impotentia quadam morali irretiuntur, tum singuli ut bonum quod velint non faciant, tum consequenter omnes simul sumpti ut socialiter et historice regnum quoddam peccati constituant et sub potestate tenebrarum, mortis, diaboli versentur.

*Ordinate* denique inimicis communicatur divina amicitia secundum liberum Dei consilium divina sapientia conceptum et divina bonitate electum.

Quia ergo liberum est hoc consilium, a placitis rationalistarum et semirationalistarum recedendum est; et ideo neque rationes necessariae sunt a nobis quaerendae cur Deus homo, neque vel convenientes rationes quae perfecte a nobis intelliguntur. Quod enim ab infinita Dei sapientia unico intuitu comprehenditur atque concipitur, a nobis nisi multis seorsum rationibus non apprehenditur, neque adaequatis et propriis sed analogicis, neque perfecte intellectis sed imperfecte (DB 1796). Et cum ipsum consilium divina sapientia conceptum divinam voluntatem ad unum non determinet sed eam liberam relinquat ut etiam alia consilia pari sapientia concepta et pari bonitate eligibilia consideret, multo minus analogica et imperfecta nostra divini consilii intelligentia convenientiam quandam excedere potest.

Quod si termini iam satis innotescunt quid sibi velint, magis particulariter declarare oportet quale fuerit liberum hoc divinum consilium secundum quod Filius est homo factus. Quod quo clarius et ordinatius fiat, primo principia quaedam declaramus et deinde eadam applicamus.

Principia vero sunt tria, nempe, causae, continuitatis, et diffundendae amicitiae.

Principium causae dicimus secundum quod Deus per causas secundas agere solet, et ideo conveniens fuit ut inter homines homo exsisteret propter quem divina amicitia inimicis hominibus communicetur.

Principium continuitatis dicimus secundum quod Deus agere solet secundum convenientiam naturae creatae, et ideo conveniebat ut ipsa divinae amicitiae communicatio fieret non per eversionem quandam communis

Now this friendship is *communicated* to intellectual creatures contingently and in time: first of all, in hope, through the possession of the indwelling Holy Spirit as a pledge of their inheritance, and secondly, in heaven, when, being confirmed in grace, they rejoice in the immediate vision of God.

The *enemies of God*, however, are sinners, tainted as they are by mortal sin whether original or actual and therefore held to be not only morally culpable but also liable to punishment both in this life and in the next. And so, enmeshed in a moral impotence, individually they fail to do the good they want to do, and as a consequence all acting together socially and historically set up a reign of sin and live subject to the power of darkness, of death, and of the devil.

Finally, God's friendship is communicated to these enemies of his *in due order*, following the free plan conceived by his wisdom and chosen by his goodness.

Because this plan is freely chosen, it is far removed from the notions of the rationalists and semi-rationalists, and therefore we must not look for necessary reasons why God became man, or even for reasons of fittingness that we can perfectly understand. What divine wisdom comprehends and conceives in a single vision can be apprehended by us only through many separate reasons that are not adequate and proper but analogous, and are understood, not perfectly, but imperfectly (DB 1796, [DS 3016, ND 132]). And since this plan conceived by divine wisdom does not restrict the divine will to one alternative but leaves it free to consider other plans conceived with equal wisdom and choiceworthy with equal goodness, it is all the more impossible for our analogical and imperfect understanding of God's plan to arrive at anything beyond reasons of fittingness.

Now if the meaning of these terms is sufficiently understood, we must explain more in detail the nature of this free divine plan according to which the Son became man. To do this in a clearer and more orderly fashion, we shall first state certain principles and then go on to apply them.

The principles are these three: the principle of cause, the principle of continuity, and the principle of the diffusion of friendship.

We call the principle of cause that principle according to which God customarily acts through secondary causes; therefore it was fitting that in the whole human race there should exist a human being because of whom God's friendship might be communicated to those who are his enemies.

We call the principle of continuity that principle whereby God customarily acts in accordance with what is fitting to a created nature; thus it was fitting that divine friendship be communicated not through some disruption

rerum cursus (secundum placita quaedam eschatologica, apocalyptica, hebraica), sed servato generali rerum cursu et, ut in pluribus, stantibus omnibus legibus tum naturalibus tum humanis sive psychologicis sive socialibus sive historicis.

Principium diffundendae amicitiae dicimus secundum quod amicus amici amicos diligit. Quod quidem principium eo extendit ut propter amicum etiam inimici diligantur. Uti enim docet S. Thomas: 'Et tanta potest esse dilectio amici quod propter amicum diligantur hi qui ad ipsum pertinent etiam si nos offendant vel odiant. Et hoc modo amicitia caritatis se extendit etiam ad inimicos, quos diligimus ex caritate in ordine ad Deum, ad quem principaliter habetur amicitia caritatis.'[35]

Applicantur deinde haec principia concludendo, et primo quidem circa terminum ad quem, postea autem circa terminum a quo; et in utroque casu, cum ipsa principia non sint nisi convenientes, etiam necessario deductae conclusiones nisi convenientes non erunt.

Et circa termimum ad quem, quatenus applicantur principia causae et diffundendae caritatis, requiritur homo qui est intermedius amicus, amicus scilicet Dei secundum divinam amicitiam et amicus etiam hominum ut propter eum ad caeteros homines extendatur divina amicitia.

Iam vero ut homo sit amicus Dei secundum amicitiam divinam, actu ordinari debet in bonum Dei infinitum possidendum; et ideo gratia sanctificante et virtutibus infusis et Spiritus sancti donis ornari debet eiusdemque Spiritus motionibus illuminari atque illustrari.[36] Sed haec omnia absolute supernaturalia sunt et proportionem cuiuslibet substantiae finitae excedunt. Quare nulla mera creatura iure quodam suo est amicus Dei secundum amicitiam divinam.

Praeterea, potest quidem mera creatura esse amica Dei sive ex puro beneplacito divino sive ex merito alterius. Sed si ponitur intermedius qui ex puro beneplacito divino est Dei amicus, relinquitur principium causae.

of the ordinary course of events (which would have satisfied certain Jewish eschatological and apocalyptic expectations), but in continuity with the normal course of events and, for the most part, letting laws, both natural and human – psychological, social, and historical – stand.

We call the principle of the diffusion of friendship that principle according to which a friend loves his friend's friends. This principle itself even goes so far as to loving one's enemies for the sake of one's friend. As St Thomas puts it, 'It is possible to have so much love for a friend as to love for his sake those who are connected with him, even if they offend or hate us. In this way the friendship of charity extends even to one's enemies, whom we love out of charity ordered to God, for whom above all we have the friendship of charity.'[35]

Next, we apply these principles by drawing conclusions from them, first with regard to the *terminus ad quem*, then with regard to the *terminus a quo*; and in both instances, since the principles themselves are only what is fitting, the conclusions necessarily deduced from them will state only what is fitting.

With regard to the *terminus ad quem*, when applying the principles of cause and of the diffusion of charity, some human being is required who is a friendly intermediary, that is, a friend of God according to divine friendship and also a friend of all the others, so that because of him divine friendship may be extended to other human beings.

Now to be a friend of God according to divine friendship, one must be actually ordered to the possession of God as infinite good; therefore one must be endowed with sanctifying grace and the infused virtues and the gifts of the Holy Spirit, and be enlightened and illumined[36] by the movements of this same Holy Spirit. But all of these are absolutely supernatural and exceed the proportion of any finite substance whatsoever. Therefore no mere creature is in its own right a friend of God according to divine friendship.

Furthermore, it is true that a mere creature can be a friend of God either out of God's sheer pleasure or because of the merit of someone else. But if we posit an intermediary who is a friend of God out of God's sheer pleasure,

35 Ibid. 2-2, q. 23, a. 1, ad 2m.
36 [Latin, *illuminari atque illustrari*. Lonergan may have intended to write 'illuminari atque inspirari,' 'enlightened and inspired,' for he usually speaks of the movements of the Holy Spirit as illuminations (of the intellect) and inspirations (of the will); see, for example, on p. 597, above: '... movements of the Holy Spirit by which our minds are enlightened and our wills inspired.' Besides, *illuminari* and *illustrari* are synonymous terms.]

Et si ponitur intermedius qui merito alterius est Dei amicus, incipitur regressus in infinitum. Quare, ut salventur tum principium causae tum principium diffundendae caritatis, requiritur homo qui iure quodam suo est Dei amicus.

Sed superius habitum est nullam meram creaturam iuro quodam suo esse Dei amicam secundum amicitiam divinam. Sequitur principia tum causae tum diffundendae caritatis non salvari nisi intermedius amicus sit persona divina in humana natura subsistens.

Praeterea, si ponitur persona divina in humana natura subsistens, ponitur homo qui iure suo est Dei amicus. Ponitur homo, quia in humana natura subsistit. Ponitur qui iure suo est Dei amicus, nam persona divina iure suo gaudet amicitia divina.

Prima ergo ratio cur Deus homo est ut habeatur homo qui iure suo sit Dei amicus secundum divinam amicitiam.

Cui rationi statim adiungitur alia. Qui enim iure suo divinam amicitiam habet, si homo est, etiam omnia dona supernaturalia iure suo habet; et ideo exsistit causa exemplaris proportionata secundum quam haec dona aliis hominibus communicari possunt.

Obici tamen potest quod divina amicitia debetur divinae personae qua in divina natura subsistente, non autem qua in humana natura subsistente.

Respondetur amicitiam esse mutuum amorem benevolentiae, neque hanc benevolentiam diminui eo quod persona amica aliam naturam assumit. Quare Deus Pater diligit Filium, non solum qua Deum sed etiam qua hominem, Amore procedente qui est ipse Spiritus sanctus, uti in baptismo Christi manifestatur.

Sed ulterius considerandum est quod amicus intermedius non solum Dei amicus esse debet sed etiam amicus hominum; unde ipse homines diligere debet et homines ipsum. Quorum primum sequitur ex dictis sed alterum addit super ea. Nam amicus Dei caritate perfunditur et ideo, sicut diligit Deum super omnia, ita propter Deum diligit proximum. Homines autem Deo sunt inimici atque peccatores, et ideo Dei amicum non diligunt sed odio habent. 'Omnis enim qui male agit odit lucem et non venit ad lucem, ut non arguantur opera eius' (Io 3.20), et 'Non potest mundus odisse vos; me autem odit, quia ego testimonium perhibeo de illo quod opera eius mala sunt' (Io 7.7). Quare ut amicus Dei sit amicus intermedius, homines convertere debet ex inimicitia in amicitiam ut diligentes hominem qui Deus est, in dilectionem Dei perveniant.

we abandon the principle of cause. And if we posit an intermediary who is a friend of God because of the merit of someone else, we initiate an infinite regress. In order, then, to safeguard both the principle of cause and the principle of the diffusion of friendship, we require a human being who in his own right is a friend of God.

But we said above that no mere creature in its own right is a friend of God according to divine friendship. It follows that neither the principle of cause nor the principle of the diffusion of friendship is safeguarded unless the intermediary friend is a divine person subsisting in a human nature.

Besides, if we posit a divine person subsisting in a human nature, we are positing a human being who in his own right is a friend of God. The one we posit is human, because he subsists in a human nature. The one we posit is in his own right a friend of God, for a divine person in his own right enjoys divine friendship.

The first reason, therefore, for God becoming human is to have a human being who in his own right is a friend of God according to divine friendship.

To this reason we immediately add another. One who in his own right enjoys God's friendship, if he is human, also enjoys by his own right all the supernatural gifts, and there is, therefore, a proportionate exemplar cause according to which these gifts can be communicated to others.

Yet it may be objected that divine friendship is owed to a divine person as subsisting in a divine nature but not as subsisting in a human nature.

To this we would reply that friendship is mutual love of benevolence, and that this benevolence is not lessened because the befriended person assumes a human nature. Hence the Father loves the Son, not only as God but also as human, with that proceeding Love which is the Holy Spirit himself, as was manifested at Christ's baptism.

Now we must go on to consider that the intermediary friend must be a friend not only of God but also of human beings; hence he must love them and they must love him. The first requirement follows from what we have been saying, but the second is a further point. For a friend of God is filled to overflowing with charity and therefore, as he loves God above all else, so also he loves his neighbor for God's sake. Human beings, however, are sinners, enemies of God, and so do not love God's friend, but rather hate him. 'For all who do evil hate the light and do not come to the light, so that their deeds may not be exposed' (John 3.20), and 'The world cannot hate you, but it hates me because I testify against it that its works are evil' (John 7.7). Therefore, in order that the friend of God be an intermediary friend, he must turn others from hostility to friendship, so that loving the human being who is God, they may come to have love for God.

Unde elucet tertia ratio cur Deus homo. Si enim divina persona est homo, dilectio huius hominis est dilectio personae divinae. Sicut enim persona divina facta homo est amicus intermedius propter quem Deus diligit homines etiam inimicos, ita etiam idem homo, quia est persona divina, est intermedius per quem homines in dilectionem Dei perveniunt. Quare non solum dicitur, 'Dilexisti eos sicut et me dilexisti' (Io 17.23, 17.26), sed etiam, 'Qui autem diligit me, diligetur a Patre meo' (Io 14.21, 14.23) et, 'Pater amat vos quia vos me amastis' (Io 16.27).

Attamen considerari oportet quemadmodum intermedius inimicos in amicitiam convertere debeat. Et secundum principium continuitatis hoc fieri convenit, non per eversionem communis rerum cursus, sed servato generali hoc cursu et stantibus, ut in pluribus, legibus tam humanis quam naturalibus.

Iam vero, uti primo capite habitum est, homines a Deo alienati ita regno quodam peccati et tenebrarum potestate concluduntur ut, quamvis bonum velle possint, non tamen ita velint ut faciant et, quamvis bonum ordinis humanum tam culturale quam exterius ad magnam quandam perfectionem perducere possint, ipsum hoc bonum peccatis suis pervertant et in causam malorum semper augentium commutent. Quare, si leges humanae et psychologicae et sociales non suspenduntur, id quod vetat continuitatis principium, e malis in bonum converti non possunt homines nisi secundum rationem crucis ut, scilicet, ipsa sua mala agnoscant atque sustineant, et bona, patienti, perseveranti voluntate evincant, et divinae providentiae benedictionem implorent.

Quod si homines secundum rationem crucis ex inimicitia in amicitiam sunt convertendi, multipliciter convenit ipsum amicum intermedium non solum legem crucis docere atque praecipere sed etiam secundum mysterium crucis opus proprium peragere, ut inimicorum odio feriatur, et haec mala in bonis vincat, et magna sua victoria demonstret quam sit verum diligentibus Deum omnia cooperari in bonum.

Convenit enim intermedium legem crucis docere atque praecipere, quia ex hypothesi decretum est hac et non alia via homines esse in salutem perducendos.

Convenit etiam intermedium secundum mysterium crucis opus peragere proprium. Nam homines Deo inimici sunt stulti et tardi corde, et ideo magis exemplo quam verbis erudiuntur et saepius ducentem sequuntur atque imitantur quam praecipientem audiunt eique obediunt.

From this, a third reason for God becoming human becomes clear. If a divine person is human, love of this human is love of a divine person. Just as a divine person become human is an intermediary friend because of whom God loves all people, even his enemies, so also this same man, being a divine person, is an intermediary through whom human beings come to have love for God. Therefore he not only said, 'You have loved them even as you have loved me' (John 17.23, 17.26), but also, 'Those who love me will be loved by my Father' (John 14.21, 14.23), and, 'The Father himself loves you, because you have loved me' (John 16.27).

Still, we must consider how the intermediary has to turn enemies into friends. It is fitting that this be done in accordance with the principle of continuity, not by interrupting the normal course of events, but by generally maintaining this course and without abrogating, for the most part, the laws of the human or of the natural order.

Now, as we mentioned in the first chapter, human beings estranged from God are imprisoned by the reign of sin and the power of darkness, so that although they are able to want what is good, they do not will to do it, and although they are capable of bringing the human good of order, both external and cultural, to a high degree of excellence, they subvert this good by their wickedness and turn it into a source of ever-increasing evils. Therefore, unless human psychological and social laws are suspended – contrary to the principle of continuity – people cannot be turned from evil to good except according to the meaning of the cross: that they acknowledge and endure the evils that beset them, conquer them by patient and persevering good will, and implore the blessing of divine providence.

But if they are to be turned from hostility to friendship according to the meaning of the cross, it is fitting in many ways that the intermediary friend himself not only teach and prescribe the law of the cross but also perform his proper work according to the mystery of the cross, that he himself be struck down by the hatred of his enemies, conquer these evil deeds by bringing good out of them, and by his great victory demonstrate how true it is that for those who love God all things work together unto good.

It is fitting that the intermediary teach and prescribe the law of the cross, because, in our supposition, God has decreed that in this way and no other are we to be brought to salvation.

It is fitting also that the intermediary perform his proper work according to the mystery of the cross. All who are hostile to God are foolish and sluggish of heart, and so learn by example more than by words, and more often follow and imitate a leader than listen to and obey one who issues commands.

Praeterea, ipse intermedius perfectissima caritate Deum super omnia diligit et proximum propter Deum. Sed qui vere diligit non solum de suis bonis dare vult, sed etiam mala quae amicus sustinere debet non aliena reputat sed quodammodo sua. Quare patiente amico compatitur, et si quomodocumque utile est, ipsa amici mala participare vult.

Praeterea, 'nulla est maior ad amorem invitatio quam praevenire amando; et nimis durus est animus qui dilectionem, si nolebat impendere, nolit rependere.'[37] Sed opus intermedii est homines inimicos ad amicitiam convertere; quem in finem nulla est efficacior via quam praevenire amando; et ideo convenit intermedium et maximum exhibere amorem et modum adhibere maxime efficacem ad eum exhibendum. Convenit ergo intermedium secundum mysterium crucis opus peragere proprium, secundum illud, 'Maiorem hac dilectione nemo habet quam ut animam suam ponat pro amicis suis' (Io 15.13) et, 'Ego si exaltatus fuero, omnia traham ad me ipsum' (Io 12.32).

Praeterea, ipsa haec amoris exhibitio atque ad amorem provocatio non sufficiunt nisi in initialem quandam atque dispositivam dilectionem in hominibus causandam. Aliud enim est personam divinam hominem factam ut hominem diligere et aliud eandem ut personam divinam diligere. Ad illam dilectionem sufficiunt humana amoris exhibitio atque ad amorem provocatio; ad hanc autem dilectionem ulterius requiruntur supernaturalia gratiae dona; et ideo dicitur, 'Nemo potest venire ad me nisi Pater qui misit me traxerit eum' (Io 6.44). Quapropter cum intermedius secundum principium causae etiam supernaturalia dona causare debeat, secundum illud, 'Nemo venit ad Patrem nisi per me' (Io 14.6), ulterius considerandum est quemadmodum intermedius in hominibus iisque Deo inimicis dona supernaturalia causet.

Iam vero, uti supra habitum est, intermedius homo est persona divina et ideo eum divina quadam animi magnitudine atque munificentia agere oportet. Quare, 'ubi abundavit delictum, superabundavit gratia' (Rom 5.20).

Sed in primis superabundat gratia si divina persona non solum facit ut homines pro se faciant sed etiam ipsa pro iis agit, sicut caput pro membris, sacerdos pro populo, pastor pro ovibus, rex pro subditis, vicarius pro repraesentatis, amicus pro amicis. Quod quidem fieri convenit, tum quia homines communiter non per se sed per alios agunt, tum quia in peccata

Besides, it is with the highest degree of love that the intermediary himself loves God above all things and his fellow human beings for God's sake. But one who really loves is not only willing to give of the goods that he has but also looks upon the evils his friend has to endure not as another's but as in some way his own. Thus when his friend suffers some evil, he suffers with him, and, if it will help in any way, he will share in those evils himself.

Moreover, 'there is no more pressing invitation to love than to show love first; and that heart is hard indeed which, if reluctant to love, still refuses to requite love.'[37] But the work of the intermediary is to turn enemies into friends, and there is no more effective way to do this than to show love first. It is fitting therefore that the intermediary show the greatest love and show it in the most effective way possible. Thus it is fitting that he perform his proper work by way of the mystery of the cross, in accordance with the words, 'No one has greater love than this, to lay down one's life for one's friends' (John 15.13), and also, 'And I, when I am lifted up from the earth, will draw all to myself' (John 12.32).

Still further, this display of love and challenge to love in return is sufficient only to make others initially disposed to love. For it is one thing to love an incarnate divine person as human and another to love him as a divine person. For the former love, a human display of love and challenge to love will suffice; but for the latter there is an additional need for the supernatural gifts of grace; hence the statement, 'No one can come to me unless drawn by the Father who sent me' (John 6.44). Therefore, since the intermediary must also produce supernatural gifts in keeping with the principle of cause, according to the words, 'No one comes to the Father except through me' (John 14.6), we must further consider how the intermediary produces supernatural gifts in others, those who are enemies of God.

As we said above, the human intermediary is a divine person and so must act with divine magnanimity and lavishness. Hence, 'where sin increased, grace abounded all the more' (Romans 5.20).

But grace is above all superabundant if a divine person brings it about not only that they work for themselves but also that he acts on their behalf, as the head for the members, a priest for his people, a shepherd for his sheep, a king for his subjects, a vicar for those whom he represents, a friend for his friends. This is indeed fitting, because we ordinarily do

37 Augustine, *De catechizandis rudibus,* IV, no. 7; ML 40, 314.

impelluntur non solum suis vitiis sed etiam alienis, tum quia ipsi pro se etiam gratia elevati atque adiuti nisi imperfecte non agunt.

Convenit ergo amicum intermedium superabundanter pro peccatis satisfacere.

not act by ourselves but through others, because we fall into sin not only through our own vices but also through the sins of others, and because, even when elevated and assisted by grace, our actions on our own behalf fall short of perfection.

It was fitting, therefore, that an intermediary friend should make superabundant satisfaction for sin.

# Appendix[1]

**Articulus XLIV: De fine Incarnationis**

Cum finis sit bonum cuius gratia aliud vel est vel fit vel habetur, ante de divisione bonorum et de finibus dicendum est quam de fine incarnationis inquiratur.

Per essentiam ergo bonum est quod ipsa boni essentia seu quidditas est; quod quidem est solus Deus (Mc 10.19).

Ex bono autem per essentiam procedit bonum dupliciter: uno modo per participationem, et sic bona est omnis simplex creatura; alio modo per communicationem sive ab aeterno sive ex tempore; ab aeterno quidem inquantum bonitas divina a Patre in Filium et a Patre Filioque in Spiritum sanctum communicatur; ex tempore autem inquantum Verbum Dei factum est homo, et Spiritus sanctus iustis datur, et ipsa divina essentia mentibus beatis immediate videnda illabitur.[2]

# Appendix[1]

## Article 44: The purpose of the incarnation

Since a purpose or end is a good for the sake of which something else exists or is done or possessed, we ought to say something about the kinds of goods and about ends before going on to inquire into the end or purpose of the incarnation.

The good by essence, then, is that which is itself the very essence or quiddity of goodness; and that is God alone (Mark 10.18).

From the good by essence, good proceeds in two ways: by participation, the way in which every simple creature is good, and by communication, whether eternally or in time. Eternally, the divine goodness is communicated from the Father to the Son and from the Father and the Son to the Holy Spirit; in time, when the Word of God became human, and the Holy Spirit is bestowed upon the just, and the divine essence itself enters into the minds of the blessed for their immediate vision of it.[2]

1 [The following is a translation of the eleven pages at the end of file 674, titled Articulus XLIV: De fine incarnationis. It seems to be a first draft of an article (44) De fine incarnationis (The purpose of the incarnation), which was then rewritten and divided into two articles, 44, De fine incarnationis and 45, Cur Deus homo (Why did God become man?). The manuscript ends at half-sentence at the end. The autograph may be found on the website www.bernardlonergan.com at 25470DTL060.]

2 Thomas Aquinas, *Summa theologiae*, 1, q. 12, aa. 4 and 5.

Quare, cum Verbum incarnatum dicat neque solum bonum per essentiam neque solum bonum per participationem, sed utrumque includat, bonum per communicationem dici potest; et similiter Spiritus sanctus inhabitans et divina essentia intellectui creato illapsa et coniuncta bonum infinitum dicunt creaturae communicatum.

Qua in communicatione distinguendum est inter id quod communicatur et id quo communicatur, ut id quod communicatur sit infinitum, ipsum nempe Dei Verbum, ipse Spiritus sanctus, ipsa divina essentia, sed id quo communicatur sit finitum, puta esse secundarium in Verbo incarnato, et gratia sanctificans in Spiritu sancto inhabitante, et lumen gloriae in visione Dei immediata.

Proinde in omni bono distinguuntur ratio actus et ratio ordinis. Ita Deus trinus ratione actus est perfectione infinitus, et ratione ordinis qui inter personas viget tantam habet perfectionem quanta maior cogitari nequit.[3] Similiter in bonis per participationem, singulae creaturae eatenus bonae sunt quatenus actu sunt et actu perficiuntur; et omnes simul ratione ordinis sunt optimum in rebus creatis,[4] si quidem bonum ordinis universi perfectius participat bonitatem divinam et repraesentat eam quam alia quaelibet creatura.[5] Denique in bonis per communicationem idem discernitur: nam ratione actus, quoad id quod communicatur, invenitur actus infinitus, et quoad id quo communicatur, inveniuntur excellentissima inter entia absolute supernaturalia; et ratione ordinis, inquantum Filius a Patre mittitur et Spiritus sanctus ab utroque, habetur ipse ordo trinitarius, si quidem missiones divinae ipsis divinis originis relationibus constituuntur;[6] et praeterea ordinantur actualis assumptio naturae humanae in dona gratiae, et dona gratiae in coronam gloriae.

Bonum ergo dividitur in bonum per essentiam, bonum per participationem, et bonum per communicationem; et in singulis inveniuntur tum ratio actus tum ratio ordinis.

Since, therefore, the incarnate Word is that which is good neither only by essence nor only by participation but in both ways, he can be said to be good by communication. In the same way the indwelling of the Holy Spirit and the insertion of the divine essence into and union with a created intellect denote infinite good communicated to a creature.

In this communication we must distinguish between that which is communicated and that by which it is communicated, where that which is communicated is infinite, namely, the divine Word, the Holy Spirit, and the divine essence, whereas that by which they are communicated is a finite reality, that is, the secondary act of existence in the incarnate Word, sanctifying grace in the indwelling of the Holy Spirit, and the light of glory in the immediate vision of God.

Further, in every good there is a distinction between the formality of act and the formality of order. Thus, the triune God by reason of act is infinite in perfection, and by reason of the order that obtains among the three persons has such a high degree of perfection that no greater degree can be thought of.[3] Similarly, in the case of what is good by participation, each creature is good to the extent that it is in act and is perfected by act; and all creatures taken together constitute by reason of their order that which is the very best in creation,[4] since the good of order of the universe participates more perfectly in the divine goodness and more perfectly reflects it than any other creature whatsoever.[5] Finally, the same can be seen in the case of what is good by communication. For by reason of act, as to that which is communicated, we find infinite act, and as to the means by which it is communicated, the most excellent of all absolutely supernatural realities. And by reason of order, in the sending of the Son by the Father and the sending of the Holy Spirit by both, there we find the order of the Trinity itself, since the divine missions are constituted by the divine relations of origin.[6] Moreover, the actual assumption of a human nature is ordered to the bestowal of the gifts of grace, and the gifts of grace are ordered to the crown of glory.

Thus the good is divided into good by essence, good by participation, and good by communication; and in each of these there is the formality of act and the formality of order.

3 Lonergan, *Divinarum personarum* 187–95. [*De Deo trino: Pars systematica* 208–15; *The Triune God: Systematics* 420–35.]

4 Thomas Aquinas, *Summa theologiae,* 1, q. 15, a. 2.

5 Ibid. q. 47, a. 1.

6 Lonergan, *Divinarum personarum* 206–12. [*De Deo trino: Pars systematica* 226–32; *The Triune God: Systematics* 454–67.]

Proinde, cum finis sit bonum, eadem in finibus viget divisio; et similiter in iis tum ad rationem actus tum ad rationem ordinis attendendum est.

Ea autem quae ad finem sunt dividuntur secundum quod finis est vel iam habitus vel acquirendus. Et quod ad finem acquirendum est nominatur medium et eatenus eligitur quatenus in finem acquirendum conducit. Quod autem ad finem iam habitum est nomen proprium non habet sed eligitur ex superabundantia dilectionis erga ipsum finem ut bonitas eius participetur, manifestetur, communicetur. Quod maxime in ipso Deo conspicitur qui, ex condescendentia suae bonitatis et ex superabundantia suae dilectionis erga ipsam divinam bonitatem, et mundum creavit et bonum infinitum creaturis communicat et iis missionibus infinitum bonum communicat quibus manifestatur ipse ordo divinarum personarum.

Praeterea, ea quae ad finem ordinantur multipliciter ad ipsum finem se haberi possunt. Ordinantur enim potentia vel naturali vel obedientiali; iam in finem proficiunt vel a fine inveniuntur aversi; et ipsa haec aversio tantummodo in quibusdam individuis est aut adeo extenditur ut malum quoddam ordinis omnia fere corrumpens constituat. Sed, ut mere hypothetica omittamus, homo lapsus ad finem vitae aeternae se habet ut potentia non naturalis sed obedientialis, neque ut proficiens sed ut a fine aversus, neque ut in paucioribus aversus sed universaliter per privationem originalis iustitiae et per consequentem corruptionem boni ordinis tam exterioris quam culturalis. Imo, etsi homo hunc in statum miserrimum libero suo arbitrio descenderit, ex eodem statu per idem arbitrium liberum ascendere non potest, tum propter impotentiam physicam relate ad bona supernaturalia, tum propter impotentiam moralem, socialem, historicam relate ad bona naturalia, uti in primo capite dictum est.

Quibus praemissis, cum Filius Dei homo factus sit propter nostram salutem (DB 54), finis incarnationis considerari debet tum secundum terminum ad quem, tum secundum terminum a quo, tum secundum modum quo ex uno termino in alium proceditur.

Primo, ergo, secundum terminum ad quem, Filius Dei homo factus mediator est. Quia enim Filius etiam homo est, dilectio Patris infinita, cum ad personam Filii terminetur, ex ipsa incarnatione extenditur ex Christo qua Deo in Christum qua hominem. Quod maxime in baptismo Christi configuratur, ubi Deus Pater exprimit suam dilectionem, tum voce de caelo delapsa,

Accordingly, since an end is a good, the same division applies to ends; and attention must likewise be paid to the formalities of act and of order in them.

Those things that are ordered to an end are divided according to whether the end is already possessed or is still to be attained. That which is ordered to the attainment of an end is called a means, and is chosen precisely insofar as it is conducive to the attainment of that end. That which is ordered to an end already possessed has no special name but is chosen out of superabundant love for the end itself in order that its goodness may be participated in, manifested, and communicated. This is most clearly seen in God himself, who, out of his gracious goodness and out of the superabundance of his love towards the divine goodness itself, created the world, communicates infinite good to his creatures, and does so by those missions by which the very order of the divine persons is manifested.

Further, those things that are ordered to an end can be related to that end in many ways. They can be ordered by either natural or obediential potency; they can progress towards the end or can be found withdrawing from it, and this withdrawal itself can either be limited to certain individuals or be so widespread as to constitute an evil of order that corrupts almost everything. However – leaving aside purely hypothetical speculation – humanity in its fallen state is related to its end, eternal life, not by natural but by obediential potency, not as advancing towards it but rather turning away from it, and this not in just a few instances but universally by the privation of original justice and the consequent corruption of the good of order, both external and cultural. In fact, although the human race by its own free will has descended to this most wretched state, it cannot raise itself out of it by that same free will, because of physical impotence with respect to goods of the supernatural order and moral, social, and historical impotence concerning goods of the natural order, as we saw in the first chapter.

In view of this, since the Son of God became man for our salvation (DB 54, [DS 125–26, ND 7–8]), the purpose of the incarnation needs to be looked at according to the 'terminus to which,' *terminus ad quem*, the 'terminus from which,' *terminus a quo*, and the way of proceeding from one to the other.

First, then, as to the *terminus ad quem*, the incarnate Son of God is mediator. Because the Son is also human, the Father's infinite love, terminating in the person of the Son, extends by reason of the incarnation from Christ as God to Christ as human. This is symbolized most of all at his baptism, when God the Father expressed his love by the voice from heaven and the

tum manifestatione Spiritus sancti sub specie columbae (Mc 1.10–11). Unde, cum amicus diligat amicos amici, fundamentum positum est ex quo nos, Filio homini facti amici, eadem dilectione ac Filius diligamur, filii adoptionis fiamus, in Spiritu dato clamemus, 'Abba, Pater,' et heredes Dei, coheredes autem Christi accipiamur. Quam ob causam, agnoscitur Filius ideo nostrae naturae particeps esse factus ut nos naturae divinae participes et communicantes fiamus.

Deinde, secundum terminum a quo, Filius Dei homo factus redemptor est. Ideo enim ex regno peccati in regnum Filii dilectionis suae transferimur, quia Filius homo (1) per modum exemplaris determinavit quid in nobis efficiendum sit, (2) per modum capitis pro nobis et obediendo meruit, et patiendo satisfecit, et ipse sacerdos se hostiam sacrificium perfectum semel obtulit, et iugiter in caelis pro nobis intercedit, (3) per modum agentis historici quasi per proprium corpus propriaque membra per ecclesiam, sacramenta, doctrinam, legislationem, et ipsum suae vitae mysterium iugiter influit, et (4) per modum mediatoris caelestis denique sacerdos aeternus per proprium sanguinem vultui Dei apparet pro nobis, ut cum fiducia ad Patrem adeamus, appropinquemus, accedamus.

Tertio, secundum modum quo ex uno termino in alium proceditur, totum mysterium divinae sapientiae atque iustitiae exhibetur. Agit enim Deus pro sua sapientia liberaque electione sua per causas secundas et secundum convenientiam ipsarum harum causarum.

Quia ergo Deus agit secundum convenientiam naturae creatae, non ideo ex malis in bonum producimur quia leges vel naturales vel humanae suspendantur ad mentem eschatologicam, apocalypticam, hebraicam, sed stantibus iisdem legibus naturalibus et humanis (si relative pauca quaedam excipias miracula), secundum rationem, legem, mysterium, iustitiam crucis, per victoriam bonae patientisque voluntatis, mala et vincuntur et in bonum transformantur.

Quia autem Deus per creaturas agit, hominem voluit qui, tamquam causa proportionata atque actualis, efficeret tum ut a malis recedamus tum ut in bonum, idque infinitum, perveniamus. Qui sane homo, cum merus homo esse non potuerit, Filius Dei erat homo factus, uti multipliciter concluditur.

Nisi enim persona divina in natura humana subsisteret, mediator non esset ut divina divinae personae dilectio in nos terminaret, secundum illud, 'Dilexisti eos sicut et me dilexisti' (Io 17.23, 17.26). Qua mediatione

appearance of the Holy Spirit in the form of a dove (Mark 1.10–11). Thus, since a friend loves his friend's friends, the foundation was established whereby we, having become friends of the Son as human, are loved with the same love as the Son is loved, become children by adoption, and cry out in the Spirit given to us, 'Abba, Father,' and are accepted as heirs of God and co-heirs with Christ. For this reason, we know the Son was made to share in our nature so that we might become sharers and communicants of the divine nature.

Second, as to the *terminus a quo*, the incarnate Son of God is redeemer. We are transferred from the reign of sin into the kingdom of his beloved Son because the Son as human (1) as exemplar has determined what is to be accomplished in us; (2) as head has by his obedience merited for us, by his suffering made satisfaction for us, and as priest offered himself once for all as victim in a perfect sacrifice and in heaven continues for ever this intercession on our behalf; (3) as a historical agent exercises a continuing influence, as through his own body and members, through the church, the sacraments, doctrine, legislation, and the mystery of his life itself; and (4) as celestial mediator and eternal priest, through his blood presents himself on our behalf before the face of God so that we too may approach with confidence and have access to the Father.

Third, the whole mystery of God's wisdom and justice is displayed by the way of proceeding from one terminus to the other. For in his wisdom and by his free decision God acts through secondary causes and in accord with what is fitting to these causes.

Since, therefore, God acts in a manner suited to a created nature, we are not brought from evil to good by the suspension of human laws or laws of nature, as an eschatological, apocalyptic, or Hebraic mentality would have it. Instead, without abrogating any physical or human laws (apart from a relatively few miracles), in accordance with the meaning, the law, the mystery, and the justice of the cross, evils are conquered and transformed into good through the victory of a good and patient will.

Because God acts through creatures, he called for a human being who, as a proportionate and actual cause, would bring it about that we should turn away from evil and arrive at what is good, indeed, infinite good. Since no merely human being could be such a one, the Son of God became that human being, as we may conclude in several ways.

For were there no divine person subsisting in a human nature, there would be no mediator whereby the divine love for a divine person would have us also as its term, according to the words, 'You have loved them as you

sublata, non fuisset inter homines ratio seu causa cur adoptionem filiorum et inhabitationem Spiritus et divinae hereditatis pignus acciperemus, ut in caelestem civitatem Deum videntium produceremur.

Praeterea, virtutes infusae et dona motionesque Spiritus sancti et lumen gloriae, cum proportionem cuiuslibet substantiae finitae excedant, ad eum tantummodo iure pertinere possunt qui persona divina est et in natura assumpta operatur. Nisi ergo divina persona in natura humana subsisteret, non fuisset exemplar cur nobis haec bona absolute supernaturalia donaretur; sed Filio Dei pro nobis tradito, fieri quodammodo non potuit ut cum illo non omnia donarentur (Rom 8.32).

Praeterea, ordo universi est proprius quidam effectus Dei, si quidem omnis creatura est agens secundum et instrumentum quod a Deo dirigi et applicari et usurpari debet, ut finis a divina sapientia ordinatus et a divina bonitate electus attingatur.[7] Sed finis incarnationis est ut ordo universi peccato disruptus et deformatus non solum restauretur sed etiam in summam quandam perfectionem producatur, secundum quod omnia in Christo instaurantur (Eph 1.10) atque reconciliantur (Col 1.20). Cui fini non proportionatur ulla mera creatura, et ideo oportebat divinam personam in natura humana subsistere.

Ulterius, ideo Deus redemptionem nostram decrevit quia dives erat in misericordia et nimia sua caritate dilexit nos (Eph 2.4). Praeterea, per ipsam hanc caritatem suam modo humano manifestatam voluit nos ad se convertere,[8] secundum illud: 'Commendat autem caritatem suam Deus in nobis, quoniam cum adhuc peccatores essemus, secundum tempus Christus pro nobis mortuus est' (Rom 5.8), et 'Deus erat in Christo mundum reconcilians sibi' (2 Cor 5.19), et 'Nos ergo diligamus Deum, quoniam Deus prior dilexit nos' (1 Io 4.19), et 'Quae autem maior est causa adventus Domini nisi ut ostenderet Deus dilectionem suam in nobis, commendans eam vehementer?'[9] Sed quis praeter personam divinam hominem factam dilectionem divinam modo humano adaequate ostendere posset?

have loved me' (John 17.23, 17.26). Without such mediation we human beings should have no grounds or reason for receiving adoptive filiation, the indwelling of the Holy Spirit, and the pledge of a divine inheritance, and so be brought to the celestial city of those who look upon the face of God.

Furthermore, infused virtues, the gifts and movements of the Holy Spirit, and the light of glory, since they exceed the proportion of any finite substance, can belong by right only to him who is a divine person operating in an assumed nature. If, therefore, there were no divine person subsisting in a human nature, there would be no exemplar for our being endowed with these absolutely supernatural gifts; but when the Son of God has been given up for our sake, it was, in a way, impossible that all things not be given to us along with him (Romans 8.32).

Again, the order of the universe is a proper effect of God, since every created thing is a secondary agent and instrument that has to be directed and applied and used by God in order that the end ordained by divine wisdom and chosen by the divine will may be attained.[7] But the purpose of the incarnation is not only to restore the order of the universe that has been disrupted and deformed by sin, but also to bring it to the highest perfection, in which all things are gathered up (Ephesians 1.10) and reconciled to God (Colossians 1.20) in Christ. No mere creature is proportionate to this purpose, which requires a divine person subsisting in a human nature.

In addition, God chose to redeem us because he was rich in mercy and loved us immensely (Ephesians 2.4). But also, through manifesting his love in a human way he wanted to convert us to himself,[8] according to the words, 'God shows his love for us in that while we were still sinners, Christ died for us' (Romans 5.8), and 'God was in Christ reconciling the world to himself' (2 Corinthians 5.19), and 'Let us, then, love God, because God has first loved us' (1 John 4.19), and 'What greater reason was there for the Lord's coming if not that God should reveal his love for us, displaying it so forcefully?'[9] But who could adequately manifest divine love in a human way except a divine person made human?

7 [Lonergan added simply 'GO,' a reference to his dissertation on 'gratia operans' and/or the articles based on it that appeared in *Theological Studies* in 1941–42. As was mentioned previously, the dissertation and the series of articles are available now in *Grace and Freedom.*]
8 Thomas Aquinas, *Summa theologiae,* 3, q. 49, a. 1.
9 Augustine, *De catechizandis rudibus,* IV, nos. 7; ML 40, 314.

Praeterea, uti supra habitum est, secundum rationem, legem, mysterium, iustitiam crucis, iniusti et inimici et peccatores ad salutem eramus conducendi. Sed quamvis iustum fuerit per viam crucis nos salvari, quod iustum est iniusti facere nolunt. Quare, ut iniusti ad iustitiam crucis acceptandam commoveremur, salvatorem oportebat iustum nostram crucem suam facere. Sed, 'Vix pro iusto quis moritur' (Rom 5.7). Quis ergo pro iniustis iustus crucem ferret, nisi homo divina caritate repletus? Et quis iure suo divina caritate repleri posset nisi divina persona homo factus?

Praeterea, cum divino consilio oportuerit hominem esse adaequatum salutis principium, illum oportuit hominem suo iure omnia dona gratiae et gloriae merere. Sed tale meritum habere non potuit nisi divina persona homo factus.

Praeterea, quia divino consilio oportebat superabundare gratiam ubi abundavit delictum (Rom 5.20) ut sit ecclesia gloriosa non habens maculam aut rugam aut aliquid huiusmodi sed sancta et immaculata (Eph 5.27), requirebatur homo qui quam perfectissime Dei bonitatem et peccati malitiam cognosceret, et Deum summopere nosque propter Deum diligeret, qui sacerdos esset sanctus, innocens, impollutus, a peccatoribus segregatus, qui se hostiam offerret ad conscientiam emundandam ab operibus mortuis, et qui superabundanter pro omnibus peccatis satisfaceret. Quae omnia facere non potuit homo nisi maximis Dei donis ornatus; neque ullus homo maximis his donis suo iure ornatur nisi divina persona homo factus.

Quibus rationibus multae et aliae addi possunt; sed dictae sufficiant, cum satis demonstrent eum esse incarnationis finem qui in Christo et per Christum perficitur sive relate ad terminum a quo salvamur, sive relate ad modum quo renovamur, sive relate ad terminum in quem producimur.

Obici tamen potest nos potius esse propter Christum quam Christus propter nos. Nam illud est alicuius quod in eum ordinatur tamquam in finem, sicut servus est domini, sed liber est causa sui.[10] Iam vero, 'Omnia enim vestra sunt, vos autem Christi, Christus autem Dei' (1 Cor 3.21–23). Quia ergo Christi sumus, in Christum ordinamur et non e converso, sicut dominus non est servi.

Besides, as we said above, it was according to the meaning, the law, the mystery, and the justice of the cross that we unjust and sinful enemies of God were to be brought to salvation. But although it was just that we be saved through the cross, those who are unjust do not want to do what is just. Therefore, in order that we the unjust might be moved to accept the justice of the cross, it was necessary that a just savior should make our cross his own. And yet, 'Hardly anyone would die even for a good person' (Romans 5.7); what just person, then, would bear the cross for the unjust if not one filled with divine love? And who could in his own right be filled with divine love if not a divine person become man?

Moreover, since according to the divine plan it was necessary that a human being be a sufficient principle of salvation, that human being would have had to merit in his own right the gifts of grace and glory. But only a divine person become human could have such merit.

Again, because the divine plan called for grace to be superabundant where sin had been abundant (Romans 5.20), in order that the church might be glorious and without spot or wrinkle or anything of the kind, but holy and without blemish (Ephesians 5.27), there was required one who would have the fullest possible knowledge of both the goodness of God and the malice of sin, and have the greatest love for God and for us because of God, who would be a holy priest, innocent, undefiled, separated from sinners, offering himself as a victim to purify our conscience from dead works and make superabundant satisfaction for all sins. No human being could do this without being endowed with God's greatest gifts, and no one is so endowed in his own right except a divine person become human.

There are many other reasons that can be adduced here. But let those we have mentioned suffice, since they amply demonstrate that this is the purpose of the incarnation achieved in Christ and through Christ, with respect to the terminus from which we are being saved, the manner in which we are renewed, and the terminus to which we are being brought.

One could object here that it is rather we who exist for Christ rather than he who exists for us. For that which is ordered to someone as to its end belongs to that person, as, for example, a slave belongs to his master, whereas a free man exists for his own sake.[10] Now, 'All things are yours, ... and you belong to Christ, and Christ belongs to God' (1 Corinthians 3.21–23). Since, therefore, we belong to Christ, we are ordered to him and not vice versa, as a master does not belong to his slave.

10 Thomas Aquinas, *Summa theologiae*, 1, q. 21, a. 1, ad 3m.

Respondetur fieri posse alia et alia ratione tum Christum tum nos esse finem. Quatenus enim bene vocamus Iesum Dominum et Magistrum (Io 13.13), nos sumus Christi et Christus est finis. Quatenus autem venit Filius hominis, non ut ministraretur ei sed ut ministraret et daret animam suam redemptionem pro multis (Mc 10.45), egit in bonum nostrum tamquam in finem. Quapropter alibi dicitur Christus esse caput et in omnibus primatum tenens (Col 1.18), et alibi dicitur esse a Patre missus ut eos qui sub lege erant redimeret ut adoptionem filiorum reciperemus (Gal 4.4–5).

Deinde, in Christo homine distinguendum est inter personam divinam et naturam assumptam. Quod vero divina persona ad nos mittitur, duo importat: (1) ipsam divinam relationis originem[11] et (2) terminum ad extra convenientem. Sed secundum primum habetur non propria finis ratio sed tantummodo ille ordo trinitarius Deo intraneus secundum quem Filius a Patre est et Spiritus ab utroque. Quantum autem ad secundum attinet, non subordinatur Filius termino creato sed potius terminus Filio subordinatur; venit enim Filius ad nos ex condescendentia suae bonitatis, neque ad acquirendum sed ad suam bonitatem communicandam, sicut et de Deo creante dicitur (DB 1783). Et similiter ratiocinandum est de missione Spiritus sancti et de ordine inter missionem Filii et missionem Spiritus; quibus manifestatur ordo trinitarius Deo intraneus, et divinae personae suo ordine connexae ordinem universi perficiunt.

Tertio, circa fines quod intendit voluntas Christi humana, alius est finis primarius et alius secundarius. Et finis quidem primarius est ipsa divina bonitas quae propter se ipsam diligitur. Finis autem secundarius est ordo universi restaurandus, secundum quod in Christo omnia instaurantur (Eph 1.10) et reconciliantur (Col 1.20). Et eligitur finis secundarius propter primarium, secundum ordinem caritatis ut Deus super omnia diligatur et quaecumque alia propter Deum. Praeterea, hic finis secundarius eligitur non ut medium sed ut obiectum secundarium ex superabundante dilectione: eligi enim ut medium non potuit, si quidem Christus iam finem suum habuit, neque sui erat redemptor sed nostri; eligi autem ut obiectum secundarium ex superabundante dilectione debuit quia, sicut ipse Deus

We can answer this objection by stating that both Christ and we ourselves are ends, but in different ways. Inasmuch as we quite properly call Christ our Lord and Teacher (John 13.13), we belong to Christ and he is our end. But inasmuch as the Son of man came not to be served but to serve and give his life as a ransom for many (Mark 10.45), the end or purpose of his action was our good. For that reason we read in one passage that Christ is head and has first place in everything (Colossians 1.18), and in another passage that he was sent by the Father to redeem those who were subject to the law so that we might receive adoptive filiation (Galatians 4.4–5).

Second, in the human Christ we must distinguish between the divine person and the assumed human nature. The fact that the divine person is sent to us entails two elements: (1) a divine relation of origin[11] and (2) an appropriate external term. But the first of these includes no notion of end in the proper sense but only that immanent Trinitarian order in God according to which the Son is from the Father and the Holy Spirit from both. As to the second element, the Son is not subordinated to the created term, but vice versa; for the Son came to us out of his condescending goodness, not to gain anything for himself but to communicate his own goodness, as also is said about God in his work of creation (DB 1783, [DS 3002, ND 412]). The same must be said about the sending of the Holy Spirit and of the order between the sending of the Son and the sending of the Spirit; these missions manifest the immanent order of the Trinity, and the divine persons, in their order among themselves, perfect the order of the universe.

Third, with regard to the ends intended by Christ in his human will, one is primary and the other secondary. The primary end is the divine goodness itself, which is loved for its own sake. The secondary end is the restoration of the order of the universe through the gathering up of all things in Christ (Ephesians 1.10) and their reconciliation in him (Colossians 1.20). This secondary end is chosen for the sake of the primary, in accordance with the order of love whereby God is loved above all things and all else loved for the sake of God. Furthermore, this secondary end is chosen not as a means but as a secondary object out of superabundant love. It could not be chosen as a means, since Christ already possessed his end and did not redeem himself but us. It had to be chosen as a secondary object out of superabundant love, because just as God himself wills the order of the universe in this way, so

11 [The autograph typescript reads 'divinam relationis originem'; but this should surely be 'divinam relationem originis.']

hoc modo vult ordinem universi, ita etiam persona divina in natura humana subsistens et modo quodam divino operans velle debuit.

Quarto, circa perfectionem ipsius Christi humanitatis, recolendum est duas esse perfectionis rationes, nempe, et actus et ordinis. Quae quidem duae rationes in una Dei trini realitate uniuntur, sed in creaturis nisi divisim esse non possunt. Quapropter duo et diversa dicuntur esse maxime perfecta in rebus creatis, nempe, et ipse universi ordo[12] et illa Dei imago quae in creatura intellectuali invenitur[13] et eo perfectior est quo magis ad exemplar divinum accedit.[14] Quibus in duobus magis perspicitur ratio ordinis in universo, qui tamen ordo esse non potest sine ordinandis actu exsistentibus; et magis perspicitur ratio actus in imagine Dei, quae tamen imago sine ordine non habetur, si quidem multi sunt actus in uno homine qui et inter se ordinari debent et praeterea modo debito tum ad Deum tum ad reliquas creaturas referri. Quam ob causam, mutuo inter se dependent et ordo universi et imago Dei in creaturis rationalibus; nam deformata imagine, corrumpitur ordo universi; e contra, corrupto ordine universi, iam exsistit illa diaboli potestas seu peccati regnum quo maxime in singulis hominibus impeditur vera et clara Dei imago.

Quibus praemissis, munus Verbi incarnati elucet. Cum enim Verbum proprie imago Dei nominetur,[15] convenientur … [16]

also a divine person subsisting in a human nature and operating in a divine manner had to will it in this way.

Fourth, with regard to the perfection of Christ's humanity, recall here that perfection has two formalities, namely, act and order. These two formalities are one in the one reality that is the triune God, but in creatures they can exist only separately. This is why there are said to be two different realities that are the most perfect in all creation, the order of the universe itself[12] and the image of God present in an intellectual creature,[13] which is all the more perfect the more closely it resembles the divine exemplar.[14] In these two realities the formality of order appears more clearly in the universe, though this order cannot exist apart from the actually existing things that are to be ordered. The formality of act is more clearly to be seen in the image of God, which image, however, does not exist without an order, since there are many acts in one human being that need to be ordered among themselves and also to be related in the right way both to God and to all other creatures. Hence the order of the universe and the image of God in rational creatures are mutually dependent, for when that image is marred, the order of the universe is disrupted. Conversely, with the disruption of the order of the universe, the power of the devil and the reign of sin now exists, strongly preventing the appearance of a true and clear image of God in every human being.

In the light of all the foregoing, the function of the incarnate Word becomes very clear. For since the Word is properly named the image of God,[15] fittingly …[16]

12 Thomas Aquinas, *Summa theologiae,* 1, q. 15, a. 2; q. 47, a. 1.
13 Ibid. 1, q. 93, a. 2, ad 3m.
14 Ibid. a. 8, ad 3m.
15 Ibid. 1, q. 35, a. 2.
16 [At this point the typescript breaks off.]

# Abbreviations

| | |
|---|---|
| AAS | *Acta Apostolicae Sedis* |
| ASS | *Acta Sanctae Sedis* |
| DB | Henricus Denzinger, Karl Rahner, et al. *Enchiridion Symbolorum: definitinum et declarationum de rebus fidei et morum.* 31st ed. Freiburg im Breisgau: Herder, 1960. |
| DBS | Louis Pirot, André Robert, and Henri Cazelles. *Dictionnaire de la Bible: contenant tous les noms de personnes, de lieux, de plantes, d'animaux mentionnés dans les Saintes Écritures, les questions théologiques, archéologiques ...: Supplément.* Paris: Letouzey et Ané, 1928–. |
| DS | Henricus Denzinger and Adolfus Schönmetzer. *Enchiridion Symbolorum: definitinum et declarationum de rebus fidei et morum.* 32nd ed. Freiburg im Breisgau: Herder, 1963 |
| DTC | *Dictionnaire de théologie catholique* |
| ML | *Patrologie cursus completus ... Series Latina.* Ed. Jacques-Paul Migne. 221 vols. Paris: J.P. Migne, 1844–55, 1862–65 |
| ND | Josef Neuner and Jacques Dupuis, eds. *The Christian Faith in the Doctrinal Documents of the Catholic Church.* 7th ed. New York: Alba House, 2001. |
| TDNT | *Theological Dictionary of the New Testament.* Ed. Gerhard Kittel. Trans. and ed. Geoffrey W. Bromiley. Grand Rapids, MI: Wm. B. Eerdmans Publishing Co., 1964–76 |
| TWNT | *Theologisches Wörterbuch zum Neuen Testament.* Ed. Gerhard Kittel, Otto Bauernfeind, and Gerhard Friedrich. Stuttgart: W. Kohlhammer, 1932 |

# Bibliography of Modern Authors


a Conchas, Daniel, '"Redemptio acquisitionis" ad Historiam Exegeseos Eph 1:14b et Loc. Par.' *Verbum Domini* 30 (1952) 14–29, 81–91, 154–69.

Bea, Augustin, et al., eds. *Cor Iesu: Commentationes in Litteras Encyclicas PII PP.* XII *'Haurietis Aquas'*: vol. 1: *Pars Theologica*; vol. 2: *Pars Historica et Pastoralis.* Rome: Herder, 1959.

Bertetto, Domenico. *Gesù redentore: cristologia.* Florence: Libreria Editrice Fiorentina, 1958.

Billot, L. *De Verbo incarnato: Commentarius in tertiam partem S. Thomae,* 7th ed. Rome: Gregorian University Press, 1927.

Bonnefoy, Jean-François. *La Primauté du Christ selon l'écriture et la tradition.* Rome: Herder, 1959. English translation: *Christ and the Cosmos,* ed. and trans. Michael D. Meilach. Paterson, NJ: St Anthony Guild Press, 1965.

Cazelles, Henri. 'Les poèmes du serviteur: leur place, leur structure, leur théologie.' *Recherches de science religieuse* 43 (1955) 5–55.

Cremer, Hermann. 'Der germanische Satisfaktionsbegriff in der Versöhnungslehre.' *Studien und Kritiken* (1893) 316–45.

– 'Die Wurzeln des Anselmischen Satisfaktionsbegriffs.' *Studien und Kritiken* (1880) 7–21.

Crowe, Frederick E. *Christ and History.* Toronto: University of Toronto Press, 2015.

d'Alès, Adhémar. *De Verbo incarnato.* 2nd ed. Paris: Gabriel Beauchesne, 1930.

Deden, D. 'Le "mystère" paulinien.' *Ephemerides theologicae Lovanienses* 13 (1936) 405–42.

Deneffe, August. 'Das Wort *satisfactio.*' *Zeitschrift für katholische Theologie* 43 (1919) 158–75.

Dupont, Jacques. *Gnosis: la connaissance religieuse dans les Épitres de Saint Paul.* Bruges and Paris: Desclée de Brouwer, 1949.

Durrwell, François-Xavier. *La résurrection de Jésus, mystére de salut; étude biblique.* Le Puy and Paris: Xavier Mappus, 1950; 2nd ed., rev. and augm., 1954–55. In English, *The Resurrection: A Biblical Study,* trans. Rosemary Sheed. New York: Sheed and Ward, 1960; 10th ed. of French, 'entièrement refondue,' Paris: Éditions du Cerf, 1976.

Edwards, D.M. *Bannau'r Ffydd.* Wrexham: Hughes & Son, 1929.

Franks, Robert S. *The Atonement.* Oxford: Oxford University Press, 1934.

– *A History of the Doctrine of the Work of Christ in Its Ecclesiastical Development.* 2 vols. London, New York, Toronto: Hodder & Stoughton, 1918.

Galtier, Paul. *De incarnatione ac redemptione.* New ed. Paris: Beauchesne, 1947.

– 'Satisfaction.' DTC XIV (27) 1129–1210.

González Ruiz, José María. '"Muerto por nuestros pecados y resucitado por neustra justificación."' *Biblica* 40 (1959) 837–58.

Heinrichs, Ludwig. *Die Genugtuungstheorie des hl. Anselmus von Canterbury.* Paderborn: Schöningh, 1909.

Hughes, Thomas Hywel. *The Atonement: Modern Theories of the Doctrine.* London: George Allen Unwin, 1949.

Jaspers, Karl. *Basic Philosophical Writings: Selections,* ed. and trans. Edith Ehrlich, Leonard H. Ehrlich, and George B. Pepper. Athens, OH: Ohio University Press, 1986.

– *Vom Ursprung und Ziel der Geschichte.* Munich: R. Piper; Zürich: Artemis-Verlag, 1949; 9th ed., Munich and Zürich: R. Piper, 1988. In English, *The Origin and Goal of History,* trans. Michael Bullock. New Haven: Yale University Press, 1953; 4th ed., 1968; reprint ed., Westport, CT: Greenwood Press, 1976.

– *Von der Wahrheit.* Vol. 1 in *Philosophische Logik.* Munich: R. Piper, 1947.

*Library of Christian Classics.* Vol. 10, *A Scholastic Miscellany: Anselm to Ockham,* ed. and trans. Eugene R. Fairweather. Philadelphia: Westminster, 1956. 284.

Lindblom, Johannes. *The Servant Songs in Deutero-Isaiah: A New Attempt to Solve an Old Problem.* Lund: C.W.K. Gleerup, 1951.

Lonergan, Bernard. *De Deo trino I: Pars dogmatica.* Rome: Gregorian University Press, 1964.

– *De Deo trino II: Pars systematica.* Rome: Gregorian University Press, 1964.

– *Divinarum personarum conceptionem analogicam evolvit Bernardus Lonergan, S.I.* Rome: Gregorian University Press, 1959.

– *De Verbo incarnato.* Rome: Gregorian University Press, 1964.

– *Early Works on Theological Method 1.* Vol. 22 in Collected Works of Bernard Lonergan. Ed. Robert M. Doran and Robert C. Croken. Toronto: University of Toronto Press, 2010.

– *Early Works on Theological Method 3.* Vol. 24 in Collected Works of Bernard Lonergan. Trans. Michael G. Shields, ed. Robert M. Doran and H. Daniel Monsour. Toronto: University of Toronto Press, 2013.

– 'Finality, Love, Marriage.' In *Collection.* Vol. 4 in Collected Works of Bernard Lonergan. Ed. Frederick E. Crowe and Robert M. Doran. Toronto: University of Toronto Press, 1988. 17–52.

– 'God's Knowledge and Will.' In *Early Latin Theology*. Vol. 19 in Collected Works of Bernard Lonergan. Trans. Michael G. Shields, ed. Robert M. Doran and H. Daniel Monsour. Toronto: University of Toronto Press, 2011. 256–411.

– *Grace and Freedom: Operative Grace in the Thought of St Thomas Aquinas*. Vol. 1 in Collected Works of Bernard Lonergan. Ed. Frederick E. Crowe and Robert M. Doran. Toronto: University of Toronto Press, 2000.

– *The Incarnate Word*. Vol. 8 in Collected Works of Bernard Lonergan. Trans. Charles Hefling, ed. Robert M. Doran and Jeremy D. Wilkins. Toronto: University of Toronto Press, 2016.

– *Insight: A Study of Human Understanding*. Vol. 3 in Collected Works of Bernard Lonergan. Ed. Frederick E. Crowe and Robert M. Doran. Toronto: University of Toronto Press, 1992.

– 'The Mediation of Christ in Prayer.' In *Philosophical and Theological Papers 1958–1964*. Vol. 6 in Collected Works of Bernard Lonergan. Ed. Robert C. Croken, Frederick E. Crowe, and Robert M. Doran. Toronto: University of Toronto Press, 1996. 160–82.

– 'On God and Secondary Causes.' In *Collection*. Vol. 4 in Collected Works of Bernard Lonergan. Ed. Frederick E. Crowe and Robert M. Doran. Toronto: University of Toronto Press, 1988. 53–65.

– *The Ontological and Psychological Constitution of Christ*. Vol. 7 in Collected Works of Bernard Lonergan. Trans. Michael G. Shields, ed. Frederick E. Crowe and Robert M. Doran. Toronto: University of Toronto Press, 2002.

– *A Second Collection*. Vol. 13 in Collected Works of Bernard Lonergan. Ed. Robert M. Doran and John D. Dadosky. Toronto: University of Toronto Press, 2016.

– 'St. Thomas' Theory of Operation.' *Theological Studies* 3 (1942) 375–402.

– *Topics in Education*. Vol. 10 in Collected Works of Bernard Lonergan. Ed. Robert M. Doran and Frederick E. Crowe. Toronto: University of Toronto Press, 1993.

– *The Triune God: Doctrines*. Vol. 11 in Collected Works of Bernard Lonergan. Trans. Michael G. Shields, ed. Robert M. Doran and H. Daniel Monsour. Toronto: University of Toronto Press, 2009.

– *The Triune God: Systematics*. Vol. 12 in Collected Works of Bernard Lonergan. Trans. Michael G. Shields, ed. Robert M. Doran and H. Daniel Monsour. Toronto: University of Toronto Press, 2007.

– *Verbum: Word and Idea in Aquinas*. Vol. 2 in Collected Works of Bernard Lonergan. Ed. Frederick E. Crowe and Robert M. Doran. Toronto: University of Toronto Press, 1997.

Lyonnet, Stanislas. 'De "Iustitia Dei" in Epistola ad Romanos 1, 17 et 3, 21–22.' *Verbum Domini* 25 (1947) 23–34.

– 'De "Iustitia Dei" in Epistola ad Romanos 10, 3 et 3, 5.' *Verbum Domini* 25 (1947) 118–21.

– 'De "Iustitia Dei" in Epistola ad Romanos 3, 25–26.' *Verbum Domini* 25 (1947) 129–44, 193–203, 257–63.

– 'De notione emptionis seu acquisitionis.' *Verbum Domini* 36 (1958) 257–69.

– 'De notione redemptionis.' *Verbum Domini* 36 (1958) 129–46.
– 'De notione salutis in Novo Testamento.' *Verbum Domini* 36 (1958) 3–15.
– *De peccato et redemptione.* Vol. 1, *De notione peccati.* Rome: Pontifical Biblical Institute, 1957; vol. 2, *De vocabulario redemptionis.* Rome: Pontifical Biblical Institute, 1960.
– *Exegesis Epistulae ad Romanos, cap. I ad IV.* 3rd ed. rev and augm. Rome: Pontifical Biblical Institute, 1963. 294–96
– *Exegesis epistulae secundae ad Corinthios.* Rome: Pontifical Biblical Institute, 1955–56.
– 'La valeur sotériologique de la résurrection du Christ selon saint Paul.' *Gregorianum* 39 (1958) 295–318
– *Theologia biblica Novi Testamenti: De peccato et redemptione.* Rome: Pontifical Biblical Institute, 1956.
Lyonnet, Stanislas, and Léopold Sabourin. *Sin, Redemption, and Sacrifice: A Biblical and Patristic Study.* Rome: Pontifical Biblical Institute, 1970.
Mersch, Emile. *Le corps mystique du Christ: Études de théologie historique.* 2 vols., 2nd ed., rev., corr., and considerably augm. Paris: Desclée de Brouwer, 1936; 3rd ed., rev. and augm., 1951.
– *The Whole Christ: The Historical Development of the Doctrine of the Mystical Body in Scripture and Tradition.* Trans. John R. Kelly. London: Dennis Dobson, and Milwaukee: Bruce Publishing Co., 1938; reprint Dennis Dobson, 1962.
Monsour, H. Daniel. 'The Halesian *Summa*'s Specification of the Relation between Uncreated and Created Grace within the Speculative Development of Medieval Theology.' Unpublished essay. Toronto, 1999.
Moraldi, Luigi. *Espiazione sacrificale e riti espiatori: nell'ambiente biblico e nell'Antico Testamento.* Rome: Pontifical Biblical Institute, 1956.
– 'Sensus vocis ἱλαστήριον in Rom. 3, 25.' *Verbum Domini* 26 (1948) 257–76.
North, Christopher R. *The Suffering Servant in Deutero-Isaiah: An Historical and Critical Study.* Oxford: Oxford University Press, 1950.
Novel, Charles. *Essai sur le développement de l'idée biblique de rédemption.* [Doctoral] thesis, Faculté de Théologie de Lyon, 1954, mimeographed.
Oakley, Francis, 'The Absolute and Ordained Power of God and the King in the Sixteenth and Seventeenth Centuries: Philosophy, Science, Politics, and Law.' *Journal of the History of Ideas* 59 (1998) 669–90.
Oggioni, Giulio. 'Il mistero della redenzione.' In *Problemi e orientamenti di teologia dommatica,* vol. 2. Milan: Marzorati, 1957. 237–343.
Parente, P. *L'Io di Cristo.* Brescia: Morcelliana, 1951, 1955.
Pesch, C. *Das Sühneleiden unseres göttlichen Erlösers.* Freiburg im Breisgau: Herder, 1916.
Philippe de la Trinité. *La Rédemption par le Sang.* Paris: Libraire Arthème Fayard, 1959.
– *What Is the Redemption?* Trans. Anthony Armstrong. New York: Hawthorn Books, and London: Burns & Oates, 1961.

Pohle, Joseph, *God: The Author of Nature and the Supernatural,* trans. and ed. Arthur Preuss. St Louis: Herder, 1916.

Prat, Ferdinand, *La théologie de S. Paul.* Vol. 2. Paris: Gabriel Beauchesne, Éditeur, 1929.

– *The Theology of Saint Paul.* Vol. 2. Trans. John L. Stoddard from the 10th French edition. Westminster, MD: Newman Bookshop 1952.

Prümm, K. 'Mystères.' DBS VI, 151–225.

– 'Zur Phänomenologie des paulinischen Mysterion und dessen seelischer Aufnahme. Eine Übersicht.' *Biblica* 37 (1956) 135–61.

Rashdall, Hastings. *The Idea of Atonement in Christian Theology.* Bampton Lectures, 1915; London: Macmillan, 1925.

Réville, Albert. *De la rédemption: Études historiques et dogmatiques.* Paris: Joel Cherbuliez, 1859.

Richard, Louis. *Le mystère de la Rédemption.* Tournai: Desclée, 1959. English translation: *The Mystery of the Redemption,* trans. Joseph Horn, with a foreword by Frank B. Norris. Baltimore and Dublin: Helicon Press, 1966.

Ritschl, Albrecht. *The Christian Doctrine of Justification and Reconciliation: The Positive Development of the Doctrine,* trans. and ed. H.R. Mackintosh and A.B. Macaulay. Edinburgh: T.&T. Clark, 1900.

– *Die christliche Lehre von der Rechtfertigung und Versöhnung,* 3 vols. Bonn: A. Marcus, 1870–74.

– *Unterricht in der christlichen Religion.* Bonn: A. Marcus, 1875. There is a more recent German version edited from the first, 1875 edition by Gerhard Ruhbach: Gütersloh: Gütersloher Verlagshaus Gerd Mohn, 1966.

Rivière, Jean 'Chronique d'Apologétique et de Théologie' *Revue du clergé français* 100 (15 Nov. 1919) 277–300.

– *The Doctrine of the Atonement: A Historical Essay.* Vol. 1. Trans. Luigi Cappadelta. London: Kegan Paul, Trench, Trübner & Co., and St Louis, MO: B. Herder, 1909.

– *Le dogme de la Rédemption dans la théologie contemporaine.* Albi: Chanoine Lombard, 1948.

– *Le dogme de la Rédemption: Essai d'étude historique.* Paris: Victor Lecoffre, 1905.

– *Le dogme de la Rédemption: Études critiques et documents.* Louvain: Bureaux de la Revue, 1931.

– *Le dogme de la Rédemption: Etude théologique.* Paris: J. Gabalda, 1914.

– 'Hétérodoxie des Pélagiens en fait de rédemption?' *Revue d'Histoire Ecclésiastique* 41 (1946) 5–43.

– 'Rédemption.' DTC XIII (26) 1912–2004.

Sabatier, Auguste. *The Doctrine of the Atonement and Its Historical Evolution.* New York: Putnam, 1904.

– *Le dogme de l'expiation et son évolution historique.* Paris: Librairie Fischbacher, 1903.

Sabourin, Léopold. *Rédemption sacrificielle: Une enquête exégétique.* Bruges and Paris: Desclée de Brouwer, 1961.

San Pablo, Basilio de. 'Irenismo en soteriología. Un caso típico de relativismo dogmático.' In *Semana Española de Teología, XI, 17–22 Sept., 1951: La encíclica 'Humani generis'*. Madrid: Consejo Superior de Investigaciones Científicas, Instituto 'Francisco Suárez,' 1952. 455–503.

– 'El Doctor Juan Rivière, Teólogo de la Redención.' *Revista Española de Teología* 14 (1954) 79–103.

Schmitt, F.S. 'Anselm v. Canterbury.' *Lexikon für Theologie und Kirche,* I (Freiburg: Herder, 1957) 592–94.

Solano, Jesús. 'Actualidades cristológico-soteriológicas.' *Estudios eclesiásticos* 24 (1950) 43–69.

– *De Verbo incarnato.* Vol. 3 in *Sacrae Theologiae Summa.* 3rd ed. Matriti: Biblioteca de Autores Cristianos, 1956.

– 'El sentido de la muerte redentora de Nuestro Señor Jesucristo y algunas corrientes modernas.' *Estudios eclesiásticos* 20 (1946) 399–414.

Spicq, Ceslaus, 'Médiation – IV: Dans le Nouveau Testament.' DBS V, 1020–83.

Stamm, Johann Jakob. *Erlösen und Vergeben im Alten Testament: Eine begriffsgeschichtliche Untersuchung.* Bern: A. Francke, 1940.

Stanley, David M. 'Ad historiam exegeseos Rom 4, 25.' *Verbum Domini* 29 (1951) 257–74.

– 'The Theme of the Servant of Yahweh in Primitive Christian Soteriology and Its Transposition by St. Paul.' *Catholic Biblical Quarterly* 16 (1954) 385–425.

Stierli, Josef, ed. *Heart of the Saviour: A Symposium on Devotion to the Sacred Heart.* Trans. Paul Andrews. New York: Herder and Herder, 1957.

Swing, Albert Temple. *The Theology of Albrecht Ritschl, Together with Instruction in the Christian Religion.* London and New York: Longmans, Green, 1901.

Vawter, Bruce. 'Resurrection and Redemption.' *Catholic Biblical Quarterly* 15 (1953) 12–23.

Vernet, F. 'Hughes de Saint-Victor.' DTC VII (13) 240–308.

Vogt, E. '"Mysteria" in textibus Qumrān.' *Biblica* 37 (1956) 247–57.

Weis, Earl Augusto. *The Anselmian Tradition in William of Auvergne's De Causis Cur Deus Homo.* Rome: Gregorian University Press, 1958.

Wright, John H. *The Order of the Universe in the Theology of St. Thomas Aquinas.* Rome: Gregorian University Press, 1957.

Xiberta, Bartholomeus M. *Enchiridion de Verbo incarnato, fontes quos ad studia theologica collegit.* Madrid: Consejo Superior de Investigaciones Cientificas, Instituto "Francisco Suárez," 1957.

– *Tractatus de Verbo Incarnato.* Vol. 2: *Soteriologia.* Madrid: Consejo Superior de Investigaciones Científicas, Instituto 'Franciscus Suárez,' 1954.

Zedda, Silvero. *L'adozione a figli di Dio e lo Spirito santo: storia dell'interpretazione e teologia mistica di Gal. 4, 6.* Rome: Pontifical Biblical Institute, 1952.

# Scriptural Passages


1 Corinthians 1.18–31 231, 233
1 Corinthians 1.18–2.16 469
1 Corinthians 1.21 567
1 Corinthians 1.23–24 23, 231, 451, 467, 525, 527
1 Corinthians 1.23–25 247, 459, 467
1 Corinthians 1.26–29 342
1 Corinthians 1.29 367, 387
1 Corinthians 1.29–31 481
1 Corinthians 1.30 25, 29, 35, 57, 231, 419, 429, 467, 565
1 Corinthians 2.7 25, 231, 467
1 Corinthians 2.7–10 469
1 Corinthians 2.8 557
1 Corinthians 2.9 231, 463
1 Corinthians 2.10–16 231, 233, 247, 467, 623
1 Corinthians 2.12–16 459
1 Corinthians 2.16 249
1 Corinthians 3.18–19 469
1 Corinthians 3.21–23 655
1 Corinthians 3.22–23 625
1 Corinthians 4.20 567
1 Corinthians 5.7 57, 429
1 Corinthians 6.9 567
1 Corinthians 6.9–11 567
1 Corinthians 6.11 47, 75, 227, 445
1 Corinthians 6.15–17 465, 489, 617
1 Corinthians 6.15–20 41, 421
1 Corinthians 7.11 77, 623
1 Corinthians 7.22–23 41, 421, 617
1 Corinthians 7.32 451
1 Corinthians 8.11 45, 417, 439
1 Corinthians 9.27 227, 525 n. 61
1 Corinthians 10.21 621
1 Corinthians 11.25 53, 57, 427
1 Corinthians 11.26 227, 416, 417, 539
1 Corinthians 12 617
1 Corinthians 12.12–31 571, 599
1 Corinthians 12.26 625
1 Corinthians 13 571
1 Corinthians 15.3 19, 45, 413, 417, 437, 439
1 Corinthians 15.17 71, 443
1 Corinthians 15.20 463
1 Corinthians 15.20–22 225
1 Corinthians 15.21 365
1 Corinthians 15.21–22 147, 461, 473, 609
1 Corinthians 15.22 235
1 Corinthians 15.26 147

1 Corinthians 15.45 71, 155, 443
1 Corinthians 15.47 325
1 Corinthians 15.49 235, 459 n. 5
1 Corinthians 15.50 567
1 Corinthians 15.52 235
1 Corinthians 15.54 183, 225, 463
1 Corinthians 15.54–55 473
1 John 1.7 57, 431
1 John 2.1 67, 75, 445, 621
1 John 2.2 47, 57, 429
1 John 2.25 569
1 John 3.2 75
1 John 3.5 57, 429
1 John 3.10 545
1 John 3.16 597
1 John 3.21 569, 623
1 John 4.9 467, 531
1 John 4.10 47, 57, 159, 245, 429
1 John 4.17 569, 623
1 John 4.19 159, 653
1 John 4.20 545
1 John 5.14 569, 623
1 Peter 1.2 59, 431, 443
1 Peter 1.18 43
1 Peter 1.18–19 41, 421
1 Peter 1.19 51, 57, 421, 441, 489, 525, 529
1 Peter 2.3–6 571
1 Peter 2.5 75
1 Peter 2.9 33, 491, 571
1 Peter 2.10 571
1 Peter 2.18–24 183
1 Peter 2.18–25 127, 229
1 Peter 2.19–23 525
1 Peter 2.19–24 23, 415, 457, 475, 477, 535
1 Peter 2.22 489, 525, 529
1 Peter 2.22–25 49, 441
1 Peter 2.23 529
1 Peter 2.24 51, 89, 147, 441, 461, 505, 553
1 Peter 2.25 607
1 Peter 3.9 39, 421
1 Peter 3.18 45, 71, 75, 243, 416, 417, 439, 443, 445, 461, 487, 529
1 Peter 4.13 229, 245, 459
1 Peter 5.3 39, 419, 457
1 Peter 5.5 343
1 Peter 5.10 231, 455
1 Thessalonians 1.9–10 567
1 Thessalonians 1.10 529
1 Thessalonians 2.12 567
1 Thessalonians 2.16 531
1 Thessalonians 5.9 529, 565, 571
1 Thessalonians 5.10 45, 417, 439
1 Thessalonians 5.15 39, 421
1 Timothy 1.15 567
1 Timothy 2.4–6 421
1 Timothy 2.5 35, 37, 67 n. 21, 443 n. 27
1 Timothy 2.5–6 37, 41, 621
1 Timothy 2.6 25, 29, 37 n. 9, 45, 439
1 Timothy 3.16 247, 465
2 Corinthians 1.20 569
2 Corinthians 3.18 595
2 Corinthians 4.4 593
2 Corinthians 4.7–14 245, 459 n. 5
2 Corinthians 4.10 245
2 Corinthians 4.17 231
2 Corinthians 5.6 237, 347
2 Corinthians 5.10 377, 611
2 Corinthians 5.14–15 245, 459 n. 5, 461, 597
2 Corinthians 5.15 45, 417, 439, 617
2 Corinthians 5.16 71, 443
2 Corinthians 5.17 363
2 Corinthians 5.18–19 77
2 Corinthians 5.18–20 623
2 Corinthians 5.19 47, 159, 175, 227, 247, 417, 467, 531, 653
2 Corinthians 5.21 51, 183, 243, 441, 487, 489, 525, 529
2 Corinthians 6.3–10 245

2 Corinthians 6.4 533
2 Corinthians 6.6–7 533
2 Corinthians 6.16–18 569, 571
2 Corinthians 7.1 569
2 Corinthians 7.10 543
2 Corinthians 13.4 243, 487
2 Peter 1.4 569
2 Peter 1.11 567
2 Peter 1.16–18 463
2 Peter 2.1 41, 423
2 Peter 2.9 567
2 Peter 3.9–10 569
2 Peter 3.13 569
2 Thessalonians 1.5 567
2 Thessalonians 2.7 471
2 Timothy 1.1 569
2 Timothy 3.12 231
2 Timothy 4.18 567
Acts 1.4 569
Acts 1.6 201, 231, 365, 459
Acts 1.8 231, 459
Acts 1.16 623
Acts 2.1–4 231
Acts 2.17–18 569
Acts 2.21 567
Acts 2.23 19, 67 n. 21, 413, 437
Acts 2.31 69
Acts 2.32–36 519
Acts 2.33 75, 251, 569, 623
Acts 2.34–35 227
Acts 2.37–38 441
Acts 2.38 47, 227, 571
Acts 2.39 569
Acts 3.18 19, 413, 439
Acts 3.19 571
Acts 3.25 481, 569
Acts 4.12 111, 501, 527, 567, 601
Acts 4.25 623
Acts 4.28 19, 413, 437
Acts 5.31 571
Acts 5.32 623
Acts 5.41 231, 245, 459
Acts 7.35 27, 31, 419
Acts 8.32 57, 429
Acts 8.32–36 49, 439
Acts 11.18 571
Acts 13.23 569
Acts 13.32 569
Acts 13.33 71, 443
Acts 14.22 565
Acts 15.10 567
Acts 15.11 567
Acts 15.28 623
Acts 17.27 569, 621
Acts 17.30 571
Acts 20.21 571
Acts 20.28 59, 431, 571, 623
Acts 26.6 569
Acts 26.20 571
Acts 26.28 247, 467
Acts 28.25 623
Colossians 1.12–13 227
Colossians 1.13 23, 77, 263, 473, 491, 529, 567, 615
Colossians 1.14 29, 33, 47, 57, 175, 225, 227, 419, 429, 563, 567
Colossians 1.15 593
Colossians 1.18 217, 441, 493, 599, 625, 657
Colossians 1.18–25 571
Colossians 1.20 57, 217, 429, 521, 623, 627, 653, 657
Colossians 1.20–22 417
Colossians 1.21 451, 567
Colossians 1.22 569, 623
Colossians 1.24 179, 203, 229, 245, 459, 597
Colossians 1.24–29 617
Colossians 1.27–28 247, 467
Colossians 2.2 467
Colossians 2.2–3 247
Colossians 2.12 227, 461
Colossians 2.14 185 & n. 39
Colossians 2.14–15 263

Colossians 2.20 461
Colossians 3.1–4 227
Colossians 3.3 71
Colossians 3.3–4 597
Colossians 3.4 75
Colossians 3.6 529
Colossians 3.9–11 245, 459 n. 5
Colossians 3.10 593
Colossians 3.17 625
Deuteronomy 7.6–10 571
Deuteronomy 7.8 25
Deuteronomy 9.26 25
Deuteronomy 13.5 25
Deuteronomy 14.2 571
Deuteronomy 15.15 25
Deuteronomy 21.8 25
Deuteronomy 21.23 51, 441
Deuteronomy 24.18 25
Deuteronomy 26.18–19 571
Ephesians 1.4 517
Ephesians 1.7 25, 29, 33, 47, 57, 175, 225, 227, 419, 429, 563, 567
Ephesians 1.9 467
Ephesians 1.9–10 247, 267, 363, 467
Ephesians 1.10 201, 441, 565, 615, 627, 653, 657
Ephesians 1.13 569
Ephesians 1.13–14 33, 565
Ephesians 1.14 29, 31, 33, 419, 571, 623
Ephesians 2.3 223, 529, 567
Ephesians 2.4 653
Ephesians 2.4–5 159, 245, 467, 531
Ephesians 2.4–6 473, 597
Ephesians 2.5 567
Ephesians 2.5–8 567
Ephesians 2.11–21 569
Ephesians 2.12 451, 567, 569
Ephesians 2.12–22 617
Ephesians 2.13 57, 429, 621
Ephesians 2.16 417, 623, 625
Ephesians 2.17 621
Ephesians 2.18 625
Ephesians 2.21 267
Ephesians 3.3–4 247
Ephesians 3.6 247, 467, 569
Ephesians 3.10 347, 467, 479, 523
Ephesians 3.12 467, 569, 621
Ephesians 3.16–19 249
Ephesians 4.17–19 569
Ephesians 4.22–24 245, 459 n. 5
Ephesians 4.23–24 593
Ephesians 4.24 615
Ephesians 4.30 29, 31, 33, 419, 565
Ephesians 5.2 45, 57, 175, 183, 227, 423, 429, 439
Ephesians 5.6 529
Ephesians 5.25 45, 155, 423, 439
Ephesians 5.25–26 143
Ephesians 5.25–27 225, 535
Ephesians 5.25–30 245, 489
Ephesians 5.27 655
Ephesians 5.28 607
Ephesians 5.32 465
Ephesians 6.12 263
Exodus 19.5–6 571
Exodus 24.8 53, 425
Exodus 29.18 57
Ezekiel 20.41 57
Galatians 1.4 45, 423, 439
Galatians 2.19–20 245, 459 n. 5
Galatians 2.20 45, 417, 423, 439, 517, 617, 619
Galatians 2.21 567
Galatians 3 183
Galatians 3.8 481
Galatians 3.10 567
Galatians 3.13 41, 51, 423, 441, 567
Galatians 3.13–14 183, 243, 487
Galatians 3.14–22 569
Galatians 3.16–18 481
Galatians 3.19–20 427
Galatians 3.20 35, 53

Galatians 3.23–25 565
Galatians 3.24 325, 365, 615
Galatians 3.26–28 245, 459 n. 5
Galatians 3.27 593
Galatians 3.29 481, 569
Galatians 4.4 201, 227, 243, 365, 487, 551, 565, 615
Galatians 4.4–5 59, 431, 625, 657
Galatians 4.5 41, 423, 529, 567
Galatians 4.5–6 491, 571
Galatians 4.6 75, 445, 623
Galatians 4.19 245, 459 n. 5, 593
Galatians 4.21–31 481
Galatians 4.23 569
Galatians 6.2 129
Genesis 2.17 147, 183, 223, 471, 503
Genesis 3.1–15 261
Genesis 3.19 147, 183, 223, 471, 503
Genesis 4.10 443
Hebrews 1.2–3 55, 427
Hebrews 1.3 57, 429
Hebrews 1.13 427
Hebrews 2.3 57, 429
Hebrews 2.8 427
Hebrews 2.9 45, 65, 225, 227, 417, 435, 439, 273, 491
Hebrews 2.10 55, 63, 177, 239, 243, 417, 427, 433, 435, 487
Hebrews 2.11 243, 487
Hebrews 2.14 55, 61, 183, 243, 263, 417, 427, 435, 461, 465, 473, 487, 551
Hebrews 2.14–15 45, 77, 147, 225
Hebrews 2.15 473, 567
Hebrews 2.17 47, 55, 61, 243, 427, 429 n. 14, 435, 487
Hebrews 2.18 55, 427
Hebrews 3.2–6 55, 427
Hebrews 4.1 569
Hebrews 4.15 55, 61, 243, 427, 435, 489, 525, 529
Hebrews 4.16 569, 621
Hebrews 5.1–2 53
Hebrews 5.2 55, 427
Hebrews 5.3 55, 427
Hebrews 5.4–6 55, 427
Hebrews 5.7 243, 487
Hebrews 5.8 19, 63, 177, 239, 243, 413, 435, 487
Hebrews 5.8–9 39, 55, 417, 427, 433
Hebrews 5.9 35, 179, 205, 237, 251, 525, 527, 601
Hebrews 5.9–10 445
Hebrews 6.12–20 569
Hebrews 6.20 69, 73, 443
Hebrews 7.1–14 427
Hebrews 7.3 55, 427
Hebrews 7.6 569
Hebrews 7.8 73, 443
Hebrews 7.11 55, 427
Hebrews 7.16 55, 73, 427, 443
Hebrews 7.17 55, 427
Hebrews 7.18–19 55, 427
Hebrews 7.19 73, 445, 569
Hebrews 7.20 55, 427
Hebrews 7.21 55, 427, 621
Hebrews 7.22 53, 55, 57, 155, 427, 443 n. 27, 621
Hebrews 7.23 55, 427
Hebrews 7.24 55, 69, 73, 427, 445, 621
Hebrews 7.24–25 601
Hebrews 7.24–28 69
Hebrews 7.25 67, 75, 445, 569, 621, 623
Hebrews 7.26 55, 427
Hebrews 7.26–27 489, 525, 529
Hebrews 7.27 55, 131, 427, 429
Hebrews 7.28 55, 69, 73, 427, 443
Hebrews 8.1–2 73, 443, 621
Hebrews 8.6 35, 53, 57, 73, 427, 443 & n. 27, 569, 621
Hebrews 8.8–12 27, 35, 53, 425, 571
Hebrews 8.12 429 n. 14

Hebrews 9.5–14 429 n. 14
Hebrews 9.6–7 55, 427
Hebrews 9.9 55, 429, 569
Hebrews 9.9–14 177
Hebrews 9.10 55, 429
Hebrews 9.12 25, 29, 31, 73, 243, 419, 443, 487, 563
Hebrews 9.13 55, 429
Hebrews 9.14 55, 73, 429, 443, 569
Hebrews 9.15 25, 29, 33, 35, 53, 55, 57, 417, 419, 427, 429, 443 n. 27, 569, 621
Hebrews 9.19–21 53, 425
Hebrews 9.22 45, 139, 623
Hebrews 9.24 69, 73, 443, 621
Hebrews 9.24–26 55, 427
Hebrews 9.25 55, 427
Hebrews 9.26 55, 429
Hebrews 9.28 57, 429, 487
Hebrews 10.1 55, 429, 621
Hebrews 10.1–2 55, 429
Hebrews 10.1–4 177
Hebrews 10.4 55, 429, 569
Hebrews 10.5 61, 435, 551
Hebrews 10.5–7 19, 55, 61, 429, 433
Hebrews 10.5–10 65
Hebrews 10.10 55, 429, 433
Hebrews 10.10–14 177
Hebrews 10.11 55, 429
Hebrews 10.12 57, 429, 621
Hebrews 10.14 57, 177, 621
Hebrews 10.17 89
Hebrews 10.17–18 57, 429
Hebrews 10.18 47
Hebrews 10.19 569
Hebrews 10.22 569, 623
Hebrews 10.23 569
Hebrews 10.36–37 569
Hebrews 11.9 569
Hebrews 11.11 569
Hebrews 11.13–17 569
Hebrews 11.35 25, 27
Hebrews 12.2 39, 421
Hebrews 12.22 623
Hebrews 12.22–24 571
Hebrews 12.24 35, 53, 57, 59, 74, 427, 431, 443 & n. 27
Hebrews 12.26 569
Hebrews 13.12 57, 429
Hosea 1.6–9 571
Hosea 2.1 571
Hosea 2.23 571
Hosea 13.9 23, 261, 521
Isaiah 6.1–5 27
Isaiah 6.2–3 261
Isaiah 6.9–10 247, 467
Isaiah 40.1–5 27
Isaiah 42.1–7 27
Isaiah 43.1 25, 27
Isaiah 43.3–4 27
Isaiah 43.14 25
Isaiah 43.20–21 571
Isaiah 44.22 27
Isaiah 45.1 27
Isaiah 45.4–5 27
Isaiah 49.1–6 27
Isaiah 50.1 27
Isaiah 50.4–9 27
Isaiah 52.3 27
Isaiah 52.13–53.12 27
Isaiah 53.4 543
Isaiah 53.4–12 49, 439, 543
Isaiah 53.5 49, 439
Isaiah 53.6 49, 439
Isaiah 53.7 49, 51, 57, 429, 439
Isaiah 53.8 49, 439
Isaiah 53.9 49, 439
Isaiah 53.10 49, 439
Isaiah 53.11 39, 49, 421, 439
Isaiah 53.12 49, 439
Isaiah 54.5–8 27
Isaiah 55.3–8 27
Isaiah 55.9 381
James 1.12 569

James 2.5 569
James 2.10 567
James 4.6 343
James 4.8 569, 621
Jeremiah 31.7–11 25
Jeremiah 31.31–34 27, 53, 427
Jeremiah 31.34 57 n. 16, 429
John 1.9 17, 413
John 1.9–10 377
John 1.11 365
John 1.13 571
John 1.14 61, 243, 435, 487, 551
John 1.17 529
John 1.29 47, 51, 57, 429, 441
John 3.5 445
John 3.17 567
John 3.17–21 277
John 3.19–21 17, 413
John 3.20 637
John 3.36 529
John 4.23–24 493
John 4.34 59, 431
John 5.16–18 17, 413 n. 3
John 5.18 413 n. 3
John 5.30 59, 431
John 5.36–46 17, 413
John 6.38 59, 431
John 6.44 641
John 6.44–45 19, 413
John 6.52–53 17, 413 n. 3
John 6.57 621
John 6.60 17, 413 n. 3
John 6.62–63 443
John 6.62–64 71
John 6.65 19, 413
John 6.66 17, 413 n. 3
John 6.70 17, 413 n. 3
John 7.7 17, 413, 637
John 7.12–13 17, 413 n. 3
John 7.16–18 59, 431
John 7.20 17, 413 n. 3
John 7.31–32 17, 413 n. 3
John 7.39 75, 445
John 7.45–49 17, 413 n. 3
John 7.51–52 17. 413 n. 3
John 8.12 17, 413
John 8.28 59, 431
John 8.29 59, 431
John 8.37 17, 413, 459
John 8.37–47 19, 413
John 8.44 261, 517
John 8.47 459
John 8.48–59 17, 413 n. 3
John 8.59 413 n. 3
John 9.16 17, 413 n. 3
John 9.22 17, 413 n. 3
John 9.30–34 17, 413 n. 3
John 9.41 19, 413
John 10.9 567
John 10.11 39, 419, 607
John 10.15 39, 419
John 10.17 17, 63, 69, 225, 419
John 10.17–18 59, 431, 435, 459, 467, 517
John 10.18 19, 69, 227, 413, 461
John 10.19–21 17, 413 n. 3
John 10.31 17, 413 n. 3
John 10.39 17, 413 n. 3
John 11.46–53 17, 413 n. 3
John 11.49–50 463
John 11.51–52 417, 607
John 11.52 441
John 11.56 17, 413 n. 3
John 12.19 17, 413 n. 3
John 12.24–25 229, 457
John 12.27 63, 435
John 12.31 517
John 12.32 245, 489, 619, 641
John 12.39–40 413
John 12.39–41 19
John 12.40 247, 467
John 12.42–43 17, 413 n. 3
John 12.46–48 377
John 12.47 567

John 12.49 59, 431
John 13.2 263, 517
John 13.13 657
John 13.27 263
John 14.6 641
John 14.17 231, 251
John 14.21 639
John 14.23 639
John 14.24 59, 431
John 14.26 569
John 14.30 131, 517
John 15.1–6 251
John 15.5 601, 621
John 15.10 59, 61, 431
John 15.12 571
John 15.12–13 535
John 15.13 63, 245, 489, 545, 553, 641
John 15.18–19 231
John 15.24–25 19
John 15.26 251, 569
John 16.7 75, 445, 623
John 16.11 517
John 16.13 251, 569, 623
John 16.27 251, 639
John 17.1–5 75, 45
John 17.5 445
John 17.6–19 445
John 17.10 489
John 17.11–12 75, 445
John 17.12 607
John 17.14 459
John 17.19 57, 75, 445
John 17.20 445
John 17.21–22 445
John 17.22 445
Jonn 17.23 251, 445, 465, 485, 595, 625, 639, 653
John 17.24 445
John 17.26 251, 445, 465, 485, 595, 625, 639, 653
John 18.36 565
John 18.37 17
John 18.37–38 463
John 19.11 19, 181, 413
John 19.30 61, 431
John 20.22–23 75, 445
John 20.23 47
Lamentations 1.12 547
Luke 1.37 479
Luke 1.68 25, 29, 31, 419
Luke 1.68–79 31, 563
Luke 2.32 563
Luke 2.38 25, 28, 31, 419, 563
Luke 6.38 221, 455
Luke 7.47 123
Luke 9.23 229, 338, 339
Luke 9.24 229
Luke 11.11 39, 421
Luke 12.50 63, 435
Luke 17.3–4 123
Luke 19.10 235, 567
Luke 21.23 531
Luke 21.28 25, 29, 31, 419, 565
Luke 22.3 263
Luke 22.15 63, 435
Luke 22.20 53, 57, 427
Luke 22.37 49, 441
Luke 22.53 23, 45, 183, 261, 517
Luke 23.34 49
Luke 24.21 25, 29, 31, 201, 231, 419, 459, 563
Luke 24.25 245, 489
Luke 24.26 19, 49, 51, 413, 437, 441
Luke 24.45–46 51
Luke 24.46 19, 49, 51, 413, 437, 441
Luke 24.49 569
Malachi 3.17 571
Mark 1.10 465
Mark 1.10–11 595, 651
Mark 1.11 463
Mark 1.14–15 565
Mark 1.15 201, 441, 571, 615
Mark 4.11 565

Mark 4.11–12 247, 467
Mark 4.26–29 565
Mark 8.34 229, 237, 475
Mark 8.34–35 457, 535
Mark 8.35 229
Mark 8.37 41, 421, 425
Mark 9.1 565
Mark 9.2–10 463
Mark 9.7 465
Mark 9.12 19, 51, 413, 441
Mark 9.31 19, 51, 413, 441
Mark 9.47 565
Mark 10.14 565
Mark 10.18 343, 495, 645
Mark 10.23 565
Mark 10.33–34 19, 51, 413, 441
Mark 10.42–45 229, 457, 477, 485, 535
Mark 10.45 25, 29, 37 & n. 9, 39, 41, 45, 51, 67 n. 21, 201, 227, 419, 439, 441, 475, 625, 657
Mark 11.25–26 123
Mark 12.34 565
Mark 14.21 17, 411
Mark 14.24 53, 57, 427
Mark 14.25 565
Mark 14.34 63, 435, 547
Mark 14.36 19, 31, 413, 433, 437, 545, 553
Mark 14.38 433
Mark 14.43 17, 411
Mark 14.55–64 17, 411
Mark 15.11 497
Mark 15.11–14 17, 411
Mark 15.15 17
Mark 15.16 17, 411
Mark 15.21–24 17, 411
Mark 15.28 49, 441, 531
Mark 15.29–31 17, 411
Mark 15.31 411
Mark 15.43 565
Matthew 1.21 567
Matthew 2.22 39, 421
Matthew 3.7 531
Matthew 5.10–12 23, 415
Matthew 5.11–12 229
Matthew 5.23–26 123
Matthew 5.28–48 229
Matthew 5.29–30 523 n. 59
Matthew 5.38 39, 117, 421
Matthew 5.38–48 23, 127, 415, 455, 475, 535
Matthew 6.12 89, 123, 177
Matthew 6.13 567
Matthew 6.14–15 123
Matthew 6.23 451, 453
Matthew 6.24 337
Matthew 6.30–32 379
Matthew 6.33 299, 367, 613
Matthew 7.7–11 379
Matthew 7.11 491
Matthew 7.16 251
Matthew 7.17–18 463
Matthew 7.18 249
Matthew 8.17 49, 439
Matthew 10.6 49, 439
Matthew 10.22 567
Matthew 10.28 523 n. 59
Matthew 11.29 201
Matthew 13.31 365
Matthew 13.43 565
Matthew 16.13 567
Matthew 16.23 241
Matthew 16.24 203, 229
Matthew 16.25 229, 567
Matthew 16.26 41, 421, 425
Matthew 17.27 39, 421
Matthew 18.21–35 123, 127
Matthew 18.35 127
Matthew 20.25–28 229, 457
Matthew 20.28 25, 29, 39, 41, 45, 67 n. 21, 227, 419, 439
Matthew 25.31–46 611
Matthew 25.40 377

Matthew 25.41 317, 523 n. 59
Matthew 25.45 377
Matthew 26.28 47, 53, 57, 427
Matthew 26.31 607
Matthew 26.38–44 227
Matthew 26.39 413
Matthew 26.39–44 63
Matthew 26.45–27.50 207
Matthew 26.53 467, 589
Matthew 26.53–54 51, 63, 435, 437, 441, 517
Matthew 26.54 19
Matthew 27.24 531
Matthew 27.46 517
Philippians 1.21 225, 473, 617
Philippians 2.3 457
Philippians 2.6 243
Philippians 2.6–8 229
Philippians 2.7 243, 487
Philippians 2.7–8 457
Philippians 2.7–11 417
Philippians 2.8 19, 61, 65, 381, 413, 433
Philippians 2.8–9 227, 491
Philippians 2.8–11 69
Philippians 2.9 65, 225, 227, 435, 473
Philippians 2.12 19, 71
Philippians 3.8 421
Philippians 3.9–11 229
Philippians 3.10–11 245, 459
Philippians 3.13–14 565
Philippians 3.18 233, 463
Philippians 3.19 233
Philippians 3.20–21 229, 459 n. 5, 461, 595
Proverbs 3.34 343
Psalm 21 [EVV 22] 27
Psalm 21.1 [EVV 22.1] 543
Psalm 39.7 [EVV 40.6] 57, 61, 429
Psalm 50.6 [EVV 51.4] 27
Psalm 73.2 [EVV 74.2] 25
Psalm 76.16 [EVV 77.16] 25
Psalm 77.35 [EVV 78.35] 25
Psalm 78.13[EVV 79.13] 571
Psalm 142.2 [EVV 143.2] 481
Revelation 1.5 57, 429
Revelation 5.6–12 621
Revelation 5.9 41, 57, 423, 429
Revelation 6.16–17 531
Revelation 7.14 51, 57, 429, 441
Revelation 11.18 529
Revelation 12.11 51, 59, 431, 441
Revelation 13.8 621
Revelation 14.3 41, 423
Revelation 14.4 41, 423
Revelation 14.10 529
Revelation 14.15–20 531
Revelation 16.19 529
Revelation 19.15 531
Romans 1.3 243, 487, 551
Romans 1.4 71, 73, 443
Romans 1.16 567
Romans 1.16–17 571
Romans 1.18 529
Romans 1.18–32 473, 615
Romans 1.18–3.20 137, 161, 323, 460, 461, 481, 567
Romans 1.21–22 341
Romans 1.28–31 341
Romans 1.32 17, 411
Romans 2.4–9 473
Romans 2.5 529
Romans 2.6 377
Romans 2.8 529
Romans 2.24 163
Romans 3.5 529
Romans 3.20 325, 481, 567
Romans 3.21 137
Romans 3.21–22 481
Romans 3.21–26 103
Romans 3.21–28 481
Romans 3.22 571
Romans 3.24 25, 29, 35, 227, 565
Romans 3.24–25 419

Romans 3.25 47, 57, 429, 571
Romans 3.25–26 247, 467, 481, 569
Romans 3.26 161, 185, 565
Romans 3.27–28 571
Romans 3.28 227
Romans 3.30 571
Romans 4.13–20 569
Romans 4.15 529
Romans 4.20–21 481
Romans 4.21 569
Romans 4.25 45, 49, 69, 71, 183, 225, 423, 439, 441, 443
Romans 5.1 227
Romans 5.1–2 467, 569, 571
Romans 5.2 621
Romans 5.5 251
Romans 5.6 45, 417, 439
Romans 5.6–8 47
Romans 5.7 655
Romans 5.8 45, 159, 247, 417, 439, 467, 531, 567, 653
Romans 5.8–10 467
Romans 5.9 57, 429, 529, 567
Romans 5.10 175, 225, 227, 473, 517, 567
Romans 5.10–11 77, 417, 623
Romans 5.12 147, 183, 223, 461, 471, 473, 503
Romans 5.12–21 225, 235, 609
Romans 5.15 17
Romans 5.19 19, 61, 65, 227, 413, 433, 435, 491
Romans 5.20 179, 337, 557, 567, 641, 655
Romans 5.21 327, 461
Romans 6.3 417, 539
Romans 6.4 227, 461, 465
Romans 6.5 231
Romans 6.6 243, 487
Romans 6.9 67 n. 21
Romans 6.9–11 243, 487
Romans 6.11 227
Romans 6.12–23 231
Romans 6.16 461
Romans 6.21 471
Romans 6.21–23 223
Romans 6.23 147, 183, 471, 503
Romans 7.4–25 460, 461
Romans 7.14 567
Romans 7.14–24 223
Romans 7.22–23 337, 567
Romans 7.23 337
Romans 7.24 567
Romans 8.1 227
Romans 8.2 567
Romans 8.3 51, 89, 227, 243, 441, 487, 537
Romans 8.3–4 59, 195, 431
Romans 8.5–17 231
Romans 8.6 461
Romans 8.11 227, 597
Romans 8.13 227, 461
Romans 8.15 75, 445, 623
Romans 8.15–16 571
Romans 8.17 203, 229, 245, 459, 597
Romans 8.17–18 231, 465
Romans 8.23 25, 29, 31, 419, 565, 567
Romans 8.24 31, 567
Romans 8.28 203, 221, 231, 343, 455, 519
Romans 8.29 71, 203, 229, 245, 459, 465, 593
Romans 8.32 23, 45, 47, 49, 249, 423, 439, 467, 485, 517, 531, 571, 653
Romans 8.34 67, 75, 445, 621
Romans 8.35–39 245, 459 n. 5
Romans 9.3–4 487
Romans 9.4–5 243
Romans 9.5–8 569
Romans 9.21 149, 505
Romans 9.22 529

Romans 9.25–26 571
Romans 9.30 571
Romans 10.9 567, 571
Romans 10.13 567
Romans 11.15 77
Romans 11.17 251
Romans 11.25–32 247, 467
Romans 11.33 385, 469
Romans 11.33–36 249, 403
Romans 12.2 459 n. 5, 593
Romans 12.5 571, 599, 617, 621
Romans 12.17 39, 421
Romans 12.21 235, 239, 449
Romans 13.13–14 459 n. 5
Romans 13.14 593
Romans 14.7–9 461
Romans 14.8 617
Romans 14.9 417
Romans 14.15 35, 417, 439
Romans 14.17 567
Romans 15.8 569
Romans 15.8–9 407 n. 53
Romans 16.25–26 247, 465
Romans 16.27 493, 521
Sirach 15.14 367
Titus 1.2 569
Titus 2.14 25, 29, 33, 45, 67 n. 21, 225, 419, 423, 439, 565, 567, 571
Titus 3.5 445
Wisdom 2.24 147, 183, 223, 261, 471, 503
Wisdom 8.1 407

# Index


Abelard, Peter, 11, 77, 209
Aberration: cultural a., 297, 311–17; and transposition of symbolic apprehension, 171
A Conchas, Daniel, 33, 45, 419 n. 8, 421 n. 10
Action and passion: and death of Christ, 19, 181 & n. 37, 475
*Actus humanus* and *actus hominis*, 549 & n. 84
Agent(s): of economy of salvation, 223; a. through nature and a. through intellect compared, 573, 575; God as historical a., 581; historical a., 581–87; social a., 577–81. *See also* Cause(s)
Alexander IV, Pope, 145 n. 28
Alexander of Hales, 145 & n. 27. *See also* John of Rupella
Alienation: and cultural aberration, 311–17; and evil, 315; from God, 327, 343; and sin, 315, 325
Ambrose, 37
Analogy: and God, 269, 347, 349, 389, 403, 425, 469, 471, 475; inadequacy of, 405; sacramental a. for understanding satisfaction, 79, 95, 185–91, 495, 507, 537–43
Anselm, 15, 87 & n. 7, 91, 93, 107–9, 111, 113, 121, 137, 143, 145, 147, 149, 151, 153, 163 & n. 35, 173, 175, 185 & n. 40, 193, 195, 207, 209, 215, 495, 497, 499 & nn. 3–10, 501 & n. 12, 505, 511, 515, 519 n. 53, 527, 537, 539
Anthropomorphism, 381, 383, 387, 391, 405
Aristotle, 85 n. 6, 129, 133, 135, 181, 219, 241, 253, 279 n. 8, 311 n. 22, 325 n. 29, 359 n. 24, 489 n. 28
Arminius, Jacob, 97, 509
Athanasius, 37
Atonement: pagan and OT meaning of a. contrasted, 47; sacrifice of, 47, 57, 247, 429, 467, 569, 609. *See also* Propitiation
Augustine, 37, 107, 111, 135, 147, 151, 153, 159, 201, 241, 243, 245, 249, 287 n. 15, 309, 311 n. 21, 381 & n. 36, 387 n. 44, 479 & n. 20, 483 n. 22, 485 n. 24, 487 n. 26, 489 & n. 29, 493 n. 34, 499, 501 n. 12,

505, 515, 517 & n. 51, 521 & n. 54, 533 n. 66, 543 & n. 79, 597 n. 17, 603, 619 & n. 28, 641 n. 37, 653 n. 9
Authenticity: as philosophical topic, 325
Axial period (Jaspers), 321 & n. 27, 615

Bañez, D., 359 n. 24, 583
Bea, Augustin, 129 & n. 24
Bellarmine, Robert, 99, 181, 511
Bertetto, Domenico, 5
Billot, L., 99 & n. 9
Blood of Christ: and redemption as mediation, 5, 29, 33, 53–59
Bonaventure, 99, 181, 511
Bonnefoy, Jean-François, 215 & n. 6
Bossuet, Jacques-Bénigne, 101
Bourdaloue, Louis, 101
Brutality: and cruelty, 105 & n. 15, 151, 507; and savagery, 123

Caiaphas, 463
Cajetan, 209
Calvin, Jean, 13, 95, 97, 99, 163, 509, 529
Causality: efficient c., 77, 599; efficient c. of Christ, 213, 447, 597, 599, 609, 611; exemplary c., 599, 603; historical c., 17, 19; and human cooperation, 573; and intelligible dependence, 573, 597, 599; and intentionality, 575; and necessity, 573; c. of sacraments, 95; and symbolic mentality, 169
Cause(s): actual c., 577, 579, 581, 651; agent (efficient) c., 223, 259, 573; antecedent moving c., 437; Aristotle's four c. and salvation, 219–23; conserving c., 581; destructive c., 581; efficient c., 599, 601; exemplar c., 237, 259, 593, 637; extrinsic c., 257, 259, 399, 631; and fate, 349; final c., 219–21, 259, 573, 631; form as c., 221–23; God as first c. of restoration, 143; and historical agent, 581; and influence, 571, 573; intrinsic c., 257, 259, 573, 631; matter as c., 219–21; originating c., 581; principal and instrumental c., 73; principle of c. and why God became man, 633, 635–37; proportionate c., 307, 309, 357, 363, 577, 579, 581, 651; proximate c., 411; restorative c., 581; secondary c., 17, 19, 359, 363, 365, 367, 583, 633, 651; c. of sin, 257–63, 521. *See also* Agent(s)
Cazelles, Henri, 51, 439 n. 23
Charity: diffusion of c., 635; and law of the cross, 205, 241; and love of enemies, 635; and redemption as end, 31; and satisfaction, 129, 131, 151; and sorrow, 81; and wisdom, 221, 241, 247
Chastisement: system of, 103; distinction of c., expiation, reparation (Rivière), 101, 115, 511, 513; and condemnation, 115, 117, 137, 141, 157, 161
Christ: action/agency of C. in general as God and as man, 587–93; and atoning sacrifice, 27–28; and axial period, 361; cause of grace, 207; cause of redemption, 237, 251, 255; death of, *see* Death of Christ; C. a divine person subsisting in a human nature, 37, 79, 131, 631, 637, 651, 653, 659; effect of C.'s historical work threefold, 611; effect directly and indirectly intended by, 611–15; efficient causality of C. in two modes, 609–11; as exemplar, 477, 593–99, 603, 609, 651; and fault, 153–55; freedom of, 343–47; as greatest historical agent, 587;

as head, 71, 141, 143, 153, 155, 157, 161, 199, 203, 205, 221, 225, 227, 235, 237, 251, 255, 485, 491, 535, 555, 561, 593, 599–609, 615, 625, 627, 629, 641, 651, 657; as historical agent, 609–21; historical work of distinguished by effect and way, 611, 615; and human good of order, 611; impeccability of, 133, 165, 223, 525, 533, 589, 591; and Isaian servant, 27, 39, 49, 51, 421, 439 & n. 23; as last Adam, 155, 203, 225; as light, 17, 377, 413; as mediator, 5, 15, 35, 37, 41, 53, 55, 57, 111, 227, 235, 237, 427, 429, 435 n. 21, 441, 443, 481, 485, 487, 501, 545, 571, 593, 621–25, 649, 651; as ministerial instrument, 591; as most historical agent, 587, 613; obedience of, *see* Obedience of Christ; as priest, 5, 7, 53–59, 67, 69, 71, 73, 75, 235, 427, 429, 443, 445, 463, 489, 491, 641, 651, 655; as priest and victim, 7, 49, 53, 57, 65, 429, 437, 523, 601, 609, 651; punished according to God's justice but not according to God's retributive justice, 99, 103, 105, 143, 161, 163, 165, 167, 189; and redemption as mediation, *see* Redemption: r. as mediation and ... ; as restorative historical agent, 615; as total historical agent, 613; vicarious satisfaction of, 109, 127–33, 153, 491, 533, 555; vicarious suffering of, *see* Vicarious suffering: of Christ; as victim, 7, 49, 53, 57, 59, 175, 429, 437, 441, 477, 523, 555, 609, 621, 651, 655; whole C. as supreme good, 199; and two operations ordered through command and obedience, 59, 431, 587; has two principles of action, 587

'Christus Victor Mortis,' 69, 183, 443 n. 26

Clement VI, Pope, 113, 179, 503, 555

Clement VIII, Pope, 13

Coherence: problem of c. and doctrine of satisfaction, 153–67

Communication: and expression, 551; of God's friendship, 631; goods by c., 199, 221, 269 n. 2, 645, 647; and signs, 293

Concreteness: principle of, 289, 293, 295

Condemnation: punishment after c., 117, 137, 141, 157, 161; of a sin and of a person, 535, 537

Conformation: degrees of, 291; and law of the cross, 455, 459, 461 n. 6; principle of, 289, 291, 293

Contexts for paying penalty for sin: two c., 85, 87, 155–57. *See also* Fault-offense-punishment; Satisfaction-pardon-remission of punishment

Contingent predication, 391, 407 n. 51.

Continuity: principle of c. and why God became man, 633, 635, 639

Conversion: and alienation, 313; and God's will, 179; and good from evil, 317, 453, 481; and signs, 293; of will, 121, 591

Cooperation: and human causality, 549, 573; and particular goods/good of order, 275, 277

Covenant: and blood of Christ, 53, 249; as foundation of sacrifice, 53, 249; old and new c., 53–57, 425–31

Cremer, Hermann, 185 & n. 40

Cross: c. of Christ and c. of followers, 205, 237–41, 475, 477; c. of Christ is our c., 239, 241, 489; and death, 225–31; divine aspect of, 477; enemies of, 233, 463; as fact, precept, and example, 449; fruits of, 463,

465; and God's intention and salvific activity, 481; and God's wisdom, goodness, freedom, and justice, 479; intellectual aspect of, 475; justice of, 479–93, 527, 531, 535, 537, 541; law of, *see* Law of the cross; meaning of c. and justice, 453, 455; meaning of c. pervasive, 459–63; meaning, law, mystery, justice of, 493, 519, 521, 525, 527, 651, 655; mystery of, *see* Mystery: of cross/law of cross; providential aspect of, 477; and resurrection, 463, 465; as revelation of God, 477; as symbol, 473, 475; twofold morality of, *see* Action and passion; volitional aspect of, 475. *See also* Divine wisdom: and cross; Transformation: of evil into good

Crowe, Frederick, 563 n. 1

Culture: primitive and higher c., 275, 281–89

Cyril of Alexandria, 37

d'Alès, A., 101 & n. 12, 111 & n. 18, 467 n. 8, 501 n. 12, 515 n. 46, 539 n. 68

Death: and cross, 225–31; and punishment/penalty for sin, 147, 183, 223, 471, 473, 503, 505, 515, 523, 527; as source of salvation, 183, 225–31, 473; transformation of, 183, 203, 225–31

Death of Christ: and action/passion, 19, 181 & n. 37, 475; commonly acknowledged aspects of, 16–25; and culpable evil, 21, 23, 45, 181, 203, 491; as example, 23, 97, 183, 203, 229, 235, 415, 449, 455, 457, 477, 509, 535; historical causality of, 17; immanent effects of, 417; near inevitability of, 17; and payment of price, 33, 39–45, 419–25; and plan, foreknowledge, intention of God, 19, 49, 247, 413, 437, 439, 467, 469, 475, 477, 497, 523, 545, 553; proximate causes of, 411; and punishment for sin, 51, 89, 91, 103, 105, 117, 133, 147, 149, 151, 153, 163, 165, 167, 189, 203, 237, 239, 501, 507, 515–37 passim (*see also* Contexts; 'Either satisfaction or punishment'; 'Either pardon or punishment'; Fault-offense-punishment; Punishment; Satisfaction-pardon-remission of punishment); and secondary causes, 17, 19; as source/means of salvation, 183, 203, 237, 441, 473; and transformation, *see* Transformation; universal effect of, 227, 417; as voluntary, 19, 125, 127, 181, 225, 415

Decline, 313, 317, 327, 367

Deden, D., 247, 469 n. 9

Deneffe, A., 115, 127

Dependence: intelligible d. and causality, 573, 597, 599

Desire(s): four natural d., 281, 283, 311, 613; intellectual d./pure d. to know, 285, 329; natural d. to see God, 613; and particular good, 271

Detestation: defined, 79; Christ's d. of sin and satisfaction, 191, 195, 535, 537, 547, 555, 557

Devil: and justice, 483; and ransom, 43, 45, 167, 425, 499; role of in passion, 183, 263, 517, 519

d'Hulst, Maurice Le Sage d'Hautroche, 101

Divine goodness: communication of, 645, 649; and d. justice, 157, 359, 407; and d. wisdom, 21, 63, 133, 157, 197, 201, 205, 241, 259, 273, 295, 317, 343, 359, 361, 367, 379, 381, 385, 403, 407, 477, 479, 491,

559, 583, 587, 591, 627, 633; and end of creation/ultimate end, 295, 361, 363, 367, 379, 627; and good by essence, 645; and order of universe, 253, 275, 627, 629, 631, 647, 657; and permitting evil, 481, 491; our sharing in, 299

Divine justice, 133–39, 347–409 passim; as applied to human affairs, 365–69; and cross, 409, 449, 453, 469, 479–93 (*see also* Cross: justice of); and d. goodness, 157, 359, 407; and d. goodness, d. generosity, and d. mercy, 407; and d. providence, 157; and d. wisdom, 119, 133, 135, 137, 139, 143, 157, 205, 347, 351, 353, 359, 365, 385, 393, 397, 403, 405, 407, 523, 527, 605, 611, 651; and evil, 363; four orderings within d.j., 135–39; general nature of, 361; general principles of, 479, 481; general principles of applied, 481–93; and good from evil, 137; historical and personal orders of, 365–79, 611; and mystery, 379, 385, 403; as related to punishment and satisfaction, 159, 161; restoration of order of, 139–43; retributive, redemptive, severe, 117; and secondary causes, 359, 363 (*see also* Cause(s): secondary c.); and two contexts, 85, 87, 155–57; two kinds of, 185. *See also* Fault-offense-punishment; Justice: retributive j. and sufferings of Christ; Satisfaction-pardon-remission of punishment

Divine power: and d. justice and wisdom, 133, 273, 295, 351, 353, 379, 397, 401, 497, 405

Divine providence: considered in two ways, 141; and divine governance, 351; and divine justice/wisdom, 139, 157, 357, 365; and human good, 365; and Old Testament, 377; and order, 351, 359, 407; and prayer, 389; and predestination/reprobation, 139; and reason and will, 365; and restoration, 141; and victory over evil, 455, 639

Divine will: and divine wisdom, 133, 139, 205, 351, 379, 397, 401, 405, 605, 653; and evil, 511; follows intellect, 393, 395; d.w. just, 351; mystery of, 247, 379, 385

Divine wisdom, 201; and charity, 241; Christ expression of, 35, 527; and cross, 205, 241, 477, 535; and d. goodness, 21, 63, 133, 157, 197, 201, 205, 241, 259, 273, 295, 317, 343, 359, 361, 367, 379, 381, 385, 403, 407, 477, 479, 491, 559, 583, 587, 591, 627, 633; and d. justice, 119, 133, 135, 137, 139, 143, 157, 205, 347, 351, 353, 359, 365, 385, 393, 397, 403, 407, 495, 523, 527, 605, 611, 651; and d. love, 249; and d. power, 133, 273, 295, 351, 353, 379, 479; and d. providence, *see* Divine providence: and d. justice and wisdom; and d. will, 133, 139, 205, 351, 379, 397, 401, 405, 605, 653; and evil, 383, 401, 407, 477, 491, 521, 525; and necessity, 581, 605; proper fittingness of, 247

Divinity of Christ: and instrumentality of Christ's humanity, 591, 593, 619, 621; and mysteries of his life, 471; our sharing in, 485; and understanding his work, 11

Divinization, 207

Dupont, Jacques, 571 n. 2

Durandus, 177

Durrwell, François-Xavier, 67 & n. 21, 69, 441 n. 26

Easter Vigil: and good from evil, 137
Economy of salvation: agent of, 223; and Aristotle's four causes, 219; Christ as exemplar of, 595; extrinsic end of, 221; form of, 221; intrinsic end of, 221; and law of the cross, 201, 203, 455, 459, 473; matter of, 219; not necessary but possible, 395; and transformation of evil into good, 449. *See also* Redemption
Edwards, D.M., 17
'Either pardon or punishment,' 113–17
'Either punishment or punishment,' 109
'Either satisfaction or punishment,' 107, 109, 111, 113, 117, 187, 249, 495, 501, 503, 515, 527, 537
Enemies: of cross, 233, 463; of God, 451, 537, 545, 567, 623, 631, 633, 637, 641, 655; love of, 23, 229, 415, 455, 467, 631, 635, 639, 641
Entitative/terminative distinction, *see* Contingent predication
Eucharist: and Christ as heavenly mediator, 621; and proclaiming death of Lord, 417, 539; and sacrifice of new covenant, 57
Evil: and alienation, 315; for Aquinas, *see* Thomas Aquinas: on evil; and basic sin, 21 n. 5, 343; common (public) e., 337; conquering e., 453, 461, 465, 477, 481, 639, 651 (*see also* Victory of will); culpable e., 21 & n. 5, 23, 45, 135, 137, 139, 151, 157, 181, 199, 203, 257, 259, 343, 383, 385, 387, 401, 415, 451, 453, 477, 491, 521 (*see also* Fault); cultural e., 303, 317, 327, 367; detestation of, 79; and divine permission, 23, 363, 387, 389, 415, 481, 491, 521 (*see also* Permit); endurance of, 161, 235, 237, 239, 243, 321, 453, 515; e. for e., 421; e. from e., 135, 137, 203; e. from good, 135; and fault, 119; and God, 383, 385, 491, 515, 521; good from e., 135, 137, 143, 181, 197, 199, 203, 221, 225, 239, 249, 251, 261, 317–25, 339, 367, 387, 401, 449, 455, 473, 475, 477, 481, 493, 519, 521, 525, 639, 651; good or e., 371, 373, 379; greatest e., 367; has no positive reality, 301; and human impotence, *see* Impotence; and incarnation, 77; e. inevitable, 327, 337; e. irrational, 307; and law of cross, 203, 237, 239, 249; and love of darkness, 17, 327, 413; moral e., 21 n. 5; of natural defect, 21, 135, 139, 157, 181, 383, 385, 401, 415, 451, 477; e. of order, 303, 317, 323, 325, 327, 367, 383, 649; originated e., 303; originating e., 303; particular e., 303, 317, 321, 325, 327, 367, 383, 385; as privation of good, 119, 199, 523; e. of punishment, 21, 45, 103, 135, 137, 139, 151, 157, 181, 199, 203, 225, 237, 239, 383, 385, 401, 415, 451, 453, 477, 523; and redemption, 5, 39, 135, 161, 203, 475; and retribution, 39; and sin, 9, 71, 79, 179, 257, 523, 535; and sorrow, 81, 515; suffering e. for justice's sake, 23; as what is opposed to good, 301
Expiation: and chastisement, 511 (*see also* Chastisement); penal/punitive e., 171, 513, 515, 537; and reparation, 511 (*see also* Reparation); and satisfaction, 83, 173, 191, 209; system of e., 181, 187; vicarious e., 83
Expression: and communication, 551; satisfaction as e., 191–95, 495, 553, 555; as sensible manifestation, 79

Falsity: ontological f., 257, 259, 387, 477, 491
Fate, 349
Fault, 21 n. 5; and Christ, 103, 105, 117, 133, 151, 153, 155, 159, 165, 167, 189, 237, 239, 505; defined, 21 n. 5, 119; and guilt, 103, 119, 121; and offense, 119; original f., 119, 121; personal f., 119, 121; and punishment, 151, 181, 451. *See also* Evil: culpable e.; Fault-offense-punishment
Fault-offense-punishment: as one set of notions or one context for penalty, 115, 117–23, 175, 187
First Vatican Council, 81, 85, 103, 155, 331, 469
Fittingness, 65, 77, 107, 113, 125, 127, 139, 151, 197, 203, 205, 207, 209, 213, 217, 219, 223, 233, 235, 241–51, 345, 395, 397, 405, 479, 481, 487, 499, 503, 551, 553, 605, 607, 609, 633, 635, 639, 641, 643
'For us and for our salvation/sins,' 97, 105, 207, 251, 439, 497, 509, 515, 547, 625, 631
Forgiveness: and redemption, *see* Sin: forgiveness of and redemption; and remission, *see* Remission: r./forgiveness of sins
Fouard, C.H., 101
Francis de Sales, 99, 511
Franks, Robert S., 9, 11, 13, 15, 95, 97, 145, 147 n. 29, 185 & n. 40, 215, 475 n. 12, 509 nn. 33–36
Franzelin, Johann Baptist, 103
Freedom: and personal order of justice, 369–79
Friendship, 129, 131, 631; f. with God, 75, 131, 315, 489, 631, 633, 635, 637, 639
Galtier, Paul, 81 & n. 5, 99 & n. 11, 105, 113, 209, 539 n. 67
Gay, Charles Louis, 101
Gelin, A., 531 n. 65
God, *see* Divine goodness; Divine justice; Divine power; Divine providence; Divine will; Divine wisdom
González Ruiz, José María, 73
Good: for Aristotle, 253; and being, 61, 197, 241, 269, 273, 301; common g., 275, 339, 607; g. by communication, 199, 221, 269 n. 2, 645, 647; g. concrete, 269, 301; converting evil into g., *see* Evil: good from e.; created g., 271, 273; created g. and human g. composed of potential, formal, and actual elements, 297; cultural g., 281, 287–95, 297, 299, 303, 311, 313, 315, 317, 319, 327, 337, 365, 367, 577, 581, 585, 611, 613; g. by essence, 199, 221, 269, 271, 341, 343, 363, 491, 627, 645, 647; and friendship, 631; God directly wills g., 21, 23, 135, 157; g. from g., 135, 367, 375; hierarchy of g., 297; human g., 277, 279, 281, 283, 289, 297 & n. 17, 309, 327, 365, 611; as object of will, 383, 393, 415; g. of order, 199, 253, 255, 267, 271, 273, 275, 277, 279, 281, 283, 287, 295, 297, 299, 301, 303, 307, 309, 311, 313, 315, 317, 321, 323, 327, 337, 349, 365, 367, 369, 385, 577, 579, 581, 585, 611, 613, 615, 623, 649; originating and originated g., 297, 299, 303; g. by participation, 199, 269, 341, 343, 645, 647; particular g., 199, 241, 253, 255, 271, 273, 277, 279, 297, 299, 303, 307, 327, 337, 365, 585, 611, 625; real g. and conceptual g., 197; relatively g.,

627; and signs, 289, 313; supreme g., 199; and values, 297
Good from evil, *see* Evil: good from e. *See also* Transformation: of evil into good
Grace: in Christ, 177, 211, 239; Christ cause of all g., 207; created and uncreated g., 447, 465, 595; distinction of habitual and actual g., 13; and divine friendship, 635; and effects of redemption, 597, 611, 647; and good of order/cultural good, 301; need for g. and redemption, 11; and redemption as end, 37; g. superabundant, 179, 655
Gregory of Nazianzus, 37
Gregory of Nyssa, 37
Grimal, Julius Leo, 101
Grotius, Hugo, 97, 99, 509
Guilt: and fault, 103, 119, 121

Habit(s): as first act, 63; forming and changing h., 331, 333; and good of order, 275, 279, 303, 369, 611, 623
Harnack, Adolf von, 185
Heinrichs, Ludwig, 117 & n. 20
Hell: views on Christ and punishments of h., 95, 97, 99, 163, 509, 511, 529
Hilary, 37
Holy Spirit: and good by communication, 199, 221, 301, 645, 647; and love of Father for Son both as God and as man, 447, 463, 595, 625, 637; mission of, and redemption, 75; and redemption as end, 5, 31, 423
Hope: and indwelling Holy Spirit, 633
Hugh of St Victor, 93, 145
Hughes, Thomas Hywel, 3, 17
*Humani generis*, 213
Image: of God, 297, 299, 301, 315, 451, 593, 615, 659; of Son, 203, 229, 245, 459, 465, 593, 595, 597
Impotence: human/moral i., 7, 77, 327–43, 367, 607, 615, 633, 649; intellectual i., 309
Incarnate spirit: contrasted with rational animal, 283
Incarnation: and analogy for God, 469; and assimilation and union, 487; and Christ's mediation, 37; fittingness of, 77, 209, 215, 217; and good by communication, 199; ways of understanding i. and redemption, 207; and hypothetical necessity, 101, 107, 109, 207, 209, 211, 213; purpose of, 207, 215, 217, 251–55, 625–59 passim
Influence: and body, 575; and cause, 571, 573; of Christ, 611, 613, 651; and circular movement in human situations, 277, 309; and dependence, 571, 573; and historical agents, 581; intelligible i., 573; and social agents, 585, 587; and space and time, 575; theory of moral i., 11; three kinds of, 573. *See also* Cause(s)
Information: principle of, 289, 291, 293, 295
Innocent II, Pope, 11
Innocent X, Pope, 99
Intelligibility: extrinsic i., 237; intrinsic i., 237, 241, 259
Intelligible: i. in act and in potency, 309, 397; divided into necessary and possible or fitting, 233, 393, 395, 573; and form, 399; i. in itself and in other, 399, 401; and reduction of finite being to extrinsic causes, 259; and understanding and wisdom, 397, 401, 407; and wisdom, choice, and action of God, 397, 401

Interpersonal relations: and the human good, 199, 279, 301, 369, 611; and redemption, 7, 73, 75, 623, 625; and satisfaction, 89
Intervention: and redemption as mediation, 5, 7, 481

Jaspers, Karl, 321 n. 27, 325 n. 30, 615 n. 25
John Chrysostom, 37
John of Rupella, 93, 111, 145, 501 n. 12
Judgment: and failure of intelligence, 305, 307; j. of God on sin, 51, 195; and intellectual development, 291, 299; last j., 135, 371, 377; and natural consequence, 377; and understanding, 399; j. of value, 79, 307
Justice: commutative j., 121, 133, 135, 349; and cross, *see* Cross: justice of; distributive j., 133, 135, 349; j. of God, *see* Divine justice; j. of judge and j. of cross, 527, 531, 533, 535, 537, 541; historical j. and positive j., 375; legal j., 133, 349; j. in metaphorical sense, 135 & n. 25; and penalties, 85; and reconciliation and forgiveness, 85, 87, 161; repairing order of divine j., 85, 139–43, 161; retributive/vindictive j., 85, 89, 99, 103, 105, 117, 121, 141, 143, 159, 161, 163, 165, 167, 179, 185, 189; social j., 349. *See also* Contexts for paying penalty for sin; Divine justice
Justification: given gratis, 137, 419, 481; and good from evil, 135 & n. 25; and redemption as end, 31, 227; and sanctification, 71; and servant, 49; and superabundant satisfaction, 179. *See also* Merit: and justification/satisfaction

Kingdom of God: and redemption/salvation, 507

Law: of cross, *see* Law of the cross; l. of effect, 319; eternal l., 139, 157, 183, 351, 353; natural l., 139, 353; Germanic l., 75 & n. 2, 185 n. 40; Jewish l., 35, 41, 51, 55, 137, 139, 229, 243, 325, 365, 423, 429, 433, 487, 529, 565, 567, 615, 617, 657; and new covenant, 53, 127, 455, 459, 619; l. of retaliation, 23, 117, 415, 531; Roman l., 75 & n. 2, 121; several meanings of, 233
Law of the cross, 197; comprises three steps, 203, 205; does not have universality of empirical law, 233; and economy of salvation, 201, 203, 455, 459, 473; as effective, 235; as essence of redemption, 237; as fitting, 235, 241–51; as found in Christ, 203, 205, 251; as found in Christ's members, 203, 205, 251; a general law, 203; and good from evil, 249, 493; as intrinsic intelligibility of redemption, 237; as just, 205; as law of redemption, 233–41, 459; as meaning of cross in New Testament expressed by way of precept, example, conformation, association, and law of economy of salvation, 455–65; as mysterious, *see* Mystery: of cross/law of cross; not absolutely necessary, 233; and new covenant, 455, 459; presents two antitheses, 231; and sin and death, 223; and transformation of death, 225, 227; universality of, 235; verified differently in head and members, 237, 239, 251; why called a law, 203. *See also* Death of Christ; Evil: good from; Punishment:

and law of cross; Redemption; Transformation
Laws: circular or serial complex of, 353–61; statistical l., 361
Leo the Great, Pope, 37, 475 n. 12
Leo XIII, Pope, 81
Le Saint, W.P., 115 n. 22
*Lex talionis, see* Retaliation: law of
Liberals: and understanding of redemption, 9, 11, 13, 15, 315, 511, 531
Life: to give one's l. and price, 7, 33, 35, 43, 47, 175, 423, 437, 491
Lindblom, Johannes, 51 n. 14
Lombard, Peter, 19, 93, 111, 145, 147, 149, 153, 415 n. 4, 501 n. 12, 505 & n. 20, 515, 539 & n. 69
Lonergan, Bernard, works referred to: *De Deo trino: Pars dogmatica*, 323 n. 28; *De Deo trino: Pars systematica*, 59, 75, 199, 431 n. 16, 465 n. 7, 647 nn. 3 and 6; *De Verbo incarnato*, xv, xvi, 37 n. 10, 65, 197 n. 1, 421 n. 9, 443 n. 26; *Divinarum personarum*, 59, 75, 199, 431 n. 16, 465 n. 7, 647 nn. 3 and 6; *Early Works on Theological Method 1*, 623 n. 29; *Early Works on Theological Method 3*, 311 n. 22; 'God's Knowledge and Will,' 157 n. 32; *Grace and Freedom*, 21 n. 5, 157 n. 32, 181 n. 37, 261, 349 n. 5, 359 n. 24, 363 n. 28, 653 n. 7; *The Incarnate Word*, xv, 37 n. 10, 65 and n. 20, 211, 223, 227, 235, 239, 251, 261, 381 n. 35, 467 n. 8, 549 n. 84, 587 n. 5; *Insight*, 21 n. 5, 199 & n. 2, 277 n. 7, 319 n. 24, 327 n. 21, 339 n. 38, 357 nn. 22–23, 359 nn. 24–25, 361 nn. 26–27, 363 n. 29, 583 n. 3; 'The Mediation of Christ in Prayer,' 357 n. 22; 'On God and Secondary Causes,' 359 n. 24; *The Ontological and Psychological Constitution of Christ*, 391 n. 45, 631 n. 33; *A Second Collection*, 197 n. 1; 'St. Thomas' Theory of Operation,' 359 n. 24, 363 n. 28; *Topics in Education*, 271 n. 3; 'The Transition from a Classicist World-View to Historical-Mindedness,' 197 n. 1; *The Triune God: Doctrines*, 323 n. 28; *The Triune God: Systematics*, 59 n. 19, 75, 85 n. 6, 199, 391 n. 45, 431 n. 16, 465 n. 7, 623 n. 29, 647 nn. 3 and 6; *Verbum*, 85 n. 6, 471 n. 10
Loofs, Friedrich, 185
Love: l. of benevolence, 631; of enemies, 23, 229, 415, 455, 467, 631, 635, 639, 641; l. of God first, 47, 159, 245, 531, 619; mutual l. of benevolence, 631, 637; as principle of satisfaction, 131, 193; 'to love' defined, 241, 275, 631. *Editor's note*: It could be argued that the overriding theme of this work is love. To do justice to the category 'love' would entail referencing most pages. Thus, under the entry love' only limited sub-categories appear.
Luther, Martin, 95
Lutherans/Lutheranism, 9, 97, 99, 153
Lyonnet, Stanislas, 27, 31, 33, 41, 43, 47, 51, 71, 103, 137, 185 & n. 39, 421 n. 9, 441 nn. 24 and 26, 481 n. 21

Maldonado, Juan, 99
Marx, Karl, 233, 375, 463
Mediation, 357 n. 22; principle of, 289, 291, 293; redemption as m., 5, 7, 11, 29, 35–75 passim, 211, 213, 241, 251, 423 n. 11, 479, 621, 653; and reconciliation, 77
Melanchthon, Philip, 95, 509

Merit: basis of, 375; defined, 9, 65; and grace, 211; and Isaian servant, 49; and justification/satisfaction, 81, 109, 131, 143, 155, 195, 213, 235, 241, 383, 439, 497, 499, 537, 603, 605, 609, 615; and obedience of Christ, 5, 7, 29, 65, 69, 251, 411, 431–35, 437, 441, 491, 563, 589, 601, 609, 651; and original sin, 111, 501; and personal order of justice, 369–79; and remission of punishment, 89
Mersch, Emile, 37 & n. 11
Messianism: Jewish m., 201
Method: philosophical and theological m. contrasted, 13, 109; and ways of understanding incarnation and redemption, 207, 213–19, 605
'Miserentissimus Redemptor,' 129, 161, 167
Mission, divine: constituted by relations of origin, 647; manifest order of divine persons, 649, 657
Mission of Holy Spirit, 75, 629
Mission of Son: and human acts of Son, 59, 431; and obedience, 61–63, 431; and person of Son, 59, 431; and procession, 59, 431; and reconciliation, 623
Modernists, 9, 17, 511, 531
Monsabré, Jacques-Marie Louis, 101
Monsour, H. Daniel, 145 n. 28
Moral impotence, *see* Impotence: human/moral
Moral influence: theory of, 11
Moraldi, Luigi, 47
Mystery: and belief, 9; of cross/law of cross, 7, 247, 295, 449, 451, 465–77, 479, 481, 489, 493, 519, 521, 525, 527, 639, 641, 651, 655; and divine justice, 403; of divine will/wisdom, 247, 249, 267, 379, 385, 467; eucharistic m., 621; of iniquity/lawlessness, 205, 471; m. kept secret, 465, 467, 617; of kingdom, 467; and life of Christ, 205, 651; and rosary, 469; and understanding, 125, 197, 403, 601, 603, 609; and vicarious suffering, 9

Natural consequence: and justice, 377
Necessity: conditioned/hypothetical n., 197, 209, 211, 213, 215, 257, 581, 583, 589; and divine causality, 573, 581; and divine wisdom, 393; n. versus fittingness, 107, 113, 125, 139, 197, 205, 207, 209, 219, 239, 405, 499, 501, 503, 605, 633; and intelligibility, 393, 395, 573
Nestorianism, 11
Nicholas of Autrecourt, 397
Nietzsche, Friedrich, 233, 463
Nominalism, 177, 509
North, Christopher R., 49, 443 n. 26
Novel, Charles, 27

Obedience of Christ: for Aquinas, 65, 77, 151, 153, 165, 175, 179, 183, 251; and dependence, 431; directly willed by God, 23; and diversity of wills, 19; and exterior bodily action, 61, 433, 557; free, 63, 191, 435, 589; and law of cross, 203; meritorious, 5, 7, 29, 65, 69, 411, 431–35, 437, 441, 497, 563, 589, 601, 609, 651; and mission of Son, 59; in New Testament, 19, 39, 55, 61, 63, 65, 69, 185, 225, 227, 239, 243, 247, 413, 417, 427, 433, 435, 487, 491; as passive, 437; and redemption as mediation, 59–65, 563; and simultaneity in truth, 591; and two operations, 587, 629
Ockham, William of, 397

Offense: and context of fault and punishment, *see* Fault-offense-punishment; o. against God (sin), 9, 71, 77, 79, 81, 87, 91, 179, 315, 443, 535 (*see also* Detestation: Christ's d.; Sin(s)); and satisfaction, 79, 89, 91, 153, 173, 175, 179, 513, 539 (*see also* Satisfaction-pardon-remission); and vicarious satisfaction, 127

Oggioni, Giulio, 5, 95, 101, 103, 171, 187

Order: good of o., *see* Good: g. of order; historical o. of justice, 365–69; and justice/wisdom/will/power of God, 133–37, 157, 205, 353–63, 407; natural and supernatural o., 109, 131; personal o. of justice, 369–79; reintegration of o. of divine justice, 85, 87, 139–43, 155, 161, 255; of universe, 21, 221, 253, 275, 349, 351, 353, 357, 359, 361, 373, 403, 405, 407, 627, 653, 659; o. of wisdom and o. of understanding, 397, 399, 407

Parente, P., 99 & n. 10

Pardon, *see* Satisfaction-pardon-remission of punishment

Paul, 17, 23, 47, 57, 61, 65, 75, 137, 223, 229, 235, 245, 247, 248, 325, 341, 347, 403, 417, 421, 433, 435, 457, 459, 461, 467, 469, 481, 489, 607, 609, 625

Paul IV, Pope, 13

Paying the penalty for sins: two contexts for, *see* Contexts

Pelagianism, 11, 131, 143, 601

Penance: sacrament of, 79, 143, 147, 159, 167, 189, 497, 505, 529

Permit: God wills to p. culpable evil, 23, 49, 135, 157, 181, 203, 257, 259, 261, 363, 387, 389, 391, 401, 407, 415, 477, 481, 491, 521, 523, 525; and good from evil, 185, 481, 491, 521, 525. *See also* Evil: and divine permission; Evil: good from

Pesch, C., 101 & n. 12, 515, n. 46

Philippe de la Trinité, 105 & n. 16, 165

Physical predetermination, 583

Pius XI, Pope, 129

Pius XII, Pope, 81, 129 n. 24, 159 n. 34

Prat, Ferdinand, 75 & n. 26

Premotion, 359 n. 24

Price: payment of, *see* Death of Christ: and payment of price. *See also* Ransom

Progress: automatic p., 325; and decline, 313; and good of order, 277–81

Propitiation, 47, 159, 481, 601; pagan and OT meaning of p. contrasted, 47. *See also* Atonement: sacrifice of

Protestants: early P. and punishment of Christ, 93, 95–99, 105, 113, 163, 511, 527, 529; and spiritual alienation, 315

Prümm, K., 247, 469 n. 9

Punishment: in broader and stricter sense, 119; and Christ, *see* Christ: punished according to God's justice but not according to God's retributive justice; and death of Christ, *see* Death of Christ: and punishment for sin; contracted and assumed, 151, 153, 161; and divine justice, 159, 161; evil of p., *see* Evil: e. of punishment; and God's will, 21, 45, 103, 135, 139, 157, 181, 383, 385, 401, 415, 477; and guilt, 121; kinds of p., 147; and law of cross, 225, 237, 453; medicinal p., 121, 165, 319 n. 25, 375, 507,

525; and redemption, 5, 423; and satisfaction, 91, 125, 127, 133, 157, 175, 177, 195, 507, 525; p. simply so called and with qualification, 119, 121, 177, 507. *See also* Contexts; 'Either satisfaction or punishment'; 'Either pardon or punishment'; Fault-offense-punishment; Satisfaction-pardon-remission of punishment

Quenstedt, Johann Andreas, 97, 511

Rahner, Hugo, 129 n. 24
Ransom, 25 & n. 7, 27, 37, 39, 41, 43, 45, 107, 167, 227, 419, 421, 425, 439, 457, 477, 485, 499, 621, 625, 657. *See also* Price
Rashdall, H., 15, 17
Rationalism, 7, 9, 13, 169, 339, 603, 633
Reconciliation: and purpose of incarnation, 215, 217, 251; and redemption as mediation, 77, 125; and work/mission of Christ, 87, 623. *See also* Contexts
Redemption: and converting evils into good, *see* Evil: good from; effects of, 563–643 passim; as end, 5, 7, 29, 31–35, 43, 71, 423, 441, 563; and law of cross, *see* Law of the cross; as mediation/means, 5, 7, 29, 35–75 passim, 423, 441, 563, 601, 603; modes and effects of r., 77; and purpose of incarnation, 207, 251, 255, 625–43, 645–59; as restoration of fallen order, 255; and transformative principle, 183–85
'Redemption': words used for r. in New Testament, 25–29 & n. 7, 419–25
Rejoicing in one's sufferings: as paradox proper to Christians, 245
Relations, interpersonal: and grace, 73, 75; and human good/good of order, 199, 277, 279, 301, 303, 369, 611, 623; and satisfaction, 89
Remission: of fault/guilt, 84, 175, 189, 541; of offense, 125, 127, 189; of punishment, 84, 99, 115, 123–27, 175, 187, 189, 541; r./forgiveness of sins, 11, 15, 29, 33, 47, 57, 87, 95, 97, 109, 117, 149, 161, 175, 185, 189, 225, 383, 391, 407, 409, 419, 427, 429, 447, 499, 501, 509, 563, 573, 615. *See also* Satisfaction-pardon-remission of punishment
Reparation: distinction of chastisement, expiation, and r., 101, 115, 511, 513; expiative r., 115; and satisfaction, 139, 141, 143, 147, 217, 541; two contexts of, 87 (*see also* Contexts)
Resurrection: as example, 231; power of r., 441–47; and redemption as end, 5, 423; and redemption in general, 67, 69
Retaliation: law of, 23, 117, 415, 531
Retribution: licit and illicit r., 123
Revelation: relative necessity of, 331
Réville, Albert, 15
Richard, Louis, 5, 9, 11, 13, 15, 27, 37, 45, 77, 79 n. 2, 81 & n. 4, 95, 97, 101, 115 & n. 19, 173, 183, 203, 209
Ritschl, Albrecht, 15 & nn. 3–4
Rivière, Jean, 3, 11, 17, 45, 77, 95, 99, 101 & n. 12, 103, 113, 115 & n. 19, 173, 181, 185, 187, 201, 209, 511 & nn. 38 and 40, 513 nn. 41 and 43, 515 & n. 50, 539 n. 68, 541 n. 76
Rondet, Henri, 129 n. 24
Rupert of Deutz, 207, 215, 217

Sabatier, Auguste, 15
Sabourin, Léopold, 27, 53, 185

Sacrifice: action of, 53, 425; agent of, 53, 425; atoning s., 47, 57, 247, 429, 467, 569, 609; and covenant, 53, 411; effects of, 53, 425; elements in, 53, 425; foundation of, 53, 425; s. of old and new covenants, 55, 57, 177, 427, 429, 433; recipients of effects of s., 53, 425; s. of reconciliation, 251; and redemption as mediation, 5, 7, 35, 53–59. *See also* Covenant

San Pablo, Basilio de, 103, 515 n. 46

Sanctifying grace, 301, 595, 597, 611, 635, 647

Satisfaction: and compensation, 89, 91; condign s., 79, 177, 179, 209, 213, 503; considered formally and materially, 83, 87, 173–77, 191, 193, 195, 499; defined, 79, 125; and detestation and sorrow regarding sin, 191–95, 545, 547, 553, 555, 557; and divine justice, 159, 161; and expiation, 83, 173, 191, 209; God directly wills Christ's s., 103, 181, 183, 515, 517; and merit, *see* Merit: and justification/satisfaction; and sacramental analogy, *see* Analogy: sacramental a.; superabundant s., 79, 113, 179, 181, 495, 503, 555–61; vicarious s., 127–33, 153, 193, 491, 501, 533, 551, 555, 603. *See also* 'Either satisfaction or punishment'; Justice: j. of judge and j. of cross

Satisfaction-pardon-remission of punishment: as one set of notions or one context for paying penalty, 87, 115, 123–27, 143, 157, 187

Satispassion, 93, 95, 101, 169, 171, 187

Schleiermacher, Friedrich, 13, 15

Schmitt, F.S., 87 & n. 7, 107

Schwendimann, Friedrich, 129 n. 24

Scotus, John Duns/Scotists, 91, 111, 177, 209, 215, 255, 397, 501 n. 12

Secondary causes, 17, 19, 359, 363, 365, 367, 583, 633, 651

Semi-rationalism, 109, 603, 633

Sens: Council of, 11

Servant: suffering s., 27, 39, 49, 51, 421, 439, 443

Signs: and culture, 283–87, 313; denotative and expressive s., 291, 549, 551, 619; division of s., 293; and human good, 289–95, 313; and mystics, 283; and principle of concreteness, 289; and principle of conformation, 289, 291; and principle of information, 291; and principle of mediation, 291, 293; technical knowledge of s., 285, 287; and Word of God made flesh, 295

Simultaneity in truth, 583, 589, 591

Sin(s): and alienation, 315, 325; basic s., 21 n. 5; and death of Christ, *see* Death of Christ: and punishment for s.; defined, 9, 79; detestation of, *see* Detestation; forgiveness of and redemption, 5, 29, 31, 33, 47, 53, 57, 71, 161, 225, 429; formal element of formal s., 21 n. 5, 257, 399; interior s., 23; law of s., 337, 453, 567; liberation from s., 27; mortal and venial, 89, 141; as offense, *see* Offense; original s., 111, 161, 165, 199, 343, 345, 501, 609; as privation of being and good, 257, 259; question of (extrinsic and intrinsic) cause of s., 257–63; reign of s., 337, 453, 633, 639, 651, 659

Skepticism, 313, 397

Socinians, 9, 13, 511, 531

Solano, Jesús, 101 n. 12, 103, 105 & n. 17, 115 & n. 21, 515 n. 46, 523 n. 60
Solidarity: and human good of order, 279, 281
Sorrow, *see* Satisfaction: and detestation and sorrow regarding sin
Sozzini, Fausto, 13, 97, 509
Sozzini, Lelio, 13
Spicq, Ceslaus, 35, 53, 427 n. 13, 443 n. 27
Stamm, Johann Jakob, 27
Stanley, David M., 51, 73, 439 n. 23
Stierli, Josef, 159 n. 34
Suárez, Francisco, 3, 45, 91, 99, 101, 111, 113, 181, 501 n. 12, 511
Substitution: and pagan overtones, 43; and satispassion, 93, 95, 101, 169, 187; as symbolic apprehension, 169, 171
*Summa fratris Alexandri,* 111, 145 & nn. 27–28, 147, 501 n. 12, 505 & n. 21, 515, 539
Supernatural: absolutely s., 131, 137, 239, 469, 557, 597, 635, 647, 653; and Christ, 637, 653; and economy of salvation, 219, 221, 301; s. gifts, 641; s. good of order, 623; s. love, 143; theorem of, 13; theorem of and shortcomings in Anselm, 109, 499 n. 10
Swing, Albert Temple, 15 n. 3
Symbolic mentality: and substitution and satispassion, 169, 171; and transposition to logical categories, 169, 171
Systematic theology, 83

Tertullian, 109, 115 & n. 22, 117, 137
Theodore of Mopsuestia, 11
Thomas Aquinas: on abstracting, 67; action and passion in, 19, 415, 475; and Christ in history, 615, 619, 653; on Christ as mediator, 37; on Christ's love and obedience, 65, 165, 431, 587; on Christ's satisfaction, 113, 149, 153, 155, 173, 177, 179, 181, 193, 195, 209, 423, 503, 513, 515, 539, 555, 603, 607; on Christ's sorrow, 543; and cultural good, 365; on divine wisdom, 379, 393, 477, 605; on divinization, 207; on evil, 21 n. 5, 181, 301, 451, 507; on falsity, 257, 477, 491; on Father's love for Son, 463, 625; and fittingness, 503, 605; and God's choice of universe, 381; and God's mercy, 409; on God's willing, 157, 257, 261, 415, 477, 491, 521; and good by communication, 645; on good out of evil, 493; on impotence, 331; on incarnation, 207, 215, 217; on intellectual virtues, 85 n. 6; on justice, 125 n. 35, 533 n. 66; on justice in redemption, 209, 503; and love of enemies, 635; on merit of Christ, 65; on modes and effects of redemption, 77; on natural desire for God, 283; on natural law, 353; on obedience of Christ, *see* Obedience of Christ: for Aquinas; on operative grace, 371; on order of universe, 253, 275, 349, 351, 353, 363, 405, 659; on punishment, 507, 515, 539; and punishment suffered by Christ, 91, 151, 165, 515, 525; on 'take upon oneself' and 'incur,' 103, 149; on union of wills through love, 127, 129, 243; on wisdom, 85
– Works: *De malo,* 21 n. 5, 121, 143, 331 n. 33, 371 n. 31; *De substantiis*

*separatis*, 363 n. 28; *De veritate*, 133, 331 n. 33, 393 n. 48, 605 n. 19; *In Boethium de Trinitate*, 67; *In III Phys.*, 19; *Summa contra Gentiles*, 129 & n. 23, 143, 177, 197, 293 n. 10, 353 n. 20, 393 n. 49, 409 n. 55, 555 n. 85; *Summa theologiae*, 19, 21 & n. 5, 23, 35, 37, 59, 63, 65, 77, 79, 85 & n. 6, 91, 103, 105, 111, 113, 117, 119, 121, 123, 125, 127, 131, 133, 135 & n. 25, 139, 143, 145, 149, 151, 153, 155, 159, 165, 173, 175, 177, 179, 181, 183, 193, 197, 199, 201, 203, 205, 207, 209, 211, 215, 217, 221, 239, 243, 247, 249, 251, 253, 257, 259, 261, 275 nn. 4–6, 283 nn. 10–12, 301 n. 19, 349 nn. 3–8, 351 nn. 9–18, 353 nn. 19 and 21, 365 n. 30, 379 n. 34, 381 nn. 35 and 37–41, 385 n. 42, 387 nn. 43–44, 393 n. 47, 405 n. 50, 407 nn. 52–53, 409 nn. 54–55, 415 nn. 4–5, 423 n. 11, 431 nn. 17–18, 451 n. 2, 465 n. 7, 475 n. 11, 477 nn. 13–16, 479 nn. 17–19, 489 n. 29, 491 nn. 31–33, 493 n. 34, 501 n. 12, 503 nn. 13–17, 507 nn. 26–32, 511 n. 39, 513 n. 42, 515 nn. 47–49, 517 n. 52, 521 nn. 55–56, 523 nn. 57–58, 525 nn. 61–63, 539 nn. 70–72, 541 nn. 73–75, 543 nn. 77–78 and 80–81, 545 n. 82, 547 n. 83, 549 n. 84, 555 nn. 85–86, 557 n. 87, 587 nn. 6–7, 589 nn. 8–9 and 11, 591 n. 12, 593 n. 13, 595 nn. 14–16, 605 nn. 18 and 20–21, 607 nn. 22–23, 615 n. 26, 619 n. 27, 625 nn. 30–31, 627 n. 32, 631 n. 34, 635 n. 35, 645 n. 2, 647 nn. 4–5, 653 n. 8, 655 n. 10, 659 nn. 12–15

Transcendence: theorem of, 261

Transformation: of death, 183, 203, 225–31; of evil into good, 203, 249, 449–55, 473, 475, 481, 493, 519, 525, 639, 651; t. principle in redemption, 185. *See also* Law of the cross

Trent, Council of, 81, 99, 111, 163, 167, 189, 435, 511, 537

Truth: contingent t. about God, 391, 581; and evidence, 307, 315; and intellectual virtues, 85; logical and ontological t., 351; simultaneity in t., 583, 591

Understanding: increase in u. and wisdom, 397; and intelligibility, 397; order of u. and order of wisdom, 397–401, 407; as pivot between sense-imagination and concepts, 399; and sensitive apprehension, 291; theological u., 85; versus proof, 397; as virtue of speculative intellect, 85 & n. 6

Unitarians, 13

Value: and actual element of good, 297; and cultural good, 297

Vásquez, Gabriel, 209

Vawter, Bruce, 73

Vernet, F., 145

Vicarious: v. acting, 7, 45, 47, 69, 437, 439; v. (passion and) death, 29, 45, 53, 127, 173, 191, 195, 441, 497; v. expiation, 83; meaning of v., 5, 437; v. satisfaction, 109, 127–33, 153, 193, 491, 501, 533, 551, 555, 603; v. sorrow, 555; v. suffering, 7, 9, 11, 35, 47, 49, 191, 195, 411, 437–41, 491, 541, 551, 553, 555, 563, 601

Victory of will, 449, 453, 461, 465, 473, 475, 477, 481, 651

Virtues: v. of speculative intellect, 85 n. 6
Vogt, E., 247, 469 n. 9
Voluntarism, 91, 255, 393–401, 503

Weis, Earl Augusto, 145 & n. 26
William of Auvergne, 93, 145
Wisdom: and basic terms, 85; and charity, 241; and cultural good, 297, 337; w. defined, 85; and fittingness, 241, 247; w. of God, *see* Divine wisdom; human w. and understanding of understanding, 305; as intellectual virtue, 85 n. 6; and judgment, 397; and mystery of divine will, 241; order of w., 397, 399, 407; stages in attainment of, 221; theological w., 85.
Wright, John H., 139

Xiberta, B.M., 3, 45, 513 & n. 44

Zedda, Silvero, 445 n. 28